THE FINANCIAL SERVICES AND MARKETS ACT 2000:
A GUIDE TO THE NEW LAW

THE FINANCIAL SERVICES AND MARKETS ACT 2000:
A GUIDE TO THE NEW LAW

Alistair Alcock MA, FSI, Barrister

Professor of Corporate Law and Acting Pro Vice-Chancellor,
The University of Buckingham
Former Director Corporate Finance, UBS Phillips & Drew

J O R D A N S
2000

Published by
Jordan Publishing Ltd
21 St Thomas Street
Bristol BS1 6JS

British Library Cataloguing-in-Publication Data
A catalogue record for this book is available from the British Library.

ISBN 0 85308 563 3

Typeset by Mendip Communications Ltd, Frome, Somerset
Printed at MPG Books Ltd, Bodmin, Cornwall

PREFACE

Until now, I have been a reader rather than an author of commentaries on new legislation. As such, I have tended to criticise them for falling into one of two categories:

(1) policy discussions which fail to give sufficient detail about the actual legislation; or
(2) detailed descriptions that do little more than reorder and paraphrase the legislation.

Here, I have sought to steer a middle course, pulling together disparate parts of the legislation into more coherent topics and trying to put those topics into some sort of context. Perhaps unusually for this type of book, I have also provided extensive footnotes to assist readers in tracking down sources, since the Financial Services and Markets Act 2000 (FSMA) is not an easy piece of legislation to explain. For all its length, it sets out only a framework for regulating the UK financial services industry. In these post *Pepper v Hart* days, I have tried to highlight important guidance and explanations given by Government Ministers during the FSMA's passage through Parliament. I have also relied heavily on the Treasury's draft statutory instruments and the Financial Services Authority's first 60 Consultation Papers and other publications which now give a fairly clear picture of what the all-important *FSA Handbook* will look like. The drafts and documents discussed in this book are those available up to 31 July 2000.

Between now and the FSMA coming into force, the Treasury and the FSA still have a lot of tidying up to do; but given the amazing level of scrutiny this reform has been subjected to over the last three years, I am reasonably confident that the arrangements described here will be those operating in 2001. What I am less confident about, given the speed of change in this industry, is how long those arrangements will last.

I must particularly thank Richard Hudson and Stephen Honey of Jordans, my publishers, for commissioning and then seeing this project through. Of course, any remaining errors (and with 1,500 amendments to the Bill, I am sure there are some) are entirely down to me. Indeed, may I express my admiration for the Parliamentary draftsmen who have had to produce all these amendments in record time. I have only had to comment on them.

Finally, I would like to dedicate this book to Sheena and Philip, whose lives have taken such a battering from the FSMA over the last two years.

ALISTAIR ALCOCK
Buckingham
September 2000

CONTENTS

Preface   v
Table of Cases   xiii
Table of Statutes   xvii
Table of Statutory Instruments and Codes   xxvii
Table of European Legislation   xxxi
Glossary of Abbreviations   xxxiii

Chapter 1   **BACKGROUND**   1
             INTRODUCTION   1
             HOW WERE UK FINANCIAL SERVICES REGULATED?   2
             The Stock Exchange   2
             The Society of Lloyd's   3
             The Takeover Panel   3
             The Bank of England   3
             The Department of Trade and Industry   4
             The regulation of Friendly Societies   4
             THE FORCES FOR CHANGE   5
             THE FINANCIAL SERVICES ACT 1986   6
             The structure   6
             Control of financial services after Big Bang   8
             Developments under the 1986 Act   8
             THE BIRTH OF A 'SUPER REGULATOR'   9
             The scope of the Financial Services Authority   10
             Interim arrangements   12
             Internal structure   12
             PROBLEMS AND RISKS   13
             The challenge for a Super Regulator   15
             THE SCENIC ROUTE   16

Chapter 2   **THE EUROPEAN FRAMEWORK**   17
             INTRODUCTION   17
             THE DEVELOPMENT OF THE EUROPEAN PASSPORT   18
             Insurers   18
             Credit institutions   19
             Investment firms   20
             Other mutual recognition   22
             Gaps in the Passport regimes   23
             PROBLEMS OF IMPLEMENTATION   23
             Regulatory arbitrage   23
             Host State regulation   24
             Conduct of business rules   25
             Problems for a single regulator   26
             THE EUROPEAN CONVENTION   27

Chapter 3   **THE FINANCIAL SERVICES AUTHORITY AND THE**
                  TRIBUNAL   31
                  BACKGROUND   31
                  STATUS OF THE FINANCIAL SERVICES AUTHORITY   32
                  FINANCIAL SERVICES AUTHORITY'S DUTIES   34
                     The objectives   35
                     The principles   38
                  ACCOUNTABILITY   39
                     Practitioners and consumers   40
                     The Treasury   41
                     Competition issues   43
                     Complaints scheme and immunity   46
                  FINANCIAL SERVICES AND MARKETS TRIBUNAL   48
                     Structure and proceedings   48

Chapter 4   **THE SCOPE OF THE FINANCIAL SERVICES AND**
                  MARKETS ACT 2000   51
                  BACKGROUND   51
                  THE NEED FOR AUTHORISATION   52
                     Exempt persons   53
                     Regulated activities   54
                     Financial promotion   56
                  STATUTORY INSTRUMENTS   59
                     The Exemption Order   59
                     The draft Financial Services and Markets Act (Regulated
                       Activities) Order   59
                     Exclusions under the draft Financial Services and
                       Markets Act (Regulated Activities) Order   62
                     Wholesale markets and corporate activities   64
                     The Financial Promotions Exemptions Order   65

Chapter 5   **AUTHORISATION AND APPROVAL**   69
                  BACKGROUND   69
                  OBTAINING AUTHORISATION   69
                     Threshold Conditions for Authorisation 71
                     UK permission   73
                     Permission procedure   74
                     European Economic Area authorisation   75
                     Treasury intervention   77
                     Significant control over authorised firms   78
                     Transfer of banking and insurance business   80
                  OBTAINING APPROVAL   81
                     The Financial Services Authority's approach   83
                     The responsibilities of senior management   85

Chapter 6   **THE FINANCIAL SERVICES AUTHORITY'S**
                  LEGISLATIVE FUNCTIONS   87
                  BACKGROUND   87
                  RULE-MAKING FOR AUTHORISED FIRMS   88

Additional rule-making powers 89
Effect of the Financial Services Authority rules and
waivers 91
Evidential provisions and guidance 93
Procedural provisions 94
THE FINANCIAL SERVICES AUTHORITY'S APPROACH
TO RULE-MAKING 96
The Financial Services Authority's Principles for
Businesses 96
Definitions of clients 98
Conduct of business rules 100
OTHER PROVISIONS 102
Prudential Sourcebook 102
Client assets rules 104
Stabilisation rules 105
Training and Competence Sourcebook 106
THE FINANCIAL SERVICES AUTHORITY'S
STATEMENTS OF PRINCIPLE 107
The approach of the Financial Services Authority 107

Chapter 7 **MARKET MISCONDUCT** 111
BACKGROUND 111
MISLEADING STATEMENTS AND PRACTICES 112
Economical with the truth 113
Market manipulation 113
INSIDER DEALING 114
Relevant dealings 115
Insiders 115
Inside information 116
Defences 117
MARKET ABUSE 118
The three categories 119
Who is vulnerable? 121
THE MARKET CODE 122
Regular user test 123
Misuse of privileged information 124
False or misleading impression 125
Distortion 127
MONEY LAUNDERING 128

Chapter 8 **COMPLAINTS AND COMPENSATION** 131
BACKGROUND 131
A single complaints system 132
A single compensation system 133
THE OMBUDSMAN 134
Compulsory and voluntary schemes 134
The approach of the Financial Services Authority and
the Financial Ombudsman Scheme Limited 137
Procedures and funding 138
COMPENSATION SCHEME 140
The proposals of the Financial Services Authority 142

**Chapter 9   ENFORCEMENT (1): DISCIPLINING THE
                UNAUTHORISED, THE AUTHORISED AND THE
                APPROVED**   145
                BACKGROUND   145
                POLICING THE PERIMETER   146
                  Prosecutions   146
                  Civil enforcement   147
                DISCIPLINING THE AUTHORISED AND APPROVED   148
                  Disciplinary and supervisory procedures   150
                  Disciplinary proposals of the Financial Services
                      Authority   154
                  Prohibition of individuals   155
                  Fines and costs   156
                  Injunctions and restitution   158
                  Varying or cancelling a permission   159
                  Co-operating with overseas regulators   161
                INSOLVENCY   163
                  Powers of the Financial Services Authority   163
                  The rights of the Financial Services Authority   164
                  Insurers   165

**Chapter 10   ENFORCEMENT (2): INVESTIGATIONS, MARKET
                MISCONDUCT AND PRIVATE ACTIONS**   167
                PERIMETER INVESTIGATIONS   167
                INVESTIGATING THE AUTHORISED AND APPROVED   168
                  Compulsion and confidentiality   172
                AUDITORS AND ACTUARIES   174
                MARKET MISCONDUCT   174
                  Use of its powers   175
                  Injunctions and restitution   177
                  Money laundering   178
                PRIVATE ACTIONS   178
                  Outside the perimeter   178
                  Within the perimeter   179

**Chapter 11   SPECIAL CASES: EXCHANGES, CLEARING HOUSES,
                LLOYD'S AND THE PROFESSIONS**   181
                BACKGROUND   181
                RECOGNISED INVESTMENT EXCHANGES AND
                    RECOGNISED CLEARING HOUSES   182
                  Recognition requirements   183
                  Insolvency arrangements   184
                  Applications and enforcement   185
                  Competition issues   186
                  The Financial Services Authority's approach   188
                  The future   188
                LLOYD'S   189
                  The approach of the Financial Services Authority   192
                PROFESSIONAL FIRMS   194
                  The Designated Professional Bodies regime   195

The approach of the Financial Services Authority 197

Chapter 12 **PUBLIC OFFERS AND LISTINGS** 199
BACKGROUND 199
THE UK LISTING AUTHORITY 201
ADMISSION TO LISTING FOR UK COMPANIES 202
  Prospectuses and other applications for listing 204
  Continuing obligations 205
  Separating out the UKLA 205
THE FINANCIAL SERVICES AND MARKETS ACT 2000
  AND SANCTIONS 207
  Reprimands, fines and crimes 208
  Compensation 209
  Persons responsible 211
  Common-law actions 212
UNLISTED SECURITIES 212
  Private placements 214

Chapter 13 **MARKETING IN GENERAL AND COLLECTIVE**
    INVESTMENT SCHEMES 217
MARKETING IN GENERAL 217
  Commercial companies 217
  Exempt businesses 218
  Authorised firms 219
THE BACKGROUND TO COLLECTIVE INVESTMENT
  SCHEMES 220
  The approach of the Financial Services Authority 221
MARKETING COLLECTIVE INVESTMENT SCHEMES 222
AUTHORISED AND RECOGNISED SCHEMES 224
  Authorised unit trusts 224
  Authorised open-ended investment company 226
  Recognised schemes 229
  Exempt and unregulated schemes 230
INVESTIGATING COLLECTIVE INVESTMENT
  SCHEMES 231

Chapter 14 **CONCLUSION** 233

Appendix **THE FINANCIAL SERVICES AND MARKETS ACT 2000** 237

INDEX 545

TABLE OF CASES

References are to paragraph numbers.

A Solicitor, Re [1993] QB 69 — 2.4
Al Nakib Investments (Jersey) Ltd v Longcroft [1990] 3 All ER 321 — 12.4.4
Albert and Le Compte v Belgium (1983) Ser A No 58 — 2.4
Alpine Investment BV v Minister van Financien (Case C384/93) [1995] ECR
    I-1141, [1995] 2 CMLR 209 — 2.3.2, 2.3.3, 2.3.4
APB v IRMO (Appl 30552/96) 15 January 1998 — 2.4
Attorney-General for Hong Kong v Reid [1994] 1 All ER 1 — 7.1

Basic v Levinson 485 US 224 (1988) — 7.5.2, 12.4.2
Benham v United Kingdom (1996) 22 EHRR 293 — 2.4
British Eagle International Airlines v Cie National Air France [1975] 1 WLR 758 — 11.2.2
Brown v United Kingdom (1998, unreported) — 2.4

Commission v France [1986] ECR 3663 — 2.1
Commission v Germany [1986] ECR 3755 — 2.1

Daniels v Anderson (1995) 16 ACSR 607 — 5.3.2
De Moor v Belgium (1994) Ser A No 292 — 2.4
Demicoli v Malta (1992) 14 EHRR 47 — 2.4
Derbyshire County Council v Times Newspapers Ltd [1992] 1 QB 770, *affirmed* in
    [1993] AC 534 — 2.4
Derry v Peek (1889) 14 App Cas 337 — 12.4.4

Elliot v Southwark LBC [1976] 1 WLR 499 — 9.3.1
Engel v The Netherlands (1976) 1 EHRR 647 — 2.4
Ernst and Ernst v Hochfelder 425 US 185 (1976) — 9.3.4
Escott v Bar-Chris Construction 283 F Supp 643 (SDNY 1968) — 12.4.3, 12.5

Gluckstein v Barnes [1900] AC 240 — 7.1
Guchez v Belgium (1984) 40 DR 100 — 2.4

Hornal v Neuberger [1957] 1 QB 247, CA — 2.4

Keck and Mithouard (Cases C-267/91 and C-268/91), (1995) 72 CMLR 101 — 2.3.2, 2.3.4
Kelly v Cooper [1992] AC 205 — 6.2.1
Kokkinakis v Greece (1993) 17 EHRR 397 — 2.4
Konig v Germany (1978) Ser A No 27 — 2.4

Lauko v Slovakia (2 September 1998, unreported) — 2.4

Meridian Global Funds Management Asia Ltd v Securities Commission [1995] 2
    AC 550 — 4.2.1
Murray v United Kingdom (1996) 22 EHRR 29 — 2.4

Oriel Ltd, Re [1986] 1 WLR 180   4.2.2
Osman v UK [1999] FLR 193   2.4, 3.4.4
Ozturk v Germany (1984) 6 EHRR 409   2.4

Percival v Wright [1902] 2 Ch 421   7.1
Peter James West and Paul Bingham, *In the matter of* (published decision, 18
     November 1994)   2.4
Possfund Custodian Ltd v Diamond [1996] 2 All ER 774   12.4.2, 12.4.4, 12.5
Poyser and Mills' Arbitration, Re [1964] 2 QB 467   9.3.1
Prince Jefri Bolkiah v KPMG [1999] 1 All ER 517   6.2.1
Pudas v Sweden (1988) 10 EHRR 380   2.4

Ravnsborg v Sweden (1994) 18 EHRR 38   2.4
Regal (Hastings) Ltd v Gulliver [1942] 1 All ER 378   7.1
R v Dacorum Gaming Licensing Committee, ex p EMI Cinemas and Leisure Ltd
     [1971] 3 All ER 666   3.3
R v de Berenger (1814) 105 Eng Rep 536   7.1
R v Ghosh [1982] QB 1053   7.2.1
R v Immigration, ex p Khan [1983] QB 790   9.3.1
R v Maidstone Crown Court, ex p Olson [1992] COD 496   2.4
R v Panel on Takeovers and Mergers, ex p Datafin plc [1987] QB 815   3.4
R v Secretary of State for the Home Department, ex p Brind [1991] 1 AC 696   2.4
R v Secretary of State for Trade and Industry, ex p R [1989] 1 WLR 372   10.2
R v Secretary of State for Transport, ex p Factortame (No 2) [1991] 1 All ER 70   2.4
R v Spens [1991] 4 All ER 421   7.2.1
R v The International Stock Exchange of the United Kingdom and the Republic
     of Ireland Limited, ex p Else (1982) Ltd [1993] BCC 11, CA   12.3, 12.4
Rewe-Zentral AG v Bundesmonopolverwaltung für Branntwein (Case 120/78)
     [1979] ECR 649, [1979] 3 CMLR 494   2.1
Rowe and Davis v United Kingdom (Case 28901/95) (16 February 2000,
     unreported)   2.4, 9.3.1

Sager v Dennemayer [1991] ECR I-4229   2.2
Salabiaku v France (1988) 13 EHRR 379   2.4
Salamon v Warner (1891) 65 LT 132   7.1
Saunders v United Kingdom (1996) 23 EHRR 313   2.4, 10.2.1
Scher v Policyholders Protection Board [1993] 3 All ER 384   2.2.1
Scott v Brown, Doering, McNab & Co [1892] 2 QB 724   7.1
Selangor United Rubber Estates Ltd v Cradock (No 3) [1968] 2 All ER 1073   7.1
SIB v Lloyd Wright [1993] 4 All ER 210   9.2.2
SIB v Pantell [1990] Ch 426   9.2.2, 9.3.5
SIB v Pantell SA (No 2) [1993] 1 All ER 134   9.2.2
SIB v Scandex Capital Management [1998] 1 WLR 712   9.2.2, 9.3.5
Silicon Graphics Inc, In re 970 F. Supp 746 (1997)   9.3.4
Smith New Court Services Ltd v Scrimgeour Vickers (Asset Management) Ltd
     [1996] 4 All ER 769   12.4.4

Three Rivers District Council v Bank of England (No 3) [1996] 3 All ER 558   3.4.4
Tinnelly and McElduff v United Kingdom (1966) 22 EHRR CD 62   2.4

Van Binsbergen v Bestuur van de Bedrijfsvereniging Voor de Metaalnijverheid
[1974] ECR 1299
2.1

Wickramsinghe v United Kingdom (Appl 31503/96) 8 December 1997 2.4
Wings v Ellis [1985] AC 272 9.2.1

US v O'Hagan 117 S Ct 2199 (1997) 7.1, 7.3.2

X v United Kingdom (Appl 28530/95) 18 January 1998 2.4

TABLE OF STATUTES

References are to paragraph numbers.

Bank of England Act 1998	3.1, 4.2.1	s 60	
s 3	3.2	(1)	7.3.1
s 31	1.4.1, 1.5.3	(2)	7.3.3
Banking Act 1979	1.2.4	(4)	7.3.3
Banking Act 1987	1.2.4, 1.5.1, 3.1, 4.3.1,	s 61	7.3
	4.3.2, 6.1, 6.4.1, 9.2.1	s 62	7.3.1
s 35	7.1	s 63(2)	7.1, 7.3
s 39	10.2	Sch 1	7.5.2
Sch 3	5.2.1, 6.3	para 5(1)	6.4.3
Borrowing (Controls and			
Guarantees) Act 1946	1.2.4		
Building Societies Act 1986	1.2.6, 3.1,		
	5.2.7, 6.4.1	Data Protection Act 1998	8.2.1
Companies Act 1980	7.1	European Communities Act 1972	2.4, 8.3
Companies Act 1985	3.2, 12.1, 13.3	s 2(2)	2.2
s 432	10.1, 10.2	Exchange Control Act 1947	1.2.4
s 741	3.2		
Companies Act 1989			
Part VII	11.2.2		
s 170	11.2.2	Fair Trading Act 1973	3.4.3
Competition Act 1998	11.2.4	Financial Services Act 1986	1.3, 1.4, 1.4.1,
s 2	3.4.3		1.5.1, 3.1, 4.1, 4.2, 4.3.1, 4.3.2,
s 3	3.4.3		5.1, 6.1, 7.1, 8.1, 9.2.2
s 18	3.4.3	s 1	4.2.2
s 19	3.4.3	(3)	2.3.2
Sch 3, para 5	3.4.3	s 2	4.2.2
Consumer Credit Act 1974	1.2.4, 4.1,	s 3	4.1
	4.3.2, 5.2.4	s 31	5.2.4
Credit Unions Act 1979	3.1	s 32	5.2.4
Criminal Justice Act 1993		ss 36–42	11.1
Part V	7.1, 9.3, 10.4	s 47	7.2.2
s 52(1)–(2)	7.3	(1)	7.1
(3)	7.3.1	(2)	7.1
s 53	7.3.2	s 56	2.3.2, 4.2, 4.2.3
(3)(a)	7.3, 7.3.4	s 57	2.3.2, 4.1, 4.2, 4.2.3
s 54(2)	7.3.1	(2)	4.2.3
s 55	7.3.1	s 58	4.2, 4.2.3
s 56	7.3.3	s 62	6.2.2, 7.1
s 57	7.3.2	s 62A	6.2.2
s 58		s 76	13.3, 13.4.4
(1)	7.3.4	s 83	6.2.1
(2)	7.3.3, 7.5.2	s 105	10.2
(3)	7.3.3, 7.5.3	s 130	4.2
(6)	7.3.4	s 131	4.2
s 59	7.3.1, 9.2.2	s 133	7.1

Financial Services Act 1986 – *cont*

s 136	4.2.3
s 137	4.2.3
s 142	
(6)	1.5.1
(7)	12.4.3
s 152(1)(a)–(e)	12.4.3
(2)–(5)	12.4.3
s 154A(b)	12.4.3
s 177	10.1, 10.2
s 191	4.2.2, 4.3.4
s 200	7.2.2
s 207	
(2)	4.2.3
(3)	4.2.3
Sch 1, Part IV	2.3.2, 12.1

Financial Services and Markets Act

2000	1.5.2, 1.6.1, 1.7
s 2	1.6, 6.1
(1)	3.3
(2)	3.3
(3)	3.3
(g)	3.3.2
(4)	3.3
(5)	3.3
(6)	3.3
s 3	1.6
s 4	1.6
s 5	1.6, 3.4.2, 6.3.2
(2)(a)	3.3.1
(b)	3.3.1
(d)	3.3.1
(3)	3.3.1, 3.4.1
s 6	1.6
(1)	3.3.1, 7.6
(2)	3.3.1
(3)	3.3.1, 7.6
(4)	3.3.1
(5)	3.3.1
s 7	3.2
s 8	3.4.1
s 9	3.4.1
s 10	3.4.1
s 12	3.4.2
s 13	3.4.2
s 14	3.4.2
(3)	12.2
s 15	3.4.2
s 16	3.4.2
s 17	3.4.2
s 18	3.4.2
s 19	4.2, 4.2.2, 9.2

s 20	4.2.1, 5.1, 10.5.2
s 21	1.2.3, 4.2, 4.2.3, 6.2.1, 9.2, 12.5.1, 13.1.1, 13.1.3, 13.3
(4)–(15)	4.2, 4.2.3
(13)	13.1.2
(22)	4.2
s 22	4.2.2, 4.2.3
s 23	4.2.1, 6.2.3, 9.2.1
(1)	10.1
s 24	6.2.3, 9.2.1
s 25	6.2.3, 9.2.1, 13.1.2, 13.3
(1)	10.1
s 26	6.2.3, 10.5.1
(4)	10.5.1
s 27	6.2.3, 10.5.1
s 28	6.2.3, 10.5.1
(8)	10.5.1
s 29	6.2.3, 10.5.1
(1)	11.2.3
(5)	11.2.3
(6)	11.2.3
s 30	6.2.3, 10.5.1, 13.1.2
(13)	10.5.1
s 31	5.2
s 32	5.2
s 33	5.2, 9.3
s 34	5.2
s 35	5.2
s 36	5.2
s 37	5.2.4
s 38	4.2.1
(2)	4.2.1
s 39	4.2.1
(1)	4.2.1
(a)	4.2.1
(6)	4.2.1
s 40(1)	5.2.1
(2)	5.2.2
(3)	5.2
s 41	5.2.1
(3)	5.2.1
s 42	5.2.1, 5.2.2
(3)–(5)	4.2.1
s 43	5.2.2, 6.2.2
s 44	5.2.2, 5.2.3
(4)	5.2
s 45	6.2.2, 9.3
(1)	9.3.6
(2)	9.3.6
(3)	9.3, 9.3.6
(4)	9.3.6
s 47(1)–(6)	9.3.7
s 48	5.2.2, 9.3.6
s 49	5.2.2, 9.3.6

Financial Services and Markets Act
2000 – *cont*

s 49(1)	5.2.1
(2)	5.2.1
(3)	5.2.1
s 50	5.2.4, 9.3.6
(1)	5.2
s 51	5.2.3
s 52	5.2.3
(4)	5.2.3
(5)	5.2.3
s 53	9.3.1, 9.3.6
s 54	9.3.1, 9.3.6
s 55	6.2.2, 9.3.1
(1)	5.2.3
s 56	9.2.2, 9.3, 11.4.1
s 57	9.3.1, 9.3.3
s 58	9.3.1, 9.3.3
s 59(1)	5.3
(2)	5.3
(3)–(9)	5.3
(10)	5.3
(11)	5.3
s 60	5.3
s 61	5.3
(1)	5.3
(2)	5.3
s 62	5.3, 9.3.1, 9.3.3
s 63	9.3, 9.3.1
s 64	5.4, 6.5
(2)	6.2.3
(3)	6.5.1
(7)	6.5.1
(8)	10.5.2
s 65	6.1, 6.5
s 66	2.4, 6.5
(1)	9.3.4
(b)	9.3
(2)	9.3.4
(b)	6.2.2
s 67	9.3.1, 9.3.4
s 68	9.3.1
(1)	9.3.1
s 69	9.3.4
(2)	9.3.4
s 70	9.3.4
s 71	10.5.2
(2)	10.5.2
s 72	12.2
s 73	12.2
s 74	
(1)–(3)	12.2
(4)	12.3
s 75	12.3

s 75(6)	12.3.1
s 76	12.3
s 77	12.4
s 78	9.3.1, 12.4
s 79	12.3
(1)(b)	12.3.1
(3)	12.4.3
s 80	12.4.2
(1)–(4)	12.3, 12.5
s 81	12.3, 12.4.2
s 82	12.3, 12.4.2
s 83	12.3
(3)–(4)	12.4.1
s 84	12.3.1
s 85(1)–(3)	12.4.1
(5)	12.4.2
s 86	12.3, 12.3.1
s 88	9.3.1, 12.4
s 89	9.3.1, 12.4, 12.4.1
s 90	12.4.2
(1)(b)	12.4.2
(2)	12.4.2
(6)	12.4.2
(7)	12.4.2
(8)	12.4.2
s 91	2.4, 12.4.1
s 92	9.3.1, 12.4.1
s 93	9.3.4, 12..4.1
(2)	9.3.4
s 94	9.3.4, 12.4.1
s 95	12.2
s 96	12.4
s 97	12.4.1
s 98	12.3
(2)–(5)	12.4.1
s 99	12.2
s 100	12.4.1
s 101	12.3
s 102	12.2
s 103(1)	12.3
s 104	5.2.7
s 105	5.2.7
s 106	5.2.7
s 107	5.2.7
s 108	5.2.7
s 109	5.2.7
s 110	5.2.7
s 111	5.2.7
s 112	5.2.7
s 113	5.2.7
s 114	5.2.7
(8)	10.4.1

Financial Services and Markets Act
   2000 – *cont*

s 115	5.2.7
s 116	5.2.7
s 117	5.2.7
s 118	
(1)	7.3.4
(c)	10.4.1
(2)	7.4
(3)	7.4
(4)	7.4
(5)	7.4
(6)	7.4
(7)	7.4.1
(8)	6.4.3, 7.4, 7.4.1
(9)	7.4
(10)	7.4, 10.4.1
s 119(1)–(3)	7.5
s 120	7.5
s 121	6.1
s 122	7.5, 10.4.1
s 123	1.6, 10.4
(1)	7.4, 7.4.2
(2)	7.4.1, 10.4.1
(3)	7.4, 7.4.1
s 124	7.4.2, 10.4.1
(2)	9.3.4, 10.4.1
s 125	10.4.1
s 126	9.3.1, 10.4.1
s 127	9.3.1, 10.4.1
s 128	10.4
s 129	10.4.1
s 130	10.4
s 131	10.4.2
s 132	3.5, 3.5.1
s 133	3.5, 3.5.1, 9.3.1
(1)	3.5.1
(a)	9.3.1
(2)	3.5.1
(9)	9.3.1
s 134	3.5.1, 10.4.1
s 135	3.5.1, 10.4.1
s 136	3.5.1, 10.4.1
s 137	3.5, 9.3.1, 10.4.1
s 138	6.2, 11.4.1
(1)(a)	6.2
(b)	6.2, 6.31
(4)	6.2
(5)	6.2, 6.3.1
(6)	6.2
(7)	3.3.1
(a)	6.2
(b)	6.2

s 138(7)(c)	6.2
s 139	6.2
s 140	6.2.1, 13.4.1
s 141(1)–(4)	6.2.1
s 142	6.2.1
s 143	6.2.1
(7)	6.2.4
(8)	6.2.4
s 144	6.2.1, 6.4.3
(3)	6.4.3
s 145	4.2.3, 13.1.3
s 146	6.2.1, 7.6, 9.3, 10.4.2
s 147	6.2.1, 9.3.1
s 148	13.4.1
(6)–(8)	6.2.2
s 149	6.2.3
s 150	6.2.2, 7.6, 10.5.2, 13.3
(4)	12.4.2
s 151	6.2.2, 6.2.3, 10.5.2
(2)	6.2.2
s 152	6.2.3
s 153	6.2.3
s 154	6.2.4
s 155	6.1
(1)–(12)	6.2.4
s 156	6.2.4
s 157(1)	6.2.3
(2)	6.2.3
(3)	6.1
(4)	6.2.4
(5)	6.2.3
s 158	6.2.4
s 159	3.4.3
s 160(1)	3.4.3
s 161	3.4.3
s 162(1)	3.4.3
s 163	3.4.4
s 164	3.4.3
s 165	10.2
(4)	10.2
(7)	10.2
(8)	10.2
(11)	10.2
s 166	10.2
(5)–(6)	10.2
s 167	10.2
(2)	10.2
(4)	10.2
s 168	10.1, 10.2
(2)	10.2
(b)–(c)	10.1
(3)	10.1
s 169	9.3.7

Financial Services and Markets Act		s 209(1)	9.3.1
2000 – *cont*		s 210	9.3.4
s 169(1)	9.3.7	(2)	9.3.4
s 170	10.2	s 212	8.3
s 171	10.2	s 213	8.3
s 172	10.2	(10)	8.3
(2)	10.2	s 214	8.3
s 173	10.1	(5)	8.3
s 174	10.2.1	(6)	8.3
(1)	10.2.1	s 215	8.3
(2)	10.4.1	s 216	8.3
s 175	10.2	s 217	8.3
s 176	10.1, 10.2	s 218	8.3
(4)	10.1	s 219	8.3
s 177	10.1, 10.2	s 220	8.3
s 178(2)	5.2.6	s 221	8.3
s 179	5.2.6	s 222	8.3
s 180	5.2.6	s 223	8.3
s 181	5.2.6	s 224	8.3
s 182	5.2.6	s 225	8.2
s 183	5.2.6	s 226	8.2.1
s 184	5.2.6	s 227	8.2.1
s 185	5.2.6	s 228	8.2.1
s 186	5.2.6	s 229	8.2.1
(2)	5.2.6	s 230	8.2.1
(3)	5.2.6	s 231	8.2.1
s 187	5.2.6	s 232	8.2.1
(3)	5.2.6	s 233	8.2.1, 8.3
s 188	5.2.6	s 234	8.2.1, 8.2.3
s 189	5.2.6	s 235	13.3
s 190	5.2.6	s 236	13.4.2
(2)	5.2.6	(4)	13.3, 13.4
s 191	5.2.6	s 237(1)	13.4.1
s 192	5.2.6	(2)	13.4.2
s 193	9.3.7	s 238	6.2.2, 13.1.3, 13.3
s 194	9.3.7	(3)	13.3
s 195	9.3.7	s 239(1)–(3)	13.4.4
(4)	9.3.7	(4)–(5)	13.4.4
s 196	9.3.7	s 240	13.3
s 197	9.3.1, 9.3.7	s 241	10.5.2, 13.3
s 198	9.3.7	s 242	13.4.1
s 199	9.3.7	s 243	13.4.1, 13.4.2
s 200	9.3.1, 9.3.7	(2)	13.4.1
s 201	9.3.7	s 244	13.4.1
s 202	10.5.2	s 245	9.3.1, 13.4.1
(2)	10.5.2	s 246	13.4.1
s 203	9.3.7	s 247	13.4.1
s 204	9.3.7	s 248	13.4.1
s 205	6.2.2, 9.3	s 249	9.3.1
s 206	6.2.2, 9.3	s 250	13.4.1, 13.4.2
(2)	9.3	s 251	13.4.1
s 207	9.3.1, 9.3.4	s 252	9.3.1, 13.4.1
s 208	9.3.1, 9.3.4	s 253	13.4.1
s 209	9.3.1	s 255	9.3.1

Financial Services and Markets Act
  2000 – *cont*
s 256   13.4.1
s 257   13.4.1
s 258   13.4.1
s 259   9.3.1, 13.4.1
s 260   9.3.1, 13.4.1
s 261   9.3.1, 13.4.1
s 262(1)–(3)   13.4.2
s 263   13.4.2
s 264   5.2.4, 13.4.3
s 265   9.3.1, 13.4.3
s 266   13.4.3
s 267   13.4.3
s 268   9.3.1, 13.4.3
s 270   13.4.3
s 271   9.3.1, 13.4.3
s 272   13.4.3
s 273   13.4.3
s 274   13.4.3
s 275   13.4.3
s 276   9.3.1, 13.4.3
s 277   13.4.3
s 278   13.4.3
s 279   13.4.3
s 280   9.3.1, 13.4.3
s 281   13.4.3
s 282   9.3.1, 13.4.3
s 283   13.4.3
s 284   13.5
s 285   4.2.1, 11.2, 11.2.3
s 286   11.2, 11.2.2
s 287   11.2.3
s 288   11.2.3
s 289   11.2.3
s 290   11.2.3
s 291   11.2
s 292   11.2
s 293   11.2.3
   (8)   11.2
s 294   11.2.3
s 295   11.2.3
s 296   11.2.3
s 297   11.2.3
s 298   11.2.3
s 299   11.2.3
s 300   11.2.1
s 301   5.2.5
s 302(1)   11.2.4
s 303(1)   11.2.4
   (2)   11.2.4
   (3)   11.2.4
   (4)   11.2.4
s 304   11.2.4

s 305   11.2.4
s 306   11.2.4
s 307   11.2.3, 11.2.4
s 308   11.2.4
s 309   11.2.4
s 310   11.2.4
s 311   11.2.4
s 312   11.2.4
s 313(1)   11.2
s 314   11.3
s 315   4.2.1, 5.1, 11.3
   (3)   11.3
s 316   4.2.1, 11.3
   (4)   11.3
   (9)–(11)   11.3
s 317   11.3
s 318   11.3
   (4)   11.3
   (7)–(9)   11.3
s 319   4.2.1, 11.3
s 320   11.3
s 321   9.3.1, 11.3
s 322   11.3
s 323   5.2.7
s 324   11.3
s 325   11.4.1
s 326   11.4.1
s 327(6)   11.4.1
   (7)   4.2.1
s 328   11.4.1
s 329   11.4.1
s 330   11.4.1
s 331   9.3.1, 11.4.1
s 332   11.4.1
s 333   9.2.1, 11.4.1
s 334   3.1
s 338   3.1
s 339   3.1
s 340   10.3
s 341   10.3
s 342   10.3
s 343   10.3
s 344   10.3
s 345   9.3.1, 10.3
s 346   10.3
s 347   5.2, 5.2.1, 5.3, 5.3.1, 9.3.4, 13.4
s 348   10.2.1
s 349   10.2.1
s 350   10.2.1
s 351   3.4.3
s 352   10.2.1
s 353   10.2.1
s 354   10.2.1

Financial Services and Markets Act
2000 – *cont*

s 355	9.4.3
s 356	9.4.1
s 357	9.4.1
s 358	9.4.1
s 359	9.4.1
(1)(c)	9.2.2
s 360	9.4.3
s 362	9.4.2
s 363	9.4.2
s 364	9.4.2
s 365	9.4.2
s 366	9.4.2, 9.4.3
s 367	9.4.1, 9.4.2
(1)(c)	9.2.2
s 368	9.4.1
s 369	9.4.3
s 370	9.4.2
s 372	9.3.6
(1)	9.2.2
(7)(b)	9.2.2
s 373	9.4.2
s 374	9.4.2
s 376	9.4.3
s 377	9.4.3
s 378	9.4.3
s 379	9.4.3
s 380	9.2.2, 9.3.5, 9.3.6, 10.4, 10.4.1
(2)	9.2.2, 9.3.5
(3)	9.2.2, 9.3.5
(6)	9.2.2
s 381	9.3.4, 10.4, 10.4.1
s 382	9.2.2, 9.3.4, 9.3.6, 10.4, 12.4.1, 12.5.1
(1)	9.2.2, 9.3.5, 10.4.2
(3)–(8)	9.3.5
(9)	9.2.2
s 383	9.3.4, 10.4, 10.4.1
(1)	10.4.2
(b)	9.3.5
(3)	10.4.2
(5)–(10)	9.3.5
s 384	6.2.2, 9.3, 9.3.4, 10.4, 12.4.2
(1)	9.3.5, 10.4.2
(2)(b)	9.3.5
(5)	9.3.5
(6)	9.3.5, 10.4.2
s 385	9.3.1, 9.3.5, 10.4
s 386	9.3.1, 9.3.5, 10.4
s 387	9.3.1
(1)(c)	9.3.1
s 388	9.3.1
(1)(b)	9.3.1
s 388(3)–(5)	9.3.1
s 389	9.3.1
s 390	9.3.1
s 391(8)	9.3.1
s 392	9.3.1, 9.3.4, 9.3.5, 9.3.6, 10.3, 10.4, 12.4, 12.4.1, 13.4.3
s 394	9.3.1
s 395	9.3.1
(2)–(4)	9.3.1
(11)–(12)	9.3.1
(13)	9.3.1
s 396	9.3.1
s 397	1.6, 7.1, 7.3.4, 9.2.1, 10.4
(1)(a)–(c)	7.2
(2)	7.2
(3)	7.2.2
(4)	6.4.3
(5)	6.4.3, 7.2.2
(b)–(c)	6.4.3
(6)	7.2.2
(7)	7.2.2
(9)	7.2
(10)	7.2, 7.2.2
(11)	7.2, 7.2.2
s 398	7.2.2, 9.3
s 399	3.4.3
s 400	7.2.2, 9.2.1
s 401	1.6, 9.3, 10.4
(2)	7.2
(5)	9.2.2
(6)	9.2.2
s 402	1.6, 9.2.1, 9.3, 10.4
(1)	10.4.3
(a)	7.3
(b)	7.6
s 404	3.4.2, 9.3.6
s 405	5.2.5
s 406	5.2.5
s 407	5.2.5
s 408	5.2.5
s 409	5.2
s 410	5.2.5
s 411	3.2, 3.5.1, 8.3
s 412	10.5.2
s 413	3.4.2, 3.4.3, 8.2.1, 8.3, 13.5
s 415	3.3.2
s 416	3.1
s 417	4.2.1
s 418	4.2.2
s 419	4.2.2
s 420	5.2.1
s 421	5.2.1
s 422	5.2.6, 9.2.1, 10.2
s 424	3.1

Financial Services and Markets Act
  2000 – *cont*
  s 426   3.4.2, 5.2
  s 427   5.2
  s 429(1)   3.4.2, 13.4.2
        (a)   4.2.2
      (3)   4.2.3
      (5)   4.2.1
  Sch 1   3.2
      para 1   3.2
          (2)   6.1
      para 2   3.2
      para 3   3.2
          (1)   3.2
      para 4   3.2
      para 5   3.2
          (2)   6.1, 6.2.3
      para 6   3.2
          (2)   3.3.2
      para 7   3.4.4
      para 8   3.4.4
          (1)   3.4.4
          (3)   3.4.4
          (5)   3.4.4
          (9)   3.4.4
      para 9   3.4.2
      para 10   3.4.2, 6.1
          (4)   3.2
      para 11   3.4.2
      para 12   3.4.2
      para 13   3.2
      para 16   3.2
      para 17   9.3.4
      para 19   2.4, 3.4.4
      para 20   3.2
      para 21   3.2
  Sch 2   4.2.2
      Parts I and II   4.2.2, 7.3.1
  Sch 3
      para 15   9.3.7
      para 17   5.2.4
      para 18   5.2.4
      para 21   5.2.4
      para 22   5.2.4
  Sch 4   2.2.3, 5.2.5
  Sch 5   5.2.5
  Sch 6   11.4.2
      paras 1–5   5.2.1
  Sch 7   12.2
      para 2   12.2
  Sch 9   12.3.1
  Sch 10, paras 1–8   12.4.2, 12.5
      para 12   13.1.1
  Sch 11, paras 1–25   12.3.1

Sch 12, Parts I, II and III   5.2.7
Sch 13, paras 1–5   3.5.1
      para 6   3.5.1
      para 7   3.5.1
      paras 8–12   3.5.1
      para 13   3.5.1
Sch 16   9.3.7
Sch 17, para 2   8.2
      para 3   8.2
      para 4   8.2
      para 5   8.2
      para 6   8.2
      para 7   8.2
      para 8   8.2.1
      para 9   8.2
      para 10   8.2
      para 11   8.2
      para 12   8.2.1
      para 13   8.2.1, 8.2.3
      para 14   8.2.1
      para 15   8.2.1, 8.2.3
      para 16   8.2.1
      paras 17–22   8.2.1
Sch 18, Parts I and II   3.1
Sch 19   3.4.3
Sch 20   3.1, 3.5.1
Friendly Societies Act 1793   1.1, 3.1
Friendly Societies Acts 1974, 1981,
  1984   3.1
Friendly Societies Act 1992   1.2.6, 3.1,
                                    5.2.7
  s 56   6.2.1

Glass-Steagall Act 1933   1.1

Human Rights Act 1998
  s 2   2.4
  s 3(1)–(2)   2.4
  s 4   2.4
  s 6   2.4
  s 19   2.4

Income and Corporation Taxes
  Act 1988
  s 842   13.2
Industrial Assurance Acts 1923–
  1948   3.1
Industrial and Provident Societies
  Act 1979   1.2.6, 3.1
Insider Dealing Act 1985   7.1
Insurance Brokers (Registration)
  Act 1977   1.2.5, 3.1
Insurance Companies Act 1982   1.2.5, 1.3,
            1.4.3, 1.5.1, 3.1, 4.3.2, 6.4.1

Insurance Companies Act 1982 –
   cont
   s 3   1.4
   s 6   2.2.1
   s 16   6.2.1
   s 29   6.2.1
   s 56   1.4, 6.2.1
   s 57   1.4
   s 114   1.4.1
   Sch 2A   6.3
Investment Advisers Act 1940   1.1
Investment Company Act 1940   1.1

Lloyd's Act 1982   1.3

Police and Criminal Evidence Act
   1984   3.4.2, 10.2.1
Policyholders Protection Act 1975   1.6,
    3.1, 6.4.1
   s 4(1)   2.2.1
Policyholders Protection Act 1997   3.1,
    8.3.1
   s 2(1)   2.2.1
Prevention of Fraud (Investments)
   Act 1939   1.2.5, 13.2
   s 13   7.1
Prevention of Fraud (Investments)
   Act 1958   1.3, 1.4

s 7   5.1
Public Utility Holding Company
   Act 1935   1.1

Restrictive Trade Practices (Stock
   Exchange) Act 1984   1.3

Sale of Goods Act 1979
   s 14   3.3.1
Securities Act 1933   1.1
   s 11   12.4.3
   (b)   12.4.3, 12.5
Securities Exchange Act 1934   1.1

Taxation of Chargeable Gains Act
   1992
   s 100   13.2
Theft Act 1968
   s 1   7.1
   s 15   7.1
   s 17   7.1
Trade Descriptions Act 1968   9.2.1
Tribunal and Inquiries Act 1992
   s 8(1)   3.5.1
Trust Indenture Act 1939   1.1

TABLE OF STATUTORY INSTRUMENTS AND CODES

References are to paragraph numbers.

Statutory Instruments

Banking Act 1987 (Exempt Transactions) Regulations 1997, SI 1997/817	4.3.4
Banking Act (Advertisements) Regulations 1988, SI 1988/645	4.1
Financial Markets and Insolvency (Settlement Finality) Regulations 1999, SI 1999/2979	11.2.6
Financial Services Act 1986 (Delegation Order) 1987, SI 1987/942	1.4.1
Financial Services Act 1986 (Restriction of Right of Action) Regulations 1991, SI 1991/489	10.5
Financial Services Act 1986 (Single Property Schemes) (Exemption) Regulations 1989, SI 1989/28	13.4.4
Insider Dealing (Securities and Regulated Markets) Order 1994, SI 1994/187	7.3.1
Insurance Companies (Accounts and Statements) Regulations 1996, SI 1996/943	6.4.1
Insurance Companies Regulations 1994, SI 1994/1516	4.1, 6.4.1
Insurance Companies (Reserves) Regulations 1996, SI 1996/946	6.4.1
Money Laundering Regulations 1993, SI 1993/1933	7.6, 9.3, 10.4.3
Official Listing of Securities (Change of Competent Authority) Regulations 1991, SI 1991/2000	1.5.1
Official Listing of Securities (Change of Competent Authority) Regulations 2000, SI 2000/968	12.1
Open-Ended Investment Companies (Investment Companies with Variable Capital) Regulations 1996, SI 1996/2827	2.2.4, 13.4.2
reg 3	13.4.2
reg 4	13.4.2
reg 5	13.4.2
reg 6	13.4.2
reg 7	13.4.2
reg 8	13.4.2
reg 9	13.4.2
reg 10	13.4.2
reg 11	13.4.2
reg 12	13.4.2
reg 13	13.4.2
reg 14	13.4.2
reg 15	13.4.2
reg 21	13.4.2
reg 23	13.4.2
reg 24	13.4.2
reg 25	13.4.2

Open-Ended Investment Companies (Investment Companies with Variable
  Capital) Regulations 1996 – *cont*
  reg 26–29   13.4.2
  reg 30   13.5
  reg 34(4)(b)   13.4.2
Open-Ended Investment Companies (Investment Companies with Variable
  Capital) Regulations 1997, SI 1997/1154   13.4.2

Public Offers of Securities Regulations 1995, SI 1995/153   12.1
  reg 3   12.5
  reg 4(1)–(2)   12.5
  reg 5   12.5
  reg 6   12.5
  reg 7(2)(k)   13.1.1
  reg 8(4)–(6)   12.5
  reg 9(1)   12.5
  reg 10   12.5
  reg 11   12.5
  reg 14   12.5
  reg 16   12.5
  Sch 4   12.5
Public Offers of Securities (Amendment) Regulations 1999, SI 1999/734   12.1
  reg 2   12.5
  reg 3   12.4.3
Public Offers of Securities (Amendment) (No 2) Regulations 1999, SI 1999/
  1146   12.5.1

Tracked Securities (Disclosure) Regulations 1994, SI 1994/188
  Art 3   11.2.1
Transfer of Functions (Financial Services) Order 1992, SI 1992/1315   1.4.1

Codes

City Code on Takeovers and Mergers   1.2.3, 1.4.3, 6.2.1, 6.3, 7.4.2
  rule 2.2   7.3.3
Code of Market Conduct   6.3.1, 6.3.2, 7.4, 7.5, 7.5.1
Code for Crown Prosecutors   9.2.1, 10.4.1
Code for Non-Investment Products   6.3.2
Common Unsolicited Calls Regulations 1991   4.3.5

Financial Services (Change of Name of Designated Agency) Rules 1997, SIB,
  20 October 1997   1.5
Financial Services (Client Money) Regulations 1991   6.4.2
Financial Services (Dedesignation) Rules and Regulations 1994   1.4.3
Financial Services (Notification of Recognised Bodies) Regulations 1995   11.2.5
Financial Services (Open-Ended Investment Companies) (Amendment) (No 1)
  Regulations 2000   13.2.1

Inter-Professional Code   6.3.1

Money Laundering Rules
  rule 1   7.6
  rule 2   7.6
  rule 3   7.6
  rule 4   7.6
  rule 5
    5.1   7.6
    5.2   7.6
  rule 6   7.6
  rule 7   7.6
  rule 8.1   7.6
  rule 9   7.6

Substantial Acquisition Rules   6.2.1

TABLE OF EUROPEAN LEGISLATION

References are to paragraph number.

Treaties

EC Treaty 1957 (Treaty of Rome)	2.4
Art 49	2.1, 2.3.4
Art 81	3.4.3
European Convention on Human Rights and Fundamental Freedoms	2.4
Art 6	2.4
(1)	2.4, 3.5, 8.1.1, 8.2.1, 9.3, 10.2.1
(2)	2.4
(3)(a)–(c)	2.4
Art 7	2.4
(1)	2.4

Directives

Directive 73/239/EEC (first non-life insurance)	1.2.5, 2.2.1
Art 15	9.3.7
Art 16(3)	9.3.7
Art 17	9.3.7
Art 20(5)	9.3.7
Art 29b(4)	5.2.5
Directive 77/780/EEC (first banking co-ordination)	1.2.4, 2.2.2
Directive 79/267/EEC (first life insurance)	1.2.5, 2.2.1
Art 17	9.3.7
Art 19	9.3.7
Art 20	9.3.7
Art 24(5)	9.3.7
Art 32b(4)	5.2.5
Directive 79/279/EEC (European admission)	2.2.4, 12.1
Directive 80/390/EEC (listing particulars)	2.2.4, 12.1
Art 7	12.3
Directive 82/121/EEC (interim reports)	2.2.4, 12.1
Directive 85/61/EEC (collective investment in transferable securities)	13.2
Directive 85/592/EEC (European listings)	
Art 7	2.2.4
Directive 88/220/EEC (undertakings for collective investment of transferable securities)	2.2.4, 2.2.5, 13.2
Directive 88/357/EEC (second non-life insurance)	1.2.5, 2.2.1
Directive 89/298/EEC (public offers)	2.2.4, 12.1
Directive 89/299/EEC (own funds)	2.2.2
Directive 89/592/EEC (insider dealing)	7.1
Directive 89/646/EEC (second banking directive)	2.2.2, 2.2.5, 2.3.3, 4.3.4, 5.2.4, 6.3.2, 9.3.7
Art 7(1)	9.3.7
Art 9(4)	5.2.5
Art 23(3)	9.3.7
Art 24(2)	9.3.7

Directive 89/647/EEC (solvency)	2.2.2
Directive 90/619/EEC (second life insurance)	1.2.5, 2.2.1
Directive 91/308/EEC (money laundering)	10.4.3
Directive 92/30/EEC (consolidated supervision)	2.2.2
Directive 92/49/EEC (third non-life insurance)	1.2.5, 2.2.1
Directive 92/96/EEC (third life insurance)	1.2.5, 2.2.1
Directive 92/121/EEC (large exposures)	2.2.2
Directive 93/6/EEC (capital adequacy)	1.6.1, 2.2.3
Directive 93/22/EEC (investment services)	2.2.3, 2.2.5, 2.3.3, 9.3.7
Art 1	2.2.3
Art 2.2(c)	11.4.1
Art 3	2.2.3
Art 5	6.4.2
Art 7(5)	5.2.5
Art 10	2.2.3, 6.4.2
Art 11	2.2.3, 2.3.3
Art 14	2.2.3
Art 15	2.2.3
Art 21	2.2.3
Art 24(2)	9.3.7
Annex A	2.2.3
Annex B	2.2.3
Annex C	2.2.3
Directive 94/19/EC (deposit guarantee)	2.2.2
Directive 95/26/EC (post BCCI)	2.3.1, 5.2.1, 10.2
Directive 97/9/EC (investors compensation)	2.2.3
Directive 98/26/EC (settlement finality)	11.2.6

GLOSSARY OF ABBREVIATIONS

1986 Act	Financial Services Act 1986
1994 Order	Insider Dealing (Securities and Regulated Markets) Order 1994
2BCD	Second Banking Coordination Directive 1989
Affirmative resolutions	Requirement that statutory instruments be subject to debates and votes of both Houses of Parliament before coming into force
AIM	Alternative Investment Market, the Stock Exchange's 'second market' for smaller non-listed companies
ATS	Alternative trading system (electronic rivals to RIEs)
BA 1987	Banking Act 1987
Basle Accord	Basle Committee on Banking Regulations and Supervisory Practices *International Convergence of Capital Measurement and Capital Standards*, July 1988
BSC	Building Societies Commission
CAD	Capital Adequacy Directive 1993
CAO	Company Announcements Office at the Stock Exchange
Cartel prohibition	Chapter I of the Competition Act 1998, prohibition of 'agreements preventing, restricting or distorting competition'
CAT	Voluntary approved standards of charges, access and terms for financial products
CIS	Collective investment scheme (eg a unit trust or OEIC)
CJA 1993	Criminal Justice Act 1993
Code of Practice	FSA evidential rules on Statements
COBS	*Conduct of Business Sourcebook*, part of the FSA's *Handbook*
COMC	Code of Market Conduct, FSA evidential rules on market abuse
Convention	European Convention on Human Rights
CREST	CRESTCo Ltd, an RCH settling trades in UK equities, gilts and money market instruments
Cruickshank Reports	*Competition and Regulation in Financial Services: Striking the Right Balance*, HM Treasury, July 1999; *Competition in UK Banking: A Report to the Chancellor of the Exchequer*, Stationery Office, March 2000
DGD	Deposit Guarantee Directive 1994
DIB	Designated investment business, regulated

	and ancillary activities excluding deposit-taking, general insurance and long-term pure protection insurance; approximately what was investment business under the 1986 Act
DPB	Designated professional body, exempts members only marginally involved in regulated activities from the FSMA
DTI	UK Department of Trade and Industry
ECHR	European Court of Human Rights in Strasbourg
ECJ	European Court of Justice in Luxembourg
EEA	European Economic Area, comprising the EU plus Iceland, Liechtenstein and Norway
EU	European Union, comprising Austria, Belgium, Denmark, Finland, France, Germany, Greece, Holland, Ireland, Italy, Luxembourg, Portugal, Spain, Sweden, and the UK
European Passport	Right of a financial services firm authorised in one EEA country to conduct business in other EEA countries created by the FS Directives
Exemption Order	Draft Financial Services and Markets Act (Exemption) Order
Forum	Financial Services Practitioner Forum
FOS	Financial Ombudsman Scheme
FPE Order	Draft Financial Services and Markets Act (Financial Promotion Exemptions) Order
FSA	Financial Services Authority, formerly the SIB
FSC	Friendly Societies Commission
FSCS	Financial Services Compensation Scheme Limited
FS Directives	Financial Services Directives, creating European Passports for credit institutions, insurance and other investment businesses
FSMA	Financial Services and Markets Act 2000
HRA 1998	Human Rights Act 1998
IBRC	Insurance Brokers Registration Council, an RPB
ICA 1982	Insurance Companies Act 1982
ICD	Investor Compensation Directive 1997
ICS	Investors Compensation Scheme under the 1986 Act
IFA	Independent Financial Adviser, not tied to any provider
IMRO	Investment Management Regulatory Organisation, an SRO
Insurers	Insurance companies and mutuals
Intermediate customers	Larger businesses and expert individuals protected by parts of the COBS

IOSCO	International Organization of Securities Commissions
IPC	Inter-Professionals Code, largely guidance on conduct with market counterparties
ISD	Investment Services Directive 1993
ISMA	International Securities Markets Association, for secondary dealings in eurobonds
ISSRO	International Securities Self-Regulating Organisation under the 1986 Act, ISMA is the only one
JMLSG	Joint Money Laundering Steering Group, producing guidance notes on the ML Regulations
Joint Committee	Joint Committee of the House of Commons and the House of Lords on Financial Services and Markets
LCH	London Clearing House Limited, an RCH for derivatives
LIFFE	London International Financial Futures and Options Exchange Limited, an RIE for financial derivatives
Listing Directives	Admission Directive 1979, Listing Particulars Directive 1980 and Interim Reports Directive 1982
Listing Rules	Listing Rules based on the Listing Directives' requirements as added to by the UKLA
Lloyd's	Society (and, where relevant, Corporation) of Lloyd's
Market counterparty	Professional clients, usually authorised, that are not protected by the COBS (except client assets rules)
ML Regulations	Money Laundering Regulations 1993, implementing the Money Laundering Directive 1991
MLRO	Money Laundering Reporting Officer
ML Rules	FSA's Money Laundering Rules
Monopoly prohibition	Chapter II of the Competition Act 1998 prohibition of 'abuse of a dominant position in a market'
Names	Individual members of Lloyd's supplying capital
NASDAQ	National Association of Securities Dealers Automated Quotations System, the US quote-driven equities market
New Basle Accord	Proposals to replace the Basle Accord due to be published in late 2000
NYSE	New York Stock Exchange, the main US order-driven equities market
OEIC	Open-ended investment company
OFT	Office of Fair Trading (including the Director-General)

OM London	OM London Exchange Limited, derivatives market owned in conjunction with the Swedish Stock Exchange
OTC	Over-the-counter, that is off-market
PACE	Police and Criminal Evidence Act 1984
PFB	Principle for businesses, a high-level FSA rule applying to authorised firms
PIA	Personal Investment Authority, an SRO
PII	Professional indemnity insurance
POS (Amendment) Regulations	Public Offers of Securities (Amendment) Regulations 1999
POS Regulations	Public Offers of Securities Regulations 1995
Private customer	Individuals and other small businesses fully protected by the COBS
RA Order	Draft Financial Services and Markets Act (Regulated Activities) Order
RBC system	Risk-based capital system, the capital requirement approach being developed for financial services
RCH	Recognised Clearing House
RIE	Recognised Investment Exchange
RNS	Regulatory News Service, run by the CAO
RPB	Recognised professional body under the 1986 Act
RR Regulations	Draft Recognition Requirements Regulations
SARs	Substantial Acquisition Rules of the Takeover Panel
SEC	US Securities and Exchange Commission
SFA	Securities and Futures Authority, an SRO
SIB	Securities and Investments Board, which has become the FSA
SRO	Self-regulating organisation under the 1986 Act
Statement	Statement of Principle, a high-level FSA requirement applying to approved persons (mainly individuals)
Stock Exchange	London Stock Exchange Limited
Takeover Code	City Code on Takeovers and Mergers
Takeover Panel	UK Panel on Takeovers and Mergers
TCA	Threshold Condition for Authorisation for a firm
Tradepoint	Tradepoint Financial Networks plc, order-driven RIE competitor of the Stock Exchange
Transparency Rules	Pre-and post-transaction disclosure rules in respect of market dealings
Tribunal	Financial Services and Markets Tribunal
UCITS Directive	Undertakings for Collective Investment in Transferable Securities Directive 1985
UKLA	UK Listing Authority, the competent authority under the Listing Directives, now the FSA

Vol   *Hansard* Volume
Yellow Book   The old listing rules based on the Listing
                        Directives' requirements as added to by the
                        Stock Exchange

Chapter 1

BACKGROUND

1.1 INTRODUCTION

One of the most striking monuments in the gardens at Stowe, Buckinghamshire, is the Temple of British Worthies. It was designed in 1735 by William Kent for the Whig leader, Lord Cobham and displays the busts of 14 Whig heroes including Elizabeth I, William III, Shakespeare, Milton, Newton and Sir John Barnard MP. The claim of Sir John to stand amongst such notable company is explained in the inscription above his bust:

> 'Sir John Barnard who distinguished himself in Parliament by an active and firm Opposition to the pernicious and iniquitous Practice of Stock-jobbing...'[1]

The fate of Sir John's 1734 'Act to Prevent the Infamous Practice of Stock-Jobbing' is perhaps instructive for present-day financial regulators. After some initial popularity, it quickly became a dead letter as its restrictions were either avoided or evaded.

The enthusiasm to regulate financial services but the difficulty in doing so effectively was, and remains, inherent in the intangible nature of securities and other financial instruments. The ease of creating and dealing in these complex bundles of rights makes it hard to capture them within any regulatory system but, at the same time, makes it only too easy to confuse or mislead consumers involved in such dealings. Eighteenth-century Britain did not have the State enforcement powers that twenty first-century Britain has; but neither did it face the power of IT systems and the availability of offshore financial centres. Also in the eighteenth century, only the Government and the very rich were involved with financial services. But that was to change during the following century, with a number of notable firsts: the Friendly Societies Act of 1793; the Ruthwell Savings Bank in 1810; the Woolwich Equitable Building Society in 1847; and the Foreign and Colonial Investment Trust in 1868. All of these involved new institutions aimed at investors of modest means[2].

By the beginning of the twentieth century, London (together with Edinburgh) was the leading financial centre dealing in securities and organising insurance for a rapidly industrialising world. Although the ravages of the Great War and the stagnation of the 1920s caused it to lose this position, first to New York and later, for a time, to Tokyo, London has remained the leading financial centre in Europe. However, despite their continuing importance, there was no serious attempt to regulate UK financial services by statute until the 1980s. This was in sharp contrast to the USA where the Great Depression had inspired a set of federal statutes separating out commercial banking, insurance and the securities industry and

---

1   The full text, by Edward Batchelor, was not inscribed there until 1763. Due to a misunderstanding, however, the bust by Peter Scheemakers was not even of the unfortunate Sir John, but of his successor as Lord Mayor of London, Alderman Perry!

2   *A History of Money – From Ancient Times to the Present Day*, Glyn Davies (University of Wales Press, 1999).

bringing the last named under the supervision of the Securities and Exchange Commission (SEC)[1].

1.2   HOW WERE UK FINANCIAL SERVICES REGULATED?

Although there was little statutory regulation, there was a high level of self-regulation imposed by four bodies, the London Stock Exchange (Stock Exchange), the Society of Lloyd's (Lloyd's), the Panel on Takeovers and Mergers (Takeover Panel) and the Bank of England. The Government Department most involved in financial regulation was the Department of Trade, which became the Department of Trade and Industry (DTI).

1.2.1   The Stock Exchange

The Stock Exchange was, in effect, a private members club holding on trust for its members a number of buildings. These provided facilities for dealing in publicly held UK securities in which trade Stock Exchange members had a virtual monopoly. The Exchange was run by a Council, most of whom were elected from amongst those members. Tight discipline was maintained by allowing only members, and the staff of firms controlled by members, to deal on the Exchange. Stock Exchange member firms were, therefore, forced to remain independent partnerships or small director-owned companies.

The Stock Exchange was proud of its record in consumer protection, which was based on three central tenets.

(1) *The Listing Agreement* was a private contract whereby, in return for the Exchange allowing an issuer's securities to be traded regularly by its members, the issuer (usually a company) agreed to publish far more information about itself and its trading performance than was required by law[2].

(2) *Single Capacity Dealing* meant that, to avoid conflicts of interest, member firms were divided into jobbers (principals) who made prices in the listed securities and brokers (agents) who acted for investors and negotiated on their behalf with the competing jobbers.

(3) *Unlimited Liability* of all members for the debts not only of their own firm, but of any other member firm (through the Stock Exchange Compensation Fund). This protected investors dealing through the Stock Exchange from the default of any member firm.

However, the system had its critics. It was a cosy, inward-looking monopoly which excluded international players like the banks. It was also an expensive method of dealing – at least for the major investment houses – because, to limit defaults, the Stock Exchange required all stockbrokers to charge their clients a minimum level of commission.

---

1   Glass-Steagall Act 1933; Securities Act 1933; Securities Exchange Act 1934; Public Utility Holding Company Act 1935; Trust Indenture Act 1939; Investment Company Act 1940; Investment Advisers Act 1940.

2   The Stock Exchange's detailed rules appeared in its *Admission of Securities to Listing* usually referred to as the 'Yellow Book', which added to the requirements which now principally appear in the Companies Act 1985, Parts VII, XI and XII.

1.2.2　The Society of Lloyd's

Like the Stock Exchange, Lloyd's was a form of club, in this case offering facilities to rich individuals (called 'names') to use their personal wealth to provide backing for insurance. To spread their risks, these names were organised by members' agents into different syndicates. The premiums received by these syndicates were invested by managing agents until needed to pay claims. Business was brought to the syndicates by Lloyd's brokers.

Like members of the Stock Exchange, names had unlimited personal liability and Lloyd's required each name to deposit funds with it as a form of margin which it then invested under trust. It also ran a Central Fund to which all names contributed to meet claims against any defaulting name. However, unlike Stock Exchange members, names were passive investors reliant on the skills of their professional agents to manage the risks they were taking.

Although Lloyd's was incorporated under statute in 1871, it remained a largely self-regulated market run by a Council dominated by representatives of its managing and members' agents. With the relaxation of the wealth requirements and a favourable tax regime, the number of Lloyd's names rose from 6,000 in 1970 to a peak of 34,000 in 1989. In effect, this meant that a considerable number of retail investors were exposed to a high risk derivatives-type investment. Then the losses which hit a small number of syndicates from asbestosis and other claims led to a crisis, the forcible reinsuring of these risks, the introduction of corporate members with limited liability and a collapse in the number of individual names back to below 6,000.

1.2.3　The Takeover Panel

The Takeover Panel was, and still remains, a remarkable example of self-regulation. From its creation in 1968, the Panel has consisted of appointees of the Bank of England and representatives of various City interest groups[1]. It has developed an elaborate City Code on Takeovers and Mergers (Takeover Code). This lays down the circumstances and terms on which a bid for a UK public company may be made and the tactics the parties may and may not use.

The Takeover Panel has never had any statutory backing but has been almost impossible to circumvent because bidders and targets have required the services of City firms to launch and defend bids and those firms are bound by their own regulators to enforce the Code[2].

1.2.4　The Bank of England

Although nationalised in 1946, the Bank of England's supervision of the City remained more a matter of convention than statute. Its representatives on the Council of the Stock Exchange and the Takeover Panel ensured its influence was felt. As lender of last resort, it had for years informally supervised the UK commercial banks. From the beginning of the Second World War, as the operator

---

1　Detailed in Introduction to the City Code on Takeovers and Mergers.
2　Principally through the requirement that investment advertisements can be issued or approved only by authorised parties, now FSMA, s 21.

of the Exchange Control System and the New Issue Queue[1], it had a more direct control over the merchant banks involved in raising capital in the UK.

However, with the development in the 1960s of secondary banks outside the traditional circle, this method of control was beginning to break down. The financial crisis which hit these operators in 1973–74 and the need to meet the requirements of the European Union's (EU's) First Banking Co-ordination Directive of 1977[2], led to the Banking Act 1979 and then the Banking Act 1987 (BA 1987). These gave the Bank of England formal powers to regulate deposit-taking, but the overall supervision of banks still depended to a considerable extent on the 'Governor's raised eyebrow'[3].

1.2.5   The Department of Trade and Industry

Between the World Wars, the development of unit trusts and financial advisers outside the control of the Stock Exchange and the Bank of England did lead to the passing of the Prevention of Fraud (Investments) Act 1939. This gave responsibility for authorising unit trusts and licensing dealers in securities to the DTI. However, firms which were considered to be well regulated, like banks and Stock Exchange member firms, were exempt.

The DTI also had responsibility under the Insurance Companies Act 1982 (ICA 1982) for authorising UK insurance companies. Although there had been growing statutory regulation of insurance companies since 1870, the need to formalise an authorisation system arose from a series of European Directives establishing the right of authorised life and non-life insurers (whether companies or mutuals) to operate throughout the EU and subsequently the European Economic Area (EEA)[4]. Insurance brokers were not regulated by the ICA 1982, although to use the title 'insurance broker' they had to be registered with the Insurance Brokers Registration Council (IBRC)[5]. Members of Lloyd's were exempt from the ICA 1982 and Lloyd's brokers were automatically registered with the IBRC.

1.2.6   The regulation of Friendly Societies

To complete the regulatory picture requires a brief look at friendly societies. A friendly society has been defined as 'a voluntary association of individuals unincorporated or incorporated, subscribing for provident benefits'[6]. Traditionally these organisations have been important in providing financial services to

---

1   The emergency wartime regulations were extended by the Borrowing (Controls and Guarantees) Act 1946 and the Exchange Control Act 1947.

2   1977/780/EEC.

3   It is deposit-taking and not lending which has required authorisation in the UK. Loans to consumers of up to £25,000, however, are regulated by the Consumer Credit Act 1974.

4   First Non-Life Insurance Directive 73/239/EEC; First Life Directive 79/267/EEC; Second Non-Life Directive 88/357/EEC; Second Life Directive 90/619/EEC; Third Non-Life Directive 92/49/EEC; Third Life Directive 92/96/EEC. The EEA consists of the 15 countries of the EU plus Norway, Iceland and Liechtenstein.

5   Insurance Brokers (Registration) Act 1977.

6   *Halsbury's Laws of England* (4th edn) vol 19(1), para 103.

retail investors, although their importance has declined in the last decade[1]. A Registrar of Friendly Societies was established in the nineteenth century, but with the increasing regulation of credit institutions, the regulation of building societies was hived off to a Building Societies Commission (BSC)[2]. A Friendly Societies Commission (FSC) was then created for the remainder except for unregistered friendly societies which were confined to providing death benefits and credit unions that were registered as industrial and provident societies[3].

1.3 THE FORCES FOR CHANGE

In the 1970s and 1980s, the stock market was remarkably scandal free, unlike Lloyd's. The ICA 1982 did give the DTI some oversight of Lloyd's solvency and the Lloyd's Act 1982 strengthened the power and independence of the Lloyd's Council. Otherwise the Wilson Committee reported in 1980 that the system of self-regulation in the City was generally working well. Despite the outward calm, however, there were forces for change developing.

Self-regulation does depend on the existence of monopolies. The development of businesses outside the control of the Stock Exchange and the Bank of England had already led to statutory intervention. Whole new markets were now developing, for example Eurobonds and financial derivatives. Many felt that the Prevention of Fraud (Investments) Act 1958, and the DTI's licensing activities under it, were inadequate to deal with these developments.

Another pressure for statutory intervention was coming from the EU which was producing directives and draft directives in the financial services field. This had already required the formalisation of banking supervision in 1979. Indeed, 1979 was to prove a fateful year for two other reasons. In February 1979, the Stock Exchange's rule book was referred to the Restrictive Practices Court and in October 1979 there was perhaps an even more important change – the removal, after nearly 40 years, of exchange controls. All at once the UK domestic securities market became only a small part of a rapidly developing global system. A system of securities regulation, which depended on cosy domestic relationships, seemed doomed.

In 1983, the Restrictive Practices Court action was stopped in return for major voluntary reforms to the Stock Exchange's rulebook[4]. These changes led to 'Big Bang' on 27 October 1986, which consisted of:

(1) the removal of minimum commissions and with it single capacity dealing, ie member firms could now act as brokers and jobbers;

(2) the creation of a screen based dealing system (based on the American NASDAQ system) which soon replaced all floor dealings; and

---

1   There are now approximately 70 building societies, 3,500 friendly societies and 11,000 industrial and provident societies according to the Financial Secretary in Standing Committee A, 7 December 1999, c 1186.

2   Building Societies Act 1986; although the Chief Registrar of Friendly Societies and the First Commissioner of the BSC remained the same individual.

3   Friendly Societies Act 1992; Industrial and Provident Societies Act 1979.

4   This accord required legislation in the form of Restrictive Trade Practices (Stock Exchange) Act 1984.

(3) the opening up of membership to corporate bodies, particularly overseas banks, and with it the end of unlimited liability.

These changes brought down the cost of dealing for institutions but also the level of protection for consumers. Still, they were probably inevitable if the Stock Exchange was to compete successfully in the new global securities market. Whether the Bank of England and the Stock Exchange could have developed a self-regulatory system which embraced all the new, and in most cases, foreign players will never be known; for the Government had decided to introduce a regulatory framework to cover most investment activity. This was in response, partly to a detailed report by Professor Gower[1], and partly to scandals like the one involving the firm that had financially advised the exchange control staff laid off by the Bank of England. Thus the Financial Services Act 1986 (the 1986 Act) came into being.

1.4 THE FINANCIAL SERVICES ACT 1986

At first glance, the 1986 Act seemed to follow the precedent of the Prevention of Fraud (Investments) Act 1958, in making it illegal for any person to engage in an investment business or advertise or solicit investments unless authorised under, or exempt from, its provisions[2]. However:

(1) the activities covered were far wider, including advising on, managing, and dealing in, most forms of investment except land, goods and banking deposits;
(2) there were no exemptions for stockbrokers, banks or insurers except the supposedly reformed Lloyd's. Others involved in only occasional investment advice, like solicitors, accountants and insurance brokers still required authorisation by their professional bodies; but
(3) individual licences for each employee or tied agent were no longer required. Authorisation was given to the firm, although a form of individual licensing was reintroduced later by the principal regulatory bodies.

1.4.1 The structure

Under the 1986 Act, financial services appeared to be regulated first by the DTI, and later by the Treasury[3]. In fact, most of the powers were delegated to the Securities and Investments Board (SIB)[4]. But even that body did not directly regulate financial services. Its main functions were to create and develop a framework of rules and regulations for the industry and to grant recognition to other self-regulating organisations (SROs) and recognised professional bodies (RPBs) who were prepared to enforce such rules and regulations on their members. The SIB did authorise some firms directly; it took over the authorisation

---

1   *Review of Investor Protection – A Discussion Document* (HMSO, 1982) followed by the first report in January 1984, 1984 Cmnd 9125, which led to a White Paper *Financial Services in the United Kingdom: A New Framework for Investor Protection*, 1985 Cmnd 9432, and a further report from Professor Gower in March 1985 (HMSO, 1985).
2   1986 Act, ss 3, 56 and 57.
3   Transfer of Functions (Financial Services) Order 1992, SI 1992/1315.
4   1986 Act, s 114; Financial Services Act 1986 (Delegation Order) 1987, SI 1987/942.

of unit trusts from the DTI and it was the body principally responsible for enforcement actions against non-authorised firms illegally conducting investment business ('policing the perimeter'). Technically, the SIB was only a private company financed by the bodies it recognised or authorised and could have had its functions removed by the DTI at any time. In practice, it was a governmental quango, the governing body of which was appointed by the Secretary of State and (until June 1998) the Governor of the Bank of England[1].

The main self-regulating bodies at the heart of the new system were the five SROs originally recognised by the SIB, although eventually these were reduced to three:

(1) *the Securities and Futures Authority (SFA)* whose members were primarily dealers in money market instruments, domestic and international securities but also included dealers in money market instruments, futures and options in securities and commodities, and the providers of corporate finance advice;

(2) *the Investment Management Regulatory Organisation (IMRO)* whose members were primarily involved in portfolio management, be it private clients, pension funds, or collective investment schemes; and

(3) *the Personal Investment Authority (PIA)* whose members were primarily engaged in the production and selling of life assurance, collective investment schemes and other investment services to private clients.

SROs could not authorise their members to engage in investment activities beyond the area of competence of that SRO[2]. This required some financial conglomerates to seek authorisation from more than one SRO. The complexity of the system could particularly be seen from the case of unit trusts which had to be authorised by the SIB, whose managements were generally authorised by IMRO, but whose units were generally sold by PIA members.

Where investment business was truly incidental to the conduct of a profession, a firm or sole practitioner did not need to seek authorisation from an SRO, but could obtain it from an RPB. The SIB recognised as RPBs the various accountancy institutes, law societies, the Institute of Actuaries and the IBRC. Organisers of market places and investment transfer facilities like the Stock Exchange, London International Financial Futures and Options Exchange Ltd (LIFFE), the London Clearing House Ltd (LCH) and CRESTCo Ltd (CREST) also required to be recognised by the SIB as Recognised Investment Exchanges or Recognised Clearing Houses (RIEs or RCHs), but once recognised, their activities were exempt.

---

1   Amended by the Bank of England Act 1998, s 31.
2   1986 Act, Sch 2, para 1.

1.4.2   Control of financial services after Big Bang

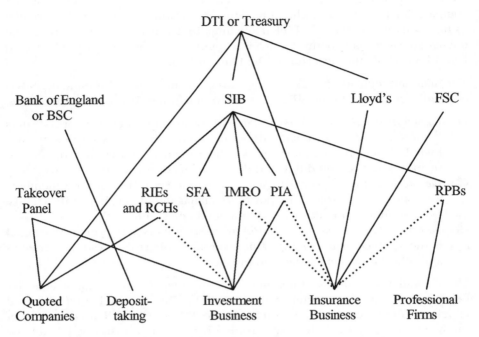

1.4.3   Developments under the 1986 Act

The complex structure created by the 1986 Act was an attempt to preserve some of the self-regulatory elements of the old system within a statutory framework. Indeed, the Stock Exchange originally hoped to be an SRO continuing to enforce its own prudential and conduct of business rules on its members as the New York Stock Exchange (NYSE) still does in the United States. Instead, at the insistence of the SIB, the Membership Department of the Exchange was spun out to form the nucleus of what became the SFA. At least, the SFA had this nucleus of experienced regulators. The other SROs were largely starting from scratch, which was part of the reason for the prescriptive approach initially taken by the SIB over the SROs' rulebooks.

The original rules drawn up by the SIB were very detailed and legalistic. That approach was abandoned in 1990, at least for the conduct of business rules. The new SIB rule book consisted of general principles and core rules of conduct along the lines of the Takeover Code. The detailed 'third tier' conduct of business rules for particular business areas were left to the SROs. In effect, all members of SROs were subject to:

(1)   the SIB's principles;
(2)   the SIB's standardised rules covering certain areas; and
(3)   the SIB's core rules as amended by the member's SRO in its third tier rules.

In 1994 the SIB went further and 'dedesignated' nearly all the core rules, leaving the SROs greater freedom to adapt them without seeking formal waivers from the

SIB[1]. The core rules still provided general guidance to the SROs about what the SIB required of their rulebooks.

This relaxation of detailed control over the SROs marked a growing acceptance that the SROs were themselves changing from being trade associations to becoming professional regulators. Although their boards had elected members, they also had increasing numbers of public interest representatives. Another mark of this changing relationship was the SROs' requirement that the senior management of member firms and those directly dealing with customers should be individually 'registered', often after passing examinations. This requirement allowed the SROs to discipline individual employees and not just firms. The Stock Exchange had always imposed this and the SFA inherited the practice. IMRO followed suit, but it was not until the creation of the PIA in 1994 that the employees of the investment firms dealing most often with private customers had the requirement imposed on them.

The SROs' ability to adapt and amend the relationship between them and their member firms and those firms' employees arose because their enforcement powers were based upon contract, that is the right to conduct investment business in return for the promise to follow the SRO's rules. This allowed the SROs to develop a disciplinary system that could issue warnings, fines or ultimately expel firms and individuals. Ironically, the SIB, solely dependent on its statutory powers, could not fine the few firms it authorised and seldom operated its power to ban individuals from involvement with investment business. Indeed, the SIB was keen to lose its power to authorise firms directly and so leave enforcement 'within the perimeter' to the SROs. It could then concentrate on 'policing the perimeter', determining overall regulatory policy and regulating the standards of supervision[2]. Also, for all its complexity, the UK regulatory system had one great virtue. It was, by international standards, cheap[3].

Why then did the Chancellor of the Exchequer surprise the financial world by announcing on 20th May 1997 that, far from developing the SROs:

(1) responsibility for bank supervision was to be moved from the Bank of England to the SIB; and
(2) the two tier system of regulating investment business was to be abandoned with the SIB taking over direct responsibility for authorising and supervising firms?

1.5 THE BIRTH OF A 'SUPER REGULATOR'

The initial impetus to create a 'Super Regulator' was probably brought about by the need to avoid a different type of monster, namely an independent bank that remained responsible for supervising the banking system. Moving the Bank of

---

1   Financial Services (Dedesignation) Rules and Regulations 1994.
2   *Financial Services Regulation – Making the Two Tier System Work,* SIB May 1993.
3   Based on the figures compiled for the Wallis Commission in Australia by National Mutual and the Boston Consulting Group, *The Cost of Complying with Financial Services Regulation,* August 1996. The total costs of the regulators in 2000 should be less than £200m, *Plan and Budget 2000/01,* FSA, February 2000. More recent comparisons are given in the *FSA Annual Report 1999/2000,* FSA, July 2000, p 84.

England's supervisory role to the SIB and merging the regulation of most of the rest of the financial services industry with it had two other advantages:

(1) consumers would have only one regulator with whom to register any complaints and from whom to seek any information; and
(2) suppliers increasingly offering a range of financial services would also only have to deal with the one regulator[1].

Both points were touched on by the Chancellor in his original announcement. The other motive that emerged from that announcement was a deep distrust of 'self-regulation'. In particular, the difficulties all the City regulators had had in resolving the problems created by the misselling of personal pensions left many, whether rightly or wrongly, blaming the complexity and supposed self-interest of the self-regulatory system for the mess. However, it seemed that the Chancellor had no prepared blue print for the new system and the overall plan only emerged from a series of announcements from Treasury Ministers and the SIB, now renamed the Financial Services Authority (FSA)[2], over the following six months.

1.5.1   The scope of the Financial Services Authority

It became clear that the aim of the Government was to transform the SIB from being a statutory overseer of self-regulating organisations sharing regulatory responsibility with a number of other statutory regulators, into being the single direct statutory regulator of the whole sector[3]. This was to be achieved by the SIB, or rather the FSA, taking on some or all of the responsibilities of 18 other regulators, namely:

Supervision and Surveillance Division of the Bank of England
Insurance Directorate of the DTI (later the Treasury)
Lloyd's
BSC
FSC
Registry of Friendly Societies
Three SROs being the PIA, SFA and IMRO
Nine RPBs being:
    Law Society of England and Wales
    Law Society of Scotland
    Law Society of Northern Ireland
    Institute of Chartered Accountants in England and Wales
    Institute of Chartered Accountants in Scotland
    Institutes of Chartered Accountants in Ireland
    Chartered Association of Certified Accountants
    Institute of Actuaries
    IBRC

---

1   As Lord Lipsey pointed out, the need for a single regulator has been as universally accepted as the need for a Child Support Agency was – hardly an auspicious precedent, vol 610 HL, 21 February 2000, c 59.
2   Financial Services (Change of Name of Designated Agency) Rules 1997, SIB, 20 October 1997.
3   The best summary of the original proposals is to be found in *Financial Services Authority: an outline*, FSA, October 1997 (*FSA Outline*). To achieve this, the new legislation will largely replace three principal pieces of legislation, the ICA 1982, the 1986 Act and the BA 1987.

These proposals still left a slightly ragged edge to the FSA's potential area of responsibilities. For example, the FSA was to be responsible for policing the solvency of most financial services institutions, but not apparently occupational pension funds[1]. It was to authorise the financial services business currently authorised by RPBs, but would probably leave the policing of professionals to those RPBs[2]. It was to authorise Lloyd's and its managing and members' agents but, likewise would leave day-to-day supervision to Lloyd's itself. Because the FSA was not to authorise co-operatives, it would not take over the Co-operative Deposit Protection Scheme, but would run other deposit compensation arrangements[3]. Although it was to be responsible for the information produced by friendly and other mutual societies, the FSA would not be responsible for the information produced by companies with publicly traded securities[4]. The Treasury initially announced that the 'competent authority' for the making and enforcing of the Listing Rules, ie the UK Listing Authority (UKLA), would remain the Stock Exchange[5]. Company documents would still be filed with Companies House and general responsibility for companies would remain with the DTI. The FSA would also not police the conduct of takeovers which would remain a matter for the Takeover Panel[6].

Subsequently, the Treasury has changed its mind on the exact boundary of the FSA's responsibilities. In July 1998 the IBRC was derecognised as an RPB and its members required to be fully authorised (mainly by the PIA). By contrast, most other RPB members only incidentally engaged in investment business will no longer need to be authorised at all under the new regime. The other dramatic change was the announcement on 4 October 1999, that the FSA would take over as the UKLA from the Stock Exchange. This change resulted from the Exchange's decision to demutualise, become a proprietary 'for-profit' organisation and seek links with European exchanges, principally the Frankfurt Stock Exchange.

It is clear that the FSA's responsibilities will be enormous. When fully established, it will employ up to 3,000 people at its Canary Wharf headquarters and will be directly or indirectly regulating over 20,000 financial services firms and supervising another 3,000 or so listed companies and other bodies[7]. The UK will not be the only country to have just one major financial services regulator – this is the pattern, for example, in Scandinavia – but where there is one regulator elsewhere,

---

1   This is the responsibility of the Occupational Pensions Regulatory Authority which has its own Pensions Ombudsman to deal with complaints.
2   *FSA Outline* at p 6, para 8.
3   Consultation Paper 5, FSA December 1997 at p 13, para 35.
4   This contrasts with the position of the Securities and Exchange Commission (SEC) in the USA.
5   Financial Services Act 1986, s 142(6); Official Listing of Securities (Change of Competent Authority) Regulations 1991, SI 1991/2000.
6   The current government seems to be as intent as its predecessors in retaining a non-statutory Panel, despite the draft 13th Company Law Directive, COM (95) 655.
7   '600 banks, 70 building societies, 850 insurance companies, 4,200 providers of retail financial services, 1,300 securities and derivatives firms, 1,100 investment management and fund management firms, not to mention dozens of professional bodies and 15,000 solicitors and accountants' Lord Saatchi at vol 610 HL, 21 February 2000, c 19, although only about 2,000 solicitors and accountants firms should need to be authorised. *Financial Services and Markets Bill: Regulatory Impact Assessment*, HM Treasury, June 1999; cf Consultation Paper 30, FSA, October 1999, Part 1. Authorised firms will have over 150,000 approved individuals working for them, Consultation Paper 53, FSA, June 2000, Section 8; see **5.3.1**.

the financial services sector it is responsible for tends to be small and concentrated within a few banks and/or insurance companies. The sheer width of the FSA's responsibilities contrasts sharply with that of the nearest comparable body, the SEC in the USA. Although the latter has about 4,000 employees, it only regulates the issuing of, and investing in, securities, and not banking, insurance or even futures dealings.

1.5.2   Interim arrangements

This new Super Regulator is coming into existence in two stages. In 1998, the Bank of England Act transferred responsibility for banking supervision to the FSA. Technically, the other regulators remain separate bodies until the Financial Services and Markets Act 2000 (FSMA) comes into force. However, the FSA was keen to establish its position before then and agreed with the three SROs and subsequently the other regulators (except the RPBs), to take on all their staff and contract them back for the remainder of their existence. A similar arrangement has brought together the staff of the eight existing dispute resolution schemes into one Ombudsman Scheme prior to its legal creation under the FSMA.

In July 1998, the FSA derecognised the IBRC as an RPB, granting interim authorisation to its members that needed it, pending most obtaining full authorisation from the PIA. Until now, apart from these insurance brokers, the FSA has only been technically responsible for regulating deposit-taking, wholesale money market business and collective investment schemes (eg unit trusts). Authorising, supervising and enforcing regulations on other financial services businesses has remained the responsibility of the old regulators. Indeed, the FSA stated that it would 'aim at least during the initial phase of the transitional period to maintain broad continuity of individual firms' relationships with regulatory staff where possible, notwithstanding the organisational integration envisaged'[1]. So what was envisaged?

1.5.3   Internal structure

The structure adopted by the FSA was a board appointed by the Treasury[2] consisting of up to 11 non-executive directors, the executive chairman and three, later only two, managing directors responsible for three divisions:

(1)   the FSA's internal organisation including finance, personnel, information technology and premises;
(2)   authorisations, enforcement, consumer relations and industry training;
(3)   supervision under whom there are separate directors responsible for:

Insurance and Friendly Societies;
Banks and Building Societies;
Investment Businesses;
Complex Groups;
Markets and Exchanges;

---

1   *FSA Outline*, p 17 at para 37.
2   Bank of England Act 1998, s 31.

Pensions Review; and

the UKLA[1].

This structure reveals a certain internal tension. Authorisation is organised on an industry-wide basis but supervision is still divided to some extent by type of business. When supervising financial conglomerates, the FSA continues, in most cases, to appoint a lead regulator to coordinate the efforts of the various regulators looking at the different types of business done[2]. This appearance of a single façade, behind which the old divisions of deposit-taking, insurance and other investment business still exist can also be seen in the proposed arrangements for single ombudsman and compensation schemes[3]. This highlights a pervasive problem, that the risks created by different types of financial services business are not the same.

1.6 PROBLEMS AND RISKS

There is no single goal of financial services regulation[4]. The FSA originally adopted three 'high-level aims'[5], which have been expanded into four regulatory objectives in the FSMA, namely:

(1) market confidence;
(2) public awareness;
(3) the protection of consumers; and
(4) the reduction of financial crime[6].

However, these simple aims disguise a complex web of regulatory techniques that arise from the different risks the FSA is trying to deal with.

(1) The most fundamental risk is of a systemic banking collapse. Banks inevitably carry large open positions with their fellow banks. They are also inherently vulnerable institutions because they 'borrow short and lend long'. A default by one or two can be perceived to threaten fellow banks and this can produce a 'run on the banks'. The most spectacular example of this was the US Crash of 1929. Some now argue that with global banking and derivatives markets, this risk has spread far beyond any domestic banking system. Techniques for reducing this risk include:

---

1   Howard Davies, as Chairman, has responsibility for the first (with Paul Boyle as a non-board Chief Operating Officer), Phillip Thorpe for the second and Michael Foot for the third. It is proposed to reinstate a third managing director who will take responsibility for retail regulation and consumer education, FSA Press Release 96/2000.

2   *FSA Outline*, p 21 paras 55–57 although the FSA is piloting multi-discipline supervisory teams, *FSA Plan & Budget 1998–99*, p 16 para 9. The Complex Group Division has single team supervision for eight groups, but otherwise lead regulators are determined by whether the group is predominantly an insurance group (general or life), a deposit-taking institution (eg commercial bank) or an investment business (eg stockbroker or US investment bank).

3   See **Chapter 8**.

4   For example, Michael Taylor, *Regulatory Leviathan: Will Super-SIB Work?*, p 42 (CTA Financial Publishing, October 1997).

5   *Report to the Chancellor on the Reform of the Financial Regulatory System*, SIB July 1997, section 1 and *FSA Outline* p 30 App 1 para 2 gave:
      to protect consumers of financial services;
      to promote clean and orderly markets; and
      to maintain confidence in the financial system.

6   FSMA, ss 2–6.

(a) creating a strong central bank as a lender of last resort;
(b) enforcing investment limitations to maintain liquidity and spread risk; and
(c) creating mutual compensation systems to discourage consumer panics.

The Bank of England remains the lender of last resort, but to obtain detailed information about individual banks it will have to co-operate very closely with the FSA which is now responsible for (b) and (c)[1].

(2) In reducing systemic risk, the above techniques inevitably offer a high level of protection for the funds of consumers transferred to banks. However, banks are no longer the only, nor indeed the main, instruments of investment intermediation for consumers. Others like building societies, insurance companies, pension funds and unit trusts all take in consumers' funds as principals, but because they do not create major systemic risks, regulators concentrate on protecting consumers through various investment limitations, ie prudential rules. Nevertheless, mutual compensation schemes have crept into these areas as well[2]. Most of these arrangements will now be the responsibility of the FSA.

(3) Where consumers are dealing with a financial services firm as an agent, regulators are less concerned about the firm's solvency. Instead they concentrate on the risks of fraud and misselling. These risks are not confined to dealing with agents. The most striking examples recently, like the pensions misselling scandal, have often been with institutions acting as principals, selling their own products. Regulatory techniques in this area have included:

(a) registration of individuals and firms to test their fitness and propriety;
(b) requirements to disclose conflicts and remuneration bases; and
(c) restrictions on marketing like suitability enquiries, risk warnings and cooling-off periods.

Although it is firms that will continue to be authorised, the FSA will be required to approve key personnel within such firms as the SROs presently do[3]. As for the conduct of business rules, perhaps one of the most unenviable tasks the FSA has been faced with is the rationalisation of the various existing sets[4].

(4) Finally, regulators are concerned with the integrity of the markets in which securities dealings take place. Most securities are risky. However, measures can be taken to try to establish some fairness in such dealings. As the value of any security should be its expected future cash flows discounted to their present value by the cost of money and the assumed risk factor[5], foreknowledge of information that might affect those expectations or assumptions is valuable; and as the market price is established by those expectations and assumptions leading investors to buy or sell the security, foreknowledge of information about those dealings is also valuable. Exploitation of that foreknowledge has been discouraged by:

---

1   See *Financial Services Authority: an outline*, App 2, 'Memorandum of Understanding between HM Treasury, the Bank of England and the FSA'.
2   The earliest scheme was probably the London Stock Exchange's own Mutual Compensation Fund and the first statutory one, the Policyholders Protection Act 1975.
3   FSMA, Parts IV and V.
4   Consultation Paper 8, FSA, April 1998; Consultation Paper 45, FSA, February 2000.
5   Based on the Capital Asset Pricing Model devised by William Sharpe, John Lintner and Jack Treynor, *Capital Asset Prices: A Theory of Market Equilibrium under Conditions of Risk* (1964) 19 Journal of Finance 425.

(a) disclosure requirements on companies etc (Listing Rules);

(b) disclosure requirements on market dealers (Transparency Rules); and

(c) criminal (and in the US, civil) liability for insider dealing and market manipulation.

Despite the publicity that this last area receives, in the UK most consumers are affected only to the extent that the institutions through which their investments are intermediated are affected. Nevertheless, the FSA is being given both criminal and civil 'prosecution' powers in this area[1].

1.6.1   The challenge for a Super Regulator

A single regulator faced with this variety of risks is bound to be tempted to apply a standardised regulatory regime. Indeed, even some of the regulated may encourage the regulator to do this because they fear that regulation which sharply distinguishes between different risks may give some competitors a regulatory advantage. The dangerous logic of creating the mythical 'level playing field' has, inter alia, entrenched unnecessary European-wide prudential rules for much of the financial services industry[2].

Over-regulation can be just as damaging as under-regulation.

(1) It can be anti-competitive, raising high entry barriers to new operators and products which customers might want. Much intellectual effort can also be wasted by existing operators seeking to persuade the regulator to a course of action that gives them a regulatory advantage[3].

(2) It can drive operations overseas to less heavily regulated jurisdictions, ie regulatory arbitrage[4]. Various directives have been passed to try to stop this happening within the EEA, but even European-wide rules do not stop some 'supervisory arbitrage', ie the tendency to head for the lightest and/or cheapest enforcement regime.

(3) It can create economic 'moral hazard'. Standardised regulation and generous compensation schemes can encourage customers to ignore risks and seek the highest apparent return. This in turn encourages reckless behaviour by the suppliers of financial services[5].

---

1   FSMA, ss 123, 397, 401 and 402. Although the administrative power to fine is modelled on the SEC's powers in the USA, all criminal prosecutions under the US federal securities legislation are the sole responsibility of the Federal Department of Justice.

2   Capital Adequacy Directive, 1993/6/EEC.

3   Referred to by economists as 'rent seeking'. For a study of such behaviour in the banking sector, see *Competition and Regulation in Financial Services: Striking the Right Balance*, HM Treasury, July 1999, and *Competition in UK Banking: A Report to the Chancellor of the Exchequer*, Stationery Office March 2000 ('Cruickshank Reports').

4   One example of regulatory arbitrage in the financial services area was the development of the offshore Eurodollar bond market to escape SEC regulation (and US federal taxes).

5   This was part of the explanation of the Savings and Loan (ie Building Societies) crisis in the USA 10 years ago.

The FSA's management is clearly aware of these dangers[1]. However, the political pressure on the FSA is strong. The Chancellor of the Exchequer, when announcing the creation of a single regulator to the House of Commons on 20 May 1997, said: 'The current system of self-regulation will be replaced by a new and fully statutory system, which will put the public interest first and increase public confidence in the system.' The clear implication of this statement and of the four regulatory objectives laid out in the FSMA is that the current system has been dominated by producer interests at the cost of consumers. The FSMA has been shaped to change this, but not without considerable amendments being made to it between the original draft Bill and the eventual Act.

1.7   THE SCENIC ROUTE

Howard Davies, the Chairman of the FSA, has described the FSMA as 'following an unusual and scenic route from the Treasury to Buckingham Palace'[2]. It has been subject to an unprecedented amount of pre-legislative scrutiny. An incomplete draft was published in July 1998 followed by a period of open consultation. The Treasury Select Committee published a report in February 1999[3] and the Government responded with a Progress Report in March[4] and missing draft sections for the Bill in April. A Joint Committee of Lords and Commons sat for just eight weeks, but published two Reports, one in April and one in May (the Joint Committee Reports)[5] to which the Government responded[6]. The Bill was eventually presented to Parliament in June 1999 and was the first Public Bill to be carried over to the following session under a procedure proposed by the 1997 Modernisation Committee[7]. Despite this pre-legislative scrutiny, the Bill was much amended during its passage through Parliament. It received Royal Assent on 14 June 2000, but is not expected to come into force until at least mid-2001. Over the last three years, the FSA has produced over 60 Consultation Papers on key areas of its proposed responsibilities under the FSMA, which in turn have led to Response Papers and Policy Statements. Before looking in detail at the FSMA, however, it is necessary to examine the restrictions imposed on the Government's freedom of action in this area by the European Framework.

1   *FSA Outline*, p 10 para 16; *A new regulator for the new millennium*, FSA January 2000, paras 4–7. Lord Saatchi has pointed out how tenuous the UK's hold on financial services might be. 'Britain has no God-given right to 55% of global trading in non-UK companies. It has no particular right to 25% of the global marine insurance market. These shares can disappear. In 1900 we had a 42% share of world shipping. In 1979, it was 7%; today it is 1%', vol 612 HL, 13 April 2000, c 336.

2   Chancery Bar Association and Combar Spring Lecture [1999] CfiLR 1.

3   Third Report from the Treasury Committee, Session 1998–99, *Financial Services Regulation, Volumes I and II*, HC 73.

4   Fourth Special Report from the Treasury Committee, Session 1998–99, *Financial Services Regulation: The Government's Response to the Third Report*, HC 347.

5   Joint Committee on Financial Services and Markets, *Draft Financial Services and Markets Bill, First Report*, HL Paper 50, HC 328 and *Second Report*, HL Paper 66, HC 465.

6   *Financial Services and Markets Bill: Government Response to the Reports of the Joint Committee on Financial Services and Markets*, HM Treasury, June 1999.

7   Vol 336 HC, 25 October 1999, c 737.

Chapter 2

THE EUROPEAN FRAMEWORK

2.1 INTRODUCTION

The regulation of any international service is fraught with difficulties. First, there is the complexity of how the business is conducted. Firms can:

(1) set up (or take over) a separate local company as a subsidiary;
(2) operate from the home-based firm (cross-border services); or
(3) set up a local office/branch as part of the home-based firm.

In case (1), the local company can be regulated by the host State like any other locally-based firm, although there is the additional risk of it being ruined by the collapse of its overseas trade parent. In case (2), customers in the host State ought to be aware that they are dealing with an overseas firm regulated by its home State. The host State should, at most, impose its marketing rules on the firm[1]. In case (3), customers in the host State may well believe that the firm is local and subject to local regulation, but the most the host State can impose is:

(a) its conduct of business rules;
(b) membership of its compensation scheme; and
(c) possibly some branch liquidity requirements.

Another problem is the differing attitudes home and host States may take to structural safeguards isolating risks. For example, Germany has required life and non-life insurers to be separately incorporated and to offer only pre-agreed products, whereas the UK has allowed the creation of composite insurers and the freedom to create virtually any insurance product. On the other hand, German universal banks have conducted a wide range of investment services whereas UK banks have kept their investment businesses separately incorporated, mainly for regulatory convenience. Can a host State impose its structural requirements on overseas branches and cross-border business?

One response to these problems is to create one central regulator (like the SEC) or, at least, centrally standardised regulation enforced by each home State regulator. Although that may cut down the scope for regulatory arbitrage and confusion, in a large multi-lingual area such as Europe, it is unlikely to lead to close and effective local (ie host State) supervision.

When trying to create a Single Market in financial services, the European Commission must have felt that it would have been 'better not to start from here'. Both the business structures and the regulatory frameworks in the different Member States were so varied that any effort to harmonise them through some central regulation would almost certainly have failed. An alternative would have been to challenge individual restrictive arrangements through the European Court of Justice (ECJ) as being in breach of the freedoms enshrined in the Treaty of Rome. In particular, the direct effect of Art 49 with its freedom to provide

---

1   With such cross-border business, there is also the difficult definitional problem of whether activities should count as business within that host State at all.

services without unnecessary restrictions imposed by a host state has been upheld in a number of cases[1]. To have established this throughout the financial services area, however, would have been a painfully slow and haphazard operation, although it is still a tactic open to the Commission outside the scope of the existing financial services directives (FS Directives).

Instead, building on the *Cassis de Dijon* principle[2], the Commission developed the concept of mutual recognition throughout the EU (and more recently the EEA), of financial services firms and their products and services that have been authorised in any one Member State. This is colloquially referred to as the 'European Passport'. To meet any objections that the consumers of one Member State could be confused, misled or otherwise put at risk by a firm or product authorised in another, perhaps rather lax Member State, the Commission has had to negotiate minimum prudential rules to be enforced by all authorising home States. Meanwhile, it has left conduct of business rules largely to the determination of host States, subject always to the European principle of the 'general good'[3].

2.2   THE DEVELOPMENT OF THE EUROPEAN PASSPORT

In its 1985 White Paper, the European Commission hoped to have the Single Market in financial services created by 1 January 1993[4], and although rather late, the principal elements are now in place. Given the starting position, this is no mean feat. As the UK in the 1980s was already an open market for financial services, the FS Directives have generally required the formalisation and adaptation only of existing authorisation procedures and regulations[5]. In other EEA countries, they have required the opening up of closed systems and the creation of authorisation procedures and regulations from scratch.

2.2.1   Insurers

The opening up of the European financial services market started before the Single Market project with the First Non-Life Insurance Directive of 1973,[6] which gave the freedom to any non-life insurer authorised in one EU country to establish branches and agencies in others. Home State regulators had to ensure that

---

1   For example, *Van Binsbergen v Bestuur van de Bedrijfsvereniging Voor de Metaalnijverheid* [1974] ECR 1299; *Commission v France* [1986] ECR 3663; *Commission v Germany* [1986] ECR 3755.

2   Case 120/78, *Rewe-Zentral AG v Bundesmonopolverwaltung fur Branntwein* [1979] ECR 649, [1979] 3 CMLR 494.

3   This principle was enunciated clearly in *Sager v Dennemayer* [1991] ECR I-4229 in the judgment at para 15, 'the freedom to provide services may be limited only by the rules which are justified by imperative reasons relating to the public interest and which apply to all persons or undertakings pursuing an activity in the State of destination, insofar as that interest is not protected by the rules to which the person providing the services is subject in the Member State in which he is established. In particular, those requirements must be objectively necessary in order to ensure compliance with professional rules and to guarantee the protection of the recipient of services and they must not exceed what is necessary to attain those objectives'.

4   Completing the Internal Market COM (85) 310 final.

5   Usually by Regulations under the European Communities Act 1972, s 2(2).

6   1973/239/EEC.

insurers authorised by them maintained at least a minimum solvency margin. The First Life Insurance Directive of 1979[1] extended the arrangement to life insurers. Existing UK composites were grandfathered, but any new life insurers had to be separately incorporated[2].

The Second Non-Life and Life Insurance Directives[3] added to the freedom of establishment, the freedom to provide cross-border services which became a full European Passport with the Third Non-Life and Life Directives of 1992[4]. These directives allowed home States that pre-vetted the policies of their authorised insurers to continue to do so, but not to increase those requirements nor impose them on insurers authorised by more liberal home States. The special position of Lloyd's was recognised. The prudential requirements of these directives have been strengthened recently by the Insurance Groups Directive[5].

Although an insurance compensation scheme is not required by European directive, the UK has operated one since 1975 which has covered all UK authorised insurers and their customers wherever they were resident[6]. Because the insurance directives have granted European insurers a passport, many are no longer authorised in the UK. This has required the scheme to be amended and in future policies will be covered by the compensation scheme only if either:

(1) they are issued in the UK by a UK authorised insurer protecting risks anywhere in the EEA; or

(2) they are issued in the EEA by a UK or EEA authorised insurer protecting risks in the UK[7].

2.2.2 Credit institutions

As with insurers, an early start was made on creating a European-wide banking market. The First Banking Co-ordination Directive of 1977[8] laid down some common minimum standards for granting licences to 'credit institutions', defined in Art 1 as 'an undertaking whose business is to receive deposits or other repayable funds from the public and to grant credits for its own account'[9]. In the UK, this definition clearly covered building societies as well as banks. Indeed, as the business of building societies expanded, many were becoming like banks, some even requiring authorisation for their investment business under the 1986 Act. Others abandoned mutuality altogether to become fully fledged banks.

---

1 1973/239/EEC.
2 Now ICA 1982, s 6.
3 1988/357/EEC and 1990/619/EEC.
4 1992/49/EEC and 1992/96/EEC.
5 1997/78/EC, implementation of which is discussed in Consultation Paper 50, FSA, May 2000. In supervising the solvency of insurers, home State regulators must now consider intra-group transactions and the risks to the insurer from the rest of its group.
6 Policyholders Protection Act 1975, as interpreted by *Scher v Policyholders Protection Board* [1993] 3 All ER 384.
7 Policyholders Protection Act 1975, s 4(1) as inserted by Policyholders Protection Act 1997, s 2(1). There is a special regime for the Channel Islands and the Isle of Man. This section has not been brought into force yet, but the FSA is expected to follow its terms.
8 1977/780/EEC.
9 The European definition and thus the European Passport only covers institutions that both accept deposits *and* grant credit. The UK legislation regulates deposit-taking, not the making of loans, see **1.2.4**.

A European Passport for credit institutions was created slightly earlier than for insurers with the Second Banking Co-ordination Directive of 1989 (2BCD) and the associated Own Funds and Solvency Directives[1]. Establishing minimum prudential rules was not difficult as most Member States were already parties to the Basle Accord of 1988[2]. The scope of the Passport, however, turned on a structural issue. As German banks conducted a wide variety of investment as well as banking businesses, the passport for credit institutions and their guaranteed subsidiaries authorised in one Member State was extended to cover any activities listed in the Annex, which included:

> '7. Trading for own account or customer account in . . .
>   a money market instruments (cheques, bills, CDs, etc)
>   b foreign exchange
>   c financial futures and options
>   d exchange and interest rate instruments
>   e transferable securities.
> 8. Participation in share issues and the provision of services related to such issues.
> 9. Advice to undertakings on capital structure, industrial strategy and related questions and advice and services relating to mergers and purchase of undertakings.
> 10. Money broking.
> 11. Portfolio management and advice.
> 12. Safekeeping and administration of securities . . .
> 14. Safe-custody services.'

Prudential supervision and rules were tightened up by the Consolidated Supervision and Large Exposures Directives[3] and, more controversially, a Deposit Guarantee Directive (DGD) was adopted in 1994[4]. To encourage the enforcement of prudential rules, this directive required all credit institutions to belong to the guarantee scheme of their home State, unless a host State's scheme was more generous, in which case a credit institution could voluntarily enter that scheme as a top up for business done in that State.

2.2.3   Investment firms

With credit institutions passported to do most types of investment business, it was believed that other investment firms should have such a Passport. The banks, however, did not want competition from such firms if they were to be subject to less stringent prudential rules. Also, many EEA countries had no existing system of authorising and regulating investment firms, although the UK had had one since the 1980s. This is why the Investment Services Directive (ISD) and the associated Capital Adequacy Directive (CAD) were not adopted until 1993 and the Investors Compensation Directive (ICD) only in 1997[5].

To obtain the Passport, an investment firm had to be incorporated, authorised and have its head office in an EEA country and be involved in one or more of the following activities for third parties, namely:

---

1   1989/646/EEC, 1989/299/EEC and 1989/647/EEC.
2   Basle Committee on Banking Regulations and Supervisory Practices, *International Convergence of Capital Measurement and Capital Standards*, July 1988. This is due to be replaced by a New Basle Accord, a firm draft of which should be published later in 2000.
3   1992/30/EEC and 1992/121/EEC.
4   1994/19/EC.
5   1993/22/EEC, 1993/6/EEC and 1997/9/EC.

(a) receiving and transmitting orders in;
(b) dealing as principal or agent in;
(c) managing discretionary portfolios of; and
(d) underwriting or placing any type of

transferable securities, money market instruments or financial derivatives (including swaps). The firm also must not fall within a number of excluded categories[1].

However, just as the 2BCD Passport could cover activities beyond deposit-taking and money-lending, the ISD Passport could extend beyond the four principal activities to cover:

(1) safekeeping and administration in relation to any securities or financial derivatives;
(2) safe custody services;
(3) granting credits or loans to allow him to carry out a transaction in any securities or financial derivatives where the firm granting the credit or loan is involved in the transaction;
(4) advice to undertakings on capital structure, industrial strategy and related matters and advice and service relating to mergers and the purchase of undertakings;
(5) services related to underwriting;
(6) investment advice concerning any securities or financial derivatives; and
(7) foreign exchange services where these are connected with the provision of investment services[2].

This list was not identical to that in the 2BCD, being wider and narrower in different areas. Unless a credit institution separately incorporated its investment businesses in non-guaranteed subsidiaries, it continued to rely upon its 2BCD passport. Still the CAD rules and some parts of the ISD applied to credit institutions providing investment services[3]. Indeed, the ISD went further than the 2BCD in a number of respects, in that it required:

(1) home States to impose 'ring fencing' rules on credit institutions and investment firms to protect clients' investment money and assets[4];
(2) host States to impose conduct of business rules for inward investment business as well as domestic business[5]; and
(3) open access to and transparency of dealings in all EEA regulated financial markets[6].

---

1   ISD Art 1 and Annexes A and B. The excluded categories are considered in **4.3.3**.
2   ISD Annex Section C.
3   In particular, capital adequacy rules in respect to the trading book and foreign exchange risk, ISD Art 3. The two activities passported under the ISD but not under the 2BCD (the receipt and transmission of customers' orders and the arranging of transactions in existing securities) have been added by the UK to the inward Passports of EEA credit institutions until now. The Government has seemed reluctant to confirm that this will continue, perhaps under an 'informal Passport', FSMA, Sch 4; vol 611 HL, 21 March 2000, c 153; see **5.2.4**.
4   ISD Art 10. Deposits, of course, cannot be ring-fenced as they are the principal capital of banks.
5   ISD Art 11.
6   ISD Arts 14, 15 and 21.

2.2.4   Other mutual recognition

The first FS Directive to rely on the principle of home State authorisation was in fact the Undertakings for Collective Investment in Transferable Securities (UCITS) Directive of 1985[1], which required mutual recognition of certain collective investment schemes (CISs) authorised to be marketed to the public in their home States (eg most UK authorised unit trusts). This eventually led to the UK allowing the domestic use of open-ended investment companies (OEICs)[2], which, as they are the accepted continental vehicle, may come to replace unit trusts. The UCITS Directive, however, has not been a great success because:

(1) it restricts the types of CISs that can qualify for a Passport;
(2) it requires very detailed scheme particulars to be given to every potential subscriber;
(3) it allows host State marketing rules to be applied;
(4) it requires a permanent establishment or at least a local paying and redemption agent in each State where the CIS is being marketed;
(5) it requires management companies to confine their activities to managing such CISs and does not give them an ISD Passport; and
(6) it does not compel fair tax treatment for inwardly passported CISs.

The UCITS Directive is due to be completely revised with three aims:

(1) to extend the types of schemes that can qualify for a Passport to cash funds, funds of funds and futures and options funds;
(2) to allow the operators of schemes to obtain a Passport to run funds and individual portfolios throughout the EEA; and
(3) to allow the production of simplified scheme particulars for investors[3].

Another example of mutual recognition was introduced by the Public Offers Directive[4]. Subject to the important qualifications of translations and tax explanations, a prospectus authorised in one Member State for the public offer of listed or non-listed securities could be used to offer those securities throughout the EEA and, if wanted, to obtain a local listing for them. That required the acceptance of minimum standards of disclosure. For listed companies, this had already been adopted in the European Listing Directives[5]. The Public Offers Directive imposed similar, though far less detailed initial disclosure requirements for non-listed securities. This Directive (unlike the Listing Directives) imposed no continuing disclosure requirements, although the Insider Dealing Directive did require non-listed companies traded on a market to keep the market informed of all new price-sensitive developments[6]. Indeed, although not concerned with mutual recognition, the Insider Dealing Directive was itself a further significant example of imposing a minimum regulatory standard for the whole European financial services industry.

---

1   1985/61/EEC amended by 1988/220/EEC.
2   Open-Ended Investment Companies (Investment Companies with Variable Capital) Regulations 1996, SI 1996/2827.
3   COM (1998) 449 and 451 final.
4   1989/298/EEC.
5   European Admission Directive 1979/279/EEC; Listing Particulars Directive 1980/390/EEC; Interim Reports Directive 1982/121/EEC.
6   1985/592/EEC Art 7.

2.2.5 Gaps in the Passport regimes

The development of the FS Directives has been piecemeal and not all financial services firms authorised, for example, under the FSMA qualify for a European Passport to conduct regulated activities elsewhere in the EEA. Single property schemes and certain authorised unit trusts that do not invest entirely in transferable securities do not qualify under the UCITS Directive as presently drafted. Dealers in commodity futures and options do not qualify for a Passport under any of the Directives.

Some activities, such as giving investment advice and providing custody services, can be passported as ancillary activities under a 2BCD or ISD Passport, but do not qualify for a passport as pure activities by themselves. The investment activities covered by these two Passports are also not identical[1]. As for the provision of pension schemes, this is so entangled with the taxation regimes of the various European countries that no Single Market is likely to develop in them for some time.

2.3 PROBLEMS OF IMPLEMENTATION

For a developed financial services market such as the UK, the concept of mutual recognition of firms, products and services from perhaps rather less developed markets raises two fundamental questions.

(1) To what extent can the regulation of UK authorised firms, products and services be stricter than the minimum required by other EEA regulators, now that their firms, products and services have open access to the UK?
(2) To what extent can UK regulations still be applied to those other EEA authorised (ie inwardly passported) firms, products and services?

2.3.1 Regulatory arbitrage

The first problem is sometimes referred to as the Delaware Effect[2]. The European Commission has been concerned that firms will set up 'brass-plate' headquarters in what might be perceived as weakly regulated or supervised jurisdictions and through opaque structures avoid effective regulation altogether, as happened in the BCCI Affair. The ISD already had stricter authorisation requirements to try to avoid this, but the Post-BCCI Directive of 1995[3] placed an obligation on all home States to refuse authorisation to insurers, credit institutions or investment firms employing such structures.

Nevertheless, the pressure to lower regulatory requirements to the minimum required by any Directives is intense. It can be seen particularly in the case of the Stock Exchange's Listing Rules. When the Listing Directives first came into effect, the Stock Exchange continued to impose a large number of extra disclosure rules

---

1   This was discussed at length in vol 343 HC, 1 February 2000, cc 972 and 973.
2   Because the tiny State of Delaware has director-friendly Corporation Laws, over half of the major listed companies in the USA are incorporated there, even if they have no other connection with the State.
3   1995/26/EC.

on companies with their primary listing in London, but faced with mutual recognition of EEA companies listed elsewhere, these have been steadily reduced.

Another example of the difficulty has arisen in the area of market transparency. Under pressure from the SIB, the Stock Exchange adopted a high level of pre- and post-transaction transparency, at least for the most regularly traded securities[1]. However, there has been concern that the current attempt to merge with other European Exchanges could lead to deals being directed through whichever system has the lightest transparency rules.

2.3.2   Host State regulation

A European Passport can only be claimed for a type of business if:

(1)   the claimant is authorised to conduct that type of business in its home State; and
(2)   that type of business falls within the lists of businesses covered by one of the FS Directives.

Therefore, it is possible for a firm to claim a Passport for some of its activities, but have to be authorised for others by the host State[2]. However, it is unclear whether the host State can apply all of its regulations, at least to non-passported cross-border activities, because where the firm is well regulated by its home State, this might be a breach of the freedom to provide services[3]. This 'informal passporting' of activities outside the scope of the FS Directives is a developing area of European law.

Another definitional problem with providing cross-border services (eg by telephone or through the Internet), is whether the business is being done in the home State of the firm or in the host State of the customer. If it is the former, the host State may not have a right to enforce any rules. In determining whether investment business was being done in the UK, the 1986 Act concentrated on whether an overseas firm had solicited or marketed to a non-professional customer in the UK, and in particular whether the strict marketing and cold-calling rules under ss 56 and 57 of the Act had been breached[4]. However, although the ECJ has considered host State marketing rules as an exception to the freedom to provide goods[5], it has rejected such an exception to the freedom to provide services[6].

To try to clarify this area, the European Commission produced an Interpretative Communication dealing with the cross-border services of credit institutions which is probably applicable to investment firms as well[7]. The exact legal standing of the

---

1   Transparency is the ability of investors to see the best prices available before transacting and the price at which the most recent deals have been transacted.
2   For example a French investment firm dealing in commodities futures in the UK, which are not covered by the ISD but which do require authorisation under the FSMA.
3   The ECJ does seem to favour home State regulation, for example allowing a home State to ban its authorised firms from cold-calling even in EEA countries where it was allowed, Case C384/93 *Alpine Investment BV v Minister van Financien* [1995] ECR I-1141, [1995] 2 CMLR 209.
4   1986 Act, s 1(3) and Sch 1, Part IV.
5   *Keck and Mithouard* (Cases C-267/91 and C-268/91) (1995) 72 CMLR 101.
6   *Alpine Investment BV v Minister van Financien.*
7   *Freedom to Provide Services and the Interest of the General Good in the Second Banking Directive* [1997] OJ C209/6. Eric Ducolombier of DGXV has expressed the view that it also applies to the ISD.

Communication is unclear because, although the ECJ may find it persuasive, it would not be bound to follow its advice.

For the purposes of a bank having to notify regulators that it is going to provide cross-border services, the Commission dismissed any test based on the originator of the initiative or a customer's place of residence. It maintained that:

> 'in order to determine where an activity was carried on, the place of what may be termed the 'characteristic performance' of the service, ie the essential supply for which payment is due, must be determined'.[1]

That test would suggest that a lot of apparently cross-border business would be treated as business conducted in the home State alone. However, curiously the Commission did not consider that that would bar the host State from imposing its conduct of business rules on this home State business! It relied, inter alia, on the Rome Convention on the law applicable to contractual obligations[2] which adopts a similar approach to the 1986 Act. As the Commission put it:

> '. . . a banking contract concluded with a consumer, must, therefore, observe at least the mandatory rules of the law of the consumer's country if the consumer was first canvassed in the consumer's country or if the order for the service was received there'.[3]

However, faced with growing Internet trade, the whole area of distance selling of financial services is under review.

Even where it is clear that passported business has been done in the host State, there remains a further definitional problem of what is a conduct of business rule as against a prudential rule, and then the application problem of which conduct of business rules may still be applied by a host State without overstepping the concept of the general good.

2.3.3 Conduct of business rules

Although the ECJ disapproves of duplicatory rules, its decision in *Alpine Investments BV v Minister van Financien* allowing a home State to impose cold-calling prohibitions on cross-border business, did highlight the difficult line to be drawn between prudential and conduct of business rules[4]. The confusion also appears in Art 11 of the ISD. This requires member States to adopt conduct of business rules applying to all investment business conducted in that State which meet the general principles laid down in the Article. These include the principle that a firm 'has and employs effectively the resources and procedures that are necessary for the proper performance of its business activities', which looks like a prudential requirement.

An acute example of this grey area in the UK was the requirement that key personnel conducting investment business must be individually registered with their regulator. When the 2BCD and ISD were implemented, the SFA removed its

---

1   Interpretative Communication Part 1B(2).
2   [1980] OJ L266/1.
3   Interpretative Communication Part 2C(2).
4   In its judgment at paras 41 and 43, the ECJ seemed to accept that the prohibition both safeguarded the reputation of the Netherlands financial markets (a quasi-prudential home State matter) and protected the investing public (a conduct of business host State matter).

requirement that overseas passported firms and their personnel prove that they were fit and proper persons to conduct investment business. Nevertheless, individual registration was retained as the SFA viewed this as a matter not just of prudential regulation, but also of the effective enforcement of conduct of business rules. The FSA is taking a more cautious approach[1].

The Interpretative Communication did consider the application of the general good principle to host State regulations and concluded that such regulations had to comply with six criteria, namely 'non-discrimination, absence of prior harmonisation, existence of an imperative reason relating to the interest of the general good, non-duplication, necessity and proportionality'. In practice, these may still allow considerable scope for host State regulation as the current enthusiasm for relying on distant home State regulation as against close host State supervision could fade in the face of any serious cross-border selling scandal.

2.3.4   Problems for a single regulator

One problem for the FSA created by the European regime is the latter's untidy nature. The European Passports created by the various FS Directives are not identical. Notification requirements, compensation arrangements, prudential requirements and scope definitions differ. Some of these problems are inherent in the nature of the firms covered, others arose because of the extended period over which the Passports were negotiated and compromises struck. The main confusion, however, probably arises because the European Commission and ECJ have failed to make a clear distinction between the freedom to provide services (true cross-border business) and the freedom of establishment (branches, etc). If the former were just subject to host State marketing rules[2], the latter could be subject to a far wider range of host State rules within the principle of the general good.

The European Commission is aware that the FS Directives need to be updated. An Action Plan has been put forward for implementation over the next five years and a Financial Services Policy Group has been looking at particular problems. So far, however, the only draft Directives to appear have been on collective investment schemes, distance selling of financial services and electronic money[3]. In the meantime, Art 59 of the Treaty of Rome on freedom of services still has direct effect and can be used to challenge any host State regulations that may not meet the 'general good' test, so that the FSA can not necessarily impose all its rules on EEA-based financial services firms just because they do not qualify for a European Passport.

---

1   SFA Rule 1-14. In Consultation Paper 53, paras 4.16–4.21, overseas directors will not be subject to approval but senior managers will be in respect of money laundering and designated investment business, ie approximately what constituted investment business under the 1986 Act, see **6.3.3**.

2   For example, if the decision in *Keck and Mithouard* had been applied in *Alpine Investments BV v Minister van Financien*. The rise of the Internet may require even host State marketing rules to be abandoned for pure home State regulation.

3   For further details, see DG XV, Release 17, July 1999.

2.4   THE EUROPEAN CONVENTION

One final problem is not created by the Treaty of Rome, but by the European Convention on Human Rights (the Convention). This could make the whole regulatory and decision-making process under the FSMA more legalistic and subject to far closer judicial review[1]. Although one of the original signatories after the Second World War, the UK has not until now made the Convention part of its domestic law[2]. However, under the Human Rights Act 1998 (HRA 1998), all public bodies, including courts and tribunals, are bound by the provisions of the Convention. Those provisions can override statutory instruments and common law but not primary legislation[3]. The courts will nevertheless have to construe primary legislation as far as possible in compliance with the Convention, and will be able to make a public declaration of non-compliance when they feel unable to do so[4]. To try to ensure that such situations do not arise too frequently, the Government Minister introducing new legislation is required to make a declaration that it complies with the Convention[5]. As a public administrative body, the FSA will itself be bound by the Convention and, therefore, potentially liable in damages for harm arising from any breach of its provisions. The Government has accepted that this liability under the Convention must override any statutory immunity from damages[6].

In incorporating the Convention into UK law, the Government is, in practice, adopting the accrued jurisprudence of the European Court of Human Rights (ECHR). Of particular importance for financial services regulation, the ECHR has refused to accept the argument that just because State regulation of particular activities is in the public interest, private commercial activities may be curtailed by such regulation without the protections of Arts 6 and 7 of the Convention[7]. Article 6(1) applies to all civil and criminal procedures and lays down that 'everyone is entitled to a fair and public hearing within a reasonable time by an independent and impartial tribunal established by law...' The remainder of Art 6 and Art 7(1) appear only to apply to criminal proceedings. They require that a defendant:

(1)   can have reasonably foreseen the legal consequences of his actions because the offence is sufficiently defined[8];

---

1   Human Rights Act 1998 and, in particular, Arts 6 and 7 of the Convention.
2   The courts already consider the Convention when interpreting ambiguities in statutes: *R v Secretary of State for the Home Department, ex p Brind* [1991] 1 AC 696, and when determining undecided issues at common law: *Derbyshire County Council v Times Newspapers Ltd* [1992] 1 QB 770, affirmed on other grounds [1993] AC 534.
3   HRA 1998, ss 2, 3(2) and 6, cf the position under the Treaty of Rome and the European Communities Act 1972; *R v Secretary of State for Transport, ex parte Factortame (No 2)* [1991] 1 All ER 70. The HRA 1998 comes into force in England and Wales on 2 October 2000 (it is already in force in Scotland).
4   HRA 1998, ss 2, 3(1) and 4.
5   HRA 1998, s 19.
6   FSMA, Sch 1, para 19, cf *Tinnelly and McElduff v United Kingdom* (1966) 22 EHRR CD 62. The extent of this exception to any immunity is not clear, *Osman v UK* [1999] FLR 193.
7   *Pudas v Sweden* (1988) 10 EHRR 380.
8   Article 7(1) as interpreted in *Kokkinakis v Greece* (1993) 17 EHRR 397.

(2) is presumed to be innocent until proved guilty[1];
(3) is properly informed of the nature of any charge and has time and facilities to prepare his defence[2];
(4) is allowed to defend himself or to be legally represented (free when the interests of justice so require)[3]; and
(5) can summon his own witnesses and cross-examine those against him[4].

The obligations imposed on criminal proceedings are thus more specific than those on civil or disciplinary proceedings. However, the ECHR has not accepted that a Contracting State can escape these extra obligations by merely defining certain proceedings as civil or disciplinary[5]. In the Memorandum from HM Treasury supplied to the Joint Committee[6], the Court's current position was summarised as follows:

> 'Although the jurisprudence is still developing and may be subject to interpretation, there are a number of factors which are relevant to the characterisation of proceedings as civil or criminal for Convention purposes. The first factor is the characterisation of the proceedings in domestic law, although a civil categorisation in domestic law is not conclusive for the Convention[7]. Second, there is the nature of the conduct at which the provisions are directed and, in particular, the overlap with the criminal law. Third, there is the question of whether the measure is directed at the population as a whole, like tax or road traffic laws, or whether, on the contrary, it is aimed at a particular group of persons possessing a special status the regulation of which is justified to preserve the proper and orderly functioning of the group[8]. Fourth, there is the nature and level of any penalty. The more punitive and severe the penalty, the more likely it is that the proceedings will be characterised as criminal under the Convention.'

The Government maintains that the disciplinary regimes for individuals and firms under Parts IV, V, VI and XIV of the FSMA will be classified as civil proceedings[9]. Certainly in recent admissibility cases, the Commission on Human Rights has viewed professional disciplinary proceedings as civil, including those of the IMRO[10]. However, in their Joint Opinion to the same Committee, Lord Lester and Javan Herberg pointed out that these decisions concerned only the banning of unfit persons[11]. They did not consider the deterrent use of unlimited fining powers for serious breaches of regulations. That situation might be viewed differently[12]. Subsequently, Lord Lester has pointed to the recent decisions by the

---

1   Convention, Art 6(2), including the privilege against self-incrimination, *Murray v United Kingdom* (1996) 22 EHRR 29; for example compelled statements, *Saunders v United Kingdom* (1996) 23 EHRR 313.
2   Convention, Art 6(3)(a).
3   Convention, Art 6(3)(b).
4   Convention, Art 6(3)(c).
5   *Engel v Netherlands* (1976) 1 EHRR 647. It has also suggested that some of rights specified for criminal proceedings may also apply in some civil proceedings, see below.
6   Joint Committee, Second Report, Minutes of Evidence, p 2, para 9.
7   *Benham v United Kingdom* (1996) 22 EHRR 293.
8   *Ozturk v Germany* (1984) 6 EHRR 409; *Ravnsborg v Sweden* (1994) 18 EHRR 38.
9   Joint Committee, Second Report, Minutes of Evidence, p 2, para 10.
10   *APB v IMRO* Appl 30552/96, 15 January 1998; *X v United Kingdom* Appl 28530/95, 18 January 1998; *Wickramsinghe v United Kingdom* Appl 31503/96, 8 December 1997.
11   Joint Committee, First Report, Annex C, p 84, paras 24–28.
12   FSMA, ss 66, 91 and 206; *Lauko v Slovakia* 2 September 1998 at para 56; *Demicoli v Malta* (1992) 14 EHRR 47.

French Courts that for the purpose of Art 6, the fining powers of the Commission des Operations de Bourse are criminal in nature[1]. On the other hand, the Government has pointed to the decision of the ECHR treating a £10,000 fine imposed on a solicitor by his professional body as a civil matter[2]. It has, therefore, continued to treat the disciplinary procedures under the FSMA as civil in nature, despite the unlimited fining power and the sheer numbers of firms and individuals potentially subject to that penalty.

By contrast, the Government has reluctantly accepted that the power to impose 'civil fines' for market abuse, contained in Part VIII of the FSMA, may indeed be viewed as criminal in nature. This is because such fines can be applied to all market participants and because 'there are significant similarities between the market abuse regime and the criminal offences of insider dealing and market manipulation...'[3] This has led the Government to accept that the use of previously compelled statements must be limited in market abuse proceedings, that legal aid will be available for them where necessary and that greater certainty be given to the scope of market abuse by the creation of 'safe harbours'[4]. There is, nevertheless, still concern that the market abuse regime could be challenged for uncertainty[5]. Also, if market abuse proceedings are criminal in nature, there is the potential for 'double jeopardy', where a defendant is pursued for market abuse and prosecuted for misleading statements or insider dealing. If, as is expected, the UK ratifies the seventh Protocol of the Convention, such double jeopardy will become a breach of that Convention.

Whether proceedings are categorised as criminal or not, they must still meet the requirement of Art 6(1) for a fair, public hearing before an independent tribunal. That does seem to be largely met by having the right to a full hearing before the Financial Services and Markets Tribunal (the Tribunal) of any disciplinary or market abuse matter not settled with the FSA. However, more could be required if other requirements of Art 6 are treated as mere examples of the requirements for a fair civil as well as criminal trial[6].

There remains the issue of the standard of proof to be applied by the Tribunal. Even if disciplinary or market abuse matters are categorised by the Convention as criminal, that does not automatically impose 'proof beyond reasonable doubt'[7]. In English law, where disciplinary proceedings are essentially criminal, the courts

---

1   Joint Committee, Second Report, Appendix 2, paras 12 and 13.

2   *Brown v United Kingdom* (1998 unreported) referred to in Joint Committee, Second Report, Minutes of Evidence, p 6, para 3; also *Konig v Germany* (1978) Ser A No 27 (practice of medicine), *Guchez v Belgium* (1984) 40 DR 100 (architecture) and *De Moor v Belgium* (1994) Ser A No 292 (advocates), all referred to in Joint Committee, Second Report, Minutes of Evidence, p 8, para 5.

3   Joint Committee, Second Report, Minutes of Evidence, p 3, paras 12 and 13.

4   Joint Committee, Second Report, Minutes of Evidence, p 3, paras 14–17.

5   For example, the opinions of Lord Steyn, Herbert Smith and Clifford Chance in Joint Committee, Second Report, App 3–5.

6   *Albert and Le Compte v Belgium* (1983) Ser A No 58, para 30. This seems to have been the ECHR's approach in more recent, albeit criminal, cases such as *Saunders v United Kingdom* (1996) 23 EHRR 313 and *Rowe and Davis v United Kingdom* Case 28901/95 (16 February 2000 unreported). The requirements for legal aid and full disclosure of evidence, for example, may apply to all FSA proceedings even if they are viewed as civil, vol 351 HC, 5 June 2000, c 53.

7   *Salabiaku v France* (1988) 13 EHRR 379.

have not been clear on the standard to be applied[1]. The old Financial Services Tribunal used to apply the usual civil standard of the 'balance of probabilities' but raising it on a sliding scale for more serious cases[2] and this is probably sufficient to meet any Convention requirement on this point.

Despite the remaining uncertainties in this area, the Chancellor of the Exchequer and Lord McIntosh of Haringey, as the sponsoring Ministers, have been prepared to make the statement under the HRA 1998, s 19, that in their view the FSMA is compatible with the Convention[3].

1   *Re A Solicitor* [1993] QB 69, cf *R v Maidstone Crown Court, ex p Olson* [1992] COD 496.
2   *In the matter of Peter James West and Paul Bingham* (published decision, 18 November 1994) following *Hornal v Neuberger* [1957] 1 QB 247, CA.
3   Stated on the cover of the original Bill as ordered to be printed on 17 June 1999 and on subsequent editions.

Chapter 3

THE FINANCIAL SERVICES AUTHORITY
AND THE TRIBUNAL

3.1 BACKGROUND

Although, in theory, a single regulator for the financial services industry will be created only when the FSMA comes into force, in practice it already exists. The Bank of England Act 1998 only added banking supervision to the limited responsibilities the FSA already had from its former incarnation as the SIB. However, in the interregnum, the FSA has taken on the staff of most of the other regulators and moved them to its Canary Wharf headquarters. A new unified management structure has been created, even if technically decisions are still being made in the name of the old regulators[1].

On the FSMA coming into force, the FSA will have direct responsibility for supervising banks, building societies, insurance businesses (including mutuals and Lloyd's) and most of the investment businesses presently requiring authorisation under the 1986 Act. It will not regulate occupational pensions, which remain the responsibility of the Occupational Pensions Regulatory Authority and any complaints about them will continue to be dealt with by the Pensions Ombudsman. The justification for this separate regime is that regulation of, and complaints about, occupational pensions generally involve non-authorised companies or trustees and collective interests in multi-million pound funds which require special arrangements. However, it has been admitted that this will cause the new stakeholder pensions to be subject to both the pensions and financial services regimes[2].

The consequences of the FSMA for other regulators will vary. The Bank of England will continue to act as the central bank responsible for the stability of the monetary system and is exempt from the provisions of the FSMA[3]. Lloyd's will continue to run its insurance market, but will, as an authorised person, be subject to FSA supervision[4]. Its members who supply capital will remain unregulated, but its professional agents will need FSA authorisation[5]. The SROs will be wound up and the RPBs will no longer be responsible for the authorisation of their members' financial activities (and in the case of the IBRC, will cease to exist)[6]. However, the remaining RPBs will be reborn as Designated Professional Bodies (DPBs), and the majority of the members that they formerly authorised will continue to be regulated by them as exempt persons[7]. The registration and supervisory functions of the BSC, the FSC and the Registry of Friendly Societies will be transferred to the FSA, but the other functions (eg the regulation of such

---

1   For further details, see **1.5.3**.
2   Vol 344 HC, 9 February 2000, cc 262 and 263.
3   Draft Exemption Order, Sch, Part I, see **4.2.1**.
4   FSMA, Part XIX.
5   Draft Regulated Activities Order, Arts 20 and 22, see **4.3.2**.
6   FSMA, s 416. Transitional provisions for the subsidiarisation and then winding up of SROs are contained in the FSMA, Sch 20.
7   See **11.4**.

societies' constitutions) may be transferred to the Treasury so that these three regulators can be wound up as well[1].

A single statutory regulator will end the last vestiges of self-regulation[2]. The FSA has a responsibility for the whole financial services industry, but is clearly on the side of the investor. Authorised firms will no longer be directly represented, although they will be regularly consulted. As a private company, the FSA will have quite remarkable powers of rule-making, investigating, enforcing and fining – all exercised under a statutory immunity from damages.

3.2   STATUS OF THE FINANCIAL SERVICES AUTHORITY

Schedule 1 to the FSMA sets out the status and the basic constitution of the FSA. Although a form of quango, the FSA does not act on behalf of the Crown, and its members, staff and officers are not Crown servants. It is a private company limited by guarantee[3]. However, its chairman and governing board are appointed and removed by the Treasury. The board, the majority of whose members must be non-executive, may delegate all but its legislative functions to committees, sub-committees, officers and employees. Legislative functions include rule-making and issuing statements, codes, directions and general guidance[4].

There was a sustained Opposition campaign to build in a presumption that the role of the executive chairman should be split into a non-executive chairman and a chief executive, as is recommended by the Combined Code for listed

---

1   FSMA, Part XXI. To achieve this, the Treasury has a wide power to make orders that can even override primary legislation, FSMA, s 339. The statutory restrictions on a friendly society changing its activities or forming subsidiaries and joint ventures will be replaced by FSA supervision, FSMA, s 334 and Sch 18, Parts I and II; vol 344 HC, 9 February 2000, cc 354–356. Similarly, some restrictions on credit unions are being relaxed: FSMA, s 338 and Sch 18, Pt V. The Treasury may by statutory instrument lay down regulations for insurance contracts: FSMA, s 424. As a result of these changes, not only will the ICA 1982 and the 1986 Act be repealed and the BA 1987 be largely repealed, but also the Policyholders Protection Acts 1975 and 1997, the Industrial Assurance Acts 1923 and 1948 and the Insurance Brokers (Registration) Act 1977 together with sections of the Industrial and Provident Societies Act 1965, Credit Unions Act 1979, the Building Societies Act 1986 and the Friendly Societies Acts 1974 and 1992: FSMA, s 416 and Schs 18 and 20.
2   The involvement of practitioners on the Authorisation and Enforcement Committees could be seen as vestiges of 'self-enforcement', but these practitioners, like those on the Practitioner Panel below, will be appointees of the FSA. It could also be said that the FSA's emphasis on general standard-setting, risk-based supervision and greater responsibility on senior management is passing some self-enforcement down to the level of the individual firms.
3   FSMA, s 1 and Sch 1, para 13. Because of its status, the FSA is exempt by paras 14 and 15 from using 'limited' as part of its name unless the Treasury requires it. By para 10(4), the Treasury can also force compliance with any of the audit and other requirements of the Companies Act 1985 not otherwise required of a company limited by guarantee.
4   FSMA, Sch 1, paras 1, 2, 3(1) and 5. Curiously, although the Treasury appoints the board, it is the FSA's responsibility to ensure that the majority are non-executive; an effort, perhaps, to ensure that the FSA does not buy off board members with jobs! (vol 610 HL, 16 March 2000, c 1741). Board members are disqualified from sitting as MPs or Members of the Northern Irish Assembly: the FSMA, Sch 1, paras 20 and 21.

companies[1]. The Government pointed to the fact that this is not done for other financial regulators round the world and that the FSA is not an ordinary company answerable to shareholders. But, as the Opposition spokesman, Lord Saatchi said:

> 'Under our proposals, the City .... would have in the chairman someone whom it could approach with its anxieties, someone who, if not instantly responsible for the issues, could take them up with the chief executive, enabling the whole system to be seen to work. The BBC is a good example of how this system works in practice .... If the BBC was to be accused of political bias of a serious nature, or of some gross invasion of privacy, or of not meeting its programming obligations in a serious way, it would be clear that someone other than the chief executive responsible for the allegedly offending decisions would become the court of appeal.'[2]

The Opposition's proposal was defeated, still leaving it open to split the functions in the future. In the meantime, the Government inserted a requirement on the FSA to 'have regard to such generally accepted principles of good governance as it is reasonable to regard as applicable to it'. It was pointed out that by justifying an executive chairman in its accounts and having a non-executive deputy chairman, the FSA did meet the current principles in the Combined Code[3].

There is also to be a special committee of non-executive members appointed by the FSA, but with its chairman appointed by the Treasury. This committee is charged specifically with:

(1) reviewing how economic and efficient the FSA is in using its resources;
(2) reviewing the financial controls of the FSA;
(3) determining the remuneration of the chairman and the executive members; and
(4) reporting on all three in the FSA's annual report to the Treasury.

The efficiency review may not be delegated but the other two can be to sub-committees. The 'housekeeping' nature of this committee does not limit the general role of the non-executive members[4]. As the Government spokesman in the Lords has said:

> 'The non-executive directors of the FSA are not there as representatives of individual disciplines within the financial markets, but as wise persons with knowledge of a wide range of financial markets, able to contribute to the work of the authority .... We expect the non-executives, led by the deputy chairman, to play a full role in the board, providing an independent perspective on the scrutiny of the executives and the FSA's overall performance.'[5]

---

1   Vol 343 HC, 27 January 2000, cc 600–617; vol 610 HL, 16 March 2000, cc 1687–1721; vol 612 HL, 13 April 2000, cc 291–306. This was also the view of the Joint Committee and of the Cruickshank Reports. The current Combined Code is to be found at the end of *The Listing Rules*.
2   Vol 612 HL, 13 April 2000, c 300.
3   FSMA, s 7; Lord McIntosh in vol 613 HL, 18 May 2000, c 378 and the Economic Secretary in vol 351 HC, 5 June 2000, c 44.
4   FSMA, Sch 1, paras 3 and 4; the FSA's governing board and committee structure is modelled on that of the Court of the Bank of England: Bank of England Act 1998, s 3. However, the members are clearly directors of a company: Companies Act 1985, s 741, as confirmed by Lord McIntosh, vol 612 HL, 13 April 2000, c 303.
5   Lord McIntosh, vol 610 HL, 16 March 2000, cc 1741 and 1744.

The FSA must maintain arrangements to monitor compliance with, and enforce, the regulatory system. The monitoring, but not the enforcement function can be contracted out to competent parties[1].

The curious status of the FSA arises from a desire not to fund it from the public purse. It has the power to charge fees to meet its expenses, to repay its existing and any future borrowings and to maintain adequate reserves. It may not charge fees for administering applications to use inward or outward European Passports, nor for granting approval for key personnel in authorised firms. In effect, this leaves it to charge the authorised firms and other bodies that it regulates. What it may not do is use fines that it levies to meet its general expenses[2]. The FSA must devise a scheme, subject to public consultation, that applies the proceeds of these penalties for the benefit of authorised firms[3].

3.3   FINANCIAL SERVICES AUTHORITY'S DUTIES

In the 1986 Act, Sch 8 did lay down the principles to be applied by the SIB when rule-making, but the FSMA now goes much further. It prescribes a set of regulatory objectives that apply to all of the FSA's general functions, which are:

(1) rule-making;
(2) preparing and issuing codes;
(3) giving general written guidance; and
(4) determining its general policy and principles by reference to which it performs its other functions[4].

The first three functions are to be 'considered as a whole' and the fourth is 'general', drafting which suggests that the objectives cannot easily be used to challenge any *particular* ruling of the FSA. This is further reinforced by the subjective duty to 'so far as reasonably possible, act in a way . . . . which the *Authority*

---

1   FSMA, Sch 1, para 6; for example, monitoring the compliance of authorised professional firms could be delegated to DPBs but enforcement could not be. In fact, the FSA has decided against such contracting out, *Response Paper to CP30*, FSA, June 2000, para 11.2.

2   FSMA, Sch 1, paras 17 and 18. The FSA's current fee proposals to try and minimise cross-subsidy by keeping separate fee-paying blocks are contained in Consultation Paper 56, FSA, June 2000.

3   FSMA, Sch 1, para 16. The consultation procedures are the same as for the complaints scheme below. The scheme to pass back the benefit of penalties can distinguish between different classes of authorised firms. However, at the end of the day, fines levied against offending firms will reduce the total cost of regulation for others. The FSA is also responsible for levying authorised firms to meet legal aid for market abuse cases, see below. Provision is made for the tax treatment of all these levies as allowable expenses and refunds as taxable receipts: FSMA, s 411.

4   FSMA, s 2(4) and (5). To be general, guidance must be given at least to a class of regulated persons.

considers most appropriate for the purpose of meeting those objectives'[1]. Nevertheless, in the unlikely event of the FSA embarking on rule-making or policies outside these objectives, it would be acting *ultra vires* and be subject to judicial review, although whether such rules or policies would be declared void might depend on how clearly outside the objectives they were[2].

The four objectives, in no particular order of priority[3], are:

(1) maintaining confidence in the financial system in the UK;
(2) promoting public understanding of that financial system;
(3) securing the appropriate degree of protection for consumers; and
(4) reducing the extent to which businesses within and without the perimeter may be used for a purpose connected with financial crime[4].

However, in pursuing these potentially costly objectives, the FSA is restrained by the following seven principles:

(1) the efficient and economic use of resources;
(2) the responsibilities of the managers of authorised firms;
(3) the burden being proportionate to the benefit;
(4) the desirability of facilitating innovation;
(5) the maintenance of international competitiveness;
(6) the need to minimise adverse effects on competition; and
(7) the desirability of facilitating competition[5].

To some extent, the tension between the objectives and the restraining principles internalises within the FSA the previous tension between the SIB, regulating the regulators and seeking the best objectives and the SROs, representing market operators and reflecting business realities[6].

3.3.1   The objectives

The Joint Committee looked in detail at these objectives and principles[7] and noted with some concern that the management of systemic risk, was not

---

1   FSMA, s 2(1) (emphasis added). This type of subjective 'self-reference' clause is found throughout the FSMA, vol 343 HC, 1 February 2000, cc 936–947. There is a loose objective test that the Authority's actions should also 'be compatible with the regulatory objectives'. However, the Economic Secretary admitted that it was the Government's aim to protect the FSA from judicial review of particular decisions: Standing Committee A, 8 July 1999, cc 57 and 62. She did, however, give an example where an overseas bank might apply for judicial review, challenging a discriminatory application of capital adequacy rules by the FSA at cc 72 and 75.

2   *R v Dacorum Gaming Licensing Committee, ex p EMI Cinemas and Leisure Ltd* [1971] 3 All ER 666.
3   Treasury Progress Report, March 1999, para 4.15.
4   FSMA, ss 2(2) and 3–6.
5   FSMA, s 2(3).
6   The objectives and restraining principles have encouraged the FSA to review its whole approach to risk assessment and regulation: *A new regulator for a new millennium*. That document does reveal another tension between devoting resources towards regulating the large firms likely to create systemic risk as against smaller retail firms likely to missell to ordinary consumers.
7   Joint Committee, First Report, Part III.

mentioned specifically[1]. Instead, the first objective refers to maintaining confidence in the financial system which is confined to the UK, but:

> '*includes*—
> (a)   financial markets and exchanges;
> (b)   regulated activities; and
> (c)   other activities connected with financial markets and exchanges'.[2]

The listed items do not cover all banking activities, but they are not a comprehensive list and the term 'financial system' must presumably do so. The objective is to maintain the standards of the system as a whole, but again that must cover the management of systemic risk[3]. When pressed on the importance of systemic risk, the FSA pointed to its Memorandum of Understanding with the Treasury and the Bank of England as being adequate[4].

The FSA has already embarked upon a programme to meet the second objective, producing a Consultation Document and a Policy Statement[5] and setting up a Consumer Education Department with an inquiry line taking about 2,000 calls a week. Booklets have been produced on key issues and programmes developed to raise financial literacy, including Town Hall Meetings. Although worthy, it was noted that attendees at these meetings were generally experienced investors and it was observed in the evidence given to the Joint Committee that the impact of league tables and other information already produced 'is not a lot'[6]. It may not be immediately obvious that this objective has much to do with financial regulation. However, the FSA is following the example of the SEC's Office of Investor Education and Assistance which has become the main two-way link between retail investors and the SEC, not just giving out advice, but encouraging complaints in return which provide the basis for nearly a quarter of all SEC regulatory investigations. Faced with the enormous difficulties of educating people about financial matters, there is a danger that this objective could become very costly. It can also prove very controversial, as the FSA has found in trying to set up Comparative Tables for the most common retail products to be made available over the internet[7].

In the third objective, what amounts to 'the appropriate degree of protection for consumers' produced sharp disagreement amongst those giving evidence to the Joint Committee. 'Consumers' here covers anyone (including authorised firms) who might be directly or indirectly affected by the FSMA regulated services,

---

1   Joint Committee, First Report, para 43; see also **1.6**.
2   FSMA, s 3(2) (emphasis added).
3   The Economic Secretary's explanation, Standing Committee A, 13 July 1999, c 182.
4   *FSA: an outline*, App 2; Joint Committee, First Report, paras 43 and 44. A standing committee of representatives from the three institutions meets monthly to review this area. Also, the FSA's chairman sits on the Court of the Bank of England and the Bank's deputy governor sits on the FSA's board. The Treasury, however, can veto any bank rescue package.
5   Consultation Paper 15, FSA, November 1998; Policy Statement *Consumer Education: A strategy for promoting public understanding of the financial system*, FSA, May 1999.
6   Joint Committee, First Report, para 57.
7   Consultation Paper 28, FSA, October 1999 and *Response to Consultation Paper 28*, FSA, June 2000. In particular, the FSA has taken the advice of Bacon and Woodrow that past investment performance should not be included as it is such a poor indicator of future performance. The Government refused to add a further objective of dealing with social exclusion, although the FSA is conducting research into this area: vol 344 HC, 9 February 2000, cc 263–268 and *FSA Plan and Budget 2000/01* para 50.

whether offered by authorised or non-authorised firms[1]. All agreed that given this startlingly wide definition, the FSA must have regard to the different risks of different investments and the different experience and expertise of different investors[2]. There was disagreement as to whether 'the general principle that consumers should take responsibility for their decisions'[3] (in effect *caveat emptor*) should ever apply to private customers. The FSA took the view that 'while they would do all they could to prevent misselling, they could not in the end prevent "mis-buying"'.[4] This view seems to have prevailed, although some further protection was added by requiring consideration of 'the needs that consumers may have for advice and accurate information'.[5] This endorses the existing type of 'suitability rule' without importing the sale of goods concept of 'fitness for the purpose'.[6] That would have suggested moving to a general system of 'product regulation' with the danger of reducing competition and being misunderstood as product endorsement by the FSA[7]. No one of these factors that the FSA 'must have regard to' overrides any others and the mix of factors leaves the FSA a relatively free hand to define different types of customer and the protection they should receive.

For the final objective, financial crimes are defined as any acts, *wherever* committed, that would have amounted to the offences of fraud, dishonesty, insider dealing, misleading or manipulating a market or handling the proceeds of crime, if done in the UK[8]. This is a recognition of the international nature of such crimes. The FSA's responsibilities were originally confined to trying to reduce the use of those that it regulates (ie authorised persons, RIEs and RCHs) for such criminal purposes, but this was extended to cover those who were not but should have been authorised[9]. As well as the increased investigative and prosecutorial roles given to it under the FSMA[10], the FSA has some responsibility for those it regulates being aware of the risk of being used in financial crime and adopting practices and devoting sufficient resources to prevent, detect and monitor it[11]. Concern was expressed about the burden that the FSA might impose upon UK firms and markets by this, and the drafting was changed so that the measures taken

---

1   FSMA, ss 5(3) and 138(7). The coverage of operations that are not authorised, even if they
     should have been, emphasises the FSA's responsibility for 'policing the perimeter' as part of
     its consumer protection activities. The width of the definition of 'consumers' is considered
     further in **6.2**.
2   FSMA, s 5(2)(a) and (b).
3   FSMA, s 5(2)(d).
4   Joint Committee, First Report, para 36. The issue was also considered by the House of Lords
     at vol 611 HL, 20 March 2000, cc 32–43.
5   FSMA, s 5(2)(c).
6   Sale of Goods Act 1979, s 14.
7   Joint Committee, First Report, paras 38–41. This fear is borne out by the problems of
     approved Charges, Access and Terms (CAT) for ISAs. Product regulation is largely confined
     to CISs, see **13.2**. The Cruickshank Reports also came out strongly against product regulation.
8   FSMA, s 6(3) and (4).
9   FSMA, s 6(1) and (5).
10   FSMA, Parts XI and XXVII.
11   FSMA, s 6(2). The particular duty is weakly worded as having to 'have regard to the
     desirability of' these outcomes. The Economic Secretary disingenuously claimed that this
     section does not impose obligations on regulated persons, but the FSA must impose some
     obligations if it is to show that it does desire such outcomes, Standing Committee A, 15 July
     1999, c 240; see, for example, Consultation Paper 46, FSA, April 2000, on money-laundering
     rules.

need only be 'appropriate' rather than 'adequate'. There remains a concern that the FSA could use this objective to justify sub-contracting its policing functions to authorised firms, but this objective, like the other three, has to be read in conjunction with the restraining principles.

3.3.2   The principles

The principles are not elaborated upon in the FSMA, but the Joint Committee was concerned about the burden of regulation and compliance and its effect on competitiveness. Indeed, the Treasury Select Committee, some of the Joint Committee, the Opposition in Parliament and most recently, Don Cruickshank in his Banking Review Reports, wished to make the fostering of competition and competitiveness a fifth objective. The Interim Cruickshank Report was particularly forceful on this point:

> 'The FSA should have a primary competition objective, in addition to its regulatory objectives .... Getting the regulator's primary statutory duties right is essential .... A competition objective that is weak relative to the regulator's other objectives is unlikely to be delivered effectively.'[1]

However, that has been resisted by both the Government and the FSA as confusing the regulator's role with that of the Office of Fair Trading (OFT) and putting the FSA in a difficult position when trying to co-operate with regulators from jurisdictions against whom it would then be required to forward the UK's interests. So international competitiveness and competition have remained restraining principles, albeit with competition split into two and subject to external scrutiny by the OFT and the Competition Commission[2].

The FSA need only 'have regard' to these principles in discharging its general functions whereas the FSA 'must, so far as is reasonably possible, act in a way .... which is compatible' with the objectives. Although the Economic Secretary refused to be drawn in Committee on the relative weight to be attached to the principles as against the objectives, the drafting does give the latter greater prominence[3]. It seems unlikely that any action of the FSA could be declared void

---

1   *Competition and Regulation in Financial Services: Striking the Right Balance* p 13 and Annex 3. In the covering letter to the Chancellor of the Exchequer of 22 July 1999, Don Cruickshank went even further saying: 'Our priority should be to develop a strategy for striking the optimal balance between competition and necessary regulation. In the search for higher sustainable growth rate for the UK beyond a stable low inflation macro-economic climate, there is in my view nothing more worthwhile for government to do than to get this balance right'.

2   Joint Committee, First Report, paras 46–51; Standing Committee A, 8 July 1999, cc 42–77; vol 343 HC, 27 January 2000, cc 645–667. For the special competition regime, see below. It has been pointed out that the wording of the second competition principle (FSMA, s 2(3)(g)) does look suspiciously like an objective, albeit one that the FSA only has to have 'regard to': Lord Taverne, vol 610 HL, 21 February 2000, c 27; cf the Utilities Bill which has as a primary objective the protection of the consumer 'wherever appropriate, by promoting effective competition'. Lord McIntosh tried to explain the distinction at vol 611 HL, 20 March 2000, cc 25 and 26. In his Final Report, Don Cruickshank has called for a review of the workings of these competition arrangements after two years: *Competition in UK Banking: A Report to the Chancellor of the Exchequer*, para 2.135.

3   The Economic Secretary, however, said: 'The fact that the principles are stated with great economy does not detract from their importance', Standing Committee A, 8 July 1999, c 77.

just because it offended one of the principles. As the Economic Secretary said, defending the drafting:

> 'We want something that requires the FSA to give proper weight to the principles and to ensure that it takes them properly into account but, at the same time, does not expose the regulators to tactical litigation on individual regulatory decisions. Exploration of these issues has led us to the conclusion that the current formulation strikes the right balance.'[1]

Still, considerations of proportionality, innovation and competitiveness should keep the FSA focused on the question, 'Is this policy, regulation or change really necessary?' Of less comfort to the regulated may be consideration of managers' responsibilities. The aim is to allow the regulator to hold back from detailed regulation of a firm because it is able to rely on effective management. This has led to a considerable emphasis on senior management arrangements and responsibilities[2].

Some FSA officials have pointed out that enforcement is not an independent objective and so should probably only be directed at meeting the market confidence and consumer protection objectives. It is also interesting that the closer the FSA has got to acquiring its new powers, the more it has emphasised the limits of regulation:

> 'In practice the FSA is not aiming to maintain a "zero failure" regime as regards failure, or lapses in conduct, by firms. This is neither possible nor desirable given the costs and moral hazard involved in such a system. To do so would be uneconomic from a cost/benefit point of view, would hinder competition and innovation and would create an unacceptable level of moral hazard both on firms and consumers.'[3]

3.4 ACCOUNTABILITY

The Joint Committee was very concerned about the accountability of the new 'Super Regulator'[4] and changes were made to the original proposals in the light of its comments. As a body conducting public functions, the FSA is subject to judicial review[5] and given its enormous powers over an industry employing well over a million people, one might imagine that a regular stream of such cases could arise. However, the whole drafting of the FSMA is designed to limit such resorts to the courts and to provide alternatives[6]. For example, although the objectives and principles that must guide the FSA in discharging its general functions do not

---

1   Vol 343 HC, 27 January 2000, cc 646 and 647. The principles do tend to stand a step behind the objectives in Ministerial Statements and the FSA's Consultation Papers, a tendency also noted by Howard Flight MP, vol 343 HC, 27 January 2000, c 653.

2   Consultation Paper 26, FSA, July 1999, and Consultation Paper 35, FSA, December 1999; see **5.3.2**.

3   Consultation Paper 38, FSA, January 2000, Annex A. As has already been noted, FSMA, Sch 1, para 6(3) only requires the FSA to 'maintain arrangements for enforcing'.

4   Joint Committee, First Report, Part V.

5   *R v Panel on Takeovers and Mergers, ex parte Datafin plc* [1987] QB 815. Although a registered company in England and Wales, the FSA may have actions brought against it in Scotland and Northern Ireland: FSMA, s 415.

6   The Financial Secretary has openly admitted to this being the design: vol 343 HC, 1 February 2000, c 946.

seem to provide much of a basis for court action, the FSA does have to consult about, and explain how, it has applied them.

3.4.1   Practitioners and consumers

The governing boards of the original SROs largely consisted of practitioners, but as they became arm's length regulators, the boards became a mixture of executive regulators, and non-executive practitioner and user representatives. Under the FSMA, the Treasury is under no obligation to appoint practitioners or consumer representatives to the board of the FSA; but even before a draft Bill was published, the FSA realised that some form of practitioner and consumer involvement would have to be developed. In the first two Consultation Papers it produced, the FSA proposed to create a Consumer Panel (based on the existing PIA Consumer Panel) and a slightly looser Practitioner Forum (Forum)[1]. These were set up in November 1998.

The FSMA now imposes a general duty on the FSA to consult practitioners and consumers 'on the extent to which its general policies and practices are consistent with its general duties' which covers both the objectives and the principles[2]. The consultation arrangements must at least include a Practitioner Panel and a Consumer Panel, with members the FSA considers appropriate and which it appoints, albeit with the appointment or dismissal of the Chairmen subject to Treasury approval. The members of the Practitioner Panel must themselves be authorised or represent authorised firms, RIEs and RCHs. The members of the Consumer Panel must be consumers or represent consumer interests. To avoid overlap with the interests represented by the Practitioner Panel, 'consumers' here do not include authorised firms but can include, for example, major corporations. Although not representing authorised firms, members of the Panel can still themselves be authorised or approved; however, the FSA must also include fair representation for individual private customers[3].

The FSMA does not lay down any further terms of reference for these Panels[4], but it is natural that the Practitioner Panel will concentrate on the restraining principles and the Consumer Panel on the consumer protection and public understanding objectives. This is reflected in the current FSA terms of reference for the Forum and Consumer Panel[5]. Clearly, the two are likely to have very different views on certain issues and the FSA must consider their representations and explain to them in writing where it disagrees with their views. The FSA is not required to carry statements from these Panels in its annual report to the Treasury, nor is it required to make specific resources available to them beyond, at

---

1   Consultation Papers 1 and 2, FSA, October 1997.
2   FSMA, s 8. To this must be added the detailed consultation provisions (including cost-benefit analyses) that apply in relation to the FSA's legislative functions, see **6.2.4**. Indeed, Lord McIntosh has said: 'We expect the panel[s] to be consulted on proposals for rules' (vol 611 HL, 20 March 2000, c 63).
3   FSMA, ss 9 and 10, cf the definition in the FSMA, s 5(3); see also Standing Committee A, 20 July 1999, cc 271 and 272.
4   Terms of reference were recommended by the Joint Committee, First Report, paras 133 and 134.
5   *FSA Annual Report 1998/99*, App 3.

least, the general obligation to 'maintain *effective* arrangements for consulting'[1]. In fact there were brief statements in the last report and, at least in respect of the Consumer Panel, a promise to continue to publish such reports and to fund the Panel so that it can commission work and research as necessary. The Forum has produced its own separate annual reports. It does not have its own staff or a regular budget from the FSA, but the FSA did finance its benchmark survey of industry opinion of regulation[2].

3.4.2 The Treasury

The FSA is obliged to keep satisfactory and safe records of its decisions and to report at least once a year to the Treasury on:

(1) the discharge of its functions;
(2) the extent to which its regulatory objectives have been met;
(3) its consideration of the restraining principles; and
(4) any other matters required by the Treasury.

This report must also contain the non-executive committee's review of efficiency, etc. It must be laid before Parliament and within three months a public meeting must be held to allow discussion of the report and questions to be put to the FSA on its performance. A further report on the proceedings of that meeting must then be published[3].

Although the contents of the report are stated in very general terms, the *FSA Annual Report 1998/99* was a 130-page document and was accompanied by an extremely long list, agreed with the Treasury, of items to be covered in future reports under the FSMA[4]. In particular, they will give an assessment of the regulatory burdens and compliance costs both of UK markets compared with overseas jurisdictions and of the changes to the UK system made during the year[5]. They will also give details of complaints made against the FSA and its response to the independent investigator's findings and of enforcement actions, including fines, costs and significant judgments of the Tribunal (see **3.5**).

The Treasury may, at its expense, appoint someone it considers independent from the FSA to compile a written report on any element of the economy, efficiency and effectiveness of the FSA, but not on its general policies, principles or functioning as the UKLA. The exact scope of any report is to be determined by

---

1   FSMA, s 8 (emphasis added). Lord McIntosh commented on this obligation to fund at vol 611 HL, 20 March 2000, c 70. The Economic Secretary confirmed that there was no obligation on the FSA to publish any dialogue between the Panels and itself: vol 351 HC, 5 June 2000, c 45.

2   *FSA Annual Report 1998/99*, p 64 and App 3; The Forum's Annual Report 1999, January 2000. The survey, which cost the FSA £100,000, showed opinion evenly split on whether the new regime would be better or worse for practitioners. The main concern was expressed by firms currently regulated by the BSC and FSC, which were both highly rated.

3   FSMA, Sch 1, paras 9–12. It is expected that the Treasury Select Committee will review these reports and take evidence from consumers and practitioners: vol 344 HC, 9 February 2000, c 343.

4   FSA Press Release 64/99. The *FSA Annual Report 1999/2000* is also 130 pages long and includes a costs comparison, p 84.

5   The Government's initial estimate was that after one-off set-up costs, the new regime would be less expensive than the old, *Financial Services and Markets Bill: Regulatory Impact Assessment*, HM Treasury, June 1999. As the original scope of the FSA's responsibilities has been extended by the Government, this now seems less likely.

the Treasury. If such a report is ever commissioned, it must be laid before Parliament and may be published[1]. All documents in the custody or control of the FSA that might reasonably be required can be called for, together with explanations from those responsible for them[2].

Furthermore, the Treasury may, again at its expense, appoint a person to conduct a full independent inquiry if it believes that:

(1) a grave risk to the financial system or significant damage to the interests of consumers (or a risk of either) has arisen because of a serious failure in the system or in its operation in relation to CISs and regulated activities (whether being conducted legally or not); or

(2) significant damage to the holder of listed securities (or a risk of it) has arisen because of a serious failure in the system for regulating listed securities or in its operation[3].

The Treasury is to determine the scope of the inquiry, but within those limits the inquiry has the powers that the High Court would have to order the production of documents and compel evidence and may ask that court to hold anyone obstructing the inquiry in contempt of court[4]. The Treasury may publish all or any part of the report and must lay that before Parliament. It may not, however, publish any part that would seriously prejudice any particular person (eg in subsequent criminal or disciplinary proceedings) or which would be breach of any international obligations[5].

Finally, if the FSA reports to the Treasury that there has been a widespread breach of its rules by authorised firms and private persons have suffered, or will do so, the Treasury may require the FSA to establish and operate a past business review and compensation scheme by statutory instrument, subject to affirmative resolutions of both Houses of the Parliament. This power has been introduced to try to overcome the problems all the existing regulators have had dealing with the pensions misselling scandal[6].

Clearly, as the body appointing and dismissing the FSA's governing board and to whom that board has to report, the Treasury remains ultimately responsible for the regulatory system. To that end, it (and, indeed any appropriate Minister of the Crown) has fairly sweeping reserve powers, unrestricted by any provision of the FSMA, 'to make such incidental, consequential, transitional or supplemental provision as [it considers] necessary or expedient for the general purposes, or any

1   FSMA, s 12. In practice, efficiency and policy may be hard to disentangle, but as the commissioning and scope of any report is entirely at the Treasury's discretion, this provision is terribly weak: Standing Committee A, 20 July 1999, cc 273–288; vol 343 HC, 1 February 2000, c 960. The Government rejected regular reviews: vol 611 HL, 20 March 2000, c 94.

2   FSMA, s 13. Legal privilege can still be claimed: FSMA, s 413.

3   FSMA, s 14. This gives a statutory basis for inquiries such as those that looked into the BCCI and Barings Affairs. Consumer interests have the same very wide definition as in FSMA, s 5.

4   FSMA, ss 15, 16 and 18. Here as elsewhere in the FSMA, the High Court means the Court of Session in Scotland. Legal privilege is protected throughout the FSMA on the same terms as in the Police and Criminal Evidence Act 1984 (PACE): FSMA, s 413.

5   FSMA, s 17; see also Standing Committee A, 20 July 1999, c 309.

6   FSMA, ss 404 and 429(1). It will also give backing to the FSA's review of the selling of free-standing additional voluntary contributions, Consultation Paper 27, FSA, August 1999 and *Response to Consultation Paper 27*, FSA, May 2000.

particular purpose, of this Act ...'[1] In the current climate of judicial interventionism, however, any major amendment of the FSMA by statutory instrument is likely to be subjected to close scrutiny. As the Economic Secretary has pointed out, 'Necessity and expediency are governed by the earlier requirement that provisions be incidental, consequential, transitional or supplemental'.[2] Nevertheless, the Government rejected a proposal to subject the Treasury to similar objectives, principles or consultation procedures to those imposed on the FSA when using its powers[3].

3.4.3 Competition issues

There is an inevitable tension between maximising competition and regulating a market. As the Economic Secretary has said:

> 'To take an extreme example, it could be argued that the entire system of authorisation is a barrier to competition, in that it prevents firms that might otherwise do so from entering the financial services industry. However, no one would seriously argue that authorisation should be abandoned for that reason.'[4]

Following the chaotic challenge to the Stock Exchange's rulebook through the Restrictive Practices Court, a special competition regime was introduced for investment business under the 1986 Act[5]. This is now being amended and applied to the whole financial services area. The Competition Act 1998 is restricted in its application in three ways:

(1) as a statutory body, the FSA's rule-making functions are not subject to the prohibitions on 'agreements preventing, restricting or distorting competition' and 'abuse of a dominant position in a market' ('cartel' and 'monopoly' prohibitions)[6];

(2) those subject to the FSA's rules have a defence against these prohibitions if their behaviour is required by the FSA's rules[7]; and

(3) the defence in (2) is extended by the FSMA to behaviour 'encouraged by any of the Authority's regulating provisions,' ie rules, statements, codes and general guidance[8].

In response to the Interim Cruickshank Report, the extension in (3) is narrower than under the 1986 Act, in that it does not excuse behaviour encouraged merely by the FSA's practices. That it has been retained at all is because:

---

1 FSMA, s 426. There was a very late amendment to give any Minister of the Crown this power 'of last resort', rather than just the Treasury which holds nearly all the specific statutory instrument making powers under the FSMA. Treasury Ministers are still the most likely to exercise it.

2 Standing Committee A, 9 December 1999, c 1258.

3 Vol 343 HC, 27 January 2000, cc 672–675; vol 611 HL, 20 March 2000, cc 125–128.

4 Standing Committee A, 9 November 1999, c 812. Howard Flight MP noted that 'The large players welcome regulation. It raises the threshold of entry enormously. The innate tendency of regulation is towards consolidation and cartels': vol 343 HC, 27 January 2000, c 652 – a view shared by the Cruickshank Reports. It is also supported by a survey of industry views that showed that the FSA was viewed far more favourably by large organisations than small ones: Forum's Annual Report 1999, p 26.

5 1986 Act, Part I, Chapter XIV.

6 The FSA is not an 'undertaking' for the purposes of the Competition Act 1998, ss 2 and 18.

7 Competition Act 1998, ss 3, 19 and Sch 3, para 5.

8 FSMA, s 164.

'The FSA may issue guidance or codes of conduct which do not require anyone to do anything, but which indicate a course of action which the FSA thinks is the acceptable way of complying with the rule or with the statute. If people act in accordance with options afforded in guidance or a code, then it would not be fair if they could be penalised under the Competition Act. In addition, guidance which represents the FSA's considered view as to acceptable ways of complying with rules would be undermined if those who follow it could be penalised. ....'[1]

Although the Government rejected making competition and international competitiveness objectives of the FSA, they are still restraining principles and the Economic Secretary has said:

'that the FSA should be committed to choosing the regulatory solutions that appear to it to have the least anti-competitive outcome that is consistent with the need to protect consumers.'[2]

This is backed up by the special competition regime. The OFT is to keep both the rules and practices of the FSA under review for any 'significantly adverse effect on competition'.[3] The scope of this external scrutiny is wide. The definition:

'brings within the regime all rules, standing guidance, statements of principle or practice, or codes issued by the FSA .... The competition scrutiny arrangements also cover the "practices" of the FSA, which in this respect mean the procedures and methods that the FSA may adopt in carrying out its functions .... Those practices may not necessarily be written down, but may emerge over time as a result of the way in which the FSA approaches its tasks. Clearly, effect will be given to such internal policies .... through the FSA's practices. As such, they will be already susceptible to competition scrutiny. Therefore, the competition scrutiny regime will cover those practices that reflect policy and principles formally set out by the FSA, as well as any informal practices.'[4]

Any of the above have a significantly adverse effect on competition if directly or indirectly 'they have or are intended or likely to have' that effect including 'the effect of requiring or encouraging exploitation of the strength of a market position'.[5] The wording deliberately differs from that of the Competition Act 1998, based as that Act is on Art 81 of the Treaty of Rome. This is to avoid the application of the ECJ's jurisprudence:

'There are two reasons why it concerns us. First, the jurisprudence has developed in the context of commercial undertakings. There is always a risk that this would have unforeseen, and possibly unwelcome, consequences if applied in a different context. Secondly, we do not want the external competition scrutiny arrangements to turn on legal issues .... The key question that we want the competition regulators to address is whether the FSA, in discharging its general duties, has struck the right balance between competition and regulation. The answer to that should turn more on economic than legal arguments.'[6]

---

1   Lord McIntosh, vol 611 HL, 27 March 2000, c 598. The defence no longer extends to behaviour merely in response to the FSA's practices, although those practices are subject to the special regime, see below.
2   Standing Committee A, 9 November 1999, c 813.
3   FSMA, s 160. The FSMA in fact refers throughout to the Director General of Fair Trading. The original proposal for the OFT to check every change to an FSA rule was dropped.
4   The Economic Secretary explaining what is now FSMA, ss 159 and 160(1), Standing Committee A, 9 November 1999, cc 814 and 815.
5   FSMA, s 159. In assessing their likely effect, it may be presumed that rules, etc will be obeyed.
6   Lord McIntosh, vol 611 HL, 27 March 2000, c 572.

However, the scrutiny is confined to domestic competition and not issues of international competitiveness. The Economic Secretary maintained:

> 'We do not think that the FSA should be subject to formal OFT scrutiny of the effect of its actions on UK international competitiveness. There is not another statutory body with an equivalent role for the other principles. That does not mean that the FSA will not want to take into account the views of consultees and the producer and consumer panels on this issue. In the end, the FSA itself should be responsible for how it takes account of international competitiveness, but that is different from competition.'[1]

For its investigations, the OFT may demand documents from anyone, and information from anyone carrying on a business, if it considers them relevant, on pain of contempt of court[2]. Non-public information obtained, however, is confidential unless it can be revealed under a complex set of gateways modelled on those in the Competition Act 1998[3].

If the OFT believes after investigation that there is a significantly adverse effect on competition, the Director General *must* publish a report and send it to the Treasury, the Competition Commission and the FSA. The Competition Commission is then required to consider the matter. If the OFT concludes that there is not such an effect, a report *may* still be published and/or sent to the Treasury, the Competition Commission and the FSA. Even where the OFT believes there is not such an effect, it can still require the Competition Commission to consider the matter. The published reports should exclude any material seriously prejudicial to an individual or body, but they have absolute privilege from defamation actions[4].

Where the Commission is required to consider the matter, it has similar powers and duties to those it has under the Fair Trading Act 1973 and Competition Act 1998. It must consider representations made to it by any substantially interested party and any cost/benefit analyses that have been prepared by the FSA. The Treasury is empowered to provide the Commission with assistance in obtaining information. Again non-public information obtained is confidential unless subject to one of the gateways.

If the Commission concludes that there is no adverse effect on competition, the Commission's view is final. If, however, it concludes that there is such an effect, the Commission must go on to consider whether it can be justified, bearing in mind the FSA's functions and obligations under the FSMA. The Commission must then make a reasoned report to the Treasury, the FSA and the OFT, unless there is a change in circumstances that renders that pointless (eg the rule or practice has already been abandoned), in which case it must make a statement to that effect. The report should explain whether there is a significantly adverse effect on competition, whether it is unjustified and if so what action the FSA should take. The report should also be published, but again the published version should exclude any material seriously prejudicial to an individual or body[5].

---

1   Standing Committee A, 9 November 1999, c 821.
2   FSMA, s 161. This does not override any legal privilege: FSMA, s 413. Misleading the OFT is a criminal offence under the Competition Act 1998: FSMA, s 399.
3   FSMA, s 351 and Sch 19.
4   FSMA, ss 160 and 162(1).
5   FSMA, s 162 and Sch 14. The Commission must determine the mode of publishing 'best calculated to bring it to the attention of the public'.

If the Commission concludes that there is an unjustifiable effect, the Treasury must (after appropriate consultation with the FSA and other interested parties) issue directions to the FSA to correct it unless:

(1) the FSA has already done so; or
(2) 'exceptional circumstances .... make it inappropriate or unnecessary'.

This Treasury override can also operate the other way around where, although the Commission believes an adverse effect to be justified, the Treasury can in 'exceptional circumstances' still direct the FSA to make a change (again after appropriate consultations). The Treasury must give its reasons for overriding the Commission[1]. Of this override, the Economic Secretary has said:

> 'The Competition Commission's conclusions will not be subject to routine second-guessing by Ministers. They will stand, except where the Treasury considers that exceptional circumstances cause it to reach a different view. We can envisage a Treasury override being triggered when it is necessary to meet our international obligations – for example to give effect to European Community legislation – or when the Treasury thinks that there would be significant implications for the operation of the financial system as a whole if the changes were to be made. In the unlikely event of exercising that override, the Treasury will have to publish a statement of its reasons and lay that before Parliament.'[2]

There has to be some concern that, for dealing with a fast-moving international business, this is a remarkably cumbersome process still open to a degree of political interference.

3.4.4   Complaints scheme and immunity

To deal with individual complaints made against itself[3], the FSA must set up its own procedures to deal quickly with complaints about the performance of its functions (other than its legislative function). This must include an independent investigator whose appointment or dismissal is subject to Treasury approval. Setting up and amending these procedures is subject to a basic public consultation exercise that requires the FSA to:

(1) publish draft proposals and to ask for representations by a specified time;
(2) consider those representations and publish a general account of them and of any significant changes to the proposals; and
(3) publish the scheme or up-dated scheme and give the Treasury a copy without delay[4].

Although the procedures may allow initial investigations to be conducted by the FSA itself, such investigations must generally then be referred to a permanent independent investigator whose appointment and removal must be approved by the Treasury. The investigator should have the means to investigate fully and fairly the complaints referred to him. The FSA must then respond to any criticisms

---

1   FSMA, s 163. In particular, the FSA cannot be required to do what it is not otherwise empowered to do, or what would be incompatible with its functions or obligations under the FSMA.
2   Vol 343 HC, 27 January 2000, c 645.
3   As against authorised firms, see **8.2**.
4   FSMA, Sch 1, para 7. The FSA must determine the mode of publishing 'best calculated to bring it to the attention of the public', but it may charge a reasonable fee for copies.

made by the investigator and he may publish his findings (and require the FSA to publish its response)[1].

The Government did not accept the Joint Committee's suggestion that the investigator have the power to award compensation. Indeed, the FSA, the independent investigator, their officers and their employees are exempt from liability in damages unless shown to be acting in bad faith or in breach of the Convention[2]. Immunities, other than for bad faith, were given to some of the old regulators, including the Bank of England and the SROs, but this one has proved controversial[3]. In particular, the extent of the Convention exception is not clear. The Economic Secretary has said 'We believe that a statutory immunity would be vulnerable only if it deprived a person of access to the court for a breach of some other convention right.'[4]

This is an attempt to explain away the decision of the ECHR in *Osman v UK*, where a blanket common-law immunity for policemen was not accepted by the court. The ECHR's reasoning is very far reaching and appears to challenge a State's right to determine its substantive law of obligations. If the court took a similar view of the immunities under the FSMA, their effectiveness could be severely limited[5]. None of this, however, precludes the FSA board from making *ex gratia* payments and the Opposition defeated the Government to include in the independent investigator's specific powers, one to recommend, although not to order, such payments[6].

Criticism may be levelled that the independent investigator cannot really be very effective if he is appointed by the FSA, if complaints cannot be made directly to him and if he can only recommend compensation[7]. Indeed, if the FSA reasonably considers that a complaint is better dealt with by other means (eg the Tribunal or legal proceedings), it is not obliged to institute the complaints procedure at all. It must, nevertheless, inform the independent investigator of this decision, and the

---

1   FSMA, Sch 1, para 8.
2   FSMA, Sch 1, para 19. The immunity does not extend to their agents who presumably must try to seek contractual indemnities. A proposal to add a further exception to the immunity for recklessness was rejected at the Report Stage (vol 343 HC, 27 January 2000, cc 625–632) and in the House of Lords (vol 612 HL, 13 April 2000, cc 324–335).
3   See Joint Committee, First Report, paras 137 and 138, though it was commented at para 139: 'If the FSA are vulnerable to suit in the event of business failure, they will go as far as possible to avoid all failures; this will be a recipe for over-regulation'. This may explain the traditional reluctance of UK courts to find any bad faith by regulators causing losses ('misfeasance in public office'), for example the BCCI case: *Three Rivers District Council v Bank of England (No 3)* [1996] 3 All ER 558.
4   Standing Committee A, 13 July 1999, c 151.
5   *Osman v United Kingdom* [1999] FLR 193.
6   FSMA, Sch 1, para 8(5). The concept of *ex gratia* payments being recommended and paid had already been accepted by the FSA in *Independent Investigation of Complaints against the FSA*, FSA, March 2000, paras 10 and 11.
7   Indeed independence is only defined as terms and conditions that will secure '*in the opinion of the Authority* ... that he will be free at all times to act independently ... without favouring the Authority': the FSMA, Sch 1, para 7(4) (emphasis added). In *Independent Investigation of Complaints against the FSA*, paras 7–9, the FSA proposed a panel to recommend an investigator and neither he nor his staff should be connected to (or have offices with) the FSA. The Government did belatedly insert into FSMA that the investigator could not use FSA staff to conduct an investigation: FSMA, Sch 1, para 8(9).

investigator does have the power to override it[1]. All of this, however, is a reflection of the limited occasions that the independent investigator is likely to be called upon. Most complaints will involve regulatory matters and any proposal the FSA makes to refuse an authorisation or approval or to publicly reprimand or impose a penalty may be referred by the affected party to the Tribunal[2].

3.5   FINANCIAL SERVICES AND MARKETS TRIBUNAL

Unlike its predecessor, the Financial Services Tribunal, the new Tribunal is central to the regulatory system. Only decisions made by the old SIB could be referred to the old Tribunal, and as most authorisations and disciplinary matters were dealt with by the SROs and RPBs, such references were rare. Now the Tribunal will hear any cases not settled with the FSA *de novo* and treat the decision of the FSA merely as a recommendation[3]. An appeal from a final decision by the Tribunal may be made, with leave, to the Court of Appeal and ultimately the House of Lords, but only on a point of law[4].

As the Economic Secretary has pointed out:

> 'A wide range of regulatory decisions will be subject to the Tribunal. They will include: the refusal of an application for a new permission; the use of the authority's own initiative powers to restrict an authorised person's business or to withdraw his authorisation; disciplinary measures against authorised firms; objections to control-lers; the refusal of an application for or withdrawal of approval under Part V; the making of a prohibition order; and the imposition of financial penalties for market abuse.'[5]

The relationship between the FSA's Enforcement Committee and the Tribunal gave the Joint Committee great concern, not least because of the need to meet the requirement of Art 6(1) of the Convention for a fair, public hearing by an independent and impartial tribunal[6]. This led to revised proposals being put to the Committee by the Treasury and the FSA which are described in **9.3**.

3.5.1   Structure and proceedings

The Tribunal will be run as part of the Court Service and the Lord Chancellor is responsible for the terms and conditions (including remuneration) of members of the Tribunal and must appoint:

(1)   a panel of chairmen for the Tribunal, each a lawyer of at least seven years' standing (and at least one qualified in Scotland) with a president and, if the work load warrants it, a deputy president, each a lawyer of at least 10 years' standing; and

---

1   FSMA, Sch 1, para 8(1), (3) and (5).
2   Indeed, Lord Donaldson of Lymington felt that the whole concept of a complaints scheme was inappropriate where there was an effective appeals procedure: vol 610 HL, 21 February 2000, c 66.
3   FSMA, ss 132 and 133.
4   FSMA, s 137; in Scotland, the Court of Session and the House of Lords. There is no appeal from an interlocutory decision.
5   Standing Committee A, 4 November 1999, c 710.
6   See **2.4**.

(2) a lay panel of 'persons ... qualified by experience or otherwise to deal with matters of the kind that might be referred to the Tribunal'.[1]

The president and any deputy president will be full-time judicial appointments subject to the normal judicial retirement and pension arrangements, the others may be full-time or part-time and will be paid, in effect, piece rates[2]. To enable the Tribunal to be created quickly, it has been suggested that the Lord Chancellor may appoint members from the current full-timers and part-timers of the Special Commissioners for Income Tax and the VAT and Duties Tribunal[3].

The Lord Chancellor is also responsible for the appointment and terms and conditions of any support staff[4]. However, the president is responsible for the arrangements determining the membership of the Tribunal for each case. The Tribunal must include one member of the panel of chairmen plus other members of either panel as appropriate. Experts may also be appointed where there are facts of 'special difficulty'[5].

The Government resisted a minimum requirement of three on a panel, although the Economic Secretary did say:

> 'We have no difficulty with the proposition that the Tribunal should normally consist of three members, with the idea that one of those people should normally be a member of the lay panel and, if possible, have relevant experience ... When interlocutory matters arise ... it may be appropriate for a single member of the chairman's panel to rule on the matter [or] in relatively straightforward cases ...'[6]

The Tribunal is subject to the scrutiny of the Council on Tribunals[7]. The basic rules of procedure including when and where the Tribunal should meet are a matter for the Lord Chancellor (in consultation with the Council); but detailed directions as to practice and procedure may be made by the President. The Tribunal has the power to summon witnesses and documents (other than privileged communications) and take evidence under oath. Refusal to comply is an offence punishable by up to two years' imprisonment and an unlimited fine. The Tribunal may consider any evidence, whether or not it was available to the FSA. It must then come to a determination and remit the matter back to the FSA with appropriate directions (if any) that are within the FSA's powers under those procedures, which the FSA must then follow. The Tribunal may also make recommendations on the FSA's regulating provisions. Tribunal decisions may be made by a majority, but must be recorded giving reasons and sent to the parties

---

1   FSMA, Sch 13, paras 1–5. It has been confirmed that the Lord Chancellor will consult 'the Lord Advocate, representing the Scottish Executive, the Law Societies of England and Wales, Northern Ireland and Scotland, the Bar Council and many others: Lord McIntosh in vol 612 HL, 18 April 2000, c 689.
2   FSMA, Sch 20; they too will be disqualified from sitting as MPs or Members of the Northern Irish Assembly.
3   Standing Committee A, 4 November 1999, c 731; vol 343 HC, 1 February 2000, c 956.
4   FSMA, Sch 13, para 6.
5   FSMA, Sch 13, para 7.
6   Standing Committee A, 4 November 1999, c 735.
7   Tribunals and Inquiries Act 1992, s 8(1).

and the Treasury. They may be enforced as a county court (or Court of Session) order[1].

Referrals to the Tribunal should normally be made within 28 days which is a tight time constraint. The Lord Chancellor can vary that time-limit and, subject to any rules he may make, the Tribunal can in particular cases, waive it[2]. Still, there remains the practical issue of how effective the Tribunal can be as a body if, particularly for individuals disciplined by the FSA, it is too costly to use. To meet this point, costs may be awarded against a party only if it has acted vexatiously, frivolously or unreasonably. All or part of the costs incurred may be awarded against the FSA if its decision was unreasonable, but not just because its decision is overturned by the Tribunal[3].

Legal aid is restricted to market abuse cases and, even then, may only be awarded from when a defendant refers the matter to the Tribunal. The Lord Chancellor will determine the eligibility criteria. Although market abuse cases may be brought against anyone, any legal aid will be funded by the Lord Chancellor requiring the FSA to levy authorised firms and pay the proceeds to the Consolidated Fund. The Financial Secretary has justified this on the grounds that it is principally authorised firms that will benefit from the reduction of market abuse, but the administration is convoluted and, curiously, leaves the FSA to determine exactly how this tax is to be raised and any refunds distributed[4].

---

1   FSMA, ss 132 and 133 and Sch 13, paras 8–12. The Tribunal cannot direct the FSA to take an action under the procedures (eg supervisory) that would have required different procedures (eg disciplinary) to have been instigated; see **9.3**.

2   FSMA, s 133(1) and (2).

3   FSMA, Sch 13, para 13. The costs are presumably only those incurred from referral to the Tribunal.

4   FSMA, ss 134–136; vol 343 HC, 27 January 2000, c 636. Tax treatment is again determined by FSMA, s 411. Refunds may be set off against other non-legal aid debts owed to the FSA, such as outstanding fees.

Chapter 4

THE SCOPE OF THE FINANCIAL SERVICES AND MARKETS ACT 2000

4.1 BACKGROUND

As Chapters 1 and 2 have shown, the pressure formally to authorise and supervise an ever wider range of financial services businesses has been both domestic and European. On a number of occasions, the Government has expressed its intention neither to expand the types of businesses needing authorisation (with the notable exception of Lloyd's and its managing and members' agents), nor to expand the types subject to conduct of business as well as prudential regulation[1]. After all, the original aim of the FSMA was just to concentrate responsibility for regulating UK financial services business on the FSA, at least as far as European obligations would allow.

However, having proposed this reform, the Government has found itself under continuing pressure to widen the scope of the FSMA, and, in particular, to extend regulation to mortgage advice, credit unions, pre-paid funeral plans and advice on long-term care insurance, if not general insurance[2]. Credit unions are to be brought into the new regime, and advice on long-term care insurance probably will be[3]. This leaves mortgages – a huge market to bring under statutory regulation. Although there are only approximately 120 lenders (most of whom are already authorised as banks or building societies), their 4,500 products are being sold to nearly 2 million consumers each year by about 50,000 advisers employed by those lenders and some 14,000 intermediary firms[4]. The sheer level of regulatory resources required is presumably why the Government proposes to take 18 months just to bring lending of over £25,000 against first mortgages of residential premises into the statutory regime. Arranging and advising on mortgages will still not be regulated, in the same way as the provision of general insurance is regulated but arranging and advising on it is not[5].

---

1 For example *Regulated Activities – A Consultation Document*, HM Treasury, February 1999, para 1.2; the Economic Secretary, Standing Committee A, 22 July 1999, c 382; Lord McIntosh, vol 610 HL, 21 February 2000, c 15.

2 Joint Committee, First Report, Part IV. Long-term care insurance is being examined by a working party set up by the Department of Health.

3 Credit unions do raise a funding issue as at present the Government pays for their regulation. It now appears that the rest of the industry will do so, FSA, Press Release 118/1999. On long-term insurance, the Government expects its current investigations to recommend regulation. Lord McIntosh, vol 612 HL, 18 April 2000, c 581.

4 *A cost-benefit analysis of statutory regulation of mortgage advice*, FSA October 1999, pp 9 and 10. The Government has admitted that cost and delay is why it has not yet made mortgage advice a regulated activity and why it has concentrated instead on a CAT regime to make the products easier to understand. Lord McIntosh, vol 612 HL, 18 April 2000, c 576.

5 *Regulation of Mortgages – a discussion document by HM Treasury*, HM Treasury, July 1999 and *Evidence of consumer damage reported during the Treasury Mortgage Consultation*, HM Treasury, January 2000; vol 344 HC, 9 February 2000, cc 345–352. Advice on endowment mortgages is already regulated as they involve long-term life assurance. Otherwise the Government will be relying, as it does in the general insurance market, on the provision of clear information by the providers to protect consumers. This will leave the FSA regulating mortgage lenders and

In line with this limited regulation of general insurance and banking, there has been little or no regulation of the advertising of general insurance or banking products and services. By contrast, the 1986 Act created a sweeping restriction on non-authorised persons advertising other investment products and services (including certain long-term insurance contracts), and authorised or non-authorised persons cold calling to market them[1].

The other marketing issue the Government has had to grapple with increasingly is how to regulate the cross-border promotions of financial products and services. The rise of cheap telecommunications and computers has enabled cross-border services to expand from the wholesale to the retail market with all the issues of consumer protection which that entails. The Government is keen to encourage such e-commerce, but is reluctant to remove any domestic consumer protection in order to reduce multiple regulation of such business.

4.2 THE NEED FOR AUTHORISATION

As was the case with the 1986 Act, the FSMA sets the boundary between lawful and unlawful financial services activities with two principal provisions:

(1) a general prohibition against carrying on, or purporting to carry on, any regulated activity by way of business in the UK unless:
 (a) the firm is authorised, or
 (b) it is exempt; and
(2) a restriction on engaging in financial promotion in the course of a business unless:
 (a) the firm is authorised,
 (b) the communication is approved by an authorised firm, or
 (c) an exemption applies.

Breach of either provision may lead to any contract made in consequence being unenforceable and can amount to a criminal offence[2].

There are important differences between these two provisions and their predecessors in the 1986 Act[3], but the key distinction remains whether a firm is authorised or not. The different authorisations required for deposit-taking, insurance and other investment businesses are now replaced by one authorisation, creating one perimeter. The responsibility for defining that perimeter lies with the Treasury[4]. Within that perimeter, a firm may have permission to conduct only certain regulated activities. If it strays outside that permission, the firm

---

their advertising, the DTI regulating mortgages up to £25,000 under the Consumer Credit Act 1974 and the Council of Mortgage Lenders regulating mortgage advice under the existing voluntary Mortgage Code. The Government may require that advising on and arranging mortgages be authorised in the future: Lord McIntosh, vol 612 HL, 18 April 2000, c 577.

1 Insurance Companies Regulations 1994, SI 1994/1516; Banking Act (Advertisements) Regulations 1988, SI 1988/645; 1986 Act, ss 56–58, 130 and 131. The FSA determined what cold calling would be permitted.

2 FSMA, Part II. The consequences of any breach are dealt with in **9.2** and **10.5**.

3 FSMA, ss 19 and 21, cf 1986 Act, ss 3 and 57.

4 FSMA, ss 21(4)–(15) and 22.

remains authorised, its contracts remain valid, it does not commit a criminal offence, but it will have contravened a requirement under the FSMA and may be subject to FSA disciplinary procedures and private civil actions[1].

4.2.1   Exempt persons

A statutory instrument subject to affirmative resolutions may provide that certain exempt persons can conduct all or some regulated activities without needing authorisation, for example the Bank of England. The Treasury has published a first draft Financial Services and Markets Act (Exemption) Order (Exemption Order). In addition, RIEs and RCHs such as the Stock Exchange and CREST are exempt persons when acting in those capacities. Lloyd's is authorised, but its members are exempt[2]. Exempt status for permitted persons and listed money market institutions will no longer exist. The use of the former has dwindled away and the FSA is already responsible under the Bank of England Act 1998 for firms claiming the latter, nearly all of whom, in any case, will need authorisation for their other activities.

The largest exempt group, however, will be members and firms controlled by members of DPBs but whose regulated activities are only incidental to the provision of their professional services. This arrangement aims to exempt the majority of accountants and lawyers currently authorised by their RPBs from having to be authorised by the FSA and is considered in greater detail in **11.4**[3].

The next largest group will be appointed representatives. These are firms or self-employed individuals contracted to conduct regulated activities (normally as selling agents) for authorised firms like unit trust managers and insurers (ie insurance companies and mutuals). Those authorised firms have to accept responsibility in writing for the acts or omissions of their appointed representatives while conducting the agreed activities, in effect just as though they were employees of the firms[4]. However, an appointed representative's knowledge or intentions will not be attributed to his principal for the purposes of criminal liability, unless it is reasonable in all the circumstances[5]. The Treasury has the power to limit the types, and prescribe the terms, of activities that may be conducted under this exemption. The Economic Secretary has confirmed that the 'activities will be drawn wide enough to cover existing appointed representatives'.[6]

---

1   FSMA, s 20, cf s 23; for the position under the old regime see Standing Committee A, 20 July 1999, c 319. The Treasury will determine by statutory instrument what breaches can give rise to a civil action.

2   FSMA, ss 38, 285, 417 and 429(5), cf ss 315 and 316; Although exempt, Lloyd's members and DPB members are not defined as 'exempt persons' because their exemption may be removed by the FSA: Lord McIntosh, vol 612 HL, 18 April 2000, c 564; see **11.3** and **11.4**. Generally, exempt persons cannot also be authorised and, if they become so later, their exemptions lapse; but RIEs, RCHs and Lloyd's members can seek permission to conduct other regulated activities and keep their exempt status: FSMA, ss 38(2) and 42(3)–(5).

3   FSMA, Part XX.

4   FSMA, s 39.

5   FSMA, s 39(6). This may limit the effect of the decision in *Meridian Global Funds Management Asia Ltd v Securities Commission* [1995] 2 AC 500.

6   FSMA, s 39(1)(a); Standing Committee A, 21 October 1999, c 464. A professional firm may be exempt for some activities as a member of a DPB and exempt for others as an appointed representative: FSMA, s 327(7).

By making insurers and other principals answerable for their agents, this arrangement reduces the number of firms the FSA has to authorise and supervise directly. However, these principals will still have to seek FSA approval for some of the managers and employees of their appointed representatives, as they currently do from the SROs[1]. There is, however, one significant change from the previous regime. Within UK banking groups and other financial conglomerates, subsidiaries authorised under the 1986 Act have often appointed other parts of the group as their appointed representatives to avoid the latter having to be authorised as well. This cannot now continue if the other parts conduct their own regulated activities (such as banking or insurance) as a person cannot be both an appointed representative and authorised[2].

Exempt status only removes the requirement to be authorised imposed by the general prohibition. The restriction on financial promotion still applies unless the promotion has been approved by an authorised firm or it falls within a specific exemption (see below).

4.2.2   Regulated activities

Because the FSMA is to regulate deposit-taking and insurance as well as other investment business, the concept of 'regulated activities' was bound to be wider than the concept of 'investment business' in the 1986 Act. The lists of investments and activities in relation to them have been expanded and the limiting notes contained in the 1986 Act removed. However, these lists are only indicative. The initial perimeter of regulated activities (and any subsequent extension) is to be determined by statutory instrument subject to confirmation by resolutions of both Houses of Parliament[3]. The Treasury has published a first draft Financial Services and Markets Act (Regulated Activities) Order (RA Order).

This perimeter can be extended beyond the listed activities and investments, as was the case under the 1986 Act[4]. However, this power is wider than its predecessor, because regulated activities no longer have to constitute a business themselves, just be carried on 'by way of business' and can relate to any property, not just assets, rights or interests that might be viewed as investments[5]. The Financial Secretary explained the new 'business' test thus:

> 'Our approach is intended to catch ... along with any mainstream activity, any activity that falls short of constituting a business in its own right, but which should be

---

1   See **5.3**.

2   FSMA, s 39(1). If an appointed representative is later authorised, the exemption lapses: FSMA, s 42(3).

3   FSMA, Sch 2, Parts I and II, cf 1986 Act, Sch 1, Parts I and II. The aim is to make the statutory instrument the sole determinant of regulated activities. Most of the notes will reappear in it. The unusual confirmation resolutions (cf prior affirmative resolutions) are because amendments may be needed urgently: Lord McIntosh, vol 612 HL, 18 April 2000, c 570.

4   FSMA, s 22 and Sch 2, Part III, cf 1986 Act, s 2 and Sch 1 which was much amended, Standing Committee A, 22 July 1999, c 380. The justification for this approach is to allow flexibility in the face of changing markets combined with ease of use by having a comprehensive definition in one statutory instrument, Standing Committee A, 19 October 1999, c 408. As Lord McIntosh has pointed out, the Government's decision to include mortgage lending as a regulated activity in due course requires no amendment to Sch 2: vol 611 HL, 20 March 2000, c 111.

5   FSMA, ss 19 and 22, cf 1986 Act, s 1.

regulated under the Bill . . . It has never been proposed that the incidental provision of financial services should be generally exempt from the authorisation requirement.'[1]

The Treasury, nevertheless, has the power to redefine what may or may not fall within this business definition, by statutory instrument subject to affirmative resolutions[2].

As the basic definition of regulated activities is now to appear in one, or possibly two statutory instruments, what is the purpose of the lists in the FSMA? The Economic Secretary has explained that:

> 'We will not be able to stray too far from what is set out in the schedule. The test will be whether an activity is the same kind of activity as those activities set out in the indicative list.'[3]

This 'four corner' limitation still seems to leave the Treasury able to specify as regulated, any activity conducted by way of business which relates to any investment or property, provided it is 'carried on in the UK'.

The concept of an activity carried on in the UK is itself difficult. There are both outward ('from the UK') and inward ('in and into the UK') elements. In respect of the outward element, a firm is deemed to be conducting a regulated activity in the UK if:

(1) it has its registered (or head) office *within* the UK and carries on an outwardly passported activity (including a manager promoting passported CISs) in an EEA country;
(2) it has its registered (or head) office *within* the UK and carries on a non-passported regulated activity anywhere outside the UK, *but only if* 'the day-to-day management' of it is the responsibility of a UK establishment; and
(3) it has its head office *outside* the UK and carries on a regulated activity outside the UK, *but only if* it is 'carried on from' a UK establishment[4].

Case (1) exists because the FS Directives make authorisation and prudential regulation the responsibility of the home State. In cases (2) and (3), there is no reference to the establishment having to be permanent, but occasional hotel visits do not seem to be enough[5]. Case (3) in particular, gives rise to potential regulatory duplication, as the home State will generally be authorising and regulating the UK branch as well. It is left to the FSA to determine which of its rules should apply to such business conducted with non-UK customers[6]. Justifying the retention of this potential 'double hit' in the FSMA, the Financial Secretary said:

> 'Although I would certainly expect an appropriately light touch to be maintained [by the FSA] so that unnecessary double regulation is avoided, making special provision

1   Vol 343 HC, 1 February 2000, c 1005. However, the RA Order does exclude incidental provision: see below.
2   FSMA, ss 419 and 429(1)(a). Managing an occupational pension fund may be specifically included as 'by way of business' as special provision was made for it under the 1986 Act, s 191: see below.
3   Standing Committee A, 22 July 1999, c 381 described as the 'four corners concept' at c 384 and in Standing Committee A, 19 October 1999, c 414.
4   FSMA, s 418.
5   Economic Secretary, Standing Committee A, 9 December 1999, c 1245; on the meaning of 'establishment', see *Re Oriel Ltd* [1986] 1 WLR 180.
6   Economic Secretary, Standing Committee A, 9 December 1999, c 1246.

in the Bill is another matter. That could prevent the FSA from applying rules to businesses in unusual cases in which it might be appropriate to apply them. For example, there may be merit in the FSA applying limited conduct of business rules to overseas branches of firms to make it clear to customers that, in conducting business through the overseas branch, the firm is not acting in accordance with the FSA's detailed UK rules and regulations . . .'[1]

As to the second inward element, *prima facie* any regulated activity carried on in or into the UK requires authorisation. Where the activity is carried on may be where the provider, rather than the customer is based, for example investment management or bank deposits repayable outside the UK. However, even in these cases, promoting such an overseas activity to UK customers is going to require authorisation, approval by an authorised person or an exemption under the restriction on financial promotion. An exemption will be given to firms which do not have a permanent place of business in the UK and whose regulated activities in the UK do not amount to a business. There is also, in effect, a special exemption for overseas banks involved in the London inter-bank market[2].

4.2.3   Financial promotion

The new concept of 'financial promotion' is wider than the former concept of 'investment advertising', as it covers what until now was treated as cold calling and solicited calls (which have not been covered before), albeit only by non-authorised persons[3]. Authorised persons involved in financial promotion (either themselves or when approving others) will be subject to any rules the FSA may make on the subject, although the Treasury intends to restrict such rules in the case of deposits and general insurance[4]. The aim of the restriction on financial promotion is to avoid any arbitrary distinctions between different media used to market financial products and services; but distinctions between the promotion of banking or general insurance and other investment business will continue.

The restriction on financial promotion can only apply to communications 'in the course of business'[5]. Therefore, discussions between private individuals about investments (eg internet chatrooms) are not covered, although the Treasury can

---

1   Vol 343 HC, 1 February 2000, c 933.
2   RA Order, Part IV and Sch 4, para 2(2)(a).
3   FSMA, s 21, cf 1986 Act, ss 56–58, 136 and 137. With the internet and other electronic developments, the distinction between 'advertising' and 'calling' has become hard to maintain. Under the old regime, the prohibition on cold calling applied to authorised and non-authorised persons and contracts contravening the prohibition were unenforceable but the call was not a criminal offence. The Financial Secretary has said, 'The guiding principles have been to make the new regime future-proof and technologically neutral': vol 344 HC, 9 February 2000, c 275.
4   FSMA, s 145; *Financial Promotion – A Consultation Document*, HM Treasury, March 1999, Part One, para 3.4. Authorised means any person authorised under the FSMA, including formally and informally passported firms and Lloyd's.
5   This seems to be a narrower test than 'by way of business' used in respect of regulated activities: FSMA, s 21, cf s 22.

redefine by statutory instrument what is 'in the course of business'[1]. Also, to reduce the need for all the exemptions that were created under the 1986 Act, the definition of financial promotion is to 'communicate [or cause to be communicated] an *invitation or inducement* to engage in investment activity'[2]. This suggests that a company's publication of general information about itself (eg interim reports, annual accounts or discussions at analysts meetings) will not amount to financial promotion, but more positive attempts to sell its shares will. As the Government spokesman in the House of Lords has said:

> 'The Government do not believe that "inducement", as used in the Bill, will catch communications where the effect has been to prompt an investment decision regardless of the motivation of the communicator. We are convinced that 'inducement', in its Bill usage, already incorporates an element of design or purpose on the part of the person making the communication ... There must be an element of persuasion contained in the communication.'[3]

However, care must be still be taken, for example, over hyperlinks to information on others' web-sites:

> 'If A's web-site contains a simple (not of itself promotional) link to B's web-site, A may, nevertheless, breach the ... prohibition if B's web-site contains material amounting to an unlawful financial promotion if A has in fact "caused" the unlawful financial promotion on B's web-site to be communicated.'[4]

The exact definition of 'engaging in investment activity' is again left to secondary legislation. It includes exercising any right to acquire, dispose of, underwrite or convert any controlled investment; but principally it is 'entering or offering to enter into an agreement the making or performance of which by either party is a controlled activity' where the definition of controlled activity does not have to coincide with regulated activities[5]. The Treasury has said:

> 'The intention is that "controlled activities" will generally equate to regulated activities ... but without the additional exclusions proposed in the Regulated Activities Order for certain kinds of investments or activities. This is the basic approach taken in relation to the scope of the advertising regime under the Financial Services Act.'[6]

The initial definitions of controlled investments and activities and of the general exemptions will be contained in a statutory instrument subject to affirmative resolutions, as will be any amendments that then expand the scope of financial promotion. General exemptions can be made subject to compliance with specific

---

1   FSMA, s 21(4). The Financial Secretary did give a general definition of business as 'an activity in which people engage regularly with a view to making a profit', and said of the power that 'it is not generally our intention to reinvent or redefine what may be "in the course of business"': Standing Committee A, 22 July 1999, c 353. See also *Financial Promotion – Second Consultation Document*, HM Treasury, October 1999, Part One, para 4.6. The numerous taxation cases on the issue may provide guidance.

2   FSMA, s 21(1) and (13) (emphasis added). The definition of 'investment advertisement' in the 1986 Act, ss 57(2) and 207(2) was notoriously wide.

3   Lord McIntosh, vol 613 HL, 18 May 2000, c 387.

4   *Financial Promotion – Second Consultation Document*, Part Two, para 2.25.

5   FSMA, s 21(8)–(15).

6   *Financial Promotion – Second Consultation Document*, Part Three, para 7: draft Financial Services and Markets Act (Financial Promotion Exemptions) Order, Sch 1.

FSA rules. The Treasury has published a first draft Financial Services and Markets Act (Financial Promotion Exemptions) Order (FPE Order)[1].

As with regulated activities, there are difficult issues as to the territorial scope of the UK law on financial promotions, with the potential for confusing multiple regulation of cross-border promotions. In respect of both 'outward' and 'inward' promotions, the FSMA seems to be wider than the 1986 Act. The restriction applies to any promotion from the UK, even if it is only directed overseas. This is logical where regulated activities arising from such a promotion require authorisation (see above). Indeed it allows for financial promotion to be purely a matter for home State regulation within the EEA which is what is being proposed in draft Directives on Distance Marketing of Consumer Financial Services and on Electronic Commerce[2].

On the other hand, communications originating outside the UK are *prima facie* still subject to the restriction if they are 'capable of having an effect in the UK'. This no longer automatically excludes advertisements in newspapers and other periodicals principally circulating outside the UK. It also covers any overseas Internet web-sites accessible in the UK unless the owner is stringent in not accepting any responses from the UK[3]. The Treasury does intend to limit the restriction, by statutory instrument, to communications 'directed at' the UK, but has resisted going any further towards pure home State regulation for the time being[4]:

> 'In taking that view, the Government has considered various relevant factors, including consumer protection, common regulatory standards for authorised persons and whether or not particular types of investment or activity are yet regulated consistently in Member States ... It is worth noting in this context that the proposal for a Distance Marketing Directive on Financial Services, which would apply to sales of financial services at a distance, is still at an early stage of discussion within the EU.'[5]

However, the Treasury has taken the power to adopt home State regulation in the future[6].

---

1   FSMA, ss 21(4), (5), (8) to (15) and 429(4). FPE Order, Sch 1 does follow the pattern of the RA Order. In the future, and subject to the 'four corners concept', advertising a house or any goods to rent or buy could be classified as a 'controlled activity' as it is not limited by Sch 2 and 'investment' covers any asset, right or interest. The Financial Secretary denied any intention to catch such activities, Standing Committee A, 22 July 1999, c 354.

2   COM (98) 46 final amended by COM (99) 385 final and COM (98) 586 amended by SEC (2000) 386 final.

3   FSMA, s 21(3), cf 1986 Act, s 207(3). The exemptions for overseas broadcasts and publications do reappear in the FPE Order, see **4.3.5**.

4   *Financial Promotion – A Consultation Document*, Part Two, para 1.2; Financial Secretary in Standing Committee A, 22 July 1999, c 351. In *Financial Promotion – Second Consultation Paper*, Part Two, para 2.12, the Treasury proposes a non-exhaustive list of four *indicia* but a safe harbour if those four are met, see **4.3.5**.

5   *Financial Promotion – Second Consultation Document*, Part Two, paras 2.20 and 2.21.

6   FSMA, s 21(6) and (7).

4.3   STATUTORY INSTRUMENTS

As has been noted above, the exact scope of the FSMA will be determined by three key statutory instruments to be prepared by the Treasury. At the time of writing, drafts of these orders have been prepared, but they will need to be amended to deal with subsequent changes announced by the Government. For example, to regulate mortgage lending will require lending against a domestic mortgage to be added to the list of regulated activities.

4.3.1   The Exemption Order

This order will continue to grant exempt person status to a number of parties that would otherwise need to obtain authorisation for their regulated activities. The proposed exemptions are basically the same as under the old regime. They fall into four categories:

(1) persons exempt in respect of all regulated activities except insurance, which include the Crown Agents, the Bank of England, other EU central banks, the principal EU institutions and a number of international banking institutions such as the IMF – all these were covered by exemptions under the BA 1987 and the 1986 Act;

(2) persons exempt only in respect of deposit-taking, including the National Savings Bank, local authorities, various municipal banks and industrial and provident societies – all these were covered by exemptions under the BA 1987;

(3) persons exempt in respect of all regulated activities except deposit-taking and insurance, which include various government agencies ranging from the National Debt Commissioners to the English Tourist Board, the National Grid, the Courts, Universities and Colleges and EEA-regulated markets (as respects providing trading facilities) – CREST is also exempted for activities beyond its existing exempt status as an RCH and all these were covered by exemptions under the 1986 Act; and

(4) persons exempt in respect of specific regulated activities – this is a strange assortment including Regional Development Agencies facilitating deals, BG plc as the public gas transporter, trade unions and employers' associations offering provident or strike benefits and UK vehicle breakdown services that generally use their own personnel[1].

4.3.2   The draft Financial Services and Markets Act (Regulated Activities) Order

Regulated activities are largely an amalgam of the activities previously regulated under the ICA 1982, the 1986 Act and the BA 1987, but with some amendments and clarifications. In general, activities may only be regulated if they relate to one or more of the following:

(1) deposits (in any currency or ECUs);

---

1   Exemption Order contained in *Regulated Activities – A Consultation Document*, Part Two. The exemption for credit unions, as industrial and provident societies, presumably will be removed in the final version.

(2) rights under general insurance contracts covering:

accident	sickness
land vehicles	railway rolling stock
aircraft	ships
goods in transit	fire and natural forces
damage to property	motor vehicle insurance
aircraft liability	liability of ships
other general liability	credit
suretyship	loss of business or other financial loss
legal expenses	assistance while abroad or otherwise

(3) rights under long-term insurance contracts covering:

life and annuity	marriage and birth
investment linked	permanent health
tontines	capital redemption
pension fund management	collective insurance
social insurance	

(4) additional friendly societies contracts covering:

funeral expenses	sickness or distressed circumstance

(5) securities, derivatives, etc being:

shares or stock in share capital (not OEICs),

instruments creating or acknowledging indebtedness,

government and public securities,

warrants, etc entitling to subscribe to any of the above three,

certificates representing any of the above four,

units in CISs (including OEICs),

financial, currency and precious metal options,

futures contracts in any commodity or property,

contracts for differences (including swaps, spread bets and rolling spot forex), and

certain long-term insurance contracts;

(6) Lloyd's syndicate capacity and membership; and

(7) any other rights to or interests in the above investments (except benefits under an occupational pension scheme)[1].

The most notable investments that are not included are real and tangible property and currencies, although futures contracts in any of them are included, as are options over currencies, palladium, platinum, gold or silver[2]. Other exceptions are carried forward from the existing regime, for example certain shares in building societies and industrial and provident societies, debts under contracts for the supply of goods and services, cheques, bank statements, and futures contracts made for commercial purposes. Investments generally do not appear under more than one heading[3].

However, certain long-term insurance contracts (such as life insurance and pension contracts) which are currently treated as investments under the 1986 Act

---

1   RA Order Parts I, III and Sch 1 contained in *Regulated Activities – A Consultation Document*, Part Two, as expanded by Consultation Paper 29, FSA, October 1999, Annex A.

2   Some loans secured on land (a type of investment that already appears in the FSMA, Sch 2 indicative list) will have to be added to the RA Order list in due course.

3   RA Order, Sch 4.

as well as insurance contracts continue to be categorised as both[1]. This allows activities relating to these types of insurance to be subject to the FSA's conduct of business rules, which do not otherwise apply to insurance. It also means that brokers giving advice about them rather than confining their advice to general insurance will continue to require authorisation (eg advising on endowment mortgages).

The regulated activities in relation to the above investments are:

(1) accepting deposits
(2) insurance business:
    effecting contracts of insurance,
    carrying out contracts of insurance;
(3) other investment business:
    establishing, operating or winding up a CIS of any property,
    acting as trustee or depositary of a CIS of any property,
    acting as sole director of an OEIC of any property,
    making a market in securities (not derivatives),
    buying such securities with a view to selling,
    regularly soliciting the public to deal in such securities or assign certain long-term insurance contracts,
    dealing as principal in derivatives or rights under certain long-term insurance contracts,
    dealing as agent in securities, derivatives or rights under certain long-term insurance contracts,
    arranging deals for others in securities, derivatives or certain long-term insurance contracts,
    making arrangements enabling or facilitating deals in securities, derivatives, Lloyd's syndicates or certain long-term insurance contracts,
    safeguarding and administering (or arranging them) for securities, derivatives or certain long-term insurance contracts,
    sending dematerialised instructions relating to securities (not derivatives),
    causing dematerialised instructions to be sent relating to such securities,
    discretionary management of assets that include securities, derivatives or certain long-term insurance contracts,
    investment advice on dealing in particular securities, derivatives or certain long-term insurance contracts,
    agreeing to engage in any of the activities under the heading of other investment business;
(4) activities in the Lloyd's market:
    advising on being a member of a Lloyd's syndicate,
    being the managing agent of a Lloyd's syndicate,
    agreeing to engage in either of the above two; and
(5) the Society of Lloyd's own activities:
    arranging deals in contracts of insurance written at Lloyd's,
    arranging deals in participation in Lloyd's syndicates,
    activities in connection with, or for the purpose of either of the two above[2].

---

1   1986 Act, Sch 1, para 10; RA Order, Part I, definition of 'contractually based investment'.
2   RA Order, Parts I and II.

This list basically combines the activities listed under the ICA 1982, the 1986 Act and the BA 1987, and adds Lloyd's activities (other than acting as a Lloyd's name). There are some other minor changes. The definitions of arranging, managing investments and investment advice have been tightened up. Dealing as a principal under the 1986 Act has been split under different heads to make the application of different exemptions easier. The principal aim, however, remains the same, namely to allow an exemption for dealing directly as a principal in securities, even to the extent of it being a business, provided one does not act like a market-maker or broker (so, for example, a day trader does not need to be authorised); but not to allow such an exemption for similar dealing in derivatives or certain long-term insurance contracts unless the dealing is done through an authorised or exempt firm (so locals in the derivatives markets and corporates such as oil and electricity supply companies that also deal in derivatives do need authorisation)[1].

It should be noted that although accepting deposits (other than on a casual basis) is a regulated activity, lending money has not been until now. Consumer loans up to £25,000 have been regulated by the Consumer Credit Act 1974, but making loans against a domestic first mortgage (which will cover most consumer loans over £25,000) is expected to become a regulated activity by the end of 2001[2].

It should also be noted that offering to carry out investment business is no longer a regulated activity. Agreeing to do so is a separate head of regulated activities. However, this may make little difference as purporting to carry it out or falsely holding oneself out as doing so are crimes and where an offering is targeted at the UK, it will be covered by the financial promotion regime.

There is a general exemption for anyone engaged in regulated activities that:

(1)   do not amount to a business anywhere; or
(2)   do not amount to a business in the UK and the person does not have a permanent place of business in the UK[3].

The RA Order was produced before the 'by way of business' test was inserted into the FSMA, but if the wider exclusion in (1) above were removed, it would broaden the scope of regulated activities to cover activities that did not amount to banking, insurance or investment business before.

4.3.3   Exclusions under the draft Financial Services and Markets Act (Regulated Activities) Order

Following the pattern of the 1986 Act, there is a long list of other exclusions from what amount to regulated activities; but those exclusions cannot be claimed by any firms that fall within the definition of an 'investment firm' for the purposes of the ISD. These are firms acting in a professional capacity for third parties which:

(a)   receive, transmit or execute orders for others;

---

1   RA Order, Sch 3, paras 6–8, cf para 9.
2   Only loans secured against land appear as investments in the FSMA, Sch 2, para 23.
3   RA Order, Part IV. Article 38 makes it clear that without a permanent place of business in the UK, a person can only need authorisation if his regulated activities nevertheless constitute carrying on a business in the UK and likewise art 39 makes it clear that an exempt person only needs authorisation if regulated activities falling outside the exemption are done by him in the course of business.

(b) deal for their own account;

(c) manage discretionary portfolios; or

(d) underwrite or place issues

in transferable securities (including units in CISs and money market instruments) and financial derivatives (including forward interest-rate agreements and swaps) and which are not:

(1) firms only providing certain investment services to other group companies and/or in administering employee participation schemes;

(2) regulated professional firms only providing such investment services incidentally in the course of their professional activities;

(3) firms providing such investment services as a necessary part of their commodities trading business;

(4) 'locals' in the futures and options markets;

(5) firms that only receive and pass on orders in securities (not derivatives) to other regulated financial businesses and do not themselves hold client funds or securities;

(6) insurance undertakings and CISs (including their depositaries and managers);

(7) European Central Banks and others managing public debt; and

(8) Danish pension fund associations and Italian *agenti do cambio*[1].

Only firms that do not do any of (a)–(d) or, if they do, fall within (1)–(8), can claim the benefit of any of the RA Order exclusions. The sheer complexity of this arrangement can be seen in the case of 'locals'. Under the ISD they deal for their own account – (b) above – although it is questionable whether they are really acting in a professional capacity for third parties. Nevertheless they are specifically excluded by an ISD exception – (4) above. However, under the RA Order they are engaged in a business dealing as a principal and, as has already been noted, the exclusion for dealings in derivatives does not cover direct dealings, only dealings through authorised or exempt firms[2]. So, although locals do not need to be authorised by the ISD and cannot benefit from a European Passport, they still need to be authorised by the FSA to do business in the UK.

Other exemptions under the RA Order include:

(1) dealings intra-group or between participators in a joint venture;

(2) dealings related to the sale of goods or supply of other services;

(3) running an employees' share scheme;

(4) the purchase or sale as a principal of a body corporate;

(5) acting on the instructions of another as a bare trustee;

(6) an overseas person acting through an authorised (or exempt) firm;

(7) an overseas person acting for a person in the UK either unsolicited or without breaching the restriction on financial promotion;

(8) advice given by professionals as part of their professional activities; and

(9) advice given in the media (excluding tip sheets).

The overall net effect of the changes to the definitions and exclusions is to reduce the need for the precautionary authorisations that were obtained under the 1986

---

1   RA Order, Part II, art 3(3)(5) and Schs 2 and 5.

2   RA Order, Sch 3, para 9.

Act, particularly by professionals such as accountants and solicitors[1]. This has been done by clarifying:

(1) that 'generic' advice (eg advice from professionals about the types of investment to consider) does not constitute investment advice;
(2) that paid trustees or personal representatives do not automatically need to be authorised;
(3) that the holding of unquoted company shares (eg as part of providing company secretarial services) does not make a firm a custodian;
(4) that the authorisation requirement for arranging deals in investments does not include purely administrative arrangements (eg preparing legal documentation);
(5) that a person does not carry on a regulated activity simply by buying and selling investments for his client using the services of an authorised person; and
(6) the definitions for the sale and acquisition of a body corporate, so as to distinguish better between the acquisition of shares in a company by way of an investment, and the acquisition of such shares as a means to a person acquiring the business and assets of the company[2].

Given the sheer difficulty of determining the exact boundary line between regulated and non-regulated activities, anyone in any doubt as to whether he needs authorisation or not should seek advice from the FSA[3].

4.3.4   Wholesale markets and corporate activities

Although the exemption for listed money market institutions has gone, the FSA has promised to continue the light touch regulation of wholesale markets. The old regime did cover certain activities such as spot and forward commercial forex and bullion dealing which are not regulated activities (even though dealing in derivatives based on forex and bullion are). The FSA will not regulate these activities, but expects market participants to arrange self-regulation.

This does raise the issue of the rather difficult boundary between regulated and non-regulated activities in this area. Dealing in commodity futures is regulated, but dealing in commodity options is not. Of course in the normal course of trading, companies are regularly entering into contracts to buy goods in the future and these commercial 'futures' contracts must be excluded. The complex *indicia* used in the 1986 Act to distinguish commercial from investment contracts have been carried forward[4].

This exclusion, and many of the others, have been devised to avoid having to authorise the activities of commercial companies that are not involved in financial services as a principal business. However, with disintermediation, commercial

---

1   Provided always that such professionals avoid being investment firms under the ISD by not offering investment services (a)–(d) above other than 'incidentally'.
2   *Regulated Activities – A Consultation Document* para 3.6.
3   As part of its *Authorisation Manual*, the FSA is providing additional guidance on the types of investment activities which do and do not require authorisation, *Response to Consultation Paper 25*, FSA, December 1999, para 6.
4   RA Order, Sch 4, para 8, although the loophole of stipulating delivery within seven days, whatever in fact was intended, is being closed.

companies have become direct players in the wholesale markets. The RA Order, proposes to replace the complex exceptions under the Banking Act 1987 (Exempt Transactions) Regulations 1997 with a simple exception so that deposits accepted by companies issuing stock certificates or other instruments are not treated as deposits and so such companies issuing them do not require to be authorised as banks[1]. The actual issuing of such instruments is also not a regulated activity (except for OEICs) and so is only subject to the prospectus and promotion protections. The problem with this simple solution is that it does not seem to be compatible with the European Banking Directives[2].

Most companies that only occasionally issue or buy-in their own securities are presumably not engaging in these activities 'in the course of business' and so they are not regulated activities within the terms of the RA Order, Part IV. There is one important exception to this business test, namely managing the funds of an occupational pension scheme. Even if it can be argued that this activity is not being conducted as a business, it remains a regulated activity unless:

(1) the day-to-day management has been contracted to an authorised (or exempt) person; or
(2) it is a small self-managed or insurance/annuity based scheme[3].

4.3.5   The Financial Promotions Exemption Order

By narrowing the basic definition of financial promotion to invitations and inducements made in the course of business, the number of exemptions from the restriction has been reduced compared to the 1986 Act. The FPE Order will also reduce the territorial scope of the restriction to promotions 'directed at' the UK[4]. On the other hand, the Government remains particularly concerned about unsolicited real-time communications, namely personal visits, telephone calls or electronic interactions that are not made on the initiative of the customer. This is a wider definition of 'unsolicited' than under the Common Unsolicited Calls Regulations 1991 and, although the exemptions like those for promoting management buy-ins or occupational pension schemes have been retained, a number of others have been removed because it is felt that the promotion should be made by or with the approval of an authorised firm[5].

---

1   RA Order, Sch 3, para 3.
2   2BCD, Art 3 in the light of the First Banking Coordination Directive's 9th recital.
3   RA Order, Part IV, art 37, repeating the exception in the 1986 Act, s 191; the draft *Conduct of Business Sourcebook*, Chapter 11 contains a special regime for firms set up to manage the funds of a company's occupational pension scheme.
4   FPE Order, art 15. Broadcasts and publications principally for overseas markets are exempt. In addition, four non-exhaustive *indicia* are specified which, if they are all met, amount to a safe harbour. They are that, in respect of UK persons:
    (1) it states it is not addressed to them;
    (2) it states it must not be relied upon by them;
    (3) it is not referred to, or accessible from, another communication directed at them; and
    (4) there are effective procedures to stop them contracting, etc.
5   SIB Release 101/1991; FPE Order, arts 14 and 65–67. With this tightening up, for example, ticking a box to receive further calls will not be sufficient to make those subsequent calls solicited.

The proposed exemptions still run to over 60 and largely follow the pattern of the previous legislation. They will now be contained in one statutory instrument and apart from (1) below, will be cumulative[1]. They include:

(1)   promoting deposit-taking or general insurance where appropriate information about the provider is given – *all* real-time communications in these two areas are exempt, as is *any* promotion of reinsurance and large-risk insurance[2];

(2)   solicited real-time communications which are not part of a coordinated promotional strategy, or if they are, are made by an overseas person[3];

(3)   promotions by overseas persons to existing overseas customers, including unsolicited real-time calls provided the customer expects such calls and has had risk warnings – overseas persons can make unsolicited calls on others sufficiently knowledgeable to understand the risks, again provided risk warnings have been issued[4];

(4)   promotions by RIEs, RCHs and other exempt persons of their exempt activities[5];

(5)   generic promotions of a type or category of investment rather than a particular investment[6];

(6)   introductions to authorised third parties[7];

(7)   passive communications providers such as Internet Service Providers and telecommunications companies[8];

(8)   listing particulars, prospectuses, certain promotions connected to them and other announcements made through approved markets[9];

(9)   purchases, sales and takeovers of control of private companies[10];

(10)   statements in or accompanied by a directors' report and annual accounts[11];

(11)   certain unit trusts and OEIC promotions[12];

(12)   certain warm-up communications that are not part of a coordinated promotional strategy[13];

(13)   safe harbours for communications directed at investment professionals, high net-worth companies or common interest groups[14];

---

1   FPE Order, art 13.
2   FPE Order, Part II. This means that banking and general insurance advisers do not need to be authorised.
3   FPE Order, arts 16 and 22.
4   FPE Order, art 21. Overseas persons may still, of course, be subject to marketing restrictions applied by their home State regulator.
5   FPE Order, arts 28 and 29. This allows exchanges to market their services, but not specific investments and allows appointed representatives to operate within their exemptions.
6   FPE Order, art 17. This exempts a lot of less specific advice given by solicitors, accountants, trade associations, etc.
7   FPE Order, art 19. This covers much of the promotion done by solicitors and accountants.
8   FPE Order, art 23. It is the web-site owners that may be promoting.
9   FPE Order, arts 58–64. This exempts official announcements of quoted companies.
10   FPE Order, arts 54–57. This exempts negotiations about such sale and purchase contracts.
11   FPE Order, art 51. This is the most likely document to promote private companies.
12   FPE Order, arts 33 and 37; for details on CISs, see **13.2**.
13   FPE Order, art 49. Limited testing of a proposal is exempt, but not telephone campaigns, etc.
14   FPE Order, arts 39, 42 and 44.

(14) promotions of shares and debentures with suitable warnings to high net-worth investors[1]; and

(15) promotions of investments to sophisticated investors, namely those certified by an authorised person as being in a position to understand the risks[2].

These last two are new and are aimed at allowing informal promotions to business angels. As the Financial Secretary explained:

> 'Other jurisdictions, such as the United States of America, recognise that some private investors are sufficiently sophisticated so that they do not need to benefit from the full protections on securities offers. Such a system can be especially helpful to start-up companies which may find it difficult to meet the expense of a regulated offer document, whether a prospectus or approved promotional document . . . Therefore, we are proposing an exemption so that, for example, companies or entrepreneurs who seek capital may make available unapproved share offer documents to a defined group of private investors.'[3]

The practical effects of these exemptions are examined in greater detail in **13.1**.

---

1   FPE Order, arts 41 and 42. The proposed tests are a minimum of £70,000–£100,000 income or £200,000–£300,000 net assets excluding main residence, pension and life assurance.
2   FPE Order, art 43. This and the previous two exemptions are to cover business angels.
3   Standing Committee A, 22 July 1999, c 353.

Chapter 5

AUTHORISATION AND APPROVAL

5.1 BACKGROUND

As has already been noted, the separate authorisation arrangements for deposit-taking, insurance and other investment business are now being replaced by a single authorisation. In practice, however, a firm will still have to apply not for a general authorisation but for permission to conduct specific activities. It will then have to reapply if it wishes to extend the scope of those activities. If it strays outside its current permission, the firm remains authorised, its contracts remain valid, it does not commit a criminal offence, but it will have contravened a requirement under the FSMA and be subject to disciplinary action[1].

The 1986 Act required only the authorisation of firms and not individual employees[2]; but the SROs gradually introduced registration requirements for senior managers and personnel dealing with customers, which meant that these key personnel could be pre-vetted and thereafter regulated contractually. Lloyd's applied similar arrangements to employees of its managing and members' agents. The statutory regulators of insurance companies, banks and mutuals, however, only vetted senior managers and then after they had taken up their posts. With the concept of approved persons, the SROs' approach will become statutory and be applied by the FSA to the key personnel of all authorised firms.

It should be noted that in the rest of this chapter, and indeed throughout the book, although individuals can be authorised as sole traders and functions requiring approval can be carried out by firms, to keep the basic distinction clear, references will generally be to authorised firms and approved individuals[3].

5.2 OBTAINING AUTHORISATION

There are three basic ways a firm can be authorised under the FSMA, namely by obtaining:

(1) permission directly from the FSA to carry on one or more regulated activities in the UK;

(2) authorisation from the EEA State in which it is headquartered and using a European Passport or other right under the Treaty of Rome to carry on one or more regulated activities in the UK[4]; or

---

1   FSMA, s 20; for the position under the old regime see Standing Committee A, 20 July 1999, c 319. The chairman of the FSA has likened these authorisations to a general driving licence 'with a list of permissions in it – all those things that the regulator allows you to do', FSA Press Release 80/2000.

2   Unlike the licensing arrangements under the Prevention of Fraud (Investments) Act 1958, s 7.

3   The FSA itself has tended to keep this terminology in its Consultation Papers.

4   FSMA, s 31. Certain other bodies are automatically authorised, for example Lloyd's (FSMA, s 315) and the operators, trustees and depositaries of recognised overseas CISs plus UK authorised OEICs (being their own operators) (FSMA, Sch 5). Firms authorised in Gibraltar

(3) grandfathered status by having been authorised to conduct what are now regulated activities under the previous regimes[1].

Because an EEA authorisation may not cover all the regulated activities a firm intends to conduct in the UK, some EEA firms will have to seek an additional permission for those other activities from the FSA[2]. However a firm obtains authorisation, the FSA must enter the details of it into the register it keeps of authorised firms[3].

The FSA must cancel a UK authorisation if the firm no longer has a permission to conduct any regulated activities. However, the FSA can delay cancelling an authorisation by retaining an 'empty permission'[4]. This strange concept was explained by the Financial Secretary:

> 'The benefit of keeping an empty permission in force is that it will allow the FSA to retain its jurisdiction over the firm involved. For example, it may be investigating a possible disciplinary matter or it may be necessary for the firm to complete a past business review ... The FSA has to cancel the firm's permission once the FSA is satisfied that it is no longer necessary ... The FSA's refusal of an application to cancel a firm's permission will be subject to the usual procedural safeguards.'[5]

A firm relying purely upon its EEA authorisation will automatically lose its UK authorisation if its home State authorisation or Passport to conduct branch or cross-border activity in the UK is withdrawn. It may otherwise ask the FSA to cancel its authorisation if it no longer wishes to conduct regulated activities in the UK[6]. Authorisation of a unincorporated partnership or association is unaffected if the membership of the firm alters or even if the firm is dissolved, provided its successor has substantially the same members and business[7].

---

may claim a European Passport under the FS Directives to operate anywhere in the EEA except the UK. The Treasury may, by statutory instrument, extend such a passport to the UK although the firms can seek UK authorisation instead (FSMA, s 409). Until now, this optional passport into the UK has applied only to credit institutions and insurers, but it will be extended to other investment firms: Lord McIntosh, vol 611 HL, 30 March 2000, c 1046.

1   FSMA, ss 426 and 427. Grandfathering may be permitted by statutory instrument and the FSA has expressed a general intention to grandfather all firms authorised by the existing regulators. In practice, this will be vital to allow the FSA to concentrate on vetting those firms being authorised for the first time. The Treasury's order may allow the FSA to refuse grandfathering or require a reapplication in particular cases, but even where grandfathering is allowed, there is going to be a practical problem lining up the new permission categories with existing authorisations: see **5.2.2**; FSA Press Release 80/2000.

2   FSMA, s 50(1), but such a firm may not apply for a UK permission for what can be covered by such a Passport to ensure that responsibility for passportable activities remains with the home State regulator, FSMA, s 40(3).

3   FSMA, s 347. The general requirement for the FSA to issue a definitive certificate has been dropped.

4   FSMA, ss 33 and 44(4).

5   Vol 344 HC, 9 February 2000, c 288. Such a refusal is subject to the FSA's rejection procedures, see **9.3.1**.

6   FSMA, ss 34–36. The operators, trustees and depositaries of recognised overseas CISs may also ask the FSA to cancel their authorisations. If a firm has an additional UK permission, it will remain authorised.

7   FSMA, s 32. This even applies to Scottish partnerships but not incorporated partnerships outside the UK.

5.2.1   Threshold Conditions for Authorisation

A firm making any initial application for, or subsequent variation to, a permission to carry on regulated activities, must meet and thereafter continue to meet five Threshold (originally Qualifying) Conditions for Authorisation (TCAs), namely:

(1) legal status;
(2) location of offices;
(3) close links;
(4) adequate resources; and
(5) suitability[1].

The two principal ones are whether the applicant has adequate resources for its activities and is suitable, ie 'a fit and proper person', to conduct those activities. The former is not confined to financial resources but covers systems to manage risk, in both cases not just of the applicant, but of the group of which it is a member. The FSA will be setting out detailed financial resources and systems requirements in its *Prudential Sourcebook*[2]. The FSA is also publishing guidance on this and other TCAs which will form part of the *Authorisation Manual.* As well as examining the applicant's capital adequacy (including professional indemnity insurance (PII)), risk management systems and business plans, the FSA will use its discretion to consider *any* relationships the applicant has and to look at whether other members of its group or anyone else might pose financial risks for the applicant or have been the subject of receivership, administration, winding-up or bankruptcy proceedings[3].

Likewise, when considering an applicant's suitability, the FSA must have regard to all the circumstances, including the applicant's connections, the nature of its proposed activities and the need to ensure sound and prudent management. The FSA proposes to publish quite detailed guidance on this TCA[4]. Clearly, there is close relationship between this guidance and the Principles for Businesses (PFBs) the FSA has produced[5], but as the FSA has explained:

'The [TCAs] are relevant to the FSA's decision about authorisation, withdrawal of authorisation and intervention. The Principles, on the other hand, as "requirements" under the legislation, are in addition relevant to decisions about discipline, as well as these other matters.

In practice, of course, the general kind of behaviour needed to meet the [TCAs] will also be required by the Principles, and vice versa. Thus, in determining if a firm

---

1   FSMA, s 41 and Sch 6, paras 1–5. The concept of overarching qualifying conditions has been taken from the BA 1987, Sch 3.
2   FSMA, Sch 6, para 4. The definitions of group, parent, subsidiary, etc are contained in FSMA, ss 420 and 421. The FSA will continue to rely on the current prudential requirements until a fully revised *Prudential Sourcebook* can be produced. However, the room for any simplification or change on minimum capital adequacy requirements is severely constrained by international obligations like the CAD and the Basle Accord, see **6.4.1**.
3   FSMA, s 49(1); Consultation Paper 20, FSA, March 1999, p 14.
4   FSMA, Sch 6, para 5; Consultation Paper 20, pp 15–18. The guidance will cover two areas, whether the firm:
         (1) can conduct its business with integrity and in compliance with high standards; and
         (2) has competent and prudent management and exercises due skill, care and diligence.
     The Economic Secretary has said that the application of this condition will be the same as under the 1986 Act: Standing Committee A, 21 October 1999, c 476.
5   See **6.3.1**.

satisfies the [TCAs], the FSA will also take into consideration whether a firm is ready, willing, and organised to comply, on a continuing basis, with the Principles and other Rules of the FSA.'[1]

In addition to these two key TCAs, the FSA must uphold three others to meet its obligations as a home State regulator under the FS Directives, particularly following the BCCI affair[2]. It must be satisfied that any close links an applicant has with another person (being part of the same group, or holding or having held in it 20% of any voting rights) will not prevent effective supervision of that applicant. Like the previous two TCAs, this is a subjective test and the FSA may issue some guidance[3].

The other two conditions are absolute. Although an individual, body corporate (including a mutual), partnership or unincorporated association may apply for a permission, insurance business may only be conducted by a body corporate, a registered friendly society or a member of Lloyd's and deposit-taking by a body corporate or a partnership. Finally, all firms incorporated in the UK must have their head office and registered office (if any) in the UK. Partnerships and sole traders with their head offices in the UK must carry on business in the UK[4].

Authorisation frees a firm from the general prohibition and the restriction on financial promotion in relation to regulated activities other than the promotion of unregulated CISs[5]. Nevertheless, an applicant can only show that it meets the TCAs (eg on financial resources) by stipulating the type and quantity of business it proposes to do. Therefore, behind the 'blanket' authorisation, the FSA has a wide discretion to limit the regulated activities an applicant can conduct[6]. It can also allow an authorised firm to be in breach of the TCAs 'in order to secure its regulatory objective of the protection of consumers', an override that has been explained by the Financial Secretary thus:

'The threshold conditions are conditions which should be met at all times and they are constant points of reference for the FSA. Important though meeting the conditions always is, however, maintaining constant strict adherence may be temporarily subordinated in the interest of consumers.

For instance, the FSA could permit an authorised insurer which no longer met the conditions to continue to carry on some limited insurance activities in order to protect the position of existing policyholders, but at the same time might prevent it from engaging in new business. The end result would still need to be either that the company met the conditions again for the activity it had permission to carry on, or that the permission was withdrawn and authorisation ended.'[7]

---

1   *Feedback Statement on Responses to Consultation Paper 20*, FSA, October 1999 and repeated in *Response on Consultation Paper 13*, FSA, October 1999, para 14.

2   Post-BCCI Directive 1995/26/EC.

3   FSMA, Sch 6, para 3; *Feedback Statement on Responses to Consultation Paper 20*, p 8. If the applicant is part of a group containing an EEA firm that would qualify for a European Passport, its home regulator must also be consulted: FSMA, s 49(2) and (3).

4   FSMA, s 40(1) and Sch 6, paras 1 and 2. The original sub-paragraphs that excluded overseas sole traders and some overseas partnerships being authorised in the UK were removed; but the FSA can consider the legal structure of any applicant under the suitable TCA.

5   For the marketing of CISs, see **13.3**.

6   FSMA, s 42.

7   FSMA, s 41(3) as explained in vol 343 HC, 1 February 2000, c 974.

5.2.2 UK permission

Technically, under these arrangements a firm applies to the FSA for permission to carry on regulated activities in the UK and authorisation automatically flows from that permission. The FSA must stipulate what activities it is giving permission for and from what date. These may be narrower or wider than those the applicant sought (which allows the FSA to standardise its permissions). Limitations may be attached or requirements specified, including those about any non-regulated activities the applicant may conduct and about the group of which it is a member[1]. Limitations reducing the scope of a permission will generally be imposed to bring the firm within a specific light regulatory regime (eg locals on a derivatives market); but requirements will be attached where the FSA has concerns about the firm (eg limiting the quantity of business done by a new firm, requiring more regular financial returns or compliance reviews). These requirements can even restrict disposals and other dealings in the assets of the firm and/or its customers and require customers' assets to be held by a trustee approved by the FSA[2]. In considering any application, the FSA may have regard to anyone that might have a relationship with the applicant[3].

An authorised firm may only have one permission, but once it has been granted, it can seek to extend, reduce or cancel it. When varying a permission, the FSA must still consider all the TCAs and may refuse an application if it considers that it would adversely affect the interests of consumers or potential consumers[4]. The FSA proposes that a firm's permission will consist of three parts:

(1) the activities from the RA Order it may undertake;
(2) the investments from the RA Order it may offer; and
(3) the customers (market counterparty, intermediate or private) with which it may deal.

All these details should be available on the Internet[5]. This approach, of specifying the range of activities permitted rather than offering a single global permission or requiring separate permissions for each and every line of business, follows the current SRO practice and is an attempt to balance consumer protection and keep the UK internationally competitive[6].

The FSA intends to mirror exactly the categories of investments and activities listed in the RA Order[7], except that:

(1) in the investment categories, commodities futures and options, spread bets and rolling spot forex contracts will be separated out from other derivatives investments;

---

1   FSMA, ss 42 and 43. This allows the FSA to specify how the business may be done and the mix or quantity perhaps in the initial years, as insurance regulators have done until now. Unregulated activities that FSA might wish to restrict are investment businesses running a casino or money lending, or being part of a group that does either: Standing Committee A, 21 October 1999, c 479.
2   FSMA, s 48; Consultation Paper 29, paras 2.12–2.16.
3   FSMA, s 49.
4   FSMA, ss 40(2) and 44. 'Consumers' remain undefined here.
5   Consultation Paper 29, paras 2.1–2.5 and 6.1.
6   Consultation Paper 29, Section 9.
7   See **4.3.2**.

(2) in the categories of regulated activities, giving advice on pension transfers and opt-outs will be kept separate from other advice and involvement in regulated as against unregulated CISs will be kept separate; and

(3) ISA, PEP and broker fund management and operating an investment trust savings scheme, which have significant regulatory and consumer protection implications but involve a combination of many of the investments and regulated activities may be categorised separately[1].

5.2.3 Permission procedure

The FSMA leaves the FSA to determine the detailed procedure for applications, but does stipulate that requests for information must be reasonable and that an application must be determined within six months of being complete and, in any case, within 12 months of the initial submission[2]. These seem very wide time-limits, particularly for applications to vary an existing permission. The FSA has stated that 'it expects that most applications will be processed well within the time-limits set out in [the FSMA]'.[3] The procedures for initial applications will be contained in the *Authorisation Manual* and for subsequent variations or cancellations in the *Supervision Manual.*

For initial applications, the FSA will produce detailed application packs to be completed and returned with the appropriate non-returnable application fee. The FSA will then determine whether the applicant meets the TCAs and is ready, willing and organised to comply with the regulatory requirements which will apply to their proposed activities. This may require requests for further information and a dialogue with the applicant. As has already been noted, a permission may be granted for more or fewer activities than those applied for and may be subject to limitations or requirements. If the FSA grants an initial application in whole or in part, it must give the applicant a written notice of when the permission will operate and keep a formal record of the permission. The firm may then use the permission given even if it is continuing to object to any restriction or limitation on it[4].

If the FSA is minded to refuse an application or to restrict or vary its width or attach limitations or requirements, it must follow its rejection procedures. The matter will presumably be passed to the Enforcement Committee to consider. If it agrees, the Committee will issue a warning notice to the applicant so that it can make representations. If the Committee remains unpersuaded by such representations, it must issue a decision notice which must also offer the right to refer any grievance to the Tribunal. This procedure does not apply if the application has been rejected as falling within a potential European Passport, because the FSA has no right to consider such an application under the FS Directives[5].

For subsequent variations, the FSA will generally not require such a formal application and the application should be made to the firm's supervision team. The FSA expects most will be dealt with informally and quickly.

---

1   Consultation Paper 29, paras 2.6–2.11.
2   FSMA, ss 51 and 52.
3   Consultation Paper 29, para 3.2.
4   FSMA, ss 52(4) and (5) and 347.
5   FSMA, ss 51, 52 and 55(1). Consultation Paper 29, paras 3.2 and 3.8–3.14. The Consultation Paper was produced before the procedural provisions of FSMA were settled by the Government. Although granting an initial permission is viewed as a supervisory matter by the

'However, the length of the process will relate directly to the complexity of variation requested. A small variation in a firm's permission is likely to take much less time than an application for an independent financial adviser to become a bank.'[1]

A firm can apply to:

(1) undertake further regulated activities;
(2) reduce the number of regulated activities it is permitted to undertake;
(3) vary the FSA's description of its regulated activities;
(4) cancel any limitation or requirement imposed by the FSA;
(5) vary any limitation or requirement imposed by the FSA; or
(6) cancel its whole permission and authorisation.

As has already been noted, the FSA can delay the cancellation of an authorisation by retaining an empty permission[2]. In deciding whether to:

'... the FSA will determine, *inter alia*, whether there are outstanding complaints, whether client money or deposits or property has been returned, whether the firm has unsettled or unexpired liabilities to its customers, and whether all debts to the FSA have been settled.'[3]

As with initial applications, the FSA may refuse, or alter the width of, subsequent variations or attach limitations or requirements. This is subject to the same rejection procedures with warning and decision notices and the right to refer any grievance to the Tribunal[4].

5.2.4   European Economic Area authorisation

A firm authorised in another EEA State to conduct banking, insurance or investment services within the terms of the appropriate FS Directive may:

(1) obtain consent from its home State regulator to set up a branch in the UK; or
(2) notify its home State regulator of its intention to conduct cross-border business into the UK[5].

Generally, the home State regulator must notify the FSA of the activities such a firm will be conducting in the UK and the FSA then has two months to prepare for the firm's supervision and to inform the firm of the UK regulations that will apply to it. Permission to conduct these activities is automatic, but the date from which it runs depends upon whether the activities will be conducted from a branch or cross-border, and in the latter case, under which FS Directive the firm is claiming its Passport. If the firm wishes to conduct activities not covered by its European Passport (eg dealing in commodities derivatives), an additional UK permission

---

Government, because there is no pressing urgency, the warning and decision procedures have been retained but without all the other disciplinary protections: vol 611 HL, 30 March 2000, cc 1026 and 1031. This is explained in greater detail in **9.3**.

1   Consultation Paper 29, para 3.4.
2   FSMA, s 44.
3   Consultation Paper 29, paras 3.3–3.6.
4   FSMA, ss 52 and 55(1). For interventions on the FSA's own initiative to vary or cancel a permission, see **9.3.6**.
5   For the development of these Directives and the scope of the European Passports, see **2.2**. Currently, approximately 200 firms have used a Passport to establish branches in the UK and 400 to undertake cross-border business into the UK.

may have to be applied for (but see below)[1]. A similar process in reverse applies to a UK firm seeking to use a European Passport to set up a branch in, or conduct cross-border business into, another EEA State[2].

As the various Directives came into effect at different times, there are slight procedural differences for the three types of business covered by European Passports. The Treasury will make regulations to deal with subsequent variations to, and cancellations of, these passported permissions and arrangements[3].

To take advantage of an inward or outward European Passport, a firm must conduct one of the core activities covered by the FS Directives. Thus, many financial services firms throughout the EEA cannot rely on these formal passporting procedures at all. Others may be able to claim a passport for some, but not all, of their activities. However, rather than have to apply for separate authorisation for any branch or cross-border activity in another EEA State, the firm may be able to rely upon the general freedoms of establishment and to provide services under the Treaty of Rome[4].

To meet this informal passporting obligation, the FSA must authorise a firm from another EEA country and permit it to conduct a regulated activity through a branch in, or cross-border into, the UK if:

(1) the firm is authorised to conduct the activity in question by its home State regulator;
(2) that regulator imposes minimum European standards or equivalent consumer protection to that applied in the UK for that activity (certifiable by the Treasury);
(3) the activity as it is conducted is not already covered by a European Passport;
(4) the home State regulator has informed the FSA in writing that the firm is authorised; and
(5) the firm has given the FSA seven days' formal notice of its intention to conduct the activity.

---

1   FSMA, s 50 and Sch 3, Part II. Inwardly passported credit institutions do not require a licence under the Consumer Credit Act 1974 to offer loans to UK consumers. For a discussion of the complications surrounding a permission's commencement, see vol 611 HL, 21 March 2000, cc 146–150 and vol 613 HL, 18 May 2000, c 394. If such a firm enters into contracts before any commencement of its permission, those contracts remain enforceable: FSMA, Sch 3, para 16.

2   FSMA, s 37 and Sch 3, Part III. If the FSA is minded to refuse to consent to an outward Passport, it must follow its rejection procedures. As guaranteed subsidiaries of banks can claim a 2BCD Passport even though they themselves are not regulated by the FSA, there is a specific crime to deter them from not applying to the FSA for their outward Passport: FSMA, Sch 3, para 21. If a UK authorised person does not apply properly for an outward Passport, the FSMA does not make its contracts unenforceable. This was one of the reasons given by the Economic Secretary for maintaining the enforceability of contracts made by inwardly passported firms that have not complied with the technicalities: vol 351 HC, 5 June 2000, c 129.

3   FSMA, Sch 3, paras 17, 18 and 22.

4   An example was given by the Financial Secretary: 'A mortgage provider that did not finance its business by accepting deposits from the public would not be a credit institution as defined by the Second Banking Directive. Lending on property is an activity that is passportable under the Second Banking Directive, but not under the Investment Services Directive. An Investment Services Directive investment firm that was authorised for mortgage lending in its home State might therefore have treaty rights that extended beyond its directive rights' (Standing Committee A, 19 October 1999, c 443).

If a firm claiming this right already has a UK permission to conduct the activity, the seven-day notice period does not apply. However, on the transfer, the FSA must cancel that permission unless there are good reasons not to. Breach of the notice provision or the supply of false or misleading information in respect of it is a criminal offence punishable with a fine[1]. As this is a developing area of European law, the FSMA does not define the scope of this informal passporting arrangement. It is ironic that this procedure is considerably less bureaucratic than those under the European Passports[2].

Finally, the operators, trustees and depositaries of inwardly passported CISs are automatically authorised and have permission to conduct their respective functions in relation to the scheme. This is to allow these European Passports, that attach to the scheme itself rather than those who are running it, to be effective. Before marketing itself in the UK, such a scheme has to give the FSA two months' notice. The FSA can refuse recognition only if the proposed marketing does not comply with UK marketing rules[3].

5.2.5 Treasury intervention

As part of European Passport arrangements, the EU reserves the right to instruct Member States not to authorise firms, or permit the take-over of authorised firms by firms from non-EEA countries. This power could be invoked if the non-EEA country is obstructing EEA firms from conducting financial services in that country[4]. In fact, since 1 March 1999, this power can be used only against countries that are not World Trade Organisation members. To meet this now limited EU requirement, the Treasury may direct the FSA to:

(1) refuse or put on hold any application for a UK permission from a firm from the offending country; or
(2) object to such a firm taking a 50% or more stake (whether direct or indirect) in a UK authorised firm.

The FSA does not have to comply with the normal warning and decision notices, but does have to notify the firm of the intervention and the reasons for it. Although a referral to the Tribunal is not specifically excluded, it would appear to be pointless if the matter is ultimately an EU decision[5]. If an inwardly passported subsidiary of a firm from an offending country has been authorised in an EU country, the passport may not be disturbed; but if the subsidiary has been authorised in one of the three additional EEA countries the passport may be removed[6].

---

1   FSMA, Sch 4. Equivalent arrangements existed under the 1986 Act, ss 31 and 32, although no certificate of 'equivalent' protection was ever asked for. Refusal to cancel a UK permission is most likely if there are outstanding disciplinary issues.
2   This informal passporting might cover inwardly passported credit institutions involved in the receipt and transmission of customers' orders or the arranging of transactions in existing securities which are not covered by the 2BCD, see **2.2.3**.
3   FSMA, s 264 and Sch 5. The Schedule also automatically authorises UK OEICs as their own operators. For further details, see **13.4.2**.
4   ISD, Art 7(5); 2BCD, Art 9(4); First Non-life Insurance Directive, Art 29b(4); First Life Insurance Directive, Art 32b(4).
5   FSMA, ss 405–407. In (2) any breach of the notice of objection is a criminal offence and can also lead to a share freeze and compulsory sale.
6   FSMA, s 408.

Finally, the Treasury has a general power to direct the FSA, RIEs, RCHs and the Ombudsman Scheme to comply with any European or other international obligations[1].

5.2.6   Significant control over authorised firms

The FS Directives require home State regulators to vet any persons that might be acquiring a significant degree of control over firms that could claim a European Passport. To that end, the Directives require regulators to be notified of such interests and of any significant changes in them. For the sake of ease and consistency, the FSMA extends that system to *all* authorised firms incorporated or formed in the UK (other than sole traders and partnerships). Indeed, where 'controller' is referred to in the FSMA, the term can be rather deceptive as what is meant is any holder above this notification threshold[2].

The definition of the notification threshold is complicated, but can be summarised as:

(1)   10% of the shares or votes in the firm or its parent; or
(2)   significant influence over the management of the firm or its parent by virtue of some lower number of shares or votes

that are held by one party or a set of associates taken together (eg different companies in a group). There are then further thresholds at 20%, 33%, 50% or otherwise becoming the direct or indirect parent of the firm. The Treasury can amend these requirements by statutory instrument and the Government has declared its intention to use the Treasury's powers to deal with two problems that arise from these notification requirements:

(1)   as prior assent must be obtained from the FSA, defining what steps are sufficient to trigger the need to give a notification; and
(2)   given the very wide definition of notifiable interests, how multiple confusing notifications are going to be avoided[3].

If a party (or set of associates) proposes a step that would raise its influence through one of these thresholds, it must notify the FSA in writing, which is then given three months to consider the proposal (including consulting the home State regulator of the party or others in the group). If the three months lapses, approval is automatic. If actual approval is given, the party must be notified immediately in writing and told the date by when the step must be taken (and if not, within one year), otherwise the approval lapses. The party must then give the FSA a further notice when it actually takes the step[4].

The FSA has to be satisfied that:

(1)   the acquirer is a 'fit and proper person' to have such control;
(2)   the interests of the firm's or any other firm's customers (or potential customers) are not threatened; and

---

1   FSMA, s 410. The power also extends to anyone subject to the special set-off arrangements under FSMA, s 301, see **11.2.2**.
2   FSMA, ss 178 and 422. Control over overseas firms that have authorised branches in the UK is no longer a matter for the UK authorities but is left to the overseas firms' home regulators.
3   FSMA, ss 179, 180, 192 and 422; vol 612 HL, 9 May 2000, c 1467.
4   FSMA, ss 178 and 182–184.

(3) in the light of the control, the TCAs are or would continue to be met[1].

The test in (2) above is very wide and authorised firms subject to a takeover bid could use it as a basis to have the FSA intervene (as well as the competition authorities) not just where the takeover might damage the firm's customers but also where it might damage the wider market in some way.

The FSA has to remain satisfied that the three tests above continue to be met. As the Financial Secretary has said:

> 'The regime is based on the fact that a person must not only meet the approval requirements to acquire control, but continue to meet those requirements through-out the period in which they have control ... If it were necessary to meet the requirements only once, most of the advantages of effective regulation and consumer protection would be lost.'[2]

Whether or not it has received a notification, if the FSA is minded to object or attach conditions to an acquisition or a continuing position, it must follow its rejection procedures. The FSA must make clear any remedial measures that would meet its objections[3]. Breach of a notice of objection or of a condition allows the FSA to issue a restriction notice effectively freezing any shares concerned pending a court order to sell the shares and to distribute the proceeds to the beneficial owners[4].

A party that proposes a step that would reduce his influence through one of these thresholds must still notify the FSA of the proposal and then of the event, but the FSA has no power to object[5]. Sometimes a party may involuntarily acquire influence (eg shares are inherited or other shares are bought in) or have his influence reduced (eg new shares are issued to others). In those circumstances, the FSA must be notified within 14 days of the party realising its position. The FSA can still object to an acquisition and seek to have shares sold[6].

Failure to notify the FSA of proposals to pass through a threshold (up or down) or acquire influence before its approval has been given, is punishable by up to a level 5 fine. There is a defence of not knowing of the circumstances that required a notification, but as with involuntary increases or reductions of influence, once the party knows, he has 14 days to make a declaration and failure to make one is also punishable by up to a level 5 fine. Acquisitions in breach of a notice of objection, however, are viewed more seriously and are punishable with up to two years' imprisonment and an unlimited fine[7].

---

1   FSMA, s 186(2) and (3). Consumers include not just customers of that firm, but customers or potential customers of any firms and their appointed representatives carrying on regulated activities. The Financial Secretary explained that 'threatened' was used instead of 'prejudiced' because the latter might cover minor changes in trading terms whereas what was aimed at was 'the less likely more but serious risk' including systemic risk that might affect not just customers of the particular authorised firm: Standing Committee A, 25 November 1999, cc 945 and 946.

2   Standing Committee A, 25 November 1999, c 945; FSMA, s 187(3).

3   FSMA, ss 183 and 185–188. Such procedures are discussed in **9.3**.

4   FSMA, s 189.

5   FSMA, ss 181 and 190.

6   FSMA, ss 178(2), 189 and 190(2).

7   FSMA, s 191.

5.2.7   Transfer of banking and insurance business

The FSA can exercise some control over the takeover or merger of most deposit-taking, insurance and other investment firms through the above sections on control. The Government has also taken the opportunity of the FSMA to rationalise control of the transfer of banks' and insurers' business[1]. Such transfers can take place after a takeover or merger has gone through (eg the Lloyds and TSB businesses being merged into one corporate entity) or as part of a rationalisation or spin-off of activities, sometimes associated with rescue packages. Because depositors and policyholders may be adversely affected by such transfers, particularly if assets and liabilities are not transferred together, they are subject to court approval. Application may be made by either the transferor or transferee and may be subject to Treasury regulations, particularly on the type of notice that must be given[2].

The FSA and any party that might be adversely affected (including employees) are entitled to be heard by the court. The court may approve the transfer only if it is satisfied that the scheme is appropriate, which in the case of insurance transfers, requires a report on the scheme in a form, and by a person, approved by the FSA. The court must also be satisfied that the transferee:

(1)   has the necessary authorisation to conduct the transferred business; and
(2)   has a certificate from the FSA or its home State regulator that it will meet any solvency or capital adequacy requirements imposed on it.

Other certificates may be required where the transfer involves other EEA States[3].

The court has a wide discretion about the orders it may make to transfer assets and liabilities, including amending the terms of any insurance policies, although this can, at the request of the FSA, be subject to an independent actuary's report[4]. Some EEA countries allow policyholders to cancel insurance policies on such transfers, so unless the transferor qualifies for a European Passport, notices must be issued in States affected to allow policyholders the opportunity to cancel. If an inwardly passported insurer transfers UK policies under the terms of the Insurance Directives, the transfer will operate automatically and not be subject to the agreement or consent of UK policyholders. The FSA can certify the margin of solvency of a UK transferee of insurance business from an EEA (or Swiss general) insurer[5].

Exactly which transfers fall within these arrangements is complicated. In the case of deposit-taking, the transfer of any business from an authorised UK firm and the transfer of UK-based business from any other firm is covered unless:

(1)   the transferor is a building society or credit union (for which there are alternative arrangements); or

---

1   Transfer of building societies' and other friendly societies' business is covered separately by the Building Societies Act 1986 and the Friendly Societies Act 1992. Bank transfers have until now required Private Acts of Parliament.
2   FSMA, ss 104, 107 and 108. The transfer of a few contracts, assets or liabilities would probably not amount to a transfer of business: vol 612 HL, 18 April 2000, c 663.
3   FSMA, ss 109–111 and Sch 12, Parts I and II.
4   FSMA, ss 112 and 113.
5   FSMA, ss 114–116 and Sch 12, Part III.

(2) the transfer is part of a court-approved scheme of arrangement anyway[1].

In the case of insurance, the arrangements apply only to transfers to establishments within the EEA, but otherwise the transfer of any UK- or EEA-based business from an authorised UK firm, the transfer of UK-based business from a non-passported firm and the transfer of reinsurance business conducted from a UK branch of a passported firm, is covered unless:

(1) the transferor is a friendly society (for which there are alternative arrangements);

(2) the transfer is of EEA-based reinsurance business from an authorised UK firm and has already been approved by another EEA court or regulator;

(3) the transfer is of non-EEA-based business from an UK authorised firm and has already been approved by a non-EEA court or regulator; or

(4) all the policyholders have consented to the transfer of a whole business which is either solely reinsurance business or is to a firm controlled by those policyholders.

In cases (2)–(4), the transferor and transferee may nevertheless apply for court sanction. Although a transfer may also be part of a court-approved scheme of arrangement, that does not exclude this further court sanction in the case of insurance[2]. The Treasury retains the power to modify these transfer requirements and to make provision for the transfer of any Lloyd's business, both by statutory instrument[3].

5.3 OBTAINING APPROVAL

Unless the FSA's prior approval has been obtained, authorised firms must take reasonable care to ensure that no individual performs a controlled function under any arrangements:

(1) the firm enters into (eg contracts of employment or service); or

(2) a contractor of the firm (eg an appointed representative) enters into[4].

The reference to 'functions' and 'arrangements' is to ensure that under whatever contractual or other basis key tasks are carried out, an authorised firm needs to seek approval for the individual (or other person) performing them. The original drafting of this section emphasised approval of the arrangements, which was amended to emphasise the individual and his performance instead. This was in response to fears that the FSA could use the section to try to control remuneration of key personnel, although the Government maintains that remuneration packages are still a legitimate interest of the FSA[5].

Whereas for authorisation, the definition of 'regulated activities' is left to the Treasury, for approved status, the definition of 'controlled functions' is to be

---

1 FSMA, s 106.

2 FSMA, s 105.

3 FSMA, ss 117 and 323.

4 FSMA, s 59(1), (2) and (10). It has been pointed out that, in practice, the obligation under (2) could be difficult to ensure where controlled functions have been delegated to another authorised firm: vol 612 HL, 18 April 2000, 614–617.

5 Standing Committee A, 26 October 1999, c 531.

determined by the FSA. To be controlled, however, the function must fall into one of three categories:

(1) senior managers – those with a 'significant influence on the conduct' of the firm's affairs relating to regulated activities;

(2) customer contacts – those 'dealing with customers' (including those contemplating being customers) of the firm in its regulated activities; or

(3) asset controllers – those 'dealing with property of customers' of the firm in its regulated activities[1].

In cases (2) and (3), the dealings have to be 'substantially connected' with carrying on regulated activities so that 'someone in a purely administrative back office role would not be covered, whereas someone in a more influential position ... would be covered'.[2]

Nevertheless, the three categories remain very wide and potentially give the FSA power to interfere with the appointment of senior and quite junior staff within authorised firms.

Occasionally, some of these functions may be conducted by bodies corporate rather than individuals, in which case the firm (and possibly its management) will have to be approved[3]. The approval procedure cannot be applied to all key personnel of inwardly passported firms, as fitness and propriety is primarily a prudential matter reserved to the home State regulator[4].

It is for the authorised firm (or the firm applying for its initial authorisation) to seek the FSA's approval for those it intends to use in these functions and the FSA is left to determine the exact procedures[5]. The FSA has three months to consider any application, although the clock stops running during any period from when the FSA has asked for further information until it is produced. An application can be withdrawn at any stage, but only with the consent of the candidate and his employer (if it is not the applicant)[6]. If the application is granted, a written notice must be sent to the candidate, the applicant firm and the employer (if different) and a formal record kept of the approved person, the firm and the employer (if different). If the FSA is minded to refuse the application, it must follow its rejection procedures[7]. Because an approval is job specific and there is no procedure to vary it, any change in an approved individual's job or functions technically will require a new application.

The FSA has to be satisfied that the candidate is a 'fit and proper person' to perform the relevant functions and may require, inter alia, formal qualifications, training or proof of competence[8]. Concern has been expressed that firms faced with the death or sudden departure of approved individuals could face

---

1   FSMA, s 59(3) to (9) and (11).
2   Financial Secretary at Standing Committee A, 26 October 1999, c 558.
3   Consultation Paper 26, FSA July 1999, para 59.
4   FSMA, s 59(8); see **2.3.3**.
5   FSMA, s 60.
6   FSMA, s 61. There appears to be no sanction on the FSA if it takes longer than three months: vol 343 HC, 1 February 2000, c 989. If an applicant firm quarrels with a candidate who does not consent to withdraw and approval is given, this could affect claims for constructive or wrongful dismissal.
7   FSMA, ss 62 and 347; for procedural details, see **9.3**.
8   FSMA, s 61(1) and (2).

unacceptable delays if temporary approvals pending further enquiries could not be given by the FSA. Despite the wider scope of the approval regime for which the FSA will be responsible, the Government refused to give it this power, but then admitted that the FSA could, in any case, give rapid approval for temporary appointments[1]. The FSA has itself promised that it will publish service standards setting out how long it expects applications to take and will publish its performance against those standards[2].

5.3.1   The Financial Services Authority's approach

The FSA has indicated that it will consider three key factors when assessing fitness and propriety:

'(1)   honesty, integrity and reputation – no individual can be approved unless the FSA is satisfied that he intends to be open and honest in his dealings with consumers, professional market participants and with regulators and that he is willing to comply with the requirements imposed upon him and his firm by or under [the FSMA];

(2)   competence and capability – the FSA expects the individual to have the necessary skills to carry out the function which he is performing or will be performing; and

(3)   financial soundness – If an individual is in financial difficulty, he may be tempted to put his interests above those of his customers to boost his own earnings.'[3]

These three factors can be seen as the equivalent of the five TCAs for a firm seeking authorisation, and just as the FSA expects firms to show that they will abide by the continuing PFBs, the FSA expects these individuals to show that they will abide by the Statements of Principle for Approved Persons and the associated Code of Practice[4].

The FSA has suggested a number of factors that it will consider, such as the candidate's criminal record (even if spent), civil proceedings against him, disciplinary findings against him, disqualification orders, bankruptcy orders, outstanding judgment debts as well as whether he satisfies the Training and Competence regime and whether 'he has been candid and truthful in all his dealings with any regulatory body'. The FSA has said a precise list is impossible because:

'. . . a person who is regarded as fit and proper for a particular role within a firm may not necessarily be considered fit and proper for any other role that he may wish to take up at a later date, either within the same firm or with a new employer. When considering each application for approval or when seeking to withdraw approval, the FSA may have regard to current, past and prospective matters.'[5]

Determining which positions should fall within the approved person regime is not easy. If it is cast too widely, the sheer numbers involved become impractical. The SROs currently approve over 150,000 individuals and merely extending their

---

1   Standing Committee, 26 October 1999, cc 532–547.
2   Consultation Paper 26, para 43. Initial standards are set out in Consultation Paper 53, FSA, June 2000, section 7.
3   Consultation Paper 26, para 91.
4   FSMA, s 64; see **6.5**.
5   Consultation Paper 26, Annex A, Criteria for assessing the fitness and propriety of approved persons, amended in *High level standards for firms and individuals*, FSA, June 2000, Annex C.

regime unaltered to all other authorised firms could add substantially to that. The FSA, however, hopes to keep the total number about the same.

The FSA considers all board directors (executive and non-executive) or their equivalent to be senior management. In partnerships, limited partners and, in very large partnerships, those not involved in the senior management caucus, will be excluded. In mutuals, where board members are elected by the membership, vetting will take place between election and the new member taking up his position[1].

Below board level, only those to whom functions of 'significant influence' have been delegated will also be included. These include not just heads of any large business units (eg corporate lending, underwriting, private banking, proprietary trading), but also those in specific positions including the Money Laundering Reporting Officer (MLRO), the Appointed Actuary for insurers and the Compliance Officer for those conducting designated investment business. It does not matter that some of these functions are not managed on a legal entity basis, but by function. These 'matrix managers' are included, whoever technically employs them[2].

Where an EEA firm is relying upon a European Passport to conduct business in the UK, the FSA is taking the view that the vetting of its board members is a matter for the home State regulator but staff in UK branches involved in designated investment business, plus the MLRO, must be approved. Other firms doing business cross-border into, or through branches in the UK are the FSA's responsibility. However, even in these cases, the FSA will have to bow to the practicalities of the situation and practise a similar policy. It cannot require prior approval of the board members of overseas firms. After initial authorisation, it only asks to be notified of board changes, but if anything then comes to light, action can still be taken on the grounds that the firm no longer satisfies the TCAs[3].

Where UK firms have significant branches overseas (in or outside the EEA), the branch managers will be treated as senior managers, but staff dealing with overseas residents will not generally need to be approved. Indeed, to keep the numbers needing approval down, the FSA is contemplating a less comprehensive regime than the current SROs. Proprietary traders (currently registered with the SFA) may be excluded unless they are also senior managers. Where individuals deal with customers, the FSA is considering factors such as the complexity of the product and the level of reliance and sophistication of the customer. Introducers and execution-only traders will be excluded[4].

Increasingly, authorised firms sub-contract activities to other firms which may themselves be:

(1) authorised, so their key personnel ought already to be approved and further approval would probably be duplicative;

---

1   Consultation Paper 26, paras 57–60. Small friendly societies may need only their CEO approved, Consultation Paper 53, para 4.30.

2   Consultation Paper 26, paras 61–64 as amended by Consultation Paper 53, paras 4.9–4.12. For designated investment business, see 6.3.

3   FSMA, s 59(8); Consultation Paper 26, paras 68 and 69 confirmed in Consultation Paper 53, chapters 4 and 6.

4   Consultation Paper 26, paras 70–77. A summary list appears in Consultation Paper 53, chapter 5. Others that no longer need approval include company secretaries, audit officers and training officers.

(2) exempt as appointed representatives, in which case the firms which appoint them should seek approval for the representatives' senior management and staff dealing with customers as though they were direct employees (appointed representatives should not be holding customers assets); and

(3) neither authorised nor exempt, in which case none of the delegated activities should be 'regulated' – even then, the senior management of the authorised firm must take responsibility in the same way as if the function were conducted in-house[1].

Although most regulated activities are conducted by firms, individuals can conduct some as sole traders and they will not need to be approved as well as authorised unless they employ individuals that require approval[2].

One area of concern is the requirement to be re-approved every time an individual changes job. It is expected that this, together with new recruits, will lead to about 2,000 applications being submitted to the FSA's Individual Vetting and Registration Department every month[3]. The Government reluctantly conceded that basic details of approvals will have to be formally recorded by the FSA as part of the public record. As the Government spokesman in the House of Lords explained:

> 'The particular difficulty arises because of the grandfathering arrangements that are proposed for employees of authorised firms. Our intention is that, for the purposes of Part V of the Bill, people should automatically be treated as having been approved for any controlled functions that they were performing when the Bill is brought into force. The process will be automatic and we cannot be sure that the authority will have all the information in time for the public record to go live on day one.
>
> However, we agree that it would be desirable to remove uncertainty on the question of the coverage of the register, and we have now brought forward amendments which require certain information to be included. That is the minimum that must be included. The authority may add to that such other information as it sees fit. The authority proposes also to include information about the controlled functions for which the person has approval.'[4]

5.3.2   The responsibilities of senior management

The principal responsibility of senior management is to implement PFB 3, which states 'A firm must take reasonable care to organise and control its affairs responsibly and effectively, with adequate risk management'. The FSA has produced a detailed Consultation Paper on this subject which highlights a particular view of how this should be done[5]. It has said:

> 'For the business and affairs of the firm as a whole to be responsibly and effectively organised and controlled at senior management level ... there should be a clear division of labour among the firm's senior managers. Each senior manager's sphere of

---

1   Consultation Paper 26, paras 81–85.
2   Consultation Paper 26, paras 86 and 87 amended by Consultation Paper 53, para 3.60.
3   Standing Committee A, 26 October 1999, c 574.
4   FSMA, s 347; vol 612 HL, 9 May 2000, c 1526. The SROs and Lloyd's will have reasonably complete lists of those currently performing the likely 'controlled functions', apart from some managers of assets. However, the regulators of general insurance and deposit-taking businesses will not have them as they have not imposed this sort of requirement before.
5   Consultation Paper 35, FSA, December 1999. Draft rules now appear in *High level standards for firms and individuals*, Annex A.

personal responsibility should be delineated by the firm and understood within it . . . While this requirement is directed to the firm, the FSA considers that responsibility for the division of labour at the top of the firm should *also* fall on a firm's most senior executive officer, or an appropriate number of its executives . . . There will need to be some visible evidence of compliance with the apportionment requirement.'[1]

The CEO or his team are also to be responsible for 'overseeing the establishment of systems and controls . . . as are appropriate to the scale, nature and complexity of its business'[2].

On the other hand, the Consultation Paper seeks to calm the fears of non-executive directors that the requirement that they be approved individuals will extend their duties and liabilities beyond:

(1) assisting in setting and monitoring the firm's strategy;
(2) providing an independent perspective; and
(3) carrying out specific responsibilities such as membership of the audit or remuneration committees[3].

The FSA suggests that this management specialisation is in line with the Combined Code on Corporate Governance which authorised firms listed in the UK will be expected to comply with anyway[4]. However, as the reaction to that Code has highlighted, this is not accepted by everyone as the best approach to management, nor is it entirely compatible with the more 'shared responsibility' approach of traditional UK company and partnership law[5]. All this seems to be a direct response to the perceived failings of management in the Barings affair. Indeed, as the illustrative examples given in the Consultation Paper itself demonstrate, this approach seems more appropriate in the case of a listed bank than a small Independent Financial Adviser (IFA)[6].

---

1   Consultation Paper 35, paras 2.1–2.3. *High level standards for firms and individuals*, para 3.15 makes it clear that responsibility for the allocation can be shared but should include the CEO if there is one. Inwardly passported forms are not required to allocate responsibility, para 3.29.
2   Consultation Paper 35, para 2.4..
3   Consultation Paper 35, Part 4. Approval of non-executive directors will largely be a matter of 'knowing nothing against', Consultation Paper 53, para 3.20.
4   Annex to the Listing Rules; this is also the view expressed in *Daniels v Anderson* (1995) 16 ACSR 607.
5   Indeed, the Combined Code itself does emphasise collective responsibility. However, 'it would be wholly wrong, in a *regulatory* context, for one director to be variously liable for the misdeeds of another or for there to be any form of "guilt by association",' *High level standards for firms and individuals*, para 2.21.
6   Consultation Paper 35, Annex E; a point also made by Lord Hunt of Wirral at vol 610 HL, 21 February 2000, c 37.

Chapter 6

THE FINANCIAL SERVICES AUTHORITY'S LEGISLATIVE FUNCTIONS

6.1 BACKGROUND

Chapter 1 examined the tensions between the SIB and the SROs about rule-making under the 1986 Act. The creation of a single regulator would have achieved little in the way of simplifying the regulation of financial services if it did not manage to produce some consolidation and standardisation of the rules that are applied to authorised firms and the individuals working for them. Nevertheless, in trying to bring a variety of regulatory systems together, there is a very real danger of over-regulation by applying an accumulation of all the previous regulators' rules to all authorised firms and approved individuals.

The most obvious example would be to apply the conduct of business rules (currently applied to investment businesses under the 1986 Act) to deposit-taking or general insurance (which includes purely protective long-term insurance) where there have been no such rules under the ICA 1982 and the BA 1987. The Government and the FSA have said repeatedly that there is no intention of making such a dramatic change[1]. That still leaves plenty of scope for regulatory creep in the name of simplification and standardisation.

The FSA has given much consideration to the 'architecture' of the new *Handbook* and what is emerging are five sections:

(1) high-level principles:
    (a) TCAs, and PFBs,
    (b) Criteria, Statements and Code of Practice for Approved Persons,
    (c) Fitness and Propriety,
    (d) Senior Management Responsibilities, Systems and Controls;
(2) business standards:
    (a) *Prudential Sourcebook,*
    (b) *Conduct of Business Sourcebook,*
    (c) *Market Conduct Sourcebook,*
    (d) *Training and Competence Sourcebook,*
    (e) *Money Laundering Sourcebook;*
(3) regulatory processes:
    (a) *Authorisation Manual,*
    (b) *Supervision Manual,*
    (c) *Enforcement Manual;*
(4) redress:
    (a) Complaints,
    (b) Compensation; and

---

1   For example, *Response to Consultation Paper 13,* FSA, October 1999, p 19, para 2. The FSA has maintained this position through the concept of 'designated investment business', see **6.3.3**.

(5) specialist sourcebooks: collective investment schemes, unit-linked life regulations, credit unions, RIEs and RCHs, Lloyd's, market service providers, etc[1].

The TCAs and the Criteria for Approval have already been dealt with in Chapter 5. This chapter will look at the statutory powers to impose requirements (particularly the high-level standards) on authorised firms and approved individuals. The FSA's proposed structure of high-level principles, detailed rules and guidance will follow that established by the SROs rather than the 'prudential guidance notes' used by the regulators of deposit-taking and insurance.

The complexity of the *Handbook* reflects the variety of delegated powers the FSA has to impose or adapt requirements under the FSMA. Such delegation is quite remarkable, but as the House of Lords Delegated Powers and Deregulation Committee commented:

> 'In this unusual situation, there is probably no sensible alternative to the approach set out in the draft Bill. We have been supported in forming this view by having regard to the reality that it will be the Authority which will have the closest understanding of market conditions, and will, consequently be best placed to deal with the detailed issues, including many technical issues, which will need to be covered in regulations.'[2]

Still, as the FSA will be operating under statutory powers, it will be somewhat more constrained than the SROs were under the previous contractual arrangements. The Board of the FSA cannot delegate its legislative functions which include rule-making and issuing statements, codes, directions and general guidance[3]. The legislative functions, considered as a whole, are governed by the four objectives and the seven restraining principles[4]. Also in its agreement with the Treasury over the contents of its annual report, the FSA will be required to 'contain an account of the way in which it has exercised its rule-making powers in the year in question'[5]. Throughout the FSMA, there are obligations on the FSA to consult appropriately and its general legislative functions are subject to detailed consultation procedures, including cost-benefit analyses[6]. It is to be hoped that all this will encourage the FSA to develop a more open regulatory style than the SROs.

6.2   RULE-MAKING FOR AUTHORISED FIRMS

The FSA's powers to make general rules governing authorised firms seem quite sweeping. Such rules can be made only if they appear to the FSA to be 'necessary or expedient' to protect those who might use the services of authorised firms or

---

1   *Response to Consultation Paper 13*, Annex C as adapted by *Handbook development*, FSA, December 1999, which makes it clear that the *Handbook* will be available in hard copy, on CD-Rom and via the Internet, confirmed in *FSA Annual Report 1999/2000*.

2   Joint Committee, First Report, Annex B, para 13.

3   FSMA, Sch 1, paras 1(2) and 5(2) as explained by the Economic Secretary, Standing Committee A, 4 November 1999, c 752.

4   FSMA, s 2; see **3.3**.

5   FSMA, Sch 1, para 10 as explained by the Economic Secretary, Standing Committee A, 4 November 1999, c 751.

6   FSMA, ss 65, 121, 155 and 157(3); see below for details.

their appointed representatives carrying on regulated activities[1]. However, the general rules:

(1) may protect any consumers from professionals to private persons,
(2) who have used as well as who might use such firms[2],
(3) even if the relationship with the firm is indirect[3],
(4) indeed, where there is no real relationship in issue[4],
(5) may also cover the non-regulated activities of firms[5],
(6) may extend to the regulated and non-regulated activities of other members in the firm's group[6], but
(7) may not prohibit or prudentially regulate inwardly passported activities[7].

In making rules about clients' money, the FSA can require such money to be held on trust, treat multiple accounts as one and order when interest must or must not be distributed. The holder of such money can only be liable as a constructive trustee for its wrongful payment if he knows the payment is wrong or deliberately failed to make reasonable enquiry. The FSA can also continue to make rules requiring a 'cooling-off' period after agreeing to enter into certain contracts (eg long-term insurance contracts)[8].

Despite the width of these general rule-making powers[9], a number of specific powers found in the previous legislation have been carried forward.

6.2.1 Additional rule-making powers

The FSA may restrict authorised unit trust managers and insurers from conducting all or any other activities, whether regulated or not[10]. In the case of insurance, the FSA has an additional power to prohibit or amend long-term insurance policies linked to particular underlying investments[11]. Where the FSA

---

1   FSMA, s 138.
2   FSMA, s 138(1)(a) and (7)(a); for example reviews of past misselling.
3   FSMA, s 138 (7)(b) and (c); for example indirect customers, beneficiaries under the trust being managed or third party beneficiaries of an insurance contract. Considerable concern was expressed that a power to make rules to protect 'rights and interests which ... may be adversely affected' might extend to almost anything. However, the Government accepted an amendment confining them to those of persons behind agents or fiduciaries.
4   FSMA, s 138(4); for example general rules to further market integrity or lessen systemic risk.
5   FSMA, s 138(1)(b); for example rules on systems, financial resources, Chinese walls. In particular, this power allows the FSA to continue to impose financial resources and large exposure rules on a bank's unregulated lending business to protect its regulated deposit-taking business. However, Lord McIntosh emphasised that 'the FSA will have power to make rules only about non-regulated activities if it considers that it is necessary or expedient to do so in order to protect the consumers of regulated activities': vol 611 HL, 27 March 2000, c 529.
6   FSMA, ss 138(5); for example the threat one Baring subsidiary posed all the others. See also the PFBs 4 and 11 at **6.3.1**.
7   FSMA, s 138(6).
8   FSMA, s 139.
9   This includes a general discretion to make different rules for different cases or classes of cases and any supplemental, consequential or transitional provisions: FSMA, s 156.
10 FSMA, ss 140 and 141(1) and (2) re-enacting 1986 Act, s 83 and ICA 1982, s 16. This is to meet obligations under the UCITS and Insurance Directives.
11 FSMA, s 141(3) and (4) re-enacting ICA 1982, s 56 and Friendly Societies Act 1992, s 56. Although such intervention is aimed at protecting investors from taking out highly volatile

makes asset identification rules for insurers aimed at protecting the funds backing long-term insurance business, the Treasury can continue to supplement that protection by regulating the behaviour of any non-authorised parents of such companies, to prevent the disposal or dissipation of such funds. In particular, it can prohibit dividend payments and the creation of mortgages or charges, declaring any that are created, void. As these regulations apply to non-authorised parties, breach of them is a criminal offence (rather than a disciplinary matter) punishable by up to a level 5 fine[1].

The FSA may 'endorse' all or part of the Takeover Code and the Substantial Acquisition Rules (SARs), that is treat them and any Panel requirements and rulings about them as though they were FSA rules applying to all or some authorised firms and approved individuals.

> 'The arrangements are therefore designed to ensure that authorised persons seek to procure their own clients' compliance with the Takeover Code and SARs and, in practice, to ensure that the adviser will cease to act for a bidder or target which does not comply with the endorsed provisions. Disciplinary or intervention powers in respect of endorsed provisions would only be taken by the Authority if the Takeover Panel has requested it to do so.'[2]

Provided the FSA is satisfied by the Panel's consultation procedures, any subsequent alteration made by the Panel to an endorsed provision will automatically be endorsed, although the FSA may revoke its endorsement at any time. The FSA has no power to endorse any other codes.

Subject to any restrictions imposed by the Treasury, the FSA may make rules about when and how authorised firms can stabilise the prices of particular investments. It can also endorse equivalent overseas rules and, provided it has notified the overseas regulator that it is satisfied with its consultation procedures, all subsequent alterations by that regulator will automatically be endorsed. The significance of these price stabilising rules is that compliance with them is a defence to the crimes of market manipulation and insider dealing and to penalties for market abuse[3].

The FSA may also make rules requiring authorised firms to create Chinese walls restricting information being passed within a firm and/or allowing it to be withheld from customers. The Government spokesman in the House of Lords commented:

> 'Those rules will continue to protect the interests of the clients of such a firm by ensuring that information which relates to a particular person in relation to a particular activity does not reach another part of the firm. They also protect the firms themselves, establishing a firm regulatory framework within which the firm must control the flow of information, both internally and externally ...'

---

policies, the special power is designed to protect the FSA if it turns out that the investors would have done better if it had not intervened! Standing Committee A, 4 November 1999, c 769.

1   FSMA, s 142 re-enacting ICA 1982, s 29.
2   Explanatory Notes to the Financial Services and Markets Bill, House of Commons, 17 June 1999, para 196. FSMA, s 143 as explained by Lord McIntosh, vol 611 HL, 27 March 2000, c 554.
3   FSMA, s 144; see also **Chapter 7**.

Compliance can be a defence to misleading statements, market manipulation and market abuse[1]. Also in the area of market misconduct, the FSA may make rules applying to authorised firms to supplement, and make compliance with, the Money Laundering Regulations a regulatory obligation[2].

Although because of their status, authorised firms cannot breach the restriction on financial promotions, the FSA may make rules about them issuing or approving such promotions and promoting collective investment schemes, again subject to any restrictions imposed by the Treasury[3].

A power to impose specific financial resources requirements on individual firms was removed from the Bill by the Government, because this could be done just as well through a requirement attached to a firm's permission. However, this will mean that such an imposition will now be able to be referred to the Tribunal like any other grievance about a requirement[4].

6.2.2 Effect of the Financial Services Authority rules and waivers

Although the FSA will be using these rule-making powers to issue its Principles for Businesses (PFBs) as well as detailed rules, as far as the FSMA is concerned, they are all rules. As authorised firms are operating within the perimeter, a breach by such a firm of any such FSA rule is not a criminal offence but a contravention of a requirement under the FSMA and, as such, subject to the FSA's disciplinary procedures. These can lead to public censure, a fine, a restitutionary order and, in an extreme case, to a restriction or cancellation of the firm's permission to conduct regulated activities[5]. Although these rules apply to authorised firms rather than approved individuals, if such an individual 'has been knowingly concerned in a contravention ... of a requirement' by the firm that obtained his approval, the individual may also be subject to the FSA's disciplinary procedures[6]. This is dealt with in greater detail in **9.3**.

The civil consequences of breaches of SROs' rules under the 1986 Act are generally continued under the FSMA[7]. Breach of an FSA rule does not make any transaction void or unenforceable, but does, *prima facie*, make an authorised person liable to private persons for any loss caused. This does not apply to financial resources rules or listing rules and the FSA can exclude other rules from this regime. It expects to do this in the case of the high-level principles, so that breach of one of the PFBs alone will not give rise to civil liability. On the other hand, the FSA can also make breaches of certain rules (eg against insider dealing) actionable by *anyone* who has suffered loss[8].

1   FSMA, s 147; Lord McIntosh, vol 612 HL, 9 May 2000, c 1405. The FSA's rules can act as a defence against civil actions for breach of fiduciary duties, cf *Fiduciary Duties and Regulatory Rules* 1995 Law Comm No 236; *Kelly v Cooper* [1992] AC 205; *Prince Jefri Bolkiah v KPMG* [1999] 1 All ER 517.
2   FSMA, s 146.
3   FSMA, s 145. The rules may only apply to promotions that, if issued by an non-authorised person, would contravene FSMA, s 21 and would not contravene FSMA, s 238 on the promotion of CISs.
4   FSMA, ss 43 and 55.
5   FSMA, ss 45, 151(1), 205, 206 and 384.
6   FSMA, s 66(2)(b).
7   1986 Act, ss 62 and 62A.
8   FSMA, ss 150 and 151(2), see **10.5.2**.

Most of these rules (and the rules covering actuaries and auditors) can be waived or modified by the FSA, but only on the application or with the consent of the firms affected and where the FSA is satisfied:

(1) compliance 'would be unduly burdensome or not achieve the purpose for which the rules were made'; and
(2) no 'undue risks' to those intended to be protected would arise.

The Government has admitted that these are quite demanding tests and may involve the FSA in lengthy investigations. Waivers and modifications can be for a period or indefinite, can be subject to conditions and can be varied or revoked. Breach of any condition attached is, in effect, a breach of the original rule[1]. There are no formal procedures imposed on the FSA regarding waivers and, in particular, no right to refer a rejection to the Tribunal.

This power is seen as a part answer to the SEC's no action letter. The Economic Secretary has emphasised its importance:

'The effect will be that, if the FSA agrees to issue a direction that a particular rule will not apply, the person to whom the direction has been issued will not be in breach of the relevant rule. The FSA will not be able to take action for breach of a particular rule if someone has acted in accordance with a waiver, and individual customers' rights to take action in respect of non-compliance with that rule could be severely limited.

In practice it is vital that the FSA is ready and willing to grant waivers or modifications on request to develop the open and flexible regulatory regime that we intend. Its recent policy paper in September this year on giving guidance and waivers discusses the waiver power; we fully expect that the FSA will make good use of it.'[2]

In its policy document, the FSA pointed out that this waiver power is far wider than that contained in the 1986 Act. Also, where a waiver has been given to one firm, other firms in the same situation do not all have to formally apply for the same waiver but may consent to it applying to them[3]. However:

'Since waivers can alter the legal rights of third parties, including private consumers, it is vital that their interests should be fully considered, and that the exercise of the waiver power should not leave their rights obscure. For this reason we regard it as very important that both the fact of a waiver and its effects should be fully transparent.'[4]

That is why the FSA is required to publish all waivers or modifications, unless it is inappropriate or unnecessary to do so. Before agreeing to keep a waiver confidential, the FSA must consider its effect on any rights to sue, and even where publication may unreasonably prejudice the commercial interests of a firm or breach international obligations, whether that could be met by not disclosing the identity of the authorised firm[5].

Although the Government may view waivers as the equivalent of no-action letters, the FSA may be rather more concerned about them being used in the same way. The SEC currently deals with some 3,000 no-action letters a year! Instead, the FSA may rely on more informal guidance.

---

1   FSMA, s 148; vol 612 HL, 9 May 2000, c 1412.
2   Standing Committee A, 4 November 1999, c 777.
3   *The FSA's approach to giving guidance and waivers to firms*, FSA, September 1999 (Guidance and Waiver Statement), para 28.
4   Guidance and Waiver Statement, para 29.
5   FSMA, s 148(6)–(8).

6.2.3 Evidential provisions and guidance

The FSA may issue evidential provisions and guidance. An evidential provision is technically a rule, but one where the FSA has specified that contravention of it is not itself a disciplinary 'offence'. However, the FSA can only do this if it also specifies that:

(1) such contravention is evidence of the contravention of another rule; and/or
(2) compliance with it is evidence of compliance with another rule.

This power enables the FSA to develop a code for guiding authorised firms on the application of the PFBs in the same way as it is required to produce a Code of Practice to guide approved individuals on the application of its Statements[1].

Guidance may be issued, not just with respect to the operation of any FSA rules, but generally in respect of the operation of the FSMA and of the FSA within it, including the regulatory objectives. Guidance also includes any recommendations the FSA may give generally (eg consumer advice) or to any class of persons regulated by the FSA[2]. The Economic Secretary has admitted that this power covers an amazing variety of circumstances:

> 'At one extreme, it may be guidance in the wide sense – directed not only at authorised firms, but more generally at consumers. That might be regarded as a kind of public information service ... Which would tell consumers what to look out for ... At the other extreme, the FSA will issue guidance to individual firms on how to comply with the rules, or how to include certain information on one of its standard forms.'[3]

Partly because of this sheer width, guidance (unlike evidential provisions) appears to have no particular legal status. The Government rejected any idea that following guidance should provide a general safe harbour, not least for fear that it 'could create an overly legalistic and formal approach'[4]. The FSA has been slightly more forthcoming. It distinguishes between general and individual guidance and believes that general guidance will play 'a major role' in the new *Handbook*. It has said:

> 'Most [general] guidance is designed to throw light on a particular aspect of regulatory requirements, not to be an exhaustive statement of firms' obligations. *But if a firm acts in accordance with the general guidance in the circumstances contemplated by that guidance, then the FSA will proceed on the footing that it has complied with the aspect of the rule to which the guidance refers.*'[5]

In distinguishing such general guidance from an evidential provision, the FSA has said:

> 'Unlike an evidential provision, however, it does not create an expectation that a firm must follow the guidance to show compliance with the rule, and it does not throw the burden of proof on the firm.'[6]

---

1 FSMA, ss 64(2) and 149.
2 FSMA, s 157(1) and (5).
3 Standing Committee A, 9 November 1999, c 802.
4 Standing Committee A, 9 November 1999, cc 808 and 809; vol 343 HC, 1 February 2000, c 933.
5 Guidance and Waiver Statement, paras 5 and 9 (emphasis as original).
6 The *Handbook* will distinguish between rules, evidential provisions and general guidance by marking paragraphs with R, E and G respectively, Consultation Paper 45a, FSA, February 2000, Part I, paras 4.8 and 4.10.

On the other hand, following guidance will not prove compliance with the rules or the FSMA. It may still help non-authorised firms to claim due diligence defences for any contraventions of the general prohibition or restriction on financial promotions. The FSA may also refrain from bringing disciplinary actions against authorised firms; but firms will still be subject to private civil actions for damages[1].

In regard to individual guidance, the FSA has been more cautious.

> 'A number of factors are relevant, including the degree of formality that attended the formulation of the query and the giving of the guidance, the lapse of time and the alteration of circumstances since the guidance was given, and the extent to which the interests of third parties such as customers, or the wider market, are at stake. It can be said, however, that *the FSA would not take regulatory action against a firm for behaviour in line with current written guidance to it in the circumstances contemplated by the guidance.*'[2]

The FSA may pay third parties to provide guidance and may charge parties for the guidance that it gives[3]. However, it is the FSA's current intention to continue to give individual guidance on a relatively informal basis and without charge. The charging provision is there in case demand for guidance, perhaps from just one sector, rises to the point that issues of overall cost and cross-subsidisation arise[4].

The other issue on guidance that the FSA has considered is the degree of publicity it should receive. The FSA has made it clear that all general guidance will be published first in electronic and paper bulletins and then will appear with the rules (including evidential rules) in the *Handbook*. The FSA 'will not operate on the basis of unwritten rules or unpublished standards'.[5] On the other hand, the FSA will not publish individual guidance except 'in highly exceptional circumstances ... However, *responses of general and lasting significance will be converted into general guidance and published as such,* after due consultation and cost-benefit analysis'.[6] This last point is part of the whole procedural arrangements for creating and publishing rules and guidance.

6.2.4 Procedural provisions

To be effective, an FSA rule must be decided on by the Board, made by an instrument in writing which stipulates under what power it is being made, printed and made available to the public (although a reasonable fee may be charged). A written copy must also be given to the Treasury. If proof of a rule is needed in legal proceedings, the staff of the FSA will certify a copy[7].

Unless there is an 'exceptional' situation requiring the immediate protection of consumers, the FSA must conduct quite an elaborate consultation procedure before adopting a new rule (which includes revoking or altering an existing one). It must first publish a draft of the rule giving a period of time for representations to be made. The draft must also be accompanied by:

(1) an explanation of the purpose of the proposed rule;

---

1   FSMA, ss 23–30 and 150, as explained by Lord McIntosh, vol 612 HL, 9 May 2000, cc 1413 and 1414.
2   Guidance and Waiver Statement, para 20 (emphasis as original).
3   FSMA, s 157(2) and (4)
4   Standing Committee A, 9 November 1999, c 806.
5   Guidance and Waiver Statement, para 6.
6   Guidance and Waiver Statement, para 22 (emphasis as original).
7   FSMA, ss 152–154 and Sch 1, para 5(2).

(2) the reasons the FSA believes it is compatible with its statutory objectives and restraining principles; and

(3) a cost-benefit analysis[1].

The cost-benefit analysis does not have to be produced where:

(1) the proposed rule is the imposition of fees or charges, when the FSA must produce the expenditure proposals relating to the fees instead;

(2) the FSA considers the proposal would reduce or at worst minimally increase the current costs of those complying with its rules[2].

The FSA must consider any representations and if it then changes the proposed rule in any significant way, it must publish a statement of the difference with a new cost-benefit analysis. When it publishes the final rule, it must also publish a general statement about the representations it received, but it is not expected to deal with every individual representation[3]. As would be expected, rules may make different provisions for different cases and may provide for consequential and transitional arrangements[4].

These procedural measures are clearly aimed at deterring the FSA from over-regulating. As was said by the Opposition in the Standing Committee, regulators:

> '... see regulation as what economists call a free good, because the costs are borne elsewhere, often invisibly ... There is a natural suspicion in the market that these cost-benefit analyses will be self-serving to some extent, and that the FSA will produce them to justify its own actions.'[5]

The Government rejected as too cumbersome any US style 'sunset regulation' requiring a rolling three-year review of the FSA's existing rules (including those grandfathered from the former regime) to subject them to cost-benefit analyses as well[6]. Even so, given the consultation experience to date, whatever else may be achieved, the FSA will remain busy as a major publishing house.

Since evidential provisions are rules, these detailed consultation requirements apply to them as well. The consultation procedures do not apply to waivers or modifications, but they have been extended to general guidance the FSA issues about any of its rules. As the Economic Secretary explained:

> 'Clearly, consultation will not be appropriate for some forms of general or, indeed, specific guidance. [It] therefore focuses on guidance on the FSA's own rules, which is given to regulated persons generally, or to a class of them. There is a good reason for such a focus – guidance on rules can impose burdens in a similar way to the rules themselves.'[7]

---

1   FSMA, s 155(1), (2), (7), (10) and (12). The Economic Secretary considered the emergency override would be used only in 'exceptional circumstances': Standing Committee A, 9 November 1999, c 799. As with the more basic consultation described in **3.4.4**, it is left to the FSA to determine how best to bring the proposals to the public's attention and it may charge a fee for copies of the proposal.

2   FSMA, s 155(3), (8), (9) and (11).

3   FSMA, s 155(4)–(6).

4   FSMA, s 156.

5   Standing Committee A, 9 November 1999, cc 785 and 794 and vol 611 HL, 27 March 2000, 566.

6   Vol 343 HC, 1 February 2000, cc 932 and 933.

7   Standing Committee A, 9 November 1999, c 802; FSMA, s 157(3).

Once issued, copies of this sort of guidance, together with any other general guidance (eg consumer advice) must be given in writing to the Treasury without delay[1].

The FSA must follow a similar procedure (but without any cost-benefit analyses) before it can endorse the Takeover Code and the associated SARs or notify the Panel that it is satisfied with the latter's consultation procedures to allow automatic endorsement of any amendments[2].

6.3   THE FINANCIAL SERVICES AUTHORITY'S APPROACH TO RULE-MAKING

There is neither the space, nor (at the time of writing) sufficient certainty about the FSA's eventual *Handbook* to look at the rules and guidance in great detail. Various elements of the *Handbook* are being consulted upon and the full version will not be published until end-2000. What follows is a review of some of the key issues that have confronted the FSA and it must be emphasised that all the rules and guidance referred to are subject to amendment.

At an early stage, the FSA set itself five design principles in creating its new *Handbook*, namely that there should be:

(1)   a succinct authoritative statement of high-level principles, stating the fundamental obligations of regulated businesses;
(2)   a solid backbone of further rules to cater for enforceability and other needs;
(3)   a major role for guidance;
(4)   a presumption against differentiation except on policy grounds; and
(5)   regulatory standards that focus on firms' outputs and on the adequacy of internal systems and controls, rather than on detailed prescription of internal arrangements[3].

A Consultation Paper was produced in September 1998 on the possible high-level principles, in which the FSA declared that 'the Principles will be a keystone in the FSA *Handbook*' not just for disciplinary purposes but also for 'throwing light on what is required for a firm to be fit and proper'. The aim was that they 'should be formulated at a level of generality which will enable them to be durable without amendment'.[4] In devising these PFBs, the FSA looked to the numerous existing models, including the SIB principles, the criteria in BA 1987, Sch 3 and ICA 1982, Sch 2A and international guidance given by the Basle Committee on Banking Supervision and IOSCO.

6.3.1   The Financial Services Authority's Principles for Businesses

Following the consultation, the FSA produced a Policy Statement with revised PFBs which are still open to amendment[5]. These are:

---

1   FSMA, s 158.
2   FSMA, s 143(7) and (8).
3   Consultation Paper 8, FSA, April 1998, Part V.
4   Consultation Paper 13, FSA, September 1998, paras 6 and 7.
5   *Response to Consultation Paper 13*, FSA, October 1999, para 4, reconsidered in Consultation Paper 57, FSA, July 2000, section 4. The Forum's Annual Report 1999 concluded from its

(1)   a firm must conduct its business with integrity[1];

(2)   a firm must conduct its business with due skill, care and diligence;

(3)   a firm must take reasonable care to organise and control its affairs responsibly and effectively, with adequate risk management systems[2];

(4)   a firm must maintain adequate financial resources[3];

(5)   a firm must observe proper standards of market conduct[4];

(6)   a firm must pay due regard to the interests of its customers and treat them fairly[5];

(7)   a firm must pay due regard to the information needs of its clients and communicate information to them in a way which is clear, fair and not misleading[6];

(8)   a firm must manage conflicts of interest fairly, both between itself and its customers and between one customer and another[7];

(9)   a firm must take reasonable care to ensure the suitability of its advice and discretionary decisions for any customer who is entitled to rely upon its judgment[8];

(10) a firm must arrange adequate protection for clients' assets when it is responsible for them[9]; and

(11) a firm must deal with its regulators in an open and co-operative way, and must tell the FSA promptly anything relating to the firm of which the FSA would reasonably expect prompt notice[10].

The PFBs will be accompanied by introductory guidance and supporting rules to determine their exact application and effect. In particular, the rules lay down:

(1)   the territorial scope of the PFBs, namely that for prudential supervision they apply to all activities wherever conducted (unless the business is inwardly passported, where this is generally the home State's responsibility[11]), but for conduct of business they apply only to activities in the UK; and

---

survey at p 14: 'From an industry viewpoint, the most important priority for the FSA is to establish a style of regulation that involves the application of broad principles rather than narrow rules'.

1   This may be weaker than SIB principle 1 which referred to 'high standards of integrity'.

2   This is tighter than SIB principle 9 and, since the Barings affair, this whole area has become a key issue for the FSA.

3   *Response to Consultation Paper 13*, para 28. This extends to non-regulated activities and activities of the rest of the firm's Group, as permitted by FSMA, s 138(1)(b) and (5).

4   For example the Inter-Professionals Code and the Code of Market Conduct. Again SIB principle 3 referred to 'high standards'.

5   *Response to Consultation Paper 13*, paras 32 and 33; this includes complaint handling and the concept of policyholders' reasonable expectations.

6   This duty can extend to *all* clients, but see remainder of **6.3.1** and **6.3.2**.

7   *Response to Consultation Paper 13*, para 38; this is less specific than SIB principle 6.

8   *Response to Consultation Paper 13*, para 40; this may apply even if there is no common-law fiduciary relationship and is considerably wider than SIB principle 4.

9   This is less prescriptive than SIB principle 7, but extends to *all* clients.

10 *Response to Consultation Paper 13*, paras 47 and 48; this duty extends to overseas regulators that have jurisdiction over the firm and, in some cases, to reporting on non-regulated activities and activities of the rest of the group.

11 Under the 2BCD, the FSA retains the right as a host regulator to apply liquidity requirements to UK branches of inwardly passported banks.

(2) the regulatory effect of the PFBs, namely that although breaches are subject to the FSA's disciplinary procedures (including restitutionary claims on behalf of investors) the PFBs may not be the basis for individual private actions.

The Introduction to the PFBs, although only guidance, also highlights a number of important issues. For example, in respect to deposit-taking or general insurance business (including purely protective long-term insurance), the FSA:

> '... would not expect to consider exercising the powers brought into play by a conduct of business contravention of a Principle, *unless* the contravention amounted to a serious or persistent violation which had implications for the soundness or fitness and propriety of the firm or for confidence in these sectors.'

Otherwise, the Introduction reiterates that 'breaking the Principles may call into question whether a firm already authorised is still fit and proper'. It also states that the onus is on the FSA to show that a PFB has been broken. The Introduction also makes it clear that the level of duty owed to clients under PFBs 6–10 depends on the nature of the client. Indeed, provided a firm classifies its clients between market counterparties and customers, PFBs 6, 8 and 9 are owed only to customers and PFB 7 is owed to market counterparties only in relation to misleading communications[1].

This last point raises the whole issue of the extent to which the FSAs should be involved in protecting non-private customers and, therefore, the extent to which its rules should apply to inter-professional business.

6.3.2 Definitions of clients

Clearly, the FSA is given a very wide discretion to impose rules on authorised firms. However, in so doing it is governed by the statutory objectives, which include 'securing the *appropriate* degree of protection for consumers' and, in particular, considering 'the differing degrees of experience and expertise that the different consumers may have ... and ... the general principle that consumers should take responsibility for their decisions'.[2] That is why the FSA set itself as one of its most urgent tasks the definition of different types of client and of the regime for inter-professionals dealings[3]. The FSA produced a Discussion Paper that addressed three key issues:

(1) how to define 'professional' market users and how to differentiate between categories of market user according to their relative expertise;
(2) how to structure any requirements for inter-professional business in a manner consistent with the PFBs; and
(3) what, if anything, should replace the Bank of England's old regulatory framework for dealing in products such as spot and forward foreign exchange and bullion, which are not regulated activities under the FSMA[4].

---

1   *Response to Consultation Paper 13*, pp 19 and 20, amended by Consultation Paper 57, Annex E. For the definition of counterparties, see **6.3.2**.
2   FSMA, s 5 (emphasis added).
3   This is particularly important as the exemption for operators in the money markets under the 1986 Act will no longer exist.
4   *Differentiated regulatory approaches: future regulation of inter-professional business*, FSA, October 1998.

Following responses from authorised firms, the FSA confirmed that it would follow the approach formerly adopted by the SFA in dividing clients into three categories – 'market counterparty', 'intermediate customer' and 'private customer' – and would apply these definitions as consistently as possible across the whole regulatory regime[1]. A simple authorised and non-authorised divide was rejected because certain classes of authorised firms such as independent financial advisers, small deposit takers or friendly societies, should probably be protected by some conduct of business provisions, while some sophisticated investors should probably be required to comply with market conduct provisions[2].

On further reflection, the FSA has accepted that it is easier to classify supranational organisations, countries, central banks, State investment bodies, *all* authorised and exempt firms (at least in respect of the business for which they hold that status), overseas financial services firms and possibly some corporates that 'opt up' as 'market counterparties'. That leaves the outstanding problem of how to protect the underlying customers of authorised firms and indirect customers in general[3]. The FSA proposes that authorised firms requiring protection for their customers must 'opt down' to intermediate customer status and only deal with other authorised firms prepared to accept that. Otherwise 'intermediate customers' will be confined to local authorities, listed companies plus other companies, partnerships, pension funds and trusts above a certain size and any private customers in respect of business in which they have sufficient expertise[4]. Overall, however, the principal distinction will be between private customers generally owed quasi-fiduciary duties (of establishing suitability, giving fair explanations and providing best execution) and professionals owed the normal common law duties (of avoiding deceit, negligence and misrepresentation). The final definition of customers and the terms of business and customer agreements that authorised firms will have to enter with them will form part of the *Conduct of Business Sourcebook* (COBS)[5]. The change from the various definitions used by the current regulators to a standard FSA definition will require many firms to renegotiate business terms. The FSA has proposed a 12-month transitional period.

On the second issue, the FSA has produced a draft Inter-Professionals Code (IPC), based on the current London Code of Conduct and on the SFA's approach to business between market counterparties[6]. This provides guidance on the application of PFB 5 and 'switches off' most of the COBS rules when authorised firms are dealing with market counterparties. All prudential requirements and the Code of Market Conduct (COMC) will still apply regardless of the nature of the

---

1   *Response to Comments on Discussion Paper: The Future Regulation of Inter-Professional Business*, FSA, June 1999; Consultation Paper 43, FSA February 2000. When the FSA refers to 'customers' as against 'clients', it is excluding market counterparties.

2   Ibid, p 7.

3   Consultation Paper 43, section 2 as amended by Consultation Paper 57, section 4. Insurers may elect to treat general insurance brokers (who do not require to be authorised) as market counterparties.

4   Consultation Paper 43, Sections 2–4, as amended by Consultation Paper 57, section 4. An 'expert' private customer may be treated as a 'sophisticated investor' for the purposes of FPE (see **4.3.5** and **13.1.1**). He will lose the right to use the Ombudsman Scheme but this will not affect his eligibility under the Compensation Scheme (see **8.2** and **8.3**).

5   COBS, Chapter 4.

6   Consultation Paper 47, FSA, May 2000, para 1.14.

counterparty[1]. On the third issue, the FSA confirmed that it would not be responsible, but the Bank of England has coordinated a Code for Non-Investment Products, laying down the sort of good practice expected by the IPC[2]. The IPC itself will form part of the *Market Conduct Sourcebook*.

In describing the nature and structure of the IPC, the FSA has said:

'The IPC is primarily guidance. This is in the form of

1. guidance on the Principles for Businesses and on specific rules and
2. guidance in the form of a statement of what the FSA understands to be generally regarded as market conventions and good market practice in certain areas ...

Because few detailed rules and only some of the Principles will apply in the IPC area, and because of the inherent nature of inter-professional business as self-disciplining, there is likely to be less scope for enforcement action. This does not, however, imply that a lower standard of behaviour is acceptable for inter-professional business.'[3]

Although the IPC switches off most of the COBS rules, it does not switch off the COMC and the market abuse regime[4]. The IPC applies to foreign firms' branches in the UK, but not UK firms' branches overseas. It also does not apply to deposits, insurance contracts or units in CISs. Deposit-taking and general insurance do not, in any case, fall within the COBS and so the switch-off is irrelevant. Units in CISs and some long-term insurance contracts do fall within the COBS, but as they would generally only be of interest to private customers, the IPC should not apply[5].

6.3.3   Conduct of business rules

The draft COBS is principally directed at authorised firms conducting designated investment business (DIB), which includes ancillary non-regulated activities but excludes deposit-taking, general insurance and purely protective long-term insurance[6]. It does, however, contain some financial promotion rules covering *all* regulated activities[7]. All COBS rules will apply to DIB with private customers and many will apply to DIB with intermediate customers, but the only rules that will apply to it with all market counterparties are the client assets rules. In general, dealings with market counterparties will be governed by the IPC[8].

Inwardly passported UCITS firms are only subject to the financial promotion provisions but other inwardly passported firms are subject to most of the rules except the client assets rules (which are considered under the ISD to be a prudential matter). Overseas branches of UK firms dealing with UK customers may also claim lighter regulation as though separately incorporated overseas. As

1   Consultation Paper 47, paras 1.1, 1.11 and 1.13; for the COMC, see **7.5**.
2   *Response to Comments on Discussion Paper: The Future Regulation of Inter-Professional Business*, p 12; Consultation Paper 47, para 1.10.
3   Consultation Paper 47 paras 1.17 and 1.22.
4   Consultation Paper 47, paras 1.26–1.30; see **Chapter 7**.
5   Consultation Paper 47, paras 2.1–2.9.
6   Consultation Paper 45a, FSA, February 2000, Part I, para 1.3; COBS, 1.3.3G; DIB is approximately what was defined as investment business under the 1986 Act. COBS does not apply directly to appointed representatives who are the responsibility of their principal: COBS, 1.7.1G.
7   See **13.1.3**.
8   Consultation Paper 45a, Part I, paras 2.18–2.21; COBS, 1.3.5R. OEICs are also not covered by the COBS.

the prudential regulation of outwardly passported firms is the responsibility of the FSA, the COBS client assets rules apply to them, but generally where UK firms are dealing with non-UK customers, the FSA proposes a light regime to avoid regulatory duplication[1].

There are general rules requiring fair and clear communications with customers, restricting inducements such as indirect benefits and soft commission and dealing with a firm's reliance on and responsibility for others[2]. Customers should be notified of the terms of business before dealing and where a private customer may be involved in providing margin or granting a firm discretionary powers, an agreement must be signed. Terms of business cannot exclude duties and liabilities under the FSMA and can limit a firm's liability under the general law only where that would be reasonable[3].

Concepts such as polarisation, know your customer, suitability, risk warnings, disclosure of charges and introducing the firm, have been carried forward from the SROs' old rule books and apply mainly to private customers. Know your customer remains a 'cornerstone of present regulatory standards' and together with suitability applies to discretionary private and intermediate customers and advisory private customers. Risk warnings before high-risk transactions apply only to private customers. The 'best advice' and polarisation rules still apply to the sale of packaged products such as policies and authorised or recognised CISs, although polarisation is being reconsidered following an OFT report on its anti-competitive tendencies[4]. The other live issues with packaged products (including here ISAs and Enterprise Investment Schemes) are the requirements of 'key features documents' to be issued pre- and post-sale and the rights of private customers to cancel or withdraw. The FSA proposes consolidating and simplifying both. It is also introducing product disclosure rules for other insurance contracts because the ICA 1982 will be repealed[5].

Chapters 7 and 8 of the COBS deal with the fair treatment of customers and generally follow the provisions of the old SFA rulebook on issues such as churning, dealing ahead, order priority, allocation, borrowings and margin calls. In dealing with conflicts of interest, however, the FSA proposes to drop the SFA's 'policy of independence' and leave the matter to more general evidential provisions. On timely best execution, the SFA itself has been consulting on how to cope with the growing complexities of dealing with competing exchanges and ATSs. The rules on post-transaction information have been adapted to cater for electronic confirmations and the exceptions have been rationalised. Where a portfolio is managed on a discretionary or advisory basis, periodic statements must be sent to both private and intermediate customers. The client assets rules are dealt with separately below.

Although the COBS will come into force with the FSMA, for a 12-month transitional period, authorised firms can continue to rely on the terms of existing

---

1   COBS, Table 1.4R.
2   COBS, Chapter 2. Although these do not add much to some of the PFBs, breaches of these rules give private persons the right to bring a civil action which breaches of PFBs do not. For the rules on financial promotions, see **13.1.3**.
3   COBS, Chapter 4.
4   COBS, Chapter 5 as explained by Consultation Paper 45a, Part II, Section 9. A decision on polarisation is expected in late 2000. See also London Economics, *Polarisation and Financial Services Intermediary Regulation*, FSA, July 2000.
5   COBS, Chapter 6 as explained by Consultation Paper 45a, Part II, Section 10.

client notices and agreements, on materials carrying the name of their former regulator and on promotions complying with their former regulators' require-ments[1]. Beyond these concessions, authorised firms will have little time to familiarise themselves with any changes the final version of the COBS may make to their current regulators' conduct of business rules[2].

6.4   OTHER PROVISIONS

The rationalisation of the previous regulators' rulebooks is an enormous task and the FSA will not have completed it all by the time that the FSMA comes into force. Therefore, the *Handbook* will rely upon existing rules in certain areas, particularly Prudential Rules.

6.4.1   *Prudential Sourcebook*

The FSA aims to introduce a set of integrated prudential requirements in mid-2002. These will be a risk-based capital system (RBC), organised, as far as international obligations will allow, according to the different risks run by firms, rather than by the categorisation of the firm, namely credit, market, operational and insurance risks rather than deposit-taking, insurance and investment business. The delay in implementation is partly to allow consultation with, and systems developments by, the firms affected. It is also to allow the New Basle Accord and any consequential changes to the CAD to be determined as these will affect credit institutions and other investment firms[3]. In the meantime, the existing regulators' rules will generally be continued by the FSA, although they will be reclassified into rules or guidance. Firms unhappy with the application of a rule will now have to apply formally for a waiver rather than relying on the regulator's discretion. However, there will be a limited interim harmonisation of the rules that apply to banks and building societies[4].

Indeed, on the FSMA coming into force, the whole basis of the prudential supervision of banks and building societies will change. Under the BA 1987 and the BSA 1986, there are no rule-making powers and the regulators rely upon policy and guidance. Banks and building societies will now be subject to the PFBs, which are rules, but rather than try to reclassify current policy and guidance into rules, evidential provisions, guidance, and even perhaps waivers, a small number of rules will be created to tie in harmonised requirements as guidance for the

---

1   Consultation Paper 45a, Part III, Transitional Rules.
2   The delay in bringing the FSMA into force until at least mid-2001 because of pressures at the Treasury may give firms a little more time to familiarise themselves with the COBS.
3   An outline of the FSA's current thinking may be gleaned from Occasional Paper 7, FSA, March 2000. The EU's proposals are to be found in *A Review of Regulatory Capital Requirements for EU Credit Institutions and Investment Firms*, European Commission, November 1999. However, in its *Response to Consultation Paper 31*, FSA, May 2000, para 8, the FSA has said that delays to the New Basle Accord will not be allowed to hold up the *Integrated Prudential Sourcebook*.
4   Consultation Paper 31, FSA November 1999, Section 1; Consultation Paper 54, FSA, June 2000; *A new capital adequacy framework*, Basle Committee on Banking Supervision June 1999; *FINANCIAL SERVICES: Implementing the Framework for Financial Markets: Action Plan*, European Commission, May 1999. For the continuation of the existing rules for insurance, see Consultation Paper 41, FSA, January 2000.

interim period[1]. The original interim proposal to raise banks' risk weighting for mortgages in arrears has, however, been withdrawn[2].

Prudential requirements cover not just capital adequacy, but also systems and controls. As one of the TCAs (adequate resources) and two of the PFBs (3 and 4), prudential requirements apply to all authorised firms' regulated and non-regulated activities. However, the FSA will still be able to differentiate between individual firms, not just on the basis of the risks assumed but also on the sophistication of their management. This can be done through detailed rules and guidance and by using waivers and even specific requirements attached to individual permissions[3]. This is an enormous degree of discretion.

The FSA will not have an entirely free hand, as there are a number of international minimum standards set – generally by type of firm. The FSA is aware that setting standards above these minima or applying these minima to firms not covered by them in the name of harmonisation could damage the international competitiveness of the UK financial services industry and has said 'the onus will be on justifying harmonisation rather than continued differentiation'.[4] Indeed, in this whole area, the FSA has expressed a welcome reluctance to harmonise:

> 'Capital requirements, for example, may be aimed at reducing the likelihood of failure – because failure may have a severe impact upon the market as well as on the customers of the firm; while for other types of firm, the impact of whose failure may be less severe, capital may be aimed as cushioning the firm and its customers from the adverse effects of a disorderly cessation of business; or at limiting the claims on compensation scheme funds should a firm fail with an unsettled (and uninsured) liability to compensate customers, eg for misselling of a financial product. A different approach may also be required for firms which, while not having liabilities of their own to customers, hold their money (or other assets) and where a financial resources cushion may help to prevent the client money losses that are often associated with the failure of a firm ...'
>
> In addition, our requirements will of course continue to embody different treatments for the same risks to take account of differences in the complexity of firms' business and their approaches to risk management. As far as possible, we shall aim to use differentiated requirements to provide incentives to firms to improve their risk management systems.'[5]

Such a highly differentiated system is going to make it difficult for many firms to determine exactly what prudential requirements will apply to them, although it must be said that current rules are hardly simple[6].

---

1   Consultation Paper 31, paras 5.5–5.11 as detailed in Consultation Papers 51 and 52, FSA, June 2000.

2   *Response to Consultation Paper 31*, para 39. Otherwise, where the risk weightings, etc for building societies have been higher than for banks, they are being brought down into line, Consultation Paper 51, Chapter 3.

3   FSMA, ss 43, 138, 148, 157 and Sch 6, para 4.

4   Consultation Paper 31, para 4.12, reconfirmed in *Response to Consultation Paper 31*, para 18.

5   Consultation Paper 31, paras 4.11 and 4.13, reconfirmed in *Response to Consultation Paper 31*, paras 23–28.

6   For example the draft *Interim Prudential Sourcebook* for insurance is pulling together elements from Policyholders Protection Act 1975, ICA 1982, Insurance Companies Regulations 1994, Insurance Companies (Reserves) Regulations 1996, Insurance Companies (Accounts and Statements) Regulations 1996, Insurance Directorate Prudential Guidance Notes, 'Dear Director' letter on derivatives and various 'Dear Appointed Actuary' letters, Consultation

6.4.2   Client assets rules

Client assets rules are largely designed to protect clients' money and other assets if the prudential rules have failed to prevent a default. Custody rules and client money rules aim to segregate clients' assets and money from those of the firm[1]. They have a number of unusual features:

(1) although found in the COBS, these rules are a home rather than a host State responsibility and, thus, are disapplied to inwardly passported firms[2];

(2) custody rules apply to market counterparties' assets as well as customers', as do client money rules, unless a market counterparty or intermediate customer opts out of the statutory trust protection for its money[3];

(3) client money rules cannot apply to bank deposits, of course, but if a bank conducts DIB, client money held in one of its accounts for that purpose can still be treated as a deposit, provided the client has been warned that the client money rules will not apply[4];

(4) trustees and solicitors under separate legal or professional obligations concerning clients' assets and money, may be exempt from the COBS rules[5]; and

(5) clients' collateral held by a firm is subject to these rules unless the firm has been given the right freely to dispose of it[6].

There are other exceptions to the custody rules for assets held for another part of the group which are not the assets of outside clients, for assets during settlement and for assets in transit (eg sending a certificate via an IFA). There are lighter regimes for market counterparties' assets where the market counterparties have opted out of the full regime and for arrangers of safe custody who pass the assets on to a third party custodian (who will no longer have to be FSA approved)[7].

There are also exceptions to the requirement to segregate clients' money, most notably for settlement purposes. The FSA proposes to end the requirement to have separate client accounts for different purposes, but also proposes to end any netting off of individual clients' balances, ie shift from net to gross segregation on a daily basis[8]. However, the FSA has consulted on a more fundamental overhaul of the client money rules.

The current rules require client money to be held separately on trust (other than money involved in settlement) and, on the default of the firm, this money is placed in a single pool to be distributed *pari passu* by an Insolvency Practitioner once

---

Paper 41, Section 3. This complexity partly explains the resistance to reducing the period for insurance businesses lodging their annual returns, *Response to Consultation Paper 31*, para 42.

1   They also aim to protect clients from the dishonesty of any authorised firm's employees.

2   ISD, Art 10; COBS, 9.1.4(1)R and 9.3.3(1)R, although non-ISD business remains subject to the rules of the jurisdiction where the business is done.

3   COBS, 9.3.35R. This is why the FSA refers to 'clients' rather than 'customers' in respect of these rules. ISD, Arts 5 and 10 require an opt out for ISD business to be by signed agreement even where the firm is not an ISD firm. The FSA only requires notification for non-ISD business: COBS, 9.3.14R and 9.3.18R.

4   COBS, 9.3.1R and 9.3.3(4)R.

5   COBS, 9.1.14R and 9.3.12R; Consultation Paper 45a, Part II, para 13.34.

6   COBS, 9.4.6R.

7   COBS, 9.1.4R, 9.1.8R, 9.1.10R, 9.1.12R, 9.1.26R and 9.1.27R.

8   COBS, 9.3.24R, 9.3.74R, 9.3.76R, 9.3.99R and 9.3.105R.

effective records have been reconstructed[1]. The FSA has reviewed these arrangements because, although they have not had to be operated often in recent years[2], the single pool *pari passu* principle exposes a low-risk customer to the investment risks assumed by consumers with a larger appetite for risk. On the other hand, most of such customers will be private and covered by the Compensation Scheme and any scheme making distinctions between customers will be slower and more costly to operate, as was found with the system before 1991. An alternative approach is to strengthen the prudential rules applying to firms holding clients' money and FSA is consulting on all these proposals[3]. Following the review, the FSA has decided, at least for the time being, to retain the current single pool arrangements[4].

6.4.3 Stabilisation rules

The FSA proposes to continue to provide a safe harbour against charges of misleading statements, market manipulation and insider dealing and to extend it to market abuse[5]. In guidance to the stabilisation rules, the FSA states the purpose of the rules as to prescribe:

> '... the circumstances in which lead stabilising managers and others acting with them are permitted to support the prices of new offers (including fresh offers of securities already traded in the market) for a limited period after the offer. This is to maintain an orderly initial market in the securities, and potentially therefore to facilitate new offers and reduce the costs to enterprises involved in the making of new offers in their securities. The managers are allowed to exert upward pressure on the price in the cash market, by all means permitted by the price stabilising rules, including by the repurchase of securities previously sold short.'[6]

Although mainly confined to primary issues of equities and bonds, stabilisation will continue to be allowed for quoted secondary offers over £15m. It will still be confined to the period from the announcement of the price (or for public debt, the unpriced issue) to 30 days after closing. There may be more than one stabilisation manager but there must be control exercised by the lead manager, one register of stabilising transactions and no intra-managers transactions. The FSA no longer intends to specify the exact disclosure wording required, but will require the market to be informed that stabilisation may take place. It will also require full explanations and profit declarations to be given to issuers of any 'Green Shoe' options[7].

In these days of global issues, stabilisation and its effects may not be confined to one jurisdiction. The FSA can extend the safe harbour by approving equivalent

---

1   Financial Services (Client Money) Regulations 1991.
2   Most recent defaults have been amongst investment advice firms being sued for pension misselling and they have not been holding client money.
3   Consultation Paper 38, FSA, January 2000.
4   Consultation Paper 57, Section 5.
5   FSMA, ss 118(8), 144, 397(4) and (5)(b) and (c) and the CJA 1993, Sch 1, para 5(1). The defence apparently extends to telling lies!
6   Consultation Paper 40, FSA January 2000, p 25.
7   Consultation Paper 40, Sections 2 and 3. Green Shoe options (named after a pioneering example in the USA) are to allow underwriters to purchase extra securities from the issuer after the underwriting. This protects underwriters who have gone short but the market price has not fallen. They do give rise to conflicts of interest and potential secret profits.

overseas rules. Stabilisation taking place overseas but potentially creating a 'false impression' in the UK is *prima facie* still the UK crime of market manipulation, but the UK stabilisation rules can protect stabilisation managers not authorised in the UK[1]. These rules will form part of the *Market Conduct Sourcebook.*

6.4.4   *Training and Competence Sourcebook*

The FSA is placing great emphasis on the quality of authorised firms' staff to ensure the maintenance of high standards throughout the industry. A draft *Training and Competence Sourcebook* has been produced largely carrying forward the requirements of the current regulators, except that back office supervisory staff of discretionary investment business will now be subject to exams and subsequent monitoring[2].

The FSA has confirmed that its policy will be to retain a lighter touch for business conducted with, or for, a non-private customer and to place the greater weight of regulation on business with, or for, the private customer[3].

The FSA's requirements are divided into two parts:

(1)   five commitments, being guidance applying to any firm conducting regulated activities including deposit-taking and general insurance, namely to:
  (a)   advance and maintain the competence of its employees,
  (b)   ensure that its employees remain competent for the functions they carry out,
  (c)   ensure that its employees are adequately supervised in relation to the attainment and maintenance of competence,
  (d)   ensure that the training for and competence of its employees is regularly reviewed,
  (e)   take account (in dealing with commitments (a)–(d)) of the level of competence that is necessary having regard to the nature of its business and the role of its employees; and
(2)   rules and guidance only applying to:
  (a)   certain individual employees such as those dealing in securities for private clients, specialist derivatives dealers, fund managers and those giving advice on investments (but not deposits or general insurance); and
  (b)   certain team leaders operating unit trusts, custodian arrangements and other administrative functions including, for the first time, the administration of long-term insurance contracts.

The rules and guidance impose five obligations:

(1)   recruitment – checking in particular the individual's examinations and experience and determining what further training may be required;
(2)   training – not just courses, but job learning, role-play and individual study;
(3)   attaining competence – both obtaining approved examinations and being supervised for an appropriate period of time given any previous experience;

1   FSMA, s 144(3); Consultation Paper 40, paras 2.24–2.30.
2   Consultation Paper 34, FSA, November 1999, confirmed, subject to some redrafting, in Consultation Paper 60, FSA, July 2000. IMRO already imposes training and competence requirements on back office staff.
3   Consultation Paper 60, para 4.10.

(4) maintaining competence – particularly where the individual's role develops or changes, but at least initially there are no minimum continuing professional training hours; and

(5) supervising competence – to ensure no direct dealing with customers until basically competent and thereafter continuing review and assessment until fully competent. Even then, competence still needs to be monitored[1].

The FSA will review the present approved examinations and does intend to rationalise and tighten up the requirements to pass such examinations within certain time-limits, particularly where individuals are advising private customers[2]. However, this is all part of the Approved Persons regime.

6.5 THE FINANCIAL SERVICES AUTHORITY'S STATEMENTS OF PRINCIPLE

As has already been noted, FSA rules apply to authorised firms, but approved individuals may also be disciplined by the FSA if they are 'knowingly concerned' in breaking them. However, those are not the only circumstances in which the FSA may discipline approved individuals.

The FSA can and will issue Statements for approved individuals, which must be accompanied by a Code of Practice, in effect evidential rules to help determine compliance with those Statements. Mere failure by an approved individual to comply with any Statements will be a disciplinary matter, without having to show that he was knowingly concerned with the breach of any FSA rules or other requirements under the FSMA. Such a failure does not invalidate any transaction, nor allow any individual civil action[3].

In issuing or changing Statements and the Code of Practice, the FSA is subject to its statutory objectives and restraining principles and must follow the same procedure as that for issuing or changing rules including cost-benefit analyses[4]. The Code of Practice may specify what conduct does or does not comply with the Statements and factors that may be taken into account, all of which may be relied upon 'so far as it tends to establish whether or not that conduct complies' with a Statement[5].

6.5.1 The approach of the Financial Services Authority

The FSA has published its initial thoughts on what Statements it will impose on approved individuals in their controlled functions, namely:

Principles applicable to all approved persons:
(1) individuals must act with integrity;
(2) individuals must act with due skill, care and diligence;

---

1   Consultation Paper 34, Section 2.
2   Consultation Paper 34, Section 3.
3   FSMA, ss 64 and 66. See **9.3**.
4   FSMA, s 65, subject again to the emergency override (FSMA, s 65(7)), which is expected to be used rarely (vol 612 HL, 18 April 2000, c 625), see **6.2.4**.
5   FSMA, s 64(3) and (7). Draft Statements and the Code of Practice are contained in *High level standards for firms and individuals*, Annex B.

(3) individuals must observe proper standards of market conduct; and
(4) individuals must deal with the FSA and with other relevant regulators in an open and co-operative way and must disclose appropriately any information of which the FSA would reasonably expect notice.

Additional principles applicable to senior managers:
(5) senior managers must take reasonable steps to ensure that the regulated business of their firms for which they are responsible is organised so that it can be controlled effectively;
(6) senior managers must exercise due skill, care and diligence in managing the business of their firm for which they are responsible; and
(7) senior managers must take reasonable steps to ensure that the business of their firm for which they are responsible complies with the regulatory requirements imposed on that business[1].

It could be argued that, from a disciplinary point of view, the Statements add little as they closely shadow the PFBs that are themselves FSA rules. The four Statements that apply to all approved individuals are the equivalent of PFBs 1, 2, 5 and 11. Turning to the proposed Code of Practice, although it does give some general factors to be considered particularly in connection with the Statements applying to senior managers (ie general guidance), it is largely confined to listing what conduct will not comply with the Statements (ie detailed rules) and few, if any, examples of conduct that will comply tend to show compliance, other than following the IPC and COMC under Statement 3.

Statement 1, for example, would be breached by an individual if he is:

'(a) deliberately misleading (or attempting to mislead) by act or omission:
    (i)   a customer;
    (ii) his firm (or its auditors or appointed actuary); or
    (iii) the FSA ...;
(b) deliberately recommending an investment to a customer or carrying out a discretionary transaction for a customer where he knows that he is unable to justify its suitability for that customer ...
(c) deliberately failing to inform, without reasonable cause:
    (i)   a customer;
    (ii) his firm (or its auditors or appointed actuary); or
    (iii) the FSA;
    of the fact that their understanding of a material issue is incorrect despite being aware of their misunderstanding ...
(d) deliberately preparing inaccurate or inappropriate records or returns in connection with a controlled function ...
(e) deliberately misusing the assets or confidential information of either:
    (i)   a customer; or
    (ii) his firm ...
(f) deliberately designing transactions so as to disguise breaches of regulatory requirements;

---

1   Consultation Paper 26, p 49 as amended by Annex B, chapter 2. In Statements 1–4 'individuals' can be other approved persons and in Statements 5–7 'senior managers' are defined as approved persons 'performing significant influence functions' and their duties extend to the whole business of their firm, not just the 'regulated activities'.

(g) deliberately failing to disclose the existence of a conflict of interest in connection with dealings with a customer.'[1]

Looking at this list, it is clear that in some cases an individual could be disciplined for a single act where it would require an accumulation of such acts by one or more individuals for an authorised firm to be in breach of the equivalent PFB 1. This has the ironic effect of making the disciplining of individuals easier than the disciplining of firms, although the FSA maintains that it is firms that are the principal subjects of its enforcement regime[2]. Nevertheless, the great virtue of the Statements, even with the Code of Practice, will be that they can be read and understood by approved individuals, whereas the *Handbook* as a whole is going to remain the domain of compliance officers and managers[3].

---

1   Consultation Paper 26, pp 51–54, as amended by Annex B, chapter 4. Generally, customer excludes market counterparty.
2   See **9.3**.
3   This is no doubt why practitioners are in favour of regulation by broad principles, Forum's Report and Accounts 1999, p 14.

Chapter 7

MARKET MISCONDUCT

7.1 BACKGROUND

Ever since the nineteenth century, the common law has accepted that the crime of conspiracy to defraud extends to rigging a market[1]. In 1939, a statutory offence was added of 'misleading statements' that might induce an investment transaction[2]. This was re-enacted in the 1986 Act and the crime of 'market manipulation' was added[3]. These statutory offences now appear under 'misleading statements and practices' in the FSMA[4]. However, because English law has taken a strict view of the separate personality of companies, it has not accepted that directors and employees of companies owe a fiduciary duty to individual shareholders to reveal information[5]. Therefore, these crimes have not been extended, as they have in the USA to cover insider dealing[6]; nor have they created a private civil action for affected shareholders[7].

In 1980, insider dealing was made a separate criminal offence[8], but to bring UK law into line with the European Directive on Insider Dealing[9], this legislation was replaced by Part V of the Criminal Justice Act 1993 (CJA 1993) which will remain in force. Again, the CJA 1993 did not create a civil action for shareholders affected by insider dealing[10]. That does not mean that directors, employees and others are not liable for the misuse of confidential information, but any action would lie with the company whose confidence has been abused and in practice, companies do not bring such actions[11].

Apart from these specialist crimes, City fraud has also been dealt with under the Theft Act 1968[12]. However, the Government has been dissatisfied with reliance

---

1 *R v de Berenger* (1814) 105 Eng Rep 536; *Scott v Brown, Doering, McNab & Co* [1892] 2 QB 724. It was also the only charge brought, albeit unsuccessfully, against the defendants in the *Blue Arrow* case.
2 Prevention of Fraud (Investments) Act 1939, s 13.
3 1986 Act, s 47(1) and (2). Similar provisions covering banking and insurance were created by 1986 Act, s 133 and Banking Act 1987, s 35.
4 FSMA, s 397.
5 *Percival v Wright* [1902] 2 Ch 421.
6 Rule 10b-5, most recently considered by the Supreme Court in *US v O'Hagan* 117 S Ct 2199 (1997).
7 *Salaman v Warner* (1891) 65 LT 132; under the 1986 Act, breach of s 47 does not give rise to a statutory tort under s 62, although the FSA could bring an action for compensation under s 61. The FSA does and will continue to have the power to bring restitutionary actions, see **10.4.2**.
8 Companies Act 1980, Part V re-enacted as Insider Dealing Act 1985.
9 1989/592/EEC.
10 Indeed, contracts tainted by insider dealing remain valid and enforceable. CJA 1993, s 63(2).
11 The strict liability of directors for secret profits can be seen in *Regal (Hastings) Ltd v Gulliver* [1942] 1 All ER 378 and the remedy may be proprietary: *Attorney-General for Hong Kong v Reid* [1994] 1 All ER 1. Tippers and tippees may even be liable: *Gluckstein v Barnes* [1900] AC 240, *Selangor United Rubber Estates Ltd v Cradock (No 3)* [1968] 2 All ER 1073.
12 Crimes like theft, obtaining a pecuniary advantage by deception, false accounting, see Theft Act 1968, ss 1, 15 and 17.

upon criminal sanctions. Proving the elements of these crimes 'beyond reasonable doubt' has meant that there have been few successful prosecutions. That is why the Government proposed to give the FSA the power to fine authorised and non-authorised persons for 'market abuse' based on a civil burden of proof. As the Economic Secretary put it:

> '. . . there is a gap in the protections [of the financial markets]. The criminal law covers all market participants, but only a narrow range of serious criminal offences. The regulatory regime is capable of dealing with a wider range of damaging behaviours, but applies only to the regulated community.'[1]

However, this original proposal to have a sweeping civil sanction was much criticised in the hearings of the Joint Committee and considerably revised during the FSMA's passage through Parliament[2]. The Government reluctantly accepted that the width of the power and the similarity of the circumstances in which it could be used to those for the existing criminal sanctions, might mean that it was a criminal sanction for the purposes of the Convention[3]. This led to three changes:

(1) a restriction on the use of compelled statements as evidence;
(2) the introduction of legal aid for market abuse cases; and
(3) a tightening up of what can amount to market abuse, including the introduction of safe harbours.

To appreciate the still broad scope of this new provision, however, it is necessary first to examine the continuing criminal offences.

7.2   MISLEADING STATEMENTS AND PRACTICES

As has already been noted, these are two separate crimes, 'making misleading statements' and 'market manipulation' punishable with up to seven years' imprisonment and an unlimited fine. Prosecutions may be brought by the FSA, by the Secretary of State, by the DPP or with the DPP's consent[4]. The Economic Secretary has given interesting examples of the two crimes:

> 'A person who puts out false information about a company in which he holds shares in order to boost the share price would be caught by the first offence. When the share price rises the fraudster sells out, a practice described in American parlance as "pump and dump" schemes. An example of the second offence is the classic boiler house operation where fraudsters buy and sell shares to each other, thus misleading investors into believing that there is keen market interest in the shares. Investors are

---

1   Economic Secretary, Standing Committee A, 2 November 1999, c 652. The ability of an outsider to undermine a market was demonstrated by the effect Sumitomo Bank had on the London Metal Exchange even though it was not a member of that exchange, see Lord Bagri, vol 610 HL, 21 February 2000, c 58.
2   Joint Committee, Second Report; Standing Committee A, 2 November 1999, cc 651–708. The most devastating criticism of the original proposals was that of Lord Hobhouse, Joint Committee, Minutes of Evidence, 15 April 1999, p 118, who said 'All those things when one adds them together add up to a scheme for punishing people who may be abroad, who may not be taking any active part in any market in this country, who have not done anything illegal, whose conduct is innocent, who are under no duty to act where they are accused of failing to act, and nevertheless punishing them for such conduct'.
3   See **2.4**.
4   FSMA, ss 397(8), 401(2) and (3). In Scotland, all criminal proceedings must still be decided upon by the Lord Advocate.

thereby induced to buy shares that later turn out to have little or no marketability or value.'[1]

The first crime covers not just lies, but misleading, false or deceptive statements, promises or forecasts, which the party either knows, or does not care, are such. Where positive statements have been made, no dishonest motivation for the error need be proved, but there is a defence of complying with FSA rules on price stabilisation or Chinese walls[2]. However, the crime also covers dishonestly concealing material facts[3]. In other words, it makes it a crime to be 'economical with the truth'. A person may be committing the crime if he makes a material misstatement or if he fails to reveal a material fact, either knowing or not caring that such concealment may persuade someone to enter into or refrain from dealing, or underwriting, or taking up rights or voting at a company meeting. Thus, the crime can arise from material statements made or omitted in defence documents and in telephone campaigns during takeover battles, as well as offers and other invitations to deal. It might also be extended to negotiations for contracts to manage funds or give advice on investments[4].

7.2.1 Economical with the truth

In what circumstances is it criminal to be economical with the truth? Unlike positive statements, being economical with the truth is only a crime if done dishonestly. The FSMA gives no guidance as to what is meant by dishonesty and the leading case on the subject lays down a two-stage test, whereby the court must decide whether:

(1) according to the standards of reasonable and honest people, the concealment was dishonest; and
(2) the defendant must have realised that the concealment was dishonest by those standards[5].

The problem with this test is that in a specialist area such as financial services, magistrates or jurors, acting as reasonable and honest people, have little experience of the area on which to have established any standards for themselves. Normally there is no positive duty to disclose material facts before contracting (*caveat emptor*) unless the relationship is one of confidence (eg principal and agent). Positive duties to disclose are created by the Companies Acts, the FSA's rules, the Listing Rules and the Takeover Code, but at least one case has held that no such positive duty need exist to convict[6].

7.2.2 Market manipulation

The second crime covers any deliberate acts which create a false impression as to the liquidity or price or value of security with the intent of inducing someone to

---

1 Standing Committee A, 9 December 1999, c 1230.
2 FSMA, s 397(1)(a) and (c) and (4). The defence covers deliberate but not reckless statements.
3 FSMA, s 397(1)(b). There is no defence here presumably because price stabilisation and withholding information with Chinese walls would not be dishonest behaviour.
4 FSMA, s 397(2), (9) and (10); the exact scope of relevant agreements is to be determined by the Treasury in a statutory instrument.
5 *R v Ghosh* [1982] QB 1053.
6 *R v Spens* [1991] 4 All ER 421.

enter into or refrain from dealing, underwriting, etc[1]. No dishonest motivation needs to be proved and the onus is on the defendant to argue that he reasonably believed his acts would not create a false or misleading impression. The crime is most likely to arise during corporate finance operations and raises very difficult issues, for example whether there must be public disclosure of securities left with underwriters or before the placings of 'rumps' in rights issues. Again, there is a defence of compliance with FSA rules on price stabilisation or Chinese walls[2].

The potential width of both of these crimes can be seen by asking whether taking a decision to buy a significant stake in a company (or even to take it over) and not declaring that intention before buying shares is criminal? Presumably such behaviour is not considered to be *dishonestly* economical with the truth, but is it creating a misleading impression? Here one has to rely on the failure to disclose not being treated as *engaging* in a course of conduct.

To commit either crime only really needs one element of it to be in the UK[3]. It should also be noted that the senior management or partners of a firm or individuals who are significant shareholders can be found guilty of these two offences and be subject to an unlimited fine if the firm committed them with their consent, connivance or just through their negligence[4].

There was an argument that s 200 of the 1986 Act making it a crime to 'furnish information which is false or misleading' could be used as an alternative to s 47, but the equivalent provision in the FSMA only covers information given to the FSA where no other provision makes the deception a crime[5].

7.3   INSIDER DEALING

Insider dealing is also punishable with up to seven years' imprisonment and an unlimited fine. Prosecutions may be brought by the FSA, by the Secretary of State, by the DPP or with the consent of the last two[6]. To maintain orderly settlement in the market, however, contracts made on the basis of inside information remain enforceable[7].

There are, in effect, three separate crimes created, namely that an individual who has inside information:

(1)   deals or procures another person to deal (whether as a principal or an agent);
(2)   encourages another person to deal who might reasonably be expected to do so; or

---

1   FSMA, s 397(3), (9) and (10); again the exact scope is to be determined by statutory instrument.
2   FSMA, s 397(5).
3   FSMA, s 397(6) and (7).
4   FSMA, s 400.
5   FSMA, s 398, for which the penalty is an unlimited fine.
6   CJA 1993, s 61; FSMA, s 402(1)(a); the Stock Exchange has been given consent to bring cases since 1989.
7   CJA 1993, s 63(2).

(3) discloses inside information other than in the proper performance of his duties[1],

although in the last case there is the defence that the individual did not expect anyone to deal because of the disclosure[2].

7.3.1 Relevant dealings

To cover derivatives and other short-term speculation, the definition of dealing includes merely agreeing to acquire or dispose of a security and entering into and bringing to an end a contract which creates a security[3]. However, not all dealings fall within the Act.

Dealings through any EEA securities or derivatives market, or elsewhere by or through a 'professional intermediary' are covered[4]. Thus, dealings by or through any securities broker or investment bank around the world may be caught, but private face-to-face transactions are not. Although the dealings do not have to be through an EEA exchange, the securities dealt in must, nevertheless, be listed or otherwise traded on such an exchange or be off-market derivatives based on such securities[5]. Public sector securities are included, but units in unit trusts do not appear to be covered leaving their managers free to trade in them, but not, it seems, managers of OEICs in their shares[6]. New issues that have not yet been listed or officially traded are also not covered, taking most underwriting and grey market transactions outside this legislation.

The crime of dealing (including procuring) is committed if either the perpetrator or the market/intermediary used is in the UK. The crimes of encouraging or disclosing are committed if either the tipper or tippee is in the UK[7].

7.3.2 Insiders

The primary offences can be committed only by individuals, but if an individual uses a company to deal, he will still be caught for procuring another person, ie the company, to deal[8]. However, to be guilty the individual must fall into one of two categories:

(1) anyone who has what he *knows* to be inside information through being a director, employee or shareholder of a company or other body that issues securities (not necessarily the securities affected by the information) or

---

1 CJA 1993, s 52(1) and (2). The expectation test is objective for (2) and subjective for (3) but the onus is on the defendant in (3).
2 CJA 1993, s 53(3)(a).
3 CJA 1993, s 55; on defences, see **7.3.4**.
4 CJA 1993, ss 52(3), 59 and 60(1); Insider Dealing (Securities and Regulated Markets) Order 1994, SI 1994/187 (the '1994 Order') as amended by SI 1996/1561. The list includes NASDAQ because its computer-based system can be used anywhere in the world.
5 CJA 1993, s 54(2) and Sch 2; 1994 Order. Thus, the crimes cover only quoted securities and derivatives based on such securities, not other types of investments.
6 CJA 1993, Sch 2, cf FSMA, Sch 2, Part II.
7 CJA 1993, s 62; 1994 Order amended by SI 1996/1561. For this purpose, the UK markets are the Stock Exchange, LIFFE, OM London Exchange Limited (OM London) and Tradepoint Financial Networks plc (Tradepoint).
8 CJA 1993, s 53.

anyone else who has access to the information by virtue of his position (an 'insider'); and

(2) anyone else who has what he *knows* to be inside information from an insider or whose direct or indirect source was such an insider (a 'tippee')[1].

For an insider, there does not have to be any clear connection between him and the securities about which he has information, just that the information came to him through his position[2]. For a tippee, it is not clear if he has to know the exact identity of the insider[3]. This seems to suggest that overhearing information at work makes someone an insider, but overhearing it at the pub does not, unless he knows enough about the source to make him a tippee.

7.3.3   Inside information

To be inside information, the information must meet the following tests, namely that it:

(1) relates to particular securities or issuers of securities (including information affecting their business prospects) and not to securities or issuers of securities generally;

(2) is specific or precise;

(3) has not been made public; and

(4) if it were made public would be likely to have a significant effect on the price or value of any securities[4].

The first element does give rise to a problem with public sector debt, as any information likely to have a significant effect on its price or value (interest rate changes, default threats, etc) is almost bound to affect securities generally. The second element is drafted in the alternative to prevent the defence that important but ill-defined information is not 'precise'[5]. No guidance is given as to what 'significant' means in the fourth element. A piece of information might move the price of a debt security very little, ordinary shares, say 5%, but derivatives considerably more[6]. There is guidance, however, on what is 'public' in the third element.

Information is deemed to have been made public if it is:

(1) officially published as required by a regulated market (eg through the Companies Announcement Office or its overseas equivalents);

(2) contained in statutorily required records (eg Companies House or the *Official Gazette*);

(3) readily available to those likely to deal in the relevant securities (but being prepared to speak to any analyst who rings up may not be enough); or

---

1   CJA 1993, s 57.
2   There is, thus, no need to show the breach of any fiduciary duty as there is in the USA, see *US v O'Hagan* 117 S Ct 2199 (1997).
3   Article 4 of the Directive, from which this derives, is itself ambiguous, yet exact knowledge of the source is what distinguishes 'information' from 'rumour'.
4   CJA 1993, ss 56 and 60(2) and (4).
5   The Directive only uses the word 'precise'.
6   The Takeover Panel now considers a share price movement of 5% in a single day something that may require an announcement, Takeover Code rule 2.2. note 1.

(4) derived from information that has been made public (eg analysis of a company's accounts and public statements)[1].

In addition, 'information *may* be treated as made public even though:

(1) it can be acquired only through diligence or expertise;
(2) it is communicated to only a section of the public;
(3) it can be acquired only by observation;
(4) it is communicated only on payment of a fee; or
(5) it is published only outside the UK[2].

7.3.4 Defences

There are three specific defences to dealing or encouraging another to deal:

(1) for market-makers acting in the course of their business 'in good faith' (though it is not clear if this allows the market-maker to go deliberately long or short);
(2) when stabilising new issue prices within the FSA's stabilisation rules (a defence for investment bank activities); and
(3) when the inside information is 'market information' (knowledge of the actual or contemplated acquisition or disposal of securities) and the actions are reasonable[3].

This last defence is again largely for professionals covering, inter alia, institutional shareholders (and their agents) not announcing their intentions of buying or selling securities before doing so, eg predator companies purchasing shares in targets before announcing bids or during the battle and banks underwriting or placing secondary offers of securities without giving progress reports[4]. One difficult question is whether it is illegal for individuals or a firm to 'front run' the publication of a highly regarded analyst's report in which the analyst is dramatically changing his view of a company. The report may be entirely derived from public information, but is the knowledge that institutional investors' views will be swayed by the report, itself inside information?

There are also three general defences to dealing or encouraging another to deal:

(1) he did not expect the dealing to result in a profit or the avoidance of a loss (eg buying on bad news or selling on good);
(2) he would have done what he did without the information (eg a trustee acting on professional advice or an analyst sticking to the advice he was giving before he received the inside information); and
(3) he reasonably believed that the information had been disclosed widely enough to avoid prejudice[5].

---

1   CJA 1993, s 58(2).
2   CJA 1993, s 58(3).
3   CJA 1993, Sch 1.
4   This defence is further evidence that these activities do not amount to offences under FSMA, s 397. New issues do not need this defence as the securities have not been listed or admitted to trading for the purposes the 1994 Order.
5   CJA 1993, s 53(1), (2) and (6)

Again, the last defence is hard to understand and seems to be there to cover corporate finance transactions where the parties involved know enough but the market has not yet been fully informed.

The only defences to disclosing inside information, however, are that:

(1) he did not expect any person to deal because of the disclosure; or
(2) he did not expect the dealing to result in a profit or the avoidance of a loss[1].

Although the onus, as with all the other defences, is on the defendant to establish them on the balance of probabilities, the first defence here makes it hard for the prosecution to secure a conviction for disclosing without proving collusion between the tipper and tippee, because the tipper can always argue that he did not expect the tippee to break the law by insider dealing.

7.4   MARKET ABUSE

The FSA has the power to reprimand publicly or impose an unlimited fine on authorised *and* non-authorised persons for engaging in market abuse. It is also indirect market abuse if a person requires or encourages (by action or even inaction) another to engage in behaviour that if done by the defendant would have amounted to direct market abuse. This is one of the most controversial parts of the FSMA[2]. Market abuse is basically defined as:

(1) behaviour in relation to any qualifying investments;
(2) likely to be regarded by regular users of the market as falling below the standard reasonably expected of a person in that position; and
(3) which falls within at least one of three categories[3].

(1) In theory, only one of either the behaviour or the market has to be in the UK (which can include markets electronically accessible in the UK) to constitute market abuse. In practice, the Treasury intends to limit 'qualifying' investments to those traded on the six RIEs physically in the UK[4]. However, it is recognised that this may change with the development of the Internet. 'UK markets' could easily become based anywhere as the current proposals to merge the London and Frankfurt Stock Exchanges makes clear. Nevertheless, the behaviour (which can be mere inaction) does not have to affect an investment on those UK markets directly. It may just affect the underlying subject-matter of such an investment or a derivative of it. Thus behaviour can include squeezes on underlying commodity markets and exploiting inside information by using spread bets even if done overseas, provided that it indirectly affects an investment traded on one of the UK markets. The behaviour can be that of one person or more than one acting together[5].

---

1   CJA 1993, s 53(3)
2   FSMA, s 123(1) and (3).
3   FSMA, s 118(1).
4   FSMA, s 118(3)–(5); Draft Financial Services and Markets Act (Market Abuse) (Prescribed Markets and Qualifying Investments) Order in *Market Abuse: Prescribed Markets*, HM Treasury, June 1999. The six markets are the Stock Exchange, LIFFE, OM London, Tradepoint, London Metal Exchange and International Petroleum Exchange. Investments here are not confined to securities and their derivatives.
5   FSMA, s 118(1), (5), (6), (9) and (10).

(2) This is quite a complicated concept. The standard is set by the hypothetical regular users of the market because it is their confidence that would be damaged[1]. However, as the Economic Secretary has pointed out, that standard:

'... will vary from case to case and market to market. For example, the market is likely to have higher expectations of a knowledgeable investor or an issuer than an ordinary member of the public.'[2]

Although a great improvement on the original draft, this test could, in theory, be used by 'market insiders' to impose cosy protective standards against 'market outsiders' or to excuse low but common standards of behaviour amongst such insiders[3]. Therefore, much may depend on the evidential rules and guidance produced by the FSA in its Code of Market Conduct (COMC).

(3) Finally, the behaviour itself must fall within one of three categories:

(a) it is based on information not generally available to those using the market but which if available to a regular user would be likely to be regarded by him as relevant in deciding the terms on which to deal in such investments (ie insider dealing);

(b) it is likely to give a regular user a false or misleading impression as to the market or value of such investments (ie misleading statements and practices); or

(c) it would be regarded by a regular user as likely to distort the market in such investments (ie rigging the market)[4].

7.4.1 The three categories

Although the three categories are similar to the underlying crimes, their scope is not identical. The definitions here are objective. Neither intent nor actual knowledge needs to be proved. This wide drafting is deliberate. As the Joint Committee noted on the issue of intent:

'The explanation given by the Government for the absence of an intent requirement is that the market abuse regime is concerned with the efficient operation of the market, not the moral culpability of individual players in the market: confidence in the markets can be affected by the effects of a player's conduct even if this is not the player's intention.'[5]

Where the market abuse is of the first type (based on 'insider dealing'), information which 'can be obtained by research or analysis by or on behalf of users

---

1   The official definition is 'a reasonable person who regularly deals on the market in investments of the kind in question': FSMA, s 118(10).

2   Standing Committee A, 2 November 1999, c 655. The Economic Secretary has also suggested that an overseas operator abiding by his local rules and practices, but nevertheless affecting a UK market, would be unlikely to be found to have abused the market: vol 344 HC, 9 February 2000, c 311.

3   Mr Heathcoat-Amory in Standing Committee A, 2 November 1999, c 669, cf Lord Eatwell in vol 610 HL, 21 February 2000, c 72.

4   FSMA, s 118(2).

5   Joint Committee, First Report, para 265; Standing Committee A, 2 November 1999, c 673; reiterated in vol 344 HC, 9 February 2000, c 309.

of a market' is deemed to be 'generally available'[1]. That does stop all 'inequality of information' being sufficient to prove market abuse, but information still does not have to be 'known' to be inside information. It just has to amount to an informational advantage that a regular user of the market would consider relevant and reasonable not to expect the person to exploit. In theory, the FSA could accept that regular users of markets really should expect informational advantages to be exploited unless obtained through a breach of confidence. Then this type of market abuse would be little wider in scope (albeit still easier to prove) than the crime of insider dealing. The FSA's approach to this issue can be seen from its draft COMC (see below).

A good example of the second type of market abuse was given in the Standing Committee. If an Internet user – perhaps a disgruntled employee – publishes a false announcement about a company that, for example, it is going to face a massive compensation suit, just so as to destroy the company's share price, the Economic Secretary confirmed that the person would have engaged in market abuse, whether or not he stood to gain financially[2]. The Economic Secretary herself gave some examples:

> 'If a company were to release information which misled investors, about say, its current profits or planned activities, it should be possible to take action against it if the circumstances warrant it, for example, if they were negligent. Similarly, if a trader does not care to follow market rules or conventions, on disclosure, for example, and, as a result, the market is misled, it should be possible to take action.'[3]

She also pointed out that failure to act could be market abuse:

> 'For example, a company's failure to inform the markets of a major new development as required by the market or listing laws could constitute market abuse. Similarly, someone who squeezes the market may not take any action, but, merely by continuing to hold a particular position, could be involved in an abuse.'[4]

Squeezing or cornering a market is probably the clearest example of the third type of market abuse, which otherwise tends to overlap with the second type. One particular problem here is that for commodity derivatives, the underlying market is often naturally dominated by a small number of producers. The Joint Committee and Standing Committee A raised the issue of copper prices being sharply affected by any African trade union calling for a strike of copper workers. The Economic Secretary said of the redrafted section:

> 'I make it clear that the copper miners do not have a position in relation to the market and the reasonable regular user would not regard their industrial action as a failure to observe the standard of behaviour expected of them, so they are outside the provision and that is our clear intention.'[5]

There are three general safe harbours created for a defendant, where:

---

1   FSMA, s 118(7). By contrast with the CJA 1993, information here can be about commodities, derivatives of which are dealt in on the London Metal Exchange or the International Petroleum Exchange, but not about securities (and derivatives thereof) only dealt in on EEA markets outside the UK.

2   Standing Committee A, 2 November 1999, cc 683 and 684.

3   Standing Committee A, 2 November 1999, c 656.

4   Standing Committee A, 2 November 1999, c 676.

5   Standing Committee A, 2 November 1999, c 674.

(1) his behaviour conformed to the FSA's rules that exclude market abuse (eg stabilisation, Chinese walls and certain Listing Rules)[1];

(2) he believed, on reasonable grounds, that the behaviour did not amount to direct or indirect market abuse; and

(3) he took all reasonable precautions and exercised all due diligence to avoid engaging in direct or indirect market abuse.

The onus in (2) and (3) is on the defendant in representations to show to the FSA that 'there are reasonable grounds for it to be satisfied' that the safe harbours are met, but the FSA is required to issue a policy indicating the circumstances that would satisfy it[2].

The FSA has to consult on and then publish the policy that it will follow on when and how much it will fine, which must have regard to:

(1) the seriousness of the behaviour's effect on the market;

(2) whether the behaviour was deliberate or reckless; and

(3) whether the penalty is being imposed on an individual[3].

7.4.2 Who is vulnerable?

The FSA may reprimand or fine not just for direct engagement in market abuse, but also for acts of omission or commission that require or encourage another to engage in behaviour which would be market abuse if engaged in by the defendant[4]. Some concern has been expressed that this indirect market abuse could lead to authorised firms being found 'guilty' for failing to realise that their customers were engaged in, say, insider dealing. The defence of 'all reasonable precautions and . . . all due diligence' might be hard to raise without enquiry into why any customer was proposing to deal, at least, where the deal was unusual in size or urgency.

However, the bigger danger is probably of direct market abuse actions being brought against directors of UK quoted companies. They are remarkably vulnerable under the second and third types of market abuse. Decisions on whether and when to make announcements about possible developments within their company and its markets can be very difficult. They are always open to challenge with the benefit of hindsight. Deliberately or even recklessly misleading the market is one thing, but merely failing to assess accurately what a regular user of that market would reasonably expect, which might be very different from the expectations of a reasonable director, is quite another. To point out that this would be reflected in the size of the fine, is hardly a comfort when one's professional career may have been destroyed.

Perhaps more surprisingly, the market abuse regime also threatens another regulator, the Takeover Panel, which fears that parties will resort to the FSA and the courts rather than accept informal Takeover Panel rulings on their conduct during takeover battles. The FSA has agreed to consult with the Panel before

---

1   Consultation Paper 59, section 7, the exact rules have yet to be determined.

2   FSMA, ss 118(8), 123(2) and 124(3).

3   FSMA, s 124. The consultation procedure must follow the basic pattern described for the complaints scheme described in **3.4.4**. For more details on reprimands and fines and the disciplinary procedures that must be followed before imposing them, see **Chapters 9** and **10**.

4   FSMA, s 123(1). In such indirect market abuse, the other party does not have to be 'guilty'.

exercising its market abuse powers in a way that could affect a takeover bid and refrain from intervening where the Panel can take effective action itself. In addition, the FSA may introduce into the COMC a complete or limited safe harbour for behaviour conforming to the Takeover Code, subject to Treasury approval[1]. An Opposition proposal for a definitive safe harbour which was not subject to Treasury approval and where the Takeover Panel was the arbiter of what amounted to conformity was narrowly defeated[2]. All the Government was prepared to concede was that the FSA should have regard to the Panel's views. As the Economic Secretary said:

> 'The Panel's view will be highly persuasive in takeover matters. If disagreement arises, we believe that, as the statutory regulator in respect of market abuse, the FSA's view should be the determining factor; however, we also believe that disagreement is most unlikely in such cases.'[3]

7.5   THE MARKET CODE

The FSMA defines only the outer limits of what can constitute market abuse. The FSA is required to draw up a COMC, in effect evidential rules, to help determine whether or not behaviour does amount to market abuse[4]. The purpose of the COMC is to allow the FSA the sort of flexibility that the non-statutory Takeover Panel has to adapt and amend its rules in the face of rapidly changing market practices. Like the Code of Practice in relation to Statements, the COMC may specify behaviour that does and does not amount to market abuse. It may also specify factors that will be taken into account by the FSA when deciding other cases, particularly as it may make different provisions for different persons and circumstances[5].

The exact status of the COMC was much discussed by the Joint Committee[6]. It is to 'give appropriate guidance to those determining whether or not behaviour amounts to market abuse'.[7] The FSMA does create a fourth safe harbour for behaviour which was specified in the then current COMC as 'not amounting to market abuse'. The effectiveness of this safe harbour depends upon whether the COMC is sufficiently specific about what does not constitute market abuse. Otherwise that COMC 'may be *relied* upon so far as it *indicates* whether or not that behaviour should be taken to amount to market abuse'.[8]

---

1   Consultation Paper 59, section 9.
2   FSMA, s 120.
3   Vol 351 HC, 5 June 2000, c 105. The Government were not prepared to carve out an exclusive area of responsibility for the Takeover Panel. Lord Alexander of Weedon, a former chairman of the Takeover Panel, forcibly put the argument against the Government's position, vol 613 HL, 12 June 2000, cc 1377–1380. Lord McIntosh did point out that the Panel itself might have difficulties with Art 6 of the Convention, c 1376. The chairman of the FSA has promised to use the safe harbour power to the full, FSA Press Release 78/2000 reiterated in Consultation Paper 59, para 9.7.
4   FSMA, s 119(1).
5   FSMA, s 119(2) and (3).
6   Joint Committee, First Report, Part VII.
7   FSMA, s 119(1).
8   FSMA, s 122 (emphasis added) The FSA may specify compliance with certain RIE rules which will amount to a safe harbour, Consultation Paper 59, section 8.

It is not entirely clear who is doing the relying. If it is the FSA, this might make behaviour which it has specified as being market abuse almost unarguably market abuse. However, the Economic Secretary has said:

> 'Where someone breaches the code it will not, however, be conclusive that he has committed market abuse. The FSA will have to prove that his behaviour comes within the definition as set out in [the FSMA]. In that case the code will carry evidential weight.'[1]

If the relying is by one of the persons whose behaviour is being challenged, this appears to widen the safe harbours but only if the person can show he consciously relied upon factors in the COMC that suggested that his behaviour was not market abuse.

The FSA has said:

> 'There is assymetry in the Act and the Code in that descriptions of behaviour that, in the opinion of the FSA, amount to market abuse, are not conclusive, whereas descriptions of behaviour that do not amount to market abuse are conclusive.'[2]

Before issuing or altering the COMC, the FSA has to follow the same consultation procedures as for its rules[3]. A first draft Code was produced in a Consultation Paper, but was so controversial that the FSA set up a practitioner group and a group representing RIEs and RCHs to discuss the issue and the Government's amended proposals. A second Consultation Paper taking these into account has now been produced with a redrafted Code[4].

The redrafted COMC is considerably longer and more complex than the first draft. This is partly because it incorporates the underlying provisions of the FSMA, but also because more guidance and examples have been given to try to cut down the number of inquiries the FSA will have to deal with[5]. The COMC concentrates on elucidating the 'regular user test' and the three categories of market abuse, which it refers to as 'misuse of information', 'false and misleading impressions' and 'distortion'.

7.5.1 Regular user test

The COMC treats the statutory test as being based on 'hypothetical' not 'actual' regular users. In other words, the fact that a particular market and its regular users accept behaviour that falls within one of the three categories, does not necessarily excuse the behaviour[6]. However, the FSA accepts that this will be a quite exceptional situation. The rules and normal practices of the markets (including overseas markets) will always be taken into account and will usually be taken as indicating what is legitimate behaviour. The FSA has stressed:

---

1   Standing Committee A, 2 November 1999, col 685.
2   COMC, para 1.1.5.
3   FSMA, s 121; see **6.2.4**.
4   Consultation Paper 10, FSA, June 1998; *Feedback Statement on Responses to CP 10*, FSA June 1999; Consultation Paper 59, FSA July 2000. The redrafted COMC is in Annex A.
5   Consultation Paper 59, Annex C estimates the cost of dealing with each enquiry at about £1,000.
6   COMC, para 1.3. An example of what would now be market abuse that was encouraged by a market was the distortion of London FOX's trading in property futures in 1991.

'In particular, the new market abuse regime is not intended to affect activities which form part of the normal transaction of business on prescribed markets. Such activities will include, amongst others, position-taking, market making, the execution of customer orders and hedging.'[1]

The COMC reiterates that market abuse does not generally require 'any intention or purpose to be present, although the purpose of the behaviour will be a factor when applying the reasonable user test'[2]. Behaviour can be abusive only if it falls below the reasonable user test, but that test does not impose a uniform standard. It varies according to the person's experience, skill and level of knowledge and the markets and investments concerned[3].

7.5.2 Misuse of information

To be misuse of information, four conditions have to be met.

(1) The behaviour must be based on the information, ie the information is a, but not necessarily the, reason for the behaviour[4].

(2) The information must not be generally available. The FSA does not have to show actual or even constructive knowledge of this status on the part of the user, but a list of factors similar to those in the CJA 1993, s 58(2) and (3) is given to determine whether information is objectively available. Information available by diligent research or observation of a public event, even if through lack of resources or opportunity, not available to others, is still deemed to be generally available[5].

(3) The information must be relevant. The COMC does not require information to be specific or precise or indeed price-sensitive, but they are factors that the FSA will consider along with how current and reliable (near to the source) it is and what other information is available. Where 'soft information' about the future is concerned, the significance of the information and its apparent level of certainty will be important. The information does not have to emanate from a source connected to the investments affected, for example it can be official information or information about the supplies of a commodity[6].

(4) The information must be of the type where disclosure on an equal basis would reasonably be expected either because:
   (a) there is a legal or regulatory requirement, for example listing or transparency rules (disclosable information); or
   (b) it is usually publicly announced, for example changes in interest rate or in published credit ratings (announceable information).

Information is disclosable or announceable if it is reasonably clear that it will have to be disclosed or announced at some point in the future, but information based

---

1   Consultation Paper 59, para 6.13.
2   Consultation Paper 59, para 6.14, although purpose has crept back in to a number of the definitions in the three categories under the guise of 'principal rationale'.
3   COMC, para 1.3.3.
4   COMC, para 1.5.5(1).
5   COMC, paras 1.5.5(2), 1.5.6–1.5.9. The observation of the burning factory from the train example is specifically mentioned as not amounting to abuse.
6   COMC, paras 1.5.5(3), 1.5.10–1.5.12. The US Supreme Court has also said when considering the US equivalent of market abuse, Rule 10b–5, that determining the materiality of soft information requires 'balancing of both the indicated probability that the event will occur and the anticipated magnitude of the event', *Basic v Levinson* 485 US 224 (1988) at 238.

merely on research or surveys is never disclosable or announceable[1]. This fourth condition does narrow the scope of the statutory definition. As the FSA has said:

> 'The reality of markets is that it is impossible for every piece of information to be made known on an equal and simultaneous basis to all market participants, and the regular user has no expectation that it should be.'[2]

The FSA has specified four safe harbours in respect of misuse of information.

(1) The deal was required by a legal, regulatory or contractual obligation.
(2) The deal was not based on or influenced by the information, which will be presumed if Chinese wall requirements have been met or in fact:
   (a) the individuals in possession of the information were not involved in the deal; and
   (b) they had no contact with those who were.
(3) The information is trading information (ie that someone intends to deal), unless it is about a possible takeover. Unlike the market information defence under the CJA 1993, Sch 1, the behaviour does not have to be reasonable. Front-running customers' orders (unless part of a possible takeover) will not, therefore, be market abuse, although it will be a breach of the COBS for authorised firms and possibly the crime of insider dealing.
(4) The information is market information about a possible takeover, but the dealing, be it in shares or options, is for or on behalf of the potential offeror and for the *sole* purpose of pursuing the bid. This does not allow dealing aimed at providing financial protection, for example selling a put option that will not lead to delivery of the stock to the potential offeror[3].

Finally, it should be noted that under misuse of information, it is not a defence that the person did not expect a profit to be made (or loss avoided) from the information. As the FSA has pointed out, 'the mischief being prevented is abuse of the market rather than personal gain'[4].

7.5.3 False or misleading impression

The COMC lists four categories of such behaviour:

(1) Artificial transactions – In an attempt to distinguish legitimate hedging or customer order transactions from wash trades and other fictitious transactions, the COMC has had to introduce an amazingly complex definition

---

Exactly how they are balanced off is not so clear, see *SEC Financial Reporting Release No 36* 7 Fed Sec L Rep (CCH) 501 (1989).

1 COMC, paras 1.5.5(4), 1.5.13–1.5.20. Thus mere consideration of, and certainly negotiations over, a merger, takeover or major contract can be 'disclosable' for this purpose, even though under *Listing Rules 9.1–9.5* there is no immediate obligation to disclose.

2 Consultation Paper 59, para 6.24. The FSA is currently taking the robust view that in the commodity derivatives markets, dealers who are suppliers of the underlying commodity will often have an informational advantage which has to be accepted by regular users. It also accepts front-running of research documents and, more controversially, of journalists' newspaper tips, a matter it proposes to leave to the Press Complaints Commission (paras 6.31 and 6.39–6.47).

3 COMC, paras 1.5.21–1.5.29.

4 Consultation Paper 59, para 6.55. However, as one of the conditions to be met is that the behaviour must be based on the information, in practice this may not be significant.

interestingly involving a 'principal rationale' defence. An artificial transaction is where:

'a person knows (or could reasonably be expected to know) that the principal effect of
the transaction (or series of transactions) on the market will be, or is likely to be,
artificially to inflate or depress the apparent supply of, or demand for, or the price of
value of a qualifying investment or relevant product such that a false or misleading
impression is likely to be given to a regular user, unless the principal rationale for the
transaction in question would amount to what a regular user would consider a
legitimate commercial rationale, notwithstanding the principal effect of the
transaction.'[1]

(2) Disseminating information – Here the abusive behaviour is where:

'a person knows (or could reasonably be expected to know) that the information is
false or misleading and disseminates the information in order to create a false or
misleading impression. (This need not be the sole purpose for disseminating the
information but will be an actuating purpose.)'[2]

This is an odd definition since it is difficult to see how dissemination can be
'in order to create' the impression if the person does not *actually* know that
the information is false or misleading. The problem the FSA is struggling with
is to distinguish between the inevitable passing on of market rumours and
promulgating them to mislead. In the first draft of the COMC, the behaviour
could be abusive only if the person had an interest in the investment. That is
still a factor to be considered but since disinformation may be disseminated
deliberately before an interest is acquired, it has been dropped as a
pre-condition. On the other hand, the positive obligation to take reasonable
care to ensure the accuracy of any information disseminated has been
removed, except in (3) below[3].

(3) Dissemination of information through an accepted channel – Where
information is to be disseminated, for example, through the Stock
Exchange's Regulatory News Service, the person responsible for its submission remains under a positive obligation to take reasonable care to ensure
that it is not false or misleading. Accidental misreporting of transactions or
figures could be market abuse unless the person has taken sufficient care to
try and prevent such mistakes[4].

(4) Course of conduct – The test here is similar to that in (1) above, but covers a
course of conduct other than transactions causing or likely to cause the
impression. Again, there is a principal rationale defence. This heading is
particularly relevant to commodity derivatives markets and the movements of
stocks and transport of the underlying commodity. The purpose of the
conduct and the interest of the person in the investment are relevant factors
that the FSA will consider[5].

The FSA has also specified four safe harbours in respect of false or misleading
impressions:

---

1   COMC, para 1.6.7.
2   COMC, para 1.6.12.
3   Consultation Paper 59, paras 6.62–6.66.
4   COMC, paras 1.6.16–1.6.18.
5   COMC, paras 1.6.19–1.6.22.

(1) certain regular market transactions like bed and breakfasts, arbitrage between different markets and stock-lending;
(2) reporting legitimate transactions as required by law or regulation;
(3) cross-trades under the rules of LIFFE or the International Petroleum Exchange; and
(4) maintaining price quotations under The Stock Exchange rules.

7.5.4 Distortion

As the FSA itself has admitted:

'it is difficult to define when a market is distorted . . . It is fair to say that regular users of a particular market will be familiar with the normal range or price movements that can be expected in certain market conditions, given the market's structure and the products traded on it. The FSA considers that a price is likely to be distorted when price movements deviate from such expected norms. Such a distortion may not be due to any particular course of behaviour by a market participant but may be caused instead by extreme market conditions beyond the control of market users.'[1]

The COMC lists a number of factors that the FSA will consider, but there are two circumstances which the COMC defines as abusive distortion:

(1) Abusive squeezes – where a person distorts prices by:
   (a) having a significant influence over supply or delivery mechanisms of a investment or the underlying product; and
   (b) directly or indirectly holds positions under which he expects delivery of them.
   It is the combination that can be abusive. Having a significant influence over supply, indeed extracting 'super-normal' profits thereby, is not of itself abusive. The abuse is cornering the market and then using the position to distort[2].
(2) Price-positioning – where a person enters into a transaction or a series of transactions where a, although not necessarily the, purpose is to move the price materially higher or lower, ie ramping prices of an investment or an relevant index.

The only safe harbour specified by the FSA in relation to distortion is following the rules of the London Metal Exchange as laid down in 'Market Aberrations: The Way Forward'.[3]

Given the complexity of all of these definitions of market abuse and the many factors that will be taken into account, the FSA is considering how it will be able to give informal oral advice as situations arise. It also recognises that there is a need for practitioner training in this area, although the changes created by the market abuse regime are going to be greater for non-practitioners who, until now, have only had to be concerned with the rather ineffective criminal sanctions[4].

---

1   Consultation Paper 59, para 6.72.
2   COMC, paras 1.7.8–1.7.10.
3   COMC, paras 1.7.11–1.7.15.
4   Consultation Paper 59, para 1.12 and sections 10 and 11.

7.6   MONEY LAUNDERING

Money earnt illicitly from drugs and other crimes is almost inevitably going to find itself laundered through the financial markets. One of the FSA's statutory objectives is the reduction of financial crime, ie 'reducing the extent to which it is possible for a business carried on by a regulated person . . . to be used for a purpose connected with . . . any offence involving . . . handling the proceeds of crime'.[1] To deal with this, the FSA can:

(1)   prosecute for breaches of the Money Laundering Regulations 1993[2] (ML Regulations); and
(2)   make rules in relation to the prevention and detection of money laundering[3].

The latter will make explicit obligations on firms to counter money laundering as part of their continuing 'fitness and propriety' and form the basis for enforcement procedures should they breach them.

Financial services firms are already subject to a number of anti-money-laundering obligations. Bank supervisors follow the Basle Committee's 1998 Statement on the subject and the UK has implemented the Money Laundering Directive through the ML Regulations which in turn have spawned the Joint Money Laundering Steering Group (JMLSG), industry representatives that have produced guidance notes on the Regulations[4].

As the FSA's objective extends beyond authorised firms, the FSA will review anti-money-laundering arrangements when considering the recognition of RIEs and RCHs and the continuing appropriateness of DPB regulation of professional firms. In relation to authorised firms, the FSA could have incorporated anti-money-laundering provisions in its rules on Systems and Controls. Instead, it has drafted a separate set of detailed Money Laundering Rules (ML Rules). These rules take the ML Regulations and the JMLSG's guidance notes as a starting point, but the scope cannot be the same. For example, the ML Rules cannot apply to bureaux de change which the ML Regulations do, but could apply to general insurance which the ML Regulations do not. In fact, the FSA has decided not to extend the detailed regime, for the time being, to general insurance or purely protective long-term insurance[5].

The ML Rules require:

(1)   the appointment of an appropriately senior individual as the Money Laundering Reporting Officer (MLRO), who must be an FSA-approved individual for that function[6];
(2)   procedures to establish the identity of a new customer, although where there is no suspicion, dealings can commence before identification procedures have been completed[7];

---

1   FSMA, s 6(1) and (3).
2   SI 1993/1933.
3   FSMA, ss 146 and 402(1)(b).
4   *Prevention of Criminal Use of the Banking System for the Purpose of Money-Laundering*, Basle Committee December 1998; 1991/308/EEC.
5   ML Rules, r 1.
6   ML Rules, rr 2 and 8.1.
7   ML Rules, r 3.

(3) arrangements for training staff on their responsibilities and for identifying and reporting any suspicious transactions to the MLRO[1];

(4) the MLRO to review such transactions and promptly report any that still seem suspicious to the National Criminal Intelligence Service[2]; and

(5) the MLRO to be responsible for considering FSA reports on suspicious jurisdictions, to monitor staff training and make annual reports to the firm's managers[3].

The ML Rules are simplified for sole traders and do not apply to the non-mainstream financial services activities of authorised professional firms that can be engaged in by exempt professional firms[4]. A breach of the ML Rules can be the basis of civil actions for damages by private persons[5].

---

1   ML Rules, rr 4, 5.1 and 7.
2   ML Rules, rr 5.2 and 6.
3   ML Rules, r 8.
4   ML Rules, r 9; see **11.4**.
5   FSMA, s 150.

Chapter 8

COMPLAINTS AND COMPENSATION

8.1 BACKGROUND

Before the 1986 Act, to the extent that financial services regulation was the responsibility of the DTI, it was subject to the jurisdiction of the Parliamentary Commissioner for Administration (PCA). It was the PCA who forced the DTI to pay £150m compensation to investors in Barlow Clowes for failing as the licensing authority to close the firm down. The 1986 Act largely took the area out of the PCA's remit. Instead, there were eight different schemes for resolving disputes between financial services firms and their retail customers:

(1) the Banking Ombudsman;
(2) the Building Societies Ombudsman;
(3) the Investment Ombudsman;
(4) the Insurance Ombudsman;
(5) the Personal Insurance Arbitration Service;
(6) the PIA Ombudsman Bureau;
(7) the SFA Complaints Bureau and Arbitration Service; and
(8) the FSA Direct Regulation Unit and Independent Investigator.

Some of the schemes were compulsory, some voluntary; some statutory and some based on contract; some were set up by the industry and some by the regulator; some were ombudsmen and some arbitrators. Eligibility criteria, limits on awards, terms of reference, procedures and funding all differed.

The compensation position was hardly less complicated, consisting of five principal schemes offering three types of cover for customers of defaulting institutions:

(1) the Deposit Protection Scheme and Building Societies Protection Scheme for deposit-takers, both offering to *all depositors* 90% of deposits up to a maximum payment of £18,000;
(2) the Investors Compensation Scheme (ICS) for investment firms offering to *non-professional investors* 100% up to £30,000 and 90% for the next £20,000 of assets lost and other losses caused by a breach of the COBS rules[1]; and
(3) the Policyholders Protection Scheme and Friendly Societies Protection Scheme for insurers, both offering to *all insured* 100% of compulsory insurance claims and 90% of long-term insurance claims, and generally to *individuals* 90% of other general insurance claims, without any upper limit and including the arrangement of continuing cover[2].

These differences in eligibility for, and cover of, the schemes in part reflected real differences between the three types of business. Also the Government's freedom

---

1 RPBs run their own schemes offering at least the cover offered by the ICS and the FSA runs a less generous scheme to cover the money markets.
2 For further details, see Consultation Paper 24, FSA, June 1999, App I.

to change the cover offered is constrained in the first two cases by European Directives[1].

From the first announcement of the creation of a 'Super Regulator', it was clear that the Government intended there to be one Financial Services Ombudsman and one Financial Services Compensation Scheme to reduce consumer confusion when trying to complain or seek compensation.

8.1.1   A single complaints system

The Financial Services Ombudsman is modelled on the Pensions Ombudsman and rather than being an Ombudsman like the PCA, is more a cross between a statutory tribunal and a European investigating magistrate. To ensure that this service was up and running when the FSMA came into force, the FSA put out a Consultation Paper in December 1997 followed by a Policy Statement in August 1998[2]. It created a single point for public enquiries by January 1999, incorporated the Financial Ombudsman Scheme Limited (FOS) appointed its board in February 1999 and worked to bring together the staffs of seven out of the eight existing schemes, although they will have only been employed by the FOS and in one premises since April 2000. Further Joint Consultation Papers were put out by the FSA and FOS in November 1999 and May 2000[3].

The original Consultation Paper pointed to a number of difficult issues in setting up a single scheme. The basic concept was to include all firms that would require FSA authorisation. However, such firms also conduct businesses not requiring authorisation, some of them closely related to regulated activities, such as acting as financial intermediaries, but many far removed such as giving legal advice. If the scheme were to cover at least all financial services businesses, what about unauthorised firms that conduct the same businesses? Some firms, for example stockbrokers, would be subject to the FSA's prudential and COBS rules, but others, for example commercial banks and general insurers, only to the FSA's prudential rules supplemented by voluntary codes. Unless the scheme considered behaviour against these codes, it would be difficult to make complaints about these firms. There again, some European firms doing passported business into the UK would not be authorised by the FSA, but would be subject to its COBS rules. Should they be included in the scheme?

On the other side of the arrangements, who should be eligible to use the scheme beyond individual private customers, for example unincorporated associations, small partnerships, companies, trusts, executors and receivers? What should be the maximum limit on any award and should it extend to distress and inconvenience? How should the scheme, probably the largest in the world, be funded[4]? There were also procedural and structural issues. How could the scheme be binding on authorised firms but not on claimants, remain quick and flexible

---

1   DGD and ICD, although in practice the cover in the UK has been more generous than the minimum set down by these Directives, see **2.2**.

2   Consultation Paper 4, FSA December 1997; Policy Statement *Consumer Complaints: the new Financial Services Ombudsman scheme,* FSA, August 1998.

3   Consultation Paper 33, FSA, November 1999; Consultation Paper 49, FSA, May 2000. The Personal Insurance Arbitration Service will remain separate until the FSA comes into force.

4   It has approximately 20 ombudsmen and 400 employees dealing with 200,000 enquiries and costing £20m a year.

and yet meet the requirements of Art 6(1) of the European Convention on Human Rights? How should its awards be enforced? How independent of both the FSA and its Compensation Scheme should the Ombudsman be?

8.1.2 A single compensation system

Unlike the Ombudsman, a single compensation scheme will not be created until the FSMA comes into force. Nevertheless, to ensure no delay, the FSA has issued two Consultation Papers on the subject, incorporated the Financial Services Compensation Scheme Limited (FSCS) as the scheme manager and appointed its board in February 2000[1].

In the first paper, the FSA noted that there were two separate justifications for compensation schemes:

(1) the narrow purpose of promoting consumer confidence in deposit-takers in order to reduce the systemic risk created by the failure of one or two such institutions causing a run on the others; and
(2) the wider purpose of protecting consumers who are not in a position to make an informed assessment of the riskiness of any institution that they entrust their money to (even though they may legally or practically be required to do so, for example having motor insurance or a current account).

Although the FSA espoused the second justification, it rejected the concept of a complete safety net for all consumers because of the moral hazard problem that creates[2]. 'Co-insurance' was, to varying degrees, a feature of all the old schemes and the FSA intends to maintain this feature in the new scheme[3]. Within that framework, the key issue has then been how far a single compensation scheme should standardise the eligibility of, and cover offered to, depositors, users of investment services and the insured.

To retain any differences between these three groups requires the creation of three sub-schemes. Should those sub-schemes then be funded separately by their members and should there be any further sub-divisions within the sub-schemes to limit any cross-subsidisation between contribution groups? Such sub-divisions have been a feature of the ICS, so that IMRO, SFA and PIA members have only paid for the defaults of their fellow members. Within the PIA, as it has been IFAs that have been responsible for most of the defaults, those losses have been met as to 15% by fellow IFAs and 85% by product providers who transact business via IFAs. This has eliminated cross-subsidy by product providers who sell directly to customers[4].

---

1   Consultation Paper 5, FSA, December 1997 and Consultation Paper 24; FSA Press Release 29/2000.
2   Consultation Paper 5, para 11; in any case, the ICD requires compensation to be given beyond the banking field.
3   Co-insurance is where consumers eligible to claim compensation still bear a share of their loss.
4   Consultation Paper 24, App H. Pension misselling claims have devastated the IFA sector.

8.2   THE OMBUDSMAN

The FSA is required to set up a company (in fact the FOS) to operate a scheme capable of resolving certain disputes 'quickly and with minimum formality'.[1] The FOS must be administered independently of the FSA by a board of directors appointed and dismissed by the FSA, subject in the case of the chairman, to Treasury approval. The FOS must appoint a Chief Ombudsman and a panel of ombudsmen on appropriate terms to ensure their independence[2]. However, this independence will be limited because the FSA is responsible for the scope and basic structure of the compulsory jurisdiction and even though the FOS is responsible for its procedural rules and the whole of the voluntary jurisdiction, these are generally subject to FSA approval. It is this interdependence that has produced Joint Consultation Papers from the FSA and FOS. Like the FSA, the FOS and its staff are not Crown servants, but have an immunity from liability in damages and also privilege from defamation actions[3].

Before the beginning of each financial year, the FOS must prepare an annual budget for approval by the FSA explaining its income and expenditure and distinguishing between its compulsory and voluntary jurisdictions (in practice two different schemes). The FOS must also prepare and publish an annual report for the FSA on the discharge of its functions, including a report from the Chief Ombudsman, again distinguishing between the compulsory and voluntary jurisdictions[4]. Although not specified by the Act, the report will be sent to Parliament for the Treasury Select Committee to consider and/or be submitted to Parliament as part of the FSA's annual report[5].

8.2.1   Compulsory and voluntary schemes

As has already been said, there will in effect be two schemes: a compulsory one, the scope of which will be determined by the FSA, and a voluntary one, determined by the FOS, but subject to FSA approval. The compulsory scheme is confined to authorised firms but may cover not just their regulated activities, but such non-regulated financial services as are specified by the FSA. By contrast, authorised *and* unauthorised firms conducting non-regulated financial services specified by the FOS, may join the voluntary scheme[6].

Complaints can be considered only if they are:

---

1   FSMA, s 225 and Sch 17, para 2.
2   FSMA, Sch 17, paras 3–5. The board has been appointed with Andreas Whittam Smith as Chairman. The current Insurance Ombudsman, Walter Merricks, has been appointed Chief Ombudsman and he has established a system of three principal ombudsmen, one for each of banking, insurance and investment services. The independence of the scheme is limited to its administration as the FSA has to set or consent to all its rules (see below).
3   Consultation Paper 33; FSMA, Sch 17, paras 6, 10 and 11. The immunity is in respect of the compulsory jurisdiction and does not cover bad faith and breaches of the Convention. However, the FOS will put the same immunity into the standard terms of its voluntary scheme.
4   FSMA, Sch 17, paras 7 and 9. The FSA can specify any particular contents.
5   Consultation Paper 33, para 1.13 and the Economic Secretary in Standing Committee A, 30 November 1999, c 1054.
6   Draft FOS Rules have been prepared jointly by the FSA and FOS and appear in Consultation Paper 49, Annex A.

(1) made by eligible complainants, defined by the FSA for the compulsory scheme and by the FOS for the voluntary scheme;

(2) in respect of acts or omissions covered at that time by the scheme; and

(3) in the case of the voluntary scheme, only if the respondent firm was (and remains at the time of the complaint) a member of the scheme.

However, in the case of the voluntary scheme, the FOS may require or allow the acts or omissions of current participants that occurred before the new scheme was set up to be dealt with under it. This allows for cases that could have been dealt with under a previous scheme to be dealt with under the voluntary scheme. Curiously, there does not seem to be a similar provision for the compulsory scheme if it is extended to deal with cases formerly dealt with under the voluntary scheme[1].

Under the compulsory scheme, the Ombudsman is to determine the case as he thinks 'fair and reasonable in all the circumstances' rather than confining himself to breaches of any principles, rules or guidance. One original suggestion was even wider, requiring the Ombudsman to determine all claims in favour of the claimant unless there was a good reason to do otherwise. The current wording still allows for consideration of non-statutory obligations such as the banks' voluntary code and other issues like maladministration. The Ombudsman must provide the parties with a reasoned written statement of his determination. If the complainant accepts it, the determination is final and binding on the respondent firm; but unless he does so within a specified time, the complainant will be taken to have rejected it and he remains free to take the issue to court. By contrast, the respondent firm has no right of appeal, even on a matter of law, and can only challenge a determination through judicial review of the Ombudsman's reasoned statement. This 'one-sided' arrangement will require the scheme to provide the respondent firm with some opportunity for a fair and public hearing in order to meet Art 6(1) of the Convention[2].

The Ombudsman's determination may include an award of damages up to a maximum set by the FSA under the scheme, although the Ombudsman can recommend that a firm pay more voluntarily. The FSA may also permit damages to be awarded for non-financial losses (eg damages for unnecessary delay or distress). Damages and any interest awarded may be enforced as though they had been awarded by a court. The Ombudsman may also direct the firm to take any other just and appropriate steps (whether or not a court would have had that power) and these may be enforced by injunction[3]. Apart from the cap on any compulsory award of damages, the Ombudsman has wider powers than a court and the scheme should prove an attractive forum for plaintiffs.

In order to pay for establishing and running the compulsory scheme, the FSA can impose levies on authorised firms. In addition, the FOS may charge respondent firms, but not complainants, fees for dealing with a case and may also make cost rules, allowing the Ombudsman to award costs orders against respondent firms.

---

1   FSMA, ss 226 and 227.

2   FSMA, s 228. This controversial arrangement was discussed by the Joint Committee, First Report, paras 292–296 and in Standing Committee A, 30 November 1999, cc 1059–1066, and vol 344 HC, 9 February 2000, cc 321–324. Although registered in England and Wales, the FOS can have actions brought against it in Scotland and Northern Ireland: FSMA, s 415.

3   FSMA, s 229 and Sch 17, para 16.

Cost rules may not allow awards against complainants except to meet the FOS's costs where a complainant's conduct was improper or unreasonable or was responsible for an unreasonable delay. The costs rules, like the other scheme rules made by the FOS, still require the FSA's approval[1]. These cost arrangements are a considerable victory for consumer organisations against authorised firms, which will now have to bear all their own costs, even if the complaint is frivolous or vexatious[2].

For the compulsory scheme, it is the FSA that must stipulate the time-limit in which complaints may be made to the FOS, although it can allow the Ombudsman to extend the limit. It can also require:

(1) a complainant to have given the firm a reasonable opportunity to deal with the complaint before referring it to the FOS; and

(2) require authorised firms to establish appropriate complaints resolution procedures[3].

Guidance and procedural rules for dealing with complaints are otherwise left to the FOS to decide, although draft rules must be published, representations considered and the FSA's consent obtained before such scheme rules may be made. These rules may deal with what matters may be considered, for how long and by whom. They may also determine when cases can be dismissed without consideration, including a power to transfer a complaint, with the complainant's consent, to another body[4].

Complaints under the voluntary scheme are to be dealt with under standard terms fixed by the FOS and approved by the FSA. These can include rules on levies and costs. These terms may allow the FOS to sub-contract part of the operation to another suitable scheme operator. The procedural rules for the voluntary scheme are left to the FOS. Again, these must be published in draft form and representations considered, but the FSA has only to be kept informed of changes rather than approve them. The split of responsibilities between the FSA and the FOS is somewhat confusing and, in practice, the two will have to work closely together[5].

Finally, to operate both schemes effectively, the Ombudsman has the power to demand specified information or documents from any party to the complaint, if he considers it necessary for the determination of the complaint. Liens are protected and, as elsewhere, legal privilege has to be respected. Otherwise, failure to comply with a demand from the FOS without reasonable excuse can, on application to the High Court, be treated as contempt[6].

---

1   FSMA, ss 230, 234 and Sch 17, para 15. These one-sided arrangements are designed to ensure that a complainant should not be deterred by any fear of picking up a respondent firm's costs, Standing Committee A, 30 November 1999, c 1068.

2   The original draft Bill allowed respondent firms to claim their costs in these circumstances.

3   FSMA, Sch 17, paras 12 and 13; FOS Rules, Chapter 3.

4   FSMA, Sch 17, paras 8 and 14; FOS Rules, Chapter 4.

5   FSMA, Sch 17, paras 17–22. The FOS has an exemption as a quasi-regulator from the Data Protection Act 1998, FSMA, s 233.

6   FSMA, ss 231, 232 and 413.

8.2.2 The approach of the Financial Services Authority and the Financial Ombudsman Scheme Limited

The FSA and FOS have agreed that the definition of eligible complainant should be the same for the compulsory and voluntary schemes and should extend beyond private individuals to small businesses, which are major complainants under the current banking scheme, but are not covered by the current insurance scheme. The proposal is to cover companies, unincorporated bodies and partnerships with an annual turnover of less than £1 million, whether they have a contract with the respondent firm or are merely third party beneficiaries, for example an insured person for whose benefit the policy was taken out, guarantors of mortgages, traders relying on a cheque guarantee card, recipients of bank references, and holders of units or shares in collective investment schemes or investment trusts[1]. This makes small businesses' complaints about general insurance subject to a complaints scheme for the first time.

Although the compulsory scheme will apply to all authorised firms, a few, such as listed money market institutions and reinsurers, do not deal with individuals and small businesses and, thus, should never be a respondent firm. They will be able to apply for an exemption from funding the scheme, although they will still be subject to it if they break the terms of their permission which then gives rise to an eligible complaint. Professional firms that are authorised in respect of their financial services activities and Lloyd's in respect of personal policyholders (but not Lloyd's members) will be subject to it, but inwardly passported firms conducting business on a service basis only (ie with no permanent place of business in the UK) will not be[2]. This raises the whole issue of the territorial coverage of the schemes. It is not defined in the FSMA and the FSA and the FOS propose to cover complaints about business conducted with UK and overseas customers by firms or branches in the UK (including inwardly passported branches)[3].

In considering the scope of the compulsory scheme, the FSA looked at three options. The scheme could cover authorised firms':

(1) regulated activities only;
(2) regulated activities and other financial services activities covered by existing schemes[4]; or
(3) all their financial services activities.

Although the FSA's goal is option (3), it would bring in large areas of unregulated business not currently covered, such as general insurance broking and advice

---

1 Intermediate customers and market counterparties are not eligible, so small authorised firms will not be eligible, unless their claim is in respect of dealings outside their permitted activities. All firms with turnovers between £1m and £5m are also not eligible, even though they may be private customers. Consultation Paper 49 and FOS Rules, Chapter 2 dropped the five-employee test and clarified that in the case of charities the test was £1m income and in the case of trusts £1m net assets.

2 Consultation Paper 33, paras 3.20–3.32, although Consultation Paper 49, paras 1.36 and 1.37 clarified that complaints about authorised professional firms principally concerning matters other then their mainstream financial services activities are excluded.

3 Consultation Paper 33, para 3.61, confirmed by Consultation Paper 49, para 1.46.

4 The non-regulated services covered are principally mortgage and certain other lending and general insurance services provided by banks and building societies.

conducted by authorised firms, which the scheme may not be able to cope with on day one. Also, it might lead to those businesses being hived off into separate subsidiaries to escape the scheme as such subsidiaries could remain unauthorised. What is proposed is to go for option (2) as far as the compulsory scheme is concerned, but to offer option (3) over time to authorised firms under the voluntary scheme.

In the case of unauthorised firms, the voluntary scheme will principally cover advice on mortgage lending. This will not be a major activity, as most of such advice is given by authorised firms and already falls within the compulsory scheme under option (2). Eventually it is hoped to expand the voluntary scheme to cover all the activities of mortgage and general insurance intermediaries. The voluntary scheme will follow the same rules and procedures as the compulsory one and members will have to give six months' notice if they wish to withdraw[1].

The FSA and FOS propose a £100,000 maximum per claim for both schemes to be reviewed every three years, but with no specific limit within that for awards in respect of distress, delay or inconvenience.

8.2.3   Procedures and funding

The FSA and FOS hope to keep the procedures informal. The FOS's staff will:

(1)   check that the respondent firm has been given a reasonable opportunity to consider the complaint;
(2)   check that the complaint is within their jurisdiction but, to meet the requirements of the European Convention, any dispute on this will be referred to the Ombudsman;
(3)   consider the information supplied by the parties and the possibility of conciliation (this currently disposes of more than 75% of cases), but if that is not possible,
(4)   institute a full investigation and produce an initial decision, which if rejected by either party,
(5)   refer it to the Ombudsman for a determination that will include any oral hearing, with legal representation, required to meet the requirements of the European Convention[2].

As the schemes are free to complainants, it will be necessary to have rules to dismiss complaints without consideration of their merits. Complaints will be dismissed if they involve no material loss, distress or inconvenience or if they have been, are being or should be dealt with by a court. Rather more controversially, other complaints that may be dismissed are those that concern:

(1)   exercising judgment to refuse credit or insurance;
(2)   investment performance;
(3)   employment and health and safety issues; and
(4)   exercising discretion under a will or private trust unless there has been maladministration or unfair treatment.

Ombudsmen will be left a wide discretion on what evidence may be accepted and what time-limits may be set. Any complaints about the operation (but not the

---

1   Consultation Paper 49, paras 1.32 and 1.44; FOS Rules, Chapter 4.
2   Consultation Paper 33, paras 4.3–4.10; FOS Rules, Chapter 3.

determinations) of the schemes will be heard by an independent Complaints Commissioner[1].

Initially, it is not proposed to make any costs rules and therefore any cost orders other than to meet a complainant's reasonable costs. So, the £20 million annual cost of the FOS will have to be borne by the industry. For the compulsory scheme, this may be done by:

(1) the FSA raising a levy on authorised firms; or

(2) the FOS charging respondent firms fees for processing each complaint[2].

It is proposed to use each in equal measure, the levy linked to the amount of business done by the firm that falls within the scheme, but an Industry Funding Group is considering the exact details. On the basis of £20 million total costs and 30,000 completed cases, this suggests a flat-rate fee of £300–400 per complaint to raise £10 million. The levy for the other £10 million was originally going to be linked to the FSA's regulatory charge for each firm, but as the compulsory scheme will cover unregulated as well as regulated business, this is being reconsidered. The FOS proposes to follow a similar funding arrangement for the voluntary scheme[3].

To keep the number of complaints to the FOS down, the FSA will make rules requiring firms subject to the compulsory scheme to have appropriate in-house procedures for resolving any variety of complaint. The FOS will impose similar requirements on firms joining the voluntary scheme[4]. There is some concern at the rising number of complaints being handled by the current schemes and the FSA intends to monitor the performance of authorised firms in this area. Therefore, firms will need to record and make a bi-annual report to the FSA on complaints of material loss, distress or inconvenience[5].

Timely resolution of complaints is vital. The FSA proposes that most complaints should be dealt with by firms within four weeks, with a possible four-week extension in difficult cases. Firms must then inform the complainant of the FOS procedure and, if he is dissatisfied, he will normally have six months in which to refer the matter to the FOS. Overall, a complaint should be made within six years of the act or omission giving rise to the complaint or within three years of when the complainant ought to have become aware of the grounds of complaint[6].

---

1   Consultation Paper 33, paras 4.1–4.30 confirmed by Consultation Paper 49, para 1.58.

2   FSMA, s 234 and Sch 17, para 15; Consultation Paper 49, para 1.57.

3   Consultation Paper 33, Section 5.

4   FSMA, Sch 17, para 13; Consultation Paper 33, para 6.2. British Standard 8600:1999 offers guidance on complaints management.

5   FOS Rules, Chapter 1; Consultation Paper 49, paras 1.70 and 1.83. Firms will have six months' grace from the rules coming in force before having to make reports. They will also have until January 2002 to amend stationery to draw attention to membership of the FOS.

6   Consultation Paper 33, paras 6.23–6.26. Records should be kept for six years, Consultation Paper 49, para 1.85. The Financial Secretary did admit that if an Ombudsman proceedings dragged on for any reason, a complainant would have to institute protective court proceedings to avoid them becoming statute-barred: vol 351 HC, 5 June 2000, c 121.

8.3   COMPENSATION SCHEME

The FSA is required to set up a company as the scheme manager (in fact the FSCS), and is responsible for the appointment and dismissal of its directors, subject in the case of the chairman, to Treasury approval. Nevertheless, these directors are to be appointed on terms that 'secure their independence' from the FSA 'in the operation of the compensation scheme'. Like the FSA and the FOS, the scheme manager and its staff are not Crown servants, but have a statutory immunity from liability in damages[1]. The argument for such an immunity seems less obvious for the scheme manager than for the FSA, particularly as the current compensation schemes do not enjoy it. The justification given by the Financial Secretary was:

> 'In some cases, consumers might be able to recover some, perhaps all, of their investments from the authorised business once the winding-up action is complete. That will take time, and while the winding-up is happening consumers could suffer hardship. The compensation scheme deals with that by enabling payments to be made at an early stage. To do so, the scheme manager must be able to take decisions about whether to make payments when full information about the circumstances of the failure might not be available. If the scheme manager needed to be constantly alert to the possibility of legal action . . . it could seriously interfere with the swift processing of claims.'[2]

As with the FOS, exactly how much independence the FSCS may have is not clear. It is the FSA that has the duty to set the rules establishing the scheme, which must provide the FSCS with the powers:

(1)   to assess and pay compensation within those rules for claims in respect of regulated activities of defaulting firms that were then authorised or appointed representatives; and

(2)   to raise levies on authorised persons to meet that compensation and other expenses (which may include the costs of establishing the scheme).

The scheme does not cover unauthorised firms illegitimately conducting regulated activities, but does cover authorised firms conducting regulated activities beyond their permission. The FSA's rules must 'take account of the desirability . . . so far as practicable' that the levies are raised from the class of authorised persons giving rise to the compensation claims – that is some duty to restrict cross-subsidisation. The amount of the levies that may be used to cover management expenses (ie costs in addition to paying compensation or ensuring the continuation of insurance cover) also has to be fixed[3]. The FSCS must make an annual report to the FSA in terms laid down by the FSA, although the FSCS can determine how it is published. Although not required by the Act, it is expected that the report will also be sent to Parliament for the Treasury Select Committee to consider[4].

---

1   FSMA, ss 212 and 222. Again, the immunity does not extend to bad faith or breaches of the Convention. The FSCS is also treated as a quasi-regulator for the purposes of the Data Protection Act 1998: FSMA, s 233. Although registered in England and Wales, the FSCS can have actions brought against it in Scotland and Northern Ireland: FSMA, s 415.

2   Standing Committee A, 30 November 1999, c 1022.

3   FSMA, ss 213 and 223. Levies are allowable expenses for tax purposes and any refunds are trading receipts: FSMA, s 411.

4   FSMA, s 218. Standing Committee A, 30 November 1999, c 1010.

The FSCS has the power to call for specified information or documents from a defaulting firm or any other person knowingly involved in an act or omission giving rise to a claim provided the FSCS considers it necessary for the fair determination of any claims made or expected to be made against the firm. There are also powers to inspect documents in the hands of liquidators, administrators and trustees in bankruptcy (and to a more limited extent the Official Receiver). Failure to comply with a request from the FSCS without reasonable excuse can, on application to the High Court, be treated as contempt[1].

The rest of Part XIV is permissive in nature and 'those clauses provide a framework of what might be expected in the rules'[2]. They allow the rules to determine when a firm is in default (which does not require actual insolvency), which types of claim will be covered up to what maximum, whether interim payments can be made, how and when levies will be made or repaid, whether there will be different funds. In the case of insurance, the rules may provide for organising the continuance of insurance cover and, indeed, the early intervention of the FSCS in the affairs of an insurer in 'financial difficulties' in order to protect 'eligible policyholders' (both terms to be defined by the rules)[3]. The Financial Secretary's explanation given for these extraordinary powers over insurers is that:

> 'The general view is that it would be in everyone's interest if it were possible to avoid liquidation, not to facilitate the companies carrying on as normal, but to ensure that there is a more orderly run-off and, if possible, that the liabilities for existing policies are honoured. I understand from the latest accounts of the Policyholders Protection Board that about 14 companies are currently on the books. The problems faced by policyholders will be minimised as will the liability on the compensation scheme.'[4]

Finally, the rules (and the UK insolvency rules) may provide for the FSCS, where it has paid out compensation, in effect, to step into the shoes of any claimants and make a single claim and be fully involved in any administration, winding-up or bankruptcy proceedings[5].

Although all FSA-authorised firms (and their appointed representatives) must participate in the scheme, inwardly passported credit institutions and investment firms will not be involved unless:

(1) they have an additional permission in which case the scheme applies only to those activities; or
(2) they have voluntarily joined the scheme in respect of some or all of their passported activities, in which case the scheme acts as a top-up to their home State scheme(s)[6].

---

1   FSMA, ss 219–221, 224 and 413. Liens and legal privilege are still protected. The reason that documents in the hands of liquidators etc may only be inspected is to pass the costs of photocopying to the FSCS!
2   Financial Secretary in Standing Committee A, 30 November 1999, c 998.
3   FSMA, ss 214, 216 and 217.
4   Standing Committee A, 30 November 1999, c 1006. An interesting question arises as to whether organising such interventions themselves is not a regulated activity requiring authorisation, but it is probably not being conducted as a business: Standing Committee A, 30 November 1999, c 1008.
5   FSMA, s 215.
6   FSMA, ss 213(10) and 214(5). The Treasury will require inwardly passported insurance businesses to join as some EEA countries do not have compensation schemes that cover them: Lord Bach, vol 613 HL, 18 May 2000, c 426.

Compensation has traditionally been more generous in the UK than elsewhere in the EEA, and is above the minimum levels required by the European Directives. Indeed, there is no European-wide requirement to compensate for defaulting insurers. As was pointed out in the Standing Committee, by looking at the extent to which inwardly passported credit institutions and investment firms voluntarily join the UK scheme:

> 'We will find out whether EEA firms consider that their credibility will be enhanced by joining our scheme. The strongest, single argument for the compensation scheme from the point of view of the firm is that it will benefit from the extra custom that will come from people who are reassured by the scheme's existence. If the scheme does not have that effect, EEA firms will not join it. If it does, they will vote with their feet and join it. Is not that the clearest proof of whether we have got the provision roughly right?'[1]

Even if an inwardly passported firm does belong to the UK scheme and defaults, its customers will have to seek the base compensation from the home State scheme. This can be avoided if the home State scheme (or government guarantee) allows the UK scheme to make the claim, in which case the UK scheme could make a whole or partial payment. Still, the UK scheme will not be able to intervene in the overseas insolvency proceedings to protect its position as it will be able to do in UK proceedings[2].

8.3.1   The proposals of the Financial Services Authority

Although the FSA has to work within the FSMA requirement that there should be a single compensation scheme, its approach has been conservative. As it has said:

> 'The FSA has been very conscious that we are not starting with a blank piece of paper. Many of the provisions in the existing schemes relating to the amounts of compensation to be paid and who can claim compensation have developed to reflect the features of their particular sector of the financial services industry. These different sectoral approaches have each been the subject of debate over the years and now represent workable approaches which are broadly acceptable to all interested parties.
>
> We have therefore decided not to seek harmonisation for harmonisation's sake. Our priority has been to seek to maintain the levels of consumer protection offered by the existing schemes and only propose to change these arrangements where we believe it is clearly justifiable.'[3]

Behind the FSCS and its single board, there will be three sub-schemes (for deposits, insurance and other investment business) each with separate management committees[4]. Authorised firms will participate in the sub-scheme that covers their business and, thus, some will have to belong to more than one sub-scheme[5]. In effect, the three existing types of scheme are being retained. Nevertheless, there are some changes proposed to three key features of these sub-schemes: eligibility, quantum and funding.

---

1   Andrew Tyrie MP in Standing Committee A, 30 November 1999, c 996.
2   FSMA, s 214(6). Standing Committee A, 30 November 1999, c 1000.
3   Consultation Paper 24, paras 2.2 and 2.3. Draft rules appear in Consultation Paper 58, FSA, July 2000.
4   Consultation Paper 24, Section 7.
5   Consultation Paper 24, Section 2.

The definition of 'eligible claimant' for the three sub-schemes will not be the same as the definition of 'eligible complainant' for the FOS and will differ between the sub-schemes. As with the FOS, individuals will generally qualify for all three. The DGD and ICD, however, require deposit and investor (but not insurance) compensation to extend to many businesses as well.

Deposits – The FSA proposes to follow all the exclusions permitted under the DGD, other than possibly extending cover to non-EEA currencies. This will reduce the current coverage by excluding not only deposits made by banks and financial institutions, but also larger companies (but not partnerships), that is those that do not meet at least two of: balance sheet total and turnover below 2.5 million Euros and fewer than 50 employees[1].

Investment business – Again, the proposal is to follow the exclusions permitted by the ICD. Unfortunately, these are not identical to those for deposits. Here, other financial institutions, larger companies *and* some partnerships may be excluded. The sub-scheme will not follow the ICD in one important respect. It will cover not just loss of money and assets, but also claims for negligence and breaches of FSA rules. This will generally leave the current coverage as it is.

Insurance – The geographical limitation introduced by the Policyholders Protection Act 1997 will be retained, but it is proposed to extend the cover provided to small companies but exclude large partnerships for non-compulsory general insurance. Otherwise, the cover will remain the same[2]. Lloyd's policyholders will not be covered by this scheme, but will continue to rely on Lloyd's own Central Fund[3].

On the issues of quantum, the FSA is considering extending deposit and non-compulsory insurance cover to 100% of the first £2,000 and raising the individual limits in the deposit sub-scheme from £18,000 to £31,700 but keeping the investment business limit at £48,000 and insurance unlimited[4].

Finally, on funding, the FSA is considering one contribution group for the deposit scheme (although a separate group for building societies could be retained), separate general and long-term insurance groups for the insurance scheme, and up to five separate groups for the investment business scheme. This is to retain the current arrangements (including the special funding for IFA defaults) so that cross-subsidisation is limited. One outstanding issue is whether authorised solicitors should remain part of their existing schemes which have been more generous than the investment business sub-scheme. The FSA considered and rejected the idea of levying a initial fee for any firm joining the sub-schemes[5]. Just as integrated firms may belong to more than one of the three sub-schemes, they may have to pay levies under more than one of these contribution groups. The base costs of running the FSCS would be spread across all the contribution groups.

---

1   Consultation Paper 58, Annex B, Chapter 4 details eligibility. This reduction in cover is supported by the Cruickshank Reports.

2   Consultation Paper 33, Section 3. The geographical limit is broadly UK and EEA risks assumed by UK authorised insurers, plus UK risks assumed by EEA authorised insurers, see **2.2.1**.

3   *Response Paper on Consultation Paper 16*, FSA, June 1999; see **11.3**.

4   Consultation Paper 58, Annex B, Chapter 10. Quantum will be reviewed after three years.

5   Consultation Paper 33, Sections 5 and 6. The FSCS will have about 150 staff and is expected to cost over £70 m per annum, including compensation payments.

Chapter 9

ENFORCEMENT (1): DISCIPLINING THE UNAUTHORISED, THE AUTHORISED AND THE APPROVED

9.1 BACKGROUND

The FSA's enforcement activities fall into two principal areas: 'policing the perimeter' and 'disciplining authorised firms and approved individuals'. It is also responsible for enforcing the new 'market misconduct' regime (see **10.4**).

Policing the perimeter is dealing with unauthorised persons who, by definition, will not have been:

(1) subjected to the FSA tests as to suitability and financial soundness;
(2) supervised or disciplined by the FSA;
(3) party to the Ombudsman Scheme; or
(4) covered by the Compensation Scheme.

Now that there is a single perimeter for regulated activities, the FSA has become the principal enforcer against unauthorised deposit-taking and insurance as well as other investment business. In its Consultation Paper on this, the FSA made it clear that to maintain public confidence in the UK financial system and to protect consumers from the activities of unauthorised firms, it would be one of its primary functions to use both its civil and criminal powers against such businesses. Of course, it would not just rely on those powers, but would also deal with enquiries from and provide information to:

(1) firms about regulated activities and the possible need for authorisation to avoid inadvertent illegal activities; and
(2) consumers about the authorisation status of the firms that they might be considering dealing with[1].

With the latter in mind, the FSA proposes to make its record of authorised firms available on the Internet. However, the Internet and its use in the provision of financial services will make the whole process of policing the perimeter an increasingly difficult task, requiring large resources and considerable co-operation with regulators around the globe to close down rogue operators.

By contrast, in its Consultation Paper on enforcement against authorised firms and approved persons, the FSA stressed that:

> 'Pro-active supervision and monitoring of Authorised Firms is central to promoting compliance and many instances of non-compliance will be satisfactorily addressed through dialogue with firms and without resort to formal enforcement action ... However ... the effective use of the FSA's formal powers ... will also play an important role in buttressing the FSA's pursuit of its statutory objectives.'[2]

---

1   Consultation Paper 25, FSA, July 1999, Chapter 1.
2   Consultation Paper 17, FSA, December 1998, para 4.

The impression is given that enforcement powers here are seen as a supplementary weapon to the primary measures of supervision and monitoring and this is borne out to some extent by enforcement not appearing as one of the FSA's statutory objectives.

9.2   POLICING THE PERIMETER

As has already been seen, the FSMA principally sets the boundary between lawful and unlawful financial services activities with two provisions:

(1) a general prohibition against carrying on, or purporting to carry on, any regulated activity unless an authorised person, or exempt in relation to that activity; and
(2) a restriction on engaging in financial promotion unless an authorised person, the communication is approved by an authorised person or an exemption applies[1].

The FSA is charged with policing this perimeter and for that purpose has now been given the power to prosecute in addition to its existing powers to institute civil enforcement proceedings, to prohibit individuals from involvement with regulated activities and to undertake any necessary investigations[2].

9.2.1   Prosecutions

There are, in particular, four offences associated with policing the perimeter:

(1) contravention of the general prohibition which is punishable by an unlimited fine and up to two years in prison (there is a defence of having taken all reasonable precautions and exercised all due diligence to avoid committing the offences)[3];
(2) contravention of the restriction on financial promotion which again is punishable by an unlimited fine and up to two years in prison (there is a due diligence defence and a defence of reasonably believing the communication was prepared or approved by an authorised person)[4];
(3) making false claims or otherwise holding oneself out to be authorised or exempt (this is punishable with up to a level 5 fine and six months in prison subject again to a due diligence defence)[5]; and

---

1   FSMA, ss 19 and 21. For the extent of regulated activities and the exemptions to financial promotions, see **4.3**.
2   To the extent that the FSA cannot recover all its costs in policing the perimeter, these are borne by the regulated community. Therefore, giving the FSA powers to prosecute may be a sly way of transferring costs to the industry that were previously borne by the taxpayer. The FSA has been able to prosecute under BA 1987 but has only done so once, *FSA Annual Report 1999/2000*, p 39.
3   FSMA, s 23.
4   FSMA, s 25.
5   FSMA, ss 24 and 333, which extends the crime to false claims of exempt professional firm status. This could cover just having a misleading name (eg including 'bank' in an unauthorised firm's title) and is probably a strict liability offence, cf *Wings v Ellis* [1985] AC 272 on the Trade Descriptions Act 1968. The fine can be multiplied by the number of days offending material was on public display.

(4) making false or misleading statements to induce investment agreements, punishable with an unlimited fine and up to seven years in prison[1].

As with any other offences under the FSMA, if it is committed by a body corporate or partnership, the directors, partners, managers, chief executive, company secretary and any other individuals with significant control over, or involvement in, the management also commit the crime if the firm has committed it through their consent, connivance or negligence[2].

The FSA has the power, subject to any conditions the Treasury may impose, to bring prosecutions for any of these offences in England, Wales and Northern Ireland, but not in Scotland where all criminal prosecutions are a matter for the Lord Advocate. Where it does have the power, the FSA still shares it with the Secretary of State, the Crown Prosecution Service (DPP in Northern Ireland) and the Serious Fraud Office with whom it will have to liaise[3].

To ensure a consistent approach, the FSA has said that it will follow the Code for Crown Prosecutors, which requires them to consider:

(1) whether there is sufficient evidence to provide a realistic prospect of conviction; and
(2) whether, having regard to the seriousness of the offence and all the circumstances, prosecution is in the public interest.

If the second test is in doubt but the offender admits the offence, a caution may be given instead[4].

9.2.2   Civil enforcement

In addition to these new powers to prosecute, the FSA can still seek civil intervention where there have been contraventions of the general prohibition. It can ask a court for:

(1) injunctions against likely or continuing breaches, orders to remedy such breaches and freezing orders against likely disposals of or dealings in assets[5];
(2) restitution orders for profits obtained, or losses suffered by others, from such breaches that can be distributed to those that have been affected[6]; and
(3) compulsory administration, bankruptcy or winding-up orders for inability to pay debts or, in the last case, merely because it would be just and equitable[7].

Making contraventions, rather than the offences of contravening, the principal trigger for civil enforcement avoids issues of criminal proof and any defences. The FSA can also seek injunctions, remedial orders and restitution, but not insolvency orders, for contraventions of the restriction on financial promotion and any other

---

1   FSMA, s 397. For details of this offence, see **7.2**.
2   FSMA, ss 400 and 422. Actions against unincorporated associations are to be brought as though they were bodies corporate: FSMA, s 403.
3   FSMA, s 401.
4   Consultation Paper 25, Chapter 5; the Treasury could formally impose this Code on the FSA under FSMA, s 401(5) and (6).
5   FSMA, s 380.
6   FSMA, s 382.
7   FSMA, ss 359(1)(c), 367(1)(c) and 372(1) and (7)(b).

offences which it could prosecute, including, of course, the four associated offences mentioned above[1].

Courts can make remedial orders, not just against those contravening the general prohibition or restriction on financial promotion (or committing the associated offences), but also 'any other person who appears to have been knowingly concerned in the contravention'. Freezing and restitution orders can be made against anyone who has 'been knowingly concerned in the contravention'.[2] In addition to these statutory powers, the FSA has *locus standi* to apply for common-law interlocutory relief, such as freezing orders (formerly *Mareva* injunctions), without offering security for costs[3]. Under the equivalent powers in the 1986 Act, the FSA opened over 600 cases into possible breaches of the perimeter in 1998/99. Some were referred to the DTI or the police for further investigation. Detailed investigations were carried out by the FSA into 123 cases and civil enforcement actions were started in 11[4].

As the principal purpose of all of these powers is the protection of the consumer rather than punishment, and the orders have to be obtained from a court, no difficulties should arise with the Convention. The remaining civil power, to prohibit an individual from all or any particular involvement with authorised or exempt persons, is more problematic. Such an order can be issued by the FSA itself against any individuals not considered 'fit and proper' to conduct all or some regulated activities, including those found to be in breach of the general prohibition. However, as it is as likely to be used against the employees and associates of authorised persons, it is dealt with below[5].

9.3   DISCIPLINING THE AUTHORISED AND APPROVED

In an ideal world, the pre-vetting and subsequent supervision of authorised persons should limit the need for disciplinary actions. However, as the FSA has emphasised, its objective of maintaining market confidence does not imply aiming to prevent all collapses or lapses in conduct. Its supervisory regime will have to concentrate on the risks that have a higher impact and higher probability of arising. The implementation of a single risk-based approach for use across all sectors, markets and firms is one of the FSA's first priorities and disciplinary action is viewed as just one of many regulatory tools[6].

Nevertheless, with up to 15,000 authorised firms and over 150,000 approved individuals, disciplinary action will become a significant FSA function, inherited from all the previous regulators. The FSA has the power to bring prosecutions against the authorised and approved just as it can against the non-authorised, not

---

1   FSMA, ss 380(6) and 382(9).
2   FSMA, ss 380(2) and (3) and 382(1); this included the lawyers who advised in *SIB v Pantell SA (No 2)* [1993] 1 All ER 134, but restitutionary orders will only be awarded against such accessories if they are also being sought against the primary offenders: *SIB v Scandex Capital Management* [1998] 1 WLR 712. Restitutory orders are examined in greater detail below.
3   *SIB v Pantell* [1990] Ch 426; *SIB v Lloyd Wright* [1993] 4 All ER 210.
4   Consultation Paper 25, para 2.14.
5   FSMA, s 56, based on 1986 Act, s 59.
6   For a description of the FSA's overall approach, see *A new regulator for the new millennium*, FSA, January 2000.

just for offences under the FSMA (eg misleading the FSA), but also systems offences under the money laundering regulations and the crime of insider dealing[1]. However, widespread use of criminal prosecution might prove counter-productive if it were to lead to a reluctance on the part of authorised firms and approved individuals to co-operate. It is expected that all but the most serious matters will be dealt with by the disciplinary machinery of the FSA and the nature of these disciplinary proceedings has been adapted to try and meet the requirements of Art 6(1) of the Convention[2].

In disciplining authorised firms, the FSA itself has five principal weapons:

(1) public reprimand for contravening requirements imposed under the FSMA[3];
(2) fining for the same[4];
(3) restitutionary orders for the same[5];
(4) varying or cancelling a permission to carry on one or more regulated activities in certain specified circumstances[6]; and
(5) withdrawing authorisation[7].

The last of these is really an automatic consequence of a firm no longer having permission to conduct any regulated activities (whether because of the FSA's intervention or at the request of the firm). The FSA can retain an empty permission if there are good reasons for doing so, but the FSA cannot fine a firm whose authorisation is about to be withdrawn[8].

The FSA may also discipline approved persons. The FSA has said repeatedly that it generally will pursue disciplinary actions against firms rather than individuals. However, it does consider directors and senior managers to be in a special position, responsible for ensuring their firm's compliance with regulatory requirements[9]. Where the firm has failed to comply, it may be appropriate to take disciplinary action against the individual responsible for that activity, but:

> 'Disciplinary action will only be taken if an individual is personally culpable: that is where the breach was deliberate; or where the individual's standard of behaviour was below that which the FSA could reasonably expect from an individual carrying out that particular controlled function.'[10]

In disciplining approved individuals, the FSA has four principal weapons:

---

1   FSMA, ss 398, 401 and 402; Money Laundering Regulations 1993, SI 1993/1933: CJA 1993, Part V.
2   Joint Committee, First Report, Part VI. Even offences under the money laundering regulations and the CJA 1993, when committed by authorised firms or approved individuals, are more likely to be dealt with under money laundering rules (FSMA, s 146), and market abuse (FSMA, Part VIII).
3   FSMA, s 205.
4   FSMA, s 206.
5   FSMA, s 384.
6   FSMA, s 45.
7   FSMA, s 33.
8   FSMA, ss 33, 45(3) and 206(2).
9   See **5.3.2** and **6.5.1**.
10   FSMA, s 66(1)(b); Consultation Paper 17, paras 88 and 90; Consultation Paper 26, para 13. This view was strengthened in *High level standards for firms and individuals*, paras 2.14 and 2.15 which propose fully objective tests.

(1) public reprimand for failing to comply with Statements or being knowingly concerned in a contravention of requirements under the FSMA by the firm that sought their approval;
(2) fining for the same[1];
(3) withdrawing approval if the person is no longer fit and proper to conduct the controlled functions in question[2]; and
(4) prohibiting an individual from all or particular involvement with regulated activities[3].

The Government rejected specifying the criminal burden of proof for disciplinary proceedings, leaving it for the Tribunal to determine 'according to the nature, severity and circumstances of the case'. Even if, as seems likely, these disciplinary powers are viewed as civil rather than criminal, the Convention still requires there to be a fair, public hearing before an independent tribunal[4]. This is met by fairly standard procedures laid down, with slight variations, at different points throughout the FSMA.

9.3.1   Disciplinary and supervisory procedures

Much of the FSMA outlines the various procedures the FSA must adopt when considering decisions in respect of specific persons, which, in all but one case, may be referred by them to the Tribunal[5]. The procedures apply to disciplining:

(1) authorised firms and approved individuals;
(2) inwardly passported and informally passported firms;
(3) authorised and recognised CISs;
(4) actuaries and auditors of authorised firms and CISs;
(5) exempt professional firms and ex-Lloyd's members;
(6) listed organisations, their sponsors and directors; and
(7) anyone involved in market abuse.

There are also procedures applying to the FSA's refusal (in whole or in part) to grant, vary, or in some cases cancel, various authorisations, permissions, requirements, approvals, directions and listings[6].

In a late effort to rationalise all these procedures and perhaps reduce the chances of challenges under the Convention to the more clearly disciplinary cases, the Government created a distinction between disciplinary actions subject to the full protections contained in the FSMA and other actions with lesser protections. The Government spokesman introducing the amendments said:

---

1   FSMA, s 66.
2   FSMA, s 63.
3   FSMA, s 56, formerly 1986 Act, s 59.
4   Standing Committee A, 28 October 1999, cc 594 and 596; Lord McIntosh confirmed that the Government expected a sliding scale to be applied to the burden of proof: vol 612 HL, 18 April 2000, c 628. Article 6(1) of the Convention could require legal aid and full disclosure of evidence to be available for all these proceedings; see **2.4**.
5   FSMA, s 298. Exchanges and clearing houses may not refer issues over recognitions or directions to the Tribunal; see **11.2.3**. Requests for guidance are not subject to any formal procedures; see **6.2.4**.
6   FSMA, ss 53, 54, 55, 57, 58, 62, 63, 67, 78, 88, 89, 92, 126, 127, 197, 200, 207, 208, 245, 249, 252, 255, 259–261, 265, 268, 271, 276, 280, 282, 321, 331, 345, 385 and 386 and Sch 3, Part III.

'First there will be disciplinary type decisions such as decisions to impose a penalty or make a public statement about misconduct ... For this category, there is no particular urgency for the decision to take effect. Accordingly, the warning notice and decision notice procedures ... will apply in full ... For these disciplinary decisions there will be a right of access to the evidence relied on and to evidence considered by the FSA which might undermine its case. The decision will come into effect only when the full procedure, including any judicial stages, is complete ...

We intend that the benefit of this same procedure should also be extended to certain types of case which, although not truly disciplinary in nature, involve particularly serious action by the FSA. This will include decisions by the FSA to cancel all permission (and therefore authorisation) under Part IV, to withdraw approval or make a prohibition order under Part V, and other similar types of action in relation to collective investment schemes under Part XVII, the professions under Part XX and auditors and actuaries under Part XXII. It will also cover cases where the FSA proposes to order restitution under Part XXIII.'[1]

Out of the seven disciplinary areas referred to above, the full disciplinary procedures do not cover the FSA's own initiatives to:

(1) vary the permission of authorised firms (which includes imposing requirements);
(2) intervene against inwardly passported and informally passported firms;
(3) suspend or discontinue listings;
(4) issue directions against authorised and recognised CISs; and
(5) issue directions against ex-Lloyd's members[2].

The Government spokesman said of these supervisory decisions:

'Although these decisions can have a considerable impact on the persons concerned, their main objective is to ensure that consumers are properly protected. A more flexible procedure is therefore required which will allow the FSA's decision to take effect with the urgency require by the circumstances ... In some cases it will be necessary for the decision to take effect immediately, but we will ensure that the FSA cannot set any date that comes into its head. Instead, we propose that the date would have to be reasonable having regard to the harm that might be done if the requirement did not take effect then.

The subject of [this] supervisory type decision would enjoy the rights ... to know the reasons for the decision, to make representations and to refer the matter to the tribunal. However, the rights to evidence will not apply. That is because these decisions will often be relatively routine. Full criminal style rights of access would be excessively bureaucratic and would seriously undermine the ability of the regulator to regulate responsibly and effectively.'[3]

This leaves the FSA's refusals to grant, vary or cancel various matters. Here the Government has proposed procedures following the pattern of the disciplinary procedures, but without all the protections. Of these rejection procedures, it was said:

---

1   Lord McIntosh, vol 611 HL, 21 March 2000, cc 169 and 170, in effect discussing FSMA, ss 392 and 394, which cover ss 54, 57, 63, 67, 88, 89, 92, 126, 127, 207, 208, 249, 255, 280, 331, 345, 385 and 386.
2   FSMA, s 395(13).
3   Lord McIntosh, vol 611 HL, 21 March 2000, c 170.

'Where applications are refused, granted only in part or granted subject to requirements, the applicant should be entitled to receive a warning notice setting out the reasons for the decision, the standard opportunity to make representations, a decision notice and the right to refer the matter to the tribunal if still aggrieved by the decision. However, we do not consider that it is appropriate or necessary for the right to access to evidence to apply in this category of case. Pending completion of the procedures, the FSA's decision will stand. That will ensure that the applicant can benefit from the permission or approval to the extent that it has been granted, while also ensuring that unfit applicants cannot carry on as if their applications had been granted while the judicial process runs its course.'[1]

In the Government's first category where the full disciplinary procedures apply, those procedures fall into the following five stages.

(1) If the FSA is minded to take any action, it must first issue a written warning notice to the individual or firm, detailing the proposed order (including the amount of any proposed fine) and the reasons for it. It must also inform the defendant of his right to see the material the FSA has relied on and any other which it considered or obtained in connection with the matter and which might, in the FSA's opinion, undermine its position. The defendant must be given at least 28 days to make representations to the FSA (which period the FSA may extend)[2].

(2) The FSA must then decide, within a reasonable period, if it is to proceed with or vary the proposal and a written decision notice must be sent informing the defendant of either the discontinuance of the action or the reasons for taking it, of the right to see any material and of the right and the procedure to refer the matter to the Tribunal. A decision notice may not be based on a different disciplinary action from the warning notice[3].

(3) If the defendant still disputes the order, he may refer the matter to the Tribunal, normally within 28 days, which will consider all the relevant facts and evidence, make a determination and issue appropriate directions to the FSA. During this period, the FSA may still negotiate a different decision notice with the defendant (without the defendant losing the right to refer the matter to the Tribunal) or discontinue the action[4].

(4) The defendant may appeal the Tribunal decision to the Court of Appeal (or Court of Session) and thence to the House of Lords, but only with leave and on a point of law[5].

---

1   Lord McIntosh, vol 611 HL, 21 March 2000, c 171.
2   FSMA, ss 387, 392 and 394. The FSA may exclude:
    (1)   purely comparative material from other cases and material intercepted under warrant or indicating the existence of such a warrant; and
    (2)   material on the grounds of legal privilege, public interest, lack of materiality or a third party's commercial interests, although in these cases it must inform the defendant that it has done so and why.
    Exclusions may still be open to challenge under the Convention following cases such as *Rowe and Davis v United Kingdom* Case 28901/95 (16 February 2000 unreported).
3   FSMA, ss 388, 389, 392 and 394. On the last point, Lord Bach said, 'A proposed financial penalty under Part XIV may be reduced or replaced with a public statement, but the authority cannot move from say, a warning notice that proposes disciplinary action under Part XIV for a breach of rules to a decision notice which raises allegations of market abuse under Part VII': vol 611, 30 March 2000, c 1025.
4   FSMA, ss 133, 388(3)–(5) and 389. For details of the Tribunal, see **3.5**.
5   FSMA, s 137.

(5) The FSA may not implement a decision notice until the matter is no longer open to referral or appeal. Once that is the case, the FSA must issue a final notice setting out in detail the terms of the decision, be it a reprimand, fine or other action. It must give a defendant at least 14 days notice to pay a fine, which if unpaid, is a civil debt[1].

While a decision remains open to referral or appeal, neither the FSA nor, curiously, the defendant may publish any information about the matter and the decision may not come into effect. When a decision does come into effect, the FSA must not publish information if it would be unfair to the defendant or prejudicial to consumers' interests. If the action has been discontinued, the FSA may still publish appropriate information with the defendant's and any affected third party's consent[2]; for any third party who, in the opinion of the FSA, is prejudicially identified in a notice, must be sent a copy of the notice and all subsequent notices. He must be given the right to see the FSA's materials, make representations and refer the prejudicial reference to the Tribunal in the same way as the defendant. He may also refer any alleged failure to send him a copy of a prejudicial notice[3]. The danger of a third party being prejudiced is increased by the considerable jurisprudence requiring full reasons to be given for any decisions, including any necessary findings of facts[4]. If a reprimand is eventually published, that also must be sent to any third party[5].

In the Government's second and third categories where less exacting procedures apply, a defendant does not have a right to the FSA's materials (although full reasons must be given for the proposed action), and third parties have no right to be notified of prejudicial references or to participate in the procedures[6]. Otherwise, for rejection decisions, the procedures are the same as for disciplinary decisions.

The procedures for supervisory decisions are different because of the need on occasion for the FSA to act quickly in order to protect consumers.

(1) If the FSA is minded to take action, it must issue written notices to the relevant parties detailing the proposed action and the reasons for it. It must also inform the parties of their rights to make representations within a specified period (which the FSA may extend) and the rights and the procedure to refer the matter to the Tribunal. If the FSA considers that it is necessary, the notice can specify that the action takes effect immediately or from a specified date, but otherwise cannot come into force until the matter can no longer be referred or appealed.

---

1   FSMA, s 390. Copies of public reprimands must be sent to the defendant and anyone else sent the decision notice: FSMA, ss 68 and 209.

2   FSMA, ss 133(9) and 391.

3   FSMA, ss 392–394.

4   FSMA, ss 387(1)(c) and 388(1)(b); *Re Poyser and Mills' Arbitration* [1964] 2 QB 467; *Elliott v Southwark LBC* [1976] 1 WLR 499; *R v Immigration Tribunal, ex p Khan* [1983] QB 790.

5   FSMA, ss 68(1) and 209(1). The Treasury can, by statutory instrument, make regulations allowing documents and notices to be delivered electronically and generally determining effective service: FSMA, s 414.

6   FSMA, s 392.

(2) If, after considering the representations, the FSA upholds, varies or cancels the proposed or implemented action, it must issue further notices. Where the action is upheld, it must inform the parties again of their rights and the procedure for referring the matter to the Tribunal and, where it is varied, all the information in (1) above must be given again[1].

(3) In general, parties may refer a proposed or implemented supervisory action to the Tribunal immediately, without waiting for the FSA to consider any representations[2]. The Tribunal and appeal procedures are otherwise the same as for disciplinary actions.

The FSA is obliged to publish a draft statement of procedures for stages (1) and (2) in respect of all three categories, and consult about them and any later revisions made to them, in the same way as for its complaints procedures[3]. The procedures must ensure that those involved in deciding to issue any notice have not been involved in establishing the evidence on which that decision was based. This arrangement may be overridden where urgent supervisory action needs to be taken, provided the decision to issue the notice is made by a person of a prescribed and suitably senior level. Failure to follow the statement of procedures does not automatically invalidate any decision, but can be taken into account by the Tribunal[4]. This last, rather curious, provision was justified by the Economic Secretary as follows:

> 'We would not want a minor clerical error in the drafting of a notice to be the grounds for re-opening a decision, especially at some future date. Resources would be wasted if the FSA were required to start the procedure again. There would also be a danger that vulnerable consumers could be left at risk in the interim.'[5]

As the distinction between disciplinary and other procedures was only introduced into the FSMA at a late stage, the FSA's original proposals on procedures really only deal with full disciplinary decisions.

9.3.2   Disciplinary proposals of the Financial Services Authority

In most cases, the FSA's supervision staff will initiate disciplinary proceedings, particularly as the FSA expects authorised firms to keep them informed of any problems. However, once disciplinary proceedings are being considered, responsibility for any investigation will pass to the enforcement staff, and normally the firm will be informed of this[6].

The enforcement staff will conduct the investigation and decide whether to take matters further. If the decision is to do so, their recommendation will be considered by an Enforcement Committee, consisting of a full-time chairman employed by the FSA and other members appointed by the FSA, and representing practitioner and public interest. The Committee will decide whether to issue a warning notice and the individual/firm will then have at least 28 days to exercise

---

1   FSMA, ss 53, 78, 197, 259, 268, 282, 321, 391(8) and 395.
2   FSMA, ss 133(1)(a) and 395(13). For supervisory procedures, the 28-day period for referral to the Tribunal runs from the initial or any subsequent notice, unlike for disciplinary or rejection procedures, when it only runs from a decision notice.
3   FSMA, ss 395 and 396; see **3.4.4**.
4   FSMA, s 395(2)–(4), (11) and (12).
5   Standing Committee A, 9 December 1999, c 1226.
6   *Response to Consultation Paper 17*, FSA, July 1999, paras 12–14.

his right to see all the evidence and make written and oral submissions. There will be the opportunity to settle or refer the matter to mediation before the Committee has to decide whether to issue a decision notice. If a decision notice is issued, the individual or firm may accept it or refer the matter to the Tribunal[1]. Rejection procedures and non-urgent supervisory procedures will presumably follow a similar pattern. Urgent interventions by the FSA, however, may be cleared by a suitably senior official without the delay of Enforcement Committee consideration.

The relationship between the Enforcement Committee of the FSA and the Tribunal was summarised by the Joint Committee thus:

> 'The touchstone is the nature of the decision notice issued by the FSA at the end of proceedings before the Enforcement Committee. According to the FSA, this will contain a statement of the Committee's views on the action that the FSA considers appropriate, including any proposed penalty; in that respect, the Enforcement Committee will go further than a prosecuting authority. However, according to the FSA, the notice would embody a conclusion "that there remained a case to answer", rather than a "judicial determination"; if the case went to the Tribunal, the decision notice would not be published. According to the Treasury, "That decision is intended to be an administrative decision, for which the FSA must be accountable alongside its other decisions, and which must be taken in a fair and reasonable manner". If the defendant does not exercise the right to go to the Tribunal, the decision notice will take effect . . . If he does, it will be "set aside", becoming merely "the basis of the FSA's case to be put before the first instance Tribunal".'[2]

Despite the importance attached to the Enforcement Committee, the Government rejected as too prescriptive Opposition proposals to give it a statutory basis in the FSMA[3]. Indeed, by producing an unsatisfactory arrangement to start with, it could be argued the Treasury and the FSA have ended up with an over-elaborate arrangement with potentially a full hearing by an 'internal' Enforcement Committee whose decisions may then be referred by the defendant for a further full hearing by the 'external' Tribunal. FSA staff have no right of appeal to overturn an Enforcement Committee's decision against them.

9.3.3   Prohibition of individuals

The FSA may prohibit anyone from performing any functions in relation to all or some regulated activities carried on by authorised or exempt firms (including professional firms). Thus, a prohibition order attaches to the particular function or functions, irrespective of the contractual arrangement (as a director, employee, contractor, etc) under which they may be performed. It may specify anything between a narrow disqualification based on the type of function or 'employer' through to a general ban from working in the financial services industry. Failure to comply with such an order is an offence, subject to a due diligence defence, punishable with up to a level 5 fine. Authorised and exempt firms may be disciplined and sued for negligently using anyone in breach of a such an order[4]. It should be noted that the FSA has only to specify when a prohibition

---

1   *Response to Consultation Paper 17*, paras 15–19.
2   Joint Committee, First Report, para 198.
3   Vol 612 HL, 9 May 2000, cc 1471 and 1472.
4   FSMA, ss 56 and 71.

order starts, not when it ends, but an individual may at any time apply to vary or revoke an existing prohibition order[1].

In determining the initial width of a prohibition and whether it should later be varied or revoked, the FSA has a wide discretion. It has stated:

> 'In the most serious cases, we may form the view that such an individual is not fit and proper because he has shown a serious lack of probity or general competence. In these cases we will usually seek to prohibit the individual from performing any class of relevant function in relation to any class of regulated activity. However, in less serious cases, we may form a view that an individual is unfit, but that his unfitness arises from a lack of competence in relation to particular functions or particular regulated activities. In such cases it may be appropriate only to seek to prohibit the individual from performing those functions or being involved in those particular regulated activities.'[2]

Likewise in varying or revoking an order, the FSA has highlighted the following relevant factors:

'–   the relative seriousness of the misconduct that resulted in the prohibition;
–   any steps subsequently taken by the individual to remedy that misconduct;
–   evidence as to the person's honesty and competence in the period since the prohibition order was made; and
–   where his unfitness arose from incompetence as opposed to dishonesty or lack of probity, evidence that his unfitness has been remedied, for example by the satisfactory completion of relevant training and the obtaining of relevant qualifications.'[3]

If the FSA is minded to make a prohibition order, it must follow its disciplinary procedures, but only its rejection procedures if it refuses to vary or revoke an existing order[4].

As an alternative to a prohibition order, the FSA can just seek to withdraw an approval, again subject to the disciplinary procedures[5]. Unlike a prohibition, such a withdrawal can be applied to the few cases of approved firms as well as individuals; but it is otherwise not as effective as a prohibition as it will operate only to bar the individual or firm from performing functions that require approval in the first place.

9.3.4   Fines and costs

Although the SROs have had the power to fine their members for breaches of both prudential and conduct of business rules, the FSA has not had such a power either under the 1986 Act or the BA 1987, nor has the Insurance Directorate, the BSC or the FSC. The FSA intends to use the power for breaches of its high-level principles in particular, but not exclusively if they also involve breaches of detailed rules[6]. Detailed rules do not apply directly to approved persons, but if they are 'knowingly

---

1   FSMA, ss 56(7) and 58.
2   Consultation Paper 25, para 6.14.
3   Consultation Paper 25, para 6.18.
4   FSMA, ss 57, 58 and 392. The FSA must keep a public record of prohibited individuals: FSMA, s 347.
5   FSMA, ss 63 and 392. The factors relevant for an approval are dealt with in **5.3.1** and are relevant for prohibitions as well: *Response to Consultation Paper 15*, para 16.
6   Namely PFBs and Statements; *Response to Consultation Paper 17*, para 58.

concerned' in a breach by their authorised firm, they can be publicly reprimanded or fined, but only if 'it is appropriate in all the circumstances'[1]. The FSA will also impose fines against firms for breaches of prudential requirements, provided they do not exacerbate any capital inadequacy and even though in the case of mutuals they will, inevitably, be paid at the expense of the mutuals' customers[2]. To publicly reprimand or fine an authorised firm or approved individual, the FSA must follow its disciplinary procedures[3].

There has been considerable concern about the FSA fining individuals and small firms for breaches of Statements and PFBs which are inevitably expressed at a high level of generality; but as even the Opposition admitted:

> 'The rules for small independent financial advisers need to be in the nature of the 10 Commandments. The disadvantage of such rules is that the FSA must have power to interpret them and to discipline according to that interpretation. One cannot have it both ways.'[4]

In determining the size of any fine, the FSA must have regard to the policy statements it is required to prepare and publish on this subject[5]. The Government did follow the Joint Committee's advice and amended the FSMA so that the FSA, for all its fining policies, must have regard to:

(1) the seriousness of the contravention;
(2) the extent to which it was deliberate or reckless; and
(3) whether the person to be fined is an individual[6].

The FSA had already published a more extensive, albeit non-exhaustive, list of factors which it considers relevant, namely:

> '(1) the nature and seriousness of the misconduct:
>   –   impact of the misconduct on the orderliness of financial markets, including whether public confidence in those markets has been damaged,
>   –   whether significant costs have been imposed on other market users or losses caused to customers,
>   –   whether the misconduct was deliberate or reckless,
>   –   the duration and frequency of breaches,
>   –   whether the misconduct reveals serious/systemic weakness in respect of the management systems or internal controls in relation to all or part of a firm's business;
> (2) the amount of profits accrued or loss avoided:
>   –   a firm or individual should not benefit from his misconduct,
>   –   the level of penalty should act as an incentive to comply with regulatory requirements;
> (3) the size, financial resources and other circumstances of the firm or individual:

---

1   FSMA, s 66(1) and (2). The Economic Secretary confirmed that 'knowingly concerned' did require the individual to 'be aware of the nature of the conduct in which he was involved ... although ... it is not enough for an approved person to claim not to know about FSA rules': Standing Committee A, 28 October 1999, c 591; cf the concept of *scienter* in the USA, *Ernst and Ernst v Hochfelder* 425 US 185 (1976) and *In re Silicon Graphics Inc* 970 F. Supp 746 (1997).
2   *Response to Consultation Paper 17*, para 60.
3   FSMA, ss 67, 207, 208 and 392.
4   Standing Committee A, 25 November 1999, c 965.
5   FSMA, ss 69, 93 and 210. These policy statements and any changes to them, must be subject to the same basic public consultation process as the FSA's complaints procedures: FSMA, ss 70, 94 and 211; see **3.4.4**.
6   FSMA, ss 69(2), 93(2), 124(2) and 210(2).

- whether the firm/individual would be able to pay the level of penalty associated with the particular misconduct or would be in financial difficulties if he did,
- the conduct of the firm/individual in bringing the misconduct to the FSA's attention, that is how quickly, effectively and completely,
- the degree of co-operation shown during the investigation of the breaches,
- any remedial steps taken since the breach was identified, including any steps taken to identify whether customers have suffered loss and to compensate them, and any disciplinary action taken by the firm against staff involved,
- any steps taken to ensure that similar problems do not arise in the future,
- the previous disciplinary record of the firm/individual; and

(4) other relevant factors could include:
- whether the FSA has issued any guidance in relation to the misconduct in question,
- what action the FSA has taken in relation to previous similar cases.'[1]

To meet the obligation not to allow its general costs and expenses to influence its fining policy, the FSA sets its income and expenditure budgets excluding any income from fines or recoveries of costs arising from disciplinary cases and external expenditure incurred in handling all but the most minor cases[2].

9.3.5   Injunctions and restitution

The FSA can seek, in respect of contraventions of any requirement under the FSMA (including market abuse), the ML Regulations and the insider dealing legislation:

(1) injunctions against likely or continuing contraventions, orders to remedy such contraventions and freezing orders against likely disposals of or dealings in assets; and

(2) restitution orders for profits obtained or losses suffered by others from such contraventions that can be distributed to those that have been affected[3].

As in the perimeter cases, being knowingly concerned in a contravention can create a secondary liability, but for market abuse the test is requiring or encouraging another to engage in the behaviour[4].

The High Court can make such remedial orders against *anyone*. As a new alternative, the FSA can make what it considers an appropriate restitutionary award itself, but only against *authorised firms*, subject to the usual disciplinary procedures[5]. This slightly complicated arrangement was explained by the Economic Secretary:

'If the FSA is applying to the courts anyway for an injunction in relation to an authorised person and it believes that that person should pay restitution, it makes

---

1   *Response to Consultation Paper 17*, App 1. A more up-to-date draft has been produced for the factors that will be considered before fining market abuse, see **10.4.1**.

2   FSMA, Sch 1, para 17; FSA *Plan and Budget 2000/01*, Section IV, para 23.

3   FSMA, ss 380–384. This applies even in Scotland, where responsibility for criminal prosecutions remains with the Lord Advocate alone. In most of these cases, the Secretary of State can also seek orders.

4   FSMA, ss 380(2) and (3), 382(1) and 384(1); cf ss 383(1)(b) and 384(2)(b); *SIB v Pantell SA (No 2)* [1993] 1 All ER 134; *SIB v Scandex Capital Management* [1998] 1 WLR 712.

5   FSMA, ss 384–386 and 392. For market abuse, see **10.4**.

sense for the application to the court to cover both the injunction and any restitution. However, where the FSA uses its internal disciplinary procedures in relation to a particular contravention, it makes more sense for it to have a direct power to require restitution to be paid, rather than having to pursue concurrent disciplinary and court-based proceedings in relation to one set of facts. If a reference is then made to the tribunal, it will be appraised of the overall picture and therefore better placed to reach a just decision ... In many ways, securing appropriate consumer redress and discipline in an authorised firm are two sides of the same coin.'[1]

FSA-ordered awards must be paid directly to those who have suffered the loss or to whom the profits are attributable. Court-ordered awards are paid to the FSA, which then distributes it to the parties. Those parties are not precluded from bringing their own proceedings by the FSA bringing a restitutionary claim[2]. Indeed, one can easily imagine a chaotic situation developing in a serious case where small private investors bring complaints to the Ombudsman, major institutional players start their own private actions and the FSA feels bound to launch a restitutionary claim to ensure that anyone else who has lost money can be compensated. The calculation bases of the awards, in theory, could be different in all three cases. If there has been a widespread breach of FSA rules by authorised firms affecting large numbers of private persons, the FSA may ask the Treasury to give it powers to review this past business and to devise an overall compensation scheme[3].

9.3.6 Varying or cancelling a permission

The FSA may intervene to vary or cancel an authorised firm's permission to conduct one or more regulated activities for:

(1) failing (or being likely to fail) to meet a TCA for that activity;
(2) failing to carry on that activity for the previous 12 months; or
(3) the protection of consumers' (or potential consumers') interests in relation to that activity.

If, as a result of a variation, there are no regulated activities for which the firm still has a permission, the empty permission must be cancelled once the FSA is satisfied that it is no longer necessary[4].

Variations may include the imposition of limitations or requirements. The FSA is also entitled to impose or vary a requirement of a permission if a person has acquired a significant control over an authorised firm and the likely effect of this change is uncertain. In the past, such a power has been used regularly by insurance regulators to impose limits on insurers that have been taken over by new and untested owners; but the FSA is not limited to using it in those cases[5].

Where the FSA proposes to intervene and vary a permission, it must follow its supervisory procedures. Thus, if necessary, the variation may take effect immedi-

---

1   Standing Committee A, 7 December 1999, c 1214.
2   FSMA, ss 382(3)–(8), 383(5)–(10) and 384(5) and (6).
3   FSMA, s 404; see **3.4.2**. Such a power would have helped in the pensions misselling scandal. Private persons may include fiduciaries and others prescribed by the Treasury acting for such persons.
4   FSMA, s 45(1) and (2).
5   FSMA, ss 45(3) and (4) and 46; Standing Committee A, 21 October 1999, cc 491 and 492. For the definition of significant control, see **5.2.6**.

ately. However, before cancelling an authorisation, other than at the firm's request, the FSA must follow the full disciplinary procedures[1].

The sort of factors that the FSA will take into account when considering whether to intervene immediately are:

(1) the extent of any loss, risk of loss or other adverse effect on consumers;
(2) the extent to which customer assets appear to be at risk;
(3) the nature and extent of any false or inaccurate information provided by the firm;
(4) the seriousness of any suspected breach of the requirements of the legislation or the FSA's rules and the steps that need to be taken to correct that breach;
(5) the financial resources of the firm;
(6) the risk that the firm's business may be used or has been used for the purposes of facilitating financial crime or laundering the proceeds of crime;
(7) the risk that the firm's conduct or business presents to the financial system and to confidence in the financial system;
(8) the conduct of the firm; and
(9) the impact that the intervention action will have on the firm's business and its customers[2].

The nature of the intervention will vary depending upon the above factors and may include:

(1) restraining the firm from a continuing or a threatened breach of its regulatory requirements;
(2) restricting the firm from engaging in those areas of its business giving rise to the concern;
(3) ensuring that the firm is able to meet its obligations and liabilities to its customers;
(4) safeguarding customer assets held by or to the order of the firm to trustees, where it appears that those assets may be at risk; and
(5) preventing dealings with a firm's or a customer's assets that appear to be being used in connection with financial crime[3].

The FSA has a general power to intervene and restrict disposals and other dealings in the assets of the firm and/or its customers, or transfer customers' assets to a trustee. Where the FSA restricts the disposal or dealings in the assets of the firm and gives notice of this to a third party holding some of them (eg a bank), the third party is freed from any contractual obligation it has to the firm, and is liable to the FSA for any transfer of the assets made thereafter. If the FSA orders assets to be transferred to a trustee, the firm must inform the trustee of the arrangement in writing. It is then a crime punishable by up to a level 5 fine to release those assets without the FSA's consent. Although the firm may order their conversion into other assets, it may not create a valid charge over them. However, the beneficiaries (normally the firm and/or its customers) still retain their interest in the assets[4].

---

1   FSMA, ss 53, 54 and 392.
2   Consultation Paper 17, para 29.
3   Consultation Paper 17, para 31.
4   FSMA, s 48. Although this section only specifies third-party release from contractual obligations, the intent is to release from other obligations such as fiduciary duties: Lord McIntosh, vol 611 HL, 21 March 2000, c 164 and vol 612 HL, 18 April 2000, c 602.

In the final resort, the FSA may in addition, or as an alternative, petition a court:

(1) for a winding-up order, either because the firm is unable to pay its debts or because it is just and equitable;

(2) for injunctions to restrain further contraventions or disposals of assets, breach of which would then be contempt of court; or

(3) for restitution orders, if they would be cost effective in the light of the losses suffered by consumers and the alternative remedies available[1].

When considering any intervention, the FSA may have regard to anyone that might have a relationship with the firm. If the firm is a subsidiary or fellow subsidiary of a firm authorised by another EEA State under one of the FS Directives, it must consult that State's regulator. If the firm itself is authorised by another EEA State and the intervention is in respect of an additional permission granted by the FSA, the FSA must take into account that State's regulator and any relevant Directive or Treaty obligations[2]. This is part of the growing need for international co-operation between regulators in this global market.

9.3.7 Co-operating with overseas regulators

Where the FSA itself has granted a permission to conduct regulated activities in the UK, it may use its powers to vary a permission (including attaching any requirements) not just for breaches of any requirements under the FSMA, but also at the request of, or just to assist, an overseas regulator[3]. In deciding whether to exercise the power, the FSA may generally take into account five matters:

(1) whether there would be any reciprocal assistance;

(2) whether the grounds for intervention would be recognised in the UK;

(3) the seriousness of the case and its importance to the UK;

(4) the public interest; and

(5) whether the overseas regulator will make a cost contribution[4].

However, if the request is from an EEA regulator, the FSA has to consider its European obligations and may not demand a cost contribution[5].

Of course, most firms authorised in another EEA country will be relying upon formal or informal Passports to conduct regulated activities in the UK and, therefore, will not have required any permission from the FSA. Nevertheless, even where this is the case, the FSA may exercise intervention powers to restrict or vary the firm's permission to conduct such activities as if it was authorised by the FSA,

---

1   FSMA, ss 372, 380 and 382 and common-law freezing orders (formerly *Mareva* injunctions). See also *Response to Consultation Paper 17*, para 100.

2   FSMA, ss 49 and 50.

3   FSMA, s 47(1). The Treasury will define what type of overseas regulators, but they are expected to be any that have any responsibilities equivalent to the FSA (as regulator and listing authority), the DTI under the Companies Act and the prosecuting authorities in respect of insider dealing and money laundering; cf FSMA, s 195(4).

4   FSMA, s 47(4) and (5).

5   FSMA, s 47(3) and (6). The Treasury will give guidance to the FSA about which categories of request should be regarded as mandatory.

but in a more limited set of circumstances[1]. Such interventions against EEA authorised firms, may be initiated if:

(1) it is at the request of, or to assist, the home State regulator of a passported business, when the FSA must consider its European obligations;

(2) it is at the request of, or to assist, any corporate or financial services regulator and there is no European obligation, when the FSA may consider, inter alia, the five matters above;

(3) the firm has contravened (or is likely to contravene) an obligation which is the responsibility of the FSA as host State regulator;

(4) the firm has knowingly or recklessly given the FSA materially false or misleading information;

(5) it is desirable to protect the interests of actual or potential customers; or

(6) activities by the firm (or its employees, agents, associates, significant holders or their associates), have, in the opinion of the OFT, rendered it unfit to conduct consumer credit business in the UK[2].

As with interventions against firms authorised by itself, the FSA must follow its supervisory procedures when intervening on behalf of an overseas regulator[3]. However, where an inwardly passported firm is in breach of a requirement which is the responsibility of the FSA as host State regulator ((3) above), the FSA's powers of intervention are constrained by the FS Directives. First, the FSA must usually give written notice to the firm asking it to remedy the situation. If the firm fails to do so in a reasonable time, the FSA must ask its home State regulator to intervene. Only if that fails may the FSA itself intervene. In urgent cases, the FSA can override these arrangements, but it must inform the firm's home State regulator and the European Commission and the latter can order the FSA to retract or vary its intervention if it is not satisfied with it[4].

To meet its obligations under the insurance directives, the FSA has an additional power to seek a court imposed asset freeze on inwardly passported insurance firms. This may only be done where the home State regulator has requested it because the solvency of the firm is in question[5].

The terms of any intervention may be varied or rescinded either by the FSA on its own initiative or at the request of the firm; but the former must follow the FSA's supervisory procedures whereas a refusal of the latter must follow its rejection

---

1   FSMA, ss 193 and 196. This includes restrictions on disposals and other dealings in assets and transferring customers' assets to a trustee: FSMA, s 201. If the firm has an additional permission under Part IV, the FSA may need to exercise powers under that Part as well as this: FSMA, s 47(2).

2   FSMA, ss 194 and 195. Firms inwardly passported under the 2BCD or ISD do not have to be licensed to conduct consumer credit business in the UK: FSMA, Sch 3, para 15. However, the OFT has been given special powers to restrict or prohibit such firms from doing so if they are considered to be unfit. The OFT must give 21 days for representations and there is an appeal procedure to the Secretary of State. Breaches of restrictions or prohibitions are punishable by an unlimited fine: FSMA, ss 203 and 204 and Sch 16.

3   FSMA, s 197.

4   FSMA, s 199.

5   FSMA, s 198; First Non-Life Insurance Directive, Arts 15, 16(3), 17 and 20(5); First Life Insurance Directive, Arts 17, 19, 20 and 24(5).

procedures[1]. Finally, to back these powers of intervention, the FSA may, at the request of an overseas regulator:

(1) order an authorised firm, RIE or RCH to provide any information or document reasonably required by the FSA to perform any of its functions; or
(2) appoint a person to investigate any matter[2].

In deciding whether to use these powers, the FSA must consider the same factors as when it is deciding to intervene on behalf of overseas regulators, including whether it is obliged to act under European obligations. It can order an investigator to allow the involvement of a representative of the overseas regulator in the investigation, but only if:

(1) it is satisfied that the FSMA requirements on confidentiality (which are, in general, EEA-wide obligations) will be upheld by that overseas regulator; and
(2) a statement of its policy with respect to such involvement has been approved by the Treasury and published[3].

9.4   INSOLVENCY

Clearly one of the biggest threats to investors must be firms which conduct regulated activities running into financial difficulties, particularly if those firms hold investors' funds as a principal. As has been seen, many investors will be protected by the Compensation Scheme, but it does not provide total cover and backs only authorised firms, not those contravening the general prohibition. Therefore, the FSA is given considerable powers and rights to intervene in any insolvency proceedings affecting authorised firms, appointed representatives and those that have contravened the general prohibition. The provisions fall into three basic categories:

(1) the powers of the FSA to initiate certain insolvency procedures;
(2) the rights of the FSA to be involved in insolvency procedures initiated by third parties; and
(3) the special provisions dealing with the insolvency of insurers.

Most of these provisions were to be found in the previous legislation, but certain gaps have been filled.

9.4.1   Powers of the Financial Services Authority

As many investors would not have the knowledge or resources to initiate insolvency proceedings, the FSA may petition a court to wind up any company or partnership which is or has been authorised, an appointed representative, or contravening the general prohibition, where:

(1) that firm is in default of any payment as part of a regulated activity;
(2) that firm is otherwise unable to pay its debts; or
(3) it is just and equitable to do so.

---

1   FSMA, s 200.
2   FSMA, s 169(1).
3   FSMA, s 169. Specific European obligations to investigate on behalf of a fellow EEA are to be found in Art 7.1 of the First Banking Directive and Arts 23.3 and 24.2 of the ISD.

If, in cases (1) or (2) above, it would be better for the firm to remain in existence, the FSA may ask the court to place it into administration instead. The FSA may only seek to wind up an inwardly passported or informally passported firm if asked to do so by its home State regulator, because by its very nature, insolvency is a prudential matter[1].

The FSA may now also petition for the bankruptcy of the estate of a sole trader who is or has been authorised or contravening the general prohibition, although as the Economic Secretary explained:

> 'There is no equivalent of the power to wind up a company or partnership on the ground that it is "just and equitable". The reason is that it is not meaningful to apply such a concept to sole traders. A sole trader's business is not legally distinct from the proprietor's personal finances, and thus there is no separate entity to be "wound up". So long as [an individual] can pay his debts, there is no way in which he can be declared bankrupt.'[2]

The FSA also has two intervention powers. It may, like any creditor, apply to the court:

(1)   to set aside transactions made at under value if the insolvent firm has conducted a regulated activity with any victim of the transaction; and
(2)   to intervene if the FSA believes that any voluntary arrangement an authorised firm or sole trader has agreed at a meeting of its creditors (to avoid insolvency) is improper or unfair[3].

9.4.2   The rights of the Financial Services Authority

Just as the FSA has the initiating powers of a creditor where regulated activities and/or authorised businesses have been involved, it is also given most of the rights a creditor has in such cases.

Where any company, partnership or sole trader is (or has been) authorised or contravening the general prohibition (or in the case of a company or partnership, an appointed representative), the FSA has the right to:

(1)   receive any information or proposals sent to creditors;
(2)   attend and speak at any meetings of creditors;
(3)   be represented and heard at any court hearing; and
(4)   ask the court to intervene in a compulsory winding up, administration, receivership or bankruptcy proceedings[4].

The FSA only has these rights in the voluntary winding up of an authorised firm that has not been carrying on long-term insurance business[5]. The FSA also has the

---

1   FSMA, ss 359, 367 and 368.
2   FSMA, s 372; Standing Committee A, 7 December 1999, c 1211.
3   FSMA, ss 356–358 and 375.
4   FSMA, ss 362, 363, 371 and 374.
5   FSMA, s 365. The exclusion of firms contravening the general prohibition is apparently because the FSA has the power under FSMA, s 367 to petition for it to be made a compulsory winding up on the basis that it would be 'just and equitable': Standing Committee A, 7 December 1999, c 1208. Firms carrying on long-term insurance business may not be wound up voluntarily without the FSA's consent anyway: FSMA, s 366.

right to be heard at any court hearing about a voluntary arrangement agreed by an authorised firm or sole trader[1].

The FSA, through its own supervisory activities, should know if an authorised firm or sole trader is the subject of insolvency proceedings, but it may not be aware of such proceedings concerning a business that has not been authorised and is or has been contravening the general prohibition. To that end, administrators, receivers, liquidators and insolvency practitioners are under a duty to report any apparent contraventions of the general prohibition to the FSA without delay[2].

9.4.3   Insurers

Traditionally, the regime covering the insolvency of insurers has differed from the general regime because of the special nature of such companies – many have very long-term liabilities. Until now, it has not been thought appropriate to allow such companies to be put into administration. However, with the consent of the Secretary of State, the Treasury may, and probably will, create a modified form of administration by statutory instrument that could be used by insolvent insurers[3].

Again, until now, insurers carrying on long-term insurance business (eg life assurance) could not be wound up voluntarily. This was to protect those with endowment policies who would lose their terminal bonuses. Now such a insurer may be voluntarily wound up, but *only* with the consent of the FSA. The FSA will ensure that arrangements are in place to protect the position of policyholders. Failure by the directors to inform the FSA that such a winding up has been proposed is an offence punishable with up to a level 5 fine and without the FSA's formal consent, any winding up resolution will be ineffective[4]. Indeed, to keep the FSA generally informed, any person who applies to the court for a provisional liquidator or a compulsory winding up order in respect of any insurer, must formally notify the FSA[5].

There are some special provisions where an insurer is being wound up, including the power to make special insolvency rules for insurers. The Treasury may make regulations to override the usual *pari passu* principle so that, for example, some assets may be ring-fenced to be meet long-term insurance liabilities. The courts, meanwhile, have a sweeping power to refuse a winding up if an order to reduce the value of one or more of the company's contracts can avoid insolvency. Finally, the liquidator of an insurer which conducted long-term business is under a duty to carry on that business 'with a view to its being transferred as a going concern to a person who may lawfully carry out those contracts'. He may allow the terms of the existing contracts to be varied, but he may not effect new contracts. He may apply to the court to appoint a special manager for that business and the court may also appoint an independent investigating actuary[6].

---

1   FSMA, ss 356–358. The arrangements differ slightly in Scotland.
2   FSMA, ss 361, 364, 370 and 373.
3   FSMA, ss 355 and 360. The Treasury may determine how to extend the arrangements to mutuals.
4   FSMA, s 366.
5   FSMA, s 369.
6   FSMA, ss 376–379.

Chapter 10

ENFORCEMENT (2): INVESTIGATIONS, MARKET MISCONDUCT AND PRIVATE ACTIONS

10.1 PERIMETER INVESTIGATIONS

The FSA (or indeed the Secretary of State) may appoint one or more persons to conduct investigations on its behalf, if it 'appears . . . that there are circumstances suggesting' inter alia a breach of the general prohibition or the restriction on financial promotion (including promoting CISs)[1]. By making breach of the prohibition or restriction the trigger, the FSA does not have to consider whether any of the due diligence defences to the related offences could be raised[2].

These investigators will generally be employees of the FSA, but their appointment grants them sweeping powers. They may require *any person*:

(1) to provide information or attend for interview to answer questions;
(2) to produce and explain specified documents or documents of a specified description which appear to the investigators to be relevant; and
(3) to give all reasonable assistance in connection with the investigation[3].

Failure to comply with these requirements without a reasonable excuse may be referred to the High Court and treated as a contempt of court. Destruction, falsification and concealment of documents and provision of false or misleading information are offences punishable with up to two years' imprisonment and an unlimited fine[4]. Indeed, if specified information or documents are not produced, the FSA (or the Secretary of State) can apply to justices for a warrant to enter premises where they are reasonably believed to be, in order to seize them. A pre-emptive warrant may even be obtained where no information or documents have been specified if it is reasonably believed that:

(1) relevant documents or information would not be produced or would be destroyed, removed or tampered with; and
(2) a crime such as making false or misleading statements, providing false or misleading evidence or tampering with evidence is being or has been committed[5].

The FSA does not envisage using these formal investigation powers often:

'However, the powers will fulfil a useful role in those limited cases where members of the unregulated community may be unwilling to co-operate with the FSA or where

---

1   FSMA, s 168(2)(b)(c) and (3). The 'circumstances suggesting' test comes from the 1986 Act, s 177 and the Companies Act 1985, s 432.
2   Standing Committee A, 23 November 1999, c 882. The offence of falsely holding oneself out to be authorised remains a trigger.
3   FSMA, s 173. For the status of this information in subsequent criminal proceedings, see below.
4   FSMA, s 177.
5   FSMA, s 176. By removing the offences of contravening the general prohibition (FSMA, s 23(1)) and the restriction on financial promotion (FSMA, s 25(1)) from the list in FSMA, s 168, the pre-emptive warrant cannot be issued in relation to those, FSMA, s 176(4).

obligations of confidentiality inhibit individuals from providing information on a voluntary basis.'[1]

These powers are part of the more general investigation powers the FSA has in respect of authorised firms and approved individuals.

10.2   INVESTIGATING THE AUTHORISED AND APPROVED

The FSA is not expecting to have to resort to statutory powers of investigation very often when dealing with authorised firms and approved individuals[2]. Nevertheless, the FSA does have considerable reserve powers under Part XI of the FSMA, backed by four court sanctions:

(1) failure to comply with a requirement under Part XI can be referred to the High Court and, unless there was a reasonable excuse, treated as a contempt;
(2) being involved in the suppression or falsification of documents when knowing or suspecting a statutory investigation may be conducted, is punishable by an unlimited fine and up to two years in prison;
(3) knowingly or recklessly providing materially false or misleading information, again is punishable by an unlimited fine and up to two years in prison; and
(4) intentional obstruction of the exercise of a warrant, is punishable by up to a level 5 fine and three months in prison[3].

In explaining Part XI, the Financial Secretary has said that it:

'... represents a synthesis – put together with some care – of the rather confusing array of investigative powers exercised by the existing regulators ... It provides the FSA with a single coherent set of powers, appropriate for a modern regulator dealing with developing markets, bounded by appropriate safeguards, and drawing on the best of what exists at present.'[4]

Nevertheless, the assembling of all the previous regulators' various powers has produced a complicated result. The FSA has six basic powers of investigation:

(1) to order an authorised firm, RIE or RCH to provide any information or document reasonably required by the FSA to perform any of its functions[5];
(2) to order an authorised firm, at its expense, to commission a report from an accountant or other suitably qualified person nominated or approved by the FSA, on any matter that the FSA could have required information or documents under (1) about[6];
(3) to appoint investigators to report on all or any part the business of an authorised firm or appointed representative, including its ownership or control[7];
(4) to order any third party to provide documents in their hands that could otherwise be required to be produced[8];

---

1   *Response to Consultation Paper 25*, para 13.
2   Consultation Paper 17, para 46.
3   FSMA, s 177. There is a defence to (2) of showing there was no intention to conceal facts.
4   Standing Committee A, 23 November 1999, c 843.
5   FSMA, s 165.
6   FSMA, s 166.
7   FSMA, s 167.
8   FSMA, s 175.

(5) to appoint investigators to report on possible contraventions by anyone of certain criminal and regulatory provisions under the FSMA, including insider dealing and market abuse[1]; and

(6) to apply for a warrant to enter premises to secure information[2].

The first three powers, although aimed principally at currently authorised firms, may be used to investigate firms which were previously authorised and any other firms in the group or in partnership with the firm at the relevant time. The breadth of these provisions is necessary to meet the terms of the Post-BCCI Directive. The FSA may also demand information or documents (under (1) above) from an authorised firm's managers, employees, agents or significant shareholders, but may not demand reports about them (under (2) above). On the other hand, the persons compiling reports may demand (on pain of a court injunction) assistance from anyone who has supplied services to the firm being reported upon[3]. The Economic Secretary explained this:

> 'Different circumstances can mean that different forms of practical assistance are required. For example, the person doing the report might need assistance in using the authorised person's computer systems. The important point is that the duty is limited to such assistance as the person doing the report may reasonably require.'[4]

The power to appoint investigators (under (3) above) is shared with the DTI because of that Department's overlapping responsibility for, and experience from, company investigations[5]. The power may be used 'if it appears' to either 'that there is good reason' for doing so (a fairly subjective test)[6]. It also extends to investigating non-regulated as well as regulated activities of currently and formerly authorised firms and appointed representatives, although where they are no longer authorised or appointed, only for the period when they were[7]. The fourth power is a remarkable extension of the rights of the FSA or an investigator to require documents from third parties, although the original proposal to require information as well has been dropped.

The last two powers are not confined to authorised firms and were looked at above. In addition to investigating perimeter breaches, the FSA can appoint investigators 'if it appears ... to [the Authority] that there are circumstances suggesting that' (a very subjective test):

(1) anyone has falsified or destroyed evidence, misled the FSA, auditors or actuaries, made false or misleading statements, engaged in market manipulation, been involved in insider dealing, committed market abuse, breached

---

1 FSMA, s 168.
2 FSMA, s 176.
3 1995/26/EC; FSMA, ss 165(7), (8) and (11), 166(5) and (6) and 167(2) and (4) and Sch 15. This is modelled on the Banking Act 1987, s 39. Significant shareholders are those directly or indirectly with 10% of the shares, votes or equivalent influence: FSMA, s 422.
4 Standing Committee A, 23 November 1999, c 856.
5 Although it could be any Secretary of State as explained by the Economic Secretary in Standing Committee A, 23 November 1999, c 862 .
6 The wording is found in the 1986 Act, s 105, but the Economic Secretary nearly conceded a more objective test in Standing Committee A, 23 November 1999, cc 866 and 870. The wording, however, does contrast with the clearly more objective 'only ... information or documents reasonably required' for the powers under (1): FSMA, s 165(4).
7 FSMA, s 167.

the money laundering regulations, breached the restriction on promoting CISs, etc;

(2) an authorised person has contravened a particular rule or breached the limits on its permission or without reasonable care used a prohibited individual or an non-approved individual in a controlled function;

(3) an individual has broken an existing prohibition order or may not be a fit and proper person to be involved in financial services; or

(4) an approved individual has been knowingly concerned in an authorised firm's breach of a requirement, has failed to comply with a Statement or is otherwise no longer a fit and proper person[1].

The low subjective hurdle the FSA has to meet before launching what could prove reputationally damaging investigations for those subjected to them, was much criticised in the Standing Committee, although there are precedents for such a test in setting up company and insider-dealing investigations[2]. It clearly limits any ability to challenge the FSA's decision by judicial review and does seem to be part of a general campaign to make the FSA 'review-proof'.

Any investigators appointed by the FSA (or the Secretary of State) are not independent of the appointing authority and are subject to their direction – indeed, they can be internal employees. Generally, the appointing authority is supposed to notify any persons under investigation in writing of the investigation and its scope (including any significantly prejudicial changes made later to that scope), but this need not be done if:

(1) the authority believes notification may lead to the investigation being frustrated; or

(2) the investigation is into breaches of the general prohibition or the restriction on financial promotion (including promoting CISs), falsely holding oneself out as authorised, market abuse, insider dealing, false or misleading statements or market manipulation[3].

The justifications offered for the second exception were that:

(1) the behaviour could be committed by unauthorised persons not subject to the FSA's general supervision; and

(2) in such 'market investigations' initially it may not be clear who are suspects.

However, the Economic Secretary did expect notification to be given 'in the majority of cases'.[4]

The exceptional status of these 'market investigations' extends not just to notification, but also to the powers of the investigators. They may, if they consider it relevant (a very subjective test), require *any person*:

(1) to provide information or attend for interview to answer questions;

(2) to produce and explain specified documents or documents of a specified description; and

---

1 FSMA, s 168. The Secretary of State also has the power to appoint investigators to report on anything under (1).

2 Standing Committee A, 23 November 1999, cc 878–893; 1986 Act, s 177 and Companies Act 1985, s 432.

3 FSMA, s 170.

4 Standing Committee A, 23 November 1999, cc 873 and 899.

(3) to give all reasonable assistance in connection with the investigation[1].

In all other cases, investigators must reasonably consider it relevant to the investigation (a more objective test) before they can require:

(1) *any person* to provide documents; but
(2) only *the person under investigation and those connected* to him to provide information and attend for interview[2].

If, however, the investigators are satisfied that it is necessary or expedient (yet another test!), they may still require any *unconnected* person to provide information or attend for interview. The Economic Secretary did not expect unconnected persons to be called often. These new investigation powers, however, should only be able to be used in respect of events after the FSMA comes into force[3].

The FSMA does not stipulate any period for the retention of documents, but the FSA intends to in its rules. Failure to produce any documents can be treated as a contempt of court, but having a reasonable excuse will be a defence[4]. If a document is not produced, the FSA or an investigator can require a statement of where the document is believed to be and the power to produce it extends to any third person in whose possession it is. Any lien survives such production. Banking confidence can be claimed unless:

(1) the bank or its client is the person (or part of the same group as the person) under investigation;
(2) it has consented to the production; or
(3) the investigating authority has specifically required the production[5].

Legal privilege can usually be claimed on the same terms as under PACE. The Economic Secretary, however, did confirm that:

> 'It is possible to waive privilege in respect of one party – in this case, the FSA or the investigator – without waiving it more generally. In other words, as long as the basis of disclosure is made clear, the usual protections for privilege under general law will still apply.'[6]

The problem lies in the practicalities of those revealing documents to the FSA or the investigator making it clear that they are not generally waiving any privilege or confidentiality. This is part of the general problem of confidentiality dealt with below.

---

1   FSMA, ss 168(2) and 173.
2   FSMA, s 171. Those connected include not just the managers, employees agents and significant shareholders of the authorised firm, but of any other firm in the group and of any such firms' bankers, auditors, actuaries or solicitors. Significant shareholders are those directly or indirectly with 10% of the shares, votes or equivalent influence: FSMA, s 422.
3   FSMA, s 172; Standing Committee A, 23 November 1999, c 910; *R v Secretary of State for Trade and Industry, ex p R* [1989] 1 WLR 372.
4   FSMA, s 177(2). The time-limits that the FSA has suggested are:
     (1)   pension fund transfers and opt outs – indefinite
     (2)   all other life and pensions – six years
     (3)   all other business – three years
     Consultation Paper 45a, Part I, para 4.15. Tax and money laundering regulations may impose more onerous requirements.
5   FSMA, s 175.
6   Standing Committee A, 23 November 1999, c 919.

As a final resort, a magistrate can issue a search warrant to the police (subject to PACE provisions) if the FSA, the Secretary of State or an investigator can show that there are reasonable grounds for believing (an objective test) that documents or information:

(1) which have been required but not produced are on the specified premises;
(2) which could be required and may be removed, tampered or destroyed are on the specified premises, which are those of an authorised firm or appointed representative; or
(3) which could be required and may be removed, tampered or destroyed are on the specified premises and an offence of making false or misleading statements, market manipulation, insider dealing, money laundering, breaching a control notice, providing false or misleading evidence or tampering with evidence is being or has been committed.

The documents may be held for up to three months or for the period of any proceedings, if started during that period[1].

10.2.1   Compulsion and confidentiality

The compulsion involved in these investigations does give rise to a problem with the Convention if the FSA decides to prosecute (or pursue market abuse proceedings). Following the decision in *Saunders*[2], compelled evidence cannot generally be adduced by the prosecution in later criminal proceedings, although it is still admissible if the defence alludes to it or the charge is one of providing false information[3]. This position is extended to market abuse proceedings because of their quasi-criminal nature. However, as the reasoning in *Saunders* turns on Art 6(1) of the Convention, which applies to civil as well as criminal proceedings, it may be that compelled statements of this variety are not even admissible in disciplinary proceedings[4].

Where criminal proceedings are being contemplated against a person, the FSA proposes to follow the Codes of Practice under PACE, that is voluntary interviews of that person under caution. If compelled evidence has already been obtained from a person before criminal proceedings are contemplated against him, the person should be made aware of the limited admissibility of that evidence, be given a copy of it and be able to take legal advice[5]. It is not proposed to publish the fact that the FSA is investigating a person or persons, unless it is necessary to contact or bring forward witnesses; nor is it proposed to publish conclusions unless the investigation has already become a matter of public knowledge[6].

Regulators rely not just on information that the regulated are compelled to give, but also on information that is volunteered. To encourage such information to be given, confidentiality would seem to be important and a number of European

---

1   FSMA, s 176. In Scotland, a sheriff can issue the warrant. The original proposal to allow the FSA to raid the premises of authorised firms without a warrant was dropped.
2   *Saunders v United Kingdom* (1997) 23 EHRR 313.
3   FSMA, s 174.
4   See **2.4**. The Government may be aware of this possibility which is why the proviso in FSMA, s 174(1) is drafted in such wide terms.
5   Consultation Paper 25, paras 3.15–3.17.
6   Consultation Paper 25, para 3.18; *Response to Consultation Paper 25*, paras 16 and 18.

Directives lay down duties of confidentiality. Information disclosed to the FSA, the Secretary of State, their employees and any experts appointed to report on an authorised firm, may not be disclosed unless:

(1) the informant and the person to whom it relates (if different) consent;
(2) the information has already been legitimately made public;
(3) the information does not reveal to whom it relates; or
(4) a 'gateway' in respect of public functions and permitted by statutory instrument is used[1].

But under the 1986 Act, these gateways were numerous and wide and the Economic Secretary has confirmed that this policy will be continued:

> 'We propose to make regulations that provide the widest possible gateways, consistent with our directive obligations. We believe that that is right because all the gateways are intended to assist domestic or overseas regulatory or law enforcement bodies.'[2]

Again care must be taken over legally privileged documents:

> 'When a person volunteers a privileged document to the FSA, he must make clear that he is waiving that privilege only in respect of the FSA. If he does not, he risks losing that document's privileged status ... If he has not specified that he wishes the document to retain its privileged status, it could be argued that nothing would prevent the FSA from disclosing that document through its gateways, just as it can disclose other confidential documents.'[3]

However, these gateways have not included disclosure *to* the Revenue. Information *from* the Revenue may be disclosed for the purpose of:

(1) determining whether an investigator should be appointed under the FSMA;
(2) assisting in such an investigation; or
(3) assisting in taking action (including criminal proceedings or before the Tribunal) as a result of such an investigation[4].

The Treasury has a power to permit the disclosure of confidential information held by others and prescribed by statutory instrument to be passed to the FSA. This may also allow those conducting functions under the FSMA (for example the FSCS) to disclose confidential information[5]. The FSA is under a specific duty to co-operate and share information with fellow financial regulators and others involved in the prevention or detection of financial crime, but it may not disclose information that it would otherwise be prevented from disclosing by, for example, the data protection legislation[6].

Breach of the principal obligation of confidentiality is a criminal offence punishable by up to two years' imprisonment and an unlimited fine. Breach of any restriction on a gateway is punishable by up to three months' imprisonment and a level 5 fine. There are some due diligence and honest belief defences[7].

---

1   FSMA, ss 348 and 349. There are also gateway restrictions on 'competition information' (FSMA, s 351), see **3.4.3**.
2   Standing Committee A, 7 December 1999, c 1202.
3   Standing Committee A, 7 December 1999, c 1202.
4   FSMA, s 350.
5   FSMA, s 353.
6   FSMA, s 354, as explained by Lord Bach, vol 611 HL, 30 March 2000, c 1017.
7   FSMA, s 352.

10.3   AUDITORS AND ACTUARIES

In addition to the general obligation on authorised firms to be open and honest with it, the FSA will have the power to require them to appoint actuaries and/or auditors on the terms and subject to the rules laid down by the FSA. Authorised firms may then be required to produce periodic financial information reported upon by their actuary or auditor[1]. This power was explained by the Financial Secretary:

> 'Many authorised persons will be limited companies, which are already required by the Companies Act to appoint auditors to report on their financial statements. However, their duties do not extend to financial reports required by regulators. Other firms, such as partnerships and sole traders, are not obliged by those Acts to appoint an auditor at all. Insurance companies are required under the Insurance Companies Act 1982 to appoint an actuary to report on their long-term – that is, their life assurance – business. That Act is to be substantially repealed; provision for actuaries' appointment and duties must be made by the Bill.'[2]

Those actuaries and auditors do not breach their duty of confidentiality if they reveal to the FSA any relevant information acquired, or opinion held in good faith, through acting in that capacity for the firm or any other part of the firm's Group. Indeed, the Treasury can make regulations requiring certain information to be given[3]. This power will have to be used to meet the requirements of the FS Directives.

Actuaries and auditors must inform the FSA immediately if they cease to act in that capacity for an authorised firm and of any relevant circumstances. Misleading actuaries or auditors is a criminal offence punishable with up to two years' imprisonment and an unlimited fine. Actuaries or auditors which fail to comply with any of their obligations under the FSMA (including duties under the trust deed of an authorised unit trust) can be disqualified by the FSA from acting for all or any class of authorised firms[4].

10.4   MARKET MISCONDUCT

The enforcement of the market misconduct regime is a whole new responsibility for the FSA. The substantive law has been already been examined in Chapter 7. The FSA has a choice of sanctions which can be applied to those within and without the perimeter. The basic choice is whether:

(1) to prosecute through the courts for insider dealing, making false or misleading statements or creating a false or misleading impression to the market;

(2) to publicly reprimand or impose its own fines for market abuse; or

(3) if the defendant is a member of an RIE or RCH, leave the matter to their disciplinary procedures[5].

---

1   FSMA, ss 340 and 341.
2   Standing Committee A, 7 December 1999, c 1191.
3   FSMA, ss 342 and 343.
4   FSMA, ss 249, 344–346 and 392. If the FSA seeks to disqualify an actuary or auditor, it must follow its disciplinary procedures.
5   CJA 1993, Part V; FSMA, ss 123, 397, 401 and 402. For RIEs and RCHs, see **11.2**.

The Treasury does have the power (with the consent of the Attorney-General and the Secretary of State) to give written guidance on which course to take. This is a reserve power but may be necessary as the right to prosecute is shared by a number of authorities in England, Wales and Northern Ireland, whereas the power to fine is solely the FSA's[1]. To avoid confusion, the FSA can, when it proposes to investigate or act on market abuse, order any RIE or RCH not to conduct or continue conducting an inquiry under their rules[2].

The position is complicated further by the supplementary powers the FSA has. The FSA and the Secretary of State have the power to apply to the High Court for:

(1) injunctions to prevent breaches of these criminal provisions; and
(2) restitution on behalf of those affected by any such breaches[3].

The FSA alone may apply to the High Court for injunctions, restitution or penalties in respect of market abuse, but it also has the power to order restitution for market abuse itself, subject to following its disciplinary procedures[4].

10.4.1 Use of its powers

The FSA has already considered how it intends to use these powers[5]. The first decision is whether to seek an injunction. This does not require there to have been a criminal offence or market abuse, but the court must be satisfied that there is a 'reasonable likelihood' of one, or of one continuing. The injunction may extend to anyone 'knowingly concerned' in a crime (the wide definition of market abuse does not need such an extension). It can also order an asset freeze of those who may have already been involved[6]. However, the FSA will consider seeking an injunction only if:

(1) it appears that serious misconduct has been involved;
(2) continuing damage may be done to market confidence or investors' interests; and
(3) private undertakings (or other intervention in the case of authorised firms) are not considered sufficient[7].

If the FSA does seek a court injunction, it can also ask the court to order restitution and fine the defendant if market abuse has already been committed[8].

The next decision is whether to prosecute. The FSA is negotiating a Memorandum of Understanding with the other prosecuting authorities to determine how such a decision should be taken. As with policing the perimeter, it will apply the Code for Crown Prosecutors. Given the difficulties in prosecuting these types of offences, there will be a temptation to rely on the apparently easier 'in-house' market abuse proceedings, although these are subject to the full disciplinary procedures[9].

---

1   FSMA, s 130. Again the Treasury can impose conditions or restrictions on the FSA prosecuting. In Scotland, the Lord Advocate (with the Treasury's consent) can give guidance to the FSA.
2   FSMA, s 128.
3   FSMA, ss 380 and 382.
4   FSMA, ss 381, 383–386 and 392; see **9.3.1**.
5   Consultation Paper 17, Section 6 and *Response to Consultation Paper 17*, paras 64–79.
6   FSMA, ss 380 and 381.
7   Consultation Paper 17, paras 131–134.
8   FSMA, ss 129 and 383.
9   FSMA, ss 126, 127, 137 and 392; see **9.3.1**.

The Government has also conceded that the market abuse proceedings may be viewed under the Convention as criminal in nature, has excluded the use of compelled evidence, granted safe harbours under the COMC and made some legal aid available[1]. However, it rejected the imposition of the criminal burden of proof, relying on:

> '... the appropriate civil scale ... the sliding scale takes account of the seriousness of the behaviour or failing alleged by the FSA. The more serious the behaviour, the higher the standard that will be applied.'[2]

If market abuse proceedings are really criminal in nature, then bringing such a case against an individual acquitted or found guilty in a criminal trial on basically the same facts, is double jeopardy and the FSA has accepted that it cannot use both procedures in this way. However, where the individual's actions were in the course of his employment, the FSA could still pursue his employer for market abuse, where it would be difficult (and in the case of insider dealing, impossible) to prove the necessary *mens rea* to prosecute the firm[3].

Breaches of the COMC or failure to follow guidance issued by the FSA will not automatically lead to market abuse proceedings. Above all, the FSA has to decide whether the behaviour falls within one of the three categories covered by market abuse and falls below the standard expected by 'a reasonable person who regularly deals on the market in investments of the kind in question'.[4]

The FSA is required to publish a statement of policy on fining for market abuse just as it is for fining authorised firms and approved individuals, and as with disciplinary fining, it is reluctant to produce a tariff[5].

Since the FSA produced its first draft, a statutory list of criteria was inserted into the FSMA requiring the FSA to consider when proposing a fine:

(1)   the seriousness of the behaviour's effect on the market;
(2)   whether the behaviour was deliberate or reckless; and
(3)   whether the penalty is being imposed on an individual[6].

This has led to draft provisions on sanctions for market abuse for the *Enforcement Manual*, which lists the following factors:

(1)   adverse effect on the market;
(2)   the extent to which the behaviour was deliberate or reckless;
(3)   whether the person is an individual;
(4)   the amount of profits accrued or loss accrued or loss avoided;
(5)   conduct following the contravention;
(6)   disciplinary record and compliance history;

---

1   FSMA, ss 114(8), 122, 123(2), 134–136 and 174(2).
2   Economic Secretary in Standing Committee A, 2 November 1999, c 692; see **2.4**. It will be interesting to see what view the Enforcement Committee and the Tribunal take of the level of proof required.
3   Consultation Paper 17, paras 125–129.
4   Consultation Paper 17, para 141; FSMA, s 118(1)(c) and (10).
5   FSMA, ss 124 and 125; the policy and any amendments to it are subject to the same basic public consultation procedure as for the FSA's complaints scheme and the policies for fining authorised firms and approved individuals. See also **3.4.4** and Consultation Paper 17, para 143.
6   FSMA, s 124(2).

(7) previous action taken by the FSA; and

(8) action taken by other regulatory authorities[1].

This is clearly aimed at calming some fears about the draconian nature of this power and limiting the levels of fines for individual negligence. Still, the person may be subject to a restitutionary claim.

10.4.2 Injunctions and restitution

To maintain orderly settlement in the market, the imposition of a fine does not make the transaction void or unenforceable[2]. However, for any form of market misconduct, the FSA may:

(1) apply to the High Court for an injunction and/or a restitutionary order against *anyone*; or

(2) make a restitutionary award itself against any *authorised firm*, and in the case of market abuse *anyone*, subject to its disciplinary procedures.

The FSA may only pursue such restitutionary claims for accrued profits or losses suffered 'as a result' of the contravention or market abuse on behalf of anyone 'to whom the profits ... are attributable; or who has suffered the loss or adverse effect'. There are also reasonable belief and due diligence defences[3].

Where the market has been positively misled and others deal at too high or too low a price, the claim is relatively straightforward. However, where the abuse is of misuse of information, it is often not clear who the victim is. Those dealing contemporaneously do not normally lose 'as a result' of the abuse. If anything, the price they will have obtained at that time will have been 'more accurate' than if no abuse had been taking place. Of course, the abuser may well have profited, but are those profits 'attributable' to the contemporaneous dealers?

The other possible claim could be on behalf of the party whose 'inside' information was exploited, usually, but not necessarily, the issuer of the securities. This party has not often lost anything. One case where a claim could be established is where a bidder is proposing to 'sweep the market' before launching the bid and the abuser has pre-empted it. It could then be claimed that by analogy with fiduciary duties, any profits made are attributable to the bidder.

The FSA has taken the view that:

'The rationale for the proposed market abuse regime in the UK is ... directed at protecting the integrity of market mechanisms, rather than protecting the interests of any particular group of market users ... We do not anticipate that the exercise of the FSA's restitution powers would normally be appropriate for the purposes of disgorging profits for the benefit of, for example:

● "Contemporaneous traders" – ie persons trading in the market at the same time as a person found to have been insider dealing or misusing information in a manner which constitutes market abuse.

---

1   Consultation Paper 59, Annex B.

2   FSMA, s 131.

3   FSMA, ss 382(1) and (8), 383(1), (3) and (10) and 384(1) and (6). Market abuse again includes indirect market abuse through requiring or encouraging others to engage in actions. The Secretary of State cannot seek remedial orders for insider dealing or market abuse.

- Companies or issuers whose investments have been the subject of manipulation, insider dealing or information misuse.'[1]

10.4.3   Money laundering

The ML Regulations implemented the Money Laundering Directive and impose on credit and financial institutions (who are generally authorised) and their management (who are generally approved), the obligation to have appropriate systems to detect and report suspicious transactions. This includes appointing an MLRO, who will himself have to be an approved individual[2].

The Government is clearly unhappy that there have been no prosecutions under the Regulations and has given the FSA the power to prosecute and also to create rules in relation to prevention and detection of money laundering through authorised firms[3]. Thus, as elsewhere, the FSA will have a choice in the case of authorised firms, whether to prosecute or to bring disciplinary actions for failing to implement internal systems to detect and report customers involved in money laundering. Again, restitutionary claims can be attached.

10.5   PRIVATE ACTIONS

In the USA, the ability to bring private actions for breaches of the federal securities legislation has played an important part in its enforcement. In the UK, such private resort to the courts has been much rarer. As under the 1986 Act, the right to bring such an action depends upon whether the matter arises within or without the perimeter.

10.5.1   Outside the perimeter

Where an agreement has been made by someone in consequence of a breach of the general obligation by the other party (or a third party), the other party cannot usually enforce it and will be required to hand back any money or property received under the agreement (less any benefits provided), together with compensation for any losses incurred. A court may, however, allow the other party to enforce the contract or otherwise retain the money or property if it is 'just and equitable in the circumstances of the case'. In determining this, the court must 'have regard to' whether:

(1) the other party reasonably believed that he was not contravening the general prohibition; or

(2) he did not know that a third party had contravened the general prohibition[4].

If the breach of the general obligation is deposit-taking, the contract is generally enforceable, unless the depositor is not entitled recover his deposit 'without delay'. In those circumstances, he can seek a court order for its return unless that

1   Consultation Paper 17, paras 155 and 158.
2   Money Laundering Regulations 1993, SI 1993/1933; Money Laundering Directive 91/308/ EEC; Consultation Paper 26, para 64(g).
3   FSMA, ss 146 and 402(1).
4   FSMA, ss 26–28. In a late amendment, the Government gave the court this wider discretion.

would not be just and equitable. In determining that, the court must have regard to whether the deposit-taker reasonably believed he was not contravening the general prohibition[1].

An agreement made, or obligation entered into, with someone in consequence of a breach of the restriction on financial promotion is generally unenforceable and money or property received must be handed back together with compensation for loss. Again a court may allow the contract to be enforced or the money or property retained if it is just and equitable in the circumstances, and in determining this, it must have regard to whether:

(1) the other party reasonably believed he was not in breach; or
(2) the other party did not know that a third party was in breach[2].

The fact that property may have passed to a third party in these cases will not defeat an action for its value at the time of the transfer[3].

10.5.2 Within the perimeter

Breaches of FSA permissions or rules do not make any transaction void or unenforceable; but private persons can claim damages for losses caused by an authorised firm for:

(1) negligently allowing a person to perform a function from which he was prohibited;
(2) negligently allowing an non-approved person to perform a function requiring approval, whether directly for the firm or for the firm's contractor;
(3) breaching a restriction on promoting or approving the promotion of non-authorised and non-recognised CISs;
(4) contravening an FSA rule; or
(5) contravening the terms of a permission of a UK firm or a requirement on an inwardly passported firm[4].

Case (5) applies only where the Treasury has prescribed the breach as one that gives rise to a private civil action. As the Government spokesman in the House of Lords explained:

'Only the cases that are prescribed by order will give rise to such rights. That is necessary to ensure that there is similar treatment between authorised persons who are subject to rules and to requirements with similar effects. For example, some investment firms are constrained from handling client money by SRO rules. Breach of those rules attracts rights of action. That ensures that there is a possible right of action where a person handles client money when they should not, as well as when a person who is entitled to handle client money fails to follow the applicable rules. In both cases, it is right that the consumer should have a right of action if they suffer loss.

However, it is not our intention to create rights of action in respect of requirements which are equivalent to financial resources rules; for example, individual capital ratios

---

1 FSMA, ss 26(4) and 29. As advising on or arranging deposit-taking is not a regulated activity, third parties cannot be in breach of the general prohibition in such a case.
2 FSMA, s 30.
3 FSMA, ss 28(8) and 30(13).
4 FSMA, ss 20, 71, 150, 151, 202 and 241. Despite the wording difference, indirect employment of a prohibited person may be caught in the same way as indirect employment of a non-approved person. These are all statutory torts, subject to the usual defences.

for banks, or premium income limits for insurance companies. The effect will therefore be to make it clear that breaches of these requirements do not attract rights of action.'[1]

Breaches of Listing Rules by listed companies and of Statements by approved individuals are not actionable. Breaches of the Financial Resources Rules are also excluded and the FSA can exclude other rules. It currently expects to exclude the high-level PFBs and the general rules for senior managers, systems and controls, but not the detailed COBS rules or the ML Rules. On the other hand, the Treasury can, by statutory instrument, prescribe rules and requirements, breaches of which will be actionable by non-private persons. It also has to prescribe the definition of a private person[2]. The Government has indicated that it intends to adapt the definition of private investor for the purposes of the 1986 Act, so that:

(1) individuals can generally sue unless they were carrying on regulated activities themselves;
(2) others can generally sue unless they were carrying on any type of business; and
(3) governments, local authorities and other public bodies generally cannot sue[3].

Finally, an investor could claim that some derivative contracts are unenforceable under the Gaming Acts, but provided they are entered into 'by way of business' which for one of the parties is a regulated activity specified by the Treasury, the contract will be upheld[4].

---

1   Lord McIntosh, vol 613 HL, 18 May 2000, cc 382 and 383, explaining the redrafted FSMA, ss 20 and 202.
2   FSMA, ss 20(2), 64(8), 71(2), 150 and 202(2).
3   Financial Services Act 1986 (Restriction of Right of Action) Regulations 1991, SI 1991/489.
4   FSMA, s 412.

Chapter 11

SPECIAL CASES: EXCHANGES, CLEARING HOUSES, LLOYD'S AND THE PROFESSIONS

11.1 BACKGROUND

Traditionally, formal markets have played a central role in financial services. Lloyd's was a central market for transacting non-life insurance. The Stock Exchange had a practical monopoly over the trading and settlement of UK publicly quoted companies' securities and gilt-edged stocks. LIFFE developed into the main market in UK (and many European) financial derivatives. All however, have lost out, not just to competing markets, but also to business being transacted outside the market system.

Lloyd's long ago lost its insurance leadership to the major insurance companies, although it has kept a niche position in arranging reinsurance and cover for unusual risks. When the Eurobond market developed in the 1970s and 1980s, telecommunications had developed sufficiently that trading took place over-the-counter (OTC), that is directly between brokers outside the Stock Exchange with stand-alone settlement systems such as Cedel and Euroclear. The Stock Exchange itself lost control over settlements of equities to CREST which has also taken on the settlement of gilts. The trading of such securities can also be conducted through the Alternative Trading Systems (ATSs) of major broking firms and others such as Reuters. UK futures and options (both financial and commodity) have generally been traded on markets, but have always been settled separately through the LCH. Swaps have always operated OTC and as settlement is performed by equal and opposite transactions, they have not required a settlement system. Here, however, the products are becoming increasingly standardised and the LCH has offered a counterparty facility called SWAPClear to eliminate credit risks.

Before determining how to regulate exchanges, there arises the question: what are the functions that constitute an exchange in the first place? The primary function seems to have been reduced to the promulgation of standard terms and conditions of trading with a view to facilitating price discovery and settlement. Yet even that does not clearly mark out exchanges from OTC operations when organisations such as the International Swaps and Derivatives Association (responsible for standardising swaps documentation), the International Primary Markets Association (responsible for standardising the new issue mechanics for eurobonds) and the International Securities Markets Association (ISMA) (responsible for standardising the secondary market trading terms, including checking, for eurobonds) are really fulfilling similar functions.

Under the 1986 Act, the existing Exchanges were not allowed to become SROs responsible for regulating their members and any settlement system they used[1]. Instead, separate regimes were set up for RIEs and RCHs. An exchange could not

---

[1]   This was in contrast to the position in the USA, where the two principal markets – the NYSE and NASDAQ – were SROs.

apply to be an RIE if it did not organise its own settlement or use an RCH. Likewise, a settlement system could not apply to be an RCH unless it settled transactions done on an RIE. Recognition gave an RIE or RCH exempt status and, therefore, it did not need to be authorised. Perhaps wisely, the 1986 Act did not attempt to define an exchange. Indeed there was some debate between the SIB and Tradepoint (the order-driven execution service competing with the Stock Exchange), as to whether it should be recognised as an RIE or just authorised like the owners of other ATSs.

The FSA could only grant RIE status to exchanges with a physical presence in the UK. If an overseas exchange wanted to give UK-based customers electronic access to its market, it had to apply to the Treasury for recognition. This would be granted if the Treasury was satisfied with the standard of its home State regulation and with the level of co-operation with that regulator and with that exchange. This left the anomaly of ISMA, which organised trading terms and the checking system TRAX for eurobonds, but did not take responsibility for liquidity or trading and was not regulated overseas. A special category of International Securities Self-Regulating Organisation (ISSRO) was created so that it could apply for an exemption. Lloyd's, its members and their agents were automatically exempt[1].

11.2   RECOGNISED INVESTMENT EXCHANGES AND RECOGNISED CLEARING HOUSES

Despite all the developments in this area, the regime for RIEs and RCHs is being carried forward largely unchanged. The need for RIEs and RCHs to be connected has been removed, which could eventually allow the ISMA to become an RIE as the FSMA no longer has a formal ISSRO category[2]. This may also encourage Euroclear and Cedel to become overseas RCHs. To meet the requirements of the ISD, only exchanges or clearing houses that have their head offices *and* registered offices outside the UK can be treated as overseas[3]. It is now the FSA rather than the Treasury that determines whether, in respect of such overseas applicants, there is adequate investor protection and co-operation, to which has been added a requirement for adequate procedures to deal with defaulting parties. These requirements replace the normal recognition requirements (see below) and provided the FSA is satisfied with them, such overseas RIEs and RCHs are not subject to such detailed FSA supervision[4]. The remainder of this section will deal with RIEs and RCHs based in the UK.

The current RIEs and RCHs will be grandfathered for a three-month transition period after the FSMA comes into force, although the new arrangements are not

---

1   1986 Act, ss 36–42 and Sch 1, para 25B.

2   As the ISMA continues to have structural difficulties, the Government is proposing to reintroduce the concept under the RA Order: Lord McIntosh, vol 612 HL, 9 May 2000, c 1508.

3   FSMA, s 313(1); Financial Secretary in Standing Committee A, 7 December 1999, c 1167. Cross-border mergers of exchanges put strains on this provision. Which regulator has principal responsibility for such exchanges depends upon the corporate structure adopted.

4   FSMA, ss 292 and 293(8), although an annual report on compliance with the special overseas recognition requirements and any competition issues must be submitted to the FSA, with copies to the Treasury and the OFT: FSMA, s 295.

likely to require any changes to their current practices[1]. That still leaves the question: why should domestic RIEs and RCHs apply to be exempt in respect of the regulated activities involved in running an exchange and/or clearing services rather than apply for full authorisation[2]? There are four principal benefits from recognised status:

(1) a Stamp Duty exemption for market-making within an RIE in UK equities;
(2) a statutory immunity for the recognised body, its staff and any recognised nominee for acts or omissions in the conduct of its regulatory functions;
(3) senior management and other employees of the recognised body do not have to become approved individuals subject to the FSA's direct discipline; and
(4) the FSA cannot make rules under its general rule-making powers for a recognised body[3].

However, the last benefit may be somewhat illusory. The FSA will not be able to impose detailed conduct of business rules, but to be, and to continue to be, recognised, an RIE or RCH will have to meet recognition requirements which the Treasury will determine in a statutory instrument. The first draft Recognition Requirements Regulations (RR Regulations) closely follow the requirements in the 1986 Act and read like adapted PFBs[4].

11.2.1 Recognition requirements

The RR Regulations lay down the following requirements.

(1) An RIE must operate facilities to allow transactions in investments, and RCHs to settle such transactions, in a timely manner; but the transactions do not have to be limited to investments.
(2) Both must be fit and proper persons with appropriate systems and controls for the scale of their operations and adequate rule-making and rule-reviewing procedures (cf PFBs 3 and 7).
(3) They must have adequate financial resources for their regulated (and non-regulated) activities (cf PFB 4).
(4) They must co-operate with UK and overseas regulators of regulated and other financial activities (cf PFB 11).
(5) They must be willing and able to promote high standards of integrity and fair dealing (cf PFBs 1, 7 and 8).

---

1   *Draft Recognition Requirements for Investment Exchanges and Clearing Houses*, HM Treasury, February 1999, Introduction, para 9.
2   FSMA, s 285. The FSA has devised a light authorised regime for, at present, nine specialist service companies whose activities are confined to arranging or facilitating deals and who may not deal with private customers: *The FSA's approach to regulation of the market infrastructure*, FSA, January 2000, Annex B; Consultation Paper 55, FSA, June 2000.
3   FSMA, s 291. FSMA Parts V and X generally apply to authorised firms. A fuller list of factors, including some disadvantages, appears in *The FSA's approach to regulation of the market infrastructure*, Annex B.
4   FSMA, s 286; the draft regulations are in *Draft Recognition Requirements for Investment Exchanges and Clearing Houses*. As this draft also contains default rules, they will also require the approval of the Secretary of State for Trade and Industry, as the DTI is responsible for insolvency issues.

(6)	They must have satisfactory access criteria to protect financial markets and investors, recording of transactions, monitoring and enforcement of rules, complaints procedures, and measures to prevent and detect market abuse and financial crime.

(7)	An RIE must also ensure that transactions in investments are limited to listed securities and any others in which there is a proper market and proper information. It must also be able to refuse admission, suspend trading, publicly censure and publish information itself in cases where substantially price-sensitive information has not been published by an issuer as soon as possible[1].

The Treasury is being given the power to allow referrals to the Tribunal from some RIE and RCH disciplinary proceedings. The Government spokesman in the House of Lords gave as the reason:

> 'If a person who is a member of a recognised investment exchange or recognised clearing house engages in behaviour which amounts to market abuse ... it is likely that this will also constitute a breach of the rules of the recognised body concerned. Rather than taking market abuse proceedings, the FSA might leave this to be dealt with as an internal disciplinary matter ... The problem with this is that it is conceivable that inconsistency might develop over time between the way such cases are dealt with by the recognised bodies as compared with the tribunal.'[2]

Finally, RCHs and RIEs offering their own clearing services must comply with the special insolvency arrangements applying to 'market contracts'.[3]

## 11.2.2	Insolvency arrangements

Because of the complex web of credits and debits that a major participant in a market or clearing system may have with his fellow participants, the default of one such participant can create a domino effect and threaten the whole system. This threat arises not just from the default of members of the system, but also from non-member customers if they are sufficiently large players. To reduce this threat, the various credits and debits of the defaulter need to be netted off to leave one net sum owed to (or in theory, from) the system. However, at least three general rules of insolvency obstruct this:

(1)	the closing out of individual transactions is potentially void after insolvency without the court's consent;

(2)	multi-lateral netting post-insolvency is a breach of the *pari passu* principle[4]; and

(3)	margin or other security held can be challenged as an improper preference.

1	RR Regulations, reg 4 and Sch, Parts I and II; Traded Securities (Disclosure) Regulations 1994, SI 1994/188 Art 3.

2	FSMA, s 300; Lord McIntosh, vol 613 HL, 18 May 2000, c 430. The power may also be exercised in other areas requiring consistency or to ensure compliance with the Convention.

3	RR Regulations, Sch, Parts III and IV.

4	Such an arrangement was rejected in *British Eagle International Airlines v Cie National Air France* [1975] 1 WLR 758, which encouraged the development of central clearing house systems where all credits and debits are with the system operator rather than other participants. Such an arrangement is operated by the LCH, but not CREST.

The Companies Act 1989, Part VII was passed to override the normal insolvency arrangements in the case of these market contracts[1]. The requirement that RIEs and RCHs have arrangements to net off a defaulter's contracts into a single sum will now be found in the RR Regulations[2]. An RIE may also designate non-members as part of these set-off arrangements, but only so long as their default would be likely 'adversely to affect the operations of the market'.[3]

Now that so many operators in the UK markets are overseas firms, the scope for jurisdictional clashes on the insolvency of such a participant are considerable (although the USA does have similar market contract rules). Theoretically, the DTI and the Treasury can even extend the UK rules to overseas exchanges. They can also, perhaps more realistically, extend the set-off regime to OTC contracts settled through parties listed by the FSA for that purpose (eg the LCH if it acts as a clearing house for swaps)[4].

11.2.3   Applications and enforcement

An applicant to be an RIE or RCH may be a company or an unincorporated association. The FSA must determine the procedure for an application and the applicant must produce copies of its rules and guidance and such other information that the FSA may reasonably require. RIEs must give details of any clearing arrangements they have or propose to make and the criteria for providing facilities for transactions not effected through them (if any). Likewise, RCHs must give details of arrangements they have or propose to make to clear transactions effected through RIEs and the criteria for providing such facilities outside them (if any)[5].

The FSA may ask for any further information that it reasonably considers necessary, which can vary from applicant to applicant. It may also have regard to any other information it has and considers relevant . The FSA is not required to give an answer within any particular period of time and may not grant recognition without the Treasury agreeing that the rules, guidance and arrangements of the applicant are not unjustifiably anti-competitive. If it does grant recognition, it must issue a recognition order specifying the commencement date[6].

Even if the FSA is satisfied that the recognition requirements are met, it is not compelled to grant recognition. However, if it is minded to refuse an application, it must follow a special procedure. It must give a written notice to the applicant and take steps to bring the notice to the attention of the applicant's members. The notice must give the FSA's reasons and at least two months for representations from the applicant, its members and any others likely to be affected. The FSA must consider these representations before issuing its final decision, which must be notified to the applicant and brought to the attention of its members and any others likely to be affected. The FSA is not specifically required to reveal what

---

1   For a detailed examination of Part VII, see *Financial Services Regulation: The New Regime* by S Gleeson (Sweet & Maxwell, 1999).
2   RR Regulations, Sch, Parts III and IV. These will require the Secretary of State's approval: FSMA, s 286.
3   RR Regulations, Sch, Part III, para 16.
4   Companies Act 1989, s 170; FSMA, s 301.
5   FSMA, ss 285, 287 and 288.
6   FSMA, ss 289, 290 and 307.

information it has considered and there is no referral to the Tribunal[1]. On this last point, the Financial Secretary was quite specific:

> 'Recognition establishes a different relationship with the regulator from that which exists between the regulator and the authorised community. The arrangements in the Bill take account of that. The proper forum for a recognised body and its members to challenge such a decision after they have had an opportunity to make representations is in the courts, by way of judicial review.'[2]

The FSA may impose notification rules on RIEs and RCHs. In particular, RIEs and RCHs must inform the FSA of any changes in their rules, guidance, or clearing arrangements. These notification rules can be waived or varied in individual cases, provided the FSA is satisfied they are unduly burdensome, do not achieve their purpose and the change would not result in undue risk to those intended to be protected[3].

The FSA must make arrangements to investigate any complaints about an RIE or RCH that calls into question that recognition[4]. Whether following such a complaint or otherwise, the FSA may issue an RIE or RCH with a direction (enforceable by court injunction if necessary), or in an extreme case revoke a recognition, if an RIE or RCH:

(1) has failed or is likely to fail to satisfy the recognition requirements; or
(2) has failed to comply with some other obligation under the FSMA.

As they are exempt, not many obligations under the FSMA, other than the recognition requirements, apply to RIEs and RCHs. Clearly, there are the notification rules, but also obligations under the market abuse and the investigation regimes. A revocation order (unless made at the request or with the consent of the RIE or RCH) may not come into effect for at least three months after it has been made and may contain any necessary or expedient transitional provisions[5]. The FSA must follow the same special procedure before issuing a direction or revoking a recognition (without the RIE's or RCH's consent) as when minded to refuse an application unless it is essential to issue a direction quickly[6].

11.2.4   Competition issues

The rules, guidance, clearing arrangements and trading practices of RIEs and RCHs are subject to a special competition regime, just as are the rules, guidance, statements and codes of the FSA under Part X of the FSMA[7]. However, as the Government spokesman in the House of Lords has said:

---

1   FSMA, ss 290(1), (5) and (6) and 298. This procedure does not apply if the Treasury has refused consent on competition grounds, see **11.2.4**.
2   Standing Committee A, 7 December 1999, c 1159.
3   FSMA, ss 293 and 294. Overseas RIEs and RCHs need give only annual returns: FSMA, s 295.
4   FSMA, s 299. This is not for day-to-day complaints where the RR Regulations require RIEs and RCHs to have their own procedures: vol 611 HL, 30 March 2000, c 974.
5   FSMA, ss 296 and 297; Financial Secretary in Standing Committee A, 2 December 1999, c 1152. Where an RIE's or RCH's rule has been changed because of a direction from the FSA, the recognised body is still free to alter or vary it later, although it is hard to conceive that it would do so without the FSA's informal consent.
6   FSMA, s 298.
7   FSMA, s 302(1).

'I should like to draw attention to two main differences of substance between the arrangements put in place for recognised bodies in Part XVIII and those which we have debated in respect of the FSA in Part X. These are, first, that the regime has to cover applicants for recognition, as well as bodies which are already recognised. This adds not inconsiderably to the complexity of these clauses, compared with those in Part X.

The second difference is that the recognised bodies themselves can exploit the strength of their market position. This is because, in spite of having some regulatory responsibilities, they are also commercial bodies. The FSA is not in the same position and it is therefore necessary for the competition scrutiny regime to be able to consider whether an exchange or clearing house is exploiting its strong market position, for example, to keep potential new entrants at bay. Apart from these differences, the regime put in place is the same as that which we have agreed should apply to the FSA.'[1]

This is a change from the Government's original approach in the Bill which, for competition purposes, treated RIEs and RCHs almost entirely as commercial bodies[2].

The FSA must send any applicant's regulatory provisions, namely rules, guidance, clearing arrangements and criteria, plus any other information it considers may assist, to the OFT to assess whether they have a 'significantly adverse effect on competition'.[3] The OFT must send a reasoned report to the FSA, the Competition Commission and the Treasury. The Competition Commission, in turn, must issue its own report if the OFT has found there is a significantly adverse effect or even where it has not, but still asks the Commission to investigate. As with reports on the FSA, the Competition Commission must consider whether any significantly adverse effect it finds is nevertheless justified in the light of the obligations imposed on RIEs and RCHs by the FSMA[4]. The Treasury may override the findings of the OFT and the Competition Commission and approve or even refuse to approve an application, but only in 'exceptional circumstances'. If the Treasury is minded to refuse an approval, it must allow and consider representations from the applicant and any other affected parties[5].

The OFT must also continue to keep the regulatory provisions *and* the practices of RIEs and RCHs under review. The practices subject to this regime are only those of the RIEs and RCHs in their capacities as regulators of exchanges and clearing houses. Any other commercial activities are subject to the normal competition regime. Otherwise, the powers and the review procedures of the OFT, the Competition Commission and the Treasury (including its override) are the same as for the FSA[6].

Again, to allow this special regime, the Competition Act 1998 is excluded, but because RIEs and RCHs, unlike the FSA, are not pure statutory regulators, the arrangements are slightly more complicated than in Part X, in that:

---

1   Lord McIntosh, vol 612, 9 May 2000, c 1513.
2   Standing Committee A, 7 December 1999, c 1162.
3   FSMA, ss 302 and 303(1) and (2). The test is the same as in Part X and differs from those found in the Competition Act 1998; see **3.4.3**.
4   FSMA, ss 303(3) and (4) and 306.
5   FSMA, ss 307 and 310.
6   FSMA, ss 304–306 and 308–310; see **3.4.3**.

(1) the cartel prohibition does not apply to any applicant or existing body's constitutional agreement in respect of its regulatory provisions, nor to its regulatory provisions, practices and the decisions made under them;

(2) the monopoly prohibition does not apply to its regulatory provisions and practices; and

(3) those subject to an RIE's or RCH's rules have a defence to the cartel and monopoly prohibitions if an agreement or conduct is 'required or encouraged' by its regulatory provisions, and in the case of the cartel prohibition, by its practices[1].

11.2.5   The Financial Services Authority's approach

As exempt persons, RIEs and RCHs are not subject to the FSA's rules for authorised firms; but they do have to comply with the recognition requirements and are subject to notification rules and guidance that will appear in the FSA's *Handbook*[2]. The guidance, particularly in respect of the recognition requirements, is far more detailed than before and in many cases looks remarkably like rules. For example, the guidance on fitness and properness:

> '... covers a wide range of topics including the suitability of the governing body, senior management and ownership, risk management, IT, conflicts of interest, relations with related businesses and outsourcing. The guidance is broadly based on the principles applied in assessing the fitness and properness of authorised persons ...'[3]

Likewise, the guidance on financial resources lays down detailed requirements to cover both counterparty and other operational risks. There is guidance on all the other recognition requirements although some recognition that over access to facilities and the prevention of financial crime and market abuse, RIEs and RCHs are under tremendous competitive pressure and cannot be expected to act as 'monopoly regulators'[4].

The existing notification rules have been amended slightly and the Treasury's guidance for recognised overseas exchanges incorporated, now that the FSA will be responsible for them. However, detailed supervision of such exchanges remains a matter for their home State regulator. The supervision of domestic RIEs and RCHs is being changed to a new risk-based system. The FSA will conduct a risk assessment 'under a number of broad headings such as financial resources, supervision of members, the recognised body's business environment, operational infrastructure and governance'[5]. Provided the FSA is satisfied that the RIE or RCH is low risk and that its internal review systems will ensure that the FSA is informed early of significant changes, the supervision will be a light one.

11.2.6   The future

As was noted at the beginning of this chapter, traditional markets are under severe pressure. ATSs, with their electronic order books, are offering some or all of:

---

1   FSMA, ss 311 and 312.
2   Draft rules appear in Consultation Paper 39a, FSA, January 2000, to replace the Financial Services (Notification of Recognised Bodies) Regulations 1995 and the current FSA and Treasury guidance.
3   Consultation Paper 39, FSA, January 2000, para 5.18.
4   Consultation Paper 39, para 5.5.
5   Consultation Paper 39, para 5.43.

(1) cheaper trading;

(2) non-standard settlement (particularly for private customers);

(3) crossing functionality (preserving anonymity); and

(4) preferencing arrangements (to deal with large institutional orders).

The markets in Europe, including the Stock Exchange and LIFFE, have responded more rapidly than those in the USA, going over to increasingly sophisticated electronic order books themselves. The fragmentation caused by the ATSs in the USA has not been so marked in Europe, although geographical fragmentation is only beginning to be broken down with proposals such as the merger of the London and Frankfurt Stock Exchanges. In the settlement area and the OTC markets, by contrast, the trend seems to be towards European-wide consolidation, which may in turn provide the drive towards 'straight-through (ie automated front to back) processing of trades'[1].

The FSA is conscious that, whatever the outcome of all these developments, the roles of RIEs, RCHs, ATSs, fully authorised firms and specialist service companies are becoming very blurred and that the current distinctions made between them for regulatory purposes may have to be revised[2]. As the Chairman of the FSA has said:

> '.... in a period of restructuring and uncertainty we need to be vigilant, and to ensure that market integrity is not compromised as competing trading systems seek competitive advantage. There are risks that the fragmentation of liquidity could – perhaps temporarily – harm investor interests, and that two-tier markets might develop, with less transparency and perhaps different pricing and spreads for major institutions on the one hand, and retail investors on the other ... If we then wish to propose regulatory changes, we will need to consult formally. But the time for debate on these questions is now.'[3]

11.3 LLOYD'S

The unique structure of Lloyd's was outlined in **1.2.2**. One of the problems with regulating this structure is its ambiguous nature. From the point of view of a policyholder, Lloyd's is just another 'insurer' managed by the Society and its Council. Therefore, logically, it should be authorised like all its UK competitors. However, from the point of view of the members, Lloyd's is running a market trading underwriting capacity. These members are now a mixture of names with unlimited liability who are generally outsiders advised by managing and members' agents, and limited liability companies, often insiders integrating the functions of the names and their agents.

Under the previous regime, Lloyd's, its members and their agents were all exempt from the need to be authorised. That has now changed. Under the FSMA, Lloyd's

---

1   *The FSA's approach to regulation of the market infrastructure*, para 3.20. However, it was noted that the Settlement Finality Directive 98/26/EC, implemented by the Financial Markets and Insolvency (Settlement Finality) Regulations 1999, SI 1999/2979 could encourage competing settlement systems. On the proposed London–Frankfurt merger, the FSA is in discussions with the German regulator, the Bundesaufsichtsamt für den Wertpapierhandel.

2   The whole purpose of the FSA's Discussion paper, *The FSA's approach to regulation of the market infrastructure*, is to raise the issues with the industry and seek advice on how to proceed.

3   FSA Press Release 46/2000.

itself is treated as though it was previously authorised and is now being grandfathered. The FSMA declares that Lloyd's is authorised and has a permission to:

(1) arrange deals in contracts of insurance at Lloyd's;
(2) arrange deals in participations in Lloyd's syndicates; and
(3) conduct any ancillary regulated activities[1].

As the Financial Secretary explained:

> 'Primarily, the permission will cover making arrangements which enable members to carry out contracts of insurance. The permission does not include carrying out contracts of insurance, which is done by the Society's members, not the Society itself.'[2]

Although statutorily authorised, Lloyd's will be treated as though it had applied for its permission from the FSA and be subject to the TCAs and the FSA's normal regulatory powers, including the power to vary or revoke that permission[3].

As advising underwriting members of Lloyd's and managing the underwriting capacity of a Lloyd's syndicate are to be regulated activities, managing and members' agents will all have to be authorised in the normal way[4]. However, Lloyd's members – be they names or corporate members – will be exempt in respect of their Lloyd's activities[5]. Members will continue to be regulated by the Council of Lloyd's, an arrangement curiously similar to the old SROs and their members. The FSA is, nevertheless, under a duty to keep itself informed of how activities are conducted in that market and how the Council is supervising and regulating them. This duty:

> '... could require the FSA to keep itself informed about voting arrangements in elections to the Council, charging policies of underwriting agents and, theoretically, the contents of the lunch menu at the Lloyd's restaurant.'[6]

In effect, the FSA has been given the Treasury's old watching brief over Lloyd's but with additional powers[7]. As the general prohibition is not going to apply to Lloyd's members, they:

> '... will have the benefit of an exemption, from direct supervision by the FSA, so long as they are members of the Society in relation to any insurance business that they carry on there. Because names will not for the time being be authorised persons, we need to provide mechanisms to allow the FSA to impose on them the requirements that it considers necessary. For example, the FSA will need to ensure that members comply with the solvency requirements set out in the single market Directive that relate to insurance. However, the FSA will not be limited to imposing requirements under those Directives. It will be for the FSA to decide the extent to which it needs to impose

---

1   FSMA, s 315.
2   Standing Committee A, 7 December 1999, c 1168.
3   FSMA, s 315(3).
4   RA Order, Arts 20 and 21 and Sch 3, para 5. Initially, the FSA will grandfather all the managing and members' agents currently regulated by Lloyd's.
5   FSMA, s 316. If members conduct regulated activities other than 'relating to contracts of insurance written at Lloyd's', they must be authorised, but their permission will still not cover their Lloyd's activities: FSMA, s 42(5).
6   FSMA, s 314; Financial Secretary in Standing Committee A, 7 December 1999, c 1170.
7   The cost to Lloyd's, however, will be much higher. Currently, it is charged £200,000 per annum by the Treasury, but the FSA has estimated that it will be charging Lloyd's £1.2m per annum: Consultation Paper 48, FSA, May 2000, para 2.12.

its own requirements, or whether it is satisfied that the arrangements under Lloyd's byelaws are adequate for the purpose.'[1]

In fact, the FSA is given a choice as to how to impose obligations on Lloyd's and its various types of members. It can impose full or partial 'direct rule' by issuing an 'insurance market direction' in respect of any class or the whole of the membership, to subject them to any of the following parts of the FSMA (modified as necessary):

(1) the approved person regime (including prohibition of individuals);
(2) the FSA's rule-making powers;
(3) the FSA's investigatory powers (including appointing an investigator);
(4) the FSA's disciplinary powers and procedures, including restitution orders;
(5) the FSA's control of those having shareholder influence;
(6) the appointment and duties of auditors and actuaries;
(7) the Ombudsman and Compensation Schemes;
(8) the FSA's powers to intervene in insolvency proceedings; and
(9) in the last resort, the imposition of the general prohibition and full authorisation[2].

Alternatively (or in addition), the FSA can direct the Council or the Society through the Council to impose obligations on the members and also on managing and members' agents[3]. The Council would be required to implement the direction using its powers to make and enforce byelaws under the Lloyd's Acts.

Whether the FSA intends to regulate directly or via the Council, it must issue a cost-benefit analysis, consult and publish as it does for new rules, unless such a delay would prejudice the interests of consumers[4]. In deciding whether to regulate, the FSA must have particular regard to:

(1) policyholders' and potential policyholders' interests;
(2) obligations under the FS Directives;
(3) its own obligation to regulate Lloyd's as an authorised person; and
(4) in the case of a direction to the Council, if it is just necessary or expedient to do so[5].

Finally, there are special arrangements for former underwriting members retiring since the reorganisation of the Lloyd's obligations on 24 December 1996. Such ex-members remain liable for claims against their participation after their retirement, but such a carrying out of an insurance contract will, in effect, remain exempt despite their retirement. The FSA can impose rules or specific requirements on such ex-members to protect policyholders from the risk of them defaulting. To make such rules, the FSA must follow the same consultation procedures as for directions above. The imposition of specific requirements on individual ex-members is subject to the FSA's supervisory procedures. The

1   Financial Secretary in Standing Committee A, 7 December 1999, c 1178.
2   FSMA, ss 316 and 317.
3   FSMA, s 318. The managing and members' agents will, of course, as authorised firms, already be subject to direct regulation. This, however, avoids the complication of the FSA having to operate two different systems to issue a direction that affects both members and their agents.
4   FSMA, ss 316(9)–(11), 318(7)–(9) and 319; see **6.2.4**.
5   FSMA, ss 316(4) and 318(4).

ex-member can also seek to have a requirement varied or amended and if the FSA is minded to refuse, it must follow its rejection procedures[1].

11.3.1   The approach of the Financial Services Authority

The Government does seem to expect the FSA to be cautious about intervening in the day-to-day running of Lloyd's. As the Financial Secretary has said:

> 'There is an extra dimension to regulation of Lloyd's which the FSA does not have in relation to authorised persons generally. Not only must it consider the need to exercise its powers in pursuit of its regulatory objectives and in accordance with the regulatory principles, but the FSA must also take into account the role of the Council of Lloyd's under the Lloyd's Acts and form a view about the extent to which it needs to intervene by regulating activities itself, or alternatively use its powers to make directions under this part of the Bill.'[2]

One of the problems the FSA faces is predicting how Lloyd's will develop. The traditional name, that is an individual member with unlimited liability, seems to be a threatened species, capital being increasingly supplied by integrated limited liability companies. As a response to this, Lloyd's has proposed a new vehicle for individuals, the Proportional Reinsurance Syndicate, run by a new category of authorised agent, the PRS manager[3]. In its Consultation Paper on Lloyd's, the FSA makes it clear that its 'primary concern will be the protection of policyholders'. Nevertheless, it will also have some concern for those supplying capital, not just as a matter of protecting albeit relatively wealthy consumers of advisory services, but also to try and avoid the systemic risk to the whole insurance market posed by such suppliers, whether names or corporates, threatening to default, particularly on reinsurance contracts[4].

Following the responses to that Consultation Paper, the FSA has summarised its initial approach to regulating this market[5]. Lloyd's, as an authorised body, will have to continue to satisfy the TCAs and will be subject to the FSA's PFBs and COBS in respect of custodianship and management of members' funds. It must have appropriate governance structures, clear lines of responsibility and arrangements for dealing with disciplinary matters and with conflicts of interest[6]. Its senior management will have to be approved individuals and must comply with the Statements and the Code of Practice. Anyone proposing to acquire significant influence over the Society through capital or votes, will have to seek the FSA's approval[7].

However, because Lloyd's has strengthened its Central Fund through reinsurance and that fund offers comprehensive cover, policyholders will rely upon this in the case of any default and will not be covered by the FSCS, at least for the time being. By contrast, although Lloyd's will continue to run a Complaints Department to

---

1   FSMA, ss 320–322 and 324; for procedures, see **9.3.1**.
2   Standing Committee A, 7 December 1999, c 1169.
3   *Private capital at Lloyd's: proportional reinsurance syndicates,* Lloyd's, April 1999.
4   Consultation Paper 16, FSA; November 1998, paras 51–53.
5   *Response Paper on Consultation Paper 16,* FSA, June 1999, paras 94–107; Consultation Paper 48, containing a draft *Lloyd's Sourcebook.*
6   *Lloyd's Sourcebook* Chapter 1. The COBS will apply only to a limited extent, Consultation Paper 57, section 6.
7   See **5.2.6**, **5.3** and **6.5** for the details of these requirements.

resolve policyholders' complaints against underwriters, if an eligible policyholder is not satisfied, he will still be able to resort to the FOS[1]. The FSA will not be requiring any Lloyd's members to be authorised for the time being. They will *not* have access to either the FSCS or the FOS, although Lloyd's will have to maintain its own schemes for members which will be monitored by the FSA[2]. Retiring members will be required to notify any changes of address so that the regime to enforce future claims against them can be effective.

Managing and members' agents and their staff that are currently approved by Lloyd's will be grandfathered and will not have to reapply to be authorised or approved. The FSA will still have the right to require reapplication in the first two years of the new regime. It will also require those falling within the approved persons regime but not currently vetted by Lloyd's to apply for approval within a limited period of time. New firms (including current outside advisers on participation in Lloyd's and future PRS managers) will have to be authorised by the FSA by applying for permission to conduct regulated activities in the usual way, including demonstrating that they meet the TCAs. At the same time, they will have to apply to be admitted to Lloyd's and thereby become subject to its byelaws. Their senior management will have to become approved individuals and, in some cases, be approved by Lloyd's as well[3]. COBS rules, particularly 'know your customer' obligations, will be applied to members' agents with respect to the advice that they give on syndicates, and to all agents in respect of promotion of their services or management of funds[4]. Lloyd's and the FSA will try to work together to avoid unnecessary duplication of effort on both initial applications and possible breaches of Lloyd's byelaws and FSA rules. The FSA will levy fees on managing and members' agents directly as well as its fees on the Society.

The main concern of the FSA (like the Treasury before it) will be the continuing solvency of Lloyd's as a whole, consisting of the central resources and those of its members. Although managing and members' agents will be subject to prudential rules, as they do not put their capital at risk as insurers, their capital adequacy does not affect Lloyd's overall solvency. Flexibility in this area is limited by European Directives[5]. Producing a global solvency figure for Lloyd's is too simplistic, because a member in surplus has no obligation to meet the liabilities of a member in deficit. Each member must be assessed separately and, to the extent that they fail to meet the European minimum solvency margin, that figure must be able to be met from the Central Fund without resorting to other members' surpluses[6]. This test will meet the European requirements, but as the FSA has commented:

'... [it] will not, in our view, provide by itself the level of protection for Lloyd's policyholders which the Government wishes to achieve. It does not relate capital

---

1   See **8.2.2**. The FSA requires Lloyd's to run a market in underwriting capacity and the Central Fund, but leaves the detailed rules to Lloyd's: *Lloyd's Sourcebook* Chapter 3.

2   *Lloyd's Sourcebook* Chapters 4 and 5.

3   Lloyd's proposes to absorb the outside adviser category into the members' agent category. Both will require approval, Consultation Paper 53, para 5.8.

4   Consultation Paper 57, section 6.

5   This includes the Insurance Groups Directive, 1998/78/EC to be implemented by 5 June 2000; see Consultation Paper 50, FSA, May 2000.

6   Consultation Paper 16, paras 95–97.

requirements to the types of risk assumed, as does good prudential supervision of insurance companies.'[1]

Authorised insurers in fact hold resources well above the minimum margin of solvency to meet the variety of risks that they are exposed to. Lloyd's has been developing an RBC system similar to that in the banking world, to make a more realistic assessment of risks its members face and approve and monitor their business plans and controls. This tool is in part internal control and in part overall prudential supervision. The FSA will monitor Lloyd's development of the RBC system but only intervene if necessary. It has explained this restrained overall approach as follows:

> '[Those] who argued for the "maximal" approach did not, however, in general recognise the extent to which functions characterised within Lloyd's as "regulatory" are in effect functions that in a normal insurance company would be carried out by central management or the compliance area. There are therefore strong arguments in favour of Lloyd's continuing to perform them. As with any insurance company, we shall monitor its performance to ensure that it continues to meet our high level requirements for regulated firms.'[2]

To assist it in this task, from 2001, Lloyd's will need to make the same detailed and public returns as other insurers, amended to give segmental reporting of trading performance at a syndicate level. Indeed, in general, the FSA has allowed Lloyd's a light regulatory regime in return for keeping the FSA fully informed of its activities[3].

11.4   PROFESSIONAL FIRMS

In its original proposals, the Government expected to transfer the regulation of investment business conducted by lawyers, accountants and other professionals away from their professional bodies to the FSA, in order to provide a 'level playing field'. However, the sheer impracticality of the FSA being responsible for a further 15,000 firms, most of whom are only marginally involved in regulated activities, and all of whom are regulated by their own professional bodies, became clear. The Government has therefore retreated and rebranded the RPB as Designated Professional Bodies (DPBs). The DPB regime will not be the same as its predecessor. For one thing, the IBRC has already been wound up and its members authorised temporarily by the PIA until the FSA takes direct responsibility. Of the remaining firms currently authorised by RPBs, the FSA has estimated that:

> 'The activities of most firms carrying on investment business within the Law Society (England and Wales) category 1, or categories A and B of the three institutes of chartered accountants (together with firms carrying on similar activities but regulated by other RPBs) – in all about 13,000 firms – will likely fall within the proposed terms of the exclusion. It is likely that few of these firms will be regulated by the FSA. The main exception from within this group is those few firms (perhaps less than a hundred)

---

1   Consultation Paper 16, para 99.
2   *Response Paper on Consultation Paper 16*, para 15. The 'maximal' approach would have required the FSA to charge Lloyd's £6.4m per annum compared to the £1.2m it expects to charge: Consultation Paper 48, para 2.12.
3   Lloyd's *Sourcebook* Chapters 2 and 3.

providing corporate finance services of a significant type, for example, in connection with listings.

About 2,000 firms currently authorised by the RPBs carry on investment business similar to that of firms currently regulated by the SROs. From [the FSMA coming into force] such business will be regulated by the FSA.'[1]

Whether this turns out to be correct depends on whether those professional firms are convinced that within the terms of the new regime and the exemptions from financial promotion, they do not need to seek a defensive authorisation. It is probably with this in mind that the FSA has pointed out to those contemplating authorisation that 'There will, however, be greater demands on firms than under the regulatory regimes of the RPBs and fees are likely to be higher'.[2]

11.4.1   The Designated Professional Bodies regime

In addition to any exemption it may have as an appointed representative, a professional firm may be exempt from the general prohibition if:

(1)   it is controlled or managed by a member or members of a profession;
(2)   its regulated activities are not rewarded by third-party payments or advantages (eg soft commission) not accounted to its clients;
(3)   its regulated activities are incidental to the provision of professional services;
(4)   those services are supervised and regulated by a DPB; and
(5)   its regulated activities do not extend beyond those permitted by that DPB, any other exemption or by the Treasury in a statutory instrument[3].

A vital difference between this and the previous regime is that the professional firms regulated by a DPB are exempt provided they abide by the above conditions, whereas such firms regulated by an RPB were authorised. Thus, if the firm now conducts regulated activities outside condition (5), the exemption falls and, as the firm is not authorised, *all* of its regulated activities (not just those in breach of condition (5)) are potentially in breach of the general prohibition, with all that follows in the way of criminal and civil liability. There are also difficulties with conditions (2) and (3).

Condition (2) aims to deter unauthorised professionals obtaining a separate income stream from regulated activities, and firms will have to be careful not to breach it to remain exempt. The Government spokesman in the House of Lords said:

'... Firms should be barred from retaining any commission obtained from IFAs in return for referring clients to them. We believe that, in any event, that prohibition is in line with a professional's general obligation to act in the best interests of his client where the professional is not a mainstream provider of financial services. In such cases, the source of third-party advice should be determined solely by reference to the client's needs.'[4]

Condition (3) is wording forced on the Government by Art 2.2(c) of the ISD, which only allows professional firms 'providing an investment service where that

---

1   Consultation Paper 30, FSA, October 1999, paras 1.11 and 1.12.
2   Consultation Paper 30, para 1.13.
3   FSMA, s 327. The Treasury is expected to exclude sensitive products such as life assurance: vol 343 HC, 1 February 2000, c 1007.
4   Lord Bach, vol 611 HL, 30 March 2000, c 1008.

service is provided in an incidental manner in the course of a professional activity' to be excluded from the requirement to be authorised. The Economic Secretary has said:

> 'In the investment services directive, "incidental" is used to mean ancillary, perhaps subordinate. That is the sense in which we are using it . . . Examples of an incidental activity might be advice on investments given by an accountant for tax planning purposes, or advice on investment as part of a wider portfolio of assets given by a solicitor to a couple who are negotiating a divorce settlement . . . [or] advice given in the course of probate.'[1]

Further guidance may come from the DPBs because they must make rules governing the regulated activities of its unauthorised members, including rules to limit those activities to those that 'arise out of, or are complementary to' the members' professional services. These have to be approved by the FSA, which itself may make rules to ensure that clients of such members know that they are not authorised. The offence of falsely holding oneself out as being authorised or exempt is extended to falsely holding oneself out as an exempt professional firm and is punishable by up to six months in prison and a level 5 fine[2].

The FSA has a general responsibility to 'keep itself informed' about the DPBs' supervision of their unauthorised members' regulated activities and the DPBs must co-operate with the FSA to that end. All this is to 'keep under review the desirability of' the FSA exercising its powers of intervention[3]. The FSA can intervene by issuing a direction in writing, limiting or removing the exemption in respect of some professional firms. This may be done in order to protect their clients or potential clients where, for example, the FSA is not satisfied by a DPB's arrangements, to enforce its rules, deal with complaints, offer redress for losses or co-operate with the FSA in respect of regulated activities. Before issuing such a direction, the FSA must issue a cost-benefit analysis, consult and publish as it does for new rules, unless such a delay would prejudice the interests of clients[4].

The FSA may also disapply the exemption in whole or in part from a specific firm if it is no longer a fit and proper person to conduct the regulated activities in question. Where the firm is a partnership, the order will apply to any successor firm with substantially the same business and partners. A firm may seek to have any existing order varied or revoked. Before making such an order, the FSA must follow its disciplinary procedures, but if subsequently it is minded to refuse an application to vary or revoke such an order, it must follow its rejection procedures[5].

Curiously, although the FSA will be responsible for the new DPB regime, it is left to the Treasury to actually designate the bodies in the first place and to stipulate any activities that may not be exempt. Before it does so, it must be satisfied that the body is established in the UK or another EEA State, has some statutory powers over

---

1   Vol 343 HC, 1 February 2000, c 1010.
2   FSMA, ss 332 and 333, cf s 24. There is a due diligence defence but where offending material is involved, the fine again may be multiplied by the number of days it is publicly displayed.
3   FSMA, s 325.
4   FSMA, ss 328 and 330; see **6.2.4**. Clients (which can include those behind fiduciaries) are defined in a similar way to consumers in FSMA, s 138.
5   FSMA, ss 329 and 331. For details of the procedures, see **9.3.1**. This power is in addition to the FSA's power to ban individuals under FSMA, s 56.

its members or some other form of statutory recognition and, above all, has rules governing its members' regulated activities[1]. Otherwise, the FSA will potentially have a tighter control over the new DPB regime once it is up and running than it had over the old RPBs.

11.4.2   The approach of the Financial Services Authority

In its Consultation Paper on UK professional firms, the FSA considered that those requiring authorisation from the FSA will generally be conducting at least one of the following mainstream investment businesses:

(1) investment advice on specific investment products to individuals (approximately 1,800 firms);
(2) discretionary investment management (approximately 100 firms); and
(3) major corporate finance advice (approximately 100 firms)[2].

The FSA expects to issue guidance on which firms will need to continue to be authorised, but it does not expect that firms outside these three groups will require a defensive authorisation, particularly with exclusions such as the use of authorised third parties under the proposed RA and FPE Orders[3].

The 2,000 UK firms that will still need to be authorised will be grandfathered into regulation by the FSA, but the FSA will have a reserve power for two years to require a group or groups of firms to reapply for authorisation[4]. FSA regulation for these firms will generally be more onerous than under the previous regime:

> 'The application of the conduct of business rules, the authorisation and Approved Persons regimes, training and competence requirements and the arrangements for supervision and enforcement are likely to be similar to those applicable to other FSA regulated firms.'[5]

Some concern has been expressed by overseas legal firms operating in the UK that they will not be able to benefit from this exempt status because they are not members of any of the Law Societies. The Government confirmed this position, but pointed out that in giving legal advice on corporate finance issues (their principal business), they will be able to rely on the exemptions in the RA Order which aim to keep the position the same as under the 1986 Act[6].

Although the PFBs will apply to the 2,000 FSA authorised firms, the FSA is minded not to apply the COBS to such firms' non-mainstream financial services business in order to bring them into line with exempt professional firms rather than other authorised firms, a small example of the FSA resisting 'levelling up' the playing field[7].

---

1   FSMA, ss 326 and 327(6).
2   Consultation Paper 30.
3   Consultation Paper 30, paras 2.11 and 2.13; see **4.3** and *Response to Paper CP30*, FSA, June 2000, para 2.20.
4   Consultation Paper 30, para 1.16. The FSA does not expect to use this power often, *Response Paper to CP30*, para 3.10.
5   Consultation Paper 30, para 2.24. The FSA does not propose to apply its ML Rules to non-mainstream business, ML Rules, r 9.2; but the Government rejected a statutory exception for such business: Lord McIntosh, vol 612, 18 April 2000, c 563.
6   Lord McIntosh, vol 612 HL, 9 May 2000, c 1417; see **4.3**.
7   Consultation Paper 49a, Part I, para 4.24; *Response to Paper CP30*, section 7.

Complaints are not quite so straightforward as they may involve a mixture of complaints about the professional services and regulated activities. Where this is the case, the FSA expects the complaints principally about the firm's mainstream financial services business to fall within the FOS regime but all other complaints to be a matter for the professional bodies' own arrangements. The FSA expects these authorised firms to belong to the FSCS as well as the FOS, but it is still considering the Law Societies' proposed opt-out for their members who are already required to belong to their own schemes providing at least £1 million cover per complaint[1]. That raises the whole issue of prudential rules to avoid default.

Until now, professional bodies have imposed PII requirements upon all their member firms and the FSA intends to continue that requirement for firms it authorises and ensure that the PII terms cover any awards made by the FOS. Otherwise, the RPBs have required firms that they have authorised to remain within the terms of the Art 2.2(c) of the ISD to avoid having to comply with the CAD's prudential rules. Firms now authorised by the FSA may or may not fall within the ISD exclusion and, if they do not, the FSA will have to apply at least the CAD minimum requirements. The FSA also has to be satisfied that any firm it authorises meets the continuing TCAs on adequate resources and suitability[2].

Initially, the FSA will continue the current RPB requirements, plus some sort of declaration of continuing solvency or regular returns to show positive net assets. In the longer term, the rules are likely to be tightened because:

> 'In principle, the FSA will want to set for professional firms carrying on the same types of activities as other firms the same financial resources requirement that is developed for other firms, unless the financial risks to which the professional firms are subject can be demonstrated to be markedly different. Relevant to this consideration may be any elements of the professional bodies' regimes that operate so as to secure in practice the interests of the clients of a firm that ceases to trade as a separate entity.'[3]

In due course, this must raise the issue for professional firms of whether any regulated activities that require authorisation should be conducted through a separate FSA authorised vehicle. This could, for example, limit the need for all partners (unless there is a clear management group) having to be approved by the FSA[4]. Whether or not a separate vehicle is created, the firm must clearly determine which of its personnel will be involved with clients and regulated activities so that they too can be approved. Experienced staff may be grandfathered, but otherwise the FSA will require examinations to have been passed[5].

---

1   Consultation Paper 30, Sections 9 and 12 as reconsidered in Consultation Paper 49, paras 1.34–1.37 and *Response to Paper CP30*, sections 9 and 12.
2   FSMA, Sch 6. An argument is put that the 100 solicitors firms that conduct discretionary investment management obtain an unfair advantage from not having to comply with the CAD minimum requirements, although note, not an argument that this really endangers their clients' funds, a classic example of regulatory creep justified by the 'level playing field' argument. The FSA has rejected the argument so far, *Response to Paper CP30*, para 5.19. It is also prepared to rely, in the case of solicitors, on the Law Societies' Accounts Rules to protect clients' money, para 7.19.
3   Consultation Paper 30, Sections 5 and 6 and particularly para 5.27. The requirement to produce returns showing positive net assets has, for the time being, been dropped, *Response to Paper CP30*, section 5.
4   See **5.3**.
5   The FSA's approach is discussed in *Response to Paper CP30*, section 4 and 8. For example, transfer of a grandfathered individual to a new role may require examinations to be passed.

Chapter 12

PUBLIC OFFERS AND LISTINGS

12.1 BACKGROUND

Until the decision in October 1999 to transfer responsibility for listing from the London Stock Exchange to the FSA, this area was not to be subject to significant reform because much of it is determined by European Directives. Offering corporate securities to the public in the UK used to be governed by the Companies Act 1985 and generally required the production of a prospectus[1]. If a listing was being sought, the issuer also had to sign a Listing Agreement with the Stock Exchange which required it to provide more initial information than the statutory minimum and to comply with the Exchange's continuing obligations.

In 1984, European Directives laying down minimum listing requirements were introduced[2], initially by statutory instrument and then by Part IV of the 1986 Act. These replaced the Companies Act 1985 requirements whenever a listing was being sought or had been obtained for the securities concerned. The Stock Exchange was appointed as the 'competent' or listing authority (the UKLA) to supervise such listings and ensure compliance with the European minimum requirements. These requirements were incorporated into *The Listing Rules* and marked as such in the margin to distinguish them from the additional requirements the Stock Exchange continued to impose[3]. These additions have been reduced over the years under the threat of companies seeking listings in less onerous EEA jurisdictions.

The Listing Rules generally required an issuer seeking to list securities to produce a document called listing particulars, whether or not the securities were being offered to the public. However, the requirement to produce a prospectus when making a public offer was reimposed when the Public Offers Directive was implemented in 1995 by the Public Offers of Securities Regulations 1995 (POS Regulations)[4]. For a listing accompanied by a public offer, this was a semantic change because the new prospectus requirements were the same as the existing ones for listing particulars and the document, whatever it was called, was still governed by Part IV of the 1986 Act. For a listing without a public offer (eg a company transferring from AIM to the listed market), listing particulars still had to be produced. However, for a public offer of securities already listed (eg the second tranche of a privatisation issue), no prescribed document was required, although the general rules governing the marketing of investments still applied.

---

1   Companies Act 1985, Part III.
2   Admission Directive 1979/279/EEC; Listing Particulars Directive 1980/390/EEC; Interim Reports Directive 1982/121/EEC (together the 'Listing Directives').
3   The official title of the Stock Exchange's *Yellow Book* was changed from *Admission of Securities to Listing* to *The Listing Rules* and it also included the Stock Exchange rules for listing securities not covered by the Listing Directives at all.
4   1989/298/EEC; SI 1995/153 amended by POS (Amendment) Regulations 1999, SI 1999/734.

The Public Offers Directive, however, did change the regime for securities not seeking a listing. The POS Regulations replaced Part III of the Companies Act 1985[1]. Although less prescriptive than *The Listing Rules*, they still required the production of a full prospectus where there was to be an offer of securities for the first time to the public in the UK. The Regulations included a complex set of exemptions effectively defining what did not amount to a public offer.

Although the Regulations only required a prospectus where there was a public offer, the Stock Exchange required that, if the issuer was seeking to have securities traded on AIM[2] for the first time without a public offer (eg a company transferring from OFEX, the offmarket trading facility), a document covering the same information as a prospectus must be produced. However, unlike listed securities, AIM securities not previously offered to the public (eg a controlling share-holder's) would need a prospectus if offered to the public later.

Part VI of the FSMA largely re-enacts Part IV of the 1986 Act as amended by the POS Regulations. Generally, it covers only securities that are seeking a listing. Although many of the sections are permissive in tone (eg 'the competent authority *may . . .*'), the underlying Listing Directives require such arrangements. The public offer of unlisted securities in the UK is still regulated by the main body of the POS Regulations.

From 1 May 2000, the London Stock Exchange ceased to be the UKLA and the responsibility was transferred to the FSA[3]. Under the FSMA, it is being given the power to admit any investment it considers appropriate to the Official List and to fine persons for breaches of *The Listing Rules*. However, the Treasury still retains the power to transfer all or any of the functions of UKLA, to limit what investments may be listed, to determine which persons are responsible for prospectuses and to define some of the exemptions from the prospectus regime.

As the FSA has commented:

'The transfer of the UKLA does, however, pose some important issues and provides a useful opportunity to review the current approach to listing in the UK. For example, the separation of admission to listing and admission to trading standards, in a world of multiple exchanges trading the same shares, raises the prospect of allowing some adjustment to existing Listing Rules to facilitate competition between exchanges on trading standards. It may also be appropriate to review the current role of sponsors in the listing process.'[4]

However, for the time being, the FSA has reissued *The Listing Rules* in new covers but containing the same rules with the same rule numbers as the *Yellow Book*. The principal change has been to make it a condition of listing that a security is admitted to trading on an RIE. Thus, applications must be made in tandem and the FSA kept informed of any subsequent proposed suspension or cancellation of

---

1   This was originally due to be replaced by Part V of the 1986 Act which, in fact, never came into force.
2   The AIM came into being on the same day as the POS Regulations came into force.
3   Official Listing of Securities (Change of Competent Authority) Regulations 2000, SI 2000/968.
4   Consultation Paper 37, FSA, December 1999, para 1.8.

trading by an RIE[1]. With cross-European exchange mergers, the RIE could soon be based elsewhere in Europe. As the Financial Secretary has commented:

> 'Listing is a seal of approval, ensuring that the issuers of a security will provide certain information to the markets at prescribed times. It is also an EU-wide concept; an enterprise admitted to listing in one Member State can be admitted to trading as a listed security on any stock exchange in any Member State.'[2]

12.2   THE UK LISTING AUTHORITY

The UKLA's principal task is to determine which securities meet the requirements to be admitted to and then retained on the Official List. Its new discretion to admit 'such securities and other things as it considers appropriate' should bring securities that did not fall within Part IV of the 1986 Act (eg gilts and covered warrants) into the statutory framework[3]. The Treasury retains the power to transfer all or any part of this responsibility to another body, subject to affirmative resolutions. This power can be exercised if:

(1) the FSA itself agrees in writing;
(2) the Treasury is satisfied that the performance of the functions would be significantly improved; or
(3) it is otherwise in the public interest.

The Treasury can also make the necessary consequential arrangements, such as the transfer of property and contracts and the amendment of statutes[4]. It seems that such a change would happen only if something had gone seriously awry. Indeed, the Treasury can institute an inquiry if a serious failure in the regulatory system might have caused significant damage to holders of listed (but not AIM) securities[5].

In the meantime, in its capacity as the UKLA, the FSA is not governed by the normal four objectives. The reasons given are:

> 'First, this is an area where the Directives permeate all that the competent authority does. Secondly, given its ability to transfer the functions to another body, the Treasury has a different role *vis-à-vis* the competent authority from the one it has in relation to the FSA generally. Therefore, we intend that, as now, the Treasury will continue to agree annually the competent authority's objectives and to hold regular meetings to assess progress.'[6]

The FSA also has no obligation as the UKLA to consult practitioners and consumers. However, it still has to have regard to six out of the seven restraining principles, concern for the responsibilities of senior management being excluded, and most of the rest of the FSMA applies with some minor modifi-

---

1   Listing Rules 1.23A, 3.14A, 7.5(l), 7.11(f), 7.12(e), 9.44 and 9.44A. This should satisfy the many statutory references to 'listing on a stock exchange'.
2   Vol 351 HC, 5 June 2000, c 64.
3   FSMA, s 74(1)–(3). The Treasury has a reserve power to prohibit certain instruments being listed, if for example they posed undue risk to investors.
4   FSMA, ss 72 and 429(1)(b) and Sch 8.
5   FSMA, s 14(3). For details of such inquiries, see **3.4.2**.
6   Lord McIntosh, vol 611 HL, 21 March 2000, c 186; FSMA, Sch 7, para 2.

cations[1]. For the first time, a special competition regime is going to be extended to the UKLA. The FSMA gives no details of the regime, but allows the Treasury to create it by statutory instrument. However, the arrangement was explained as follows:

> 'The reason for doing this by order is to allow flexibility to adapt the competition scrutiny regime should the power in Schedule 8 to the Bill ever be exercised to transfer the function to another body ... We intend to exercise this power to bring in the same arrangements for the competition scrutiny of the competent authority as the Bill has put in place for the Financial Services Authority.'[2]

To cover its costs, the UKLA may levy fees from issuers and sponsors in respect of applications for and the continuation of listings and approved sponsors' status. The UKLA may not take into account any fines it may levy to cover its costs, but it and its staff have an immunity from damages[3]. For the rest of this chapter, it will be assumed that the UKLA is and remains the FSA.

12.3   ADMISSION TO LISTING FOR UK COMPANIES

No application to admit securities to the Official List may be made other than by, or with the consent of, the issuer. The application must comply with the applicable Listing Rules and any other conditions imposed by the FSA. Even then the application may be refused if 'granting it would be detrimental to the interests of investors'[4]. The FSA has six months in which to consider any application, or six months from the last request for further information. If listing is granted, the applicant must be given a written notice. If, however, the FSA is minded to refuse the application, it must follow its rejection procedures which will now include an applicant's right to refer the refusal to the Tribunal. To protect investors that have dealt in listed securities, once securities are admitted, their listed status cannot then be challenged on the grounds that any requirement or condition was not complied with[5].

On the face of the FSMA, the FSA has a complete discretion to make different rules on listing for different cases and to waive or modify them in particular cases, provided they are made available in writing to the public[6]. In practice, the FSA is bound by the European minimum requirements, particularly in respect of prospectuses and listing particulars. Generally, these documents must be approved by the FSA, filed with the registrar of companies, then published and

---

1   FSMA, s 73 and Sch 7.
2   FSMA, s 95; Lord Bach, vol 612 HL, 18 April 2000, c 658; see **3.4.3**.
3   FSMA, ss 99 and 102. As usual, the immunity does not extend to bad faith or breaches of the Convention. The FSA has said it will not cross-subsidise between its functions as the UKLA and its general regulatory functions: *Response to Consultation Paper 37*, FSA, April 2000, para 6.
4   FSMA, s 75. The Treasury will prescribe private companies and old public companies as being unlistable. It will also prescribe what counts as the 'issuer', for example in the case of covered warrants and other derivatives: FSMA, s 103(1).
5   FSMA, s 76. Failure to comply with the time-limit is deemed to be a refusal so that the applicant can then refer the matter to the Tribunal. Such a referral can only be by the applicant and not at any shareholders' behest: *R v The International Stock Exchange of the United Kingdom and the Republic of Ireland Limited, ex p Else (1982) Ltd* [1993] BCC 11, CA.
6   FSMA, ss 74(4) and 101.

advertised before securities can be listed[1]. In addition to detailed information required by *The Listing Rules* and any special conditions imposed by the FSA, listing particulars:

> '... must contain all such information as investors and their professional advisers would reasonably require, and reasonably expect to find there, for the purpose of making an informed assessment of—
> a.   the assets and liabilities, financial position, profits and losses, and prospects of the issuer of the securities; and
> b.   the rights attaching to the securities.'[2]

This general obligation is not absolute. It is only information that those responsible for the particulars know or ought to have obtained through reasonable enquiries. Nor do the particulars have to restate the obvious. In determining what must be included, regard must be had to the nature of the issue, the persons likely to acquire it, the professional advice they may reasonably be expected to have, and the information already required to be available to them and such advisers[3].

The FSA has a power to dispense with or modify the application of *The Listing Rules*, but generally omission of information in listing particulars may only be authorised if the disclosure would be:

(1) contrary to the public interest (a ministerial certificate may be issued to this effect);
(2) seriously detrimental to the issuer and not essential for any likely acquirer to know in order to make an informed assessment; or
(3) unnecessary given those expected to deal in the particular type of securities[4].

If prior to dealings commencing there arises either:

(1) a significant change affecting matters already required to be included in the listing particulars; or
(2) a significant new matter that would have been included in the original particulars,

supplementary listing particulars must be submitted by the issuer for approval by the FSA and then filed and published. All those responsible for the original particulars are under an obligation to notify the issuer of any such change or new matter of which they become aware[5]. The formal notice announcing the listing must also have prior approval of the FSA and any summary particulars and other advertisements referring to the listing must be authorised (although not formally approved) by the FSA[6].

Once a class of securities has been listed, further new issues of that class still require new listing particulars to be produced, unless the issue is:

(1) a capitalisation issue;

---

1   FSMA, ss 79, 83 and 86.
2   FSMA, s 80(1) and (2).
3   FSMA, s 80(3) and (4). For those responsible, see **12.4.3**.
4   FSMA, s 82; Listing Particulars Directive, Art 7.
5   FSMA, s 81. For those responsible, see below.
6   FSMA, s 98; Listing Rules 8.23–8.27.

(2) shares on the conversion of listed convertibles or the exercise of listed warrants;

(3) shares or depository receipts for listed shares of no greater nominal value; or

(4) shares amounting to less than 10% of that class already in issue[1].

12.3.1   Prospectuses and other applications for listing

As has already been noted, a prospectus must be produced, even when securities are seeking a listing, if they are being offered to the public in the UK for the first time. An offer to the public includes an offer made to any section of the public including existing members or debenture holders of a company or clients of the offeror[2]. There are many exceptions, but in practice these exceptions are not significant because listing particulars covering identical information will still have to be published unless the issue falls into one of the four narrower exceptions for listing particulars given above. Otherwise, the rules applying to prospectuses are the same as those applying to listing particulars[3].

As the European minimum requirements for prospectuses and listing particulars do not apply to all securities that the FSA may admit to the Official List, it has the power to require other documents to be published before listing is granted[4]. These include issues under the four exceptions mentioned above and securities issued by certain CISs, States and their regional or local authorities, and certain warrants and certificates representing debt securities[5].

Overseas companies that have had a prospectus or listing particulars approved by the competent authority of another EEA country in the last three months, may use the same document as listing particulars in the UK. The document must be translated into English and provide certain tax, meeting notices and dividend payment details for UK residents. Any exemptions or derogations from the European minimum requirements must be acceptable to the FSA[6]. If the securities are already listed in the other EEA State, the FSA may refuse listing if it 'considers that the issuer has failed to comply with any obligations to which he is subject as a result of that [other] listing'.[7] This implies that, unless this is the case, the London listing should usually be granted as part of the European mutual recognition programme.

This mutual recognition of documents does mean that the FSA can approve prospectuses voluntarily submitted to it where no listing is being sought in the UK, but the issuer wishes to use the prospectus to offer shares in the UK and other Member States[8].

---

1   Listing Rules 5.27.
2   FSMA, s 84 and Sch 11, para 1.
3   FSMA, s 86 and Sch 11, paras 2–25.
4   FSMA, s 79(1)(b).
5   Listing Rules 5.26–5.30.
6   Listing Rules 17.68–17.79.
7   FSMA, s 75(6).
8   FSMA, s 87 and Sch 9.

12.3.2 Continuing obligations

Many of the existing rules on listing impose continuing obligations upon corporate issuers, of which the principal ones are the publication:

(1) of audited accounts within six months of the year end[1];
(2) of a financial report on the first half of each year within four months[2]; and
(3) 'without delay of any major new developments in its sphere of activity which are not public knowledge which may:
    (a) by virtue of the effect of those developments on its assets and liabilities or financial position or on the general course of its business, lead to substantial movement in the price of its listed securities; or
    (b) in the case of a company with debt securities listed, by virtue of the effect of those developments on its assets and liabilities or financial position or on the general course of its business, lead to substantial movement in the price of its listed securities, or significantly affect its ability to meet its commitments.'[3]

These three rules are European minimum requirements, but others on major capital transactions, transactions with related parties, financial disclosure and the obligations on the directors of listed companies are additional requirements until now imposed by the Stock Exchange. These additional requirements have not generally been imposed on overseas companies seeking a secondary listing in the UK[4].

12.3.3 Separating out the UKLA

While the Stock Exchange was the UKLA, being listed on the exchange and on the Official List meant the same thing. Now there will be a distinction between admission to listing and trading. As has been seen above, the Stock Exchange has traditionally imposed obligations over and above the minimum European listing requirements. The FSA is now going to have to decide to what extent it will continue to do so. As the competent authority:

> 'The FSA must be satisfied that the admission to listing requirements guarantee the minimum acceptable standards for securities offered to the public, in the event of an exchange deciding not to add any additional admission to trading rules.'[5]

The Stock Exchange could impose extra requirements for admission to trading as the NYSE does over the SEC's requirements or, as indeed the Stock Exchange itself does (and will continue to do), over the POS Regulations when admitting securities to the AIM. However, it is under competitive pressure from Tradepoint and others that may be prepared to impose few if any such extra requirements. As a minimum, however, there have to be arrangements to ensure that an exchange has the information from listed companies to maintain an orderly secondary market as it is required to do as an RIE[6].

---

1   Listing Rules 12.41 and 12.42.
2   Listing Rules 12.46–12.59.
3   Listing Rules 9.1. An exception is made for confidential negotiations or impending developments so long as there are no leaks: Listing Rules 9.4 and 9.5.
4   Listing Rules Chapter 17.
5   Consultation Paper 37, para 2.7.
6   Consultation Paper 37, paras 6.12–6.14.

The Stock Exchange has published its first set of admission to trading rules which it has kept short to try to limit the overlap with what are now the FSA's rules on listing[1]. Each applicant must specify a director or senior employee responsible for communicating with the Exchange and may also nominate a representative (eg its listing sponsor) as well. No later than when draft documentation is submitted to UKLA, the applicant must inform and meet with the Exchange to discuss its application. The application must be accompanied by copies of listing particulars and/or other key documents associated with the issue and cover all the classes of security seeking listing. There are special arrangements for later issues on the conversion of warrants and options or under an issuance programme. The Stock Exchange may refuse admission to trading if:

(1) '[it] may be detrimental to the orderly operation of the Exchange's markets or to the reputation of the markets as a whole'; or
(2) 'the applicant does not or will not comply with the Standards or with any special conditions'[2].

It is hard to imagine that if either of these were to arise, the FSA would have been prepared to admit the security to listing.

Under its continuing obligations, the Stock Exchange imposes the same general obligation as found in *The Listing Rules* on issuers to announce information that 'would be likely to lead to substantial movement in the price of its listed securities' and to give a timetable for dividends, issues, redemptions, etc. The only other obligations are to impose *The Listing Rules* timetable for open offers and to pay an annual fee[3]. An issuer may request the suspension of trading and the Exchange will impose one if either listing is suspended or 'the orderly operation of its markets ... may be temporarily jeopardised'. The Exchange retains an absolute discretion to cancel the right to trade. Finally, unless a private censure is agreed upon, the Stock Exchange will refer any proposal to censure an issuer or its nominated representative or to cancel trading to the Company Disciplinary Committee whose ruling may be appealed within 20 days to the Company Appeals Committee whose decisions are final[4].

The FSA has so far only made minor consequential amendments to *The Listing Rules*, partly because the Stock Exchange had just consulted comprehensively on amendments to *The Listing Rules* which were only implemented in January 2000[5]. The FSMA will require some procedural changes to be made (see below).

One problem arising from the separation of the UKLA from the Stock Exchange is the replacement of the Regulatory News Service (RNS) run by the Exchange's Company Announcements Office (CAO). To ensure orderly markets, *The Listing Rules* still require listed companies to make any significant announcements via the RNS during business hours. Out-of-hours announcements must be given to two

---

1   *Admission and Disclosure Standards*, Stock Exchange, May 2000.
2   *Admission and Disclosure Standards*, Chapters 1 and 2.
3   *Admission and Disclosure Standards*, Chapter 3, cf Listing Rules 4.24 and 9.1–9.10.
4   *Admission and Disclosure Standards*, Chapter 4.
5   The Listing Rules, FSA May 2000; *Listing Rules 2000*, London Stock Exchange, September 1999. As has already been noted, the principal change is to make listing and admission to trading on an RIE interdependent. The FSA is considering whether compliance with Listing Rules could offer a safe harbour from market abuse: *Response to Consultation Paper 37*, para 16.

newspapers and two wire services and sent to the CAO for publication when the market opens. The RNS has ensured a minimum standard of timely dissemination of information and has avoided the need for many trading halts. The RNS will be retained for a transitional period, but the FSA is considering the use of electronic filing and the commercial news services as occurs in the USA; although it must be admitted that the US news dissemination system has not been noticeably more timely and efficient than that in the UK[1]. It should be noted that although filing announcements remains the same, file copies of circulars and resolutions should now be sent to the UKLA rather than the CAO, and the UKLA will arrange a Document Viewing Facility for contracts and other documents to be put on display[2].

12.4   THE FINANCIAL SERVICES AND MARKETS ACT 2000 AND SANCTIONS

The FSMA will require some changes to the UKLA's procedures. For example, as part of the *Yellow Book* requirements, the Stock Exchange used to require all applicants for listing to use the services of a sponsoring member firm whom it could hold responsible for ensuring that the applicant complied with all its obligations. After Big Bang, that was amended to allow banks and other non-member firms to perform the same functions by joining a list of approved sponsors. Now under the FSMA, this is being put on a statutory basis. *The Listing Rules* will continue to prescribe the qualifications for and responsibilities of an approved sponsor. If the FSA is minded to refuse an application to be an approved sponsor, it will have to follow its rejection procedures; but if it is minded to cancel an existing approval, that is considered so serious, it is subject to the FSA's disciplinary procedures[3].

The Stock Exchange claimed a general power to suspend a listing 'where the smooth operation of the market is, or may be, temporarily jeopardised or where the protection of investors so requires', which if it lasted for more than six months could lead to a cancellation[4]. The FSA will continue to have a discretion to suspend a listing in such circumstances and to discontinue a listing 'if satisfied that there are special circumstances which preclude normal regular dealings in them'. As suspension or discontinuance may have to be done urgently, under the FSMA the FSA will only need to follow its supervisory procedures, but if, having suspended the listing, it refuses to cancel the suspension, it will have to follow its rejection procedures. Holders of the securities, however, cannot challenge the decisions, even through judicial review[5].

---

1   Consultation Paper 37, Part 5.
2   Listing Rules 8.4 and 9.31. The FSA has set up an Information Dissemination Advisory Group to look at the whole issue of the dissemination of regulatory announcements: *Response to Consultation Paper 37*, para 14.
3   FSMA, ss 88, 89 and 392. The FSA 'may' require sponsors, so that this obligation could be removed in future without the FSMA being amended. Sponsors may be publicly censured, but not fined; see below.
4   Listing Rules 1.19 and 1.23.
5   FSMA, ss 77 and 78; *R v The International Stock Exchange of the United Kingdom and the Republic of Ireland Limited, ex parte Else (1982) Ltd* [1993] BCC 11, CA.

The Listing Rules can specify what remedial action must be taken if an issuer fails to comply with any of its obligations and, in particular, allows the FSA to publish information itself if the issuer fails to do so[1]. Until now, it has been the Quotations Committee of the Stock Exchange that has exercised the power publicly to censure the issuer and any director involved and to suspend or cancel the listing or threaten to do so if the director remained in office[2]. There was an appeal to the Quotations Appeal Committee. The FSA has kept these Committees as part of its structure; but now the power publicly to censure, plus the new power to fine is being put on a statutory basis[3].

12.4.1   Reprimands, fines and crimes

Under the FSMA, the FSA is now acquiring the right to fine as an alternative to publicly censuring an applicant or issuer that it considers has contravened any listing rule (whether or not it is an European minimum requirement). It may also publicly censure or fine anyone who was a director at the time and was 'knowingly concerned' in the contravention. Sponsors may be censured but not fined for breaching any rules on listing imposed upon them[4]. The FSA must have regard to its current published policy on the imposition and amount of fines in this area which must not take account of the costs of running the UKLA. Like other fining policies, it must have regard to:

(1)   the seriousness of the contravention;
(2)   the extent to which it was deliberate or reckless; and
(3)   whether the person to be fined is an individual.

This policy and the associated scheme to apply the proceeds of any fines for the benefit of issuers are subject to the same basic public consultation as the FSA's complaints scheme and other policies for fining. In imposing a fine or a public reprimand, the FSA must follow its disciplinary procedures[5].

Failure to file listing particulars or a prospectus with the registrar of companies on or before the date they are published is an offence committed by the issuer and anyone knowingly a party to the publication but is only punishable by a fine[6]. Offering securities for the first time to the public in the UK before a prospectus is published is an offence punishable by up to two years' imprisonment as well as a fine[7]. Issuing advertisements in connection with the listing that have not been authorised or approved by the FSA is also punishable by up to two years in prison and a fine. There is a defence of reasonably believing that the advertisement

---

1   FSMA, s 96.
2   Listing Rules 1.8–1.10.
3   Consultation Paper 37, para 6.5.
4   FSMA, ss 89 and 91. The fine must be imposed within two years of when the FSA, from the information it had, ought to have known of the contravention.
5   FSMA, ss 89, 92 to 94, 100 and 392; for the disciplinary procedures, see **9.3.1**.
6   FSMA, s 83(3) and (4).
7   FSMA, s 85(1)–(3). Publishing an incomplete prospectus is not an offence under this section.

issued has been authorised or approved[1]. No civil liability can arise on the basis that an authorised or approved advertisement is misleading, if taken together with the listing particulars or prospectus it would not be likely to mislead those likely to consider acquiring the securities[2]. Serious errors in listing particulars or prospectuses may amount to the crime of misleading statements and practices[3].

Just as the FSA can appoint an investigator to look into suspected contraventions of FSA rules and certain criminal provisions, it can appoint an investigator 'if it appears that there are circumstances suggesting':

(1) a breach of any Listing Rules;
(2) a director of an applicant or issuer has been knowingly concerned in such a breach; or
(3) a contravention of the criminal provisions concerning prospectuses and listing particulars referred to above[4].

In addition, the FSA can launch a court action on behalf of investors for compensation and/or disgorgement of profits for the breach of any obligation under the FSMA, indeed it can directly order an authorised firm to pay without going to court[5]. However, there is a separate civil action against anyone responsible for misleading listing particulars and prospectuses.

12.4.2 Compensation

In general, breaches of *The Listing Rules* are not a statutory tort giving a private civil action for damages. However, failure to publish a prospectus before a public offer of securities in the UK is[6]. The more common problem, however, is that a prospectus has been published, but it is inaccurate. *Prima facie*, errors of omission or commission in listing particulars and prospectuses render any party responsible for the document liable for any loss caused thereby to anyone acquiring the securities covered by the document[7]. This statutory liability applies only to listing particulars and prospectuses (including supplementary ones) and not any other documents or announcements issued by listed companies.

Errors include:

(1) any untrue or misleading statement in the document; and
(2) the omission of any matter required by Listing Rules other than:
     (a) a statement that there is no such matter; or
     (b) an omission authorised by the FSA[8].

Anyone responsible can escape liability if he made such enquiries, if any, as were reasonable and reasonably believed that the statement was true and not misleading (or was properly omitted) when the document was submitted for FSA approval, provided that at the time the securities were subsequently acquired:

---

1   FSMA, s 98(2) and (3).
2   FSMA, s 98(4) and (5); see **12.4.2**.
3   See **7.2**.
4   FSMA, s 97.
5   FSMA, ss 382 and 384.
6   FSMA, ss 85(5) and 150(4).
7   FSMA, s 90.
8   FSMA, ss 82 and 90(3).

(1) he continued in that belief;
(2) it was not reasonably practicable to bring the correction to the attention of those likely to acquire them;
(3) he had taken all reasonable steps to bring a correction to their attention; or
(4) he ought reasonably to be excused because he believed it when the dealings commenced and now too much time has elapsed[1].

He is not liable for failing to call for a supplementary document if, until dealings commenced, he reasonably believed the change to be immaterial. He is also not liable if a correction notice has actually been published properly or after having taken all reasonable steps, he reasonably believes that it has been. No-one is liable if the acquirer knew of the error at the time of the acquisition[2].

Where the statement is, or purports to be, made by or on the authority of an expert (eg an accountant, valuer or engineer) and included with his consent, others responsible for the document only have to prove a reasonable belief that the expert was competent and had consented (rather than that his statements were true, etc). Any correction notice need only be to the effect that he was not competent or that he had not consented[3]. Those responsible also have no liability for statements made by public officials or in official documents, provided they have been accurately and fairly reproduced[4].

It should be noted that for any person responsible for a prospectus or listing particulars:

(1) the positive duty to make enquiries lapses when the document is submitted for, presumably, final approval;
(2) a duty to report any significant changes to the issuer and for it to produce a supplementary document continues until dealings begin; but
(3) thereafter, there remains a duty to use reasonable endeavours to get a correction notice about any significant changes at least until there has been a sufficient lapse of time that the document is no longer relevant or those responsible should be excused[5].

Acquiring securities includes contracting to acquire them or any interest in them, not just at the time of the listing but probably also in secondary dealings thereafter[6]. As the section refers only to loss suffered 'as a result of' the error, no actual reliance on an error in the document should need to be proved, just that the error caused the offer or subsequent market price to be too high[7]. However, the securities do have to be those covered by the document. So, for example, if a public offer is being made of ordinary shares prior to an initial listing for the company, the prospectus covers not just the shares being publicly offered, but also

---

1   FSMA, Sch 10, para 1.
2   FSMA, Sch 10, paras 3, 6 and 7. The duty to produce a supplementary document only lapses on dealings beginning and this presumably means official rather than grey market dealings.
3   FSMA, Sch 10, paras 2, 4 and 8. Of course, this may not be a defence against the expert suing the directors if his misstatement was caused, in part, by their misinforming him in the first place.
4   FSMA, Sch 10, para 5.
5   The overall effect of FSMA, ss 80, 81 and 90 and Sch 10.
6   FSMA, s 90(7); *Possfund Custodian Trustee Ltd v Diamond* [1996] 2 All ER 774.
7   FSMA, s 90(1)(b). The is known in the USA as 'fraud-on-the-market', where it is sufficient to establish liability; see *Basic v Levinson* 485 US 224 (1998).

all the other ordinary shares because the FSA will require them to be listed at the same time. In effect, the prospectus is listing particulars for these other shares. However, if the company already has securities listed, any later prospectus or listing particulars will only cover those securities about to be listed. This is so even though the information in the document will affect the securities already listed and if these are of the same class, it may be practically impossible to know in secondary dealings whether securities acquired are new or old. This could force the acquirer of securities back on to common-law actions which are specifically preserved, but cannot make anyone liable for non-disclosure of matters that would not have been required to be disclosed in the listing particulars or prospectus[1].

12.4.3 Persons responsible

The Treasury is to define by statutory instrument those responsible for listing particulars and prospectuses.[2] These were previously listed in the 1986 Act, ss 152 and 154A(b) and the approach will remain the same. The expected list is therefore:

(1) the issuer of the securities;
(2) the directors (and proposed directors) of the issuer;
(3) anyone named in the document as accepting responsibility for all or part of it;
(4) anyone else authorising all or part of the document; and
(5) in the case of a prospectus, anyone else offering the securities as a principal[3].

This list is not without some difficulties.

(1) In most cases the issuer is obvious, but in the case of listed covered warrants (ie warrants to acquire existing securities, which may or may not be held by the securities house) it is the securities house issuing the warrants, not the underlying company, whereas in the case of listed depositary receipts, it is the underlying company, not the depositary[4].
(2) Generally, current directors are specifically named as responsible in the document. Proposed directors are liable only if they have agreed to be named. Directors are not liable for Eurobond prospectuses or where they are specifically exempted by the UKLA. However, because banks issuing listed covered warrants are treated as the issuers, the bank's directors are responsible for such issues[5].
(3) Those accepting responsibility for part of the document, for example experts for their reports, are responsible for only that part, in the form and context that they agreed. A particular problem arises with takeovers for securities which require details of the offeree to be contained in listing particulars. They can be made the sole responsibility of the offeree and its directors with their agreement, but this cannot be obtained in contested takeovers[6].

---

1 FSMA, s 90(6) and (8), see **12.4.4**.
2 FSMA, s 79(3).
3 Economic Secretary, Standing Committee A, 28 October 1999, c 625.
4 1986 Act, ss 142(7) and 152(1)(a). It should also be noted that unlike the position in the USA under the Securities Act 1933, s 11, the issuer has the benefit of all the defences open to any other parties responsible for the document.
5 1986 Act, s 152(1)(b) and (c), (2) and (5).
6 1986 Act, s 152(1)(d), (3) and (4).

(4) It is not entirely clear whether any sponsoring bank or broker can be said to be authorising the document. Indeed, the particular liability of underwriters is not spelt out as it is in the USA[1].

(5) Underwriters may still be caught as offerors, at least if they purchase the securities to sell them on (ie an offer for sale). If, however, they merely agree to be the purchasers of last resort, the offerors are the existing shareholders (eg directors or venture capitalists) selling shares in the offer. Venture capitalists have complained about this liability for a document that they have not drafted, even though to the extent that they sell in the offer, they have benefited from the mistake. The provision has recently been amended so that where the prospectus has been drafted by the issuer or others acting for it, any others such as venture capitalists selling securities in the offer are not liable[2].

12.4.4 Common-law actions

Where the acquirer of securities has bought them directly from an offeror or issuer, the normal contractual remedies for breach of contract or misrepresentation will apply, including repudiation or rescission of the contract. However, to be able to sue others responsible for any misleading document or announcement, for example the directors, auditors and sponsors, an action would have to be for deceit or negligent misrepresentation.

To prove intentional or reckless deception is notoriously difficult, although if it can be established against any party he is liable for all the losses that naturally flowed from the deceit[3]. Negligence is easier to prove, but the party will only be liable if a duty of care was broken and the loss was within the contemplation of that duty. In *Possfund Custodian Trustee Ltd v Diamond*,[4] Lightman J seemed to consider that a duty of care may be owed to acquirers of securities in any offer and in the after-market, although it is unclear whether such acquirers need to have relied directly on the error in the prospectus or whether reliance upon the effect on the purchase price is sufficient (ie the fraud-on-the-market doctrine).

12.5 UNLISTED SECURITIES

Although not part of the FSMA, to complete the picture on controlling securities, it is necessary to look briefly at the prospectus regime for unlisted securities. The POS Regulations require that:

(1) any offering (written, oral or otherwise) by a principal for himself or another[5],

(2) to the public or a section of the public in the UK[6],

---

1   1986 Act, s 152(1)(e); Securities Act 1933, s 11(b) as interpreted in *Escott v Bar-Chris Construction* 283 F Supp 643 (SDNY 1968).

2   1986 Act, s 154A, as amended by the POS (Amendment) Regulations, reg 3.

3   *Derry v Peek* (1889) 14 App Cas 337; *Smith New Court Securities Ltd v Scrimgeour Vickers (Asset Management) Ltd* [1996] 4 All ER 769.

4   [1996] 2 All ER 774, but compare *Al Nakib Investments (Jersey) Ltd v Longcroft* [1990] 3 All ER 321.

5   POS Regulations, reg 5.

6   POS Regulations, reg 6.

(3) of shares, debentures, warrants and depositary receipts[1],

(4) can only be made for the first time after the publication of a prospectus[2],

(5) which has been registered with the appropriate registrar of companies[3],

(6) containing all the information listed in Sch 1 to the Regulations[4], and

(7) 'all such information as investors would reasonably require, and reasonably expect to find there, for the purpose of making an informed assessment of –

(a) the assets and liabilities, financial position, profits and losses, and prospects of the issuer of the securities; and

(b) the rights attaching to those securities.'[5]

Although Sch 1 is far less specific than *The Listing Rules,* the key requirements are the same as is the overall obligation in (7) above. Indeed, curiously the obligations in the Regulations seem more onerous as the obligation is not specifically restricted by the likely knowledge of any professional advisers[6].

Exemptions from the prospectus requirements can be made for rights issues and issues of under 10% of a class of shares already traded on an approved exchange (eg the AIM). Full prospectuses issued within the last 12 months can be used or referred to for a later issue of new securities (of the same or a different class) so long as updated information is provided[7]. Prospectuses approved by other EEA authorities may also be used for public offers and where no listing is being sought in the UK, do not have to be translated into English[8].

No approval for any prospectus for non-listed securities need be sought from the FSA, unless it is to be used for public offers in other EEA countries. Nor does the Stock Exchange pre-vet a prospectus in connection with an application for securities to be traded on the AIM[9]. FSA permission can be obtained to omit information in the same way as for listing particulars, except on the basis of being contrary to the public interest which requires ministerial permission[10]. The obligation to produce supplementary prospectuses is similar to that for listed securities except that the obligation extends to the closing of the offer rather than to the commencement of any dealings[11].

The criminal sanctions for offering securities to the public without a prospectus, for failing to file with the registrar or for advertising the offer without stating where a prospectus may be obtained from, are also similar[12]. As with the listed regime, there is no requirement to send a prospectus to offerees, but if the prospectus errors cause loss there are similar statutory provisions for compensation[13]. However, some doubt has been raised as to whether those acquiring

1   POS Regulations, reg 3.
2   POS Regulations, reg 4(1).
3   POS Regulations, reg 4(2).
4   POS Regulations, reg 8.
5   POS Regulations, reg 9(1).
6   FSMA, s 80(4).
7   POS Regulations, reg 8(4)–(6).
8   POS Regulations, Sch 4 as amended by POS (Amendment) Regulations, reg 2.
9   Stock Exchange Rules 16 and 17 cover AIM securities.
10   POS Regulations, reg 11.
11   POS Regulations, reg 10; See also the FSMA, Sch 10, para 4.
12   POS Regulations, reg 16.
13   POS Regulations, reg 14.

securities in secondary dealings (eg on the AIM) rather than in the original offer can sue[1].

The persons responsible for a prospectus or supplementary prospectus are:

(1)   the issuer;
(2)   the current or named prospective directors of the issuer;
(3)   those accepting responsibility for all or part of the prospectus, for that part;
(4)   any others authorising all or part of the prospectus, for that part;
(5)   the offeror where not the issuer; and
(6)   the directors of the offeror where the issue is not in association with the issuer[2].

The last two raise some difficult issues already touched on in connection with listed securities. To be an offeror, a person has to be acting as a principal[3]. Thus, if a prospectus covers shares sold by existing shareholders, the sponsor will be the offeror if it acts as a principal, but the shareholders will be offerors if the sponsor acts as an agent. Indeed, if the sponsor is only an agent, it is not clear if it is responsible for the prospectus at all, unless it can be said that the prospectus was 'authorised' by it[4]. The directors of the sponsor will not in any case be liable as that offer would still be in association with the issuer. However, the directors of securities houses offering unlisted 'covered warrants' are liable because that offer is not in association with the issuer.

12.5.1   Private placements

Although the exceptions to what amounts to a public offer are almost identical for unlisted and listed securities, they are far more significant for unlisted securities because if an offer falls within them it is treated as a private placement with no specific documentation required[5]. These exemptions are useful, not just for small domestic issues, but also for international issues. Despite the creation of a single European market, the test of whether an issue requires a prospectus is made jurisdiction by jurisdiction. So, even if a public offer of securities is being made with a prospectus in one EEA country, any limited offers being made at the same time in the UK and any other EEA countries can claim the benefit of the exemptions under the POS Regulations and the equivalent exemptions in those countries[6]. However, such a private offer in the UK is still regulated by the FSA's marketing rules[7].

Over 20 different exemptions are listed in reg 7. Certain exemptions apply to particular types of issue, for example those:

---

1   *Possfund Custodian Trustee Ltd v Diamond* [1996] 2 All ER 774, 783.
2   POS Regulations, reg 13.
3   POS Regulations, reg 5.
4   Again this contrasts with the heavy responsibility of underwriters in the USA; see Securities Act 1933, s 11(b), as interpreted in *Escott v Bar-Chris Construction* 283 F Supp 643 (SDNY 1968).
5   POS Regulations, reg 7, cf the FSMA, Sch 11. The Stock Exchange does require the equivalent of a prospectus if there is an initial application to have the securities traded on the AIM.
6   Confirmed by the Economic Secretary, Standing Committee A, 28 October 1999, c 650.
7   FSMA, s 21 outlaws financial promotion in the UK other than by or with the approval of an authorised person. Those authorised persons are generally subject to the FSA's detailed rules

(1) under 40,000 ecus in total;
(2) where the minimum investment is over 40,000 ecus;
(3) to employees, ex-employees and their immediate families;
(4) of private company securities under any pre-emption requirement; or
(5) of Euro-securities provided that they are not advertised to inexperienced investors.

Euro-securities are defined as securities offered only through financial institutions, in at least one country other than the issuer's home country, by a syndicate with members from at least two countries[1]. This exception is really a triumph of pragmatism over consistency, as although such Eurobond issues are not generally sold to private investors in the UK, they are in the rest of Europe. This mechanism of issue offers little protection to such investors and could be used perfectly well for the aggressive sale of junk bonds. It is specified only to exclude the lucrative Eurobond market from the tiresome details and liabilities involved in the issue of prospectuses.

Other exemptions generally depend upon to whom the issue is offered and are cumulative, eg issues:

(1) to investment professionals;
(2) to not more than 50 persons;
(3) to a 'sufficiently knowledgeable' restricted circle;
(4) in connection with a takeover; and
(5) of the same class and issued at the same time as securities for which a prospectus has been issued.

To avoid artificial use of these exemptions, small separate issues made within a 12-month period may be treated as one public offer. On the other hand, the use of the first three exemptions together can cover quite extensive offers, particularly as offers to investment professionals appear to allow them to take the investment for their discretionary clients. Care must be taken with the 50 limit, however, as it may be that any individual (partners counting as separate individuals) offered the securities in the last 12 months (whether or not he accepted) counts in the total.

The takeover exemption might cover not only securities issued as consideration in a public takeover, but also pre-placings with third-party investors of securities issued as vendor consideration for buying private companies. However, even if 'offered in connection with a takeover' does not cover such third-party placings, it would require a very large placing to exceed the judicious application of the first three exemptions above.

The last exemption appears to deal with the problem of an unlisted company, a minority of whose shares were sold with a prospectus and a significant number of the remainder are now to be sold. However, if that is the purpose of the exemption, the drafting is infelicitous because, for example, if the company only sold new shares to raise capital under the prospectus, the remaining shares were not 'issued at the same time' (unless most were part of a contemporaneous

---

on marketing. Breach of FSMA, s 21 may also give rise to the FSA seeking compensation or a disgorgement of profits (FSMA, s 382), see **9.2** and **13.1**.

1   POS Regulations, reg 2 as amended by POS (Amendment) Regulations, reg 2 and POS (Amendment) (No 2) Regulations 1999, SI 1999/1146.

capitalisation issue) even if they were in issue at the time. Again, reliance on the first three exemptions taken together is probably sufficient.

Chapter 13

MARKETING IN GENERAL AND COLLECTIVE INVESTMENT SCHEMES

13.1 MARKETING IN GENERAL

As was seen in Chapter 4, a vital feature of the FSMA, helping to delimit its scope, is the restriction on engaging in financial promotion, that is marketing financial products and services. This restriction applies only to promotion in the course of a business. Therefore, private recommendations, whether made over the dinner table or in an on-line chat room, are not caught, even if they are made by someone in the financial services industry, provided, of course, they are not going to generate business for him or his firm. That still leaves three broad groups which need to consider the financial promotion regime:

(1) commercial companies not conducting a financial services business;
(2) exempt businesses; and
(3) authorised firms.

13.1.1 Commercial companies

Commercial companies not directly involved in deposit-taking, insurance or other investment business in the UK (which generally require authorisation) are, nevertheless, conducting a business and must either have any communication that may be a promotion approved by an authorised firm, or rely on a specific exemption under the FPE Order[1].

Problems are most likely to arise for such non-authorised companies when they are:

(1) raising capital for themselves;
(2) buying or selling themselves or members of the group;
(3) offering financial products or services to their employees; and
(4) commenting about their financial performance.

(1) Offers of securities will require the filing of a prospectus unless the offer is not being made to the public. To be certain that an offer is private, a firm will have to make sure that the offer falls into the cumulative list of exceptions under the POS Regulations (or the more restricted set in the Listing Rules, if the securities are to be listed)[2]. Prospectuses, mini-prospectuses, formal advertisements and documents referring to the availability of the prospectus are exempt, but other promotional material surrounding a public offer will require the approval of an authorised firm[3]. A private offer will also require the approval of an authorised firm unless it is only directed at professionals and high net worth or sophisticated investors[4]. Direct approaches (eg visits or telephone calls) should only be made to

---

1   FSMA, s 21.
2   See **12.3.1** and **12.5.1**.
3   FPE Order, arts 58–64.
4   FPE Order, arts 39 and 41–43.

professional investors and high net worth firms although initial soundings of others may be possible[1].

(2) There are exemptions for promoting joint ventures, purchasing and selling small private companies and offers to take over private companies[2]. Direct approaches should only be made in respect of private sales or management buy-outs[3]. Offers made to take over quoted companies and defence documents fall within the exemption for official announcements made through exchanges[4]. However, other advertisements, telephone campaigns etc will need to be approved by an authorised firm unless they can be confined to professional investors and high net worth firms[5]. Take over offers with securities as consideration do not have to be filed as prospectuses, but if the securities are to be listed and are not less than 10% of an existing class of listed securities, listing particulars will still have to be produced[6].

(3) A company can make direct approaches to its current and former employees (and their immediate families) about employee share schemes, although any wider scheme will have to be arranged through an authorised person. It may also make direct approaches about any occupational pension scheme[7].

(4) Formal statements made by quoted companies through a stock exchange are exempt, as are other statements, advertisements or documents affecting the company's securities, provided they do not contain any specific advice, invitation or inducement to underwrite, subscribe for or deal in investments or otherwise be involved in investment business[8]. Most of these would not amount to inducements or invitations of any kind anyway. Statements by unquoted companies are even less likely to be viewed as inducements or invitations and there is a specific exemption for statements affecting the company's securities in or accompanied by the directors' reports and annual accounts, but again only if they do not contain any specific advice, inducement or invitation to underwrite, subscribe for or deal in investments, or otherwise be involved in investment business[9].

13.1.2   Exempt businesses

Promotions by RIEs and RCHs of their own and their members' services are exempt, provided they do not refer to specific investments. Appointed representatives can also issue promotions within the area of their exemption, but may not give approval to non-authorised persons' promotions[10]. However, non-authorised solicitors and accountants may not be able to rely on these general exemptions and may have to rely on others. In particular, promotions of deposits and general insurance are basically exempt, as are generic promotions of types of investments. Introducing clients to authorised firms to give specific investment advice is also

---

1   FPE Order, arts 14, 39(1)(a), 42(1)(a) and 49.
2   FPE Order, arts 33 and 54–57.
3   FPE Order, arts 14, 54 and 65.
4   FPE Order, arts 58 and 59. Indeed, defence documents are not usually promoting investment
     activity, but trying to stop it.
5   FPE Order, arts 14, 39(1)(a) and 42(1)(a).
6   FSMA, Sch 10, para 12 and POS Regulations, reg 7(2)(k); cf Listing Rule 5.27.
7   FPE Order, arts 14, 52 and 69.
8   FPE Order, arts 58–60.
9   FPE Order, art 51.
10   FPE Order, arts 28–30.

exempt, although making direct approaches for this purpose is not permitted. Direct approaches are permitted for the purposes of acting as a trustee or personal representative[1].

The position of the media is not straightforward. Newspapers and broadcasters continue not to need authorisation for giving occasional pieces of investment advice[2]. Therefore, if they then accept an advertisement which amounts to financial promotion and it has not been issued or approved by an authorised firm, they are 'causing a communication to be made' and they cannot claim the passive provider exemption since they decide which advertisements they will carry. They do have a due diligence defence against prosecution and claims for compensation[3]. There is also no specific exemption for journalists and articles must not contain 'invitations or inducements', even if they may amount to occasional investment advice.

13.1.3 Authorised firms

Authorised firms have a blanket exemption from the restriction on financial promotion. Under the 1986 Act, they were still subject in the same way as unauthorised firms to the SIB's Common Unsolicited Calls Regulations 1991. Now, however, whether issuing a promotion themselves or approving the promotions of others, they will only be subject to the FSA's rules (principally Chapter 3 of COBS) and the usual disciplinary consequences of any breach[4].

Generally, the COBS rules apply only to promotions concerning DIB directed at the UK, although they are also imposed on outward unsolicited real-time communications. The rules, however, do impose a general requirement on *any* authorised firms issuing or approving *any* promotion directed at the UK or outwardly 'to show that it believes on reasonable grounds that the promotion is fair, clear and not misleading'[5]. The FSA also proposes to incorporate the requirements of the Comparative Advertising Directive so that promotions subject to those requirements will be exempt from the Control of Misleading Advertisements (Amendments) Regulations 2000[6].

Where a firm is approving a promotion, it must use someone with 'appropriate expertise' and retain records of the approval. If the promotion is to UK private customers from overseas, the approving firm must have no reason to doubt the honesty and reliability of the overseas party and the promotion must draw attention to any reduction in protection from the FSMA and the FSCS[7].

The very simplest promotions such as 'awareness advertisements' and price lists may be exempt from the rules and leaflets, mailshots and Internet communi-

---

1   FPE Order, arts 7, 8, 14, 17, 19, 45 and 46; *Financial Promotion – Second Consultation Document* Part One, para 6.3.
2   RA Order, arts 78 and 79. Tipsheets do require authorisation, but other newspapers and magazines can still seek certification from the FSA confirming that they do not need authorisation.
3   FSMA, ss 21(13), 25 and 30; FPE Order, art 23.
4   FSMA, ss 21 and 145.
5   COBS, rules 3.1.1R, 3.8.4R and Table 3.4R. Banks and general insurers should consider their own voluntary codes.
6   1997/55/EC; SI 2000/914; Consultation Paper 57, section 7.
7   COBS, sections 3.6, 3.7 and 3.12.

cations that amount to 'teasers' are subject to only the basic requirements of fairness and clarity, but where specific investments are promoted, with perhaps past performance information, the requirements become more elaborate. Real-time communications must be at social hours and must allow any recipient to end them whenever he wishes. The FSA also gives special guidance about using the Internet and electronic media[1].

As with the SROs' old rules, the COBS rules on 'direct offer' financial promotions to private customers are the most elaborate, involving clear risk warnings and in some cases cancellation rights[2]. Unsolicited real-time communications may only be made where an exemption under the FPE Order would apply, for example deposits, general insurance, life policies, authorised CISs and to professionals or high net worth investors[3].

It is expected that the FSA will initially follow the pattern set by the previous regulators, prescribing few if any rules for the promotion of banking services or general insurance, which after all, unauthorised firms are generally free to promote; but it will lay down detailed rules for the marketing of other investments (including long-term insurance) to retail customers. The FSA's freedom to set the rules can be restricted by the Treasury and is restricted by one other feature brought forward from the 1986 Act, the restriction on even authorised firms marketing CISs[4].

13.2   THE BACKGROUND TO COLLECTIVE INVESTMENT SCHEMES

One of the problems facing private investors in the stock market is how to put small amounts of money into a variety of investments in order to spread their risk effectively. Traditionally, this has been done in the UK through two different vehicles: investment trusts and unit trusts.

Despite their name, investment trusts are not trusts but close-ended companies that do not conduct any trade but purely invest money in stocks and shares. Provided they meet certain requirements about their internal structure, spread and type of investments, distribution policy, and have their securities listed, they are not subject to corporation tax as other holding companies would be[5]. As their securities are initially marketed by issuing a prospectus and subsequently traded through the Stock Exchange like any other listed securities, they have not been subject to other regulations.

By contrast, unit trusts are open-ended trusts in which units are marketed continuously to investors who may buy and sell them from and to the fund. Ever since the Prevention of Fraud (Investments) Act 1939, unit trusts wishing to market units to the public have had to be authorised, first by the DTI and

---

1   COBS, sections 3.5, 3.8 and 3.14.
2   COBS, section 3.9. Direct offer is where the customer can accept directly by, for example, filling in an application form.
3   COBS, section 3.10.
4   FSMA, ss 145 and 238.
5   Income and Corporation Taxes Act 1988, s 842; Taxation of Chargeable Gains Act 1992, s 100(1); *Listing Rules*, Chapter 21, imposed some other conditions.

following the 1986 Act, by the SIB. As they are being marketed directly to the public and must be managed cautiously to be able to shrink and expand with fluctuations in demand, they have been subject to tighter regulation than investment trusts. In particular, unit trusts have been restricted in what they can invest in and prevented from borrowing or otherwise gearing up their risk profile. On the other hand, their open-ended nature has meant that units may be bought and sold at any time at or near the underlying asset value of the trust, whereas shares in closed-ended investment trusts are frequently trading at a significant discount to their underlying asset value.

This relatively simple choice of vehicle has become far more complex in recent years. To allow authorised unit trusts to operate tracker funds for example, they have been permitted to invest in options and futures. Limited partnerships and unit trust structures have been used to create non-authorised schemes which specialise in less tradeable investments such as natural resources and real property. Stockbrokers have also created less formal investment pools to provide a product for their discretionary clients that will spread their portfolios in a cost-efficient manner. Meanwhile, the UK has been required to recognise open-ended investment companies (OEICs), which are used instead of unit trusts on the continent and which may come to replace them in the UK[1]. Indeed, the closed-ended nature of existing UK investment trusts has become less fixed as the rules on buying in shares have been relaxed. All this has made defining the various vehicles and determining what regulatory regime should apply to each increasingly difficult. Nevertheless, the basic principle remains that open-ended vehicles being marketed continuously to the public should be subject to a special regulatory regime, a rare example of direct product regulation in the UK.

The other complication that has existed since the 1986 Act has been the authorisation of those involved in CISs. Not only must funds being marketed to the public be authorised, but also any managers, trustees, depositaries and selling agents, often by different regulators. Under the FSMA, this will all be the responsibility of the FSA[2].

13.2.1 The approach of the Financial Services Authority

In the draft COBS, the FSA has devoted two chapters specifically to rules affecting operators, trustees and depositaries of CISs. A CIS operator generally means in the case of a unit trust, the manager, and in the case of an OEIC, the OEIC itself or its authorised corporate director where that is the structure, namely the person responsible for the management of the assets. COBS, Chapter 10 pulls together the rules which apply to such asset management activities, but where the manager acts outside that capacity (eg undertakes to promote the scheme) the other appropriate COBS rules apply. Chapter 11 covers the activities of unit trust trustees and OEIC depositaries, namely the persons entrusted with the property of schemes. It also covers other trustees not exempted from authorisation by the RA Order. It pulls together the rules which apply to such custody activities, and also other rules when such persons act beyond a custody role, for example requiring

1   Undertakings for Collective Investment in Transferable Securities Directive 1985/61/EEC amended by 1988/220/EEC (UCITS Directive).

2   Indeed as the RA Order now includes acting as trustee or depositary of *any* CIS, trustees and depositaries of *unregulated* schemes need to be authorised.

them to seek 'proper advice' whenever they intend to exercise powers of investment[1].

As authorised OEICs increase in number, the FSA is clearly keen to bring their regulation into line with that of authorised unit trusts. It has, for example, proposed allowing short form accounts to be sent out to their shareholders (as unit trusts can do to their unitholders) and requiring their full accounts to be presented in a similar way to unit trusts'[2].

13.3   MARKETING COLLECTIVE INVESTMENT SCHEMES

As we have already seen, there is a restriction on engaging in financial promotion in the course of a business unless:

(1)   the firm is authorised;
(2)   the communication is approved by an authorised firm; or
(3)   an exemption applies[3].

However, that restriction is extended in the case of CISs. Even authorised firms may not engage in promoting participation in CISs nor approve communications from others doing so unless:

(1)   the scheme is authorised, exempt or recognised;
(2)   the promotion is 'otherwise than to the general public', as defined by the FSA; or
(3)   the promotion falls within a Treasury exception created by statutory instrument.

As with the restriction on financial promotion, the CIS restriction is confined to 'invitations and inducements', but otherwise this is a more comprehensive ban than under the 1986 Act, s 76, and, in particular, covers the approval of third parties' communications as well as the issue of authorised firms' own invitations or inducements[4]. Breach of this CIS restriction can lead to civil actions for damages by private persons. It is not, however, a criminal offence, although an approval of a third-party promotion in breach of the restriction is void which in turn may render that promotion an offence unless the third party can claim the defence that he believed the promotion was validly approved[5].

The other significant change made to the position under the 1986 Act is that this restriction is no longer confined to communications 'issued in the UK'. Thus, outward promotions from the UK are now caught, leaving only promotions made outside the UK which cannot have an effect within the UK excluded[6]. As the Economic Secretary explained:

---

1   Consultation Paper 45a, Part II, para 15.9. This probably only codifies an existing common-law duty.
2   Consultation Paper 36; Financial Services (Open-Ended Investment Companies) (Amendment) (No 1) Regulations 2000.
3   FSMA, s 21.
4   FSMA, ss 238 and 240. In practice, the SROs banned any member from approving communications that the member could not have issued itself.
5   FSMA, ss 21, 25, 150, 240 and 241.
6   FSMA, s 238(3).

'There is a European Union dimension to all this. Hon. Members will know of the draft e-commerce directive and the draft distance marketing directive, both of which propose a more fully home-State approach to the regulation of marketing ... Secondly, an additional, UCITS-specific angle needs to be addressed. The UCITS Directive requires the UK to prevent UK schemes that would qualify as UCITS, but which are not authorised as such, from being marketed to the rest of Europe.'[1]

Potentially, this could put UK authorised firms at a competitive disadvantage where an overseas market allows the promotion of certain schemes to the public or specified persons, but the FSA does not. No promotion (electronic or otherwise) of such schemes could be issued from the UK, even if it was clear that no UK person could participate in them. It was partly with this in mind that the Government introduced Treasury-specified exceptions which could cover:

'... promotions of specified unauthorised schemes, such as certain venture capital funds originating in the United Kingdom which could not be promoted to the UK public but which are allowed by the regulatory authorities in the target country ... [or] EU legislation could move to a full home State regime for these schemes, in which case an order specifying communications originating in EU States may become necessary ... The EU has not yet made this move and we cannot afford to leave anyone unprotected in the meantime.'[2]

CISs are defined to cover not just unit trusts and OEICs, but any arrangements (including contractual ones) where:

(1) contributions and profits are held as a single or exchangeable pools and/or property (including land and money) is managed as a whole by or on behalf of the operator;
(2) persons participate in the arrangements without having day-to-day management of the property; and
(3) no Treasury exemption applies[3].

This wide definition has been carried forward from the 1986 Act and potentially covers time shares, racing syndicates, office pools entering the National Lottery and even exotic schemes such as the once popular pooled investments in ostriches. However, in its draft Financial Services and Markets Act (Collective Investment Schemes) Order, the Treasury proposes to carry forward the exemptions currently made under the 1986 Act which include arrangements:

(1) operated otherwise than as a business;
(2) treated as other types of investment, for example deposits, contracts of insurance, depositary receipts;
(3) operated by RCHs or RIEs as clearing services;
(4) for sharing the use or enjoyment of property (including time shares);
(5) set up intra-group or to provide occupational pensions or certain employee share schemes;
(6) with primarily a commercial purpose (including franchises);
(7) operated as parallel investment management schemes for clients' portfolios (subject to certain conditions); and

---

1   Standing Committee A, 2 December 1999, c 1085.
2   Lord McIntosh, vol 611 HL, 30 March 2000, c 949.
3   FSMA, s 235.

(8) set up as UK bodies corporate (other than OEICs), for example investment trusts and companies[1].

Some concern was expressed in the Standing Committee that the effectiveness of this last exception might be damaged by the wide definition of OEICs in the FSMA. The aim is to allow the development of OEICs beyond schemes which confine their investments to transferable securities so as to qualify for a UCITS Passport. Some corporate structures used for investment companies and employee share schemes could conceivably have been treated as OEICs and so fall within the restriction on promoting CISs. The definition was redrafted, but what is clear is that closed-ended non-corporate funds such as venture capital limited partnerships and closed-ended unit trusts certainly do fall within the marketing restriction[2].

13.4 AUTHORISED AND RECOGNISED SCHEMES

The most significant exception to the restriction on marketing CISs is that for authorised, recognised and exempt schemes. Authorised firms (including inwardly passported firms) may generally promote five categories of such schemes, two domestic and three overseas:

(1) authorised unit trusts;
(2) authorised OEICs;
(3) recognised EEA schemes that comply with the UCITS Directive;
(4) recognised schemes authorised in designated countries; and
(5) individually recognised overseas schemes[3].

13.4.1 Authorised unit trusts

Unit trusts are defined as CISs under which the property is held on trust for the participants. The information required, and the procedures adopted, to apply for authorisation as a unit trust are left to the FSA. Applications must be made jointly by the (proposed) trustee and manager, who must be separate and independent of each other, but who both must:

(1) be incorporated and headquartered in an EEA country;
(2) have a place of business in the UK;
(3) be authorised and have permission to conduct that activity in the UK; and
(4) be liable for any failures 'to exercise due care and diligence' (exclusions are void).

The FSA may require the manager's business to be confined to managing CISs, which is currently a requirement for a scheme to qualify under the UCITS Directive. The scheme's name must be approved, its purposes must seem realistic and it must provide for redemption (or sale on an investment exchange) of its

---

1   *Regulated Activities – A Consultation Document*, HM Treasury, February 1999, Part Two.
2   Standing Committee A, 2 December 1999, cc 1075–1079 and 1091; FSMA, s 236(4), which specifically excludes companies buying-in shares under the Companies Act 1985 or the equivalent provisions of other EEA States being treated as OEICs.
3   FSMA, s 238(4). The FSA must keep a public record of all of these: FSMA, s 347.

units at a price 'related to the net value of the property to which the units relate'. No time-limit is mentioned in contrast to the basic definition of an OEIC (see below). The FSA must be satisfied that the scheme complies with these statutory requirements and with its own trust scheme rules and must be provided with a copy of the trust deed certified by a solicitor to that effect[1].

The FSA has six months from receipt of a completed application (and 12 months from first application) to decide whether to authorise the scheme. If the FSA accepts an application, it must issue a written notice to the applicants and where the scheme qualifies under the UCITS Directive (or for any other EU rights) it can request the FSA to issue a certificate to that effect[2]. If the FSA is minded to refuse an application, it must follow its rejection procedures which now include the right to refer the refusal to the Tribunal[3].

The FSA is given the power to lay down both trust scheme and scheme particulars rules. The trust scheme rules determine the constitutions of authorised unit trust schemes, including terms for the issue and redemption of units, for investment and borrowing, for the appointment and removal of auditors, for the production of reports and for the amendment of the scheme. These rules bind managers, trustees and participants, even if they are not repeated in the trust deed. Scheme particulars rules determine the information the manager must give about the trust in its particulars (the equivalent of its prospectus) and may determine liability for losses arising because of any errors (whether of omission or commission) contained therein[4]. The FSA has the power to modify or waive these rules in particular cases in the same way as it has for its other rules[5].

The trustee or manager of a scheme must give written notice to the FSA of a proposal to change the other. The manager must also give notice of any proposed change to the scheme. Changes must still conform to the statutory requirements and those of the FSA rules. The FSA has a month to consider whether to refuse any change which otherwise will automatically come into effect. The manager or the trustee may also seek to revoke the trust's authorisation. If the FSA is minded to refuse any of these applications, again it must follow its rejection procedures[6]. A refusal is most likely where the affairs of the trust are being investigated, but can be to protect participants or to stop a UCITS scheme converting itself into a non-UCITS scheme.

This raises the whole area of the enforcement powers of the FSA. It may:

(1) revoke a trust's authorisation;

---

1   FSMA, ss 140, 237(1), 242, 243 and 253. Many of these requirements are to be found in the UCITS Directive. Authorised unit trusts do not have to comply with all the UCITS requirements and so some are non-UCITS trusts. Nevertheless, the Government rejected any relaxation of the rules for non-UCITS trusts, so that, for example, the structure could be used for stakeholder pensions or US and Swiss banks could act as trustees or managers rather than having to form UK subsidiaries to do it, Standing Committee A, 2 December 1999, cc 1096–1100.

2   FSMA, ss 243(2), 244 and 246. This is all that remains of the original proposal that all authorised firms be issued with certificates explaining their authorisation.

3   FSMA, s 245; see **9.3.1**. The right of trustees and managers to refer FSA decisions to the Tribunal did not exist under the 1986 Act.

4   FSMA, ss 247 and 248.

5   FSMA, s 250, cf s 148.

6   FSMA, ss 251, 252 and 256; see **9.3.1**.

(2) suspend the issue and/or redemption of its units;
(3) order the manager or trustee to wind it up;
(4) seek a High Court order to replace the manager and/or trustee; or
(5) seek a High Court order to appoint an authorised person to wind it up.

Any of the above may be done if:

(1) any specific requirements attached to the authorisation are no longer satisfied;
(2) the manager or trustee has contravened or is likely to contravene any other requirements under the FSMA;
(3) either has knowingly or recklessly given false or misleading information to the FSA; or
(4) it is in the interests of participants or potential participants to do so.

The trusts' authorisation may also be revoked if it has been dormant for at least 12 months[1]. As these powers may have to be used immediately to protect investors, they are generally subject to the FSA's more flexible supervisory procedures. However, the revocation of authorisation is considered so serious that it is subject to the full disciplinary procedures[2].

Orders to suspend the issue or redemption of units or wind up the trust may later be revoked or varied. If the FSA grants such a request, it must give the applicants a written notice, but if it is minded to refuse it in whole or in part, it must follow its rejection procedures[3].

13.4.2 Authorised open-ended investment company

OEICs are defined as CISs where a company:

(1) holds and manages (or has managed for it) investments for the purpose of spreading risk for the benefit of its members; and
(2) those members may reasonably expect their interests to be realisable within a reasonable period and at a price calculated mainly by reference to their underlying net value.

The members' interests do not have to be shares, but can be some lesser instrument. Redemptions or repurchases under the general company law of an EEA State (and of any other States designated by the Treasury) do not make a company an OEIC. The Treasury can amend this definition of an OEIC by statutory instrument, subject to affirmative resolutions[4]. The Government has kept to a fairly loose definition because:

> 'Whereas Treasury regulations and FSA rules will determine the nature of OEICs that can be established in the UK, the definition has to apply to overseas established schemes as well, over whose constitution the UK authorities have no control. It is imperative that the OEIC definition is broad enough to cover a variety of such schemes that are capable of offering collective investments.'

---

1   FSMA, ss 254, 257 and 258. When considering revoking authorisation to protect participants or potential participants, the FSA can consider a wide list of parties associated with the scheme, but not apparently in the other cases.
2   FSMA, s 259, cf ss 255 and 392.
3   FSMA, ss 257, 260 and 261; see **9.3.1**.
4   FSMA, ss 236 and 429(1).

It was pointed out that condition (2) above might make investment trusts with fixed lives become OEICs as they near the end of that life. However, the Government spokesman in the House of Lords said:

> 'The answer to [the] point on the fixed life company in the last few months of its life is that what we proposed is based on the overall impression that the reasonable investor would get when he is considering investing in it ... It does not concern a particular point in time at the end of a company's life.'[1]

To allow for the creation of such vehicles in the UK, the Treasury has a sweeping general power:

> '... to make provision for—
>
> (a) facilitating the carrying on of collective investment by means of open-ended investment companies;
> (b) regulating such companies.'[2]

These regulations will determine the whole legal regime governing UK OEICs, including incorporation, registration, management, investment policies, auditing, inspection, winding up and dissolution – a sort of mini-Companies Act. However, the Treasury can delegate functions to the FSA, in particular the power to make rules about authorisation and to actually authorise and register OEICs[3]. As the Financial Secretary said:

> 'Broadly speaking, the general shape of the authorised unit trust and open-ended investment company provisions will be on all fours. Anything covered by FSA rules on authorised unit trusts will also be covered, where appropriate, by FSA rules on OEICs.'[4]

If authorised unit trusts and OEICs are to be treated similarly, there seems to be no reason other than accident of statutory history that the arrangements for authorising unit trusts are detailed in the FSMA but for authorising OEICs are to be left in a statutory instrument.

Since 6 January 1997, UK OEICs have been permitted under the Open-Ended Investment Companies (Investment Companies with Variable Capital) Regulations 1996[5]. As these Regulations were created under the limited powers of the European Communities Act 1972, s 2(2), they have only allowed authorised OEICs which would qualify for a Passport under the UCITS Directive to be created. To encourage their development, the Government has granted these OEICs the same tax transparency as authorised unit trusts[6]. It has also waived stamp duty on the conversion of existing UCITS qualifying unit trusts into OEICs and the FSA allowed such conversions without holding a members' meeting until June 2000. There has still been some reluctance to convert from one structure to

---

1   Lord McIntosh, vol 611 HL, 30 March 2000, c 944. On revisiting the issue, Lord McIntosh was cautious, only saying that it would 'probably fall to be considered as a closed-ended company throughout its life': Vol 612 HL, 9 May 2000, c 1497. The Opposition has pointed out that if this is not the case, it could have some unfortunate tax consequences for investors: vol 351 HC, 5 June 2000, c 124.

2   FSMA, s 262(1).

3   FSMA, s 262(2) and (3).

4   Standing Committee A, 2 December 1999, c 1115.

5   SI 1996/2827.

6   Open-Ended Investment Companies (Tax) Regulations 1997, SI 1997/1154.

the other, and as single pricing comes in for unit trusts, there will appear to be little difference between the two vehicles as far as investors are concerned[1].

The Treasury has published new draft Open-Ended Companies (Companies with Variable Capital) Regulations (OEIC Regulations)[2], which follow the pattern of the 1996 Regulations, but with the following key differences:

(1) the restriction on OEICs' investments to transferable securities has been removed, allowing the creation of money market and property funds and funds of funds and leaving the FSA to determine what may be authorised;
(2) the FSA will register OEICs immediately on granting authorisation[3];
(3) the FSA will have the same power to waive and modify rules as it has for authorised unit trusts[4]; and
(4) the FSA's procedures will be brought into line with those for authorised unit trusts, including the right to refer matters to the Tribunal[5].

As with authorised unit trusts, an OEIC's property must be held independently, in this case by an authorised depositary, for example a unit trust's trustee (see above); however, there is no requirement for a manager as the company is its own operator[6]. The FSA will be able to make the equivalent of trust scheme and particulars rules and lay down the procedure for applying for authorisation[7]. The OEIC Regulations do require specific details of directors to be given in an application and if there is only to be one director, it must be a corporate body authorised for the purpose. If there is to be more than one director, the FSA may still require one to be designated as the authorised corporate director responsible for the OEIC's record keeping, pricing, dealings and safeguarding the assets[8]. Before authorising an OEIC, the FSA must check the suitability of its name with the appropriate registrar of companies, and on authorisation submit the necessary registration documents; but once authorised, the company is automatically incorporated even though it does not have property or shareholders[9]. The FSA has the same powers of intervention as it has over authorised unit trusts, that is to stop the issue and redemption of securities, revoke authorisation and seek the winding up of the company or the removal of a director or depositary[10].

Now that the FSA will be responsible for determining what CISs may be authorised, it has been consulting on limited issue and limited redemption funds, be they OEICs or unit trusts[11]. However, the FSA is concerned at the erosion of the

---

1   Consultation Paper 32, FSA, November 1999, confirmed the withdrawal of the right to convert without a meeting. About 20% of CIS funds are in OEICs and the Government expects this to rise under the new regime.
2   HM Treasury, 29 March 2000.
3   OEIC Regulations, reg 4 and Part IV. The FSA will also maintain the register and OEICs are exempt from registration at Companies House under the Companies Act 1985: FSMA, s 263.
4   OEIC Regulations, reg 7, cf FSMA, s 250.
5   OEIC Regulations, regs 8 to 10, 15, 21, 23 and 26–29 shadowed the then equivalent sections in FSMA. The draft OEIC Regulations were, in fact, issued before the amendments to the FSMA creating disciplinary, supervisory and rejection procedures, but will presumably be amended to follow the same pattern.
6   OEIC Regulations, regs 5 and 14; FSMA, ss 237(2) and 243.
7   OEIC Regulations, regs 6, 11, 13 and 14.
8   OEIC Regulations, regs 12, 14 and 34(4)(b).
9   OEIC Regulations, regs 3, 4 and 17.
10   OEIC Regulations, regs 24 and 25.
11   Consultation Paper 11, FSA, June 1998.

clear distinction between open-ended and closed-ended funds. As it has commented:

> 'Increased choice could come at a cost in two related areas:
> - if the establishment of funds that limit issues and/or redemption (to any extent permitted) "dilutes" the product distinctiveness of open-ended funds in such a way that it discourages investment in collective investment schemes;
> - if a limited issue/limited redemption fund can market itself in a way that emphasises its benefits while disguising the non-monetary costs (eg limited redemption), creating investor confusion and thereby placing other collective investment funds at an unfair competitive advantage.'[1]

The Treasury has even suggested the creation of Pooled Unauthorised Companies (PUNCs), but these would be unregulated schemes and unless they were granted tax transparency, they would not be popular investment vehicles.

13.4.3 Recognised schemes

Overseas CISs may only be promoted by authorised firms to the public in the UK if they are recognised by the FSA in one of three ways.

The first category consists of UCITS passported CISs (whether trusts, OEICs or otherwise) where the operator has given the FSA not less than two months' notice of wishing to market the scheme in the UK. The FSA will require a certificate from the home State regulator confirming that the scheme qualifies under UCITS and that the scheme has set up appropriate facilities for UK participants. The UCITS Directive does require scheme particulars to be translated into the language of the country in which it is being promoted. In fact, the UCITS Directive is not specifically referred to and the Treasury is empowered to prescribe any requirements by statutory instrument. This will allow for any changes required by the expected replacement of the UCITS Directive. Otherwise, the FSA can only impose UK financial promotion rules and, in effect, may only object to an initial application for recognition or suspend subsequent promotion of the scheme because it believes that these are not being or will not be complied with. If the FSA does not issue a notice objecting to the application within two months, recognition is automatic. If the FSA does issue a notice, it must basically follow its rejection procedures. A later suspension of promotion, because it may have to be done immediately, is subject to the supervisory procedures; but a refusal, in whole or in part, to vary or revoke such a suspension is subject to the rejection procedures.'[2]

The second category consists of CISs of a class specified from an overseas country or territory designated by statutory instrument. In effect, this allows the Treasury to passport non-EEA schemes (currently from Jersey, Guernsey, the Isle of Man and Bermuda) which again give two months' notice to be recognised. If the FSA does not issue a warning notice within those two months, recognition is automatic. Before designating a new country or territory, the Treasury must call for a report from the FSA in order to be satisfied that the local laws and practice give equivalent protection to that provided by the authorisation system for unit trusts and/or OEICs in the UK[3]. The Treasury no longer has to be satisfied that the

---

1   Consultation Paper 11, para 40.
2   FSMA, ss 264–269.
3   FSMA, s 270.

designated country or territory offers reciprocal arrangements for UK-authorised schemes, as such a provision has been outlawed by the World Trade Organisation[1].

Finally, the FSA may recognise individual CISs that do not fall within the previous two categories but which meet similar requirements to those imposed upon UK-authorised schemes. The FSA is left a wide area of discretion about the structures it can accept. As the Financial Secretary commented:

> 'In practice, and as is the case with the present legislation, we wish to leave enough flexibility in the Bill for the FSA to recognise individually schemes that have a different institutional structure when appropriate. On balance, it is right that the existence of a depositary or trustee is not essential. In practice the FSA will need to satisfy itself with the matters referred to in the clause before individually recognising a scheme. It may be only in exceptional cases that it feels that it can properly take the view that the adequate protection is provided in relation to a scheme that does not have a separate trustee or depositary'[2].

This does mean that the FSA can recognise overseas schemes (eg limited partnerships) that it could not authorise if they were UK based. The FSA, however, has six months from receipt of a completed application (and 12 months from first application) to determine whether to recognise such a scheme. If it does recognise the scheme, it must issue a written notice to the applicant. Thereafter, the FSA must be given one month's notice of any proposed change to the scheme, its operator trustee or depositary[3].

If the FSA is minded to refuse an application under these last two categories, it must follow its rejection procedures[4]. As these two categories are not covered by a European Passport, the FSA has powers to determine the contents of any scheme particulars, to require facilities in the UK and to intervene and revoke the recognition of such schemes. Interventions are generally subject to the supervisory procedures but the revocation of recognition is so serious that it is subject to the full disciplinary procedures[5].

13.4.4   Exempt and unregulated schemes

The Treasury may make regulations to exempt the marketing of schemes that cover single or adjacent buildings managed as a whole by or on behalf of the operator of the scheme, provided the units in the scheme can be traded on an RIE[6]. Such an exemption already exists under the 1986 Act, s 76 and, therefore, it might be expected that such schemes would be treated for marketing purposes like authorised CISs. However, the FSA has, in practice, restricted the marketing of these specialist vehicles to professionals and insisted on them producing full

---

1   Standing Committee A, 2 December 1999, c 1122.
2   Standing Committee A, 2 December 1999, c 1127.
3   FSMA, ss 272–275 and 277.
4   FSMA, ss 271 and 276.
5   FSMA, ss 278–283 and 392. In the case of the Channel Islands and Isle of Man designated schemes, the FSA has accepted the local scheme particulars. Operators marketing these non-passported CISs are exempt from the restriction on financial promotion in the UK: FPE Order, art 33.
6   FSMA, s 239(1)–(3).

scheme particulars[1]. The FSA will continue to have such powers and unless its regulations are relaxed, such schemes will remain few and far between[2].

CISs that do not fall within any of the above six categories may not be promoted to the public, nor even to 'ordinary business investors' as was permitted under the 1986 Act[3]. However, the FSA is expected to allow authorised firms (including inwardly passported firms) to market such schemes on a restricted basis as is currently permitted under the Financial Services (Promotion of Unregulated Schemes) Regulations 1991 in the case of:

(1) tax-exempt schemes to pension funds;
(2) incentive schemes for employees or former employees; or
(3) other schemes to expert non-private customers[4].

It could be argued that as authorised firms owe private customers a duty to check the suitability of any investment, these marketing restrictions on exempt and unregulated CISs should be relaxed; but there is no sign that they will be, particularly as that would run counter to the spirit, at least, of the UCITS Directive and any proposed replacement for it.

13.5 INVESTIGATING COLLECTIVE INVESTMENT SCHEMES

The FSA and the Secretary of State can appoint a person (including an FSA employee) to investigate any CIS or its manager, operator, trustee or depositary other than a UK OEIC. OEICs are only excluded because similar powers to investigate them are contained in the OEIC Regulations. The investigation can be extended to other CISs with the same manager, operator, trustee or depositary and, indeed, any other prescribed CIS (in this case, including OEICs). The investigator has the power to call for any relevant documents and to require anyone to give assistance including attending and giving evidence under oath. Unreasonable failure to do so may be treated as a contempt of court. As with other investigations ordered by the FSA or the Secretary of State, legal privilege is protected, bank confidences may be broken only at the specific request of the FSA (or the Secretary of State) and compelled statements may not be admissible in subsequent criminal or market abuse proceedings. Overall, however, the investigator has the same wide powers as one appointed to investigate insider dealing, market abuse or a breach of the general prohibition[5].

---

1   Financial Services Act 1986 (Single Property Schemes) (Exemption) Regulations 1989, SI 1989/28 and Financial Services (Single Property Schemes) (Supplementary) Regulations 1989.
2   FSMA, s 239(4) and (5).
3   FPE Order, art 37 does exempt an OEIC marketing its own securities to its existing shareholders and creditors.
4   COBS, section 3.11 does propose similar arrangements to the current ones. The sort of CISs that might be promoted under (3). are the Isle of Man's Experienced Investor Funds.
5   FSMA, ss 284 and 413; OEIC Regulations, reg 30.

Chapter 14
CONCLUSION

After the 1986 Act came into force, successive Conservative Governments refused to revisit the subject of financial services regulation, fearing that it would be opening Pandora's box. When he launched the reform of the system in May 1997, Gordon Brown seems to have had no such qualms. Three gruelling years later, a much-amended FSMA has reached the statute book. One has to have some sympathy with the Parliamentary draftsmen involved, forced to draft over 1,500 amendments to deal with the last minute changes of mind over at the Treasury and the severe pressure applied by the Opposition parties, particularly in the House of Lords. What has emerged is a monster piece of legislation, but has it created, in the FSA, a monster?

As the Chief Secretary to the Treasury said on FSMA's third reading in the Commons:

> 'The importance of [the FSMA] is undoubted. Its purpose is to put into place modern and effective regulation for one of our most important industries. Financial services account for 7% of gross domestic product and contribute £32 billion net to the balance of payments. The United Kingdom's world-beating financial services industry is vital not only because it employs more than a million people, but because it provides a means to look after the savings of many millions more. Firms in all sectors of the economy rely crucially on it for the provision of finance.'[1]

Central to these new arrangements is the FSA as the single statutory regulator. A lot of the debates in Parliament were spent discussing how to make this body effectively accountable and yet remain responsive to the fast-changing and increasingly competitive market it will be regulating. One Opposition spokesman said without too much exaggeration:

> 'We need to be clear that we are creating a leviathan – an institution of unprecedented power and authority ... We are creating the most powerful body in this country after the Government.'[2]

However, whether the new arrangements will be so revolutionary in practice is open to question. A more balanced view has been given by the Chairman of the FSA:

> 'In many respects, the new regime will be quite like the old. For the most part [the FSMA] consolidates the existing powers and responsibilities of the financial regulators. And as we plan our implementation of the new legislation, we are keen to avoid making change for change's sake ... We nonetheless plan major changes in the way we carry out our regulatory task ... We plan to implement a risk-based approach to regulation, focusing attention on the key threats to the achievement of our statutory objectives. We will devote more resources to thematic work across the financial services sector and will place more emphasis on helping consumers make good buying decisions, which ought to reduce the amount of effort we need to spend on clearing up the consequences of misselling later, which has been an unhappy feature of the old regime.

---

1   Vol 344 HC, 9 February 2000, c 358.
2   Andrew Tyrie MP, vol 343 HC, 27 January 2000, c 608.

In addition, the scope of our work will become broader, in important ways. We shall be directly responsible for the regulation of professional firms carrying on investment business, we shall be responsible for policing the new authorisation and disclosure regime for mortgage lenders, we shall be regulating credit unions, we shall be the United Kingdom's listing authority ... And we shall be responsible for supervising the Society of Lloyd's and members' and managing agents at Lloyd's.'[1]

A gap has certainly opened up between the rather grand rhetoric of Ministers that has accompanied the creation of the FSA and the rather more modest statements emanating from the institution itself in recent months. This is no doubt due to the increasing realisation that, with the rise of e-commerce and its use for the provision of financial services, the UK share of this lucrative market is vulnerable. As has been pointed out, the UK had 42% of world shipping in 1900 and through over-regulation and restrictive practices reduced that to 1% a century later[2].

The danger of regulatory arbitrage causing lucrative business to flow away from the UK was highlighted in the dying days of the FSMA's passage through Parliament with the announcement of the proposed merger of the London and Frankfurt Stock Exchanges. The Government has made light of the change:

'... The intention is to create two pan-European equity markets. The first will be a market for blue-chip shares, based in London. It will continue to be a UK recognised investment exchange, overseen by the FSA. The second will be a proposed joint venture with NASDAQ to provide a market for growth company shares, which will operate in Frankfurt under German regulation ... This is not a unique situation. A similar arrangement already exists. The Swedish OM Group owns both the stock exchange in Stockholm, regulated by the Swedish authorities, and a derivatives exchange in London which is a UK recognised investment exchange overseen by the FSA ... The FSA is not and cannot be responsible for markets and exchanges located abroad which do not have operations in the UK. They are subject to the regulatory authorities of the jurisdiction in which they are located.'[3]

However, maintaining neat jurisdictional boundaries is not possible. If the regulatory regimes differ between the UK and Germany, companies may be able to choose where to list and still be traded on the merged exchange. Also, as has been noted at many points, the FSMA itself does not confine its reach to activities in the UK. In particular, the Treasury has reserved the right to extend the market abuse regime to behaviour affecting markets physically outside the UK[4].

Despite its length, the FSMA only provides the barest of frameworks. The period between Royal Assent and it coming into force is going to see over 80 statutory instruments drafted by the Treasury and a complete *Handbook* drafted by the FSA; but even those will only provide the regulations. What will really matter is the supervisory style of the FSA. For all the soothing words of the FSA's Chairman and the talk of evolution rather than revolution, this is a journey into the unknown[5]. As another Opposition spokesman has commented:

1   The chairman of the FSA in *FSA Plan and Budget 2000/01*, pp 3 and 4.
2   Lord Saatchi and Lord Bagri, vol 610 HL, 21 February 2000, cc 20 and 57.
3   Lord McIntosh, vol 613 HL, 18 May 2000, c 373.
4   See **7.4** and **Chapter 12**. The Chairman of the FSA has commented on the growing pressure to harmonise transparency rules across Europe, FSA Press Release 82/2000.
5   Commercial banks, building societies and insurers (including Lloyd's) are almost certainly going to notice a more formal style of supervision than they have been used to as the old SROs' style is applied to them.

'It has been said that fish swim, birds fly and regulators regulate. Governments will always find new things to regulate, and Governments come under political pressure to defend consumers, investigate and intervene in markets and to correct real or imaginary deficiencies.'[1]

The tortuously slow progress of the FSMA to the statute book may have given Ministers time to adjust their expectations and reconsider some important issues. It has certainly allowed the FSA time to find its feet before taking on full responsibility in a way that the old SROs never managed. However, it has also meant that the FSA will move straight from the production of its *Handbook* to the devising and implementation of its new risk-based supervision system. Perhaps that is just the way of the modern world. I can only hope that any political pressure to produce short-term results at the expense of longer-term stability will be fiercely resisted.

---

1   David Heathcoat-Amory MP, vol 351 HC, 5 June 2000, c 73.

Appendix

FINANCIAL SERVICES AND MARKETS ACT 2000

(2000 c 8)

ARRANGEMENT OF SECTIONS

PART I

THE REGULATOR

Section		Page
1	The Financial Services Authority	258

The Authority's general duties

| 2 | The Authority's general duties | 259 |

The regulatory objectives

3	Market confidence	259
4	Public awareness	260
5	The protection of consumers	260
6	The reduction of financial crime	260

Corporate governance

| 7 | Duty of Authority to follow principles of good governance | 261 |

Arrangements for consulting practitioners and consumers

8	The Authority's general duty to consult	261
9	The Practitioner Panel	261
10	The Consumer Panel	261
11	Duty to consider representations by the Panels	262

Reviews

| 12 | Reviews | 262 |
| 13 | Right to obtain documents and information | 262 |

Inquiries

14	Cases in which the Treasury may arrange independent inquiries	263
15	Power to appoint person to hold an inquiry	263
16	Powers of appointed person and procedure	264
17	Conclusion of inquiry	264
18	Obstruction and contempt	265

PART II

REGULATED AND PROHIBITED ACTIVITIES

The general prohibition

19   The general prohibition   265

Requirement for permission

20   Authorised persons acting without permission   265

Financial promotion

21   Restrictions on financial promotion   266

Regulated activities

22   The classes of activity and categories of investment   267

Offences

23   Contravention of the general prohibition   267
24   False claims to be authorised or exempt   267
25   Contravention of section 21   268

Enforceability of agreements

26   Agreements made by unauthorised persons   268
27   Agreements made through unauthorised persons   268
28   Agreements unenforceable by section 26 or 27   269
29   Accepting deposits in breach of general prohibition   269
30   Enforceability of agreements resulting from unlawful communications   270

PART III

AUTHORISATION AND EXEMPTION

Authorisation

31   Authorised persons   271
32   Partnerships and unincorporated associations   271

Ending of authorisation

33   Withdrawal of authorisation by the Authority   271
34   EEA firms   272
35   Treaty firms   272
36   Persons authorised as a result of paragraph 1(1) of Schedule 5   272

Exercise of EEA rights by UK firms

37 Exercise of EEA rights by UK firms   272

Exemption

38 Exemption orders   272
39 Exemption of appointed representatives   273

PART IV

PERMISSION TO CARRY ON REGULATED ACTIVITIES

Application for permission

40 Application for permission   273
41 The threshold conditions   274

Permission

42 Giving permission   274
43 Imposition of requirements   275

Variation and cancellation of Part IV permission

44 Variation etc. at request of authorised person   275
45 Variation etc. on the Authority's own initiative   276
46 Variation of permission on acquisition of control   276
47 Exercise of power in support of overseas regulator   276
48 Prohibitions and restrictions   277

Connected persons

49 Persons connected with an applicant   278

Additional permissions

50 Authority's duty to consider other permissions etc.   278

Procedure

51 Applications under this Part   279
52 Determination of applications   279
53 Exercise of own-initiative power: procedure   280
54 Cancellation of Part IV permission: procedure   281

References to the Tribunal

55 Right to refer matters to the Tribunal   281

PART V

PERFORMANCE OF REGULATED ACTIVITIES

Prohibition orders

56 Prohibition orders   281
57 Prohibition orders: procedure and right to refer to Tribunal   282
58 Applications relating to prohibitions: procedure and right to refer to
    Tribunal   282

Approval

59 Approval for particular arrangements   283
60 Applications for approval   284
61 Determination of applications   284
62 Applications for approval: procedure and right to refer to Tribunal   285
63 Withdrawal of approval   285

Conduct

64 Conduct: statements and codes   285
65 Statements and codes: procedure   286
66 Disciplinary powers   287
67 Disciplinary measures: procedure and right to refer to Tribunal   288
68 Publication   288
69 Statement of policy   288
70 Statements of policy: procedure   289

Breach of statutory duty

71 Actions for damages   289

PART VI

OFFICIAL LISTING

The competent authority

72 The competent authority   289
73 General duty of the competent authority   290

The official list

74 The official list   290

Listing

75 Applications for listing   290
76 Decision on application   291
77 Discontinuance and suspension of listing   291
78 Discontinuance or suspension: procedure   292

Listing particulars

79	Listing particulars and other documents	293
80	General duty of disclosure in listing particulars	293
81	Supplementary listing particulars	294
82	Exemptions from disclosure	294
83	Registration of listing particulars	295

Prospectuses

84	Prospectuses	295
85	Publication of prospectus	296
86	Application of this Part to prospectuses	296
87	Approval of prospectus where no application for listing	296

Sponsors

88	Sponsors	297
89	Public censure of sponsor	297

Compensation

90	Compensation for false or misleading particulars	298

Penalties

91	Penalties for breach of listing rules	298
92	Procedure	299
93	Statement of policy	299
94	Statements of policy: procedure	300

Competition

95	Competition scrutiny	300

Miscellaneous

96	Obligations of issuers of listed securities	301
97	Appointment by competent authority of persons to carry out investigations	301
98	Advertisements etc. in connection with listing applications	302
99	Fees	302
100	Penalties	303
101	Listing rules: general provisions	304
102	Exemption from liability in damages	304
103	Interpretation of this Part	304

PART VII

CONTROL OF BUSINESS TRANSFERS

104	Control of business transfers	305
105	Insurance business transfer schemes	305
106	Banking business transfer schemes	307

107 Application for order sanctioning transfer scheme   307
108 Requirements on applicants   308
109 Scheme reports   308
110 Right to participate in proceedings   308
111 Sanction of the court for business transfer schemes   308
112 Effect of order sanctioning business transfer scheme   309
113 Appointment of actuary in relation to reduction of benefits   310
114 Rights of certain policyholders   310

Business transfers outside the United Kingdom

115 Certificates for purposes of insurance business transfers overseas 311
116 Effect of insurance business transfers authorised in other EEA States 311

Modifications

117 Power to modify this Part   312

PART VIII

PENALTIES FOR MARKET ABUSE

Market abuse

118 Market abuse   312

The code

119 The code   313
120 Provisions included in the Authority's code by reference to the City Code   314
121 Codes: procedure   314
122 Effect of the code   315

Power to impose penalties

123 Power to impose penalties in cases of market abuse   315

Statement of policy

124 Statement of policy   316
125 Statement of policy: procedure   316

Procedure

126 Warning notices   317
127 Decision notices and right to refer to Tribunal   317

Miscellaneous

128 Suspension of investigations   317
129 Power of court to impose penalty in cases of market abuse   318
130 Guidance   318

131 Effect on transactions 318

PART IX

HEARINGS AND APPEALS

132 The Financial Services and Markets Tribunal 318
133 Proceedings: general provision 319

Legal assistance before the Tribunal

134 Legal assistance scheme 319
135 Provisions of the legal assistance scheme 320
136 Funding of the legal assistance scheme 320

Appeals

137 Appeal on a point of law 321

PART X

RULES AND GUIDANCE

CHAPTER I

RULE-MAKING POWERS

138 General rule-making power 321
139 Miscellaneous ancillary matters 322
140 Restriction on managers of authorised unit trust schemes 323
141 Insurance business rules 323
142 Insurance business: regulations supplementing Authority's rules 323
143 Endorsement of codes etc. 324

Specific rules

144 Price stabilising rules 325
145 Financial promotion rules 325
146 Money laundering rules 326
147 Control of information rules 326

Modification or waiver

148 Modification or waiver of rules 326

Contravention of rules

149 Evidential provisions 327
150 Actions for damages 328

151 Limits on effect of contravening rules 328

Procedural provisions

152 Notification of rules to the Treasury 328
153 Rule-making instruments 328
154 Verification of rules 328
155 Consultation 329
156 General supplementary powers 330

CHAPTER II

GUIDANCE

157 Guidance 330
158 Notification of guidance to the Treasury 331

CHAPTER III

COMPETITION SCRUTINY

159 Interpretation 331
160 Reports by Director General of Fair Trading 332
161 Power of Director to request information 333
162 Consideration by Competition Commission 333
163 Role of the Treasury 334
164 The Competition Act 1998 335

PART XI

INFORMATION GATHERING AND INVESTIGATIONS

Powers to gather information

165 Authority's power to require information 336
166 Reports by skilled persons 337

Appointment of investigators

167 Appointment of persons to carry out general investigations 337
168 Appointment of persons to carry out investigations in particular cases 338

Assistance to overseas regulators

169 Investigations etc. in support of overseas regulator 339

Conduct of investigations

170 Investigations: general 340
171 Powers of persons appointed under section 167 340
172 Additional power of persons appointed as a result of section 168(1) or (4) 341
173 Powers of persons appointed as a result of section 168(2) 341
174 Admissibility of statements made to investigators 342
175 Information and documents: supplemental provisions 342

176 Entry of premises under warrant 343

Offences

177 Offences 344

PART XII

CONTROL OVER AUTHORISED PERSONS

Notice of control

178 Obligation to notify the Authority 345

Acquiring, increasing and reducing control

179 Acquiring control 346
180 Increasing control 346
181 Reducing control 347

Acquiring or increasing control: procedure

182 Notification 347
183 Duty of Authority in relation to notice of control 348
184 Approval of acquisition of control 348
185 Conditions attached to approval 348
186 Objection to acquisition of control 349
187 Objection to existing control 349
188 Notices of objection under section 187: procedure 350

Improperly acquired shares

189 Improperly acquired shares 350

Reducing control: procedure

190 Notification 351

Offences

191 Offences under this Part 352

Miscellaneous

192 Power to change definitions of control etc. 353

PART XIII

INCOMING FIRMS: INTERVENTION BY AUTHORITY

Interpretation

193 Interpretation of this Part 353
194 General grounds on which power of intervention is exercisable 353

195 Exercise of power in support of overseas regulator   354
196 The power of intervention   355

Exercise of power of intervention

197 Procedure on exercise of power of intervention   355
198 Power to apply to court for injunction in respect of certain overseas
    insurance companies   356
199 Additional procedure for EEA firms in certain cases   356

Supplemental

200 Rescission and variation of requirements   357
201 Effect of certain requirements on other persons   357
202 Contravention of requirement imposed under this Part   358

Powers of Director General of Fair Trading

203 Power to prohibit the carrying on of Consumer Credit Act business   358
204 Power to restrict the carrying on of Consumer Credit Act business   359

PART XIV

DISCIPLINARY MEASURES

205 Public censure   359
206 Financial penalties   359
207 Proposal to take disciplinary measures   360
208 Decision notice   360
209 Publication   360
210 Statements of policy   360
211 Statements of policy: procedure   361

PART XV

THE FINANCIAL SERVICES COMPENSATION SCHEME

The scheme manager

212 The scheme manager   361

The scheme

213 The compensation scheme   362

Provisions of the scheme

214 General   363
215 Rights of the scheme in relevant person's insolvency   364
216 Continuity of long-term insurance policies   364
217 Insurers in financial difficulties   365

Annual report

218 Annual report   366

Information and documents

219 Scheme manager's power to require information   366
220 Scheme manager's power to inspect information held by liquidator etc.   367
221 Powers of court where information required   368

Miscellaneous

222 Statutory immunity   368
223 Management expenses   368
224 Scheme manager's power to inspect documents held by Official Receiver
    etc.   368

PART XVI

THE OMBUDSMAN SCHEME

The scheme

225 The scheme and the scheme operator   369
226 Compulsory jurisdiction   369
227 Voluntary jurisdiction   370

Determination of complaints

228 Determination under the compulsory jurisdiction   371
229 Awards   372
230 Costs   372

Information

231 Ombudsman's power to require information   373
232 Powers of court where information required   373
233 Data protection   373

Funding

234 Industry funding   374

PART XVII

COLLECTIVE INVESTMENT SCHEMES

CHAPTER I

INTERPRETATION

235 Collective investment schemes   374
236 Open-ended investment companies   375

237 Other definitions   375

CHAPTER II

RESTRICTIONS ON PROMOTION

238 Restrictions on promotion   376
239 Single property schemes   376
240 Restriction on approval of promotion   377
241 Actions for damages   377

CHAPTER III

AUTHORISED UNIT TRUST SCHEMES

Applications for authorisation

242 Applications for authorisation of unit trust schemes   377
243 Authorisation orders   378
244 Determination of applications   379

Applications refused

245 Procedure when refusing an application   379

Certificates

246 Certificates   379

Rules

247 Trust scheme rules   379
248 Scheme particulars rules   380
249 Disqualification of auditor for breach of trust scheme rules   381
250 Modification or waiver of rules   381

Alterations

251 Alteration of schemes and changes of manager or trustee   382
252 Procedure when refusing approval of change of manager or trustee   382

Exclusion clauses

253 Avoidance of exclusion clauses   382

Ending of authorisation

254 Revocation of authorisation order otherwise than by consent   383
255 Procedure   383

256 Requests for revocation of authorisation order 383

Powers of intervention

257 Directions 384
258 Applications to the court 384
259 Procedure on giving directions under section 257 and varying them on
   Authority's own initiative 385
260 Procedure: refusal to revoke or vary direction 386
261 Procedure: revocation of direction and grant of request for variation 386

CHAPTER IV

OPEN-ENDED INVESTMENT COMPANIES

262 Open-ended investment companies 387
263 Amendment of section 716 Companies Act 1985 388

CHAPTER V

RECOGNISED OVERSEAS SCHEMES

Schemes constituted in other EEA States

264 Schemes constituted in other EEA States 388
265 Representations and references to the Tribunal 389
266 Disapplication of rules 389
267 Power of Authority to suspend promotion of scheme 389
268 Procedure on giving directions under section 267 and varying them on
   Authority's own initiative 390
269 Procedure on application for variation or revocation of direction 391

Schemes authorised in designated countries or territories

270 Schemes authorised in designated countries or territories 392
271 Procedure 393

Individually recognised overseas schemes

272 Individually recognised overseas schemes 393
273 Matters that may be taken into account 394
274 Applications for recognition of individual schemes 394
275 Determination of applications 395
276 Procedure when refusing an application 395
277 Alteration of schemes and changes of operator, trustee or depositary 395

Schemes recognised under sections 270 and 272

278 Rules as to scheme particulars 395
279 Revocation of recognition 395
280 Procedure 396
281 Directions 396
282 Procedure on giving directions under section 281 and varying them
   otherwise than as requested 396

Facilities and information in UK

283 Facilities and information in UK   397

CHAPTER VI

INVESTIGATIONS

284 Power to investigate   398

PART XVIII

RECOGNISED INVESTMENT EXCHANGES AND CLEARING HOUSES

CHAPTER I

EXEMPTION

General

285 Exemption for recognised investment exchanges and clearing houses   399
286 Qualification for recognition   400

Applications for recognition

287 Application by an investment exchange   400
288 Application by a clearing house   400
289 Applications: supplementary   401
290 Recognition orders   401
291 Liability in relation to recognised body's regulatory functions   401
292 Overseas investment exchanges and overseas clearing houses   402

Supervision

293 Notification requirements   402
294 Modification or waiver of rules   403
295 Notification: overseas investment exchanges and overseas clearing houses 404
296 Authority's power to give directions   404
297 Revoking recognition   404
298 Directions and revocation: procedure   405
299 Complaints about recognised bodies   406
300 Extension of functions of Tribunal   406

Other matters

301 Supervision of certain contracts   406

CHAPTER II

COMPETITION SCRUTINY

302 Interpretation   407

Role of Director General of Fair Trading

303 Initial report by Director   408
304 Further reports by Director   408
305 Investigations by Director   409

Role of Competition Commission

306 Consideration by Competition Commission   410

Role of the Treasury

307 Recognition orders: role of the Treasury   411
308 Directions by the Treasury   411
309 Statements by the Treasury   412
310 Procedure on exercise of certain powers by the Treasury   412

CHAPTER III

EXCLUSION FROM THE COMPETITION ACT 1998

311 The Chapter I prohibition   412
312 The Chapter II prohibition   413

CHAPTER IV

Interpretation

313 Interpretation of Part XVIII   414

PART XIX

LLOYD'S

General

314 Authority's general duty   415

The Society

315 The Society: authorisation and permission   415

Power to apply Act to Lloyd's underwriting

316 Direction by Authority   415
317 The core provisions   416
318 Exercise of powers through Council   416
319 Consultation   417

Former underwriting members

320 Former underwriting members   418
321 Requirements imposed under section 320   418
322 Rules applicable to former underwriting members   419

Transfers of business done at Lloyd's

323 Transfer schemes   419

Supplemental

324 Interpretation of this Part   419

PART XX

PROVISION OF FINANCIAL SERVICES BY MEMBERS OF THE PROFESSIONS

325 Authority's general duty   420
326 Designation of professional bodies   420
327 Exemption from the general prohibition   421
328 Directions in relation to the general prohibition   422
329 Orders in relation to the general prohibition   422
330 Consultation   423
331 Procedure on making or varying orders under section 329   424
332 Rules in relation to persons to whom the general prohibition does not apply 424
333 False claims to be a person to whom the general prohibition does not apply   425

PART XXI

MUTUAL SOCIETIES

Friendly societies

334 The Friendly Societies Commission   425
335 The Registry of Friendly Societies   426

Building societies

336 The Building Societies Commission   426
337 The Building Societies Investor Protection Board   426

Industrial and provident societies and credit unions

338 Industrial and provident societies and credit unions   427

Supplemental

339 Supplemental provisions   427

PART XXII

AUDITORS AND ACTUARIES

Appointment

340 Appointment   428

Information

341 Access to books etc.　　　429
342 Information given by auditor or actuary to the Authority　　　429
343 Information given by auditor or actuary to the Authority: persons with close links　　　429
344 Duty of auditor or actuary resigning etc. to give notice　　　430

Disqualification

345 Disqualification　　　430

Offence

346 Provision of false or misleading information to auditor or actuary　　　431

PART XXIII

PUBLIC RECORD, DISCLOSURE OF INFORMATION AND CO-OPERATION

The public record

347 The record of authorised persons etc.　　　431

Disclosure of information

348 Restrictions on disclosure of confidential information by Authority etc.　　　432
349 Exceptions from section 348　　　433
350 Disclosure of information by the Inland Revenue　　　434
351 Competition information　　　435
352 Offences　　　436
353 Removal of other restrictions on disclosure　　　436

Co-operation

354 Authority's duty to co-operate with others　　　436

PART XXIV

INSOLVENCY

Interpretation

355 Interpretation of this Part　　　437

Voluntary arrangements

356 Authority's powers to participate in proceedings: company voluntary arrangements　　　437
357 Authority's powers to participate in proceedings: individual voluntary arrangements　　　437
358 Authority's powers to participate in proceedings: trust deeds for creditors in Scotland　　　438

Administration orders

359 Petitions   438
360 Insurers   439
361 Administrator's duty to report to Authority   439
362 Authority's powers to participate in proceedings   439

Receivership

363 Authority's powers to participate in proceedings   440
364 Receiver's duty to report to Authority   440

Voluntary winding up

365 Authority's powers to participate in proceedings   440
366 Insurers effecting or carrying out long-term contracts of insurance 441

Winding up by the court

367 Winding-up petitions   441
368 Winding-up petitions: EEA and Treaty firms   442
369 Insurers: service of petition etc. on Authority   442
370 Liquidator's duty to report to Authority   442
371 Authority's powers to participate in proceedings   443

Bankruptcy

372 Petitions   443
373 Insolvency practitioner's duty to report to Authority   444
374 Authority's powers to participate in proceedings   444

Provisions against debt avoidance

375 Authority's right to apply for an order   445

Supplemental provisions concerning insurers

376 Continuation of contracts of long-term insurance where insurer in
     liquidation   445
377 Reducing the value of contracts instead of winding up   446
378 Treatment of assets on winding up   446
379 Winding-up rules   447

PART XXV

INJUNCTIONS AND RESTITUTION

Injunctions

380 Injunctions   447

381 Injunctions in cases of market abuse 448

Restitution orders

382 Restitution orders 449
383 Restitution orders in cases of market abuse 450

Restitution required by Authority

384 Power of Authority to require restitution 451
385 Warning notices 452
386 Decision notices 452

PART XXVI

NOTICES

Warning notices

387 Warning notices 452

Decision notices

388 Decision notices 453

Conclusion of proceedings

389 Notices of discontinuance 453
390 Final notices 454

Publication

391 Publication 455

Third party rights and access to evidence

392 Application of sections 393 and 394 455
393 Third party rights 456
394 Access to Authority material 457

The Authority's procedures

395 The Authority's procedures 458
396 Statements under section 395: consultation 459

PART XXVII

OFFENCES

Miscellaneous offences

397 Misleading statements and practices 459
398 Misleading the Authority: residual cases 461

399 Misleading the Director General of Fair Trading   461

Bodies corporate and partnerships

400 Offences by bodies corporate etc.   461

Institution of proceedings

401 Proceedings for offences   462
402 Power of the Authority to institute proceedings for certain other offences   462
403 Jurisdiction and procedure in respect of offences   462

PART XXVIII

MISCELLANEOUS

Schemes for reviewing past business

404 Schemes for reviewing past business   463

Third countries

405 Directions   464
406 Interpretation of section 405   464
407 Consequences of a direction under section 405   465
408 EFTA firms   465
409 Gibraltar   466

International obligations

410 International obligations   466

Tax treatment of levies and repayments

411 Tax treatment of levies and repayments   467

Gaming contracts

412 Gaming contracts   468

Limitation on powers to require documents

413 Protected items   468

Service of notices

414 Service of notices   469

Jurisdiction

415 Jurisdiction in civil proceedings   469

Removal of certain unnecessary provisions

416 Provisions relating to industrial assurance and certain other enactments   470

PART XXIX

INTERPRETATION

417 Definitions   470
418 Carrying on regulated activities in the United Kingdom   472
419 Carrying on regulated activities by way of business   473
420 Parent and subsidiary undertaking   473
421 Group   474
422 Controller   474
423 Manager   475
424 Insurance   476
425 Expressions relating to authorisation elsewhere in the single market   476

PART XXX

SUPPLEMENTAL

426 Consequential and supplementary provision   476
427 Transitional provisions   477
428 Regulations and orders   478
429 Parliamentary control of statutory instruments   478
430 Extent   479
431 Commencement   479
432 Minor and consequential amendments, transitional provisions and repeals   479
433 Short title   479

SCHEDULES:
    Schedule 1—The Financial Services Authority
        Part I—General
        Part II—Status
        Part III—Penalties and Fees
        Part IV—Miscellaneous
    Schedule 2—Regulated Activities
        Part I—Regulated Activities
        Part II—Investments
        Part III—Supplemental Provisions
    Schedule 3—EEA Passport Rights
        Part I—Defined terms
        Part II—Exercise of Passport Rights by EEA Firms
        Part III—Exercise of Passport Rights by UK Firms
    Schedule 4—Treaty Rights
    Schedule 5—Persons Concerned in Collective Investment Schemes
    Schedule 6—Threshold Conditions
        Part I—Part IV Permission
        Part II—Authorisation
        Part III—Additional Conditions
    Schedule 7—The Authority as Competent Authority for Part VI
    Schedule 8—Transfer of functions under Part VI
    Schedule 9—Non-listing Prospectuses

Schedule 10—Compensation: Exemptions
Schedule 11—Offers of Securities
Schedule 12—Transfer schemes: certificates
      Part I—Insurance Business Transfer Schemes
      Part II—Banking Business Transfer Schemes
      Part III—Insurance business transfers effected outside the United Kingdom
Schedule 13—The Financial Services and Markets Tribunal
      Part I—General
      Part II—The Tribunal
      Part III—Constitution of Tribunal
      Part IV—Tribunal Procedure
Schedule 14—Role of the Competition Commission
Schedule 15—Information and Investigations: Connected Persons
      Part I—Rules for Specific Bodies
      Part II—Additional Rules
Schedule 16—Prohibitions and Restrictions imposed by Director General of Fair
      Trading
Schedule 17—The Ombudsman Scheme
      Part I—General
      Part II—The Scheme Operator
      Part III—The Compulsory Jurisdiction
      Part IV—The Voluntary Jurisdiction
Schedule 18—Mutuals
      Part I—Friendly Societies
      Part II—Friendly Societies: Subsidiaries and Controlled Bodies
      Part III—Building Societies
      Part IV—Industrial and Provident Societies
      Part V—Credit Unions
Schedule 19—Competition Information
      Part I—Persons and functions for the purposes of section 351
      Part II—The enactments
Schedule 20—Minor and Consequential Amendments
Schedule 21—Transitional Provisions and Savings
Schedule 22—Repeals

An Act to make provision about the regulation of financial services and markets; to provide for the transfer of certain statutory functions relating to building societies, friendly societies, industrial and provident societies and certain other mutual societies; and for connected purposes. [14th June 2000]

PART I

THE REGULATOR

1 The Financial Services Authority

(1) The body corporate known as the Financial Services Authority ('the Authority') is to have the functions conferred on it by or under this Act.

(2) The Authority must comply with the requirements as to its constitution set out in Schedule 1.

(3) Schedule 1 also makes provision about the status of the Authority and the exercise of certain of its functions.

The Authority's general duties

2   The Authority's general duties

(1) In discharging its general functions the Authority must, so far as is reasonably possible, act in a way—

(a)   which is compatible with the regulatory objectives; and

(b)   which the Authority considers most appropriate for the purpose of meeting those objectives.

(2) The regulatory objectives are—

(a)   market confidence;

(b)   public awareness;

(c)   the protection of consumers; and

(d)   the reduction of financial crime.

(3) In discharging its general functions the Authority must have regard to—

(a)   the need to use its resources in the most efficient and economic way;

(b)   the responsibilities of those who manage the affairs of authorised persons;

(c)   the principle that a burden or restriction which is imposed on a person, or on the carrying on of an activity, should be proportionate to the benefits, considered in general terms, which are expected to result from the imposition of that burden or restriction;

(d)   the desirability of facilitating innovation in connection with regulated activities;

(e)   the international character of financial services and markets and the desirability of maintaining the competitive position of the United Kingdom;

(f)   the need to minimise the adverse effects on competition that may arise from anything done in the discharge of those functions;

(g)   the desirability of facilitating competition between those who are subject to any form of regulation by the Authority.

(4) The Authority's general functions are—

(a)   its function of making rules under this Act (considered as a whole);

(b)   its function of preparing and issuing codes under this Act (considered as a whole);

(c)   its functions in relation to the giving of general guidance (considered as a whole); and

(d)   its function of determining the general policy and principles by reference to which it performs particular functions.

(5) 'General guidance' has the meaning given in section 158(5).

The regulatory objectives

3   Market confidence

(1) The market confidence objective is: maintaining confidence in the financial system.

(2) 'The financial system' means the financial system operating in the United Kingdom and includes—

(a)   financial markets and exchanges;

(b)   regulated activities; and

(c)   other activities connected with financial markets and exchanges.

4   Public awareness

(1) The public awareness objective is: promoting public understanding of the financial system.

(2) It includes, in particular—

(a)   promoting awareness of the benefits and risks associated with different kinds of investment or other financial dealing; and
(b)   the provision of appropriate information and advice.

(3) 'The financial system' has the same meaning as in section 3.

5   The protection of consumers

(1) The protection of consumers objective is: securing the appropriate degree of protection for consumers.

(2) In considering what degree of protection may be appropriate, the Authority must have regard to—

(a)   the differing degrees of risk involved in different kinds of investment or other transaction;
(b)   the differing degrees of experience and expertise that different consumers may have in relation to different kinds of regulated activity;
(c)   the needs that consumers may have for advice and accurate information; and
(d)   the general principle that consumers should take responsibility for their decisions.

(3) 'Consumers' means persons—

(a)   who are consumers for the purposes of section 138; or
(b)   who, in relation to regulated activities carried on otherwise than by authorised persons, would be consumers for those purposes if the activities were carried on by authorised persons.

6   The reduction of financial crime

(1) The reduction of financial crime objective is: reducing the extent to which it is possible for a business carried on—

(a)   by a regulated person, or
(b)   in contravention of the general prohibition,

to be used for a purpose connected with financial crime.

(2) In considering that objective the Authority must, in particular, have regard to the desirability of—

(a)   regulated persons being aware of the risk of their businesses being used in connection with the commission of financial crime;
(b)   regulated persons taking appropriate measures (in relation to their administration and employment practices, the conduct of transactions by them and otherwise) to prevent financial crime, facilitate its detection and monitor its incidence;
(c)   regulated persons devoting adequate resources to the matters mentioned in paragraph (b).

(3) 'Financial crime' includes any offence involving—

(a)   fraud or dishonesty;

(b) misconduct in, or misuse of information relating to, a financial market; or

(c) handling the proceeds of crime.

(4) 'Offence' includes an act or omission which would be an offence if it had taken place in the United Kingdom.

(5) 'Regulated person' means an authorised person, a recognised investment exchange or a recognised clearing house.

Corporate governance

7 Duty of Authority to follow principles of good governance

In managing its affairs, the Authority must have regard to such generally accepted principles of good corporate governance as it is reasonable to regard as applicable to it.

Arrangements for consulting practitioners and consumers

8 The Authority's general duty to consult

The Authority must make and maintain effective arrangements for consulting practitioners and consumers on the extent to which its general policies and practices are consistent with its general duties under section 2.

9 The Practitioner Panel

(1) Arrangements under section 8 must include the establishment and maintenance of a panel of persons (to be known as 'the Practitioner Panel') to represent the interests of practitioners.

(2) The Authority must appoint one of the members of the Practitioner Panel to be its chairman.

(3) The Treasury's approval is required for the appointment or dismissal of the chairman.

(4) The Authority must have regard to any representations made to it by the Practitioner Panel.

(5) The Authority must appoint to the Practitioner Panel such—

(a) individuals who are authorised persons,
(b) persons representing authorised persons,
(c) persons representing recognised investment exchanges, and
(d) persons representing recognised clearing houses,

as it considers appropriate.

10 The Consumer Panel

(1) Arrangements under section 8 must include the establishment and maintenance of a panel of persons (to be known as 'the Consumer Panel') to represent the interests of consumers.

(2) The Authority must appoint one of the members of the Consumer Panel to be its chairman.

(3) The Treasury's approval is required for the appointment or dismissal of the chairman.

(4) The Authority must have regard to any representations made to it by the Consumer Panel.

(5) The Authority must appoint to the Consumer Panel such consumers, or persons representing the interests of consumers, as it considers appropriate.

(6) The Authority must secure that the membership of the Consumer Panel is such as to give a fair degree of representation to those who are using, or are or may be contemplating using, services otherwise than in connection with businesses carried on by them.

(7) 'Consumers' means persons, other than authorised persons—

 (a)   who are consumers for the purposes of section 138; or
 (b)   who, in relation to regulated activities carried on otherwise than by authorised persons, would be consumers for those purposes if the activities were carried on by authorised persons.

11   Duty to consider representations by the Panels

(1) This section applies to a representation made, in accordance with arrangements made under section 8, by the Practitioner Panel or by the Consumer Panel.

(2) The Authority must consider the representation.

(3) If the Authority disagrees with a view expressed, or proposal made, in the representation, it must give the Panel a statement in writing of its reasons for disagreeing.

Reviews

12   Reviews

(1) The Treasury may appoint an independent person to conduct a review of the economy, efficiency and effectiveness with which the Authority has used its resources in discharging its functions.

(2) A review may be limited by the Treasury to such functions of the Authority (however described) as the Treasury may specify in appointing the person to conduct it.

(3) A review is not to be concerned with the merits of the Authority's general policy or principles in pursuing regulatory objectives or in exercising functions under Part VI.

(4) On completion of a review, the person conducting it must make a written report to the Treasury—

 (a)   setting out the result of the review; and
 (b)   making such recommendations (if any) as he considers appropriate.

(5) A copy of the report must be—

 (a)   laid before each House of Parliament; and
 (b)   published in such manner as the Treasury consider appropriate.

(6) Any expenses reasonably incurred in the conduct of a review are to be met by the Treasury out of money provided by Parliament.

(7) 'Independent' means appearing to the Treasury to be independent of the Authority.

13   Right to obtain documents and information

(1) A person conducting a review under section 12—

 (a)   has a right of access at any reasonable time to all such documents as he may reasonably require for purposes of the review; and
 (b)   may require any person holding or accountable for any such document to provide such information and explanation as are reasonably necessary for that purpose.

(2) Subsection (1) applies only to documents in the custody or under the control of the Authority.

(3) An obligation imposed on a person as a result of the exercise of powers conferred by subsection (1) is enforceable by injunction or, in Scotland, by an order for specific performance under section 45 of the Court of Session Act 1988.

Inquiries

14   Cases in which the Treasury may arrange independent inquiries

(1) This section applies in two cases.

(2) The first is where it appears to the Treasury that—

  (a)   events have occurred in relation to—
        (i)   a collective investment scheme, or
        (ii)   a person who is, or was at the time of the events, carrying on a regulated activity
               (whether or not as an authorised person),
        which posed or could have posed a grave risk to the financial system or caused or
        risked causing significant damage to the interests of consumers; and
  (b)   those events might not have occurred, or the risk or damage might have been
        reduced, but for a serious failure in—
        (i)   the system established by this Act for the regulation of such schemes or of such
               persons and their activities; or
        (ii)   the operation of that system.

(3) The second is where it appears to the Treasury that—

  (a)   events have occurred in relation to listed securities or an issuer of listed securities
        which caused or could have caused significant damage to holders of listed
        securities; and
  (b)   those events might not have occurred but for serious failure in the regulatory system
        established by Part VI or in its operation.

(4) If the Treasury consider that it is in the public interest that there should be an independent inquiry into the events and the circumstances surrounding them, they may arrange for an inquiry to be held under section 15.

(5) 'Consumers' means persons—

  (a)   who are consumers for the purposes of section 138; or
  (b)   who, in relation to regulated activities carried on otherwise than by authorised
        persons, would be consumers for those purposes if the activities were carried on by
        authorised persons.

(6) 'The financial system' has the same meaning as in section 3.

(7) 'Listed securities' means anything which has been admitted to the official list under Part VI.

15   Power to appoint person to hold an inquiry

(1) If the Treasury decide to arrange for an inquiry to be held under this section, they may appoint such person as they consider appropriate to hold the inquiry.

(2) The Treasury may, by a direction to the appointed person, control—

  (a)   the scope of the inquiry;

   (b)   the period during which the inquiry is to be held;

   (c)   the conduct of the inquiry; and

   (d)   the making of reports.

(3) A direction may, in particular—

   (a)   confine the inquiry to particular matters;

   (b)   extend the inquiry to additional matters;

   (c)   require the appointed person to discontinue the inquiry or to take only such steps as are specified in the direction;

   (d)   require the appointed person to make such interim reports as are so specified.

16 Powers of appointed person and procedure

(1) The person appointed to hold an inquiry under section 15 may—

   (a)   obtain such information from such persons and in such manner as he thinks fit;

   (b)   make such inquiries as he thinks fit; and

   (c)   determine the procedure to be followed in connection with the inquiry.

(2) The appointed person may require any person who, in his opinion, is able to provide any information, or produce any document, which is relevant to the inquiry to provide any such information or produce any such document.

(3) For the purposes of an inquiry, the appointed person has the same powers as the court in respect of the attendance and examination of witnesses (including the examination of witnesses abroad) and in respect of the production of documents.

(4) 'Court' means—

   (a)   the High Court; or

   (b)   in Scotland, the Court of Session.

17 Conclusion of inquiry

(1) On completion of an inquiry under section 15, the person holding the inquiry must make a written report to the Treasury—

   (a)   setting out the result of the inquiry; and

   (b)   making such recommendations (if any) as he considers appropriate.

(2) The Treasury may publish the whole, or any part, of the report and may do so in such manner as they consider appropriate.

(3) Subsection (4) applies if the Treasury propose to publish a report but consider that it contains material—

   (a)   which relates to the affairs of a particular person whose interests would, in the opinion of the Treasury, be seriously prejudiced by publication of the material; or

   (b)   the disclosure of which would be incompatible with an international obligation of the United Kingdom.

(4) The Treasury must ensure that the material is removed before publication.

(5) The Treasury must lay before each House of Parliament a copy of any report or part of a report published under subsection (2).

(6) Any expenses reasonably incurred in holding an inquiry are to be met by the Treasury out of money provided by Parliament.

18   Obstruction and contempt

(1) If a person ('A')—

(a)   fails to comply with a requirement imposed on him by a person holding an inquiry under section 15, or

(b)   otherwise obstructs such an inquiry,

the person holding the inquiry may certify the matter to the High Court (or, in Scotland, the Court of Session).

(2) The court may enquire into the matter.

(3) If, after hearing—

(a)   any witnesses who may be produced against or on behalf of A, and

(b)   any statement made by or on behalf of A,

the court is satisfied that A would have been in contempt of court if the inquiry had been proceedings before the court, it may deal with him as if he were in contempt.

PART II

REGULATED AND PROHIBITED ACTIVITIES

The general prohibition

19   The general prohibition

(1) No person may carry on a regulated activity in the United Kingdom, or purport to do so, unless he is—

(a)   an authorised person; or

(b)   an exempt person.

(2) The prohibition is referred to in this Act as the general prohibition.

Requirement for permission

20   Authorised persons acting without permission

(1) If an authorised person carries on a regulated activity in the United Kingdom, or purports to do so, otherwise than in accordance with permission—

(a)   given to him by the Authority under Part IV, or

(b)   resulting from any other provision of this Act,

he is to be taken to have contravened a requirement imposed on him by the Authority under this Act.

(2) The contravention does not—

(a)   make a person guilty of an offence;

(b)   make any transaction void or unenforceable; or

(c)   (subject to subsection (3)) give rise to any right of action for breach of statutory duty.

(3) In prescribed cases the contravention is actionable at the suit of a person who suffers loss as a result of the contravention, subject to the defences and other incidents applying to actions for breach of statutory duty.

Financial promotion

21   Restrictions on financial promotion

(1) A person ('A') must not, in the course of business, communicate an invitation or inducement to engage in investment activity.

(2) But subsection (1) does not apply if—

(a)   A is an authorised person; or
(b)   the content of the communication is approved for the purposes of this section by an authorised person.

(3) In the case of a communication originating outside the United Kingdom, subsection (1) applies only if the communication is capable of having an effect in the United Kingdom.

(4) The Treasury may by order specify circumstances in which a person is to be regarded for the purposes of subsection (1) as—

(a)   acting in the course of business;
(b)   not acting in the course of business.

(5) The Treasury may by order specify circumstances (which may include compliance with financial promotion rules) in which subsection (1) does not apply.

(6) An order under subsection (5) may, in particular, provide that subsection (1) does not apply in relation to communications—

(a)   of a specified description;
(b)   originating in a specified country or territory outside the United Kingdom;
(c)   originating in a country or territory which falls within a specified description of country or territory outside the United Kingdom; or
(d)   originating outside the United Kingdom.

(7) The Treasury may by order repeal subsection (3).

(8) 'Engaging in investment activity' means—

(a)   entering or offering to enter into an agreement the making or performance of which by either party constitutes a controlled activity; or
(b)   exercising any rights conferred by a controlled investment to acquire, dispose of, underwrite or convert a controlled investment.

(9) An activity is a controlled activity if—

(a)   it is an activity of a specified kind or one which falls within a specified class of activity; and
(b)   it relates to an investment of a specified kind, or to one which falls within a specified class of investment.

(10) An investment is a controlled investment if it is an investment of a specified kind or one which falls within a specified class of investment.

(11) Schedule 2 (except paragraph 26) applies for the purposes of subsections (9) and (10) with references to section 22 being read as references to each of those subsections.

(12) Nothing in Schedule 2, as applied by subsection (11), limits the powers conferred by subsection (9) or (10).

(13) 'Communicate' includes causing a communication to be made.

(14) 'Investment' includes any asset, right or interest.

(15) 'Specified' means specified in an order made by the Treasury.

Regulated activities

22   The classes of activity and categories of investment

(1) An activity is a regulated activity for the purposes of this Act if it is an activity of a specified kind which is carried on by way of business and—

  (a)   relates to an investment of a specified kind; or
  (b)   in the case of an activity of a kind which is also specified for the purposes of this paragraph, is carried on in relation to property of any kind.

(2) Schedule 2 makes provision supplementing this section.

(3) Nothing in Schedule 2 limits the powers conferred by subsection (1).

(4) 'Investment' includes any asset, right or interest.

(5) 'Specified' means specified in an order made by the Treasury.

Offences

23   Contravention of the general prohibition

(1) A person who contravenes the general prohibition is guilty of an offence and liable—

  (a)   on summary conviction, to imprisonment for a term not exceeding six months or a fine not exceeding the statutory maximum, or both;
  (b)   on conviction on indictment, to imprisonment for a term not exceeding two years or a fine, or both.

(2) In this Act 'an authorisation offence' means an offence under this section.

(3) In proceedings for an authorisation offence it is a defence for the accused to show that he took all reasonable precautions and exercised all due diligence to avoid committing the offence.

24   False claims to be authorised or exempt

(1) A person who is neither an authorised person nor, in relation to the regulated activity in question, an exempt person is guilty of an offence if he—

  (a)   describes himself (in whatever terms) as an authorised person;
  (b)   describes himself (in whatever terms) as an exempt person in relation to the regulated activity; or
  (c)   behaves, or otherwise holds himself out, in a manner which indicates (or which is reasonably likely to be understood as indicating) that he is—
    (i)   an authorised person; or
    (ii)   an exempt person in relation to the regulated activity.

(2) In proceedings for an offence under this section it is a defence for the accused to show that he took all reasonable precautions and exercised all due diligence to avoid committing the offence.

(3) A person guilty of an offence under this section is liable on summary conviction to imprisonment for a term not exceeding six months or a fine not exceeding level 5 on the standard scale, or both.

(4) But where the conduct constituting the offence involved or included the public display of any material, the maximum fine for the offence is level 5 on the standard scale multiplied by the number of days for which the display continued.

25   Contravention of section 21

(1) A person who contravenes section 21(1) is guilty of an offence and liable—

   (a)   on summary conviction, to imprisonment for a term not exceeding six months or a fine not exceeding the statutory maximum, or both;

   (b)   on conviction on indictment, to imprisonment for a term not exceeding two years or a fine, or both.

(2) In proceedings for an offence under this section it is a defence for the accused to show—

   (a)   that he believed on reasonable grounds that the content of the communication was prepared, or approved for the purposes of section 21, by an authorised person; or

   (b)   that he took all reasonable precautions and exercised all due diligence to avoid committing the offence.

Enforceability of agreements

26   Agreements made by unauthorised persons

(1) An agreement made by a person in the course of carrying on a regulated activity in contravention of the general prohibition is unenforceable against the other party.

(2) The other party is entitled to recover—

   (a)   any money or other property paid or transferred by him under the agreement; and

   (b)   compensation for any loss sustained by him as a result of having parted with it.

(3) 'Agreement' means an agreement—

   (a)   made after this section comes into force; and

   (b)   the making or performance of which constitutes, or is part of, the regulated activity in question.

(4) This section does not apply if the regulated activity is accepting deposits.

27   Agreements made through unauthorised persons

(1) An agreement made by an authorised person ('the provider')—

   (a)   in the course of carrying on a regulated activity (not in contravention of the general prohibition), but

   (b)   in consequence of something said or done by another person ('the third party') in the course of a regulated activity carried on by the third party in contravention of the general prohibition,

is unenforceable against the other party.

(2) The other party is entitled to recover—

   (a)   any money or other property paid or transferred by him under the agreement; and

   (b)   compensation for any loss sustained by him as a result of having parted with it.

(3) 'Agreement' means an agreement—

   (a)   made after this section comes into force; and

   (b)   the making or performance of which constitutes, or is part of, the regulated activity in question carried on by the provider.

(4) This section does not apply if the regulated activity is accepting deposits.

28 Agreements unenforceable by section 26 or 27

(1) This section applies to an agreement which is unenforceable because of section 26 or 27.

(2) The amount of compensation recoverable as a result of that section is—

(a) the amount agreed by the parties; or
(b) on the application of either party, the amount determined by the court.

(3) If the court is satisfied that it is just and equitable in the circumstances of the case, it may allow—

(a) the agreement to be enforced; or
(b) money and property paid or transferred under the agreement to be retained.

(4) In considering whether to allow the agreement to be enforced or (as the case may be) the money or property paid or transferred under the agreement to be retained the court must—

(a) if the case arises as a result of section 26, have regard to the issue mentioned in subsection (5); or
(b) if the case arises as a result of section 27, have regard to the issue mentioned in subsection (6).

(5) The issue is whether the person carrying on the regulated activity concerned reasonably believed that he was not contravening the general prohibition by making the agreement.

(6) The issue is whether the provider knew that the third party was (in carrying on the regulated activity) contravening the general prohibition.

(7) If the person against whom the agreement is unenforceable—

(a) elects not to perform the agreement, or
(b) as a result of this section, recovers money paid or other property transferred by him under the agreement,

he must repay any money and return any other property received by him under the agreement.

(8) If property transferred under the agreement has passed to a third party, a reference in section 26 or 27 or this section to that property is to be read as a reference to its value at the time of its transfer under the agreement.

(9) The commission of an authorisation offence does not make the agreement concerned illegal or invalid to any greater extent than is provided by section 26 or 27.

29 Accepting deposits in breach of general prohibition

(1) This section applies to an agreement between a person ('the depositor') and another person ('the deposit-taker') made in the course of the carrying on by the deposit-taker of accepting deposits in contravention of the general prohibition.

(2) If the depositor is not entitled under the agreement to recover without delay any money deposited by him, he may apply to the court for an order directing the deposit-taker to return the money to him.

(3) The court need not make such an order if it is satisfied that it would not be just and equitable for the money deposited to be returned, having regard to the issue mentioned in subsection (4).

(4) The issue is whether the deposit-taker reasonably believed that he was not contravening the general prohibition by making the agreement.

(5) 'Agreement' means an agreement—

(a)   made after this section comes into force; and

(b)   the making or performance of which constitutes, or is part of, accepting deposits.

30   Enforceability of agreements resulting from unlawful communications

(1) In this section—

'unlawful communication' means a communication in relation to which there has been a contravention of section 21(1);

'controlled agreement' means an agreement the making or performance of which by either party constitutes a controlled activity for the purposes of that section; and

'controlled investment' has the same meaning as in section 21.

(2) If in consequence of an unlawful communication a person enters as a customer into a controlled agreement, it is unenforceable against him and he is entitled to recover—

(a)   any money or other property paid or transferred by him under the agreement; and

(b)   compensation for any loss sustained by him as a result of having parted with it.

(3) If in consequence of an unlawful communication a person exercises any rights conferred by a controlled investment, no obligation to which he is subject as a result of exercising them is enforceable against him and he is entitled to recover—

(a)   any money or other property paid or transferred by him under the obligation; and

(b)   compensation for any loss sustained by him as a result of having parted with it.

(4) But the court may allow—

(a)   the agreement or obligation to be enforced, or

(b)   money or property paid or transferred under the agreement or obligation to be retained,

if it is satisfied that it is just and equitable in the circumstances of the case.

(5) In considering whether to allow the agreement or obligation to be enforced or (as the case may be) the money or property paid or transferred under the agreement to be retained the court must have regard to the issues mentioned in subsections (6) and (7).

(6) If the applicant made the unlawful communication, the issue is whether he reasonably believed that he was not making such a communication.

(7) If the applicant did not make the unlawful communication, the issue is whether he knew that the agreement was entered into in consequence of such a communication.

(8) 'Applicant' means the person seeking to enforce the agreement or obligation or retain the money or property paid or transferred.

(9) Any reference to making a communication includes causing a communication to be made.

(10) The amount of compensation recoverable as a result of subsection (2) or (3) is—

(a)   the amount agreed between the parties; or

(b)   on the application of either party, the amount determined by the court.

(11) If a person elects not to perform an agreement or an obligation which (by virtue of subsection (2) or (3)) is unenforceable against him, he must repay any money and return any other property received by him under the agreement.

(12) If (by virtue of subsection (2) or (3)) a person recovers money paid or property transferred by him under an agreement or obligation, he must repay any money and return any other property received by him as a result of exercising the rights in question.

(13) If any property required to be returned under this section has passed to a third party, references to that property are to be read as references to its value at the time of its receipt by the person required to return it.

PART III

AUTHORISATION AND EXEMPTION

Authorisation

31   Authorised persons

(1) The following persons are authorised for the purposes of this Act—

   (a)   a person who has a Part IV permission to carry on one or more regulated activities;
   (b)   an EEA firm qualifying for authorisation under Schedule 3;
   (c)   a Treaty firm qualifying for authorisation under Schedule 4;
   (d)   a person who is otherwise authorised by a provision of, or made under, this Act.

(2) In this Act 'authorised person' means a person who is authorised for the purposes of this Act.

32   Partnerships and unincorporated associations

(1) If a firm is authorised—

   (a)   it is authorised to carry on the regulated activities concerned in the name of the firm; and
   (b)   its authorisation is not affected by any change in its membership.

(2) If an authorised firm is dissolved, its authorisation continues to have effect in relation to any firm which succeeds to the business of the dissolved firm.

(3) For the purposes of this section, a firm is to be regarded as succeeding to the business of another firm only if—

   (a)   the members of the resulting firm are substantially the same as those of the former firm; and
   (b)   succession is to the whole or substantially the whole of the business of the former firm.

(4) 'Firm' means—

   (a)   a partnership; or
   (b)   an unincorporated association of persons.

(5) 'Partnership' does not include a partnership which is constituted under the law of any place outside the United Kingdom and is a body corporate.

Ending of authorisation

33   Withdrawal of authorisation by the Authority

(1) This section applies if—

   (a)   an authorised person's Part IV permission is cancelled; and
   (b)   as a result, there is no regulated activity for which he has permission.

(2) The Authority must give a direction withdrawing that person's status as an authorised person.

34   EEA firms

(1) An EEA firm ceases to qualify for authorisation under Part II of Schedule 3 if it ceases to be an EEA firm as a result of—

    (a)   having its EEA authorisation withdrawn; or

    (b)   ceasing to have an EEA right in circumstances in which EEA authorisation is not required.

(2) At the request of an EEA firm, the Authority may give a direction cancelling its authorisation under Part II of Schedule 3.

(3) If an EEA firm has a Part IV permission, it does not cease to be an authorised person merely because it ceases to qualify for authorisation under Part II of Schedule 3.

35   Treaty firms

(1) A Treaty firm ceases to qualify for authorisation under Schedule 4 if its home State authorisation is withdrawn.

(2) At the request of a Treaty firm, the Authority may give a direction cancelling its Schedule 4 authorisation.

(3) If a Treaty firm has a Part IV permission, it does not cease to be an authorised person merely because it ceases to qualify for authorisation under Schedule 4.

36   Persons authorised as a result of paragraph 1(1) of Schedule 5

(1) At the request of a person authorised as a result of paragraph 1(1) of Schedule 5, the Authority may give a direction cancelling his authorisation as such a person.

(2) If a person authorised as a result of paragraph 1(1) of Schedule 5 has a Part IV permission, he does not cease to be an authorised person merely because he ceases to be a person so authorised.

Exercise of EEA rights by UK firms

37   Exercise of EEA rights by UK firms

Part III of Schedule 3 makes provision in relation to the exercise outside the United Kingdom of EEA rights by UK firms.

Exemption

38   Exemption orders

(1) The Treasury may by order ('an exemption order') provide for—

    (a)   specified persons, or

    (b)   persons falling within a specified class,

to be exempt from the general prohibition.

(2) But a person cannot be an exempt person as a result of an exemption order if he has a Part IV permission.

(3) An exemption order may provide for an exemption to have effect—

    (a)   in respect of all regulated activities;

    (b)   in respect of one or more specified regulated activities;

    (c)   only in specified circumstances;

(d)   only in relation to specified functions;

(e)   subject to conditions.

(4) 'Specified' means specified by the exemption order.

39   Exemption of appointed representatives

(1) If a person (other than an authorised person)—

(a)   is a party to a contract with an authorised person ('his principal') which—
  (i)   permits or requires him to carry on business of a prescribed description, and
  (ii)   complies with such requirements as may be prescribed, and

(b)   is someone for whose activities in carrying on the whole or part of that business his principal has accepted responsibility in writing,

he is exempt from the general prohibition in relation to any regulated activity comprised in the carrying on of that business for which his principal has accepted responsibility.

(2) A person who is exempt as a result of subsection (1) is referred to in this Act as an appointed representative.

(3) The principal of an appointed representative is responsible, to the same extent as if he had expressly permitted it, for anything done or omitted by the representative in carrying on the business for which he has accepted responsibility.

(4) In determining whether an authorised person has complied with a provision contained in or made under this Act, anything which a relevant person has done or omitted as respects business for which the authorised person has accepted responsibility is to be treated as having been done or omitted by the authorised person.

(5) 'Relevant person' means a person who at the material time is or was an appointed representative by virtue of being a party to a contract with the authorised person.

(6) Nothing in subsection (4) is to cause the knowledge or intentions of an appointed representative to be attributed to his principal for the purpose of determining whether the principal has committed an offence, unless in all the circumstances it is reasonable for them to be attributed to him.

PART IV

PERMISSION TO CARRY ON REGULATED ACTIVITIES

Application for permission

40   Application for permission

(1) An application for permission to carry on one or more regulated activities may be made to the Authority by—

(a)   an individual;

(b)   a body corporate;

(c)   a partnership; or

(d)   an unincorporated association.

(2) An authorised person may not apply for permission under this section if he has a permission—

(a)   given to him by the Authority under this Part, or

(b)   having effect as if so given,

which is in force.

(3) An EEA firm may not apply for permission under this section to carry on a regulated activity which it is, or would be, entitled to carry on in exercise of an EEA right, whether through a United Kingdom branch or by providing services in the United Kingdom.

(4) A permission given by the Authority under this Part or having effect as if so given is referred to in this Act as 'a Part IV permission'.

41   The threshold conditions

(1) 'The threshold conditions', in relation to a regulated activity, means the conditions set out in Schedule 6.

(2) In giving or varying permission, or imposing or varying any requirement, under this Part the Authority must ensure that the person concerned will satisfy, and continue to satisfy, the threshold conditions in relation to all of the regulated activities for which he has or will have permission.

(3) But the duty imposed by subsection (2) does not prevent the Authority, having due regard to that duty, from taking such steps as it considers are necessary, in relation to a particular authorised person, in order to secure its regulatory objective of the protection of consumers.

Permission

42   Giving permission

(1) 'The applicant' means an applicant for permission under section 40.

(2) The Authority may give permission for the applicant to carry on the regulated activity or activities to which his application relates or such of them as may be specified in the permission.

(3) If the applicant—

  (a)   in relation to a particular regulated activity, is exempt from the general prohibition as a result of section 39(1) or an order made under section 38(1), but
  (b)   has applied for permission in relation to another regulated activity,

the application is to be treated as relating to all the regulated activities which, if permission is given, he will carry on.

(4) If the applicant—

  (a)   in relation to a particular regulated activity, is exempt from the general prohibition as a result of section 285(2) or (3), but
  (b)   has applied for permission in relation to another regulated activity,

the application is to be treated as relating only to that other regulated activity.

(5) If the applicant—

  (a)   is a person to whom, in relation to a particular regulated activity, the general prohibition does not apply as a result of Part XIX, but
  (b)   has applied for permission in relation to another regulated activity,

the application is to be treated as relating only to that other regulated activity.

(6) If it gives permission, the Authority must specify the permitted regulated activity or activities, described in such manner as the Authority considers appropriate.

(7) The Authority may—

(a) incorporate in the description of a regulated activity such limitations (for example as to circumstances in which the activity may, or may not, be carried on) as it considers appropriate;

(b) specify a narrower or wider description of regulated activity than that to which the application relates;

(c) give permission for the carrying on of a regulated activity which is not included among those to which the application relates.

43 Imposition of requirements

(1) A Part IV permission may include such requirements as the Authority considers appropriate.

(2) A requirement may, in particular, be imposed—

(a) so as to require the person concerned to take specified action; or

(b) so as to require him to refrain from taking specified action.

(3) A requirement may extend to activities which are not regulated activities.

(4) A requirement may be imposed by reference to the person's relationship with—

(a) his group; or

(b) other members of his group.

(5) A requirement expires at the end of such period as the Authority may specify in the permission.

(6) But subsection (5) does not affect the Authority's powers under section 44 or 45.

Variation and cancellation of Part IV permission

44 Variation etc. at request of authorised person

(1) The Authority may, on the application of an authorised person with a Part IV permission, vary the permission by—

(a) adding a regulated activity to those for which it gives permission;

(b) removing a regulated activity from those for which it gives permission;

(c) varying the description of a regulated activity for which it gives permission;

(d) cancelling a requirement imposed under section 43; or

(e) varying such a requirement.

(2) The Authority may, on the application of an authorised person with a Part IV permission, cancel the permission.

(3) The Authority may refuse an application under this section if it appears to it—

(a) that the interests of consumers, or potential consumers, would be adversely affected if the application were to be granted; and

(b) that is is desirable in the interests of consumers, or potential consumers, for the application to be refused.

(4) If, as a result of a variation of a Part IV permission under this section, there are no longer any regulated activities for which the authorised person concerned has permission, the Authority must, once it is satisfied that it is no longer necessary to keep the permission in force, cancel it.

(5) The Authority's power to vary a Part IV permission under this section extends to including any provision in the permission as varied that could be included if a fresh permission were being given in response to an application under section 40.

45   Variation etc. on the Authority's own initiative

(1) The Authority may exercise its power under this section in relation to an authorised person if it appears to it that—

   (a)   he is failing, or is likely to fail, to satisfy the threshold conditions;
   (b)   he has failed, during a period of at least 12 months, to carry on a regulated activity for which he has a Part IV permission; or
   (c)   it is desirable to exercise that power in order to protect the interests of consumers or potential consumers.

(2) The Authority's power under this section is the power to vary a Part IV permission in any of the ways mentioned in section 44(1) or to cancel it.

(3) If, as a result of a variation of a Part IV permission under this section, there are no longer any regulated activities for which the authorised person concerned has permission, the Authority must, once it is satisfied that it is no longer necessary to keep the permission in force, cancel it.

(4) The Authority's power to vary a Part IV permission under this section extends to including any provision in the permission as varied that could be included if a fresh permission were being given in response to an application under section 40.

(5) The Authority's power under this section is referred to in this Part as its own-initiative power.

46   Variation of permission on acquisition of control

(1) This section applies if it appears to the Authority that—

   (a)   a person has acquired control over a UK authorised person who has a Part IV permission; but
   (b)   there are no grounds for exercising its own-initiative power.

(2) If it appears to the Authority that the likely effect of the acquisition of control on the authorised person, or on any of its activities, is uncertain the Authority may vary the authorised person's permission by—

   (a)   imposing a requirement of a kind that could be imposed under section 43 on giving permission; or
   (b)   varying a requirement included in the authorised person's permission under that section.

(3) Any reference to a person having acquired control is to be read in accordance with Part XII.

47   Exercise of power in support of overseas regulator

(1) The Authority's own-initiative power may be exercised in respect of an authorised person at the request of, or for the purpose of assisting, a regulator who is—

   (a)   outside the United Kingdom; and
   (b)   of a prescribed kind.

(2) Subsection (1) applies whether or not the Authority has powers which are exercisable in relation to the authorised person by virtue of any provision of Part XIII.

(3) If a request to the Authority for the exercise of its own-initiative power has been made by a regulator who is—

   (a)   outside the United Kingdom,

(b) of a prescribed kind, and

(c) acting in pursuance of provisions of a prescribed kind,

the Authority must, in deciding whether or not to exercise that power in response to the request, consider whether it is necessary to do so in order to comply with a Community obligation.

(4) In deciding in any case in which the Authority does not consider that the exercise of its own-initiative power is necessary in order to comply with a Community obligation, it may take into account in particular—

(a) whether in the country or territory of the regulator concerned, corresponding assistance would be given to a United Kingdom regulatory authority;

(b) whether the case concerns the breach of a law, or other requirement, which has no close parallel in the United Kingdom or involves the assertion of a jurisdiction not recognised by the United Kingdom;

(c) the seriousness of the case and its importance to persons in the United Kingdom;

(d) whether it is otherwise appropriate in the public interest to give the assistance sought.

(5) The Authority may decide not to exercise its own-initiative power, in response to a request, unless the regular concerned undertakes to make such contribution towards the cost of its exercise as the Authority considers appropriate.

(6) Subsection (5) does not apply if the Authority decides that it is necessary for it to exercise its own-initiative power in order to comply with a Community obligation.

(7) In subsections (4) and (5) 'request' means a request of a kind mentioned in subsection (1).

48 Prohibitions and restrictions

(1) This section applies if the Authority—

(a) on giving a person a Part IV permission, imposes an assets requirement on him; or

(b) varies an authorised person's Part IV permission so as to alter an assets requirement imposed on him or impose such a requirement on him.

(2) A person on whom an assets requirement is imposed is referred to in this section as 'A'.

(3) 'Assets requirement' means a requirement under section 43—

(a) prohibiting the disposal of, or other dealing with, any of A's assets (whether in the United Kingdom or elsewhere) or restricting such disposals or dealings; or

(b) that all or any of A's assets, or all or any assets belonging to consumers but held by A or to his order, must be transferred to and held by a trustee approved by the Authority.

(4) If the Authority—

(a) imposes a requirement of the kind mentioned in subsection (3)(a), and

(b) gives notice of the requirement to any institution with whom A keeps an account,

the notice has the effects mentioned in subsection (5).

(5) Those effects are that—

(a) the institution does not act in breach of any contract with A if, having been instructed by A (or on his behalf) to transfer any sum or otherwise make any payment out of A's account, it refuses to do so in the reasonably held belief that complying with the instruction would be incompatible with the requirement; and

(b)   if the institution complies with such an instruction, it is liable to pay to the Authority an amount equal to the amount transferred from, or otherwise paid out of, A's account in contravention of the requirement.

(6) If the Authority imposes a requirement of the kind mentioned in subsection (3)(b), no assets held by a person as trustee in accordance with the requirement may, while the requirement is in force, be released or dealt with except with the consent of the Authority.

(7) If, while a requirement of the kind mentioned in subsection (3)(b) is in force, A creates a charge over any assets of his held in accordance with the requirement, the charge is (to the extent that it confers security over the assets) void against the liquidator and any of A's creditors.

(8) Assets held by a person as trustee ('T') are to be taken to be held by T in accordance with a requirement mentioned in subsection (3)(b) only if—

(a)   A has given T written notice that those assets are to be held by T in accordance with the requirement; or
(b)   they are assets into which assets to which paragraph (a) applies have been transposed by T on the instructions of A.

(9) A person who contravenes subsection (6) is guilty of an offence and liable on summary conviction to a fine not exceeding level 5 on the standard scale.

(10) 'Charge' includes a mortgage (or in Scotland a security over property).

(11) Subsections (6) and (8) do not affect any equitable interest or remedy in favour of a person who is a beneficiary of a trust as a result of a requirement of the kind mentioned in subsection (3)(b).

Connected persons

49   Persons connected with an applicant

(1) In considering—

(a)   an application for a Part IV permission, or
(b)   whether to vary or cancel a Part IV permission,

the Authority may have regard to any person appearing to it to be, or likely to be, in a relationship with the applicant or person given permission which is relevant.

(2) Before—

(a)   giving permission in response to an application made by a person who is connected with an EEA firm, or
(b)   cancelling or varying any permission given by the Authority to such a person,

the Authority must consult the firm's home state regulator.

(3) A person ('A') is connected with an EEA firm if—

(a)   A is a subsidiary undertaking of the firm; or
(b)   A is a subsidiary undertaking of a parent undertaking of the firm.

Additional permissions

50   Authority's duty to consider other permissions etc.

(1) 'Additional Part IV permission' means a Part IV permission which is in force in relation to an EEA firm, a Treaty firm or a person authorised as a result of paragraph 1(1) of Schedule 5.

(2) If the Authority is considering whether, and if so how, to exercise its own-initiative power under this Part in relation to an additional Part IV permission, it must take into account—

(a) the home State authorisation of the authorised person concerned;
(b) any relevant directive; and
(c) relevant provisions of the Treaty.

Procedure

51 Applications under this Part

(1) An application for a Part IV permission must—

(a) contain a statement of the regulated activity or regulated activities which the applicant proposes to carry on and for which he wishes to have permission; and
(b) give the address of a place in the United Kingdom for service on the applicant of any notice or other document which is required or authorised to be served on him under this Act.

(2) An application for the variation of a Part IV permission must contain a statement—

(a) of the desired variation; and
(b) of the regulated activity or regulated activities which the applicant proposes to carry on if his permission is varied.

(3) Any application under this Part must—

(a) be made in such manner as the Authority may direct; and
(b) contain, or be accompanied by, such other information as the Authority may reasonably require.

(4) At any time after receiving an application and before determining it, the Authority may require the applicant to provide it with such further information as it reasonably considers necessary to enable it to determine the application.

(5) Different directions may be given, and different requirements imposed, in relation to different applications or categories of application.

(6) The Authority may require an applicant to provide information which he is required to provide under this section in such form, or to verify it in such a way, as the Authority may direct.

52 Determination of applications

(1) An application under this Part must be determined by the Authority before the end of the period of six months beginning with the date on which it received the completed application.

(2) The Authority may determine an incomplete application if it considers it appropriate to do so; and it must in any event determine such an application within twelve months beginning with the date on which it received the application.

(3) The applicant may withdraw his application, by giving the Authority written notice, at any time before the Authority determines it.

(4) If the Authority grants an application for, or for variation of, a Part IV permission, it must give the applicant written notice.

(5) The notice must state the date from which the permission, or the variation, has effect.

(6) If the Authority proposes—

    (a)   to give a Part IV permission but to exercise its power under section 42(7)(a) or (b) or 43(1), or

    (b)   to vary a Part IV permission on the application of an authorised person but to exercie its power under any of those provisions (as a result of section 44(5)),

it must give the applicant a warning notice.

(7) If the Authority proposes to refuse an application made under this Part, it must (unless subsection (8) applies) give the applicant a warning notice.

(8) This subsection applies if it appears to the Authority that—

    (a)   the applicant is an EEA firm; and

    (b)   the application is made with a view to carrying on a regulated activity in a manner in which the applicant is, or would be, entitled to carry on that activity in the exercise of an EEA right whether through a United Kingdom branch or by providing services in the United Kingdom.

(9) If the Authority decides—

    (a)   to give a Part IV permission but to exercise its power under section 42(7)(a) or (b) or 43(1),

    (b)   to vary a Part IV permission on the application of an authorised person but to exercise its power under any of those provisions (as a result of section 44(5)), or

    (c)   to refuse an application under this Part,

it must give the applicant a decision notice.

53   Exercise of own-initiative power: procedure

(1) This section applies to an exercise of the Authority's own-initiative power to vary an authorised person's Part IV permission.

(2) A variation takes effect—

    (a)   immediately, if the notice given under subsection (4) states that that is the case;

    (b)   on such date as may be specified in the notice; or

    (c)   if no date is specified in the notice, when the matter to which the notice relates is no longer open to review.

(3) A variation may be expressed to take effect immediately (or on a specified date) only if the Authority, having regard to the ground on which it is exercising its own-initiative power, reasonably considers that it is necessary for the variation to take effect immediately (or on that date).

(4) If the Authority proposes to vary the Part IV permission, or varies it with immediate effect, it must give the authorised person written notice.

(5) The notice must—

    (a)   give details of the variation;

    (b)   state the Authority's reasons for the variation and for its determination as to when the variation takes effect;

    (c)   inform the authorised person that he may make representations to the Authority within such period as may be specified in the notice (whether or not he has referred the matter to the Tribunal);

    (d)   inform him of when the variation takes effect; and

    (e)   inform him of his right to refer the matter to the Tribunal.

(6) The Authority may extend the period allowed under the notice for making representations.

(7) If, having considered any representations made by the authorised person, the Authority decides—

    (a)   to vary the permission in the way proposed, or

    (b)   if the permission has been varied, not to rescind the variation,

it must give him written notice.

(8) If, having considered any representations made by the authorised person, the Authority decides—

    (a)   not to vary the permission in the way proposed,

    (b)   to vary the permission in a different way, or

    (c)   to rescind a variation which has effect,

it must give him written notice.

(9) A notice given under subsection (7) must inform the authorised person of his right to refer the matter to the Tribunal.

(10) A notice under subsection (8)(b) must comply with subsection (5).

(11) If a notice informs a person of his right to refer a matter to the Tribunal, it must give an indication of the procedure on such a reference.

(12) For the purposes of subsection (2)(c), whether a matter is open to review is to be determined in accordance with section 391(8).

54   Cancellation of Part IV permission: procedure

(1) If the Authority proposes to cancel an authorised person's Part IV permission otherwise than at his request, it must give him a warning notice.

(2) If the Authority decides to cancel an authorised person's Part IV permission otherwise than at his request, it must give him a decision notice.

References to the Tribunal

55   Right to refer matters to the Tribunal

(1) An applicant who is aggrieved by the determination of an application made under this Part may refer the matter to the Tribunal.

(2) An authorised person who is aggrieved by the exercise of the Authority's own-initiative power may refer the matter to the Tribunal.

PART V

PERFORMANCE OF REGULATED ACTIVITIES

Prohibition orders

56   Prohibition orders

(1) Subsection (2) applies if it appears to the Authority that an individual is not a fit and proper person to perform functions in relation to a regulated activity carried on by an authorised person.

(2) The Authority may make an order ('a prohibition order') prohibiting the individual from performing a specified function, any function falling within a specified description or any function.

(3) A prohibition order may relate to—

   (a)   a specified regulated activity, any regulated activity falling within a specified description or all regulated activities;

   (b)   authorised persons generally or any person within a specified class of authorised person.

(4) An individual who performs or agrees to perform a function in breach of a prohibition order is guilty of an offence and liable on summary conviction to a fine not exceeding level 5 on the standard scale.

(5) In proceedings for an offence under subsection (4) it is a defence for the accused to show that he took all reasonable precautions and exercised all due diligence to avoid committing the offence.

(6) An authorised person must take reasonable care to ensure that no function of his, in relation to the carrying on of a regulated activity, is performed by a person who is prohibited from performing that function by a prohibition order.

(7) The Authority may, on the application of the individual named in a prohibition order, vary or revoke it.

(8) This section applies to the performance of functions in relation to a regulated activity carried on by—

   (a)   a person who is an exempt person in relation to that activity, and

   (b)   a person to whom, as a result of Part XX, the general prohibition does not apply in relation to that activity,

as it applies to the performance of functions in relation to a regulated activity carried on by an authorised person.

(9) 'Specified' means specified in the prohibition order.

57   Prohibition orders: procedure and right to refer to Tribunal

(1) If the Authority proposes to make a prohibition order it must give the individual concerned a warning notice.

(2) The warning notice must set out the terms of the prohibition.

(3) If the Authority decides to make a prohibition order it must give the individual concerned a decision notice.

(4) The decision notice must—

   (a)   name the individual to whom the prohibition order applies;

   (b)   set out the terms of the order; and

   (c)   be given to the individual named in the order.

(5) A person against whom a decision to make a prohibition order is made may refer the matter to the Tribunal.

58   Applications relating to prohibitions: procedure and right to refer to Tribunal

(1) This section applies to an application for the variation or revocation of a prohibition order.

(2) If the Authority decides to grant the application, it must give the applicant written notice of its decision.

(3) If the Authority proposes to refuse the application, it must give the applicant a warning notice.

(4) If the Authority decides to refuse the application, it must give the applicant a decision notice.

(5) If the Authority gives the applicant a decision notice, he may refer the matter to the Tribunal.

Approval

59   Approval for particular arrangements

(1) An authorised person ('A') must take reasonable care to ensure that no person performs a controlled function under an arrangement entered into by A in relation to the carrying on by A of a regulated activity, unless the Authority approves the performance by that person of the controlled function to which the arrangement relates.

(2) An authorised person ('A') must take reasonable care to ensure that no person performs a controlled function under an arrangement entered into by a contractor of A in relation to the carrying on by A of a regulated activity, unless the Authority approves the performance by that person of the controlled function to which the arrangement relates.

(3) 'Controlled function' means a function of a description specified in rules.

(4) The Authority may specify a description of function under subsection (3) only if, in relation to the carrying on of a regulated activity by an authorised person, it is satisfied that the first, second or third condition is met.

(5) The first condition is that the function is likely to enable the person responsible for its performance to exercise a significant influence on the conduct of the authorised person's affairs, so far as relating to the regulated activity.

(6) The second condition is that the function will involve the person performing it in dealing with customers of the authorised person in a manner substantially connected with the carrying on of the regulated activity.

(7) The third condition is that the function will involve the person performing it in dealing with property of customers of the authorised person in a manner substantially connected with the carrying on of the regulated activity.

(8) Neither subsection (1) nor subsection (2) applies to an arrangement which allows a person to perform a function if the question of whether he is a fit and proper person to perform the function is reserved under any of the single market directives to an authority in a country or territory outside the United Kingdom.

(9) In determining whether the first condition is met, the Authority may take into account the likely consequences of a failure to discharge that function properly.

(10) 'Arrangement'—

  (a)   means any kind of arrangement for the performance of a function of A which is entered into by A or any contractor of his with another person; and
  (b)   includes, in particular, that other person's appointment to an office, his becoming a partner or his employment (whether under a contract of service or otherwise).

(11) 'Customer', in relation to an authorised person, means a person who is using, or who is or may be contemplating using, any of the services provided by the authorised person.

60   Applications for approval

(1) An appplication for the Authority's approval under section 59 may be made by the authorised person concerned.

(2) The application must—

(a)   be made in such manner as the Authority may direct; and
(b)   contain, or be accompanied by, such information as the Authority may reasonably require.

(3) At any time after receiving the application and before determining it, the Authority may require the applicant to provide it with such further information as it reasonably considers necessary to enable it to determine the application.

(4) The Authority may require an applicant to present information which he is required to give under this section in such form, or to verify it in such a way, as the Authority may direct.

(5) Different directions may be given, and different requirements imposed, in relation to different applications or categories of application.

(6) 'The authorised person concerned' includes a person who has applied for permission under Part IV and will be the authorised person concerned if permission is given.

61   Determination of applications

(1) The Authority may grant an application made under section 60 only if it is satisfied that the person in respect of whom the application is made ('the candidate') is a fit and proper person to perform the function to which the application relates.

(2) In deciding that question, the Authority may have regard (among other things) to whether the candidate, or any person who may perform a function on his behalf—

(a)   has obtained a qualification,
(b)   has undergone, or is undergoing, training, or
(c)   possesses a level of competence,

required by general rules in relation to persons performing functions of the kind to which the application relates.

(3) The Authority must, before the end of the period of three months beginning with the date on which it receives an application made under section 60 ('the period for consideration'), determine whether—

(a)   to grant the application; or
(b)   to give a warning notice under section 62(2).

(4) If the Authority imposes a requirement under section 60(3), the period for consideration stops running on the day on which the requirement is imposed but starts running again—

(a)   on the day on which the required information is received by the Authority; or
(b)   if the information is not provided on a single day, on the last of the days on which it is received by the Authority.

(5) A person who makes an application under section 60 may withdraw his application by giving written notice to the Authority at any time before the Authority determines it, but only with the consent of—

(a)   the candidate; and
(b)   the person by whom the candidate is to be retained to perform the function concerned, if not the applicant.

62   Applications for approval; procedure and right to refer to Tribunal

(1) If the Authority decides to grant an application made under section 60 ('an application'), it must give written notice of its decision to each of the interested parties.

(2) If the Authority proposes to refuse an application, it must give a warning notice to each of the interested parties.

(3) If the Authority decides to refuse an application, it must give a decision notice to each of the interested parties.

(4) If the Authority decides to refuse an application, each of the interested parties may refer the matter to the Tribunal.

(5) 'The interested parties', in relation to an application, are—

- (a) the applicant;
- (b) the person in respect of whom the application is made ('A'); and
- (c) the person by whom A's services are to be retained, if not the applicant.

63   Withdrawal of approval

(1) The Authority may withdraw an approval given under section 59 if it considers that the person in respect of whom it was given is not a fit and proper person to perform the function to which the approval relates.

(2) When considering whether to withdraw its approval, the Authority may take into account any matter which it could take into account if it were considering an application made under section 60 in respect of the performance of the function to which the approval relates.

(3) If the Authority proposes to withdraw its approval, it must give each of the interested parties a warning notice.

(4) If the Authority decides to withdraw its approval, it must give each of the interested parties a decision notice.

(5) If the Authority decides to withdraw its approval, each of the interested parties may refer the matter to the Tribunal.

(6) 'The interested parties', in relation to an approval, are—

- (a) the person on whose application it was given ('A');
- (b) the person in respect of whom it was given ('B'); and
- (c) the person by whom B's services are retained, if not A.

Conduct

64   Conduct: statements and codes

(1) The Authority may issue statements of principle with respect to the conduct expected of approved persons.

(2) If the Authority issues a statement of principle under subsection (1), it must also issue a code of practice for the purpose of helping to determine whether or not a person's conduct complies with the statement of principle.

(3) A code issued under subsection (2) may specify—

- (a) descriptions of conduct which, in the opinion of the Authority, comply with a statement of principle;

   (b)   descriptions of conduct which, in the opinion of the Authority, do not comply with a statement of principle;

   (c)   factors which, in the opinion of the Authority, are to be taken into account in determining whether or not a person's conduct complies with a statement of principle.

(4) The Authority may at any time alter or replace a statement or code issued under this section.

(5) If a statement or code is altered or replaced, the altered or replacement statement or code must be issued by the Authority.

(6) A statement or code issued under this section must be published by the Authority in the way appearing to the Authority to be best calculated to bring it to the attention of the public.

(7) A code published under this section and in force at the time when any particular conduct takes place may be relied on so far as it tends to establish whether or not that conduct complies with a statement of principle.

(8) Failure to comply with a statement of principle under this section does not of itself give rise to any right of action by persons affected or affect the validity of any transaction.

(9) A person is not to be taken to have failed to comply with a statement of principle if he shows that, at the time of the alleged failure, it or its associated code of practice had not been published.

(10) The Authority must, without delay, give the Treasury a copy of any statement or code which it publishes under this section.

(11) The power under this section to issue statements of principle and codes of practice—

   (a)   includes power to make different provision in relation to persons, cases or circumstances of different descriptions; and

   (b)   is to be treated for the purposes of section 2(4)(a) as part of the Authority's rule-making functions.

(12) The Authority may charge a reasonable fee for providing a person with a copy of a statement or code published under this section.

(13) 'Approved person' means a person in relation to whom the Authority has given its approval under section 59.

65   Statements and codes: procedure

(1) Before issuing a statement or code under section 64, the Authority must publish a draft of it in the way appearing to the Authority to be best calculated to bring it to the attention of the public.

(2) The draft must be accompanied by—

   (a)   a cost benefit analysis; and

   (b)   notice that representations about the proposal may be made to the Authority wihtin a specified time.

(3) Before issuing the proposed statement or code, the Authority must have regard to any representations made to it in accordance with subsection (2)(b).

(4) If the Authority issues the proposed statement or code it must publish an account, in general terms, of—

   (a)   the representations made to it in accordance with subsection (2)(b); and

   (b)   its response to them.

(5) If the statement or code differs from the draft published under subsection (1) in a way which is, in the opinion of the Authority, significant—

    (a)   the Authority must (in addition to complying with subsection (4)) publish details of the difference; and

    (b)   those details must be accompanied by a cost benefit analysis.

(6) Neither subsection (2)(a) nor subsection (5)(b) applies if the Authority considers—

    (a)   that, making the appropriate comparison, there will be no increase in costs; or

    (b)   that, making that comparison, there will be an increase in costs but the increase will be of minimal significance.

(7) Subsections (1) to (6) do not apply if the Authority considers that the delay involved in complying with them would prejudice the interests of consumers.

(8) A statement or code must state that it is issued under section 64.

(9) The Authority may charge a reasonable fee for providing a copy of a draft published under subsection (1).

(10) This section also applies to a proposal to alter or replace a statement or code.

(11) 'Cost benefit analysis' means an estimate of the costs together with an analysis of the benefits that will arise—

    (a)   if the proposed statement or code is issued; or

    (b)   if subsection (5)(b) applies, from the statement or code that has been issued.

(12) 'The appropriate comparison' means—

    (a)   in relation to subsection (2)(a), a comparison between the overall position if the statement or code is issued and the overall position if it is not issued;

    (b)   in relation to subsection (5)(b), a comparison between the overall position after the issuing of the statement or code and the overall position before it was issued.

66   Disciplinary powers

(1) The Authority may take action against a person under this section if—

    (a)   it appears to the Authority that he is guilty of misconduct; and

    (b)   the Authority is satisfied that it is appropriate in all the circumstances to take action against him.

(2) A person is guilty of misconduct if, while an approved person—

    (a)   he has failed to comply with a statement of principle issued under section 64; or

    (b)   he has been knowingly concerned in a contravention by the relevant authorised person of a requirement imposed on that authorised person by or under this Act.

(3) If the Authority is entitled to take action under this section against a person, it may—

    (a)   impose a penalty on him of such amount as it considers appropriate; or

    (b)   publish a statement of his misconduct.

(4) The Authority may not take action under this section after the end of the period of two years beginning with the first day on which the Authority knew of the misconduct, unless proceedings in respect of it against the person concerned were begun before the end of that period.

(5) For the purposes of subsection (4)—

    (a)   the Authority is to be treated as knowing of misconduct if it has information from which the misconduct can reasonably be inferred; and

(b)   proceedings against a person in respect of misconduct are to be treated as begun when a warning notice is given to him under section 67(1).

(6) 'Approved person' has the same meaning as in section 64.

(7) 'Relevant authorised person', in relation to an approved person, means the person on whose application approval under section 59 was given.

67   Disciplinary measures: procedure and right to refer to Tribunal

(1) If the Authority proposes to take action against a person under section 66, it must give him a warning notice.

(2) A warning notice about a proposal to impose a penalty must state the amount of the penalty.

(3) A warning notice about a proposal to publish a statement must set out the terms of the statement.

(4) If the Authority decides to take action against a person under section 66, it must give him a decision notice.

(5) A decision notice about the imposition of a penalty must state the amount of the penalty.

(6) A decision notice about the publication of a statement must set out the terms of the statement.

(7) If the Authority decides to take action against a person under section 66, he may refer the matter to the Tribunal.

68   Publication

After a statement under section 66 is published, the Authority must send a copy of it to the person concerned and to any person to whom a copy of the decision notice was given.

69   Statement of policy

(1) The Authority must prepare and issue a statement of its policy with respect to—

(a)   the imposition of penalties under section 66; and
(b)   the amount of penalties under that section.

(2) The Authority's policy in determining what the amount of a penalty should be must include having regard to—

(a)   the seriousness of the misconduct in question in relation to the nature of the principle or requirement concerned;
(b)   the extent to which that misconduct was deliberate or reckless; and
(c)   whether the person on whom the penalty is to be imposed is an individual.

(3) The Authority may at any time alter or replace a statement issued under this section.

(4) If a statement issued under this section is altered or replaced, the Authority must issue the altered or replacement statement.

(5) The Authority must, without delay, give the Treasury a copy of any statement which it publishes under this section.

(6) A statement issued under this section must be published by the Authority in the way appearing to the Authority to be best calculated to bring it to the attention of the public.

(7) The Authority may charge a reasonable fee for providing a person with a copy of the statement.

(8) In exercising, or deciding whether to exercise, its power under section 66 in the case of any particular misconduct, the Authority must have regard to any statement of policy published under this section and in force at the time when the misconduct in question occurred.

70   Statements of policy: procedure

(1) Before issuing a statement under section 69, the Authority must publish a draft of the proposed statement in the way appearing to the Authority to be best calculated to bring it to the attention of the public.

(2) The draft must be accompanied by notice that representations about the proposal may be made to the Authority within a specified time.

(3) Before issuing the proposed statement, the Authority must have regard to any representations made to it in accordance with subsection (2).

(4) If the Authority issues the proposed statement it must publish an account, in general terms, of—

   (a)   the representations made to it in accordance with subsection (2); and
   (b)   its response to them.

(5) If the statement differs from the draft published under subsection (1) in a way which is, in the opinion of the Authority, significant, the Authority must (in addition to complying with subsection (4)) publish details of the difference.

(6) The Authority may charge a reasonable fee for providing a person with a copy of a draft published under section (1).

(7) This section also applies to a proposal to alter or replace a statement.

Breach of statutory duty

71   Actions for damages

(1) A contravention of section 56(6) or 59(1) or (2) is actionable at the suit of a private person who suffers loss as a result of the contravention, subject to the defences and other incidents applying to actions for breach of statutory duty.

(2) In prescribed cases, a contravention of that kind which would be actionable at the suit of a private person is actionable at the suit of a person who is not a private person, subject to the defences and other incidents applying to actions for breach of statutory duty.

(3) 'Private person' has such meaning as may be prescribed.

PART VI

OFFICIAL LISTING

The competent authority

72   The competent authority

(1) On the coming into force of this section, the functions conferred on the competent authority by this Part are to be exercised by the Authority.

(2) Schedule 7 modifies this Act in its application to the Authority when it acts as the competent authority.

(3) But provision is made by Schedule 8 allowing some or all of those functions to be transferred by the Treasury so as to be exercisable by another person.

73 General duty of the competent authority

(1) In discharging its general functions the competent authority must have regard to—

- (a) the need to use its resources in the most efficient and economic way;
- (b) the principle that a burden or restriction which is imposed on a person should be proportionate to the benefits, considered in general terms, which are expected to arise from the imposition of that burden or restriction;
- (c) the desirability of facilitating innovation in respect of listed securities;
- (d) the international character of capital markets and the desirability of maintaining the competitive position of the United Kingdom;
- (e) the need to minimise the adverse effects on competition of anything done in the discharge of those functions;
- (f) the desirability of facilitating competition in relation to listed securities.

(2) The competent authority's general functions are—

- (a) its function of making rules under this Part (considered as a whole);
- (b) its functions in relation to the giving of general guidance in relation to this Part (considered as a whole);
- (c) its function of determining the general policy and principles by reference to which it performs particular functions under this Part.

The official list

74 The official list

(1) The competent authority must maintain the official list.

(2) The competent authority may admit to the official list such securities and other things as it considers appropriate.

(3) But—

- (a) nothing may be admitted to the official list except in accordance with this Part; and
- (b) the Treasury may by order provide that anything which falls within a description or category specified in the order may not be admitted to the official list.

(4) The competent authority may make rules ('listing rules') for the purposes of this Part.

(5) In the following provisions of this Part—

'security' means anything which has been, or may be, admitted to the official list; and 'listing' means being included in the official list in accordance with this Part.

Listing

75 Applications for listing

(1) Admission to the official list may be granted only on an application made to the competent authority in such manner as may be required by listing rules.

(2) No application for listing may be entertained by the competent authority unless it is made by, or with the consent of, the issuer of the securities concerned.

(3) No application for listing may be entertained by the competent authority in respect of securities which are to be issued by a body of a prescribed kind.

(4) The competent authority may not grant an application for listing unless it is satisfied that—

   (a)   the requirements of listing rules (so far as they apply to the application), and
   (b)   any other requirements imposed by the authority in relation to the application,

are complied with.

(5) An application for listing may be refused if, for a reason relating to the issuer, the competent authority considers that granting it would be detrimental to the interests of investors.

(6) An application for listing securities which are already officially listed in another EEA State may be refused if the issuer has failed to comply with any obligations to which he is subject as a result of that listing.

76   Decision on application

(1) The competent authority must notify the applicant of its decision on an application for listing—

   (a)   before the end of the period of six months beginning with the date on which the application is received; or
   (b)   if within that period the authority has required the applicant to provide further information in connection with the application, before the end of the period of six months beginning with the date on which that information is provided.

(2) If the competent authority fails to comply with subsection (1), it is to be taken to have decided to refuse the application.

(3) If the competent authority decides to grant an application for listing, it must give the applicant written notice.

(4) If the competent authority proposes to refuse an application for listing, it must give the applicant a warning notice.

(5) If the competent authority decides to refuse an application for listing, it must give the applicant a decision notice.

(6) If the competent authority decides to refuse an application for listing, the applicant may refer the matter to the Tribunal.

(7) If securities are admitted to the official list, their admission may not be called in question on the ground that any requirement or condition for their admission has not been complied with.

77   Discontinuance and suspension of listing

(1) The competent authority may, in accordance with listing rules, discontinue the listing of any securities if satisfied that there are special circumstances which preclude normal regular dealings in them.

(2) The competent authority may, in accordance with listing rules, suspend the listing of any securities.

(3) If securities are suspended under subsection (2) they are to be treated, for the purposes of sections 96 and 99, as still being listed.

(4) This section applies to securities whenever they were admitted to the official list.

(5) If the competent authority discontinues or suspends the listing of any securities, the issuer may refer the matter to the Tribunal.

78   Discontinuance or suspension: procedure

(1) A discontinuance or suspension takes effect—

    (a)   immediately, if the notice under subsection (2) states that that is the case;

    (b)   in any other case, on such date as may be specified in that notice.

(2) If the competent authority—

    (a)   proposes to discontinue or suspend the listing of securities, or

    (b)   discontinues or suspends the listing of securities with immediate effect,

it must give the issuer of the securities written notice.

(3) The notice must—

    (a)   give details of the discontinuance or suspension;

    (b)   state the competent authority's reasons for the discontinuance or suspension and for choosing the date on which it took effect or takes effect;

    (c)   inform the issuer of the securities that he may make representations to the competent authority within such period as may be specified in the notice (whether or not he has referred the matter to the Tribunal);

    (d)   inform him of the date on which the discontinuance or suspension took effect or will take effect; and

    (e)   inform him of his right to refer the matter to the Tribunal.

(4) The competent authority may extend the period within which representations may be made to it.

(5) If, having considered any representations made by the issuer of the securities, the competent authority decides—

    (a)   to discontinue or suspend the listing of the securities, or

    (b)   if the discontinuance or suspension has taken effect, not to cancel it,

the competent authority must give the issuer of the securities written notice.

(6) A notice given under subsection (5) must inform the issuer of the securities of his right to refer the matter to the Tribunal.

(7) If a notice informs a person of his right to refer a matter to the Tribunal, it must give an indication of the procedure on such a reference.

(8) If the competent authority decides—

    (a)   not to discontinue or suspend the listing of the securities, or

    (b)   if the discontinuance or suspension has taken effect, to cancel it,

the competent authority must give the issuer of the securities written notice.

(9) The effect of cancelling a discontinuance is that the securities concerned are to be readmitted, without more, to the official list.

(10) If the competent authority has suspended the listing of securities and proposes to refuse an application by the issuer of the securities for the cancellation of the suspension, it must give him a warning notice.

(11) The competent authority must, having considered any representations made in response to the warning notice—

(a) if it decides to refuse the application, give the issuer of the securities a decision notice;

(b) if it grants the application, give him written notice of its decision.

(12) If the competent authority decides to refuse an application for the cancellation of the suspension of listed securities, the applicant may refer the matter to the Tribunal.

(13) 'Discontinuance' means a discontinuance of listing under section 77(1).

(14) 'Suspension' means a suspension of listing under section 77(2).

Listing particulars

79   Listing particulars and other documents

(1) Listing rules may provide that securities (other than new securities) of a kind specified in the rules may not be admitted to the official list unless—

(a) listing particulars have been submitted to, and approved by, the competent authority and published; or

(b) in such cases as may be specified by listing rules, such document (other than listing particulars or a prospectus of a kind required by listing rules) as may be so specified has been published.

(2) 'Listing particulars' means a document in such form and containing such information as may be specified in listing rules.

(3) For the purposes of this Part, the persons responsible for listing particulars are to be determined in accordance with regulations made by the Treasury.

(4) Nothing in this section affects the competent authority's general power to make listing rules.

80   General duty of disclosure in listing particulars

(1) Listing particulars submitted to the competent authority under section 79 must contain all such information as investors and their professional advisers would reasonably require, and reasonably expect to find there, for the purpose of making an informed assessment of—

(a) the assets and liabilities, financial position, profits and losses, and prospects of the issuer of the securities; and

(b) the rights attaching to the securities.

(2) That information is required in addition to any information required by—

(a) listing rules, or

(b) the competent authority,

as a condition of the admission of the securities to the official list.

(3) Subsection (1) applies only to information—

(a) within the knowledge of any person responsible for the listing particulars; or

(b) which it would be reasonable for him to obtain by making enquiries.

(4) In determining what information subsection (1) requires to be included in listing particulars, regard must be had (in particular) to—

(a) the nature of the securities and their issuer;

(b) the nature of the persons likely to consider acquiring them;

(c) the fact that certain matters may reasonably be expected to be within the knowledge of professional advisers of a kind which persons likely to acquire the securities may reasonably be expected to consult; and

(d) any information available to investors or their professional advisers as a result of requirements imposed on the issuer of the securities by a recognised investment exchange, by listing rules or by or under any other enactment.

81 Supplementary listing particulars

(1) If at any time after the preparation of listing particulars which have been submitted to the competent authority under section 79 and before the commencement of dealings in the securities concerned following their admission to the official list—

(a) there is a significant change affecting any matter contained in those particulars the inclusion of which was required by—
   (i)   section 80,
   (ii) listing rules, or
   (iii) the competent authority, or

(b) a significant new matter arises, the inclusion of information in respect of which would have been so required if it had arisen when the particulars were prepared,

the issuer must, in accordance with listing rules, submit supplementary listing particulars of the change or new matter to the competent authority, for its approval and, if they are approved, publish them.

(2) 'Significant' means significant for the purpose of making an informed assessment of the kind mentioned in section 80(1).

(3) If the issuer of the securities is not aware of the change or new matter in question, he is not under a duty to comply with subsection (1) unless he is notified of the change or new matter by a person responsible for the listing particulars.

(4) But it is the duty of any person responsible for those particulars who is aware of such a change or new matter to give notice of it to the issuer.

(5) Subsection (1) applies also as respects matters contained in any supplementary listing particulars previously published under this section in respect of the securities in question.

82 Exemptions from disclosure

(1) The competent authority may authorise the omission from listing particulars of any information, the inclusion of which would otherwise be required by section 80 or 81, on the ground—

(a) that its disclosure would be contrary to the public interest;
(b) that its disclosure would be seriously detrimental to the issuer; or
(c) in the case of securities of a kind specified in listing rules, that its disclosure is unnecessary for persons of the kind who may be expected normally to buy or deal in securities of that kind.

(2) But—

(a) no authority may be granted under subsection (1)(b) in respect of essential information; and
(b) no authority granted under subsection (1)(b) extends to any such information.

(3) The Secretary of State or the Treasury may issue a certificate to the effect that the disclosure of any information (including information that would otherwise have to be included in listing particulars for which they are themselves responsible) would be contrary to the public interest.

(4) The competent authority is entitled to act on any such certificate in exercising its powers under subsection (1)(a).

(5) This section does not affect any powers of the competent authority under listing rules made as a result of section 101(2).

(6) 'Essential information' means information which a person considering acquiring securities of the kind in question would be likely to need in order not to be misled about any facts which it is essential for him to know in order to make an informed assessment.

(7) 'Listing particulars' includes supplementary listing particulars.

83   Registration of listing particulars

(1) On or before the date on which listing particulars are published as required by listing rules, a copy of the particulars must be delivered for registration to the registrar of companies.

(2) A statement that a copy has been delivered to the registrar must be included in the listing particulars when they are published.

(3) If there has been a failure to comply with subsection (1) in relation to listing particulars which have been published—

  (a)   the issuer of the securities in question, and
  (b)   any person who is a party to the publication and aware of the failure,

is guilty of an offence.

(4) A person guilty of an offence under subsection (3) is liable—

  (a)   on summary conviction, to a fine not exceeding the statutory maximum;
  (b)   on conviction on indictment, to a fine.

(5) 'Listing particulars' includes supplementary listing particulars.

(6) 'The registrar of companies' means—

  (a)   if the securities are, or are to be, issued by a company incorporated in Great Britain whose registered office is in England and Wales, the registrar of companies in England and Wales;
  (b)   if the securities are, or are to be, issued by a company incorporated in Great Britain whose registered office is in Scotland, the registrar of companies in Scotland;
  (c)   if the securities are, or are to be, issued by a company incorporated in Northern Ireland, the registrar of companies for Northern Ireland; and
  (d)   in any other case, any of those registrars.

Prospectuses

84   Prospectuses

(1) Listing rules must provide that no new securities for which an application for listing has been made may be admitted to the official list unless a prospectus has been submitted to, and approved by, the competent authority and published.

(2) 'New securities' means securities which are to be offered to the public in the United Kingdom for the first time before admission to official list.

(3) 'Prospectus' means a prospectus in such form and containing such information as may be specified in listing rules.

(4) Nothing in this section affects the competent authority's general power to make listing rules.

85 Publication of prospectus

(1) If listing rules made under section 84 require a prospectus to be published before particular new securities are admitted to the official list, it is unlawful for any of those securities to be offered to the public in the United Kingdom before the required prospectus is published.

(2) A person who contravenes subsection (1) is guilty of an offence and liable—

(a) on summary conviction, to imprisonment for a term not exceeding three months or a fine not exceeding level 5 on the standard scale;

(b) on conviction on indictment, to imprisonment for a term not exceeding two years or a fine, or both.

(3) A person is not to be regarded as contravening subsection (1) merely because a prospectus does not fully comply with the requirements of listing rules as to its form or content.

(4) But subsection (3) does not affect the question whether any person is liable to pay compensation under section 90.

(5) Any contravention of subsection (1) is actionable, at the suit of a person who suffers loss as a result of the contravention, subject to the defences and other incidents applying to actions for breach of statutory duty.

86 Application of this Part to prospectuses

(1) The provisions of this Part apply in relation to a prospectus required by listing rules as they apply in relation to listing particulars.

(2) In this Part—
(a) any reference to listing particulars is to be read as including a reference to a prospectus; and
(b) any reference to supplementary listing particulars is to be read as including a reference to a supplementary prospectus.

87 Approval of prospectus where no application for listing

(1) Listing rules may provide for a prospectus to be submitted to and approved by the competent authority if—

(a) securities are to be offered to the public in the United Kingdom for the first time;
(b) no application for listing of the securities has been made under this Part; and
(c) the prospectus is submitted by, or with the consent of, the issuer of the securities.

(2) 'Non-listing prospectus' means a prospectus submitted to the competent authority as a result of any listing rules made under subsection (1).

(3) Listing rules made under subsection (1) may make provision—

(a) as to the information to be contained in, and the form of, a non-listing prospectus; and
(b) as to the timing and manner of publication of a non-listing prospectus.

(4) The power conferred by subsection (3)(b) is subject to such provision made by or under any other enactment as the Treasury may by order specify.

(5) Schedule 9 modifies provisions of this Part as they apply in relation to non-listing prospectuses.

Sponsors

88   Sponsors

(1) Listing rules may require a person to make arrangements with a sponsor for the performance by the sponsor of such services in relation to him as may be specified in the rules.

(2) 'Sponsor' means a person approved by the competent authority for the purposes of the rules.

(3) Listing rules made by virtue of subsection (1) may—

(a)   provide for the competent authority to maintain a list of sponsors;
(b)   specify services which must be performed by a sponsor;
(c)   impose requirements on a sponsor in relation to the provision of services or specified services;
(d)   specify the circumstances in which a person is qualified for being approved as a sponsor.

(4) If the competent authority proposes—

(a)   to refuse a person's application for approval as a sponsor, or
(b)   to cancel a person's approval as a sponsor,

it must give him a warning notice.

(5) If, after considering any representations made in response to the warning notice, the competent authority decides—

(a)   to grant the application for approval, or
(b)   not to cancel the approval,

it must give the person concerned, and any person to whom a copy of the warning notice was given, written notice of its decision.

(6) If, after considering any representations made in response to the warning notice, the competent authority decides—

(a)   to refuse to grant the application for approval, or
(b)   to cancel the approval,

it must give the person concerned a decision notice.

(7) A person to whom a decision notice is given under this section may refer the matter to the Tribunal.

89   Public censure of sponsor

(1) Listing rules may make provision for the competent authority, if it considers that a sponsor has contravened a requirement imposed on him by rules made as a result of section 88(3)(c), to publish a statement to that effect.

(2) If the competent authority proposes to publish a statement it must give the sponsor a warning notice setting out the terms of the proposed statement.

(3) If, after considering any representations made in response to the warning notice, the competent authority decides to make the proposed statement, it must give the sponsor a decision notice setting out the terms of the statement.

(4) A sponsor to whom a decision notice is given under this section may refer the matter to the Tribunal.

Compensation

90   Compensation for false or misleading particulars

(1) Any person responsible for listing particulars is liable to pay compensation to a person who has—

(a)   acquired securities to which the particulars apply; and
(b)   suffered loss in respect of them as a result of—
  (i)   any untrue or misleading statement in the particulars; or
  (ii)   the omission from the particulars of any matter required to be included by section 80 or 81.

(2) Subsection (1) is subject to exemptions provided by Schedule 10.

(3) If listing particulars are required to include information about the absence of a particular matter, the omission from the particulars of that information is to be treated as a statement in the listing particulars that there is no such matter.

(4) Any person who fails to comply with section 81 is liable to pay compensation to any person who has—

(a)   acquired securities of the kind in question; and
(b)   suffered loss in respect of them as a result of the failure.

(5) Subsection (4) is subject to exemptions provided by Schedule 10.

(6) This section does not affect any liability which may be incurred apart from this section.

(7) References in this section to the acquisition by a person of securities include references to his contracting to acquire them or any interest in them.

(8) No person shall, by reason of being a promoter of a company or otherwise, incur any liability for failing to disclose information which he would not be required to disclose in listing particulars in respect of a company's securities—

(a)   if he were responsible for those particulars; or
(b)   if he is responsible for them, which he is entitled to omit by virtue of section 82.

(9) The reference in subsection (8) to a person incurring liability includes a reference to any other person being entitled as against that person to be granted any civil remedy or to rescind or repudiate an agreement.

(10) 'Listing particulars', in subsection (1) and Schedule 10, includes supplementary listing particulars.

Penalties

91   Penalties for breach of listing rules

(1) If the competent authority considers that—

(a)   an issuer of listed securities, or
(b)   an applicant for listing,

has contravened any provision of listing rules, it may impose on him a penalty of such amount as it considers appropriate.

(2) If, in such a case, the competent authority considers that a person who was at the material time a director of the issuer or applicant was knowingly concerned in the contravention, it may impose on him a penalty of such amount as it considers appropriate.

(3) If the competent authority is entitled to impose a penalty on a person under this section in respect of a particular matter it may, instead of imposing a penalty on him in respect of that matter, publish a statement censuring him.

(4) Nothing in this section prevents the competent authority from taking any other steps which it has power to take under this Part.

(5) A penalty under this section is payable to the competent authority.

(6) The competent authority may not take action against a person under this section after the end of the period of two years beginning with the first day on which it knew of the contravention unless proceedings against that person, in respect of the contravention, were begun before the end of that period.

(7) For the purposes of subsection (6)—

    (a)   the competent authority is to be treated as knowing of a contravention if it has information from which the contravention can reasonably be inferred; and

    (b)   proceedings against a person in respect of a contravention are to be treated as begun when a warning notice is given to him under section 92.

92   Procedure

(1) If the competent authority proposes to take action against a person under section 91, it must give him a warning notice.

(2) A warning notice about a proposal to impose a penalty must state the amount of the proposed penalty.

(3) A warning notice about a proposal to publish a statement must set out the terms of the proposed statement.

(4) If the competent authority decides to take action against a person under section 91, it must give him a decision notice.

(5) A decision notice about the imposition of a penalty must state the amount of the penalty.

(6) A decision notice about the publication of a statement must set out the terms of the statement.

(7) If the competent authority decides to take action against a person under section 91, he may refer the matter to the Tribunal.

93   Statement of policy

(1) The competent authority must prepare and issue a statement ('its policy statement') of its policy with respect to—

    (a)   the imposition of penalties under section 91; and

    (b)   the amount of penalties under that section.

(2) The competent authority's policy in determining what the amount of a penalty should be must include having regard to—

    (a)   the seriousness of the contravention in question in relation to the nature of the requirement contravened;

    (b)   the extent to which that contravention was deliberate or reckless; and

(c)   whether the person on whom the penalty is to be imposed is an individual.

(3) The competent authority may at any time alter or replace its policy statement.

(4) If its policy statement is altered or replaced, the competent authority must issue the altered or replacement statement.

(5) In exercising, or deciding whether to exercise, its power under section 91 in the case of any particular contravention, the competent authority must have regard to any policy statement published under this section and in force at the time when the contravention in question occurred.

(6) The competent authority must publish a statement issued under this section in the way appearing to the competent authority to be best calculated to bring it to the attention of the public.

(7) The competent authority may charge a reasonable fee for providing a person with a copy of the statement.

(8) The competent authority must, without delay, give the Treasury a copy of any policy statement which it publishes under this section.

94   Statements of policy: procedure

(1) Before issuing a statement under section 93, the competent authority must publish a draft of the proposed statement in the way appearing to the competent authority to be best calculated to bring it to the attention of the public.

(2) The draft must be accompanied by notice that representations about the proposal may be made to the competent authority within a specified time.

(3) Before issuing the proposed statement, the competent authority must have regard to any representations made to it in accordance with subsection (2).

(4) If the competent authority issues the proposed statement it must publish an account, in general terms, of—

(a)   the representations made to it in accordance with subsection (2); and
(b)   its response to them.

(5) If the statement differs from the draft published under subsection (1) in a way which is, in the opinion of the competent authority, significant, the competent authority must (in addition to complying with subsection (4)) publish details of the difference.

(6) The competent authority may charge a reasonable fee for providing a person with a copy of a draft published under subsection (1).

(7) This section also applies to a proposal to alter or replace a statement.

Competition

95   Competition scrutiny

(1) The Treasury may by order provide for—

(a)   regulating provisions, and
(b)   the practices of the competent authority in exercising its functions under this Part ('practices'),

to be kept under review.

(2) Provision made as a result of subsection (1) must require the person responsible for keeping regulating provisions and practices under review to consider—

(a) whether any regulating provision or practice has a significantly adverse effect on competition; or

(b) whether two or more regulating provisions or practices taken together have, or a particular combination of regulating provisions and practices has, such an effect.

(3) An order under this section may include provision corresponding to that made by any provision of Chapter III of Part X.

(4) Subsection (3) is not to be read as in any way restricting the power conferred by subsection (1).

(5) Subsections (6) to (8) apply for the purposes of provision made by or under this section.

(6) Regulating provisions or practices have a significantly adverse effect on competition if—

(a) they have, or are intended or likely to have, that effect; or

(b) the effect that they have, or are intended or likely to have, is to require or encourage behaviour which has, or is intended or likely to have, a significantly adverse effect on competition.

(7) If regulating provisions or practices have, or are intended or likely to have, the effect of requiring or encouraging exploitation of the strength of a market position they are to be taken to have, or be intended or be likely to have, an adverse effect on competition.

(8) In determining whether any of the regulating provisions or practices have, or are intended or likely to have, a particular effect, it may be assumed that the persons to whom the provisions concerned are addressed will act in accordance with them.

(9) 'Regulating provisions' means—

(a) listing rules,

(b) general guidance given by the competent authority in connection with its functions under this Part.

Miscellaneous

96 Obligations of issuers of listed securities

(1) Listing rules may—

(a) specify requirements to be complied with by issuers of listed securities; and

(b) make provision with respect to the action that may be taken by the competent authority in the event of non-compliance.

(2) If the rules require an issuer to publish information, they may include provision authorising the competent authority to publish it in the event of his failure to do so.

(3) This section applies whenever the listed securities were admitted to the official list.

97 Appointment by competent authority of persons to carry out investigations

(1) Subsection (2) applies if it appears to the competent authority that there are circumstances suggesting that—

(a) there may have been a breach of listing rules;

(b) a person who was at the material time a director of an issuer of listed securities has been knowingly concerned in a breach of listing rules by that issuer;

(c) a person who was at the material time a director of a person applying for the admission of securities to the official list has been knowingly concerned in a breach of listing rules by that applicant;

(d)   there may have been a contravention of section 83, 85 or 98.

(2) The competent authority may appoint one or more competent persons to conduct an investigation on its behalf.

(3) Part XI applies to an investigation under subsection (2) as if—

(a)   the investigator were appointed under section 167(1);
(b)   references to the investigating authority in relation to him were to the competent authority;
(c)   references to the offences mentioned in section 168 were to those mentioned in subsection (1)(d);
(d)   references to an authorised person were references to the person under investigation.

98   Advertisements etc. in connection with listing applications

(1) If listing particulars are, or are to be, published in connection with an application for listing, no advertisement or other information of a kind specified by listing rules may be issued in the United Kingdom unless the contents of the advertisement or other information have been submitted to the competent authority and that authority has—

(a)   approved those contents; or
(b)   authorised the issue of the advertisement or information without such approval.

(2) A person who contravenes subsection (1) is guilty of an offence and liable—

(a)   on summary conviction, to a fine not exceeding the statutory maximum;
(b)   on conviction on indictment, to imprisonment for a term not exceeding two years or a fine, or both.

(3) A person who issues an advertisement or other information to the order of another person is not guilty of an offence under subsection (2) if he shows that he believed on reasonable grounds that the advertisement or information had been approved, or its issue authorised, by the competent authority.

(4) If information has been approved, or its issue has been authorised, under this section, neither the person issuing it nor any person responsible for, or for any part of, the listing particulars incurs any civil liability by reason of any statement in or omission from the information if that information and the listing particulars, taken together, would not be likely to mislead persons of the kind likely to consider acquiring the securities in question.

(5) The reference in subsection (4) to a person incurring civil liability includes a reference to any other person being entitled as against that person to be granted any civil remedy or to rescind or repudiate an agreement.

99   Fees

(1) Listing rules may require the payment of fees to the competent authority in respect of—

(a)   applications for listing;
(b)   the continued inclusion of securities in the official list;
(c)   applications under section 88 for approval as a sponsor; and
(d)   continued inclusion of sponsors in the list of sponsors.

(2) In exercising its powers under subsection (1), the competent authority may set such fees as it considers will (taking account of the income it expects as the competent authority) enable it—

(a)   to meet expenses incurred in carrying out its functions under this Part or for any incidental purpose;

(b) to maintain adequate reserves; and

(c) in the case of the Authority, to repay the principal of, and pay any interest on, any money which it has borrowed and which has been used for the purpose of meeting expenses incurred in relation to—

   (i)   its assumption of functions from the London Stock Exchange Limited in relation to the official list; and

   (ii) its assumption of functions under this Part.

(3) In fixing the amount of any fee which is to be payable to the competent authority, no account is to be taken of any sums which it receives, or expects to receive, by way of penalties imposed by it under this Part.

(4) Subsection (2)(c) applies whether expenses were incurred before or after the coming into force of this Part.

(5) Any fee which is owed to the competent authority under any provision made by or under this Part may be recovered as a debt due to it.

100 Penalties

(1) In determining its policy with respect to the amount of penalties to be imposed by it under this Part, the competent authority must take no account of the expenses which it incurs, or expects to incur, in discharging its functions under this Part.

(2) The competent authority must prepare and operate a scheme for ensuring that the amounts paid to it by way of penalties imposed under this Part are applied for the benefit of issuers of securities admitted to the official list.

(3) The scheme may, in particular, make different provision with respect to different classes of issuer.

(4) Up to date details of the scheme must be set out in a document ('the scheme details').

(5) The scheme details must be published by the competent authority in the way appearing to it to be best calculated to bring them to the attention of the public.

(6) Before making the scheme, the competent authority must publish a draft of the proposed scheme in the way appearing to it to be best calculated to bring it to the attention of the public.

(7) The draft must be accompanied by notice that representations about the proposals may be made to the competent authority within a specified time.

(8) Before making the scheme, the competent authority must have regard to any representations made to it under subsection (7).

(9) If the competent authority makes the proposed scheme, it must publish an account, in general terms, of—

(a) the representations made to it in accordance with subsection (7); and

(b) its response to them.

(10) If the scheme differs from the draft published under subsection (6) in a way which is, in the opinion of the competent authority, significant the competent authority must (in addition to complying with subsection (9)) publish details of the difference.

(11) The competent authority must, without delay, give the Treasury a copy of any scheme details published by it.

(12) The competent authority may charge a reasonable fee for providing a person with a copy of—

(a) a draft published under subsection (6);

(b)   scheme details.

(13) Subsections (6) to (10) and (12) apply also to a proposal to alter or replace the scheme.

101   Listing rules: general provisions

(1) Listing rules may make different provision for different cases.

(2) Listing rules may authorise the competent authority to dispense with or modify the application of the rules in particular cases and by reference to any circumstances.

(3) Listing rules must be made by an instrument in writing.

(4) Immediately after an instrument containing listing rules is made, it must be printed and made available to the public with or without payment.

(5) A person is not to be taken to have contravened any listing rule if he shows that at the time of the alleged contravention the instrument containing the rule had not been made available as required by subsection (4).

(6) The production of a printed copy of an instrument purporting to be made by the competent authority on which is endorsed a certificate signed by an officer of the authority authorised by it for that purpose and stating—

(a)   that the instrument was made by the authority,
(b)   that the copy is a true copy of the instrument, and
(c)   that on a specified date the instrument was made available to the public as required by subsection (4),

is evidence (or in Scotland sufficient evidence) of the facts stated in the certificate.

(7) A certificate purporting to be signed as mentioned in subsection (6) is to be treated as having been properly signed unless the contrary is shown.

(8) A person who wishes in any legal proceedings to rely on a rule-making instrument may require the Authority to endorse a copy of the instrument with a certificate of the kind mentioned in subsection (6).

102   Exemption from liability in damages

(1) Neither the competent authority nor any person who is, or is acting as, a member, officer or member of staff of the competent authority is to be liable in damages for anything done or omitted in the discharge, or purported discharge, of the authority's functions.

(2) Subsection (1) does not apply—

(a)   if the act or omission is shown to have been in bad faith; or
(b)   so as to prevent an award of damages made in respect of an act or omission on the ground that the act or omission was unlawful as a result of section 6(1) of the Human Rights Act 1998.

103   Interpretation of this Part

(1) In this Part—

'application' means an application made under section 75;
'issuer', in relation to anything which is or may be admitted to the official list, has such meaning as may be prescribed by the Treasury;
'listing' has the meaning given in section 74(5);
'listing particulars' has the meaning given in section 79(2);
'listing rules' has the meaning given in section 74(4);

'new securities' has the meaning given in section 84(2);

'the official list' means the list maintained as the official list by the Authority immediately before the coming into force of section 74, as that list has effect for the time being;

'security' (except in section 74(2)) has the meaning given in section 74(5).

(2) In relation to any function conferred on the competent authority by this Part, any reference in this Part to the competent authority is to be read as a reference to the person by whom that function is for the time being exercisable.

(3) If, as a result of an order under Schedule 8, different functions conferred on the competent authority by this Part are exercisable by different persons, the powers conferred by section 91 are exercisable by such person as may be determined in accordance with the provisions of the order.

(4) For the purposes of this Part, a person offers securities if, and only if, as principal—

   (a)   he makes an offer which, if accepted, would give rise to a contract for their issue or sale by him or by another person with whom he has made arrangements for their issue or sale; or

   (b)   he invites a person to make such an offer.

(5) 'Offer' and 'offeror' are to be read accordingly.

(6) For the purposes of this Part, the question whether a person offers securities to the public in the United Kingdom is to be determined in accordance with Schedule 11.

(7) For the purpsoes of subsection (4) 'sale' includes any disposal for valuable consideration.

PART VII

CONTROL OF BUSINESS TRANSFERS

104   Control of business transfers

No insurance business transfer scheme or banking business transfer scheme is to have effect unless an order has been made in relation to it under section 111(1).

105   Insurance business transfer schemes

(1) A scheme is an insurance business transfer scheme if it—

   (a)   satisfies one of the conditions set out in subsection (2);

   (b)   results in the business transferred being carried on from an establishment of the transferee in an EEA State; and

   (c)   is not an excluded scheme.

(2) The conditions are that—

   (a)   the whole or part of the business carried on in one or more member States by a UK authorised person who has permission to effect or carry out contracts of insurance ('the authorised person concerned') is to be transferred to another body ('the transferee');

   (b)   the whole or part of the business, so far as it consists of reinsurance, carried on in the United Kingdom through an establishment there by an EEA firm qualifying for authorisation under Schedule 3 which has permission to effect or carry out contracts of insurance ('the authorised person concerned') is to be transferred to another body ('the transferee');

(c)   the whole or part of the business carried on in the United Kingdom by an authorised person who is neither a UK authorised person nor an EEA firm but who has permission to effect or carry out contracts of insurance ('the authorised person concerned') is to be transferred to another body ('the transferee').

(3) A scheme is an excluded scheme for the purposes of this section if it falls within any of the following cases:

CASE 1

Where the authorised person concerned is a friendly society.

CASE 2

Where—

(a)   the authorised person concerned is a UK authorised person;
(b)   the business to be transferred under the scheme is business which consists of the effecting or carrying out of contracts of reinsurance in one or more EEA States other than the United Kingdom; and
(c)   the scheme has been approved by a court in an EEA State other than the United Kingdom or by the host state regulator.

CASE 3

Where—

(a)   the authorised person concerned is a UK authorised person;
(b)   the business to be transferred under the scheme is carried on in one or more countries or territories (none of which is an EEA State) and does not include policies of insurance (other than reinsurance) against risks arising in an EEA State; and
(c)   the scheme has been approved by a court in a country or territory other than an EEA State or by the authority responsible for the supervision of that business in a country or territory in which it is carried on.

CASE 4

Where the business to be transferred under the scheme is the whole of the business of the authorised person concerned and—

(a)   consists solely of the effecting or carrying out of contracts of reinsurance, or
(b)   all the policyholders are controllers of the firm or of firms within the same group as the firm which is the transferee,

and, in either case, all of the policyholders who will be affected by the transfer have consented to it.

(4) The parties to a scheme which falls within Case 2, 3 or 4 may apply to the court for an order sanctioning the scheme as if it were an insurance business transfer scheme.

(5) Subsection (6) applies if the scheme involves a compromise or arrangement falling within section 427A of the Companies Act 1985 (or Article 420A of the Companies (Northern Ireland) Order 1986).

(6) Sections 425 to 427 of that Act (or Articles 418 to 420 of that Order) have effect as modified by section 427A of that Act (or Article 420A of that Order) in relation to that compromise or arrangement.

(7) But subsection (6) does not affect the operation of this Part in relation to the scheme.

(8) 'UK authorised person' means a body which is an authorised person and which—

(a) is incorporated in the United Kingdom; or
(b) is an unincorporated association formed under the law of any part of the United Kingdom.

(9) 'Establishment' means, in relation to a person, his head office or a branch of his.

106 Banking business transfer schemes

(1) A scheme is a banking business transfer scheme if it—

(a) satisfies one of the conditions set out in subsection (2);
(b) is one under which the whole or part of the business to be transferred includes the accepting of deposits; and
(c) is not an excluded scheme.

(2) The conditions are that—

(a) the whole or part of the business carried on by a UK authorised person who has permission to accept deposits ('the authorised person concerned') is to be transferred to another body ('the transferee');
(b) the whole or part of the business carried on in the United Kingdom by an authorised person who is not a UK authorised person but who has permission to accept deposits ('the authorised person concerned') is to be transferred to another body which will carry it on in the United Kingdom ('the transferee').

(3) A scheme is an excluded scheme for the purposes of this section if—

(a) the authorised person concerned is a building society or a credit union; or
(b) the scheme is a compromise or arrangement to which section 427A(1) of the Companies Act 1985 or Article 420A of the Companies (Northern Ireland) Order 1986 (mergers and divisions of public companies) applies.

(4) For the purposes of subsection (2)(a) it is immaterial whether or not the business to be transferred is carried on in the United Kingdom.

(5) 'UK authorised person' has the same meaning as in section 105.

(6) 'Building society' has the meaning given in the Building Societies Act 1986.

(7) 'Credit union' means a credit union within the meaning of—

(a) the Credit Unions Act 1979;
(b) the Credit Unions (Northern Ireland) Order 1985.

107 Application for order sanctioning transfer scheme

(1) An application may be made to the court for an order sanctioning an insurance business transfer scheme or a banking business transfer scheme.

(2) An application may be made by—

(a) the authorised person concerned;
(b) the transferee; or
(c) both.

(3) The application must be made—

(a) if the authorised person concerned and the transferee are registered or have their head offices in the same jurisdiction, to the court in that jurisdiction;

   (b)   if the authorised person concerned and the transferee are registered or have their head offices in different jurisdictions, to the court in either jurisdiction;

   (c)   if the transferee is not registered in the United Kingdom and does not have his head office there, to the court which has jurisdiction in relation to the authorised person concerned.

(4) 'Court' means—

   (a)   the High Court; or

   (b)   in Scotland, the Court of Session.

108   Requirements on applicants

(1) The Treasury may by regulations impose requirements on applicants under section 107.

(2) The court may not determine an application under that section if the applicant has failed to comply with a prescribed requirement.

(3) The regulations may, in particular, include provision—

   (a)   as to the persons to whom, and periods within which, notice of an application must be given;

   (b)   enabling the court to waive a requirement of the regulations in prescribed circumstances.

109   Scheme reports

(1) An application under section 107 in respect of an insurance business transfer scheme must be accompanied by a report on the terms of the scheme ('a scheme report').

(2) A scheme report may be made only by a person—

   (a)   appearing to the Authority to have the skills necessary to enable him to make a proper report; and

   (b)   nominated or approved for the purpose by the Authority.

(3) A scheme report must be made in a form approved by the Authority.

110   Right to participate in proceedings

On an application under section 107, the following are also entitled to be heard—

   (a)   the Authority, and

   (b)   any person (including an employee of the authorised person concerned or of the transferee) who alleges that he would be adversely affected by the carrying out of the scheme.

111   Sanction of the court for business transfer schemes

(1) This section sets out the conditions which must be satisfied before the court may make an order under this section sanctioning an insurance business transfer scheme or a banking business transfer scheme.

(2) The court must be satisfied that—

   (a)   the appropriate certificates have been obtained (as to which see Parts I and II of Schedule 12);

   (b)   the transferee has the authorisation required (if any) to enable the business, or part, which is to be transferred to be carried on in the place to which it is to be transferred (or will have it before the scheme takes effect).

(3) The court must consider that, in all the circumstances of the case, it is appropriate to sanction the scheme.

112   Effect of order sanctioning business transfer scheme

(1) If the court makes an order under section 111(1), it may by that or any subsequent order make such provision (if any) as it thinks fit—

    (a)   for the transfer to the transferee of the whole or any part of the undertaking concerned and of any property or liabilities of the authorised person concerned;

    (b)   for the allotment or appropriation by the transferee of any shares, debentures, policies or other similar interests in the transferee which under the scheme are to be allotted or appropriated to or for any other person;

    (c)   for the continuation by (or against) the transferee of any pending legal proceedings by (or against) the authorised person concerned;

    (d)   with respect to such incidental, consequential and supplementary matters as are, in its opinion, necessary to secure that the scheme is fully and effectively carried out.

(2) An order under subsection (1)(a) may—

    (a)   transfer property or liabilities whether or not the authorised person concerned otherwise has the capacity to effect the transfer in question;

    (b)   make provision in relation to property which was held by the authorised person concerned as trustee;

    (c)   make provision as to future or contingent rights or liabilities of the authorised person concerned, including provision as to the construction of instruments (including wills) under which such rights or liabilities may arise;

    (d)   make provision as to the consequences of the transfer in relation to any retirement benefits scheme (within the meaning of section 611 of the Income and Corporation Taxes Act 1988) operated by or on behalf of the authorised person concerned.

(3) If an order under subsection (1) makes provision for the transfer of property or liabilities—

    (a)   the property is transferred to and vests in, and

    (b)   the liabilities are transferred to and become liabilities of, the transferee as a result of the order.

(4) But if any property or liability included in the order is governed by the law of any country or territory outside the United Kingdom, the order may require the authorised person concerned, if the transferee so requires, to take all necessary steps for securing that the transfer to the transferee of the property or liability is fully effective under the law of that country or territory.

(5) Property transferred as the result of an order under subsection (1) may, if the court so directs, vest in the transferee free from any charge which is (as a result of the scheme) to cease to have effect.

(6) An order under subsection (1) which makes provision for the transfer of property is to be treated as an instrument of transfer for the purposes of the provisions mentioned in subsection (7) and any other enactment requiring the delivery of an instrument of transfer for the registration of property.

(7) The provisions are—

    (a)   section 183(1) of the Companies Act 1985;

(b)   Article 193(1) and (2) of the Companies (Northern Ireland) Order 1986.

(8) If the court makes an order under section 111(1) in relation to an insurance business transfer scheme, it may by that or any subsequent order make such provision (if any) as it thinks fit—

(a)   for dealing with the interests of any person who, within such time and in such manner as the court may direct, objects to the scheme;

(b)   for the dissolution, without winding up, of the authorised person concerned;

(c)   for the reduction, on such terms and subject to such conditions (if any) as it thinks fit, of the benefits payable under—

(i)   any description of policy, or

(ii)   policies generally,

entered into by the authorised person concerned and transferred as a result of the scheme.

(9) If, in the case of an insurance business transfer scheme, the authorised person concerned is not an EEA firm, it is immaterial for the purposes of subsection (1)(a), (c) or (d) or subsection (2), (3) or (4) that the law applicable to any of the contracts of insurance included in the transfer is the law of an EEA State other than the United Kingdom.

(10) The transferee must, if an insurance or banking business transfer scheme is sanctioned by the court, deposit two office copies of the order made under subsection (1) with the Authority within 10 days of the making of the order.

(11) But the Authority may extend that period.

(12) 'Property' includes property, rights and powers of any description.

(13) 'Liabilities' includes duties.

(14) 'Shares' and 'debentures' have the same meaning as in—

(a)   the Companies Act 1985; or

(b)   in Northern Ireland, the Companies (Northern Ireland) Order 1986.

(15) 'Charge' includes a mortgage (or, in Scotland, a security over property).

113   Appointment of actuary in relation to reduction of benefits

(1) This section applies if an order has been made under section 111(1).

(2) The court making the order may, on the application of the Authority, appoint an independent actuary—

(a)   to investigate the business transferred under the scheme; and

(b)   to report to the Authority on any reduction in the benefits payable under policies entered into by the authorised person concerned that, in the opinion of the actuary, ought to be made.

114   Rights of certain policyholders

(1) This section applies in relation to an insurance business transfer scheme if—

(a)   the authorised person concerned is an authorised person other than an EEA firm qualifying for authorisation under Schedule 3;

(b)   the court has made an order under section 111 in relation to the scheme; and

(c)   an EEA State other than the United Kingdom is, as regards any policy included in the transfer which evidences a contract of insurance, the State of the commitment or the EEA State in which the risk is situated ('the EEA State concerned').

(2) The court must direct that notice of the making of the order, or the execution of any instrument, giving effect to the transfer must be published by the transferee in the EEA State concerned.

(3) A notice under subsection (2) must specify such period as the court may direct as the period during which the policyholder may exercise any right which he has to cancel the policy.

(4) The order or instrument mentioned in subsection (2) does not bind the policyholder if—

    (a)   the notice required under that subsection is not published; or

    (b)   the policyholder cancels the policy during the period specified in the notice given under that subsection.

(5) The law of the EEA State concerned governs—

    (a)   whether the policyholder has a right to cancel the policy; and

    (b)   the conditions, if any, subject to which any such right may be exercised.

(6) Paragraph 6 of Schedule 12 applies for the purposes of this section as it applies for the purposes of that Schedule.

Business transfers outside the United Kingdom

115   Certificates for purposes of insurance business transfers overseas

Part III of Schedule 12 makes provision about certificates which the Authority may issue in relation to insurance business transfers taking place outside the United Kingdom.

116   Effect of insurance business transfers authorised in other EEA States

(1) This section applies if, as a result of an authorised transfer, an EEA firm falling within paragraph 5(d) of Schedule 3 transfers to another body all its rights and obligations under any UK policies.

(2) This section also applies if, as a result of an authorised transfer, a company authorised in an EEA State other than the United Kingdom under Article 27 of the first life insurance directive, or Article 23 of the first non-life insurance directive, transfers to another body all its rights and obligations under any UK policies.

(3) If appropriate notice of the execution of an instrument giving effect to the transfer is published, the instrument has the effect in law—

    (a)   of transferring to the transferee all the transferor's rights and obligations under the UK policies to which the instrument applies, and

    (b)   if the instrument so provides, of securing the continuation by or against the transferee of any legal proceedings by or against the transferor which relate to those rights and obligations.

(4) No agreement or consent is required before subsection (3) has the effects mentioned.

(5) 'Authorised transfer' means—

    (a)   in subsection (1), a transfer authorised in the home State of the EEA firm in accordance with—

        (i)   Article 11 of the third life directive; or

        (ii)   Article 12 of the third non-life directive; and

    (b)   in subsection (2), a transfer authorised in an EEA State other than the United Kingdom in accordance with—

        (i)   Article 31a of the first life directive; or

(ii)   Article 28a of the first non-life directive.

(6) 'UK policy' means a policy evidencing a contract of insurance (other than a contract of reinsurance) to which the applicable law is the law of any part of the United Kingdom.

(7) 'Appropriate notice' means—

(a)   if the UK policy evidences a contract of insurance in relation to which an EEA State other than the United Kingdom is the State of the commitment, notice given in accordance with the law of that State;

(b)   if the UK policy evidences a contract of insurance where the risk is situated in an EEA State other than the United Kingdom, notice given in accordance with the law of that EEA State;

(c)   in any other case, notice given in accordance with the applicable law.

(8) Paragraph 6 of Schedule 12 applies for the purposes of this section as it applies for the purposes of that Schedule.

Modifications

117   Power to modify this Part

(1) The Treasury may by regulations—

(a)   provide for prescribed provisions of this Part to have effect in relation to prescribed cases with such modifications as may be prescribed;

(b)   make such amendments to any provision of this Part as they consider appropriate for the more effective operation of that or any other provision of this Part.

PART VIII

PENALTIES FOR MARKET ABUSE

Market abuse

118   Market abuse

(1) For the purposes of this Act, market abuse is behaviour (whether by one person alone or by two or more persons jointly or in concert)—

(a)   which occurs in relation to qualifying investments traded on a market to which this section applies;

(b)   which satisfies any one or more of the conditions set out in subsection (2); and

(c)   which is likely to be regarded by a regular user of that market who is aware of the behaviour as a failure on the part of the person or persons concerned to observe the standard of behaviour reasonably expected of a person in his or their position in relation to the market.

(2) The conditions are that—

(a)   the behaviour is based on information which is not generally available to those using the market but which, if available to a regular user of the market, would or would be likely to be regarded by him as relevant when deciding the terms on which transactions in investments of the kind in question should be effected;

(b)   the behaviour is likely to give a regular user of the market a false or misleading impression as to the supply of, or demand for, or as to the price or value of, investments of the kind in question;

(c)   a regular user of the market would, or would be likely to, regard the behaviour as behaviour which would, or would be likely to, distort the market in investments of the kind in question.

(3) The Treasury may by order prescribe (whether by name or by description)—

(a)   the markets to which this section applies; and
(b)   the investments which are qualifying investments in relation to those markets.

(4) The order may prescribe different investments or descriptions of investment in relation to different markets or descriptions of market.

(5) Behaviour is to be disregarded for the purposes of subsection (1) unless it occurs—

(a)   in the United Kingdom; or
(b)   in relation to qualifying investments traded on a market to which this section applies which is situated in the United Kingdom or which is accessible electronically in the United Kingdom.

(6) For the purposes of this section, the behaviour which is to be regarded as occurring in relation to qualifying investments includes behaviour which—

(a)   occurs in relation to anything which is the subject matter, or whose price or value is expressed by reference to the price or value, of those qualifying investments; or
(b)   occurs in relation to investments (whether qualifying or not) whose subject matter is those qualifying investments.

(7) Information which can be obtained by research or analysis conducted by, or on behalf of, users of a market is to be regarded for the purposes of this section as being generally available to them.

(8) Behaviour does not amount to market abuse if it conforms with a rule which includes a provision to the effect that behaviour conforming with the rule does not amount to market abuse.

(9) Any reference in this Act to a person engaged in market abuse is a reference to a person engaged in market abuse whether alone or with one or more other persons.

(10) In this section—

'behaviour' includes action or inaction;
'investment' is to be read with section 22 and Schedule 2;
'regular user', in relation to a particular market, means a reasonable person who regularly deals on that market in investments of the kind in question.

The code

119   The code

(1) The Authority must prepare and issue a code containing such provisions as the Authority considers will give appropriate guidance to those determining whether or not behaviour amounts to market abuse.

(2) The code may among other things specify—

(a)   descriptions of behaviour that, in the opinion of the Authority, amount to market abuse;
(b)   descriptions of behaviour that, in the opinion of the Authority, do not amount to market abuse;
(c)   factors that, in the opinion of the Authority, are to be taken into account in determining whether or not behaviour amounts to market abuse.

(3) The code may make different provision in relation to persons, cases or circumstances of different descriptions.

(4) The Authority may at any time alter or replace the code.

(5) If the code is altered or replaced, the altered or replacement code must be issued by the Authority.

(6) A code issued under this section must be published by the Authority in the way appearing to the Authority to be best calculated to bring it to the attention of the public.

(7) The Authority must, without delay, give the Treasury a copy of any code published under this section.

(8) The Authority may charge a reasonable fee for providing a person with a copy of the code.

120   Provisions included in the Authority's code by reference to the City Code

(1) The Authority may include in a code issued by it under section 119 ('the Authority's code') provision to the effect that in its opinion behaviour conforming with the City Code—

(a)   does not amount to market abuse;
(b)   does not amount to market abuse in specified circumstances; or
(c)   does not amount to market abuse if engaged in by a specified description of person.

(2) But the Treasury's approval is required before any such provision may be included in the Authority's code.

(3) If the Authority's code includes provision of a kind authorised by subsection (1), the Authority must keep itself informed of the way in which the Panel on Takeovers and Mergers interprets and administers the relevant provisions of the City Code.

(4) 'City Code' means the City Code on Takeovers and Mergers issued by the Panel as it has effect at the time when the behaviour occurs.

(5) 'Specified' means specified in the Authority's code.

121   Codes: procedure

(1) Before issuing a code under section 119, the Authority must publish a draft of the proposed code in the way appearing to the Authority to be best calculated to bring it to the attention of the public.

(2) The draft must be accompanied by—

(a)   a cost benefit analysis; and
(b)   notice that representations about the proposal may be made to the Authority within a specified time.

(3) Before issuing the proposed code, the Authority must have regard to any representations made to it in accordance with subsection (2)(b).

(4) If the Authority issues the proposed code it must publish an account, in general terms, of—

(a)   the representations made to it in accordance with subsection (2)(b); and
(b)   its response to them.

(5) If the code differs from the draft published under subsection (1) in a way which is, in the opinion of the Authority, significant—

(a)   the Authority must (in addition to complying with subsection (4)) publish details of the difference; and
(b)   those details must be accompanied by a cost benefit analysis.

(6) Subsections (1) to (5) do not apply if the Authority considers that there is an urgent need to publish the code.

(7) Neither subsection (2)(a) nor subsection (5)(b) applies if the Authority considers—

(a)   that, making the appropriate comparison, there will be no increase in costs; or
(b)   that, making that comparison, there will be an increase in costs but the increase will be of minimal significance.

(8) The Authority may charge a reasonable fee for providing a person with a copy of a draft published under subsection (1).

(9) This section also applies to a proposal to alter or replace a code.

(10) 'Cost benefit analysis' means an estimate of the costs together with an analysis of the benefits that will arise—

(a)   if the proposed code is issued; or
(b)   if subsection (5)(b) applies, from the code that has been issued.

(11) 'The appropriate comparison' means—

(a)   in relation to subsection (2)(a), a comparison between the overall position of the code is issued and the overall position if it is not issued;
(b)   in relation to subsection (5)(b), a comparison between the overall position after the issuing of the code and the overall position before it was issued.

122   Effect of the code

(1) If a person behaves in a way which is described (in the code in force under section 119 at the time of the behaviour) as behaviour that, in the Authority's opinion, does not amount to market abuse that behaviour of his is to be taken, for the purposes of this Act, as not amounting to market abuse.

(2) Otherwise, the code in force under section 119 at the time when particular behaviour occurs may be relied on so far as it indicates whether or not that behaviour should be taken to amount to market abuse.

Power to impose penalties

123   Power to impose penalties in cases of market abuse

(1) If the Authority is satisfied that a person ('A')—

(a)   is or has engaged in market abuse, or
(b)   by taking or refraining from taking any action has required or encouraged another person or persons to engage in behaviour which, if engaged in by A, would amount to market abuse,

it may impose on him a penalty of such amount as it considers appropriate.

(2) But the Authority may not impose a penalty on a person if, having considered any reprsentations made to it in response to a warning notice, there are reasonable grounds for it to be satisfied that—

(a)   he believed, on reasonable grounds, that his behaviour did not fall within paragraph (a) or (b) of subsection (1), or

(b) he took all reasonable precautions and exercised all due diligence to avoid behaving in a way which fell within paragraph (a) or (b) of that subsection.

(3) If the Authority is entitled to impose a penalty on a person under this section it may, instead of imposing a penalty on him, publish a statement to the effect that he has engaged in market abuse.

Statement of policy

124   Statement of policy

(1) The Authority must prepare and issue a statement of its policy with respect to—

(a) the imposition of penalties under section 123; and
(b) the amount of penalties under that section.

(2) The Authority's policy in determining what the amount of a penalty should be must include having regard to—

(a) whether the behaviour in respect of which the penalty is to be imposed had an adverse effect on the market in question and, if it did, how serious that effect was;
(b) the extent to which that behaviour was deliberate or reckless; and
(c) whether the person on whom the penalty is to be imposed is an individual.

(3) A statement issued under this section must include an indication of the circumstances in which the Authority is to be expected to regard a person as—

(a) having a reasonable belief that his behaviour did not amount to market abuse; or
(b) having taken reasonable precautions and exercised due diligence to avoid engaging in market abuse.

(4) The Authority may at any time alter or replace a statement issued under this section.

(5) If a statement issued under this section is altered or replaced, the Authority must issue the altered or replacement statement.

(6) In exercising, or deciding whether to exercise, its power under section 123 in the case of any particular behaviour, the Authority must have regard to any statement published under this section and in force at the time when the behaviour concerned occurred.

(7) A statement issued under this section must be published by the Authority in the way appearing to the Authority to be best calculated to bring it to the attention of the public.

(8) The Authority may charge a reasonable fee for providing a person with a copy of a statement published under this section.

(9) The Authority must, without delay, give the Treasury a copy of any statement which it publishes under this section.

125   Statement of policy: procedure

(1) Before issuing a statement of policy under section 124, the Authority must publish a draft of the proposed statement in the way appearing to the Authority to be best calculated to bring it to the attention of the public.

(2) The draft must be accompanied by notice that representations about the proposal may be made to the Authority within a specified time.

(3) Before issuing the proposed statement, the Authority must have regard to any representations made to it in accordance with subsection (2).

(4) If the Authority issues the proposed statement it must publish an account, in general terms, of—

(a)   the representations made to it in accordance with subsection (2); and
(b)   its response to them.

(5) If the statement differs from the draft published under subsection (1) in a way which is, in the opinion of the Authority, significant, the Authority must (in addition to complying with subsection (4)) publish details of the difference.

(6) The Authority may charge a reasonable fee for providing a person with a copy of a draft published under subsection (1).

(7) This section also applies to a proposal to alter or replace a statement.

Procedure

126   Warning notices

(1) If the Authority proposes to take action against a person under section 123, it must give him a warning notice.

(2) A warning notice about a proposal to impose a penalty must state the amount of the proposed penalty.

(3) A warning notice about a proposal to publish a statement must set out the terms of the proposed statement.

127   Decision notices and right to refer to Tribunal

(1) If the Authority decides to take action against a person under section 123, it must give him a decision notice.

(2) A decision notice about the imposition of a penalty must state the amount of the penalty.

(3) A decision notice about the publication of a statement must set out the terms of the statement.

(4) If the Authority decides to take action against a person under section 123, that person may refer the matter to the Tribunal.

Miscellaneous

128   Suspension of investigations

(1) If the Authority considers it desirable or expedient because of the exercise or possible exercise of a power relating to market abuse, it may direct a recognised investment exchange or recognised clearing house—

(a)   to terminate, suspend or limit the scope of any inquiry which the exchange or clearing house is conducting under its rules; or
(b)   not to conduct an inquiry which the exchange or clearing house proposes to conduct under its rules.

(2) A direction under this section—

(a)   must be given to the exchange or clearing house concerned by notice in writing; and
(b)   is enforceable, on the application of the Authority, by injunction or, in Scotland, by an order under section 45 of the Court of Session Act 1988.

(3) The Authority's powers relating to market abuse are its powers—

    (a)   to impose penalties under section 123; or

    (b)   to appoint a person to conduct an investigation under section 168 in a case falling within subsection (2)(d) of that section.

129   Power of court to impose penalty in cases of market abuse

(1) The Authority may on an application to the court under section 381 or 383 request the court to consider whether the circumstances are such that a penalty should be imposed on the person to whom the application relates.

(2) The court may, if it considers it appropriate, make an order requiring the person concerned to pay to the Authority a penalty of such amount as it considers appropriate.

130   Guidance

(1) The Treasury may from time to time issue written guidance for the purpose of helping relevant authorities to determine the action to be taken in cases where behaviour occurs which is behaviour—

    (a)   with respect to which the power in section 123 appears to be exercisable; and

    (b)   which appears to involve the commission of an offence under section 397 of this Act or Part V of the Criminal Justice Act 1993 (insider dealing).

(2) The Treasury must obtain the consent of the Attorney General and the Secretary of State before issuing any guidance under this section.

(3) In this section 'relevant authorities'—

    (a)   in relation to England and Wales, means the Secretary of State, the Authority, the Director of the Serious Fraud Office and the Director of Public Prosecutions;

    (b)   in relation to Northern Ireland, means the Secretary of State, the Authority, the Director of the Serious Fraud Office and the Director of Public Prosecutions for Northern Ireland.

(4) Subsections (1) to (3) do not apply to Scotland.

(5) In relation to Scotland, the Lord Advocate may from time to time, after consultation with the Treasury, issue written guidance for the purpose of helping the Authority to determine the action to be taken in cases where behaviour mentioned in subsection (1) occurs.

131   Effect on transactions

The imposition of a penalty under this Part does not make any transaction void or unenforceable.

PART IX

HEARINGS AND APPEALS

132   The Financial Services and Markets Tribunal

(1) For the purposes of this Act, there is to be a tribunal known as the Financial Services and Markets Tribunal (but referred to in this Act as 'the Tribunal').

(2) The Tribunal is to have the functions conferred on it by or under this Act.

(3) The Lord Chancellor may by rules make such provision as appears to him to be necessary or expedient in respect of the conduct of proceedings before the Tribunal.

(4) Schedule 13 is to have effect as respects the Tribunal and its proceedings (but does not limit the Lord Chancellor's powers under this section).

133 Proceedings: general provision

(1) A reference to the Tribunal under this Act must be made before the end of—

    (a) the period of 28 days beginning with the date on which the decision notice or supervisory notice in question is given; or

    (b) such other period as may be specified in rules made under section 132.

(2) Subject to rules made under section 132, the Tribunal may allow a reference to be made after the end of that period.

(3) On a reference the Tribunal may consider any evidence relating to the subject-matter of the reference, whether or not it was available to the Authority at the material time.

(4) On a reference the Tribunal must determine what (if any) is the appropriate action for the Authority to take in relation to the matter referred to it.

(5) On determining a reference, the Tribunal must remit the matter to the Authority with such directions (if any) as the Tribunal considers appropriate for giving effect to its determination.

(6) In determining a reference made as a result of a decision notice, the Tribunal may not direct the Authority to take action which the Authority would not, as a result of section 388(2), have had power to take when giving the decision notice.

(7) In determining a reference made as a result of a supervisory notice, the Tribunal may not direct the Authority to take action which would have otherwise required the giving of a decision notice.

(8) The Tribunal may, on determining a reference, make recommendations as to the Authority's regulating provisions or its procedures.

(9) The Authority must not take the action specified in a decision notice—

    (a) during the period within which the matter to which the decision notice relates may be referred to the Tribunal; and

    (b) if the matter is so referred, until the reference, and any appeal against the Tribunal's determination, has been finally disposed of.

(10) The Authority must act in accordance with the determination of, and any direction given by, the Tribunal.

(11) An order of the Tribunal may be enforced—

    (a) as if it were an order of a county court; or

    (b) in Scotland, as if it were an order of the Court of Session.

(12) 'Supervisory notice' has the same meaning as in section 395.

Legal assistance before the Tribunal

134 Legal assistance scheme

(1) The Lord Chancellor may by regulations establish a scheme governing the provision of legal assistance in connection with proceedings before the Tribunal.

(2) If the Lord Chancellor establishes a scheme under subsection (1), it must provide that a person is eligible for assistance only if—

    (a) he falls within subsection (3); and

(b)   he fulfils such other criteria (if any) as may be prescribed as a result of section 135(1)(d).

(3) A person falls within this subsection if he is an individual who has referred a matter to the Tribunal under section 127(4).

(4) In this Part of this Act 'the legal assistance scheme' means any scheme in force under subsection (1).

135   Provisions of the legal assistance scheme

(1) The legal assistance scheme may, in particular, make provision as to—

(a)   the kinds of legal assistance that may be provided;
(b)   the persons by whom legal assistance may be provided;
(c)   the manner in which applications for legal assistance are to be made;
(d)   the criteria on which eligibility for legal assistance is to be determined;
(e)   the persons or bodies by whom applications are to be determined;
(f)   appeals against refusals of applications;
(g)   the revocation or variation of decisions;
(h)   its administration and the enforcement of its provisions.

(2) Legal assistance under the legal assistance scheme may be provided subject to conditions or restrictions, including conditions as to the making of contributions by the person to whom it is provided.

136   Funding of the legal assistance scheme

(1) The Authority must pay to the Lord Chancellor such sums at such times as he may, from time to time, determine in respect of the anticipated or actual cost of legal assistance provided in connection with proceedings before the Tribunal under the legal assistance scheme.

(2) In order to enable it to pay any sum which it is obliged to pay under subsection (1), the Authority must make rules requiring the payment to it by authorised persons or any class of authorised person of specified amounts or amounts calculated in a specified way.

(3) Sums received by the Lord Chancellor under subsection (1) must be paid into the Consolidated Fund.

(4) The Lord Chancellor must, out of money provided by Parliament fund the cost of legal assistance provided in connection with proceedings before the Tribunal under the legal assistance scheme.

(5) Subsection (6) applies if, as respects a period determined by the Lord Chancellor, the amount paid to him under subsection (1) as respects that period exceeds the amount he has expended in that period under subsection (4).

(6) The Lord Chancellor must—

(a)   repay, out of money provided by Parliament, the excess to the Authority; or
(b)   take the excess into account on the next occasion on which he makes a determination under subsection (1).

(7) The Authority must make provision for any sum repaid to it under subsection (6)(a)—

(a)   to be distributed among—
  (i)   the authorised persons on whom a levy was imposed in the period in question as a result of rules made under subsection (2); or
  (ii) such of those persons as it may determine;

(b)   to be applied in order to reduce any amounts which those persons, or such of them as it may determine, are or will be liable to pay to the Authority, whether under rules made under subsection (2) or otherwise; or

(c)   to be partly so distributed and partly so applied.

(8) If the Authority considers that it is not practicable to deal with any part of a sum repaid to it under subsection (6)(a) in accordance with provision made by it as a result of subsection (7), it may, with the consent of the Lord Chancellor, apply or dispose of that part of that sum in such manner as it considers appropriate.

(9) 'Specified' means specified in the rules.

Appeals

137   Appeal on a point of law

(1) A party to a reference to the Tribunal may with permission appeal—

(a)   to the Court of Appeal, or

(b)   in Scotland, to the Court of Session,

on a point of law arising from a decision of the Tribunal disposing of the reference.

(2) 'Permission' means permission given by the Tribunal or by the Court of Appeal or (in Scotland) the Court of Session.

(3) If, on an appeal under subsection (1), the court considers that the decision of the Tribunal was wrong in law, it may—

(a)   remit the matter to the Tribunal for rehearing and determination by it; or

(b)   itself make a determination.

(4) An appeal may not be brought from a decision of the Court of Appeal under subsection (3) except with the leave of—

(a)   the Court of Appeal; or

(b)   the House of Lords.

(5) An appeal lies, with the leave of the Court of Session or the House of Lords, from any decision of the Court of Session under this section, and such leave may be given on such terms as to costs, expenses or otherwise as the Court of Session or the House of Lords may determine.

(6) Rules made under section 132 may make provision for regulating or prescribing any matters incidental to or consequential on an appeal under this section.

PART X

RULES AND GUIDANCE

CHAPTER I

RULE-MAKING POWERS

138   General rule-making power

(1) The Authority may make such rules applying to authorised persons—

(a)   with respect to the carrying on by them of regulated activities, or

(b)   with respect to the carrying on by them of activities which are not regulated activities, as appear to it to be necessary or expedient for the purpose of protecting the interests of consumers.

(2) Rules made under this section are referred to in this Act as the Authority's general rules.

(3) The Authority's power to make general rules is not limited by any other power which it has to make regulating provisions.

(4) The Authority's general rules may make provision applying to authorised persons even though there is no relationship between the authorised persons to whom the rules will apply and the persons whose interests will be protected by the rules.

(5) General rules may contain requirements which take into account, in the case of an authorised person who is a member of a group, any activity of another member of the group.

(6) General rules may not—

   (a)   make provision prohibiting an EEA firm from carrying on, or holding itself out as carrying on, any activity which it has permission conferred by Part II of Schedule 3 to carry on in the United Kingdom;
   (b)   make provision, as respects an EEA firm, about any matter responsibility for which is, under any of the single market directives, reserved to the firm's home state regulator.

(7) 'Consumers' means persons—

   (a)   who use, have used, or are or may be contemplating using, any of the services provided by—
      (i)   authorised persons in carrying on regulated activities; or
      (ii) persons acting as appointed representatives;
   (b)   who have rights or interests which are derived from, or are otherwise attributable to, the use of any such services by other persons; or
   (c)   who have rights or interests which may be adversely affected by the use of any such services by persons acting on their behalf or in a fiduciary capacity in relation to them.

(8) If an authorised person is carrying on a regulated activity in his capacity as a trustee, the persons who are, have been or may be beneficiaries of the trust are to be treated as persons who use, have used or are or may be contemplating using services provided by the authorised person in his carrying on of that activity.

(9) For the purposes of subsection (7) a person who deals with an authorised person in the course of the authorised person's carrying on of a regulated activity is to be treated as using services provided by the authorised person in carrying on those activities.

139   Miscellaneous ancillary matters

(1) Rules relating to the handling of money held by an authorised person in specified circumstances ('clients' money') may—

   (a)   make provision which results in that clients' money being held on trust in accordance with the rules;
   (b)   treat two or more accounts as a single account for specified purposes (which may include the distribution of money held in the accounts);
   (c)   authorise the retention by the authorised person of interest accruing on the clients' money; and
   (d)   make provision as to the distribution of such interest which is not to be retained by him.

(2) An institution with which an account is kept in pursuance of rules relating to the handling of clients' money does not incur any liability as constructive trustee if money is wrongfully paid from the account, unless the institution permits the payment—

    (a)   with knowledge that it is wrongful; or

    (b)   having deliberately failed to make enquiries in circumstances in which a reasonable and honest person would have done so.

(3) In the application of subsection (1) to Scotland, the reference to money being held on trust is to be read as a reference to its being held as agent for the person who is entitled to call for it to be paid over to him or to be paid on his direction or to have it otherwise credited to him.

(4) Rules may—

    (a)   confer rights on persons to rescind agreements with, or withdraw offers to, authorised persons within a specified period; and

    (b)   make provision, in respect of authorised persons and persons exercising those rights, for the restitution of property and the making or recovery of payments where those rights are exercised.

(5) 'Rules' means general rules.

(6) 'Specified' means specified in the rules.

140   Restriction on managers of authorised unit trust schemes

(1) The Authority may make rules prohibiting an authorised person who has permission to act as the manager of an authorised unit trust scheme from carrying on a specified activity.

(2) Such rules may specify an activity which is not a regulated activity.

141   Insurance business rules

(1) The Authority may make rules prohibiting an authorised person who has permission to effect or carry out contracts of insurance from carrying on a specified activity.

(2) Such rules may specify an acivity which is not a regulated activity.

(3) The Authority may make rules in relation to contracts entered into by an authorised person in the course of carrying on business which consists of the effecting or carrying out of contracts of long-term insurance.

(4) Such rules may, in particular—

    (a)   restrict the descriptions of property or indices of the value of property by reference to which the benefits under such contracts may be determined;

    (b)   make provision, in the interests of the protection of policyholders, for the substitution of one description of property, or index of value, by reference to which the benefits under a contract are to be determined for another such description of property or index.

(5) Rules made under this section are referred to in this Act as insurance business rules.

142   Insurance business: regulations supplementing Authority's rules

(1) The Treasury may make regulations for the purpose of preventing a person who is not an authorised person but who—

    (a)   is a parent undertaking of an authorised person who has permission to effect or carry out contracts of insurance, and

    (b)   falls within a prescribed class,

from doing anything to lessen the effectiveness of asset identification rules.

(2) 'Asset identification rules' means rules made by the Authority which require an authorised person who has permission to effect or carry out contracts of insurance to identify assets which belong to him and which are maintained in respect of a particular aspect of his business.

(3) The regulations may, in particular, include provision—

    (a)   prohibiting the payment of dividends;

    (b)   prohibiting the creation of charges;

    (c)   making charges created in contravention of the regulations void.

(4) The Treasury may by regulations provide that, in prescribed circumstances, charges created in contravention of asset identification rules are void.

(5) A person who contravenes regulations under subsection (1) is guilty of an offence and liable on summary conviction to a fine not exceeding level 5 on the standard scale.

(6) 'Charges' includes mortgages (or in Scotland securities over property).

143   Endorsement of codes etc.

(1) The Authority may make rules ('endorsing rules')—

    (a)   endorsing the City code on Takeovers and Mergers issued by the Panel on Takeovers and Mergers;

    (b)   endorsing the Rules Governing Substantial Acquisitions of Shares issued by the Panel.

(2) Endorsement may be—

    (a)   as respects all authorised persons; or

    (b)   only as respects a specified kind of authorised person.

(3) At any time when endorsing rules are in force, and if asked to do so by the Panel, the Authority may exercise its powers under Part IV or section 66 as if failure to comply with an endorsed provision was a ground entitling the Authority to exercise those powers.

(4) At any time when endorsing rules are in force and if asked to do so by the Panel, the Authority may exercise its powers under Part XIII, XIV or XXV as if the endorsed provisions were rules applying to the persons in respect of whom they are endorsed.

(5) For the purposes of subsections (3) and (4), a failure to comply with a requirement imposed, or ruling given, under an endorsed provision is to be treated as a failure to comply with the endorsed provision under which that requirement was imposed or ruling was given.

(6) If endorsed provisions are altered, subsections (3) and (4) apply to them as altered, but only if before the alteration the Authority has notified the Panel (and has not withdrawn its notification) that it is satisfied with the Panel's consultation procedures.

(7) 'Consultation procedures' means procedures designed to provide an opportunity for persons likely to be affected by alterations to those provisions to make representations about proposed alterations to any of those provisions.

(8) Subsections (1), (2)(d), (4), (5), (6)(a) and (12) of section 155 apply (with the necessary modifications) to a proposal to give notification of the kind mentioned in subsection (6) as they apply to a proposal to make endorsing rules.

(9) This section applies in relation to particular provisions of the code or rules mentioned in subsection (1) as it applies to the code or the rules.

Specific rules

144   Price stabilising rules

(1) The Authority may make rules ('price stabilising rules') as to—

(a)   the circumstances and manner in which,
(b)   the conditions subject to which, and
(c)   the time when or the period during which,

action may be taken for the purpose of stabilising the price of investments of specified kinds.

(2) Price stabilising rules—

(a)   are to be made so as to apply only to authorised persons;
(b)   may make different provision in relation to different kinds of investment.

(3) The Authority may make rules which, for the purposes of section 397(5)(b), treat a person who acts or engages in conduct—

(a)   for the purpose of stabilising the price of investments, and
(b)   in conformity with such provisions corresponding to price stabilising rules and made by a body or authority outside the United Kingdom as may be specified in the rules under this subsection,

as acting, or engaging in that conduct, for that purpose and in conformity with price stabilising rules.

(4) The Treasury may by order impose limitations on the power to make rules under this section.

(5) Such an order may, in particular—

(a)   specify the kinds of investment in relation to which price stabilising rules may make provision;
(b)   specify the kinds of investment in relation to which rules made under subsection (3) may make provision;
(c)   provide for price stabilising rules to make provision for action to be taken for the purpose of stabilising the price of investments only in such circumstances as the order may specify;
(d)   provide for price stabilising rules to make provision for action to be taken for that purpose only at such times or during such periods as the order may specify.

(6) If provisions specified in rules made under subsection (3) are altered, the rules continue to apply to those provisions as altered, but only if before the alteration the Authority has notified the body or authority concerned (and has not withdrawn its notification) that it is satisfied with its consultation procedures.

(7) 'Consultation procedures' has the same meaning as in section 143.

145   Financial promotion rules

(1) The Authority may make rules applying to authorised persons about the communication by them, or their approval of the communication by others, of invitations or inducements—

(a)   to engage in investment activity; or
(b)   to participate in a collective investment scheme.

(2) Rules under this section may, in particular, make provision about the form and content of communications.

(3) Subsection (1) applies only to communications which—

(a) if made by a person other than an authorised person, without the approval of an authorised person, would contravene section 21(1);

(b) may be made by an authorised person without contravening section 238(1).

(4) 'Engage in investment activity' has the same meaning as in section 21.

(5) The Treasury may by order impose limitations on the power to make rules under this section.

146   Money laundering rules

The Authority may make rules in relation to the prevention and detection of money laundering in connection with the carrying on of regulated activities by authorised persons.

147   Control of information rules

(1) The Authority may make rules ('control of information rules') about the disclosure and use of information held by an authorised person ('A').

(2) Control of information rules may—

(a) require the withholding of information which A would otherwise have to disclose to a person ('B') for or with whom A does business in the course of carrying on any regulated or other activity;

(b) specify circumstances in which A may withhold information which he would otherwise have to disclose to B;

(c) require A not to use for the benefit of B information A holds which A would otherwise have to use in that way;

(d) specify circumstances in which A may decide not to use for the benefit of B information A holds which A would otherwise have to use in that way.

Modification or waiver

148   Modification or waiver of rules

(1) This section applies in relation to the following—

(a)   auditors and actuaries rules;

(b)   control of information rules;

(c)   financial promotion rules;

(d)   general rules;

(e)   insurance business rules;

(f)   money laundering rules; and

(g)   price stabilising rules.

(2) The Authority may, on the application or with the consent of an authorised person, direct that all or any of the rules to which this section applies—

(a)   are not to apply to the authorised person; or

(b)   are to apply to him with such modifications as may be specified in the direction.

(3) An application must be made in such manner as the Authority may direct.

(4) The Authority may not give a direction unless it is satisfied that—

(a) compliance by the authorised person with the rules, or with the rules as unmodified, would be unduly burdensome or would not achieve the purpose for which the rules were made; and

(b)   the direction would not result in undue risk to persons whose interests the rules are intended to protect.

(5) A direction may be given subject to conditions.

(6) Unless it is satisfied that it is inappropriate or unnecessary to do so, a direction must be published by the Authority in such a way as it thinks most suitable for bringing the direction to the attention of—

(a)   those likely to be affected by it; and
(b)   others who may be likely to make an application for a similar direction.

(7) In deciding whether it is satisfied as mentioned in subsection (6), the Authority must—

(a)   take into account whether the direction relates to a rule contravention of which is actionable in accordance with section 150;
(b)   consider whether its publication would prejudice, to an unreasonable degree, the commercial interests of the authorised person concerned or any other member of his immediate group; and
(c)   consider whether its publication would be contrary to an international obligation of the United Kingdom.

(8) For the purposes of paragraphs (b) and (c) of subsection (7), the Authority must consider whether it would be possible to publish the direction without either of the consequences mentioned in those paragraphs by publishing it without disclosing the identity of the authorised person concerned.

(9) The Authority may—

(a)   revoke a direction; or
(b)   vary it on the application, or with the consent, of the authorised person to whom it relates.

(10) 'Direction' means a direction under subsection (2).

(11) 'Immediate group', in relation to an authorised person ('A'), means—

(a)   A;
(b)   a parent undertaking of A;
(c)   a subsidiary undertaking of A;
(d)   a subsidiary undertaking of a parent undertaking of A;
(e)   a parent undertaking of a subsidiary undertaking of A.

Contravention of rules

149   Evidential provisions

(1) If a particular rule so provides, contravention of the rule does not give rise to any of the consequences provided for by other provisions of this Act.

(2) A rule which so provides must also provide—

(a)   that contravention may be relied on as tending to establish contravention of such other rule as may be specified; or
(b)   that compliance may be relied on as tending to establish compliance with such other rule as may be specified.

(3) A rule may include the provision mentioned in subsection (1) only if the Authority considers that it is appropriate for it also to include the provision required by subsection (2).

150   Actions for damages

(1) A contravention by an authorised person of a rule is actionable at the suit of a private person who suffers loss as a result of the contravention, subject to the defences and other incidents applying to actions for breach of statutory duty.

(2) If rules so provide, subsection (1) does not apply to contravention of a specified provision of those rules.

(3) In prescribed cases, a contravention of a rule which would be actionable at the suit of a private person is actionable at the suit of a person who is not a private person, subject to the defences and other incidents applying to actions for breach of statutory duty.

(4) In subsections (1) and (3) 'rule' does not include—

   (a) listing rules; or
   (b) a rule requiring an authorised person to have or maintain financial resources.

(5) 'Private person' has such meaning as may be prescribed.

151   Limits on effect of contravening rules

(1) A person is not guilty of an offence by reason of a contravention of a rule made by the Authority.

(2) No such contravention makes any transaction void or unenforceable.

Procedural provisions

152   Notification of rules to the Treasury

(1) If the Authority makes any rules, it must give a copy to the Treasury without delay.

(2) If the Authority alters or revokes any rules, it must give written notice to the Treasury without delay.

(3) Notice of an alteration must include details of the alteration.

153   Rule-making instruments

(1) Any power conferred on the Authority to make rules is exercisable in writing.

(2) An instrument by which rules are made by the Authority ('a rule-making instrument') must specify the provision under which the rules are made.

(3) To the extent to which a rule-making instrument does not comply with subsection (2), it is void.

(4) A rule-making instrument must be published by the Authority in the way appearing to the Authority to be best calculated to bring it to the attention of the public.

(5) The Authority may charge a reasonable fee for providing a person with a copy of a rule-making instrument.

(6) A person is not to be taken to have contravened any rule made by the Authority if he shows that at the time of the alleged contravention the rule-making instrument concerned had not been made available in accordance with this section.

154   Verification of rules

(1) The production of a printed copy of a rule-making instrument purporting to be made by the Authority—

(a) on which is endorsed a certificate signed by a member of the Authority's staff authorised by it for that purpose, and

(b) which contains the required statements,

is evidence (or in Scotland sufficient evidence) of the facts stated in the certificate.

(2) The required statements are—

(a) that the instrument was made by the Authority;

(b) that the copy is a true copy of the instrument; and

(c) that on a specified date the instrument was made available to the public in accordance with section 153(4).

(3) A certificate purporting to be signed as mentioned in subsection (1) is to be taken to have been properly signed unless the contrary is shown.

(4) A person who wishes in any legal proceedings to rely on a rule-making instrument may require the Authority to endorse a copy of the instrument with a certificate of the kind mentioned in subsection (1).

155   Consultation

(1) If the Authority proposes to make any rules, it must publish a draft of the proposed rules in the way appearing to it to be best calculated to bring them to the attention of the public.

(2) The draft must be accompanied by—

(a) a cost benefit analysis;

(b) an explanation of the purpose of the proposed rules;

(c) an explanation of the Authority's reasons for believing that making the proposed rules is compatible with its general duties under section 2; and

(d) notice that representations about the proposals may be made to the Authority within a specified time.

(3) In the case of a proposal to make rules under a provision mentioned in subsection (9), the draft must also be accompanied by details of the expected expenditure by reference to which the proposal is made.

(4) Before making the proposed rules, the Authority must have regard to any representations made to it in accordance with subsection (2)(d).

(5) If the Authority makes the proposed rules, it must publish an account, in general terms, of—

(a) the representations made to it in accordance with subsection (2)(d); and

(b) its response to them.

(6) If the rules differ from the draft published under subsection (1) in a way which is, in the opinion of the Authority, significant—

(a) the Authority must (in addition to complying with subsection (5)) publish details of the difference; and

(b) those details must be accompanied by a cost benefit analysis.

(7) Subsections (1) to (6) do not apply if the Authority considers that the delay involved in complying with them would be prejudicial to the interests of consumers.

(8) Neither subsection (2)(a) nor subsection (6)(b) applies if the Authority considers—

(a) that, making the appropriate comparison, there will be no increase in costs; or

(b) that, making that comparison, there will be an increase in costs but the increase will be of minimal significance.

(9) Neither subsection (2)(a) nor subsection (6)(b) requires a cost benefit analysis to be carried out in relation to rules made under—

(a)   section 136(2);
(b)   subsection (1) of section 213 as a result of subsection (4) of that section;
(c)   section 234;
(d)   paragraph 17 of Schedule 1.

(10) 'Cost benefit analysis' means an estimate of the costs together with an analysis of the benefits that will arise—

(a)   if the proposed rules are made; or
(b)   if subsection (6) applies, from the rules that have been made.

(11) 'The appropriate comparison' means—

(a)   in relation to subsection (2)(a), a comparison between the overall position if the rules are made and the overall position if they are not made;
(b)   in relation to subsection (6)(b), a comparison between the overall position after the making of the rules and the overall position before they were made.

(12) The Authority may charge a reasonable fee for providing a person with a copy of a draft published under subsection (1).

156   General supplementary powers

(1) Rules made by the Authority may make different provision for different cases and may, in particular, make different provision in respect of different descriptions of authorised person, activity or investment.

(2) Rules made by the Authority may contain such incidental, supplemental, consequential and transitional provision as the Authority considers appropriate.

CHAPTER II

GUIDANCE

157   Guidance

(1) The Authority may give guidance consisting of such information and advice as it considers appropriate—

(a)   with respect to the operation of this Act and of any rules made under it;
(b)   with respect to any matters relating to functions of the Authority;
(c)   for the purpose of meeting the regulatory objectives;
(d)   with respect to any other matters about which it appears to the Authority to be desirable to give information or advice.

(2) The Authority may give financial or other assistance to persons giving information or advice of a kind which the Authority could give under this section.

(3) If the Authority proposes to give guidance to regulated persons generally, or to a class of regulated person, in relation to rules to which those persons are subject, subsections (1), (2) and (4) to (10) of section 155 apply to the proposed guidance as they apply to proposed rules.

(4) The Authority may—

(a)   publish its guidance;

(b) offer copies of its published guidance for sale at a reasonable price; and

(c) if it gives guidance in response to a request made by any person, make a reasonable charge for that guidance.

(5) In this Chapter, references to guidance given by the Authority include references to any recommendation made by the Authority to persons generally, to regulated persons generally or to any class of regulated person.

(6) 'Regulated person' means any—

(a) authorised person;

(b) person who is otherwise subject to rules made by the Authority.

158 Notification of guidance to the Treasury

(1) On giving any general guidance, the Authority must give the Treasury a copy of the guidance without delay.

(2) If the Authority alters any of its general guidance, it must give written notice to the Treasury without delay.

(3) The notice must include details of the alteration.

(4) If the Authority revokes any of its general guidance, it must give written notice to the Treasury without delay.

(5) 'General guidance' means guidance given by the Authority under section 157 which is—

(a) given to persons generally, to regulated persons generally or to a class of regulated person;

(b) intended to have continuing effect; and

(c) given in writing or other legible form.

(6) 'Regulated person' has the same meaning as in section 157.

CHAPTER III

COMPETITION SCRUTINY

159 Interpretation

(1) In this Chapter—

'Director' means the Director General of Fair Trading;

'practices', in relation to the Authority, means practices adopted by the Authority in the exercise of functions under this Act;

'regulating provisions' means any—

(a) rules;

(b) general guidance (as defined by section 158(5));

(c) statement issued by the Authority under section 64;

(d) code issued by the Authority under section 64 or 119.

(2) For the purposes of this Chapter, regulating provisions or practices have a significantly adverse effect on competition if—

(a) they have, or are intended or likely to have, that effect; or

(b) the effect that they have, or are intended or likely to have, is to require or encourage behaviour which has, or is intended or likely to have, a significantly adverse effect on competition.

(3) If regulating provisions or practices have, or are intended or likely to have, the effect of requiring or encouraging exploitation of the strength of a market position they are to be taken, for the purposes of this Chapter, to have an adverse effect on competition.

(4) In determining under this Chapter whether any of the regulating provisions have, or are likely to have, a particular effect, it may be assumed that the persons to whom the provisions concerned are addressed will act in accordance with them.

160   Reports by Director General of Fair Trading

(1) The Director must keep the regulating provisions and the Authority's practices under review.

(2) If at any time the Director considers that—

(a) a regulating provision or practice has a significantly adverse effect on competition, or
(b) two or more regulating provisions or practices taken together, or a particular combination of regulating provisions and practices, have such an effect,

he must make a report to that effect.

(3) If at any time the Director considers that—

(a) a regulating provision or practice does not have a significantly adverse effect on competition, or
(b) two or more regulating provisions or practices taken together, or a particular combination of regulating provisions and practices, do not have any such effect,

he may make a report to that effect.

(4) A report under subsection (2) must include details of the adverse effect on competition.

(5) If the Director makes a report under subsection (2) he must—

(a) send a copy of it to the Treasury, the Competition Commission and the Authority; and
(b) publish it in the way appearing to him to be best calculated to bring it to the attention of the public.

(6) If the Director makes a report under subsection (3)—

(a) he must send a copy of it to the Treasury, the Competition Commission and the Authority; and
(b) he may publish it.

(7) Before publishing a report under this section the Director must, so far as practicable, exclude any matter which relates to the private affairs of a particular individual the publication of which, in the opinion of the Director, would or might seriously and prejudicially affect his interests.

(8) Before publishing such a report the Director must, so far as practicable, exclude any matter which relates to the affairs of a particular body the publication of which, in the opinion of the Director, would or might seriously and prejudicially affect its interests.

(9) Subsections (7) and (8) do not apply in relation to copies of a report which the Director is required to send under subsection (5)(a) or (6)(a).

(10) For the purposes of the law of defamation, absolute privilege attaches to any report of the Director under this section.

161   Power of Director to request information

(1) For the purpose of investigating any matter with a view to its consideration under section 160, the Director may exercise the powers conferred on him by this section.

(2) The Director may by notice in writing require any person to produce to him or to a person appointed by him for the purpose, at a time and place specified in the notice, any document which—

(a)   is specified or described in the notice; and
(b)   is a document in that person's custody or under his control.

(3) The Director may by notice in writing—

(a)   require any person carrying on any business to provide him with such information as may be specified or described in the notice; and
(b)   specify the time within which, and the manner and form in which, any such information is to be provided.

(4) A requirement may be imposed under subsection (2) or (3)(a) only in respect of documents or information which relate to any matter relevant to the investigation.

(5) If a person ('the defaulter') refuses, or otherwise fails, to comply with a notice under this section, the Director may certify that fact in writing to the court and the court may enquire into the case.

(6) If, after hearing any witness who may be produced against or on behalf of the defaulter and any statement which may be offered in defence, the court is satisfied that the defaulter did not have a reasonable excuse for refusing or otherwise failing to comply with the notice, the court may deal with the defaulter as if he were in contempt.

(7) 'Court' means—

(a)   the High Court; or
(b)   in relation to Scotland, the Court of Session.

162   Consideration by Competition Commission

(1) If the Director—

(a)   makes a report under section 160(2), or
(b)   asks the Commission to consider a report that he has made under section 160(3),

the Commission must investigate the matter.

(2) The Commission must then make its own report on the matter unless it considers that, as a result of a change of circumstances, no useful purpose would be served by a report.

(3) If the Commission decides in accordance with subsection (2) not to make a report, it must make a statement setting out the change of circumstances which resulted in that decision.

(4) A report made under this section must state the Commission's conclusion as to whether—

(a)   the regulating provision or practice which is the subject of the report has a significantly adverse effect on competition; or

(b)   the regulating provisions or practices, or combination of regulating provisions and practices, which are the subject of the report have such an effect.

(5) A report under this section stating the Commission's conclusion that there is a significantly adverse effect on competition must also—

(a)   state whether the Commission considers that that effect is justified; and
(b)   if it states that the Commission considers that it is not justified, state its conclusion as to what action, if any, ought to be taken by the Authority.

(6) Subsection (7) applies whenever the Commission is considering, for the purposes of this section, whether a particular adverse effect on competition is justified.

(7) The Commission must ensure, so far as that is reasonably possible, that the conclusion it reaches is compatible with the functions conferred, and obligations imposed, on the Authority by or under this Act.

(8) A report under this section must contain such an account of the Commission's reasons for its conclusions as is expedient, in the opinion of the Commission, for facilitating proper understanding of them.

(9) Schedule 14 supplements this section.

(10) If the Commission makes a report under this section it must send a copy to the Treasury, the Authority and the Director.

163   Role of the Treasury

(1) This section applies if the Competition Commission makes a report under section 162(2) which states its conclusion that there is a significantly adverse effect on competition.

(2) If the Commission's conclusion, as stated in the report, is that the adverse effect on competition is not justified, the Treasury must give a direction to the Authority requiring it to take such action as may be specified in the direction.

(3) But subsection (2) does not apply if the Treasury consider—

(a)   that, as a result of action taken by the Authority in response to the Commission's report, it is unnecessary for them to give a direction; or
(b)   that the exceptional circumstances of the case make it inappropriate or unnecessary for them to do so.

(4) In considering the action to be specified in a direction under subsection (2), the Treasury must have regard to any conclusion of the Commission included in the report because of section 162(5)(b).

(5) Subsection (6) applies if—

(a)   the Commission's conclusion, as stated in its report, is that the adverse effect on competition is justified; but
(b)   the Treasury consider that the exceptional circumstances of the case require them to act.

(6) The Treasury may give a direction to the Authority requiring it to take such action—

(a)   as they consider to be necessary in the light of the exceptional circumstances of the case; and
(b)   as may be specified in the direction.

(7) The Authority may not be required as a result of this section to take any action—

  (a) that it would not have power to take in the absence of a direction under this section; or

  (b) that would otherwise be incompatible with any of the functions conferred, or obligations imposed, on it by or under this Act.

(8) Subsection (9) applies if the Treasury are considering—

  (a) whether subsection (2) applies and, if so, what action is to be specified in a direction under that subsection; or

  (b) whether to give a direction under subsection (6).

(9) The Treasury must—

  (a) do what they consider appropriate to allow the Authority, and any other person appearing to the Treasury to be affected, an opportunity to make representations; and

  (b) have regard to any such representations.

(10) If, in reliance on subsection (3)(a) or (b), the Treasury decline to act under subsection (2), they must make a statement to that effect, giving their reasons.

(11) If the Treasury give a direction under this section they must make a statement giving—

  (a) details of the direction; and

  (b) if the direction is given under subsection (6), their reasons for giving it.

(12) The Treasury must—

  (a) publish any statement made under this section in the way appearing to them best calculated to bring it to the attention of the public; and

  (b) lay a copy of it before Parliament.

164   The Competition Act 1998

(1) The Chapter I prohibition does not apply to an agreement the parties to which consist of or include—

  (a) an unauthorised person, or

  (b) a person who is otherwise subject to the Authority's regulating provisions,

to the extent to which the agreement consists of provisions the inclusion of which in the agreement is encouraged by any of the Authority's regulating provisions.

(2) The Chapter I prohibition does not apply to the practices of an authorised person or a person who is otherwise subject to the regulating provisions to the extent to which the practices are encouraged by any of the Authority's regulating provisions.

(3) The Chapter II prohibition does not apply to conduct of—

  (a) an authorised person, or

  (b) a person who is otherwise subject to the Authority's regulating provisions,

to the extent to which the conduct is encouraged by any of the Authority's regulating provisions.

(4) 'The Chapter I prohibition' means the prohibition imposed by section 2(1) of the Competition Act 1998.

(5) 'The Chapter II prohibition' means the prohibition imposed by section 18(1) of that Act.

PART XI

INFORMATION GATHERING AND INVESTIGATIONS

Powers to gather information

165   Authority's power to require information

(1) The Authority may, by notice in writing given to an authorised person, require him—

(a)   to provide specified information or information of a specified description; or

(b)   to produce specified documents or documents of a specified description.

(2) The information or documents must be provided or produced—

(a)   before the end of such reasonable period as may be specified; and

(b)   at such place as may be specified.

(3) An officer who has written authorisation from the Authority to do so may require an authorised person without delay—

(a)   to provide the officer with specified information or information of a specified description; or

(b)   to produce to him specified documents or documents of a specified description.

(4) This section applies only to information and documents reasonably required in connection with the exercise by the Authority of functions conferred on it by or under this Act.

(5) The Authority may require any information provided under this section to be provided in such form as it may reasonably require.

(6) The Authority may require—

(a)   any information provided, whether in a document or otherwise, to be verified in such manner, or

(b)   any document produced to be authenticated in such manner,

as it may reasonably require.

(7) The powers conferred by subsections (1) and (3) may also be exercised to impose requirements on—

(a)   a person who is connected with an authorised person;

(b)   an operator, trustee or depositary of a scheme recognised under section 270 or 272 who is not an authorised person;

(c)   a recognised investment exchange or recognised clearing house.

(8) 'Authorised person' includes a person who was at any time an authorised person but who has ceasd to be an authorised person.

(9) 'Officer' means an officer of the Authority and includes a member of the Authority's staff or an agent of the Authority.

(10) 'Specified' means—

(a)   in subsections (1) and (2), specified in the notice; and

(b)   in subsection (3), specified in the authorisation.

(11) For the purposes of this section, a person is connected with an authorised person ('A') if he is or has at any relevant time been—

(a)   a member of A's group;
(b)   a controller of A;
(c)   any other member of a partnership of which A is a member; or
(d)   in relation to A, a person mentioned in Part I of Schedule 15.

166   Reports by skilled persons

(1) The Authority may, by notice in writing given to a person to whom subsection (2) applies, require him to provide the Authority with a report on any matter about which the Authority has required or could require the provision of information or production of documents under section 165.

(2) This subsection applies to—

(a)   an authorised person ('A'),
(b)   any other member of A's group,
(c)   a partnership of which A is a member, or
(d)   a person who has at any relevant time been a person falling within paragraph (a), (b) or (c),

who is, or was at the relevant time, carrying on a business.

(3) The Authority may require the report to be in such form as may be specified in the notice.

(4) The person appointed to make a report required by subsection (1) must be a person—

(a)   nominated or approved by the Authority; and
(b)   appearing to the Authority to have the skills necessary to make a report on the matter concerned.

(5) It is the duty of any person who is providing (or who at any time has provided) services to a person to whom subsection (2) applies in relation to a matter on which a report is required under subsection (1) to give a person appointed to provide such a report all such assistance as the appointed person may reasonably require.

(6) The obligation imposed by subsection (5) is enforceable, on the application of the Authority, by an injunction or, in Scotland, by an order for specific performance under section 45 of the Court of Session Act 1988.

Appointment of investigators

167   Appointment of persons to carry out general investigations

(1) If it appears to the Authority or the Secretary of State ('the investigating authority') that there is good reason for doing so, the investigating authority may appoint one or more competent persons to conduct an investigation on its behalf into—

(a)   the nature, conduct or state of the business of an authorised person or of an appointed representative;
(b)   a particular aspect of that business; or
(c)   the ownership or control of an authorised person.

(2) If a person appointed under subsection (1) thinks it necessary for the purposes of his investigation, he may also investigate the business of a person who is or has at any relevant time been—

(a)   a member of the group of which the person under investigation ('A') is part; or

(b)   a partnership of which A is a member.

(3) If a person appointed under subsection (1) decides to investigate the business of any person under subsection (2) he must give that person written notice of his decision.

(4) The power conferred by this section may be exercised in relation to a former authorised person (or appointed representative) but only in relation to—

(a)   business carried on at any time when he was an authorised person (or appointed representative); or

(b)   the ownership or control of a former authorised person at any time when he was an authorised person.

(5) 'Business' includes any part of a business even if it does not consist of carrying on regulated activities.

168   Appointment of persons to carry out investigations in particular cases

(1) Subsection (3) applies if it appears to an investigating authority that there are circumstances suggesting that—

(a)   a person may have contravened any regulation made under section 142; or

(b)   a person may be guilty of an offence under section 177, 191, 346 or 398(1) or under Schedule 4.

(2) Subsection (3) also applies if it appears to an investigating authority that there are circumstances suggesting that—

(a)   an offence under section 24(1) or 397 or under Part V of the Criminal Justice Act 1993 may have been committed;

(b)   there may have been a breach of the general prohibition;

(c)   there may have been a contravention of section 21 or 238; or

(d)   market abuse may have taken place.

(3) The investigating authority may appoint one or more competent persons to conduct an investigation on its behalf.

(4) Subsection (5) applies if it appears to the Authority that there are circumstances suggesting that—

(a)   a person may have contravened section 20;

(b)   a person may be guilty of an offence under prescribed regulations relating to money laundering;

(c)   an authorised person may have contravened a rule made by the Authority;

(d)   an individual may not be a fit and proper person to perform functions in relation to a regulated activity carried on by an authorised or exempt person;

(e)   an individual may have performed or agreed to perform a function in breach of a prohibition order;

(f)   an authorised or exempt person may have failed to comply with section 56(6);

(g)   an authorised person may have failed to comply with section 59(1) or (2);

(h)   a person in relation to whom the Authority has given its approval under section 59 may not be a fit and proper person to perform the function to which that approval relates; or

(i)   a person may be guilty of misconduct for the purposes of section 66.

(5) The Authority may appoint one or more competent persons to conduct an investigation on its behalf.

(6) 'Investigating authority' means the Authority or the Secretary of State.

Assistance to overseas regulators

169   Investigations etc. in support of overseas regulator

(1) At the request of an overseas regulator, the Authority may—

    (a)   exercise the power conferred by section 165; or

    (b)   appoint one or more competent persons to investigate any matter.

(2) An investigator has the same powers as an investigator appointed under section 168(3) (as a result of subsection (1) of that section).

(3) If the request has been made by a competent authority in pursuance of any Community obligation the Authority must, in deciding whether or not to exercise its investigative power, consider whether its exercise is necessary to comply with any such obligation.

(4) In deciding whether or not to exercise its investigative power, the Authority may take into account in particular—

    (a)   whether in the country or territory of the overseas regulator concerned, corresponding assistance would be given to a United Kingdom regulatory authority;

    (b)   whether the case concerns the breach of a law, or other requirement, which has no close parallel in the United Kingdom or involves the assertion of a jurisdiction not recognised by the United Kingdom;

    (c)   the seriousness of the case and its importance to persons in the United Kingdom;

    (d)   whether it is otherwise appropriate in the public interest to give the assistance sought.

(5) The Authority may decide that it will not exercise its investigative power unless the overseas regulator undertakes to make such contribution towards the cost of its exercise as the Authority considers appropriate.

(6) Subsections (4) and (5) do not apply if the Authority considers that the exercise of its investigative power is necessary to comply with a Community obligation.

(7) If the Authority has appointed an investigator in response to a request from an overseas regulator, it may direct the investigator to permit a representative of that regulator to attend, and take part in, any interview conducted for the purposes of the investigation.

(8) A direction under subsection (7) is not to be given unless the Authority is satisfied that any information obtained by an overseas regulator as a result of the interview will be subject to safeguards equivalent to those contained in Part XXIII.

(9) The Authority must prepare a statement of its policy with respect to the conduct of interviews in relation to which a direction under subsection (7) has been given.

(10) The statement requires the approval of the Treasury.

(11) If the Treasury approve the statement, the Authority must publish it.

(12) No direction may be given under subsection (7) before the statement has been published.

(13) 'Overseas regulator' has the same meaning as in section 195.

(14) 'Investigative power' means one of the powers mentioned in subsection (1).

(15) 'Investigator' means a person appointed under subsection (1)(b).

Conduct of investigations

170   Investigations: general

(1) This section applies if an investigating authority appoints one or more competent persons ('investigators') under section 167 or 168(3) or (5) to conduct an investigation on its behalf.

(2) The investigating authority must give written notice of the appointment of an investigator to the person who is the subject of the investigation ('the person under investigation').

(3) Subsections (2) and (9) do not apply if—

- (a) the investigator is appointed as a result of section 168(1) or (4) and the investigating authority believes that the notice required by subsection (2) or (9) would be likely to result in the investigation being frustrated; or
- (b) the investigator is appointed as a result of subsection (2) of section 168.

(4) A notice under subsection (2) must—

- (a) specify the provisions under which, and as a result of which, the investigator was appointed; and
- (b) state the reason for his appointment.

(5) Nothing prevents the investigating authority from appointing a person who is a member of its staff as an investigator.

(6) An investigator must make a report of his investigation to the investigating authority.

(7) The investigating authority may, by a direction to an investigator, control—

- (a) the scope of the investigation;
- (b) the period during which the investigation is to be conducted;
- (c) the conduct of the investigation; and
- (d) the reporting of the investigation.

(8) A direction may, in particular—

- (a) confine the investigation to particular matters;
- (b) extend the investigation to additional matters;
- (c) require the investigator to discontinue the investigation or to take only such steps as are specified in the direction;
- (d) require the investigator to make such interim reports as are so specified.

(9) If there is a change in the scope or conduct of the investigation and, in the opinion of the investigating authority, the person subject to investigation is likely to be significantly prejudiced by not being made aware of it, that person must be given written notice of the change.

(10) 'Investigating authority', in relation to an investigator, means—

- (a) the Authority, if the Authority appointed him;
- (b) the Secretary of State, if the Secretary of State appointed him.

171   Powers of persons appointed under section 167

(1) An investigator may require the person who is the subject of the investigation ('the person under investigation') or any person connected with the person under investigation—

(a) to attend before the investigator at a specified time and place and answer questions; or

(b) otherwise to provide such information as the investigator may require.

(2) An investigator may also require any person to produce at a specified time and place any specified documents or documents of a specified description.

(3) A requirement under subsection (1) or (2) may be imposed only so far as the investigator concerned reasonably considers the question, provision of information or production of the document to be relevant to the purposes of the investigation.

(4) For the purposes of this section and section 172, a person is connected with the person under investigation ('A') if he is or has at any relevant time been—

(a) a member of A's group;

(b) a controller of A;

(c) a partnership of which A is a member; or

(d) in relation to A, a person mentioned in Part I or II of Schedule 15.

(5) 'Investigator' means a person conducting an investigation under section 167.

(6) 'Specified' means specified in a notice in writing.

172 Additional power of persons appointed as a result of section 168(1) or (4)

(1) An investigator has the powers conferred by section 171.

(2) An investigator may also require a person who is neither the subject of the investigation ('the person under investigation') nor a person connected with the person under investigation—

(a) to attend before the investigator at a specified time and place and answer questions; or

(b) otherwise to provide such information as the investigator may require for the purposes of the investigation.

(3) A requirement may only be imposed under subsection (2) if the investigator is satisfied that the requirement is necessary or expedient for the purposes of the investigation.

(4) 'Investigator' means a person appointed as a result of subsection (1) or (4) of section 168.

(5) 'Specified' means specified in a notice in writing.

173 Powers of persons appointed as a result of section 168(2)

(1) Subsections (2) to (4) apply if an investigator considers that any person ('A') is or may be able to give information which is or may be relevant to the investigation.

(2) The investigator may require A—

(a) to attend before him at a specified time and place and answer questions; or

(b) otherwise to provide such information as he may require for the purposes of the investigation.

(3) The investigator may also require A to produce at a specified time and place any specified documents or documents of a specified description which appear to the investigator to relate to any matter relevant to the investigation.

(4) The investigator may also otherwise require A to give him all assistance in connection with the investigation which A is reasonably able to give.

(5) 'Investigator' means a person appointed under subsection (3) of section 168 (as a result of subsection (2) of that section).

174   Admissibility of statements made to investigators

(1) A statement made to an investigator by a person in compliance with an information requirement is admissible in evidence in any proceedings, so long as it also complies with any requirements governing the admissibility of evidence in the circumstances in question.

(2) But in criminal proceedings in which that person is charged with an offence to which this subsection applies or in proceedings in relation to action to be taken against that person under section 123—

(a)   no evidence relating to the statement may be adduced, and

(b)   no question relating to it may be asked,

by or on behalf of the prosecution or (as the case may be) the Authority, unless evidence relating to it is adduced, or a question relating to it is asked, in the proceedings by or on behalf of that person.

(3) Subsection (2) applies to any offence other than one—

(a)   under section 177(4) or 398;

(b)   under section 5 of the Perjury Act 1911 (false statements made otherwise than on oath);

(c)   under section 44(2) of the Criminal Law (Consolidation) (Scotland) Act 1995 (false statements made otherwise than on oath); or

(d)   under Article 10 of the Perjury (Northern Ireland) Order 1979.

(4) 'Investigator' means a person appointed under section 167 or 168(3) or (5).

(5) 'Information requirement' means a requirement imposed by an investigator under section 171, 172, 173 or 175.

175   Information and documents: supplemental provisions

(1) If the Authority or an investigator has power under this Part to require a person to produce a document but it appears that the document is in the possession of a third person, that power may be exercised in relation to the third person.

(2) If a document is produced in response to a requirement imposed under this Part, the person to whom it is produced may—

(a)   take copies or extracts from the document; or

(b)   require the person producing the document, or any relevant person, to provide an explanation of the document.

(3) If a person who is required under this Part to produce a document fails to do so, the Authority or an investigator may require him to state, to the best of his knowledge and belief, where the document is.

(4) A lawyer may be required under this Part to furnish the name and address of his client.

(5) No person may be required under this Part to disclose information or produce a document in respect of which he owes an obligation of confidence by virtue of carrying on the business of banking unless—

(a)   he is the person under investigation or a member of that person's group;

(b)   the person to whom the obligation of confidence is owed is the person under investigation or a member of that person's group;

(c)   the person to whom the obligation of confidence is owed consents to the disclosure or production; or

(d)   the imposing on him of a requirement with respect to such information or document has been specifically authorised by the investigating authority.

(6) If a person claims a lien on a document, its production under this Part does not affect the lien.

(7) 'Relevant person', in relation to a person who is required to produce a document, means a person who—

(a)   has been or is or is proposed to be a director or controller of that person;

(b)   has been or is an auditor of that person;

(c)   has been or is an actuary, accountant or lawyer appointed or instructed by that person; or

(d)   has been or is an employee of that person.

(8) 'Investigator' means a person appointed under section 167 or 168(3) or (5).

176   Entry of premises under warrant

(1) A justice of the peace may issue a warrant under this section if satisfied on information on oath given by or on behalf of the Secretary of State, the Authority or an investigator that there are reasonable grounds for believing that the first, second or third set of conditions is satisfied.

(2) The first set of conditions is—

(a)   that a person on whom an information requirement has been imposed has failed (wholly or in part) to comply with it; and

(b)   that on the premises specified in the warrant—
   (i)   there are documents which have been required; or
   (ii)   there is information which has been required.

(3) The second set of conditions is—

(a)   that the premises specified in the warrant are premises of an authorised person or an appointed representative;

(b)   that there are on the premises documents or information in relation to which an information requirement could be imposed; and

(c)   that if such a requirement were to be imposed—
   (i)   it would not be complied with; or
   (ii)   the documents or information to which it related would be removed, tampered with or destroyed.

(4) The third set of conditions is—

(a)   that an offence mentioned in section 168 for which the maximum sentence on conviction on indictment is two years or more has been (or is being) committed by any person;

(b)   that there are on the premises specified in the warrant documents or information relevant to whether that offence has been (or is being) committed;

(c)   that an information requirement could be imposed in relation to those documents or information; and

(d)   that if such a requirement were to be imposed—
   (i)   it would not be complied with; or
   (ii)   the documents or information to which it related would be removed, tampered with or destroyed.

(5) A warrant under this section shall authorise a constable—

(a) to enter the premises specified in the warrant;

(b) to search the premises and take possession of any documents or information appearing to be documents or information of a kind in respect of which a warrant under this section was issued ('the relevant kind') or to take, in relation to any such documents or information, any other steps which may appear to be necessary for preserving them or preventing interference with them;

(c) to take copies of, or extracts from, any documents or information appearing to be of the relevant kind;

(d) to require any person on the premises to provide an explanation of any document or information appearing to be of the relevnt kind or to state where it may be found; and

(e) to use such force as may be reasonably necessary.

(6) In England and Wales, sections 15(5) to (8) and section 16 of the Police and Criminal Evidence Act 1984 (execution of search warrants and safeguards) apply to warrants issued under this section.

(7) In Northern Ireland, Articles 17(5) to (8) and 18 of the Police and Criminal Evidence (Northern Ireland) Order 1989 apply to warrants issued under this section.

(8) Any document of which possession is taken under this section may be retained—

(a) for a period of three months; or

(b) if within that period proceedings to which the document is relevant are commenced against any person for any criminal offence, until the conclusion of those proceedings.

(9) In the application of this section to Scotland—

(a) for the references to a justice of the peace substitute references to a justice of the peace or a sheriff; and

(b) for the references to information on oath substitute references to evidence on oath.

(10) 'Investigator' means a person appointed under section 167 or 168(3) or (5).

(11) 'Information requirement' means a requirement imposed—

(a) by the Authority under section 167 or 175; or

(b) by an investigator under section 171, 172, 173, 175.

Offences

177   Offences

(1) If a person other than the investigator ('the defaulter') fails to comply with a requirement imposed on him under this Part the person imposing the requirement may certify that fact in writing to the court.

(2) If the court is satisfied that the defaulter failed without reasonable excuse to comply with the requirement, it may deal with the defaulter (and in the case of a body corporate, any director or officer) as if he were in contempt.

(3) A person who knows or suspects that an investigation is being or is likely to be conducted under this Part is guilty of an offence if—

(a) he falsifies, conceals, destroys or otherwise disposes of a document which he knows or suspects is or would be relevant to such an investigation, or

(b) he causes or permits the falsification, concealment, destruction or disposal of such a document, unless he shows that he had no intention of concealing facts disclosed by the documents from the investigator.

(4) A person who, in purported compliance with a requirement imposed on him under this Part—

(a)   provides information which he knows to be false or misleading in a material particular, or

(b)   recklessly provides information which is false or misleading in a material particular,

is guilty of an offence.

(5) A person guilty of an offence under subsection (3) or (4) is liable—

(a)   on summary conviction, to imprisonment for a term not exceeding six months or a fine not exceeding the statutory maximum, or both;

(b)   on conviction on indictment, to imprisonment for a term not exceeding two years or a fine, or both.

(6) Any person who intentionally obstructs the exercise of any rights conferred by a warrant under section 176 is guilty of an offence and liable on summary conviction to imprisonment for a term not exceeding three months or a fine not exceeding level 5 on the standard scale, or both.

(7) 'Court' means—

(a)   the High Court;

(b)   in Scotland, the Court of Session.

PART XII

CONTROL OVER AUTHORISED PERSONS

Notice of control

178   Obligation to notify the Authority

(1) If a step which a person proposes to take would result in his acquiring—

(a)   control over a UK authorised person,

(b)   an additional kind of control over a UK authorised person, or

(c)   an increase in a relevant kind of control which he already has over a UK authorised person,

he must notify the Authority of his proposal.

(2) A person who, without himself taking any such step, acquires any such control or additional or increased control must notify the Authority before the end of the period of 14 days beginning with the day on which he first becomes aware that he has acquired it.

(3) A person who is under the duty to notify the Authority imposed by subsection (1) must also give notice to the Authority on acquiring, or increasing, the control in question.

(4) In this Part 'UK authorised person' means an authorised person who—

(a)   is a body incorporated in, or an unincorporated association formed under the law of, any part of the United Kingdom; and

(b)   is not a person authorised as a result of paragraph 1 of Schedule 5.

(5) A notice under subsection (1) or (2) is referred to in this Part as 'a notice of control'.

Acquiring, increasing and reducing control

179   Acquiring control

(1) For the purposes of this Part, a person ('the acquirer') acquires control over a UK authorised person ('A') on first falling within any of the cases in subsection (2).

(2) The cases are where the acquirer—

   (a)   holds 10% or more of the shares in A;
   (b)   is able to exercise significant influence over the management of A by virtue of his shareholding in A;
   (c)   holds 10% or more of the shares in a parent undertaking ('P') of A;
   (d)   is able to exercise significant influence over the management of P by virtue of his shareholding in P;
   (e)   is entitled to exercise, or control the exercise of, 10% or more of the voting power in A;
   (f)   is able to exercise significant influence over the management of A by virtue of his voting power in A;
   (g)   is entitled to exercise, or control the exercise of, 10% or more of the voting power in P; or
   (h)   is able to exercise significant influence over the management of P by virtue of his voting power in P.

(3) In subsection (2) 'the acquirer' means—

   (a)   the acquirer;
   (b)   any of the acquirer's associates; or
   (c)   the acquirer and any of his associates.

(4) For the purposes of this Part, each of the following is to be regarded as a kind of control—

   (a)   control arising as a result of the holding of shares in A;
   (b)   control arising as a result of the holding of shares in P;
   (c)   control arising as a result of the entitlement to exercise, or control the exercise of, voting power in A;
   (d)   control arising as a result of the entitlement to exercise, or control the exercise of, voting power in P.

(5) For the purposes of this section and sections 180 and 181, 'associate', 'shares' and 'voting power' have the same meaning as in section 422.

180   Increasing control

(1) For the purposes of this Part, a controller of a person ('A') who is a UK authorised person increases his control over A if—

   (a)   the percentage of shares held by the controller in A increases by any of the steps mentioned in subsection (2);
   (b)   the percentage of shares held by the controller in a parent undertaking ('P') of A increases by any of the steps mentioned in subsection (2);
   (c)   the percentage of voting power which the controller is entitled to execise, or control the exercise of, in A increases by any of the steps mentioned in subsection (2);
   (d)   the percentage of voting power which the controller is entitled to exercise, or control the exercise of, in P increases by any of the steps mentioned in subsection (2); or
   (e)   the controller becomes a parent undertaking of A.

(2) The steps are—

    (a)   from below 10% to 10% or more but less than 20%;
    (b)   from below 20% to 20% or more but less than 33%;
    (c)   from below 33% to 33% or more but less than 50%;
    (d)   from below 50% to 50% or more.

(3) In paragraphs (a) to (d) of subsection (1) 'the controller' means—

    (a)   the controller;
    (b)   any of the controller's associates; or
    (c)   the controller and any of his associates.

(4) In the rest of this Part 'acquiring control' or 'having control' includes—

    (a)   acquiring or having an additional kind of control; or
    (b)   acquiring an increase in a relevant kind of control, or having increased control of a relevant kind.

181   Reducing control

(1) For the purposes of this Part, a controller of a person ('A') who is a UK authorised person reduces his control over A if—

    (a)   the percentage of shares held by the controller in A decreases by any of the steps mentioned in subsection (2),
    (b)   the percentage of shares held by the controller in a parent undertaking ('P') of A decreases by any of the steps mentioned in subsection (2),
    (c)   the percentage of voting power which the controller is entitled to exercise, or control the exercise of, in A decreases by any of the steps mentioned in subsection (2),
    (d)   the percentage of voting power which the controller is entitled to exercise, or control the exercise of, in P decreases by any of the steps mentioned in subsection (2), or
    (e)   the controller ceases to be a parent undertaking of A,

unless the controller ceases to have the kind of control concerned over A as a result.

(2) The steps are—

    (a)   from 50% or more to 33% or more but less than 50%;
    (b)   from 33% or more to 20% or more but less than 33%;
    (c)   from 20% or more to 10% or more but less than 20%;
    (d)   from 10% or more to less than 10%.

(3) In paragraphs (a) to (d) of subsection (1) 'the controller' means—

    (a)   the controller;
    (b)   any of the controller's associates; or
    (c)   the controller and any of his associates.

Acquiring or increasing control: procedure

182   Notification

(1) A notice of control must—

    (a)   be given to the Authority in writing; and
    (b)   include such information and be accompanied by such documents as the Authority may reasonably require.

(2) The Authority may require the person giving a notice of control to provide such additional information or documents as it reasonably considers necessary in order to enable it to determine what action it is to take in response to the notice.

(3) Different requirements may be imposed in different circumstances.

183   Duty of Authority in relation to notice of control

(1) The Authority must, before the end of the period of three months beginning with the date on which it receives a notice of control ('the period for consideration'), determine whether—

  (a)   to approve of the person concerned having the control to which the notice relates; or
  (b)   to serve a warning notice under subsection (3) or section 185(3).

(2) Before doing so, the authority must comply with such requirements as to consultation with competent authorities outside the United Kingdom as may be prescribed.

(3) If the Authority proposes to give the person concerned a notice of objection under section 186(1), it must give him a warning notice.

184   Approval of acquisition of control

(1) If the Authority decides to approve of the person concerned having the control to which the notice relates it must notify that person of its approval in writing without delay.

(2) If the Authority fails to comply with subsection (1) of section 183 it is to be treated as having given its approval and notified the person concerned at the end of the period fixed by that subsection.

(3) The Authority's approval remains effective only if the person to whom it relates acquires the control in question—

  (a)   before the end of such period as may be specified in the notice; or
  (b)   if no period is specified, before the end of the period of one year beginning with the date—
     (i)   of the notice of approval;
     (ii)   on which the Authority is treated as having given approval under subsection (2); or
     (iii) of a decision on a reference to the Tribunal which results in the person concerned receiving approval.

185   Conditions attached to approval

(1) The Authority's approval under section 184 may be given unconditionally or subject to such conditions as the Authority considers appropriate.

(2) In imposing any conditions, the Authority must have regard to its duty under section 41.

(3) If the Authority proposes to impose conditions on a person it must give him a warning notice.

(4) If the Authority decides to impose conditions on a person it must give him a decision notice.

(5) A person who is subject to a condition imposed under this section may apply to the Authority—

  (a)   for the condition to be varied; or
  (b)   for the condition to be cancelled.

(6) The Authority may, on its own initiative, cancel a condition imposed under this section.

(7) If the Authority has given its approval to a person subject to a condition, he may refer to the Tribunal—

    (a)   the imposition of the condition; or

    (b)   the Authority's decision to refuse an application made by him under subsection (5).

186   Objection to acquisition of control

(1) On considering a notice of control, the Authority may give a decision notice under this section to the person acquiring control ('the acquirer') unless it is satisfied that the approval requirements are met.

(2) The approval requirements are that—

    (a)   the acquirer is a fit and proper person to have the control over the authorised person that he has or would have if he acquired the control in question; and

    (b)   the interests of consumers would not be threatened by the acquirer's control or by his acquiring that control.

(3) In deciding whether the approval requirements are met, the Authority must have regard, in relation to the control that the acquirer—

    (a)   has over the authorised person concerned ('A'), or

    (b)   will have over A if the proposal to which the notice of control relates is carried into effect,

to its duty under section 41 in relation to each regulated activity carried on by A.

(4) If the Authority gives a notice under this section but considers that the approval requirements would be met if the person to whom a notice is given were to take, or refrain from taking, a particular step, the notice must identify that step.

(5) A person to whom a notice under this section is given may refer the matter to the Tribunal.

(6) 'Consumers' means persons who are consumers for the purposes of section 138.

187   Objection to existing control

(1) If the Authority is not satisfied that the approval requirements are met, it may give a decision notice under this section to a person if he has failed to comply with a duty to notify imposed by section 178.

(2) If the failure relates to subsection (1) or (2) of that section, the Authority may (instead of giving a notice under subsection (1)) approve the acquisition of the control in question by the person concerned as if he had given it a notice of control.

(3) The Authority may also give a decision notice under this section to a person who is a controller of a UK authorised person if the Authority becomes aware of matters as a result of which it is satisfied that—

    (a)   the approval requirements are not met with respect to the controller; or

    (b)   a condition imposed under section 185 required that person to do (or refrain from doing) a particular thing and the condition has been breached as a result of his failing to do (or doing) that thing.

(4) A person to whom a notice under this section is given may refer the matter to the Tribunal.

(5) 'Approval requirements' has the same meaning as in section 186.

188   Notices of objection under section 187: procedure

(1) If the Authority proposes to give a notice of objection to a person under section 187, it must give him a warning notice.

(2) Before doing so, the Authority must comply with such requirements as to consultation with competent authorities outside the United Kingdom as may be prescribed.

(3) If the Authority decides to give a warning notice under this section, it must do so before the end of the period of three months beginning—

> (a)   in the case of a notice to be given under section 187(1), with the date on which it became aware of the failure to comply with the duty in question;
> (b)   in the case of a notice to be given under section 187(3), with the date on which it became aware of the matters in question.

(4) The Authority may require the person concerned to provide such additional information or documents as it considers reasonable.

(5) Different requirements may be imposed in different circumstances.

(6) In this Part 'notice of objection' means a notice under section 186 or 187.

Improperly acquired shares

189   Improperly acquired shares

(1) The powers conferred by this section are exercisable if a person has acquired, or has continued to hold, any shares in contravention of—

> (a)   a notice of objection; or
> (b)   a condition imposed on the Authority's approval.

(2) The Authority may by notice in writing served on the person concerned ('a restriction notice') direct that any such shares which are specified in the notice are, until further notice, subject to one or more of the following restrictions—

> (a)   a transfer of (or agreement to transfer) those shares, or in the case of unissued shares any transfer of (or agreement to transfer) the right to be issued with them, is void;
> (b)   no voting rights are to be exercisable in respect of the shares;
> (c)   no further shares are to be issued in right of them or in pursuance of any offer made to their holder;
> (d)   except in a liquidation, no payment is to be made of any sums due from the body corporate on the shares, whether in respect of capital or otherwise.

(3) The court may, on the application of the Authority, order the sale of any shares to which this section applies and, if they are for the time being subject to any restriction under subsection (2), that they are to cease to be subject to that restriction.

(4) No order may be made under subsection (3)—

> (a)   until the end of the period within which a reference may be made to the Tribunal in respect of the notice of objection; and
> (b)   if a reference is made, until the matter has been determined or the reference withdrawn.

(5) If an order has been made under subsection (3), the court may, on the application of the Authority, make such further order relating to the sale or transfer of the shares as it thinks fit.

(6) If shares are sold in pursuance of an order under this section, the proceeds of sale, less the costs of the sale, must be paid into court for the benefit of the persons beneficially interested in them; and any such person may apply to the court for the whole or part of the proceeds to be paid to him.

(7) This section applies—

    (a) in the case of an acquirer falling within section 178(1), to all the shares—
        (i)   in the authorised person which the acquirer has acquired;
        (ii) which are held by him or an associate of his; and
        (iii) which were not so held immediately before he became a person with control over the authorised person;
    (b) in the case of an acquirer falling within section 178(2), to all the shares held by him or an associate of his at the time when he first became aware that he had acquired control over the authorised person; and
    (c) to all the shares in an undertaking ('C')—
        (i)   which are held by the acquirer or an associate of his,
        and
        (ii) which were not so held before he became a person with control in relation to the authorised person,
        where C is the undertaking in which shares were acquired by the acquirer (or an associate of his) and, as a result, he became a person with control in relation to that authorised person.

(8) A copy of the restriction notice must be served on—

    (a) the authorised person to whose shares it relates; and
    (b) if it relates to shares held by an associate of that authorised person, on that associate.

(9) The jurisdiction conferred by this section may be exercised by the High Court and the Court of Session.

Reducing control: procedure

190 Notification

(1) If a step which a controller of a UK authorised person proposes to take would result in his—

    (a) ceasing to have control of a relevant kind over the authorised person, or
    (b) reducing a relevant kind of control over that person,

he must notify the Authority of his proposal.

(2) A controller of a UK authorised person who, without himself taking any such step, ceases to have that control or reduces that control must notify the Authority before the end of the period of 14 days beginning with the day on which he first becomes aware that—

    (a) he has ceased to have the control in question; or
    (b) he has reduced that control.

(3) A person who is under the duty to notify the Authority imposed by subsection (1) must also give a notice to the Authority—

    (a) on ceasing to have the control in question; or
    (b) on reducing that control.

(4) A notice under this section must—

(a)   be given to the Authority in writing; and
(b)   include details of the extent of the control (if any) which the person concerned will retain (or still retains) over the authorised person concerned.

Offences

191   Offences under this Part

(1) A person who fails to comply with the duty to notify the Authority imposed on him by section 178(1) or 190(1) is guilty of an offence.

(2) A person who fails to comply with the duty to notify the Authority imposed on him by section 178(2) or 190(2) is guilty of an offence.

(3) If a person who has given a notice of control to the Authority carries out the proposal to which the notice relates, he is guilty of an offence if—

(a)   the period of three months beginning with the date on which the Authority received the notice is still running; and
(b)   the Authority has not responded to the notice by either giving its approval or giving him a warning notice under section 183(3) or 185(3).

(4) A person to whom the Authority has given a warning notice under section 183(3) is guilty of an offence if he carries out the proposal to which the notice relates before the Authority has decided whether to give him a notice of objection.

(5) A person to whom a notice of objection has been given is guilty of an offence if he acquires the control to which the notice applies at a time when the notice is still in force.

(6) A person guilty of an offence under subsection (1), (2), (3) or (4) is liable on summary conviction to a fine not exceeding level 5 on the standard scale.

(7) A person guilty of an offence under subsection (5) is liable—

(a)   on summary conviction, to a fine not exceeding the statutory maximum; and
(b)   on conviction on indictment, to imprisonment for a term not exceeding two years or a fine, or both.

(8) A person guilty of an offence under subsection (5) is also liable on summary conviction to a fine not exceeding one tenth of the statutory maximum for each day on which the offence has continued.

(9) It is a defence for a person charged with an offence under subsection (1) to show that he had, at the time of the alleged offence, no knowledge of the act or circumstances by virtue of which the duty to notify the Authority arose.

(10) If a person—

(a)   was under the duty to notify the Authority imposed by section 178(1) or 190(1) but had no knowledge of the act or circumstances by virtue of which that duty arose, but
(b)   subsequently becomes aware of that act or those circumstances,

he must notify the Authority before the end of the period of 14 days beginning with the day on which he first became so aware.

(11) A person who fails to comply with the duty to notify the Authority imposed by subsection (10) is guilty of an offence and liable, on summary conviction, to a fine not exceeding level 5 on the standard scale.

Miscellaneous

192 Power to change definitions of control etc.

The Treasury may by order—

  (a) provide for exemptions from the obligations to notify imposed by sections 178 and 190;

  (b) amend section 179 by varying, or removing, any of the cases in which a person is treated as having control over a UK authorised person or by adding a case;

  (c) amend section 180 by varying, or removing, any of the cases in which a person is treated as increasing control over a UK authorised person or by adding a case;

  (d) amend section 181 by varying, or removing, any of the cases in which a person is treated as reducing his control over a UK authorised person or by adding a case;

  (e) amend section 422 by varying, or removing, any of the cases in which a person is treated as being a controller of a person or by adding a case.

PART XIII

INCOMING FIRMS: INTERVENTION BY AUTHORITY

Interpretation

193 Interpretation of this Part

(1) In this Part—

'additional procedure' means the procedure described in section 199;
'incoming firm' means—

  (a) an EEA firm which is exercising, or has exercised, its right to carry on a regulated activity in the United Kingdom in accordance with Schedule 3; or

  (b) a Treaty firm which is exercising, or has exercised, its right to carry on a regulated activity in the United Kingdom in accordance with Schedule 4; and

'power of intervention' means the power conferred on the Authority by section 196.

(2) In relation to an incoming firm which is an EEA firm, expressions used in this Part and in Schedule 3 have the same meaning in this Part as they have in that Schedule.

194 General grounds on which power of intervention is exercisable

(1) The Authority may exercise its power of intervention in respect of an incoming firm if it appears to it that—

  (a) the firm has contravened, or is likely to contravene, a requirement which is imposed on it by or under this Act (in a case where the Authority is responsible for enforcing compliance in the United Kingdom);

  (b) the firm has, in purported compliance with any requirement imposed by or under this Act, knowingly or recklessly given the Authority information which is false or misleading in a material particular; or

  (c) it is desirable to exercise the power in order to protect the interests of actual or potential customers.

(2) Subsection (3) applies to an incoming EEA firm falling within subparagraph (a) or (b) of paragraph 5 of Schedule 3 which is exercising an EEA right to carry on any Consumer Credit Act business in the United Kingdom.

(3) The Authority may exercise its power of intervention in respect of the firm if the Director General of Fair Trading has informed the Authority that—

(a)   the firm,
(b)   any of the firm's employees, agents or associates (whether past or present), or
(c)   if the firm is a body corporate, a controller of the firm or an associate of such a controller,

has done any of the things specified in paragraphs (a) to (d) of section 25(2) of the Consumer Credit Act 1974.

(4) 'Associate', 'Consumer Credit Act business' and 'controller' have the same meaning as in section 203.

195   Exercise of power in support of overseas regulator

(1) The Authority may exercise its power of intervention in respect of an incoming firm at the request of, or for the purpose of assisting, an overseas regulator.

(2) Subsection (1) applies whether or not the Authority's power of intervention is also exercisable as a result of section 194.

(3) 'An overseas regulator' means an authority in a country or territory outside the United Kingdom—

(a)   which is a home state regulator; or
(b)   which exercises any function of a kind mentioned in subsection (4).

(4) The functions are—

(a)   a function corresponding to any function of the Authority under this Act;
(b)   a function corresponding to any function exercised by the competent authority under Part VI in relation to the listing of shares;
(c)   a function corresponding to any function exercised by the Secretary of State under the Companies Act 1985;
(d)   a function in connection with—
  (i)   the investigation of conduct of the kind prohibited by Part V of the Criminal Justice Act 1993 (insider dealing); or
  (ii)   the enforcement of rules (whether or not having the force of law) relating to such conduct;
(e)   a function prescribed by regulations made for the purposes of this subsection which, in the opinion of the Treasury, relates to companies or financial services.

(5) If—

(a)   a request to the Authority for the exercise of its power of intervention has been made by a home state regulator in pursuance of a Community obligation, or
(b)   a home state regulator has notified the Authority that an EEA firm's EEA authorisation has been withdrawn,

the Authority must, in deciding whether or not to exercise its power of intervention, consider whether exercising it is necessary in order to comply with a Community obligation.

(6) In deciding in any case in which the Authority does not consider that the exercise of its power of intervention is necessary in order to comply with a Community obligation, it may take into account in particular—

(a)   whether in the country or territory of the overseas regulator concerned, corresponding assistance would be given to a United Kingdom regulatory authority;

(b) whether the case concerns the breach of a law, or other requirement, which has no close parallel in the United Kingdom or involves the assertion of a jurisdiction not recognised by the United Kingdom;

(c) the seriousness of the case and its importance to persons in the United Kingdom;

(d) whether it is otherwise appropriate in the public interest to give the assistance sought.

(7) The Authority may decide not to exercise its power of intervention, in response to a request, unless the regulator concerned undertakes to make such contribution to the cost of its exercise as the Authority considers appropriate.

(8) Subsection (7) does not apply if the Authority decides that it is necessary for it to exercise its power of intervention in order to comply with a Community obligation.

196 The power of intervention

If the Authority is entitled to exercise its power of intervention in respect of an incoming firm under this Part, it may impose any requirement in relation to the firm which it could impose if—

(a) the firm's permission was a Part IV permission; and

(b) the Authority was entitled to exercise its power under that Part to vary that permission.

Exercise of power of intervention

197 Procedure on exercise of power of intervention

(1) A requirement takes effect—

(a) immediately, if the notice given under subsection (3) states that that is the case;

(b) on such date as may be specified in the notice; or

(c) if no date is specified in the notice, when the matter to which it relates is no longer open to review.

(2) A requirement may be expressed to take effect immediately (or on a specified date) only if the Authority, having regard to the ground on which it is exercising its power of intervention, considers that it is necessary for the requirement to take effect immediately (or on that date).

(3) If the Authority proposes to impose a requirement under section 196 on an incoming firm, or imposes such a requirement with immediate effect, it must give the firm written notice.

(4) The notice must—

(a) give details of the requirement;

(b) inform the firm of when the requirement takes effect;

(c) state the Authority's reasons for imposing the requirement and for its determination as to when the requirement takes effect;

(d) inform the firm that it may make representations to the Authority within such period as may be specified in the notice (whether or not it has referred the matter to the Tribunal); and

(e) inform it of its right to refer the matter to the Tribunal.

(5) The Authority may extend the period allowed under the notice for making representations.

(6) If, having considered any representations made by the firm, the Authority decides—

(a) to impose the requirement proposed, or

(b) if it has been imposed, not to rescind the requirement,

it must give it written notice.

(7) If, having considered any representations made by the firm, the Authority decides—

(a) not to impose the requirement proposed,

(b) to impose a different requirement from that proposed, or

(c) to rescind a requirement which has effect,

it must give it written notice.

(8) A notice given under subsection (6) must inform the firm of its right to refer the matter to the Tribunal.

(9) A notice under subsection (7)(b) must comply with subsection (4).

(10) If a notice informs a person of his right to refer a matter to the Tribunal, it must give an indication of the procedure on such a reference.

198   Power to apply to court for injunction in respect of certain overseas insurance companies

(1) This section applies if the Authority has received a request made in respect of an incoming EEA firm in accordance with—

(a) Article 20.5 of the first non-life insurance directive; or

(b) Article 24.5 of the first life insurance directive.

(2) The court may, on an application made to it by the Authority with respect to the firm, grant an injunction restraining (or in Scotland an interdict prohibiting) the firm disposing of or otherwise dealing with any of its assets.

(3) If the court grants an injunction, it may by subsequent orders make provision for such incidental, consequential and supplementary matters as it considers necessary to enable the Authority to perform any of its functions under this Act.

(4) 'The court' means—

(a) the High Court; or

(b) in Scotland, the Court of Session.

199   Additional procedure for EEA firms in certain cases

(1) This section applies if it appears to the Authority that its power of intervention is exercisable in relation to an EEA firm exercising EEA rights in the United Kingdom ('an incoming EEA firm') in respect of the contravention of a relevant requirement.

(2) A requirement is relevant if—

(a) it is imposed by the Authority under this Act; and

(b) as respects its contravention, any of the single market directives provides that a procedure of the kind set out in the following provisions of this section is to apply.

(3) The Authority must, in writing, require the firm to remedy the situation.

(4) If the firm fails to comply with the requirement under subsection (3) within a reasonable time, the Authority must give a notice to that effect to the firm's home state regulator requesting it—

(a) to take all appropriate measures for the purpose of ensuring that the firm remedies the situation which has given rise to the notice; and

(b) to inform the Authority of the measures it proposes to take or has taken or the reasons for not taking such measures.

(5) Except as mentioned in subsection (6), the Authority may not exercise its power of intervention unless satisfied—

(a) that the firm's home state regulator has failed or refused to take measures for the purpose mentioned in subsection (4)(a); or

(b) that the measures taken by the home state regulator have proved inadequate for that purpose.

(6) If the Authority decides that it should exercise its power of intervention in respect of the incoming EEA firm as a matter of urgency in order to protect the interests of consumers, it may exercise that power—

(a) before complying with subsections (3) and (4); or

(b) where it has complied with those subsections, before it is satisfied as mentioned in subsection (5).

(7) In such a case the Authority must at the earliest opportunity inform the firm's home state regulator and the Commission.

(8) If—

(a) the Authority has (by virtue of subsection (6)) exercised its power of intervention before complying with subsections (3) and (4) or before it is satisfied as mentioned in subsection (5), and

(b) the Commission decides under any of the single market directives that the Authority must rescind or vary any requirement imposed in the exercise of its power of intervention,

the Authority must in accordance with the decision rescind or vary the requirement.

Supplemental

200 Rescission and variation of requirements

(1) The Authority may rescind or vary a requirement imposed in exercise of its power of intervention on its own initiative or on the application of the person subject to the requirement.

(2) The power of the Authority on its own initiative to rescind a requirement is exercisable by written notice given by the Authority to the person concerned, which takes effect on the date specified in the notice.

(3) Section 197 applies to the exercise of the power of the Authority on its own initiative to vary a requirement as it applies to the imposition of a requirement.

(4) If the Authority proposes to refuse an application for the variation or rescission of a requirement, it must give the applicant a warning notice.

(5) If the Authority decides to refuse an application for the variation or rescission of a requirement—

(a) the Authority must give the applicant a decision notice; and

(b) that person may refer the matter to the Tribunal.

201 Effect of certain requirements on other persons

If the Authority, in exercising its power of intervention, imposes on an incoming firm a requirement of a kind mentioned in subsection (3) of section 48, the requirement has the same effect in relation to the firm as it would have in relation to an authorised person if it had been imposed on the authorised person by the Authority acting under section 45.

202   Contravention of requirement imposed under this Part

(1) Contravention of a requirement imposed by the Authority under this Part does not—

(a)   make a person guilty of an offence;
(b)   make any transaction void or unenforceable; or
(c)   (subject to subsection (2)) give rise to any right of action for breach of statutory duty.

(2) In prescribed cases the contravention is actionable at the suit of a person who suffers loss as a result of the contravention, subject to the defences and other incidents applying to actions for breach of statutory duty.

Powers of Director General of Fair Trading

203   Power to prohibit the carrying on of Consumer Credit Act business

(1) If it appears to the Director General of Fair Trading ('the Director') that subsection (4) has been, or is likely to be, contravened as respects a consumer credit EEA firm, he may by written notice given to the firm impose on the firm a consumer credit prohibition.

(2) If it appears to the Director that a restriction imposed under section 204 on an EEA consumer credit firm has not been complied with, he may by written notice given to the firm impose a consumer credit prohibition.

(3) 'Consumer credit prohibition' means a prohibition on carrying on, or purporting to carry on, in the United Kingdom any Consumer Credit Act business which consists of or includes carrying on one or more listed activities.

(4) This subsection is contravened as respects a firm if—

(a)   the firm or any of its employees, agents or associates (whether past or present), or
(b)   if the firm is a body corporate, any controller of the firm or an associate of any such controller,

does any of the things specified in paragraphs (a) to (d) of section 25(2) of the Consumer Credit Act 1974.

(5) A consumer credit prohibition may be absolute or may be imposed—

(a)   for such period,
(b)   until the occurrence of such event, or
(c)   until such conditions are complied with,

as may be specified in the notice given under subsection (1) or (2).

(6) Any period, event or condition so specified may be varied by the Director on the application of the firm concerned.

(7) A consumer credit prohibition may be withdrawn by written notice served by the Director on the firm concerned, and any such notice takes effect on such date as is specified in the notice.

(8) Schedule 16 has effect as respects consumer credit prohibitions and restrictions under section 204.

(9) A firm contravening a prohibition under this section is guilty of an offence and liable—

(a)   on summary conviction, to a fine not exceeding the statutory maximum;

(b)   on conviction on indictment, to a fine.

(10) In this section and section 204—

'a consumer credit EEA firm' means an EEA firm falling within any of paragraphs (a) to (c) of paragraph 5 of Schedule 3 whose EEA authorisation covers any Consumer Credit Act business;

'Consumer Credit Act business' means consumer credit business, consumer hire business or ancillary credit business;

'consumer credit business', 'consumer hire business' and 'ancillary credit business' have the same meaning as in the Consumer Credit Act 1974;

'listed activity' means an activity listed in the Annex to the second banking co-ordination directive or the Annex to the investment services directive;

'associate' has the same meaning as in section 25(2) of the Consumer Credit Act 1974;

'controller' has the meaning given by section 189(1) of that Act.

204   Power to restrict the carrying on of Consumer Credit Act business

(1) In this section 'restriction' means a direction that a consumer credit EEA firm may not carry on in the United Kingdom, otherwise than in accordance with such condition or conditions as may be specified in the direction, any Consumer Credit Act business which—

(a)   consists of or includes carrying on any listed activity; and
(b)   is specified in the direction.

(2) If it appears to the Director that the situation as respects a consumer credit EEA firm is such that the powers conferred by section 203(1) are exercisable, the Director may, instead of imposing a prohibition, impose such restriction as appears to him desirable.

(3) A restriction—

(a)   may be withdrawn, or
(b)   may be varied with the agreement of the firm concerned,

by written notice served by the Director on the firm, and any such notice takes effect on such date as is specified in the notice.

(4) A firm contravening a restriction is guilty of an offence and liable—

(a)   on summary conviction, to a fine not exceeding the statutory maximum;
(b)   on conviction on indictment, to a fine.

PART XIV

DISCIPLINARY MEASURES

205   Public censure

If the Authority considers that an authorised person has contravened a requirement imposed on him by or under this Act, the Authority may publish a statement to that effect.

206   Financial penalties

(1) If the Authority considers that an authorised person has contravened a requirement imposed on him by or under this Act, it may impose on him a penalty, in respect of the contravention, of such amount as it considers appropriate.

(2) The Authority may not in respect of any contravention both require a person to pay a penalty under this section and withdraw his authorisation under section 33.

(3) A penalty under this section is payable to the Authority.

207   Proposal to take disciplinary measures

(1) If the Authority proposes—

   (a)   to publish a statement in respect of an authorised person (under section 205), or
   (b)   to impose a penalty on an authorised person (under section 206),

it must give the authorised person a warning notice.

(2) A warning notice about a proposal to publish a statement must set out the terms of the statement.

(3) A warning notice about a proposal to impose a penalty, must state the amount of the penalty.

208   Decision notice

(1) If the Authority decides—

   (a)   to publish a statement under section 205 (whether or not in the terms proposed), or
   (b)   to impose a penalty under section 206 (whether or not of the amount proposed),

it must without delay give the authorised person concerned a decision notice.

(2) In the case of a statement, the decision notice must set out the terms of the statement.

(3) In the case of a penalty, the decision notice must state the amount of the penalty.

(4) If the Authority decides to—

   (a)   publish a statement in respect of an authorised person under section 205, or
   (b)   impose a penalty on an authorised person under section 206,

the authorised person may refer the matter to the Tribunal.

209   Publication

After a statement under section 205 is published, the Authority must send a copy of it to the authorised person and to any person on whom a copy of the decision notice was given under section 393(4).

210   Statements of policy

(1) The Authority must prepare and issue a statement of its policy with respect to—

   (a)   the imposition of penalties under this Part; and
   (b)   the amount of penalties under this Part.

(2) The Authority's policy in determining what the amount of a penalty should be must include having regard to—

   (a)   the seriousness of the contravention in question in relation to the nature of the requirement contravened;
   (b)   the extent to which that contravention was deliberate or reckless; and
   (c)   whether the person on whom the penalty is to be imposed is an individual.

(3) The Authority may at any time alter or replace a statement issued under this section.

(4) If a statement issued under this section is altered or replaced, the Authority must issue the altered or replacement statement.

(5) The Authority must, without delay, give the Treasury a copy of any statement which it publishes under this section.

(6) A statement issued under this section must be published by the Authority in the way appearing to the Authority to be best calculated to bring it to the attention of the public.

(7) In exercising, or deciding whether to exercise, its power under section 206 in the case of any particular contravention, the Authority must have regard to any statement published under this section and in force at the time when the contravention in question occurred.

(8) The Authority may charge a reasonable fee for providing a person with a copy of the statement.

211 Statements of policy: procedure

(1) Before issuing a statement under section 210, the Authority must publish a draft of the proposed statement in the way appearing to the Authority to be best calculated to bring it to the attention of the public.

(2) The draft must be accompanied by notice that representations about the proposal may be made to the Authority within a specified time.

(3) Before issuing the proposed statement, the Authority must have regard to any representations made to it in accordance with subsection (2).

(4) If the Authority issues the proposed statement it must publish an account, in general terms, of—

(a) the representations made to it in accordance with subsection (2); and
(b) its response to them.

(5) If the statement differs from the draft published under subsection (1) in a way which is, in the opinion of the Authority, significant, the Authority must (in addition to complying with subsection (4)) publish details of the difference.

(6) The Authority may charge a reasonable fee for providing a person with a copy of a draft published under subsection (1).

(7) This section also applies to a proposal to alter or replace a statement.

PART XV

THE FINANCIAL SERVICES COMPENSATION SCHEME

The scheme manager

212 The scheme manager

(1) The Authority must establish a body corporate ('the scheme manager') to exercise the functions conferred on the scheme manager by or under this Part.

(2) The Authority must take such steps as are necessary to ensure that the scheme manager is, at all times, capable of exercising those functions.

(3) The constitution of the scheme manager must provide for it to have—

(a) a chairman; and
(b) a board (which must include the chairman) whose members are the scheme manager's directors.

(4) The chairman and other members of the board must be persons appointed, and liable to removal from office, by the Authority (acting, in the case of the chairman, with the approval of the Treasury).

(5) But the terms of their appointment (and in particular those governing removal from office) must be such as to secure their independence from the Authority in the operation of the compensation scheme.

(6) The scheme manager is not to be regarded as exercising functions on behalf of the Crown.

(7) The scheme manager's board members, officers and staff are not to be regarded as Crown servants.

The scheme

213   The compensation scheme

(1) The Authority must by rules establish a scheme for compensating persons in cases where relevant persons are unable, or are likely to be unable, to satisfy claims against them.

(2) The rules are to be known as the Financial Services Compensation Scheme (but are referred to in this Act as 'the compensation scheme').

(3) The compensation scheme must, in particular, provide for the scheme manager—

    (a)   to assess and pay compensation, in accordance with the scheme, to claimants in respect of claims made in connection with regulated activities carried on (whether or not with permission) by relevant persons; and

    (b)   to have power to impose levies on authorised persons, or any class of authorised person, for the purpose of meeting its expenses (including in particular expenses incurred, or expected to be incurred, in paying compensation, borrowing or insuring risks).

(4) The compensation scheme may provide for the scheme manager to have power to impose levies on authorised persons, or any class of authorised person, for the purpose of recovering the cost (whenever incurred) of establishing the scheme.

(5) In making any provision of the scheme by virtue of subsection (3)(b), the Authority must take account of the desirability of ensuring that the amount of the levies imposed on a particular class of authorised person reflects, so far as practicable, the amount of the claims made, or likely to be made, in respect of that class of person.

(6) An amount payable to the scheme manager as a result of any provision of the scheme made by virtue of subsection (3)(b) or (4) may be recovered as a debt due to the scheme manager.

(7) Sections 214 to 217 make further provision about the scheme but are not to be taken as limiting the power conferred on the Authority by subsection (1).

(8) In those sections 'specified' means specified in the scheme.

(9) In this Part (except in sections 219, 220 or 224) 'relevant person' means a person who was—

    (a)   an authorised person at the time the act or omission giving rise to the claim against him took place; or

    (b)   an appointed representative at that time.

(10) But a person who, at that time—

    (a)   qualified for authorisation under Schedule 3, and

(b)   fell within a prescribed category,

is not to be regarded as a relevant person in relation to any activities for which he had permission as a result of any provision of, or made under, that Schedule unless he had elected to participate in the scheme in relation to those activities at that time.

Provisions of the scheme

214   General

(1) The compensation scheme may, in particular, make provision—

(a)   as to the circumstances in which a relevant person is to be taken (for the purposes of the scheme) to be unable, or likely to be unable, to satisfy claims made against him;

(b)   for the establishment of different funds for meeting different kinds of claim;

(c)   for the imposition of different levies in different cases;

(d)   limiting the levy payable by a person in respect of a specified period;

(e)   for repayment of the whole or part of a levy in specified circumstances;

(f)   for a claim to be entertained only if it is made by a specified kind of claimant;

(g)   for a claim to be entertained only if it falls within a specified kind of claim;

(h)   as to the procedure to be followed in making a claim;

(i)   for the making of interim payments before a claim is finally determined;

(j)   limiting the amount payable on a claim to a specified maximum amount or a maximum amount calculated in a specified manner;

(k)   for payment to be made, in specified circumstances, to a person other than the claimant.

(2) Different provision may be made with respect to different kinds of claim.

(3) The scheme may provide for the determination and regulation of matters relating to the scheme by the scheme manager.

(4) The scheme, or particular provisions of the scheme, may be made so as to apply only in relation to—

(a)   activities carried on,

(b)   claimants,

(c)   matters arising, or

(d)   events occurring,

in specified territories, areas or localities.

(5) The scheme may provide for a person who—

(a)   qualifies for authorisation under Schedule 3, and

(b)   falls within a prescribed category,

to elect to participate in the scheme in relation to some or all of the activities for which he has permission as a result of any provision of, or made under, that Schedule.

(6) The scheme may provide for the scheme manager to have power—

(a)   in specified circumstances,

(b)   but only if the scheme manager is satisfied that the claimant is entitled to receive a payment in respect of his claim—

(i)   under a scheme which is comparable to the compensation scheme, or

(ii)   as the result of a guarantee given by a government or other authority, to make a full payment of compensation to the claimant and recover the whole or part of the amount of that payment from the other scheme or under that guarantee.

215   Rights of the scheme in relevant person's insolvency

(1) The compensation scheme may, in particular, make provision—

   (a)   as to the effect of a payment of compensation under the scheme in relation to rights or obligations arising out of the claim against a relevant person in respect of which the payment was made;
   (b)   for conferring on the scheme manager a right of recovery against that person.

(2) Such a right of recovery conferred by the scheme does not, in the event of the relevant person's insolvency, exceed such right (if any) as the claimant would have had in that event.

(3) If a person other than the scheme manager presents a petition under section 9 of the 1986 Act or Article 22 of the 1989 Order in relation to a company or partnership which is a relevant person, the scheme manager has the same rights as are conferred on the Authority by section 362.

(4) If a person other than the scheme manager presents a petition for the winding up of a body which is a relevant person, the scheme manager has the same rights as are conferred on the Authority by section 371.

(5) If a person other than the scheme manager presents a bankruptcy petition to the court in relation to an individual who, or an entity which, is a relevant person, the scheme manager has the same rights as are conferred on the Authority by section 374.

(6) Insolvency rules may be made for the purpose of integrating any procedure for which provision is made as a result of subsection (1) into the general procedure on the administration of a company or partnership or on a winding-up, bankruptcy or sequestration.

(7) 'Bankruptcy petition' means a petition to the court—

   (a)   under section 264 of the 1986 Act or Article 238 of the 1989 Order for a bankruptcy order to be made against an individual;
   (b)   under section 5 of the 1985 Act for the sequestration of the estate of an individual;
   (c)   under section 6 of the 1985 Act for the sequestration of the estate belonging to or held for or jointly by the members of an entity mentioned in subsection (1) of that section.

(8) 'Insolvency rules' are—

   (a)   for England and Wales, rules made under sections 411 and 412 of the 1986 Act;
   (b)   for Scotland, rules made by order by the Treasury, after consultation with the Scottish Ministers, for the purposes of this section; and
   (c)   for Northern Ireland, rules made under Article 359 of the 1989 Order and section 55 of the Judicature (Northern Ireland) Act 1978.

(9) 'The 1985 Act', 'the 1986 Act', 'the 1989 Order' and 'court' have the same meaning as in Part XXIV.

216   Continuity of long-term insurance policies

(1) The compensation scheme may, in particular, include provision requiring the scheme manager to make arrangements for securing continuity of insurance for policyholders, or policyholders of a specified class, of relevant long-term insurers.

(2) 'Relevant long-term insurers' means relevant persons who—

(a) have permission to effect or carry out contracts of long-term insurance; and

(b) are unable, or unlikely to be unable, to satisfy claims made against them.

(3) The scheme may provide for the scheme manager to take such measures as appear to him to be appropriate—

(a) for securing or facilitating the transfer of a relevant long-term insurer's business so far as it consists of the carrying out of contracts of long-term insurance, or of any part of that business, to another authorised person;

(b) for securing the issue by another authorised person to the policyholders concerned of policies in substitution for their existing policies.

(4) The scheme may also provide for the scheme manager to make payments to the policyholders concerned—

(a) during any period while he is seeking to make arrangements mentioned in subsection (1);

(b) if it appears to him that it is not reasonably practicable to make such arrangements.

(5) A provision of the scheme made by virtue of section 213(3)(b) may include power to impose levies for the purpose of meeting expenses of the scheme manager incurred in—

(a) taking measures as a result of any provision of the scheme made by virtue of subsection (3);

(b) making payments as a result of any such provision made by virtue of subsection (4).

217 Insurers in financial difficulties

(1) The compensation scheme may, in particular, include provision for the scheme manager to have power to take measures for safeguarding policyholders, or policyholders of a specified class, of relevant insurers.

(2) 'Relevant insurers' means relevant persons who—

(a) have permission to effect or carry out contracts of insurance; and

(b) are in financial difficulties.

(3) The measures may include such measures as the scheme manager considers appropriate for—

(a) securing or facilitating the transfer of a relevant insurer's business so far as it consists of the carrying out of contracts of insurance, or of any part of that business, to another authorised person;

(b) giving assistance to the relevant insurer to enable it to continue to effect or carry out contracts of insurance.

(4) The scheme may provide—

(a) that if measures of a kind mentioned in subsection (3)(a) are to be taken, they should be on terms appearing to the scheme manager to be appropriate, including terms reducing, or deferring payment of, any of the things to which any of those who are eligible policyholders in relation to the relevant insurer are entitled in their capacity as such;

(b) that if measures of a kind mentioned in subsection (3)(b) are to be taken, they should be conditional on the reduction of, or the deferment of the payment of, the things to which any of those who are eligible policyholders in relation to the relevant insurer are entitled in their capacity as such;

(c) for ensuring that measures of a kind mentioned in subsection (3)(b) do not benefit to any material extent persons who were members of a relevant insurer when it began to be in financial difficulties or who had any responsibility for, or who may have profited from, the circumstances giving rise to its financial difficulties, except in specified circumstances;

(d) for requiring the scheme manager to be satisfied that any measures he proposes to take are likely to cost less than it would cost to pay compensation under the scheme if the relevant insurer became unable, or likely to be unable, to satisfy claims made against him.

(5) The scheme may provide for the Authority to have power—

(a) to give such assistance to the scheme manager as it considers appropriate for assisting the scheme manager to determine what measures are practicable or desirable in the case of a particular relevant insurer;

(b) to impose constraints on the taking of measures by the scheme manager in the case of a particular relevant insurer;

(c) to require the scheme manager to provide it with information about any particular measures which the scheme manager is proposing to take.

(6) The scheme may include provision for the scheme manager to have power—

(a) to make interim payments in respect of eligible policyholders of a relevant insurer;

(b) to indemnify any person making payments to eligible policyholders of a relevant insurer.

(7) A provision of the scheme made by virtue of section 213(3)(b) may include power to impose levies for the purpose of meeting expenses of the scheme manager incurred in—

(a) taking measures as a result of any provision of the scheme made by virtue of subsection (1);

(b) making payments or giving indemnities as a result of any such provision made by virtue of subsection (6).

(8) 'Financial difficulties' and 'eligible policyholders' have such meanings as may be specified.

Annual report

218　Annual report

(1) At least once a year, the scheme manager must make a report to the Authority on the discharge of its functions.

(2) The report must—

(a) include a statement setting out the value of each of the funds established by the compensation scheme; and

(b) comply with any requirements specified in rules made by the Authority.

(3) The scheme manager must publish each report in the way it considers appropriate.

Information and documents

219　Scheme manager's power to require information

(1) The scheme manager may, by notice in writing given to the relevant person in respect of whom a claim is made under the scheme or to a person otherwise involved, require that person—

(a) to provide specified information or information of a specified description; or

(b) to produce specified documents or documents of a specified description.

(2) The information or documents must be provided or produced—

(a) before the end of such reasonable period as may be specified; and

(b) in the case of information, in such manner or form as may be specified.

(3) This section applies only to information and documents the provision or production of which the scheme manager considers—

(a) to be necessary for the fair determination of the claim; or

(b) to be necessary (or likely to be necessary) for the fair determination of other claims made (or which it expects may be made) in respect of the relevant person concerned.

(4) If a document is produced in response to a requirement imposed under this section, the scheme manager may—

(a) take copies or extracts from the document; or

(b) require the person producing the document to provide an explanation of the document.

(5) If a person who is required under this section to produce a document fails to do so, the scheme manager may require the person to state, to the best of his knowledge and belief, where the document is.

(6) If the relevant person is insolvent, no requirement may be imposed under this section on a person to whom section 220 or 224 applies.

(7) If a person claims a lien on a document, its production under this Part does not affect the lien.

(8) 'Relevant person' has the same meaning as in section 224.

(9) 'Specified' means specified in the notice given under subsection (1).

(10) A person is involved in a claim made under the scheme if he was knowingly involved in the act or omission giving rise to the claim.

220   Scheme manager's power to inspect information held by liquidator etc.

(1) For the purpose of assisting the scheme manager to discharge its functions in relation to a claim made in respect of an insolvent relevant person, a person to whom this section applies must permit a person authorised by the scheme manager to inspect relevant documents.

(2) A person inspecting a document under this section may take copies of, or extracts from, the document.

(3) This section applies to—

(a) the administrative receiver, administrator, liquidator or trustee in bankruptcy of an insolvent relevant person;

(b) the permanent trustee, within the meaning of the Bankruptcy (Scotland) Act 1985, on the estate of an insolvent relevant person.

(4) This section does not apply to a liquidator, administrator or trustee in bankruptcy who is—

(a) the Official Receiver;

(b) the Official Receiver for Northern Ireland; or

(c) the Accountant in Bankruptcy.

(5) 'Relevant person' has the same meaning as in section 224.

221 Powers of court where information required

(1) If a person ('the defaulter')—

(a) fails to comply with a requirement imposed under section 219, or
(b) fails to permit documents to be inspected under section 220,

the scheme manager may certify that fact in writing to the court and the court may enquire into the case.

(2) If the court is satisfied that the defaulter failed without reasonable excuse to comply with the requirement (or to permit the documents to be inspected), it may deal with the defaulter (and, in the case of a body corporate, any director or officer) as if he were in contempt.

(3) 'Court' means—

(a) the High Court;
(b) in Scotland, the Court of Session.

Miscellaneous

222 Statutory immunity

(1) Neither the scheme manager nor any person who is, or is acting as, its board member, officer or member of staff is to be liable in damages for anything done or omitted in the discharge, or purported discharge, of the scheme manager's functions.

(2) Subsection (1) does not apply—

(a) if the act or omission is shown to have been in bad faith; or
(b) so as to prevent an award of damages made in respect of an act or omission on the ground that the act or omission was unlawful as a result of section 6(1) of the Human Rights Act 1998.

223 Management expenses

(1) The amount which the scheme manager may recover, from the sums levied under the scheme, as management expenses attributable to a particular period may not exceed such amount as may be fixed by the scheme as the limit applicable to that period.

(2) In calculating the amount of any levy to be imposed by the scheme manager, no amount may be included to reflect management expenses unless the limit mentioned in subsection (1) has been fixed by the scheme.

(3) 'Management expenses' means expenses incurred, or expected to be incurred, by the scheme manager in connection with its functions under this Act other than those incurred—

(a) in paying compensation;
(b) as a result of any provision of the scheme made by virtue of section 216(3) or (4) or 216(1) or (6).

224 Scheme manager's power to inspect documents held by Official Receiver etc.

(1) If, as a result of the insolvency or bankruptcy of a relevant person, any documents have come into the possession of a person to whom this section applies, he must permit any person authorised by the scheme manager to inspect the documents for the purpose of establishing—

(a) the identity of persons to whom the scheme manager may be liable to make a payment in accordance with the compensation scheme; or

(b) the amount of any payment which the scheme manager may be liable to make.

(2) A person inspecting a document under this section may take copies or extracts from the document.

(3) In this section 'relevant person' means a person who was—

(a) an authorised person at the time the act or omission which may give rise to the liability mentioned in subsection (1)(a) took place; or

(b) an appointed representative at that time.

(4) But a person who, at that time—

(a) qualified for authorisation under Schedule 3, and

(b) fell within a prescribed category,

is not to be regarded as a relevant person for the purposes of this section in relation to any activities for which he had permission as a result of any provision of, or made under, that Schedule unless he had elected to participate in the scheme in relation to those activities at that time.

(5) This section applies to—

(a) the Official Receiver;

(b) the Official Receiver for Northern Ireland; and

(c) the Accountant in Bankruptcy.

PART XVI

THE OMBUDSMAN SCHEME

The scheme

225 The scheme and the scheme operator

(1) This Part provides for a scheme under which certain disputes may be resolved quickly and with minimum formality by an independent person.

(2) The scheme is to be administered by a body corporate ('the scheme operator').

(3) The scheme is to be operated under a name chosen by the scheme operator but is referred to in this Act as 'the ombudsman scheme'.

(4) Schedule 17 makes provision in connection with the ombudsman scheme and the scheme operator.

226 Compulsory jurisdiction

(1) A complaint which relates to an act or omission of a person ('the respondent') in carrying on an activity to which compulsory jurisdiction rules apply is to be dealt with under the ombudsman scheme if the conditions mentioned in subsection (2) are satisfied.

(2) The conditions are that—

(a) the complainant is eligible and wishes to have the complaint dealt with under the scheme;

(b) the respondent was an authorised person at the time of the act or omission to which the complaint relates; and

    (c)   the act or omission to which the complaint relates occurred at a time when compulsory jurisdiction rules were in force in relation to the activity in question.

(3) 'Compulsory jurisdiction rules' means rules—

    (a)   made by the Authority for the purposes of this section; and
    (b)   specifying the activities to which they apply.

(4) Only activities which are regulated activities, or which could be made regulated activities by an order under section 22, may be specified.

(5) Activities may be specified by reference to specified categories (however described).

(6) A complainant is eligible, in relation to the compulsory jurisdiction of the ombudsman scheme, if he falls within a class of person specified in the rules as eligible.

(7) The rules—

    (a)   may include provision for persons other than individuals to be eligible; but
    (b)   may not provide for authorised persons to be eligible except in specified circumstances or in relation to complaints of a specified kind.

(8) The jurisdiction of the scheme which results from this section is referred to in this Act as the 'compulsory jurisdiction'.

227   Voluntary jurisdiction

(1) A complaint which relates to an act or omission of a person ('the respondent') in carrying on an activity to which voluntary jurisdiction rules apply is to be dealt with under the ombudsman scheme if the conditions mentioned in subsection (2) are satisfied.

(2) The conditions are that—

    (a)   the complainant is eligible and wishes to have the complaint dealt with under the scheme;
    (b)   at the time of the act or omission to which the complaint relates, the respondent was participating in the scheme;
    (c)   at the time when the complaint is referred under the scheme, the respondent has not withdrawn from the scheme in accordance with its provisions;
    (d)   the act or omission to which the complaint relates occurred at a time when voluntary jurisdiction rules were in force in relation to the activity in question; and
    (e)   the complaint cannot be dealt with under the compulsory jurisdiction.

(3) 'Voluntary jurisdiction rules' means rules—

    (a)   made by the scheme operator for the purposes of this section; and
    (b)   specifying the activities to which they apply.

(4) The only activities which may be specified in the rules are activities which are, or could be, specified in compulsory jurisdiction rules.

(5) Activities may be specified by reference to specified categories (however described).

(6) The rules require the Authority's approval.

(7) A complainant is eligible, in relation to the voluntary jurisdiction of the ombudsman scheme, if he falls within a class of person specified in the rules as eligible.

(8) The rules may include provision for persons other than individuals to be eligible.

(9) A person qualifies for participation in the ombudsman scheme if he falls within a class of person specified in the rules in relation to the activity in question.

(10) Provision may be made in the rules for persons other than authorised persons to participate in the ombudsman scheme.

(11) The rules may make different provision in relation to complaints arising from different activities.

(12) The jurisdiction of the scheme which results from this section is referred to in this Act as the 'voluntary jurisdiction'.

(13) In such circumstances as may be specified in voluntary jurisdiction rules, a complaint—

(a) which relates to an act or omission occurring at a time before the rules came into force, and
(b) which could have been dealt with under a scheme which has to any extent been replaced by the voluntary jurisdiction,

is to be dealt with under the ombudsman scheme even though paragraph (b) or (d) of subsection (2) would otherwise prevent that.

(14) In such circumstances as may be specified in voluntary jurisdiction rules, a complaint is to be dealt with under the ombudsman scheme even though—

(a) paragraph (b) or (d) of subsection (2) would otherwise prevent that, and
(b) the complaint is not brought within the scheme as a result of subsection (13),

but only if the respondent has agreed that complaints of that kind were to be dealt with under the scheme.

Determination of complaints

228 Determination under the compulsory jurisdiction

(1) This section applies only in relation to the compulsory jurisdiction.

(2) A complaint is to be determined by reference to what is, in the opinion of the ombudsman, fair and reasonable in all the circumstances of the case.

(3) When the ombudsman has determined a complaint he must give a written statement of his determination to the respondent and to the complainant.

(4) The statement must—

(a) give the ombudsman's reasons for his determination;
(b) be signed by him; and
(c) require the complainant to notify him in writing, before a date specified in the statement, whether he accepts or rejects the determination.

(5) If the complainant notifies the ombudsman that he accepts the determination, it is binding on the respondent and the complainant and final.

(6) If, by the specified date, the complainant has not notified the ombudsman of his acceptance or rejection of the determination he is to be treated as having rejected it.

(7) The ombudsman must notify the respondent of the outcome.

(8) A copy of the determination on which appears a certificate signed by an ombudsman is evidence (or in Scotland sufficient evidence) that the determination was made under the scheme.

(9) Such a certificate purporting to be signed by an ombudsman is to be taken to have been duly signed unless the contrary is shown.

229   Awards

(1) This section applies only in relation to the compulsory jurisdiction.

(2) If a complaint which has been dealt with under the scheme is determined in favour of the complainant, the determination may include—

   (a) an award against the respondent of such amount as the ombudsman considers fair compensation for loss or damage (of a kind falling within subsection (3)) suffered by the complainant ('a money award');

   (b) a direction that the respondent take such steps in relation to the complainant as the ombudsman considers just and appropriate (whether or not a court could order those steps to be taken).

(3) A money award may compensate for—

   (a) financial loss; or

   (b) any other loss, or any damage, of a specified kind.

(4) The Authority may specify the maximum amount which may be regarded as fair compensation for a particular kind of loss or damage specified under subsection (3)(b).

(5) A money award may not exceed the monetary limit; but the ombudsman may, if he considers that fair compensation requires payment of a larger amount, recommend that the respondent pay the complainant the balance.

(6) The monetary limit is such amount as may be specified.

(7) Different amounts may be specified in relation to different kinds of complaint.

(8) A money award—

   (a) may provide for the amount payable under the award to bear interest at a rate and as from a date specified in the award; and

   (b) is enforceable by the complainant in accordance with Part III of Schedule 17.

(9) Compliance with a direction under subsection (2)(b)—

   (a) is enforceable by an injunction; or

   (b) in Scotland, is enforceable by an order under section 45 of the Court of Session Act 1988.

(10) Only the complainant may bring proceedings for an injunction or proceedings for an order.

(11) 'Specified' means specified in compulsory jurisdiction rules.

230   Costs

(1) The scheme operator may by rules ('costs rules') provide for an ombudsman to have power, on determining a complaint under the compulsory jurisdiction, to award costs in accordance with the provisions of the rules.

(2) Costs rules require the approval of the Authority.

(3) Costs rules may not provide for the making of an award against the complainant in respect of the respondent's costs.

(4) But they may provide for the making of an award against the complainant in favour of the scheme operator, for the purpose of providing a contribution to resources deployed in dealing with the complaint, if in the opinion of the ombudsman—

   (a) the complainant's conduct was improper or unreasonable; or

   (b) the complainant was responsible for an unreasonable delay.

(5) Costs rules may authorise an ombudsman making an award in accordance with the rules to order that the amount payable under the award bears interest at a rate and as from a date specified in the order.

(6) An amount due under an award made in favour of the scheme operator is recoverable as a debt due to the scheme operator.

(7) Any other award made against the respondent is to be treated as a money award for the purposes of paragraph 16 of Schedule 17.

Information

231 Ombudsman's power to require information

231(1) An ombudsman may, by notice in writing given to a party to a complaint, require that party—

   (a)   to provide specified information or information of a specified description; or
   (b)   to produce specified documents or documents of a specified description.

(2) The information or documents must be provided or produced—

   (a)   before the end of such reasonable period as may be specified; and
   (b)   in the case of information, in such manner or form as may be specified.

(3) This section applies only to information and documents the production of which the ombudsman considers necessary for the determination of the complaint.

(4) If a document is produced in response to a requirement imposed under this section, the ombudsman may—

   (a)   take copies or extracts from the document; or
   (b)   require the person producing the document to provide an explanation of the document.

(5) If a person who is required under this section to produce a document fails to do so, the ombudsman may require him to state, to the best of his knowledge and belief, where the document is.

(6) If a person claims a lien on a document, its production under this Part does not affect the lien.

(7) 'Specified' means specified in the notice given under subsection (1).

232 Powers of court where information required

(1) If a person ('the defaulter') fails to comply with a requirement imposed under section 231, the ombudsman may certify that fact in writing to the court and the court may enquire into the case.

(2) If the court is satisfied that the defaulter failed without reasonable excuse to comply with the requirement, it may deal with the defaulter (and, in the case of a body corporate, any director or officer) as if he were in contempt.

(3) 'Court' means—

   (a)   the High Court;
   (b)   in Scotland, the Court of Session.

233 Data protection

In section 31 of the Data Protection Act 1998 (regulatory activity), after subsection (4), insert—

'(4A) Personal data processed for the purpose of discharging any function which is conferred by or under Part XVI of the Financial Services and Markets Act 2000 on the body established by the Financial Services Authority for the purposes of that Part are exempt from the subject information provisions in any case to the extent to which the application of those provisions to the data would be likely to prejudice the proper discharge of the function.'

Funding

234   Industry funding

(1) For the purpose of funding—

    (a)   the establishment of the ombudsman scheme (whenever any relevant expense is incurred), and

    (b)   its operation in relation to the compulsory jurisdiction,

the Authority may make rules requiring the payment to it or to the scheme operator, by authorised persons or any class of authorised person of specified amounts (or amounts calculated in a specified way).

(2) 'Specified' means specified in the rules.

PART XVII

COLLECTIVE INVESTMENT SCHEMES

CHAPTER I

INTERPRETATION

235   Collective investment schemes

(1) In this Part 'collective investment scheme' means any arrangements with respect to property of any description, including money, the purpose or effect of which is to enable persons taking part in the arrangements (whether by becoming owners of the property or any part of it or otherwise) to participate in or receive profits or income arising from the acquisition, holding, management or disposal of the property or sums paid out of such profits or income.

(2) The arrangements must be such that the persons who are to participate ('participants') do not have day-to-day control over the management of the property, whether or not they have the right to be consulted or to give directions.

(3) The arrangements must also have either or both of the following characteristics—

    (a)   the contributions of the participants and the profits or income out of which payments are to be made to them are pooled;

    (b)   the property is managed as a whole by or on behalf of the operator of the scheme.

(4) If arrangements provide for such pooling as is mentioned in subsection (3)(a) in relation to separate parts of the property, the arrangements are not to be regarded as constituting a single collective investment scheme unless the participants are entitled to exchange rights in one part for rights in another.

(5) The Treasury may by order provide that arrangements do not amount to a collective investment scheme—

    (a)   in specified circumstances; or

(b)   if the arrangements fall within a specified category of arrangement.

236   Open-ended investment companies

(1) In this Part 'an open-ended investment company' means a collective investment scheme which satisfies both the property condition and the investment condition.

(2) The property condition is that the property belongs beneficially to, and is managed by or on behalf of, a body corporate ('BC') having as its purpose the investment of its funds with the aim of—

(a) spreading investment risk; and
(b)   giving its members the benefit of the results of the management of those funds by or on behalf of that body.

(3) The investment condition is that, in relation to BC, a reasonable investor would, if he were to participate in the scheme—

(a)   expect that he would be able to realise, within a period appearing to him to be reasonable, his investment in the scheme (represented, at any given time, by the value of shares in, or securities of, BC held by him as a participant in the scheme); and
(b)   be satisfied that his investment would be realised on a basis calculated wholly or mainly by reference to the value of property in respect of which the scheme makes arrangements.

(4) In determining whether the investment condition is satisfied, no account is to be taken of any actual or potential redemption or repurchase of shares or securities under—

(a)   Chapter VII of Part V of the Companies Act 1985;
(b)   Chapter VII of Part VI of the Companies (Northern Ireland) Order 1986;
(c)   corresponding provisions in force in another EEA State; or
(d)   provisions in force in a country or territory other than an EEA state which the Treasury have, by order, designated as corresponding provisions.

(5) The Treasury may by order amend the definition of 'an open-ended investment company' for the purposes of this Part.

237   Other definitions

(1) In this Part 'unit trust scheme' means a collective investment scheme under which the property is held on trust for the participants.

(2) In this Part—

'trustee', in relation to a unit trust scheme, means the person holding the property in question on trust for the participants;
'depositary', in relation to—

(a)   a collective investment scheme which is constituted by a body incorporated by virtue of regulations under section 262, or
(b)   any other collective investment scheme which is not a unit trust scheme,

means any person to whom the property subject to the scheme is entrusted for safekeeping;
'the operator', in relation to a unit trust scheme with a separate trustee, means the manager and in relation to an open-ended investment company, means that company;
'units' means the rights or interests (however described) of the participants in a collective investment scheme.

(3) In this Part—

'an authorised unit trust scheme' means a unit trust scheme which is authorised for the purposes of this Act by an authorisation order in force under section 243;

'an authorised open-ended investment company' means a body incorporated by virtue of regulations under section 262 in respect of which an authorisation order is in force under any provision made in such regulations by virtue of subsection (2)(1) of that section;

'a recognised scheme' means a scheme recognised under section 264, 270 or 272.

CHAPTER II

RESTRICTIONS ON PROMOTION

238   Restrictions on promotion

(1) An authorised person must not communicate an invitation or inducement to participate in a collective investment scheme.

(2) But that is subject to the following provisions of this section and to section 239.

(3) Subsection (1) applies in the case of a communication originating outside the United Kingdom only if the communication is capable of having an effect in the United Kingdom.

(4) Subsection (1) does not apply in relation to—

   (a)   an authorised unit trust scheme;
   (b)   a scheme constituted by an authorised open-ended investment company; or
   (c)   a recognised scheme.

(5) Subsection (1) does not apply to anything done in accordance with rules made by the Authority for the purpose of exempting from that subsection the promotion otherwise than to the general public of schemes of specified descriptions.

(6) The Treasury may by order specify circumstances in which subsection (1) does not apply.

(7) An order under subsection (6) may, in particular, provide that subsection (1) does not apply in relation to communications—

   (1)   of a specified description;
   (b)   originating in a specified country or territory outside the United Kingdom;
   (c)   originating in a country or territory which falls within a specified description of country or territory outside the United Kingdom; or
   (d)   originating outside the United Kingdom.

(8) The Treasury may by order repeal subsection (3).

(9) 'Communicate' includes causing a communication to be made.

(10) 'Promotion otherwise than to the general public' includes promotion in a way designed to reduce, so far as possible, the risk of participation by persons for whom participation would be unsuitable.

(11) 'Participate', in relation to a collective investment scheme, means become a participant (within the meaning given by section 235(2)) in the scheme.

239   Single property schemes

(1) The Treasury may by regulations make provision for exempting single property schemes from section 238(1).

(2) For the purposes of subsection (1) a single property scheme is a scheme which has the characteristics mentioned in subsection (3) and satisfies such other requirements as are prescribed by the regulations conferring the exemption.

(3) The characteristics are—

(a) that the property subject to the scheme (apart from cash or other assets held for management purposes) consists of—
   (i) a single building (or a single building with ancillary buildings) managed by or on behalf of the operator of the scheme, or
   (ii) a group of adjacent or contiguous buildings managed by him or on his behalf as a single enterprise,
   with or without ancillary land and with or without furniture, fittings or other contents of the building or buildings in question; and
(b) that the units of the participants in the scheme are either dealt in on a recognised investment exchange or offered on terms such that any agreement for their acquisition is conditional on their admission to dealings on such an exchange.

(4) If regulations are made under subsection (1), the Authority may make rules imposing duties or liabilities on the operator and (if any) the trustee or depositary of a scheme exempted by the regulations.

(5) The rules may include, to such extent as the Authority thinks appropriate, provision for purposes corresponding to those for which provision can be made under section 248 in relation to authorised unit trust schemes.

240 Restriction on approval of promotion

(1) An authorised person may not approve for the purposes of section 21 the content of a communication relating to a collective investment scheme if he would be prohibited by section 238(1) from effecting the communication himself or from causing it to be communicated.

(2) For the purposes of determining in any case whether there has been a contravention of section 21(1), an approval given in contravention of subsection (1) is to be regarded as not having been given.

241 Actions for damages

If an authorised person contravenes a requirement imposed on him by section 238 or 240, section 150 applies to the contravention as it applies to a contravention mentioned in that section.

CHAPTER III

AUTHORISED UNIT TRUST SCHEMES

Applications for authorisation

242 Applications for authorisation of unit trust schemes

(1) Any application for an order declaring a unit trust scheme to be an authorised unit trust scheme must be made to the Authority by the manager and trustee, or proposed manager and trustee, of the scheme.

(2) The manager and trustee (or proposed manager and trustee) must be different persons.

(3) The application—

(a) must be made in such manner as the Authority may direct; and

(b) must contain or be accompanied by such information as the Authority may reasonably require for the purpose of determining the application.

(4) At any time after receiving an application and before determining it, the Authority may require the applicants to provide it with such further information as it reasonably considers necessary to enable it to determine the application.

(5) Different directions may be given, and different requirements imposed, in relation to different applications.

(6) The Authority may require applicants to present information which they are required to give under this section in such form, or to verify it in such a way, as the Authority may direct.

243   Authorisation orders

(1) If, on the application under section 242 in respect of a unit trust scheme, the Authority—

(a) is satisfied that the scheme complies with the requirements set out in this section,

(b) is satisfied that the scheme complies with the requirements of the trust scheme rules, and

(c) has been provided with a copy of the trust deed and a certificate signed by a solicitor to the effect that it complies with such of the requirements of this section or those rules as relate to its contents,

the Authority may make an order declaring the scheme to be an authorised unit trust scheme.

(2) If the Authority makes an order under subsection (1), it must give written notice of the order to the applicant.

(3) In this Chapter 'authorisation order' means an order under subsection (1).

(4) The manager and the trustee must be persons who are independent of each other.

(5) The manager and the trustee must each—

(a) be a body corporate incorporated in the United Kingdom or another EEA State, and

(b) have a place of business in the United Kingdom,

and the affairs of each must be administered in the country in which it is incorporated.

(6) If the manager is incorporated in another EEA State, the scheme must not be one which satisfies the requirement prescribed for the purposes of section 264.

(7) The manager and the trustee must each be an authorised person and the manager must have permission to act as manager and the trustee must have permission to act as trustee.

(8) The name of the scheme must not be undesirable or misleading.

(9) The purposes of the scheme must be reasonably capable of being successfully carried into effect.

(10) The participants must be entitled to have their units redeemed in accordance with the scheme at a price—

(a) related to the net vlaue of the property to which the units relate; and

(b) determined in accordance with the scheme.

(11) But a scheme is to be treated as complying with subsection (10) if it requires the manager to ensure that a participant is able to sell his units on an investment exchange at a price not significantly different from that mentioned in that subsection.

244   Determination of applications

(1) An application under section 242 must be determined by the Authority before the end of the period of six months beginning with the date on which it receives the completed application.

(2) The Authority may determine an incomplete application if it considers it appropriate to do so; and it must in any event determine such an application within twelve months beginning with the date on which it first receives the application.

(3) The applicant may withdraw his application, by giving the Authority written notice, at any time before the Authority determines it.

Applications refused

245   Procedure when refusing an application

(1) If the Authority proposes to refuse an application made under section 242 it must give each of the applicants a warning notice.

(2) If the Authority decides to refuse the application—

    (a)   it must give each of the applicants a decision notice; and
    (b)   either applicant may refer the matter to the Tribunal.

Certificates

246   Certificates

(1) If the manager or trustee of a unit trust scheme which complies with the conditions necessary for it to enjoy the rights conferred by any relevant Community instrument so requests, the Authority may issue a certificate to the effect that the scheme complies with those conditions.

(2) Such a certificate may be issued on the making of an authorisation order in respect of the scheme or at any subsequent time.

Rules

247   Trust scheme rules

(1) The Authority may make rules ('trust scheme rules') as to—

    (a)   the constitution, management and operation of authorised unit trust schemes;
    (b)   the powers, duties, rights and liabilities of the manager and trustee of any such scheme;
    (c)   the rights and duties of the participants in any such scheme; and
    (d)   the winding up of any such scheme.

(2) Trust scheme rules may, in particular, make provision—

    (a)   as to the issue and redemption of the units under the scheme;
    (b)   as to the expenses of the scheme and the means of meeting them;

(c) for the appointment, removal, powers and duties of an auditor for the scheme;

(d) for restricting or regulating the investment and borrowing powers exercisable in relation to the scheme;

(e) requiring the keeping of records with respect to the transactions and financial position of the scheme and for the inspection of those records;

(f) requiring the preparation of periodical reports with respect to the scheme and the provision of those reports to the participants and to the Authority; and

(g) with respect to the amendment of the scheme.

(3) Trust scheme rules may make provision as to the contents of the trust deed, including provision requiring any of the matters mentioned in subsection (2) to be dealt with in the deed.

(4) But trust scheme rules are binding on the manager, trustee and participants independently of the contents of the trust deed and, in the case of the participants, have effect as if contained in it.

(5) If—

(a) a modification is made of the statutory provisions in force in Great Britain or Northern Ireland relating to companies,

(b) the modification relates to the rights and duties of persons who hold the beneficial title to any shares in a company without also holding the legal title, and

(c) it appears to the Treasury that, for the purpose of assimilating the law relating to authorised unit trust schemes to the law relating to companies as so modified, it is expedient to modify the rule-making powers conferred on the Authority by this section,

the Treasury may by order make such modifications of those powers as they consider appropriate.

248 Scheme particulars rules

(1) The Authority may make rules ('scheme particulars rules') requiring the manager of an authorised unit trust scheme—

(a) to submit scheme particulars to the Authority; and

(b) to publish scheme particulars or make them available to the public on request.

(2) 'Scheme particulars' means particulars in such form, containing such information about the scheme and complying with such requirements, as are specified in scheme particulars rules.

(3) Scheme particulars rules may require the manager of an authorised unit trust scheme to submit, and to publish or make available, revised or further scheme particulars if there is a significant change affecting any matter—

(a) which is contained in scheme particulars previously published or made available; and

(b) whose inclusion in those particulars was required by the rules.

(4) Scheme particulars rules may require the manager of an authorised unit trust scheme to submit, and to publish or make available, revised or further scheme particulars if—

(a) a significant new matter arises; and

(b) the inclusion of information in respect of that matter would have been required in previous particulars if it had arisen when those particulars were prepared.

(5) Scheme particulars rules may provide for the payment, by the person or persons who in accordance with the rules are treated as responsible for any scheme particulars, of compensation to any qualifying person who has suffered loss as a result of—

(a)   any untrue or misleading statement in the particulars; or

(b)   the omission from them of any matter required by the rules to be included.

(6) 'Qualifying person' means a person who—

(a)   has become or agreed to become a participant in the scheme; or

(b)   although not being a participant, has a beneficial interest in units in the scheme.

(7) Scheme particulars rules do not affect any liability which any person may incur apart from the rules.

249   Disqualification of auditor for breach of trust scheme rules

(1) If it appears to the Authority that an auditor has failed to comply with a duty imposed on him by trust scheme rules, it may disqualify him from being the auditor for any authorised unit trust scheme or authorised open-ended investment company.

(2) Subsections (2) to (5) of section 345 have effect in relation to disqualification under subsection (1) as they have effect in relation to disqualification under subsection (1) of that section.

250   Modification or waiver of rules

(1) In this section 'rules' means—

(a)   trust scheme rules; or

(b)   scheme particulars rules.

(2) The Authority may, on the application or with the consent of any person to whom any rules apply, direct that all or any of the rules—

(a)   are not to apply to him as respects a particular scheme; or

(b)   are to apply to him, as respects a particular scheme, with such modifications as may be specified in the direction.

(3) The Authority may, on the application or with the consent of the manager and trustee of a particular scheme acting jointly, direct that all or any of the rules—

(a)   are not to apply to the scheme; or

(b)   are to apply to the scheme with such modifications as may be specified in the direction.

(4) Subsections (3) to (9) and (11) of section 148 have effect in relation to a direction under subsection (2) as they have effect in relation to a direction under section 148(2) but with the following modifications—

(a)   subsection (4)(a) is to be read as if the words 'by the authorised person' were omitted;

(b)   any reference to the authorised person (except in subsection (4)(a)) is to be read as a reference to the person mentioned in subsection (2); and

(c)   subsection (7)(b) is to be read, in relation to a participant of the scheme, as if the word 'commercial' were omitted.

(5) Subsections (3) to (9) and (11) of section 148 have effect in relation to a direction under subsection (3) as they have effect in relation to a direction under section 148(2) but with the following modifications—

(a)   subsection (4)(a) is to be read as if the words 'by the authorised person' were omitted;

(b)   subsections (7)(b) and (11) are to be read as if references to the authorised person were references to each of the manager and the trustee of the scheme;

(c)   subsection (7)(b) is to be read, in relation to a participant of the scheme, as if the word 'commercial' were omitted;

(d)   subsection (8) is to be read as if the reference to the authorised person concerned were a reference to the scheme concerned and to its manager and trustee; and

(e)   subsection (9) is to be read as if the reference to the authorised person were a reference to the manager and trustee of the scheme acting jointly.

Alterations

251   Alteration of schemes and changes of manager or trustee

(1) The manager of an authorised unit trust scheme must give written notice to the Authority of any proposal to alter the scheme or to replace its trustee.

(2) Any notice given in respect of a proposal to alter the scheme involving a change in the trust deed must be accompanied by a certificate signed by a solicitor to the effect that the change will not affect the compliance of the deed with the trust scheme rules.

(3) The trustee of an authorised unit trust scheme must give written notice to the Authority of any proposal to replace the manager of the scheme.

(4) Effect is not to be given to any proposal of which notice has been given under subsection (1) or (3) unless—

(a)   the Authority, by written notice, has given its approval to the proposal; or

(b)   one month, beginning with the date on which the notice was given, has expired without the manager or trustee having received from the Authority a warning notice under section 252 in respect of the proposal.

(5) The Authority must not approve a proposal to replace the manager or the trustee of an authorised unit trust scheme unless it is satisfied that, if the proposed replacement is made, the scheme will continue to comply with the requirements of section 243(4) or (7).

252   Procedure when refusing approval of change of manager or trustee

(1) If the Authority proposes to refuse approval of a proposal to replace the trustee or manager of an authorised unit trust scheme, it must give a warning notice to the person by whom notice of the proposal was given under section 251(1) or (3).

(2) If the Authority proposes to refuse approval of a proposal to alter an authorised unit trust scheme it must give separate warning notices to the manager and the trustee of the scheme.

(3) To be valid the warning notice must be received by that person before the end of the month beginning with the date on which notice of the proposal was given.

(4) If, having given a warning to a person, the Authority decides to refuse approval—

(a)   it must give him a decision notice; and

(b)   he may refer the matter to the Tribunal.

Exclusion clauses

253   Avoidance of exclusion clauses

Any provision of the trust deed of an authorised unit trust scheme is void in so far as it would have the effect of exempting the manager or trustee from liability for any failure to exercise due care and diligence in the discharge of his functions in respect of the scheme.

Ending of authorisation

254   Revocation of authorisation order otherwise than by consent

(1) An authorisation order may be revoked by an order made by the Authority if it appears to the Authority that—

   (a)   one or more of the requirements for the making of the order are no longer satisfied;
   (b)   the manager or trustee of the scheme concerned has contravened a requirement imposed on him by or under this Act;
   (c)   the manager or trustee of the scheme has, in purported compliance with any such requirement, knowingly or recklessly given the Authority information which is false or misleading in a material particular;
   (d)   no regulated activity is being carried on in relation to the scheme and the period of that inactivity began at least twelve months earlier; or
   (e)   none of paragraphs (a) to (d) applies, but it is desirable to revoke the authorisation order in order to protect the interests of participants or potential participants in the scheme.

(2) For the purposes of subsection (1)(e), the Authority may take into account any matter relating to—

   (a)   the scheme;
   (b)   the manager or trustee;
   (c)   any person employed by or associated with the manager or trustee in connection with the scheme;
   (d)   any director of the manager or trustee;
   (e)   any person exercising influence over the manager or trustee;
   (f)   any body corporate in the same group as the manager or trustee;
   (g)   any director of any such body corporate;
   (h)   any person exercising influence over any such body corporate.

255   Procedure

(1) If the Authority proposes to make an order under section 254 revoking an authorisation order ('a revoking order'), it must give separate warning notices to the manager and the trustee of the scheme.

(2) If the Authority decides to make a revoking order, it must without delay give each of them a decision notice and either of them may refer the matter to the Tribunal.

256   Requests for revocation of authorisation order

(1) An authorisation order may be revoked by an order made by the Authority at the request of the manager or trustee of the scheme concerned.

(2) If the Authority makes an order under subsection (1), it must give written notice of the order to the manager and trustee of the scheme concerned.

(3) The Authority may refuse a request to make an order under this section if it considers that—

   (a)   the public interest requires that any matter concerning the scheme should be investigated before a decision is taken as to whether the authorisation order should be revoked; or
   (b)   revocation would not be in the interests of the participants or would be incompatible with a Community obligation.

(4) If the Authority proposes to refuse a request under this section, it must give separate warning notices to the manager and the trustee of the scheme.

(5) If the Authority decides to refuse the request, it must without delay give each of them a decision notice and either of them may refer the matter to the Tribunal.

Powers of intervention

257   Directions

(1) The Authority may give a direction under this section if it appears to the Authority that—

    (a)   one or more of the requirements for the making of an authorisation order are no longer satisfied;

    (b)   the manager or trustee of an authorised unit trust scheme has contravened, or is likely to contravene, a requirement imposed on him by or under this Act;

    (c)   the manager or trustee of such a scheme has, in purported compliance with any such requirement, knowingly or recklessly give the Authority information which is false or misleading in a material particular; or

    (d)   none of the paragraphs (a) to (c) applies, but it is desirable to give a direction in order to protect the interests of participants or potential participants in such a scheme.

(2) A direction under this section may—

    (a)   require the manager of the scheme to cease the issue or redemption, or both the issue and redemption, of units under the scheme;

    (b)   require the manager and trustee of the scheme to wind it up.

(3) If the the authorisation order is revoked, the revocation does not affect any direction under this section which is then in force.

(4) A direction may be given under this section in relation to a scheme in the case of which the authorisation order has been revoked if a direction under this section was already in force at the time of revocation.

(5) If a person contravenes a direction under this section, section 150 applies to the contravention as it applies to a contravention mentioned in that section.

(6) The Authority may, either on its own intiative or on the application of the manager or trustee of the scheme concerned, revoke or vary a direction given under this section if it appears to the Authority—

    (a)   in the case of revocation, that it is no longer necessary for the direction to take effect or continue in force;

    (b)   in the care of variation, that the direction should take effect or continue in force in a different form.

258   Applications to the court

(1) If the Authority could give a direction under section 257, it may also apply to the court for an order—

    (a)   removing the manager or the trustee, or both the manager and the trustee, of the scheme; and

    (b)   replacing the person or persons removed with a suitable person or persons nominated by the Authority.

(2) The Authority may nominate a person for the purposes of subsection (1)(b) only if it is satisfied that, if the order was made, the requirements of section 243(4) to (7) would be complied with.

(3) If it appears to the Authority that there is no person it can nominate for the purposes of subsection (1)(b), it may apply to the court for an order—

    (a) removing the manager or the trustee, or both the manager and the trustee, of the scheme; and

    (b) appointing an authorised person to wind up the scheme.

(4) On an application under this section the court may make such order as it thinks fit.

(5) The court may, on the application of the Authority, rescind any such order as is mentioned in subsection (3) and substitute such an order as is mentioned in subsection (1).

(6) The Authority must give written notice of the making of an application under this section to the manager and trustee of the scheme concerned.

(7) The jurisdiction conferred by this section may be exercised by—

    (1) the High Court;

    (b) in Scotland, the Court of Session.

259 Procedure on giving directions under section 257 and varying them on Authority's own initiative

(1) A direction takes effect—

    (a) immediately, if the notice given under subsection (3) states that that is the case;

    (b) on such date as may be specified in the notice; or

    (c) if no date is specified in the notice, when the matter to which it relates is no longer open to review.

(2) A direction may be expressed to take effect immediately (or on a specified date) only if the Authority, having regard to the ground on which it is exercising its power under section 257, considers that it is necessary for the direction to take effect immediately (or on that date).

(3) If the Authority proposes to give a direction under section 257, or gives such a direction with immediate effect, it must give separate written notice to the manager and the trustee of the scheme concerned.

(4) The notice must—

    (a) give details of the direction;

    (b) inform the person to whom it is given of when the direction takes effect;

    (c) state the Authority's reasons for giving the direction and for its determination as to when the direction takes effect;

    (d) inform the person to whom it is given that he may make representations to the Authority within such period as may be specified in it (whether or not he has referred the matter to the Tribunal); and

    (e) inform him of his right to refer the matter to the Tribunal.

(5) If the direction imposes a requirement under section 257(2)(a), the notice must state that the requirement has effect until—

    (a) a specified date; or

    (b) a further direction.

(6) If the direction imposes a requirement under section 257(2)(b), the scheme must be wound up—

    (a) by a date specified in the notice; or

    (b) if not date is specified, as soon as practicable.

(7) The Authority may extend the period allowed under the notice for making representations.

(8) If, having considered any representations made by a person to whom the notice was given, the Authority decides—

    (a)   to give the direction in the way proposed, or

    (b)   if it has been given, not to revoke the direction,

it must give separate written notice to the manager and the trustee of the scheme concerned.

(9) If, having considered any representations made by a person to whom the notice was given, the Authority decides—

    (a)   not to give the direction in the way proposed,

    (b)   to give the direction in a way other than that proposed, or

    (c)   to revoke a direction which has effect,

it must give separate written notice to the manager and the trustee of the scheme concerned.

(10) A notice given under subsection (8) must inform the person to whom it is given of his right to refer the matter to the Tribunal.

(11) A notice under subsection (9)(b) must comply with subsection (4).

(12) If a notice informs a person of his right to refer a matter to the Tribunal, it must give an indication of the procedure on such a reference.

(13) This section applies to the variation of a direction on the Authority's own initiative as it applies to the giving of a direction.

(14) For the purposes of subsection (1)(c), whether a matter is open to review is to be determined in accordance with section 391(8).

260 Procedure: refusal to revoke or vary direction

(1) If on an application under section 257(6) for a direction to be revoked or varied the Authority proposes—

    (a)   to vary the direction otherwise than in accordance with the application, or

    (b)   to refuse to revoke or vary the direction,

it must give the applicant a warning notice.

(2) If the Authority decides to refuse to revoke or vary the direction—

    (a)   it must give the applicant a decision notice; and

    (b)   the applicant may refer the matter to the Tribunal.

261 Procedure: revocation of direction and grant of request for variation

(1) If the Authority decides on its own initiative to revoke a direction under section 257 it must give separate written notices of its decision to the manager and trustee of the scheme.

(2) If on the application under section 257(6) for a direction to be revoked or varied the Authority decides to revoke the direction or vary it in accordance with the application, it must give the applicant written notice of its decision.

(3) A notice under this section must specify the date on which the decision takes effect.

(4) The Authority may publish such information about the revocation or variation, in such way, as it considers appropriate.

CHAPTER IV

OPEN-ENDED INVESTMENT COMPANIES

262 Open-ended investment companies

(1) The Treasury may by regulations make provision for—

(a) facilitating the carrying on of collective investment by means of open-ended investment companies;

(b) regulating such companies.

(2) The regulations may, in particular, make provision—

(a) for the incorporation and registration in Great Britain of bodies corporate;

(b) for a body incorporated by virtue of the regulations to take such form as may be determined in accordance with the regulations;

(c) as to the purposes for which such a body may exist, the investments which it may issue and otherwise as to its constitution;

(d) as to the management and operation of such a body and the management of its property;

(e) as to the powers, duties, rights and liabilities of such a body and of other persons, including—

    (i) the directors or sole director of such a body;

    (ii) its depositary (if any);

    (iii) its shareholders, and persons who hold the beneficial title to shares in it without holding the legal title;

    (iv) its auditor; and

    (v) any persons who act or purport to act on its behalf;

(f) as to the merger of one or more such bodies and the division of such a body;

(g) for the appointment and removal of an auditor for such a body;

(h) as to the winding up and dissolution of such a body;

(i) for such a body, or any director or depositary of such a body, to be required to comply with directions given by the Authority;

(j) enabling the Authority to apply to a court for an order removing and replacing any director or depositary of such a body;

(k) for the carrying out of investigations by persons appointed by the Authority or the Secretary of State;

(l) corresponding to any provision made in relation to unit trust schemes by Chapter III of this Part.

(3) Regulations under this section may—

(a) impose criminal liability;

(b) confer functions on the Authority;

(c) in the case of provision made by virtue of subsection (2)(1), authorise the making of rules by the Authority;

(d) confer jurisdiction on any court or on the Tribunal;

(e) provide for fees to be charged by the Authority in connection with the carrying out of any of its functions under the regulations (including fees payable on a periodical basis);

(f) modify, exclude or apply (with or without modifications) any primary or subordinate legislation (including any provision of, or made under, this Act);

(g) make consequential amendments, repeals and revocations of any such legislation;

(h) modify or exclude any rule of law.

(4) The provision that may be made by virtue of subsection (3)(f) includes provision extending or adapting any power to make subordinate legislation.

(5) Regulations under this section may, in particular—

(a)   revoke the Open-Ended Investment Companies (Investment Companies with Variable Capital) Regulations 1996; and

(b)   provide for things done under or in accordance with those regulations to be treated as if they had been done under or in accordance with regulations under this section.

263   Amendment of section 716 Companies Act 1985

In section 716(1) of the Companies Act 1985 (prohibition on formation of companies with more than 20 members unless registered under the Act etc.), after 'this Act', insert 'is incorporated by virtue of regulations made under section 262 of the Financial Services and Markets Act 2000'.

CHAPTER V

RECOGNISED OVERSEAS SCHEMES

Schemes constituted in other EEA States

264   Schemes constituted in other EEA States

(1) A collective investment scheme constituted in another EEA State is a recognised scheme if—

(a)   it satisfies such requirements as are prescribed for the purposes of this section; and

(b)   not less than two months before inviting persons in the United Kingdom to become participants in the scheme, the operator of the scheme gives notice to the Authority of his intention to do so, specifying the way in which the invitation is to be made.

(2) But this section does not make the scheme a recognised scheme if within two months of receiving the notice under subsection (1) the Authority notifies—

(a)   the operator of the scheme, and

(b)   the authorities of the State in question who are responsible for the authorisation of collective investment schemes,

that the way in which the invitation is to be made does not comply with the law in force in the United Kingdom.

(3) The notice to be given to the Authority under subsection (1)—

(a)   must be accompanied by a certificate from the authorities mentioned in subsection (2)(b) to the effect that the scheme complies with the conditions necessary for it to enjoy the rights conferred by any relevant Community instrument;

(b)   must contain the address of a place in the United Kingdom for the service on the operator of notices or other documents required or authorised to be served on him under this Act; and

(c)   must contain or be accompanied by such other information and documents as may be prescribed.

(4) A notice given by the Authority under subsection (2) must—

(a)   give the reasons for which the Authority considers that the law in force in the United Kingdom will not be complied with; and

(b)   specify a reasonable period (which may not be less than 28 days) within which any person to whom it is given may make representations to the Authority.

(5) For the purposes of this section a collective investment scheme is constituted in another EEA State if—

(a)   it is constituted under the law of that State by a contract or under a trust and is managed by a body corporate incorporated under that law; or

(b)   it takes the form of an open-ended investment company incorporated under that law.

(6) The operator of a recognised scheme may give written notice to the Authority that he desires the scheme to be no longer recognised by virtue of this section.

(7) On the giving of notice under subsection (6), the scheme ceases to be a recognised scheme.

265   Representations and references to the Tribunal

(1) This section applies if any representations are made to the Authority, before the period for making representations has ended, by a person to whom a notice was given by the Authority under section 264(2).

(2) The Authority must, within a reasonable period, decide in the light of those representations whether or not to withdraw its notice.

(3) If the Authority withdraws its notice the scheme is a recognised scheme from the date on which the notice is withdrawn.

(4) If the Authority decides not to withdraw its notice, it must give a decision notice to each person to whom the notice under section 264(2) was given.

(5) The operator of the scheme to whom the decision notice is given may refer the matter to the Tribunal.

266   Disapplication of rules

(1) Apart from—

(a)   financial promotion rules, and

(b)   rules under section 283(1),

rules made by the Authority under this Act do not apply to the operator, trustee or depositary of a scheme in relation to the carrying on by him of regulated activities for which he has permission in that capacity.

(2) 'Scheme' means a scheme which is a recognised scheme by virtue of section 264.

267   Power of Authority to suspend promotion of scheme

(1) Subsection (2) applies if it appears to the Authority that the operator of a scheme has communicated an invitation or inducement in relation to the scheme in a manner contrary to financial promotion rules.

(2) The Authority may direct that—

(a)   the exemption from subsection (1) of section 238 provided by subsection (4)(c) of that section is not to apply in relation to the scheme; and

(b)   subsection (5) of that section does not apply with respect to things done in relation to the scheme.

(3) A direction under subsection (2) has effect—

(a)   for a specified period;

(b)   until the occurrence of a specified event; or

(c)   until specified conditions are complied with.

(4) The Authority may, either on its own initiative or on the application of the operator of the scheme concerned, vary a direction given under subsection (2) if it appears to the Authority that the direction should take effect or continue in force in a different form.

(5) The Authority may, either on its own initiative or on the application of the operator of the recognised scheme concerned, revoke a direction given under subsection (2) if it appears to the Authority—

(a) that the conditions specified in the direction have been complied with; or

(b) that it is no longer necessary for the direction to take effect or continue in force.

(6) If an event is specified, the direction ceases to have effect (unless revoked earlier) on the occurrence of that event.

(7) For the purposes of this section and sections 268 and 269—

(a) the scheme's home State is the EEA State in which the scheme is constituted (within the meaning given by section 264);

(b) the competent authorities in the scheme's home State are the authorities in that State who are responsible for the authorisation of collective investment schemes.

(8) 'Scheme' means a scheme which is a recognised scheme by virtue of section 264.

(9) 'Specified', in relation to a direction, means specified in it.

268 Procedure on giving directions under section 267 and varying them on Authority's own initiative

(1) A direction under section 267 takes effect—

(a) immediately, if the notice given under subsection (3)(a) states that that is the case;

(b) on such date as may be specified in the notice; or

(c) if no date is specified in the notice, when the matter to which it relates is no longer open to review.

(2) A direction may be expressed to take effect immediately (or on a specified date) only if the Authority, having regard to its reasons for exercising its power under section 267, considers that it is necessary for the direction to take effect immediately (or on that date).

(3) If the Authority proposes to give a direction under section 267, or gives such a direction with immediate effect, it must—

(a) give the operator of the scheme concerned written notice; and

(b) inform the competent authorities in the scheme's home State of its proposal or (as the case may be) of the direction.

(4) The notice must—

(a) give details of the direction;

(b) inform the operator of when the direction takes effect;

(c) state the Authority's reasons for giving the direction and for its determination as to when the direction takes effect;

(d) inform the operator that he may make representations to the Authority within such period as may be specified in it (whether or not he has referred the matter to the Tribunal); and

(e) inform him of his right to refer the matter to the Tribunal.

(5) The Authority may extend the period allowed under the notice for making representations.

(6) Subsection (7) applies if, having considered any representations made by the operator, the Authority decides—

    (a)   to give the direction in the way proposed, or

    (b)   if it has been given, not to revoke the direction.

(7) The Authority must—

    (a)   give the operator of the scheme concerned written notice; and

    (b)   inform the competent authorities in the scheme's home State of the direction.

(8) Subsection (9) applies if, having considered any representations made by a person to whom the notice was given, the Authority decides—

    (a)   not to give the direction in the way proposed,

    (b)   to give the direction in a way other than that proposed, or

    (c)   to revoke a direction which has effect.

(9) The Authority must—

    (a)   give the operator of the scheme concerned written notice; and

    (b)   inform the competent authorities in the scheme's home State of its decision.

(10) A notice given under subsection (7)(a) must inform the operator of his right to refer the matter to the Tribunal.

(11) A notice under subsection (9)(a) given as a result of subsection (8)(b) must comply with subsection (4).

(12) If a notice informs a person of his right to refer a matter to the Tribunal, it must give an indication of the procedure on such a reference.

(13) This section applies to the variation of a direction on the Authority's own initiative as it applies to the giving of a direction.

(14) For the purposes of subsection (1)(c), whether a matter is open to review is to be determined in accordance with section 391(8).

269   Procedure on application for variation or revocation of direction

(1) If, on application under subsection (4) or (5) of section 267, the Authority proposes—

    (a)   to vary a direction otherwise than in accordance with the application, or

    (b)   to refuse the application,

it must give the operator of the scheme concerned a warning notice.

(2) if, on such an application, the Authority decides—

    (a)   to vary a direction otherwise than in accordance with the application, or

    (b)   to refuse the application,

it must give the operator of the scheme concerned a decision notice.

(3) If the application is refused, the operator of the scheme may refer the matter to the Tribunal.

(4) If, on such an application, the Authority decides to grant the application it must give the operator of the scheme concerned written notice.

(5) If the Authority decides on its own initiative to revoke a direction given under section 267 it must give the operator of the scheme concerned written notice.

(6) The Authority must inform the competent authorities in the scheme's home State of any notice given under this section.

Schemes authorised in designated countries or territories

270   Schemes authorised in designated countries or territories

(1) A collective investment scheme which is not a recognised scheme by virtue of section 264 but is managed in, and authorised under the law of, a country or territory outside the United Kingdom is a recognised scheme if—

    (a)   that country or territory is designated for the purposes of this section by an order made by the Treasury;

    (b)   the scheme is of a class specified by the order;

    (c)   the operator of the scheme has given written notice to the Authority that he wishes it to be recognised; and

    (d)   either—

        (i)   the Authority, by written notice, has given its approval to the scheme's being recognised; or

        (ii)   two months, beginning with the date on which notice was given under paragraph (c), have expired without the operator receiving a warning notice from the Authority under section 271.

(2) The Treasury may not make an order designating any country or territory for the purposes of this section unless satisfied—

    (a)   that the law and practice under which relevant collective investment schemes are authorised and supervised in that country or territory affords to investors in the United Kingdom protection at least equivalent to that provided for them by or under this Part in the case of comparable authorised schemes; and

    (b)   that adequate arrangements exist, or will exist, for co-operation between the authorities of the country or territory responsible for the authorisation and supervision of relevant collective investment schemes and the Authority.

(3) 'Relevant collective investment schemes' means collective investment schemes of the class or classes to be specified by the order.

(4) 'Comparable authorised schemes' means whichever of the following the Treasury consider to be the most appropriate, having regard to the class or classes of scheme to be specified by the order—

    (a)   authorised unit trust schemes;

    (b)   authorised open-ended investment companies;

    (c)   both such unit trust schemes and such companies.

(5) If the Treasury are considering whether to make an order designating a country or territory for the purposes of this section—

    (a)   the Treasury must ask the Authority for a report—

        (i)   on the law and practice of that country or territory in relation to the authorisation and supervision of relevant collective investment schemes,

        (ii)   on any existing or proposed arrangements for co-operation between it and the authorities responsible in that country or territory for the authorisation and supervision of relevant collective investment schemes,

        having regard to the Treasury's need to be satisfied as mentioned in subsection (2);

    (b)   the Authority must provide the Treasury with such a report; and

    (c)   the Treasury must have regard to it in deciding whether to make the order.

(6) The notice to be given by the operator under subsection (1)(c)—

    (a)   must contain the address of a place in the United Kingdom for the service on the operator of notices or other documents required or authorised to be served on him under this Act; and

(b) must contain or be accompanied by such information and documents as may be specified by the Authority.

271 Procedure

(1) If the Authority proposes to refuse approval of a scheme's being a recognised scheme by virtue of section 270, it must give the operator of the scheme a warning notice.

(2) To be valid the warning notice must be received by the operator before the end of two months beginning with the date on which notice was given under section 270(1)(c).

(3) If, having given a warning notice, the Authority decides to refuse approval—

(a) it must give the operator of the scheme a decision notice; and
(b) the operator may refer the matter to the Tribunal.

Individually recognised overseas schemes

272 Individually recognised overseas schemes

(1) The Authority may, on the application of the operator of a collective investment scheme which—

(a) is managed in a country or territory outside the United Kingdom,
(b) does not satisfy the requirements prescribed for the purposes of section 264,
(c) is not managed in a country or territory designated for the purposes of section 270 or, if it is so managed, is of a class not specified by the designation order, and
(d) appears to the Authority to satisfy the requirements set out in the following provisions of this section,

make an order declaring the scheme to be a recognised scheme.

(2) Adequate protection must be afforded to participants in the scheme.

(3) The arrangements for the scheme's constitution and management must be adequate.

(4) The powers and duties of the operator and, if the scheme has a trustee or depositary, of the trustee or depositary must be adequate.

(5) In deciding whether the matters mentioned in subsection (3) or (4) are adequate, the Authority must have regard to—

(a) any rule of law, and
(b) any matters which are, or could be, the subject of rules,

applicable in relation to comparable authorised schemes.

(6) 'Comparable authorised schemes' means whichever of the following the Authority considers the most appropriate, having regard to the nature of scheme in respect of which the application is made—

(a) authorised unit trust schemes;
(b) authorised open-ended investment companies;
(c) both such unit trust schemes and such companies.

(7) The scheme must take the form of an open-ended investment company or (if it does not take that form) the operator must be a body corporate.

(8) The operator of the scheme must—

(a) if an authorised person, have permission to act as operator;
(b) if not an authorised person, be a fit and proper person to act as operator.

(9) The trustee or depositary (if any) of the scheme must—

    (a)   if an authorised person, have permission to act as trustee or depositary;

    (b)   if not an authorised person, be a fit and proper person to act as trustee or depositary.

(10) The operator and the trustee or depositary (if any) of the scheme must be able and willing to co-operate with the Authority by the sharing of information and in other ways.

(11) The name of the scheme must not be undesirable or misleading.

(12) The purposes of the scheme must be reasonably capable of being successfully carried into effect.

(13) The participants must be entitled to have their units redeemed in accordance with the scheme at a price related to the net value of the property to which the units relate and determined in accordance with the scheme.

(14) But a scheme is to be treated as complying with subsection (13) if it requires the operator to ensure that a participant is able to sell his units on an investment exchange at a price not significantly different from that mentioned in that subsection.

(15) Subsection (13) is not to be read as imposing a requirement that the participants must be entitled to have their units redeemed (or sold as mentioned in subsection (14)) immediately following a demand to that effect.

273   Matters that may be taken into account

For the purposes of subsections (8)(b) and (9)(b) of section 272, the Authority may take into account any matter relating to—

    (a)   any person who is or will be employed by or associated with the operator, trustee or depositary in connection with the scheme;

    (b)   any director of the operator, trustee or depositary;

    (c)   any person exercising influence over the operator, trustee or depositary;

    (d)   any body corporate in the same group as the operator, trustee or depositary;

    (e)   any director of any such body corporate;

    (f)   any person exercising influence over any such body corporate.

274   Applications for recognition of individual schemes

(1) An application under section 272 for an order declaring a scheme to be a recognised scheme must be made to the Authority by the operator of the scheme.

(2) The application—

    (a)   must be made in such manner as the Authority may direct;

    (b)   must contain the address of a place in the United Kingdom for the service on the operator of notices or other documents required or authorised to be served on him under this Act;

    (c)   must contain or be accompanied by such information as the Authority may reasonably require for the purpose of determining the application.

(3) At any time after receiving an application and before determining it, the Authority may require the applicant to provide it with such further information as it reasonably considers necessary to enable it to determine the application.

(4) Different directions may be given, and different requirements imposed, in relation to different applications.

(5) The Authority may require an applicant to present information which he is required to give under this section in such form, or to verify it in such a way, as the Authority may direct.

275   Determination of applications

(1) An application under section 272 must be determined by the Authority before the end of the period of six months beginning with the date on which it receives the completed application.

(2) The Authority may determine an incomplete application if it considers it appropriate to do so; and it must in any event determine such an application within twelve months beginning with the date on which it first receives the application.

(3) If the Authority makes an order under section 272(1), it must give written notice of the order to the applicant.

276   Procedure when refusing an application

(1) If the Authority proposes to refuse an application made under section 272 it must give the applicant a warning notice.

(2) If the Authority decides to refuse the application—

   (a)   it must give the applicant a decision notice; and
   (b)   the applicant may refer the matter to the Tribunal.

277   Alteration of schemes and changes of operator, trustee or depositary

(1) The operator of a scheme recognised by virtue of section 272 must give written notice to the Authority of any proposed alteration to the scheme.

(2) Effect is not to be given to any such proposal unless—

   (a)   the Authority, by written notice, has given its approval to the proposal; or
   (b)   one month, beginning with the date on which notice was given under subsection (1), has expired without the Authority having given written notice to the operator that it has decided to refuse approval.

(3) At least one month before any replacement of the operator, trustee or depositary of such a scheme, notice of the proposed replacement must be given to the Authority—

   (a)   by the operator, trustee or depositary (as the case may be); or
   (b)   by the person who is to replace him.

Schemes recognised under sections 270 and 272

278   Rules as to scheme particulars

The Authority may make rules imposing duties or liabilities on the operator of a scheme recognised under section 270 or 272 for purposes corresponding to those for which rules may be made under section 248 in relation to authorised unit trust schemes.

279   Revocation of recognition

The Authority may direct that a scheme is to cease to be recognised by virtue of section 270 or revoke an order under section 272 if it appears to the Authority—

   (a)   that the operator, trustee or depositary of the scheme has contravened a requirement imposed on him by or under this Act;
   (b)   that the operator, trustee or depositary of the scheme has, in purported compliance with any such requirement, knowingly or recklessly given the Authority information which is false or misleading in a material particular;

(c)   in the case of an order under section 272, that one or more of the requirements for the making of the order are no longer satisfied; or

(d)   that none of paragraphs (a) to (c) applies, but it is undesirable in the interests of the participants or potential participants that the scheme should continue to be recognised.

280   Procedure

(1) If the Authority proposes to give a direction under section 279 or to make an order under that section revoking a recognition order, it must give a warning notice to the operator and (if any) the trustee or depositary of the scheme.

(2) If the Authority decides to give a direction or make an order under that section—

(a)   it must without delay give a decision notice to the operator and (if any) the trustee or depositary of the scheme; and

(b)   the operator or the trustee or depositary may refer the matter to the Tribunal.

281   Directions

(1) In this section a 'relevant recognised scheme' means a scheme recognised under section 270 or 272.

(2) If it appears to the Authority that—

(a)   the operator, trustee or depositary of a relevant recognised scheme has contravened, or is likely to contravene, a requirement imposed on him by or under this Act,

(b)   the operator, trustee or depositary of such a scheme has, in purported compliance with any such requirement, knowingly or recklessly given the Authority information which is false or misleading in a material particular,

(c)   one or more of the requirements for the recognition of a scheme under section 272 are no longer satisfied, or

(d)   none of paragraphs (a) to (c) applies, but the exercise of the power conferred by this section is desirable in order to protect the interests of participants or potential participants in a relevant recognised scheme who are in the United Kingdom,

it may direct that the scheme is not to be a recognised scheme for a specified period or until the occurrence of a specified event or until specified conditions are complied with.

282   Procedure on giving directions under section 281 and varying them otherwise than as requested

(1) A direction takes effect—

(a)   immediately, if the notice given under subsection (3) states that that is the case;

(b)   on such a date as may be specified in the notice; or

(c)   if no date is specified in the notice, when the matter to which it relates is no longer open to review.

(2) A direction may be expressed to take effect immediately (or on a specified date) only if the Authority, having regard to the ground on which it is exercising its power under section 281, considers that it is necessary for the direction to take effect immediately (or on that date).

(3) If the Authority proposes to give a direction under section 281, or gives such a direction with immediate effect, it must give separate written notice to the operator and (if any) the trustee or depositary of the scheme concerned.

(4) The notice must—

(a) give details of the direction;

(b) inform the person to whom it is given of when the direction takes effect;

(c) state the Authority's reasons for giving the direction and for its determination as to when the direction takes effect;

(d) inform the person to whom it is given that he may make representations to the Authority within such period as may be specified in it (whether or not he has referred the matter to the Tribunal); and

(e) inform him of his right to refer the matter to the Tribunal.

(5) The Authority may extend the period allowed under the notice for making representations.

(6) If, having considered any representations made by a person to whom the notice was given, the Authority decides—

(a) to give the direction in the way proposed, or

(b) if it has been given, not to revoke the direction,

it must give separate written notice to the operator and (if any) the trustee or depositary of the scheme concerned.

(7) If, having considered any representations made by a person to whom the notice was given, the Authority decides—

(a) not to give the direction in the way proposed,

(b) to give the direction in a way other than that proposed, or

(c) to revoke a direction which has effect,

it must give separate written notice to the operator and (if any) the trustee or depositary of the scheme concerned.

(8) A notice given under subsection (6) must inform the person to whom it is given of his right to refer the matter to the Tribunal.

(9) A notice under subsection (7)(b) must comply with subsection (4).

(10) If a notice informs a person of his right to refer a matter to the Tribunal, it must give an indication of the procedure on such a reference.

(11) This section applies to the variation of a direction on the Authority's own initiative as it applies to the giving of a direction.

(12) For the purposes of subsection (1)(c), whether a matter is open to review is to be determined in accordance with section 391(8).

Facilities and information in UK

283   Facilities and information in UK

(1) The Authority may make rules requiring operators of recognised schemes to maintain in the United Kingdom, or in such part or parts of it as may be specified, such facilities as the Authority thinks desirable in the interests of participants and as are specified in rules.

(2) The Authority may by notice in writing require the operator of any recognised scheme to include such explanatory information as is specified in the notice in any communication of his which—

(a) is a communication of an invitation or inducement of a kind mentioned in section 21(1); and

(b) names the scheme.

(3) In the case of a communication originating outside the United Kingdom, subsection (2) only applies if the communication is capable of having an effect in the United Kingdom.

CHAPTER VI

INVESTIGATIONS

284   Power to investigate

(1) An investigating authority may appoint one or more competent persons to investigate on its behalf—

   (a)   the affairs of, or of the manager or trustee of, any authorised unit trust scheme,

   (b)   the affairs of, or of the operator, trustee or depositary of, any recognised scheme so far as relating to activities carried on in the United Kingdom, or

   (c)   the affairs of, or of the operator, trustee or depositary of, any other collective investment scheme except a body incorporated by virtue of regulations under section 262,

if it appears to the investigating authority that it is in the interests of the participants or potential participants to do so or that the matter is of public concern.

(2) A person appointed under subsection (1) to investigate the affairs of, or of the manager, trustee, operator or depositary of, any scheme (scheme 'A'), may also, if he thinks it necessary for the purposes of that investigation, investigate—

   (a)   the affairs of, or of the manager, trustee, operator or depositary of, any other such scheme as is mentioned in subsection (1) whose manager, trustee, operator or depositary is the same person as the manager, trustee, operator or depositary of scheme A;

   (b)   the affairs of such other schemes and persons (including bodies incorporated by virtue of regulations under section 262 and the directors and depositaries of such bodies) as may be prescribed.

(3) If the person appointed to conduct an investigation under this section ('B') considers that a person ('C') is or may be able to give information which is relevant to the investigation, B may require C—

   (a)   to produce to B any documents in C's possession or under his control which appear to B to be relevant to the investigation,

   (b)   to attend before B, and

   (c)   otherwise to give B all assistance in connection with the investigation which C is reasonably able to give,

and it is C's duty to comply with that requirement.

(4) Subsections (5) to (9) of section 170 apply if an investigating authority appoints a person under this section to conduct an investigation on its behalf as they apply in the case mentioned in subsection (1) of that section.

(5) Section 174 applies to a statement made by a person in compliance with a requirement imposed under this section as it applies to a statement mentioned in that section.

(6) Subsections (2) to (4) and (6) of section 175 and section 177 have effect as if this section were contained in Part XI.

(7) Subsections (1) to (9) of section 176 apply in relation to a person appointed under subsection (1) as if—

   (a)   references to an investigator were references to a person so appointed;

   (b)   references to an information requirement were references to a requirement imposed under section 175 or under subsection (3) by a person so appointed;

   (c)   the premises mentioned in subsection (3)(a) were the premises of a person whose affairs are the subject of an investigation under this section or of an appointed representative of such a person.

(8) No person may be required under this section to disclose information or produce a document in respect of which he owes an obligation of confidence by virtue of carrying on the business of banking unless subsection (9) or (10) applies.

(9) This subsection applies if—

   (a)   the person to whom the obligation of confidence is owed consents to the disclosure or production; or

   (b)   the imposing on the person concerned of a requirement with respect to information or a document of a kind mentioned in subsection (8) has been specifically authorised by the investigating authority.

(10) This subsection applies if the person owing the obligation of confidence or the person to whom it is owed is—

   (a)   the manager, trustee, operator or depositary of any collective investment scheme which is under investigation;

   (b)   the director of a body incorporated by virtue of regulations under section 262 which is under investigation;

   (c)   any other person whose own affairs are under investigation.

(11) 'Investigating authority' means the Authority or the Secretary of State.

PART XVIII

RECOGNISED INVESTMENT EXCHANGES AND CLEARING HOUSES

CHAPTER I

EXEMPTION

General

285   Exemption for recognised investment exchanges and clearing houses

(1) In this Act—

   (a)   'recognised investment exchange' means an investment exchange in relation to which a recognition order is in force; and

   (b)   'recognised clearing house' means a clearing house in relation to which a recognition order is in force.

(2) A recognised investment exchange is exempt from the general prohibition as respects any regulated activity—

   (a)   which is carried on as a part of the exchange's business as an investment exchange; or

   (b)   which is carried on for the purposes of, or in connection with, the provision of clearing services by the exchange.

(3) A recognised clearing house is exempt from the general prohibition as respects any regulated activity which is carried on for the purposes of, or in connection with, the provision of clearing services by the clearing house.

286   Qualification for recognition

(1) The Treasury may make regulations setting out the requirements—

  (a)   which must be satisfied by an investment exchange or clearing house if it is to qualify as a body in respect of which the Authority may make a recognition order under this Part; and

  (b)   which, if a recognition order is made, it must continue to satisfy if it is to remain a recognised body.

(2) But if regulations contain provision as to the default rules of an investment exchange or clearing house, or as to proceedings taken under such rules by such a body, they require the approval of the Secretary of State.

(3) 'Default rules' means rules of an investment exchange or clearing house which provide for the taking of action in the event of a person's appearing to be unable, or likely to become unable, to meet his obligations in respect of one or more market contracts connected with the exchange or clearing house.

(4) 'Market contract' means—

  (a)   a contract to which Part VII of the Companies Act 1989 applies as a result of section 155 of that Act or a contract to which Part V of the Companies (No. 2) (Northern Ireland) Order 1990 applies as a result of Article 80 of that Order; and

  (b)   such other kind of contract as may be prescribed.

(5) Requirements resulting from this section are referred to in this Part as 'recognition requirements'.

Applications for recognition

287   Application by an investment exchange

(1) Any body corporate or unincorporated association may apply to the Authority for an order declaring it to be a recognised investment exchange for the purposes of this Act.

(2) The application must be made in such manner as the Authority may direct and must be accompanied by—

  (a)   a copy of the applicant's rules;

  (b)   a copy of any guidance issued by the applicant;

  (c)   the required particulars; and

  (d)   such other information as the Authority may reasonably require for the purpose of determining the application.

(3) The required particulars are—

  (a)   particulars of any arrangements which the applicant has made, or proposes to make, for the provision of clearing services in respect of transactions effected on the exchange;

  (b)   if the applicant proposes to provide clearing services in respect of transactions other than those effected on the exchange, particulars of the criteria which the applicant will apply when determining to whom it will provide those services.

288   Application by a clearing house

(1) Any body corporate or unincorporated association may apply to the Authority for an order declaring it to be a recognised clearing house for the purposes of this Act.

(2) The application must be made in such manner as the Authority may direct and must be accompanied by—

(a)   a copy of the applicant's rules;
(b)   a copy of any guidance issued by the applicant;
(c)   the required particulars; and
(d)   such other information as the Authority may reasonably require for the purpose of determining the application.

(3) The required particulars are—

(a)   if the applicant makes, or proposes to make, clearing arrangements with a recognised investment exchange, particulars of those arrangements;
(b)   if the applicant proposes to provide clearing services for persons other than recognised investment exchanges, particulars of the criteria which it will apply when determining to whom it will provide those services.

289   Applications: supplementary

(1) At any time after receiving an application and before determining it, the Authority may require the applicant to provide such further information as it reasonably considers necessary to enable it to determine the application.

(2) Information which the Authority requires in connection with an application must be provided in such form, or verified in such manner, as the Authority may direct.

(3) Different directions may be given, or requirements imposed, by the Authority with respect to different applications.

290   Recognition orders

(1) If it appears to the Authority that the applicant satisfies the recognition requirements applicable in its case, the Authority may make a recognition order declaring the applicant to be—

(a)   a recognised investment exchange, if the application is made under section 287;
(b)   a recognised clearing house, if it is made under section 288.

(2) The Treasury's approval of the making of a recognition order is required under section 307.

(3) In considering an application, the Authority may have regard to any information which it considers is relevant to the application.

(4) A recognition order must specify a date on which it is to take effect.

(5) Section 298 has effect in relation to a decision to refuse to make a recognition order—

(a)   as it has effect in relation to a decision to revoke such an order; and
(b)   as if references to a recognised body were references to the applicant.

(6) Subsection (5) does not apply in a case in which the Treasury have failed to give their approval under section 307.

291   Liability in relation to recognised body's regulatory functions

(1) A recognised body and its officers and staff are not to be liable in damages for anything done or omitted in the discharge of the recognised body's regulatory functions unless it is shown that the act or omission was in bad faith.

(2) But subsection (1) does not prevent an award of damages made in respect of an act or omission on the ground that the act or omission was unlawful as a result of section 6(1) of the Human Rights Act 1998.

(3) 'Regulatory functions' means the functions of the recognised body so far as relating to, or to matters arising out of, the obligations to which the body is subject under or by virtue of this Act.

292   Overseas investment exchanges and overseas clearing houses

(1) An application under section 287 or 288 by an overseas applicant must contain the address of a place in the United Kingdom for the service on the applicant of notices or other documents required or authorised to be served on it under this Act.

(2) If it appears to the Authority that an overseas applicant satisfies the requirements of subsection (3) it may make a recognition order declaring the applicant to be—

    (a)   a recognised investment exchange;

    (b)   a recognised clearing house.

(3) The requirements are that—

    (a)   investors are afforded protection equivalent to that which they would be afforded if the body concerned were required to comply with recognition requirements;

    (b)   there are adequate procedures for dealing with a person who is unable, or likely to become unable, to meet his obligations in respect of one or more market contracts connected with the investment exchange or clearing house;

    (c)   the applicant is able and willing to co-operate with the Authority by the sharing of information and in other ways;

    (d)   adequate arrangements exist for co-operation between the Authority and those responsible for the supervision of the applicant in the country or territory in which the applicant's head office is situated.

(4) In considering whether it is satisfied as to the requirements mentioned in subsection (3)(a) and (b), the Authority is to have regard to—

    (a)   the relevant law and practice of the country or territory in which the applicant's head office is situated;

    (b)   the rules and practices of the applicant.

(5) In relation to an overseas applicant and a body or association declared to be a recognised investment exchange or recognised clearing house by a recognition order made by virtue of subsection (2)—

    (a)   the reference in section 313(2) to recognition requirements is to be read as a reference to matters corresponding to the matters in respect of which provision is made in the recognition requirements;

    (b)   sections 296(1) and 297(2) have effect as if the requirements mentioned in section 296(1)(a) and section 297(2)(a) were those of subsection (3)(a), (b), and (c) of this section;

    (c)   section 297(2) has effect as if the grounds on which a recognition order may be revoked under that provision included the ground that in the opinion of the Authority arrangements of the kind mentioned in subsection (3)(d) no longer exist.

Supervision

293   Notification requirements

(1) The Authority may make rules requiring a recognised body to give it—

    (a)   notice of such events relating to the body as may be specified; and

    (b)   such information in respect of those events as may be specified.

(2) The rules may also require a recognised body to give the Authority, at such times or in respect of such periods as may be specified, such information relating to the body as may be specified.

(3) An obligation imposed by the rules extends only to a notice or information which the Authority may reasonably require for the exercise of its functions under this Act.

(4) The rules may require information to be given in a specified form and to be verified in a specified manner.

(5) If a recognised body—

(a) alters or revokes any of its rules or guidance, or
(b) makes new rules or issues new guidance,

it must give written notice to the Authority without delay.

(6) If a recognised investment exchange makes a change—

(a) in the arrangements it makes for the provision of clearing services in respect of transactions effected on the exchange, or
(b) in the criteria which it applies when determining to whom it will provide clearing services,

it must give written notice to the Authority without delay.

(7) If a recognised clearing house makes a change—

(a) in the recognised investment exchanges for whom it provides clearing services, or
(b) in the criteria which it applies when determining to whom (other than recognised investment exchanges) it will provide clearing services,

it must give written notice to the Authority without delay.

(8) Subsections (5) to (7) do not apply to an overseas investment exchange or an overseas clearing house.

(9) 'Specified' means specified in the Authority's rules.

294   Modification or waiver of rules

(1) The Authority may, on the application or with the consent of a recognised body, direct that rules made under section 293 or 295—

(a) are not to apply to the body; or
(b) are to apply to the body with such modifications as may be specified in the direction.

(2) An application must be made in such manner as the Authority may direct.

(3) Subsections (4) to (6) apply to a direction given under subsection (1).

(4) The Authority may not give a direction unless it is satisfied that—

(a) compliance by the recognised body with the rules, or with the rules as unmodified, would be unduly burdensome or would not achieve the purpose for which the rules were made; and
(b) the direction would not result in undue risk to persons whose interests the rules are intended to protect.

(5) A direction may be given subject to conditions.

(6) The Authority may—

(a) revoke a direction; or

   (b)   vary it on the application, or with the consent, of the recognised body to which it relates.

295   Notification: overseas investment exchanges and overseas clearing houses

(1) At least once a year, every overseas investment exchange and overseas clearing house must provide the Authority with a report.

(2) The report must contain a statement as to whether any events have occurred which are likely—

   (a)   to affect the Authority's assessment of whether it is satisfied as to the requirements set out in section 292(3); or

   (b)   to have any effect on competition.

(3) The report must also contain such information as may be specified in rules made by the Authority.

(4) The investment exchange or clearing house must provide the Treasury and the Director with a copy of the report.

296   Authority's power to give directions

(1) This section applies if it appears to the Authority that a recognised body—

   (a)   has failed, or is likely to fail, to satsify the recognition requirements; or

   (b)   has failed to comply with any other obligation imposed on it by or under this Act.

(2) The Authority may direct the body to take specified steps for the purpose of securing the body's compliance with—

   (a)   the recognition requirements; or

   (b)   any obligation of the kind in question.

(3) A direction under this section is enforceable, on the application of the Authority, by an injunction or, in Scotland, by an order for specific performance under section 45 of the Court of Session Act 1988.

(4) The fact that a rule made by a recognised body has been altered in response to a direction given by the Authority does not prevent it from being subsequently altered or revoked by the recognised body.

297   Revoking recognition

(1) A recognition order may be revoked by an order made by the Authority at the request, or with the consent, of the recognised body concerned.

(2) If it appears to the Authority that a recognised body—

   (a)   is failing, or has failed, to satisfy the recognition requirements, or

   (b)   is failing, or has failed, to comply with any other obligation imposed on it by or under this Act,

it may make an order revoking the recognition order for that body even though the body does not wish the order to be made.

(3) An order under this section ('a revocation order') must specify the date on which it is to take effect.

(4) In the case of a revocation order made under subsection (2), the specified date must not be earlier than the end of the period of three months beginning with the day on which the order is made.

(5) A revocation order may contain such transitional provisions as the Authority thinks necessary or expedient.

298 Directions and revocation: procedure

(1) Before giving a direction under section 296, or making a revocation order under section 297(2), the Authority must—

   (a) give written notice of its intention to do so to the recognised body concerned;

   (b) take such steps as it considers reasonably practicable to bring the notice to the attention of members (if any) of that body; and

   (c) publish the notice in such manner as it thinks approprite for bringing it to the attention of other persons who are, in its opinion, likely to be affected.

(2) A notice under subsection (1) must—

   (a) state why the Authority intends to give the direction or make the order; and

   (b) draw attention to the right to make representations conferred by subsection (3).

(3) Before the end of the period for making representations—

   (a) the recognised body,

   (b) any member of that body, and

   (c) any other person who is likely to be affected by the proposed direction or revocation order,

may make representations to the Authority.

(4) The period for making representations is—

   (a) two months beginning—

      (i) with the date on which the notice is served on the recognised body; or

      (ii) if later, with the date on which the notice is published; or

   (b) such longer period as the Authority may allow in the particular case.

(5) In deciding whether to—

   (a) give a direction, or

   (b) make a revocation order,

the Authority must have regard to any representations made in accordance with subsection (3).

(6) When the Authority has decided whether to give a direction under section 296 or to make the proposed revocation order, it must—

   (a) give the recognised body written notice of its decision; and

   (b) if it has decided to give a direction or make an order, take such steps as it considers reasonably practicable for bringing its decision to the attention of members of the body or of other persons who are, in the Authority's opinion, likely to be affected.

(7) If the Authority considers it essential to do so, it may give a direction under section 296—

   (a) without following the procedure set out in this section; or

   (b) if the Authority has begun to follow that procedure, regardless of whether the period for making representations has expired.

(8) If the Authority has, in relation to a particular matter, followed the procedure set out in subsections (1) to (5), it need not follow it again if, in relation to that matter, it decides to take action other than that specified in its notice under subsection (1).

299   Complaints about recognised bodies

(1) The Authority must make arrangements for the investigation of any relevant complaint about a recognised body.

(2) 'Relevant complaint' means a complaint which the Authority considers is relevant to the question of whether the body concerned should remain a recognised body.

300   Extension of functions of Tribunal

(1) If the Treasury are satisfied that the condition mentioned in subsection (2) is satisfied, they may by order confer functions on the Tribunal with respect to disciplinary proceedings—

   (a)   of one or more investment exchanges in relation to which a recognition order under section 290 is in force or of such investment exchanges generally, or
   (b)   of one or more clearing houses in relation to which a recognition order under that section is in force or of such clearing houses generally.

(2) The condition is that it is desirable to exercise the power conferred under subsection (1) with a view to ensuring that—

   (a)   decisions taken in disciplinary proceedings with respect to which functions are to be conferred on the Tribunal are consistent with—
       (i)   decisions of the Tribunal in cases arising under Part VIII; and
       (ii)   decisions taken in other disciplinary proceedings with respect to which the Tribunal has functions as a result of an order under this section; or
   (b)   the disciplinary proceedings are in accordance with the Convention rights.

(3) An order under this section may modify or exclude any provision made by or under this Act with respect to proceedings before the Tribunal.

(4) 'Disciplinary proceedings' means proceedings under the rules of an investment exchange or clearing house in relation to market abuse by persons subject to the rules.

(5) 'The Convention rights' has the meaning given in section 1 of the Human Rights Act 1998.

Other matters

301   Supervision of certain contracts

(1) The Secretary of State and the Treasury, acting jointly, may by regulations provide for—

   (a)   Part VII of the Companies Act 1989 (financial markets and insolvency), and
   (b)   Part V of the Companies (No. 2) (Northern Ireland) Order 1990,

to apply to relevant contracts as it applies to contracts connected with a recognised body.

(2) 'Relevant contracts' means contracts of a prescribed description in relation to which settlement arrangements are provided by a person for the time being included in a list ('the list') maintained by the Authority for the purposes of this section.

(3) Regulations may be made under this section only if the Secretary of State and the Treasury are satisfied, having regard to the extent to which the relevant contracts concerned are contracts of a kind dealt in by persons supervised by the Authority, that it is appropriate for the arrangements mentioned in subsection (2) to be supervised by the Authority.

(4) The approval of the Treasury is required for—

   (a)   the conditions set by the Authority for admission to the list; and

(b)   the arrangements for admission to, and removal from, the list.

(5) If the Treasury withdraw an approval given by them under subsection (4), all regulations made under this section and then in force are to be treated as suspended.

(6) But if—

(a)   the Authority changes the conditions or arrangements (or both), and
(b)   the Treasury give a fresh approval under subsection (4),

the suspension of the regulation ends on such date as the Treasury may, in giving the fresh approval, specify.

(7) The Authority must—

(a)   publish the list as for the time being in force; and
(b)   provide a certified copy of it to any person who wishes to refer to it in legal proceedings.

(8) A certified copy of the list is evidence (or in Scotland sufficient evidence) of the contents of the list.

(9) A copy of the list which purports to be certified by or on behalf of the Authority is to be taken to have been duly certified unless the contrary is shown.

(10) Regulations under this section may, in relation to a person included in the list—

(a)   apply (with such exceptions, additions and modifications as appear to the Secretary of State and the Treasury to be necessary or expedient) such provisions of, or made under, this Act as they consider appropriate;
(b)   provide for the provisions of Part VII of the Companies Act 1989 and Part V of the Companies (No. 2) (Northern Ireland) Order 1990 to apply (with such exceptions, additions or modifications as appear to the Secretary of State and the Treasury to be necessary or expedient).

CHAPTER II

COMPETITION SCRUTINY

302   Interpretation

(1) In this Chapter and Chapter III—

'practices' means—

(a)   in relation to a recognised investment exchange, the practices of the exchange in its capacity as such; and
(b)   in relation to a recognised clearing house, the practices of the clearing house in respect of its clearing arrangements;

'regulatory provisions' means—

(a)   the rules of an investment exchange or a clearing house;
(b)   any guidance issued by an investment exchange or clearing house;
(c)   in the case of an investment exchange, the arrangements and criteria mentioned in section 287(3);
(d)   in the case of a clearing house, the arrangements and criteria mentioned in section 288(3).

(2) For the purposes of this Chapter, regulatory provisions or practices have a significantly adverse effect on competition if—

(a) they have, or are intended or likely to have, that effect; or

(b) the effect that they have, or are intended or likely to have, is to require or encourage behaviour which has, or is intended or likely to have, a significantly adverse effect on competition.

(3) If regulatory provisions or practices have, or are intended or likely to have, the effect of requiring or encouraging exploitation of the strength of a market position they are to be taken, for the purposes of this Chapter, to have an adverse effect on competition.

(4) In determining under this Chapter whether any regulatory provisions have, or are intended or likely to have, a particular effect, it may be assumed that persons to whom the provisions concerned are addressed will act in accordance with them.

Role of Director General of Fair Trading

303   Initial report by Director

(1) The Authority must send to the Treasury and to the Director a copy of any regulatory provisions with which it is provided on an application for recognition under section 287 or 288.

(2) The Authority must send to the Director such information in its possession as a result of the application for recognition as it considers will assist him in discharging his functions in connection with the application.

(3) The Director must issue a report as to whether—

(a) a regulatory provision of which a copy has been sent to him under subsection (1) has a significantly adverse effect on competition; or

(b) a combination of regulatory provisions so copied to him have such an effect.

(4) If the Director's conclusion is that one or more provisions have a significantly adverse effect on competition, he must state his reasons for that conclusion.

(5) When the Director issues a report under subsection (3), he must send a copy of it to the Authority, the Competition Commission and the Treasury.

304   Further reports by Director

(1) The Director must keep under review the regulatory provisions and practices of recognised bodies.

(2) If at any time the Director considers that—

(a) a regulatory provision or practice has a significantly adverse effect on competition, or

(b) regulatory provisions or practices, or a combination of regulating provisions and practices have such an effect,

he must make a report.

(3) If at any time the Director considers that—

(a) a regulatory provision or practice does not have a significantly adverse effect on competition, or

(b) regulatory provisions or practices, or a combination of regulatory provisions and practices do not have any such effect,

he may make a report to that effect.

(4) A report under subsection (2) must contain details of the adverse effect on competition.

(5) If the Director makes a report under subsection (2), he must—

    (a)   send a copy of it to the Treasury, to the Competition Commission and to the Authority; and

    (b)   publish it in the way appearing to him to be best calculated to bring it to the attention of the public.

(6) If the Director makes a report under subsection (3)—

    (a)   he must send a copy of it to the Treasury, to the Competition Commission and to the Authority; and

    (b)   he may publish it.

(7) Before publishing a report under this section, the Director must, so far as practicable, exclude any matter which relates to the private affairs of a particular individual the publication of which, in the opinion of the Director, would or might seriously and prejudicially affect his interests.

(8) Before publishing such a report, the Director must exclude any matter which relates to the affairs of a particular body the publication of which, in the opinion of the Director, would or might seriously and prejudicially affect its interests.

(9) Subsections (7) and (8) do not apply to the copy of a report which the Director is required to send to the Treasury, the Competition Commission and the Authority under subsection (5)(a) or (6)(a).

(10) For the purposes of the law of defamation, absolute privilege attaches to any report of the Director under this section.

305   Investigations by Director

(1) For the purpose of investigating any matter with a view to its consideration under section 303 or 304, the Director may exercise the powers conferred on him by this section.

(2) The Director may by notice in writing require any person to produce to him or to a person appointed by him for the purpose, at a time and place specified in the notice, any document which—

    (a)   is specified or described in the notice; and

    (b)   is a document in that person's custody or under his control.

(3) The Director may by notice in writing—

    (a)   require any person carrying on any business to provide him with such information as may be specified or described in the notice; and

    (b)   specify the time within which, and the manner and form in which, any such information is to be provided.

(4) A requirement may be imposed under subsection (2) or (3)(a) only in respect of documents or information which relate to any matter relevant to the investigation.

(5) If a person ('the defaulter') refuses, or otherwise fails, to comply with a notice under this section, the Director may certify that fact in writing to the court and the court may enquire into the case.

(6) If, after hearing any witness who may be produced against or on behalf of the defaulter and any statement which may be offered in defence, the court is satisfied that the defaulter did not have a reasonable excuse for refusing or otherwise failing to comply with the notice, the court may deal with the defaulter as if he were in contempt.

(7) In this section, 'the court' means—

    (a)   the High Court; or

(b)   in Scotland, the Court of Session.

Role of Competition Commission

306   Consideration by Competition Commission

(1) If subsection (2) or (3) applies, the Commission must investigate the matter which is the subject of the Director's report.

(2) This subsection applies if the Director sends to the Competition Commission a report—

(a)   issued by him under section 303(3) which concludes that one or more regulatory provisions have a significantly adverse effect on competition, or

(b)   made by him under section 304(2).

(3) This subsection applies if the Director asks the Commission to consider a report—

(a)   issued by him under section 303(3) which concludes that one or more regulatory provisions do not have a significantly adverse effect on competition, or

(b)   made by him under section 304(3).

(4) The Commission must then make its own report on the matter unless it considers that, as a result of a change of circumstances, no useful purpose would be served by a report.

(5) If the Commission decides in accordance with subsection (4) not to make a report, it must make a statement setting out the change of circumstances which resulted in that decision.

(6) A report made under this section must state the Commission's conclusion as to whether—

(a)   the regulatory provision or practice which is the subject of the report has a significantly adverse effect on competition, or

(b)   the regulatory provisions or practices or combination of regulatory provisions and practices which are the subject of the report have such an effect.

(7) A report under this section stating the Commission's conclusion that there is a significantly adverse effect on competition must also—

(a)   state whether the Commission considers that that effect is justified; and

(b)   if it states that the Commission considers that it is not justified, state its conclusion as to what action, if any, the Treasury ought to direct the Authority to take.

(8) Subsection (9) applies whenever the Commission is considering, for the purposes of this section, whether a particular adverse effect on competition is justified.

(9) The Commission must ensure, so far as that is reasonably possible, that the conclusion it reaches is compatible with the obligations imposed on the recognised body concerned by or under this Act.

(10) A report under this section must contain such an account of the Commission's reasons for its conclusions as is expedient, in the opinion of the Commission, for facilitating proper understanding of them.

(11) The provisions of Schedule 14 (except paragraph 2(b)) apply for the purposes of this section as they apply for the purposes of section 162.

(12) If the Commission makes a report under this section it must send a copy to the Treasury, the Authority and the Director.

Role of the Treasury

307   Recognition orders: role of the Treasury

(1) Subsection (2) applies if, on an application for a recognition order—

   (a)   the Director makes a report under section 303 but does not ask the Competition Commission to consider it under section 306;
   (b)   the Competition Comission concludes—
       (i)   that the applicant's regulatory provisions do not have a significantly adverse effect on competition; or
       (ii)   that if those provisions do have that effect, the effect is justified.

(2) The Treasury may refuse to approve the making of the recognition order only if they consider that the exceptional circumstances of the case make it inappropriate for them to give their approval.

(3) Subsection (4) applies if, on an application for a recognition order, the Competition Commission concludes—

   (a)   that the applicant's regulatory provisions have a significantly adverse effect on competition; and
   (b)   that that effect is not justified.

(4) The Treasury must refuse to approve the making of the recognition order unless they consider that the exceptional circumstances of the case make it inappropriate for them to refuse their approval.

308   Directions by the Treasury

(1) This section applies if the Competition Commission makes a report under section 306(4) (other than a report on an application for a recognition order) which states the Commission's conclusion that there is a significantly adverse effect on competition.

(2) If the Commission's conclusion, as stated in the report, is that the adverse effect on competition is not justified, the Treasury must give a remedial direction to the Authority.

(3) But subsection (2) does not apply if the Treasury consider—

   (a)   that, as a result of action taken by the Authority or the recognised body concerned in response to the Commission's report, it is unnecessary for them to give a direction; or
   (b)   that the exceptional circumstances of the case make it inappropriate or unnecessary for them to do so.

(4) In considering the action to be specified in a remedial direction, the Treasury must have regard to any conclusion of the Commission included in the report because of section 306(7)(b).

(5) Subsection (6) applies if—

   (a)   the Commission's conclusion, as stated in its report, is that the adverse effect on competition is justified; but
   (b)   the Treasury consider that the exceptional circumstances of the case require them to act.

(6) The Treasury may give a direction to the Authority requiring it to take such action—

   (a)   as they consider to be necessary in the light of the exceptional circumstances of the case; and
   (b)   as may be specified in the direction.

(7) If the action specified in a remedial direction is the giving by the Authority of a direction—

(a)   the direction to be given must be compatible with the recognition requirements applicable to the recognised body in relation to which it is given; and

(b)   subsections (3) and (4) of section 296 apply to it as if it were a direction given under that section.

(8) 'Remedial direction' means a direction requiring the Authority—

(a)   to revoke the recognition order for the body concerned; or

(b)   to give such directions to the body concerned as may be specified in it.

309   Statements by the Treasury

(1) If, in reliance on subsection (3)(a) or (b) of section 308, the Treasury decline to act under subsection (2) of that section, they must make a statement to that effect, giving their reasons.

(2) If the Treasury give a direction under section 308 they must make a statement giving—

(a)   details of the direction; and

(b)   if the direction is given under subsection (6) of that section, their reasons for giving it.

(3) The Treasury must—

(a)   publish any statement made under this section in the way appearing to them best calculated to bring it to the attention of the public; and

(b)   lay a copy of it before Parliament.

310   Procedure on exercise of certain powers by the Treasury

(1) Subsection (2) applies if the Treasury are considering—

(a)   whether to refuse their approval under section 307;

(b)   whether section 308(2) applies; or

(c)   whether to give a direction under section 308(6).

(2) The Treasury must—

(a)   take such steps as they consider appropriate to allow the exchange or clearing house concerned, and any other person appearing to the Treasury to be affected, an opportunity to make representations—

(i)   about any report made by the Director under section 303 or 304 or by the Competition Commission under section 306;

(ii)   as to whether, and if so how, the Treasury should exercise their powers under section 307 or 308; and

(b)   have regard to any such representations.

CHAPTER III

EXCLUSION FROM THE COMPETITION ACT 1998

311   The Chapter I prohibition

(1) The Chapter I prohibition does not apply to an agreement for the constitution of a recognised body to the extent to which the agreement relates to the regulatory provisions of that body.

(2) If the conditions set out in subsection (3) are satisfied, the Chapter I prohibition does not apply to an agreement for the constitution of—

(a)   an investment exchange which is not a recognised investment exchange, or
(b)   a clearing house which is not a recognised clearing house,

to the extent to which the agreement relates to the regulatory provisions of that body.

(3) The conditions are that—

(a)   the body has applied for a recognition order in accordance with the provisions of this Act; and
(b)   the application has not been determined.

(4) The Chapter I prohibition does not apply to a recognised body's regulatory provisions.

(5) The Chapter I prohibition does not apply to a decision made by a recognised body to the extent to which the decision relates to any of that body's regulatory provisions or practices.

(6) The Chapter I prohibition does not apply to practices of a recognised body.

(7) The Chapter I prohibition does not apply to an agreement the parties to which consist of or include—

(a)   a recognised body, or
(b)   a person who is subject to the rules of a recognised body,

to the extent to which the agreement consists of provisions the inclusion of which is required or encouraged by any of the body's regulatory provisions or practices.

(8) If a recognised body's recognition order is revoked, this section is to have effect as if that body had continued to be recognised until the end of the period of six months beginning with the day on which the revocation took effect.

(9) 'The Chapter I prohibition' means the prohibition imposed by section 2(1) of the Competition Act 1998.

(10) Expressions used in this section which are also used in Part I of the Competition Act 1998 are to be interpreted in the same way as for the purposes of that Part of that Act.

312   The Chapter II prohibition

(1) The Chapter II prohibition does not apply to—

(a)   practices of a recognised body;
(b)   the adoption or enforcement of such a body's regulatory provisions;
(c)   any conduct which is engaged in by such a body or by a person who is subject to the rules of such a body to the extent to which it is encouraged or required by the regulatory provisions of the body.

(2) The Chapter II prohibition means the prohibition imposed by section 18(1) of the Competition Act 1998.

CHAPTER IV

Interpretation

313   Interpretation of Part XVIII

(1) In this Part—

'application' means an application for a recognition order made under section 287 or 288;

'applicant' means a body corporate or unincorporated association which has applied for a recognition order;

'Director' means the Director General of Fair Trading;

'overseas applicant' means a body corporate or association which has neither its head office nor its registered office in the United Kingdom and which has applied for a recognition order;

'overseas investment exchange' means a body corporate or association which has neither its head office nor its registered office in the United Kingdom and in relation to which a recognition order is in force;

'overseas clearing house' means a body corporate or association which has neither its head office nor its registered office in the United Kingdom and in relation to which a recognition order is in force;

'recognised body' means a recognised investment exchange or a recognised clearing house;

'recognised clearing house' has the meaning given in section 285;

'recognised investment exchange' has the meaning given in section 285;

'recognition order' means an order made under section 290 or 292;

'recognition requirements' has the meaning given by section 286;

'remedial direction' has the meaning given in section 308(8);

'revocation order' has the meaning given in section 297.

(2) References in this Part to rules of an investment exchange (or a clearing house) are to rules made, or conditions imposed, by the investment exchange (or the clearing house) with respect to—

(a)   recognition requirements;

(b)   admission of persons to, or their exclusion from the use of, its facilities; or

(c)   matters relating to its constitution.

(3) References in this Part to guidance issued by an investment exchange are references to guidance issued, or any recommendation made, in writing or other legible form and intended to have continuing effect, by the investment exchange to—

(a)   all or any class of its members or users, or

(b)   persons seeking to become members of the investment exchange or to use its facilities,

with respect to any of the matters mentioned in subsection (2)(a) to (c).

(4) References in this Part to guidance issued by a clearing house are to guidance issued, or any recommendation made, in writing or other legible form and intended to have continued effect, by the clearing house to—

(a)   all or any class of its members, or

(b)   persons using or seeking to use its services,

with respect to the provision by it or its members of clearing services.

PART XIX

LLOYD'S

General

314   Authority's general duty

(1) The Authority must keep itself informed about—

(a)   the way in which the Council supervises and regulates the market at Lloyd's; and
(b)   the way in which regulated activities are being carried on in that market.

(2) The Authority must keep under review the desirability of exercising—

(a)   any of its powers under this Part;
(b)   any powers which it has in relation to the Society as a result of section 315.

The Society

315   The Society: authorisation and permission

(1) The Society is an authorised person.

(2) The Society has permission to carry on a regulated activity of any of the following kinds—

(a)   arranging deals in contracts of insurance written at Lloyd's ('the basic market activity');
(b)   arranging deals in participation in Lloyd's syndicates ('the secondary market activity'); and
(c)   an activity carried on in connection with, or for the purposes of, the basic or secondary market activity.

(3) For the purposes of Part IV, the Society's permission is to be treated as if it had been given on an application for permission under that Part.

(4) The power conferred on the Authority by section 45 may be exercised in anticipation of the coming into force of the Society's permission (or at any other time).

(5) The Society is not subject to any requirement of this Act concerning the registered office of a body corporate.

Power to apply Act to Lloyd's underwriting

316   Direction by Authority

(1) The general prohibition or (if the general prohibition is not applied under this section) a core provision applies to the carrying on of an insurance market activity by—

(a)   a member of the Society, or
(b)   the members of the Society taken together,

only if the Authority so directs.

(2) A direction given under subsection (1) which applies a core provision is referred to in this Part as 'an insurance market direction'.

(3) In subsection (1)—

'core provision' means a provision of this Act mentioned in section 317; and
'insurance market activity' means a regulated activity relating to contracts of insurance
    written at Lloyd's.

(4) In deciding whether to give a direction under subsection (1), the Authority must have
particular regard to—

- (a)   the interests of policyholders and potential policyholders;
- (b)   any failure by the Society to satisfy an obligation to which it is subject as a result of a
    provision of the law of another EEA State which—
    - (i)   gives effect to any of the insurance directives; and
    - (ii)   is applicable to an activity carried on in that State by a person to whom this
        section applies;
- (c)   the need to ensure the effective exercise of the functions which the Authority has in
    relation to the Society as a result of section 315.

(5) A direction under subsection (1) must be in writing.

(6) A direction under subsection (1) applying the general prohibition may apply it in
relation to different classes of person.

(7) An insurance market direction—

- (a)   must specify each core provision, class of person and kind of activity to which it
    applies;
- (b)   may apply different provisions in relation to different classes of person and
    different kinds of activity.

(8) A direction under subsection (1) has effect from the date specified in it, which may not
be earlier than the date on which it is made.

(9) A direction under subsection (1) must be published in the way appearing to the
Authority to be best calculated to bring it to the attention of the public.

(10) The Authority may charge a reasonable fee for providing a person with a copy of the
direction.

(11) The Authority must, without delay, give the Treasury a copy of any direction which it
gives under this section.

317   The core provisions

(1) The core provisions are Parts V, X, XI, XII, XIV, XV, XVI, XXII and XXIV, sections 384
to 386 and Part XXVI.

(2) References in an applied core provision to an authorised person are (where necessary)
to be read as references to a person in the class to which the insurance market direction
applies.

(3) An insurance market direction may provide that a core provision is to have effect, in
relation to persons to whom the provision is applied by the direction, with modifications.

318   Exercise of powers through Council

(1) The Authority may give a direction under this subsection to the Council or to the
Society (acting through the Council) or to both.

(2) A direction under subsection (1) is one given to the body concerned—

- (a)   in relation to the exercise of its powers generally with a view to achieving, or in
    support of, a specified objective; or

(b) in relation to the exercise of a specified power which it has, whether in a specified manner or with a view to achieving, or in support of, a specified objective.

(3) 'Specified' means specified in the direction.

(4) A direction under subsection (1) may be given—

(a) instead of giving a direction under section 316(1); or
(b) if the Authority considers it necessary or expedient to do so, at the same time as, or following, the giving of such a direction.

(5) A direction may also be given under subsection (1) in respect of underwriting agents as if they were among the persons mentioned in section 316(1).

(6) A direction under this section—

(a) does not, at any time, prevent the exercise by the Authority of any of its powers;
(b) must be in writing.

(7) A direction under section (1) must be published in the way appearing to the Authority to be best calculated to bring it to the attention of the public.

(8) The Authority may charge a reasonable fee for providing a person with a copy of the direction.

(9) The Authority must, without delay, give the Treasury a copy of any direction which it gives under this section.

319 Consultation

(1) Before giving a direction under section 316 or 318, the Authority must publish a draft of the proposed direction.

(2) The draft must be accompanied by—

(a) a cost benefit analysis; and
(b) notice that representations about the proposed direction may be made to the Authority within a specified time.

(3) Before giving the proposed direction, the Authority must have regard to any representations made to it in accordance with subsection (2)(b).

(4) If the Authority gives the proposed direction it must publish an account, in general terms, of—

(a) the representations made to it in accordance with subsection (2)(b); and
(b) its response to them.

(5) If the direction differs from the draft published under subsection (1) in a way which is, in the opinion of the Authority, significant—

(a) the Authority must (in addition to complying with subsection 4)) publish details of the difference; and
(b) those details must be accompanied by a cost benefit analysis.

(6) Subsections (1) to (5) do not apply if the Authority considers that the delay involved in complying with them would be prejudicial to the interests of consumers.

(7) Neither subsection (2)(a) nor subsection (5)(b) applies if the Authority considers—

(a) that, making the appropriate comparison, there will be no increase in costs; or
(b) that, making that comparison, there will be an increase in costs but the increase will be of minimal significance.

(8) The Authority may charge a reasonable fee for providing a person with a copy of a draft published under subsection (1).

(9) When the Authority is required to publish a document under this section it must do so in the way appearing to it to be best calculated to bring it to the attention of the public.

(10) 'Cost benefit analysis' means an estimate of the costs together with an analysis of the benefits that will arise—

  (a)   if the proposed direction is given; or
  (b)   if subsection (5)(b) applies, from the direction that has been given.

(11) 'The appropriate comparison' means—

  (a)   in relation to subsection (2)(a), a comparison between the overall position if the direction is given and the overall position if it is not given;
  (b)   in relation to subsection (5)(b), a comparison between the overall position after the giving of the direction and the overall position before it was given.

Former underwriting members

320   Former underwriting members

(1) A former underwriting member may carry out each contract of insurance that he has underwritten at Lloyd's whether or not he is an authorised person.

(2) If he is an authorised person, any Part IV permission that he has does not extend to his activities in carrying out any of those contracts.

(3) The Authority may impose on a former underwriting member such requirements as appear to it to be appropriate for the purpose of protecting policyholders against the risk that he may not be able to meet his liabilities.

(4) A person on whom a requirement is imposed may refer the matter to the Tribunal.

321   Requirements imposed under section 320

(1) A requirement imposed under section 320 takes effect—

  (a)   immediately, if the notice given under subsection (2) states that that is the case;
  (b)   in any other case, on such date as may be specified in that notice.

(2) If the Authority proposes to impose a requirement on a former underwriting member ('A') under section 320, or imposes such a requirement on him which takes effect immediately, it must give him written notice.

(3) The notice must—

  (a)   give details of the requirement;
  (b)   state the Authority's reasons for imposing it;
  (c)   inform A that he may make representations to the Authority within such period as may be specified in the notice (whether or not he has referred the matter to the Tribunal);
  (d)   inform him of the date on which the requirement took effect or will take effect; and
  (e)   inform him of his right to refer the matter to the Tribunal.

(4) The Authority may extend the period allowed under the notice for making representations.

(5) If, having considered any representations made by A, the Authority decides—

  (a)   to impose the proposed requirement, or

(b)   if it has been imposed, not to revoke it,

it must give him written notice.

(6) If the Authority decides—

(a)   not to impose a proposed requirement, or
(b)   to revoke a requirement that has been imposed,

it must give A written notice.

(7) If the Authority decides to grant an application by A for the variation or revocation of a requirement, it must give him written notice of its decision.

(8) If the Authority proposes to refuse an application by A for the variation or revocation of a requirement it must give him a warning notice.

(9) If the Authority, having considered any representations made in response to the warning notice, decides to refuse the application, it must give A a decision notice.

(10) A notice given under—

(a)   subsection (5), or
(b)   subsection (9) in the case of a decision to refuse the application,

must inform A of his right to refer the matter to the Tribunal.

(11) If the Authority decides to refuse an application for a variation or revocation of the requirement, the applicant may refer the matter to the Tribunal.

(12) If a notice informs a person of his right to refer a matter to the Tribunal, it must give an indication of the procedure on such a reference.

322   Rules applicable to former underwriting members

(1) The Authority may make rules imposing such requirements on persons to whom the rules apply as appear to it to be appropriate for protecting policyholders against the risk that those persons may not be able to meet their liabilities.

(2) The rules may apply to—

(a)   former underwriting members generally; or
(b)   to a class of former underwriting member specified in them.

(3) Section 319 applies to the making of proposed rules under this section as it applies to the giving of a proposed direction under section 316.

(4) Part X (except sections 152 to 154) does not apply to rules made under this section.

Transfers of business done at Lloyd's

323   Transfer schemes

The Treasury may by order provide for the application of any provision of Part VII (with or without modification) in relation to schemes for the transfer of the whole or any part of the business carried on by one or more members of the Society or former underwriting members.

Supplemental

324   Interpretation of this Part

(1) In this Part—

'arranging deals', in relation to the investments to which this Part applies, has the same meaning as in paragraph 3 of Schedule 2;

'former underwriting member' means a person ceasing to be an underwriting member of the Society on, or at any time after, 24 December 1996; and

'participating in Lloyd's syndicates', in relation to the secondary market activity, means the investment described in sub-paragraph (1) of paragraph 21 of Schedule 2.

(2) A term used in this Part which is defined in Lloyd's Act 1982 has the same meaning as in that Act.

PART XX

PROVISION OF FINANCIAL SERVICES BY MEMBERS OF THE PROFESSIONS

325   Authority's general duty

(1) The Authority must keep itself informed about—

(a)   the way in which designated professional bodies supervise and regulate the carrying on of exempt regulated activities by members of the professions in relation to which they are established;

(b)   the way in which such members are carrying on exempt regulated activities.

(2) In this Part—

'exempt regulated activities' means regulated activities which may, as a result of this Part, be carried on by members of a profession which is supervised and regulated by a designated professional body without breaching the general prohibition; and

'members', in relation to a profession, means persons who are entitled to practise the profession in question and, in practising it, are subject to the rules of the body designated in relation to that profession, whether or not they are members of that body.

(3) The Authority must keep under review the desirability of exercising any of its powers under this Part.

(4) Each designated professional body must co-operate with the Authority, by the sharing of information and in other ways, in order to enable the Authority to perform its functions under this Part.

326   Designation of professional bodies

(1) The Treasury may by order designate bodies for the purposes of this Part.

(2) A body designated under subsection (1) is referred to in this Part as a designated professional body.

(3) The Treasury may designate a body under subsection (1) only if they are satisfied that—

(a)   the basic condition, and

(b)   one or more of the additional conditions,

are met in relation to it.

(4) The basic condition is that the body has rules applicable to the carrying on by members of the profession in relation to which it is established of regulated activities which, if the body were to be designated, would be exempt regulated activities.

(5) The additional conditions are that—

(a) the body has power under any enactment to regulate the practice of the profession;

(b) being a member of the profession is a requirement under any enactment for the exercise of particular functions or the holding of a particular office;

(c) the body has been recognised for the purpose of any enactment other than this Act and the recognition has not been withdrawn;

(d) the body is established in an EEA State other than the United Kingdom and in that State—

    (i) the body has power corresponding to that mentioned in paragraph (a);

    (ii) there is a requirement in relation to the body corresponding to that mentioned in paragraph (b); or

    (iii) the body is recognised in a manner corresponding to that mentioned in paragraph (c).

(6) 'Enactment' includes an Act of the Scottish Parliament, Northern Ireland legislation and subordinate legislation (whether made under an Act, an Act of the Scottish Parliament or Northern Ireland legislation).

(7) 'Recognised' means recognised by—

(a) a Minister of the Crown;

(b) the Scottish Ministers;

(c) a Northern Ireland Minister;

(d) a Northern Ireland department or its head.

327 Exemption from the general prohibition

(1) The general prohibition does not apply to the carrying on of a regulated activity by a person ('P') if—

(a) the conditions set out in subsections (2) to (7) are satisfied; and

(b) there is not in force—

    (i) a direction under section 328, or

    (ii) an order under section 329,

    which prevents this subsection from applying to the carrying on of that activity by him.

(2) P must be—

(a) a member of a profession; or

(b) controlled or managed by one or more such members.

(3) P must not receive from a person other than his client any pecuniary reward or other advantage, for which he does not account to his client, arising out of his carrying on of any of the activities.

(4) The manner of the provision by P of any service in the course of carrying on the activities must be incidental to the provision by him of professional services.

(5) P must not carry on, or hold himself out as carrying on, a regulated activity other than—

(a) one which rules made as a result of section 332(3) allow him to carry on; or

(b) one in relation to which he is an exempt person.

(6) The activities must not be of a description, or relate to an investment of a description, specified in an order made by the Treasury for the purposes of this subsection.

(7) The activities must be the only regulated activities carried on by P (other than regulated activities in relation to which he is an exempt person).

(8) 'Professional services' means services—

(a) which do not constitute carrying on a regulated activity, and

(b) the provision of which is supervised and regulated by a designated professional body.

328 Directions in relation to the general prohibition

(1) The Authority may direct that section 327(1) is not to apply to the extent specified in the direction.

(2) A direction under subsection (1)—

(a) must be in writing;
(b) may be given in relation to different classes of person or different descriptions of regulated activity.

(3) A direction under subsection (1) must be published in the way appearing to the Authority to be best calculated to bring it to the attention of the public.

(4) The Authority may charge a reasonable fee for providing a person with a copy of the direction.

(5) The Authority must, without delay, give the Treasury a copy of any direction which it gives under this section.

(6) The Authority may exercise the power conferred by subsection (1) only if it is satisfied that it is desirable in order to protect the interests of clients.

(7) In considering whether it is so satisfied, the Authority must have regard amongst other things to the effectiveness of any arrangements made by any designated professional body—

(a) for securing compliance with rules made under section 332(1);
(b) for dealing with complaints against its members in relation to the carrying on by them of exempt regulated activities;
(c) in order to offer redress to clients who suffer, or claim to have suffered, loss as a result of misconduct by its members in their carrying on of exempt regulated activities;
(d) for co-operating with the Authority under section 325(4).

(8) In this Part 'clients' means—

(a) persons who use, have used or are or may be contemplating using, any of the services provided by a member of a profession in the course of carrying on exempt regulated activities;
(b) persons who have rights or interests which are derived from, or otherwise attributable to, the use of any such services by other persons; or
(c) persons who have rights or interests which may be adversely affected by the use of any such services by persons acting on their behalf or in a fiduciary capacity in relation to them.

(9) If a member of a profession is carrying on an exempt regulated activity in his capacity as a trustee, the persons who are, have been or may be beneficiaries of the trust are to be treated as persons who use, have used or are or may be contemplating using services provided by that person in his carrying on of that activity.

329 Orders in relation to the general prohibition

(1) Subsection (2) applies if it appears to the Authority that a person to whom, as a result of section 327(1), the general prohibition does not apply is not a fit and proper person to carry on regulated activities in accordance with that section.

(2) The Authority may make an order disapplying section 327(1) in relation to that person to the extent specified in the order.

(3) The Authority may, on the application of the person named in an order under subsection (1), vary or revoke it.

(4) 'Specified' means specified in the order.

(5) If a partnership is named in an order under this section, the order is not affected by any change in its membership.

(6) If a partnership named in an order under this section is dissolved, the order continues to have effect in relation to any partnership which succeeds to the business of the dissolved partnership.

(7) For the purposes of subsection (6), a partnership is to be regarded as succeeding to the business of another partnership only if—

- (a) the members of the resulting partnership are substantially the same as those of the former partnership; and
- (b) succession is to the whole or substantially the whole of the business of the former partnership.

330   Consultation

(1) Before giving a direction under section 328(1), the Authority must publish a draft of the proposed direction.

(2) The draft must be accompanied by—

- (a) a cost benefit analysis; and
- (b) notice that representations about the proposed direction may be made to the Authority within a specified time.

(3) Before giving the proposed direction, the Authority must have regard to any representations made to it in accordance with subsection (2)(b).

(4) If the Authority gives the proposed direction it must publish an account, in general terms, of—

- (a) the representations made to it in accordance with subsection (2)(b); and
- (b) its response to them.

(5) If the direction differs from the draft published under subsection (1) in a way which is, in the opinion of the Authority, significant—

- (a) the Authority must (in addition to complying with subsection (4)) publish details of the difference; and
- (b) those details must be accompanied by a cost benefit analysis.

(6) Subsections (1) to (5) do not apply if the Authority considers that the delay involved in complying with them would prejudice the interests of consumers.

(7) Neither subsection (2)(a) nor subsection (5)(b) applies if the Authority considers—

- (a) that, making the appropriate comparison, there will be no increase in costs; or
- (b) that, making that comparison, there will be an increase in costs but the increase will be of minimal significance.

(8) The Authority may charge a reasonable fee for providing a person with a copy of a draft published under subsection (1).

(9) When the Authority is required to publish a document under this section it must do so in the way appearing to it to be best calculated to bring it to the attention of the public.

(10) 'Cost benefit analysis' means an estimate of the costs together with an analysis of the benefits that will arise—

    (a)   if the proposed direction is given; or

    (b)   if subsection (5)(b) applies, from the direction that has been given.

(11)   'The appropriate comparison' means—

    (a)   in relation to subsection (2)(a), a comparison between the overall position if the direction is given and the overall position if it is not given;

    (b)   in relation to subsection (5)(b), a comparison between the overall position after the giving of the direction and the overall position before it was given.

331   Procedure on making or varying orders under section 329

(1) If the Authority proposes to make an order under section 329, it must give the person concerned a warning notice.

(2) The warning notice must set out the terms of the proposed order.

(3) If the Authority decides to make an order under section 329, it must give the person concerned a decision notice.

(4) The decision notice must—

    (a)   name the person to whom the order applies;

    (b)   set out the terms of the order; and

    (c)   be given to the person named in the order.

(5) Subsections (6) to (8) apply to an application for the variation or revocation of an order under section 329.

(6) If the Authority decides to grant the application, it must give the applicant written notice of its decision.

(7) If the Authority proposes to refuse the application, it must give the applicant a warning notice.

(8) If the Authority decides to refuse the application, it must give the applicant a decision notice.

(9) A person—

    (a)   against whom the Authority have decided to make an order under section 329, or

    (b)   whose application for the variation or revocation of such an order the Authority had decided to refuse,

may refer the matter to the Tribunal.

(10) The Authority may not make an order under section 329 unless—

    (a)   the period within which the decision to make to the order may be referred to the Tribunal has expired and no such reference has been made; or

    (b)   if such a reference has been made, the reference has been determined.

332   Rules in relation to persons to whom the general prohibition does not apply

(1) The Authority may make rules applicable to persons to whom, as a result of section 327(1), the general prohibition does not apply.

(2) The power conferred by subsection (1) is to be exercised for the purpose of ensuring that clients are aware that such persons are not authorised persons.

(3) A designated professional body must make rules—

    (a) applicable to members of the profession in relation to which it is established who are not authorised persons; and

    (b) governing the carrying on by those members of regulated activities (other than regulated activities in relation to which they are exempt persons).

(4) Rules made in compliance with subsection (3) must be designed to secure that, in providing a particular professional service to a particular client, the member carries on only regulated activities which arise out of, or are complementary to, the provision by him of that service to that client.

(5) Rules made by a designated professional body under subsection (3) require the approval of the Authority.

333 False claims to be a person to whom the general prohibition does not apply

(1) A person who—

    (a) describes himself (in whatever terms) as a person to whom the general prohibition does not apply, in relation to a particular regulated activity, as a result of this Part, or

    (b) behaves, or otherwise holds himself out, in a manner which indicates (or which is reasonably likely to be understood as indicating) that he is such a person,

is guilty of an offence if he is not such a person.

(2) In proceedings for an offence under this section it is a defence for the accused to show that he took all reasonable precautions and exercised all due diligence to avoid committing the offence.

(3) A person guilty of an offence under this section is liable on summary conviction to imprisonment for a term not exceeding six months or a fine not exceeding level 5 on the standard scale, or both.

(4) But where the conduct constituting the offence involved or included the public display of any material, the maximum fine for the offence is level 5 on the standard scale multiplied by the number of days for which the display continued.

PART XXI

MUTUAL SOCIETIES

Friendly societies

334 The Friendly Societies Commission

(1) The Treasury may by order provide—

    (a) for any functions of the Friendly Societies Commission to be transferred to the Authority;

    (b) for any functions of the Friendly Societies Commission which have not been, or are not being, transferred to the Authority to be transferred to the Treasury.

(2) If the Treasury consider it appropriate to do so, they may by order provide for the Friendly Societies Commission to cease to exist on a day specified in or determined in accordance with the order.

(3) The enactments relating to friendly societies which are mentioned in Part I of Schedule 18 are amended as set out in that Part.

(4) Part II of Schedule 18—

   (a)   removes certain restrictions on the ability of incorporated friendly societies to form subsidiaries and control corporate bodies; and

   (b)   makes connected amendments.

335   The Registry of Friendly Societies

(1) The Treasury may by order provide—

   (a)   for any functions of the Chief Registrar of Friendly Societies, or of an assistant registrar of friendly societies for the central registration area, to be transferred to the Authority;

   (b)   for any of their functions which have not been, or are not being, transferred to the Authority to be transferred to the Treasury.

(2) The Treasury may by order provide—

   (a)   for any functions of the central office of the registry of friendly societies to be transferred to the Authority;

   (b)   for any functions of that office which have not been, or are not being, transferred to the Authority to be transferred to the Treasury.

(3) The Treasury may by order provide—

   (a)   for any functions of the assistant registrar of friendly societies for Scotland to be transferred to the Authority;

   (b)   for any functions of the assistant registrar which have not been, or are not being, transferred to the Authority to be transferred to the Treasury.

(4) If the Treasury consider it appropriate to do so, they may by order provide for—

   (a)   the office of Chief Registrar of Friendly Societies,

   (b)   the office of assistant registrar of friendly societies for the central registration area,

   (c)   the central office, or

   (d)   the office of assistant registrar of friendly societies for Scotland,

to cease to exist on a day specified in or determined in accordance with the order.

Building societies

336   The Building Societies Commission

(1) The Treasury may by order provide—

   (a)   for any functions of the Building Societies Commission to be transferred to the Authority;

   (b)   for any functions of the Building Societies Commission which have not been, or are not being, transferred to the Authority to be transferred to the Treasury.

(2) If the Treasury consider it appropriate to do so, they may by order provide for the Building Societies Commission to cease to exist on a day specified in or determined in accordance with the order.

(3) The enactments relating to building societies which are mentioned in Part III of Schedule 18 are amended as set out in that Part.

337   The Building Societies Investor Protection Board

The Treasury may by order provide for the Building Societies Investor Protection Board to cease to exist on a day specified in or determined in accordance with the order.

Industrial and provident societies and credit unions

338   Industrial and provident societies and credit unions

(1) The Treasury may by order provide for the transfer to the Authority of any functions conferred by—

   (a)   the Industrial and Provident Societies Act 1965;
   (b)   the Industrial and Provident Societies Act 1967;
   (c)   the Friendly and Industrial and Provident Societies Act 1968;
   (d)   the Industrial and Provident Societies Act 1975;
   (e)   the Industrial and Provident Societies Act 1978;
   (f)   the Credit Unions Act 1979.

(2) The Treasury may by order provide for the transfer to the Treasury of any functions under those enactments which have not been, or are not being, transferred to the Authority.

(3) The enactments relating to industrial and provident societies which are mentioned in Part IV of Schedule 18 are amended as set out in that Part.

(4) The enactments relating to credit unions which are mentioned in Part V of Schedule 18 are amended as set out in that Part.

Supplemental

339   Supplemental provisions

(1) The additional powers conferred by section 428 on a person making an order under this Act include power for the Treasury, when making an order under section 334, 335, 336 or 338 which transfers functions, to include provision—

   (a)   for the transfer of any functions of a member of the body, or servant or agent of the body or person, whose functions are transferred by the order;
   (b)   for the transfer of any property, rights or liabilities held, enjoyed or incurred by any person in connection with transferred functions;
   (c)   for the carrying on and completion by or under the authority of the person to whom functions are transferred of any proceedings, investigations, or other matters commenced, before the order takes effect, by or under the authority of the person from whom the functions are transferred;
   (d)   amending any enactment relating to transferred functions in connection with their exercise by, or under the authority of, the person to whom they are transferred;
   (e)   for the substitution of the person to whom functions are transferred for the person from whom they are transferred, in any instrument, contract or legal proceedings made or begun before the order takes effect.

(2) The additional powers conferred by section 428 on a person making an order under this Act include power for the Treasury, when making an order under section 334(2), 335(4), 336(2) or 337, to include provision—

   (a)   for the transfer of any property, rights or liabilities held, enjoyed or incurred by any person in connection with the office or body which ceases to have effect as a result of the order;
   (b)   for the carrying on and completion by or under the authority of such person as may be specified in the order of any proceedings, investigations or other matters commenced, before the order takes effect, by or under the authority of the person whose office, or the body which, ceases to exist as a result of the order;
   (c)   amending any enactment which makes provision with respect to that office or body;

(d) for the substitution of the Authority, the Treasury or such other body as may be specified in the order in any instrument, contract or legal proceedings made or begun before the order takes effect.

(3) On or after the making of an order under any of sections 334 to 338 ('the original order'), the Treasury may by order make any incidental, supplemental, consequential or transitional provision which they had power to include in the original order.

(4) A certificate issued by the Treasury that property vested in a person immediately before an order under this Part takes effect has been transferred as a result of the order is conclusive evidence of the transfer.

(5) Subsections (1) and (2) are not to be read as affecting in any way the powers conferred by section 428.

PART XXII

AUDITORS AND ACTUARIES

Appointment

340   Appointment

(1) Rules may require an authorised person, or an authorised person falling within a specified class—

(a) to appoint an auditor, or
(b) to appoint an actuary,

if he is not already under an obligation to do so imposed by another enactment.

(2) Rules may require an authorised person, or an authorised person falling within a specified class—

(a) to produce periodic financial reports; and
(b) to have them reported on by an auditor or an actuary.

(3) Rules may impose such other duties on auditors of, or actuaries acting for, authorised persons as may be specified.

(4) Rules under subsection (1) may make provision—

(a) specifying the manner in which and time within which an auditor or actuary is to be appointed;
(b) requiring the Authority to be notified of an appointment;
(c) enabling the Authority to make an appointment if no appointment has been made or notified;
(d) as to remuneration;
(e) as to the term of office, removal and resignation of an auditor or actuary.

(5) An auditor or actuary appointed as a result of rules under subsection (1), or on whom duties are imposed by rules under subsection (3)—

(a) must act in accordance with such provision as may be made by rules; and
(b) is to have such powers in connection with the discharge of his functions as may be provided by rules.

(6) In subsections (1) to (3) 'auditor' or 'actuary' means an auditor, or actuary, who satisfies such requirements as to qualifications, experience and other matters (if any) as may be specified.

(7) 'Specified' means specified in rules.

Information

341 Access to books etc.

(1) An appointed auditor of, or an appointed actuary acting for, an authorised person—

- (a) has a right of access at all times to the authorised person's books, accounts and vouchers; and
- (b) is entitled to require from the authorised person's officers such information and explanations as he reasonably considers necessary for the performance of his duties as auditor or actuary.

(2) 'Appointed' means appointed under or as a result of this Act.

342 Information given by auditor or actuary to the Authority

(1) This section applies to a person who is, or has been, an auditor of an authorised person appointed under or as a result of a statutory provision.

(2) This section also applies to a person who is, or has been, an actuary acting for an authorised person and appointed under or as a result of a statutory provision.

(3) An auditor or actuary does not contravene any duty to which he is subject merely because he gives to the Authority—

- (a) information on a matter of which he has, or had, become aware in his capacity as auditor of, or actuary acting for, the authorised person, or
- (b) his opinion on such a matter,

if he is acting in good faith and he reasonably believes that the information or opinion is relevant to any functions of the Authority.

(4) Subsection (3) applies whether or not the auditor or actuary is responding to a request from the Authority.

(5) The Treasury may make regulations prescribing circumstances in which an auditor or actuary must communicate matters to the Authority as mentioned in subsection (3).

(6) It is the duty of an auditor or actuary to whom any such regulations apply to communicate a matter to the Authority in the circumstances prescribed by the regulations.

(7) The matters to be communicated to the Authority in accordance with the regulations may include matters relating to persons other than the authorised person concerned.

343 Information given by auditor or actuary to the Authority: persons with close links

(1) This section applies to a person who—

- (a) is, or has been, an auditor of an authorised person appointed under or as a result of a statutory provision; and
- (b) is, or has been, an auditor of a person ('CL') who has close links with the authorised person.

(2) This section also applies to a person who—

- (a) is, or has been, an actuary acting for an authorised person and appointed under or as a result of a statutory provision; and
- (b) is, or has been, an actuary acting for a person ('CL') who has close links with the authorised person.

(3) An auditor or actuary does not contravene any duty to which he is subject merely because he gives to the Authority—

  (a) information on a matter concerning the authorised person of which he has, or had, become aware in his capacity as auditor of, or actuary acting for, CL, or
  (b) his opinion on such a matter,

if he is acting in good faith and he reasonably believes that the information or opinion is relevant to any functions of the Authority.

(4) Subsection (3) applies whether or not the auditor or actuary is responding to a request from the Authority.

(5) The Treasury may make regulations prescribing circumstances in which an auditor or actuary must communicate matters to the Authority as mentioned in subsection (3).

(6) It is the duty of an auditor or actuary to whom any such regulations apply to communicate a matter to the Authority in the circumstances prescribed by the regulations.

(7) The matters to be communicated to the Authority in accordance with the regulations may include matters relating to persons other than the authorised person concerned.

(8) CL has close links with the authorised person concerned ('A') if CL is—

  (a) a parent undertaking of A;
  (b) a subsidiary undertaking of A;
  (c) a parent undertaking of a subsidiary undertaking of A; or
  (d) a subsidiary undertaking of a parent undertaking of A.

(9) 'Subsidiary undertaking' includes all the instances mentioned in Article 1(1) and (2) of the Seventh Company Law Directive in which an entity may be a subsidiary of an undertaking.

344   Duty of auditor or actuary resigning etc. to give notice

(1) This section applies to an auditor or actuary to whom section 342 applies.

(2) He must without delay notify the Authority if he—

  (a) is removed from office by an authorised person;
  (b) resigns before the expiry of his term of office with such a person; or
  (c) is not re-appointed by such a person.

(3) If he ceases to be an auditor of, or actuary acting for, such a person, he must without delay notify the Authority—

  (a) of any matter connected with his so ceasing which he thinks ought to be drawn to the Authority's attention; or
  (b) that there is no such matter.

Disqualification

345   Disqualification

(1) If it appears to the Authority that an auditor or actuary to whom section 342 applies has failed to comply with a duty imposed on him under this Act, it may disqualify him from being the auditor of, or (as the case may be) from acting as an actuary for, any authorised person or any particular class of authorised person.

(2) If the Authority proposes to disqualify a person under this section it must give him a warning notice.

(3) If it decides to disqualify him it must give him a decision notice.

(4) The Authority may remove any disqualification imposed under this section if satisfied that the disqualified person will in future comply with the duty in question.

(5) A person who has been disqualified under this section may refer the matter to the Tribunal.

Offence

346   Provision of false or misleading information to auditor or actuary

(1) An authorised person who knowingly or recklessly gives an appointed auditor or actuary information which is false of misleading in a material particular is guilty of an offence and liable—

    (a)   on summary conviction, to imprisonment for a term not exceeding six months or a fine not exceeding the statutory maximum, or both;

    (b)   on conviction on indictment, to imprisonment for a term not exceeding two years or a fine, or both.

(2) Subsection (1) applies equally to an officer, controller or manager of an authorised person.

(3) 'Appointed' means appointed under or as a result of this Act.

PART XXIII

PUBLIC RECORD, DISCLOSURE OF INFORMATION AND CO-OPERATION

The public record

347   The record of authorised persons etc.

(1) The Authority must maintain a record of every—

    (a)   person who appears to the Authority to be an authorised person;

    (b)   authorised unit trust scheme;

    (c)   authorised open-ended investment company;

    (d)   recognised scheme;

    (e)   recognised investment exchange;

    (f)   recognised clearing house;

    (g)   individual to whom a prohibition order relates;

    (h)   approved person; and

    (i)   person falling within such other class (if any) as the Authority may determine.

(2) The record must include such information as the Authority considers appropriate and at least the following information—

    (a)   in the case of a person appearing to the Authority to be an authorised person—

        (i)   information as to the services which he holds himself out as able to provide; and

        (ii)   any address of which the Authority is aware at which a notice or other document may be served on him;

    (b)   in the case of an authorised unit trust scheme, the name and address of the manager and trustee of the scheme;

    (c)   in the case of an authorised open-ended investment company, the name and address of—

        (i)   the company;

   (ii) if it has only one director, the director; and

   (iii) its depositary (if any);

 (d) in the case of a recognised scheme, the name and address of—

   (i) the operator of the scheme; and

   (ii) any representative of the operator in the United Kingdom;

 (e) in the case of a recognised investment exchange or recognised clearing house, the name and address of the exchange or clearing house;

 (f) in the case of an individual to whom a prohibition order relates—

   (i) his name; and

   (ii) details of the effect of the order;

 (g) in the case of a person who is an approved person—

   (i) his name;

   (ii) the name of the relevant authorised person;

   (iii) if the approved person is performing a controlled function under an arrangement with a contractor of the relevant authorised person, the name of the contractor.

(3) If it appears to the Authority that a person in respect of whom there is an entry in the record as a result of one of the paragraphs of subsection (1) has ceased to be a person to whom that paragraph applies, the Authority may remove the entry from the record.

(4) But if the Authority decides not to remove the entry, it must—

 (a) make a note to that effect in the record; and

 (b) state why it considers that the person has ceased to be a person to whom that paragraph applies.

(5) The Authority must—

 (a) make the record available for inspection by members of the public in a legible form at such times and in such place or places as the Authority may determine; and

 (b) provide a certified copy of the record, or any part of it, to any person who asks for it—

   (i) on payment of the fee (if any) fixed by the Authority; and

   (ii) in a form (either written or electronic) in which it is legible to the person asking for it.

(6) The Authority may—

 (a) publish the record, or any part of it;

 (b) exploit commercially the information contained in the record, or any part of that information.

(7) 'Authorised unit trust scheme', 'authorised open-ended investment company' and 'recognised scheme' have the same meaning as in Part XVII, and associated expressions are to be read accordingly.

(8) 'Approved person' means a person in relation to whom the Authority has given its approval under section 59 and 'controlled function' and 'arrangement' have the same meaning as in that section.

(9) 'Relevant authorised person' has the meaning given in section 66.

Disclosure of information

348 Restrictions on disclosure of confidential information by Authority etc.

(1) Confidential information must not be disclosed by a primary recipient, or by any person obtaining the information directly or indirectly from a primary recipient, without the consent of—

    (a)   the person from whom the primary recipient obtained the information; and

    (b)   if different, the person to whom it relates.

(2) In this Part 'confidential information' means information which—

    (a)   relates to the business or other affairs of any person;

    (b)   was received by the primary recipient for the purposes of, or in the discharge of, any functions of the Authority, the competent authority for the purposes of Part VI or the Secretary of State under any provision made by or under this Act; and

    (c)   is not prevented from being confidential information by subsection (4).

(3) It is immaterial for the purposes of subsection (2) whether or not the information was received—

    (a)   by virtue of a requirement to provide it imposed by or under this Act;

    (b)   for other purposes as well as purposes mentioned in that subsection.

(4) Information is not confidential information if—

    (a)   it has been made available to the public by virtue of being disclosed in any circumstances in which, or for any purposes for which, disclosure is not precluded by this section; or

    (b)   it is in the form of a summary or collection of information so framed that it is not possible to ascertain from it information relating to any particular person.

(5) Each of the following is a primary recipient for the purposes of this Part—

    (a)   the Authority;

    (b)   any person exercising functions conferred by Part VI on the competent authority;

    (c)   the Secretary of State;

    (d)   a person appointed to make a report under section 166;

    (e)   any person who is or has been employed by a person mentioned in paragraphs (a) to (c);

    (f)   any auditor or expert instructed by a person mentioned in those paragraphs.

(6) In subsection (5)(f) 'expert' includes—

    (a)   a competent person appointed by the competent authority under section 97;

    (b)   a competent person appointed by the Authority or the Secretary of State to conduct an investigation under Part XI;

    (c)   any body or person appointed under paragraph 6 of Schedule 1 to perform a function on behalf of the Authority.

349   Exceptions from section 348

(1) Section 348 does not prevent a disclosure of confidential information which is—

    (a)   made for the purpose of facilitating the carrying out of a public function; and

    (b)   permitted by regulations made by the Treasury under this section.

(2) The regulations may, in particular, make provision permitting the disclosure of confidential information or of confidential information of a prescribed kind—

    (a)   by prescribed recipients, or recipients of a prescribed description, to any person for the purpose of enabling or assisting the recipient to discharge prescribed public functions;

    (b)   by prescribed recipients, or recipients of a prescribed description, to prescribed persons, or persons of prescribed descriptions, for the purpose of enabling or assisting those persons to discharge prescribed public functions;

   (c)   by the Authority to the Treasury or the Secretary of State for any purpose;

   (d)   by any recipient of the disclosure is with a view to or in connection with prescribed proceedings.

(3) The regulations may also include provision—

   (a)   making any permission to disclose confidential information subject to conditions (which may relate to the obtaining of consents or any other matter);

   (b)   restricting the uses to which confidential information disclosed under the regulations may be put.

(4) In relation to confidential information, each of the following is a 'recipient'—

   (a)   a primary recipient;

   (b)   a person obtaining the information directly or indirectly from a primary recipient.

(5) 'Public functions' includes—

   (a)   functions conferred by or in accordance with any provision contained in any enactment or subordinate legislation;

   (b)   functions conferred by or in accordance with any provision contained in the Community Treaties or any Community instrument;

   (c)   similar functions conferred on persons by or under provisions having effect as part of the law of a country or territory outside the United Kingdom;

   (d)   functions exercisable in relation to prescribed disciplinary proceedings.

(6) 'Enactment' includes—

   (a)   an Act of the Scottish Parliament;

   (b)   Northern Ireland legislation.

(7) 'Subordinate legislation' has the meaning given in the Interpretation Act 1978 and also includes an instrument made under an Act of the Scottish Parliament or under Northern Ireland legislation.

350   Disclosure of information by the Inland Revenue

(1) No obligation as to secrecy imposed by statute or otherwise prevents the disclosure of Revenue information to—

   (a)   the Authority, or

   (b)   the Secretary of State,

if the disclosure is made for the purpose of assisting in the investigation of a matter under section 168 or with a view to the appointment of an investigator under that section.

(2) A disclosure may only be made under subsection (1) by or under the authority of the Commissioners of Inland Revenue.

(3) Section 348 does not apply to Revenue information.

(4) Information obtained as a result of subsection (1) may not be used except—

   (a)   for the purpose of deciding whether to appoint an investigator under section 168;

   (b)   in the conduct of an investigation under section 168;

   (c)   in criminal proceedings brought against a person under this Act or the Criminal Justice Act 1993 a a result of an investigation under section 168;

   (d)   for the purpose of taking action under this Act against a person as a result of an investigation under section 168;

   (e)   in proceedings before the Tribunal as a result of action taken as mentioned in paragraph (d).

(5) Information obtained as a result of subsection (1) may not be disclosed except—

    (a)   by or under the authority of the Commissioners of Inland Revenue;

    (b)   in proceedings mentioned in subsection (4)(c) or (e) or with a view to their institution.

(6) Subsection (5) does not prevent the disclosure of information obtained as a result of subsection (1) to a person to whom it could have been disclosed under subsection (1).

(7) 'Revenue information' means information held by a person which it would be an offence under section 182 of the Finance Act 1989 for him to disclose.

351   Competition information

(1) A person is guilty of an offence if he has competition information (whether or not it was obtained by him) and improperly discloses it—

    (a)   if it relates to the affairs of an individual, during that individual's lifetime;

    (b)   if it relates to any particular business of a body, while that business continues to be carried on.

(2) For the purposes of subsection (1) a disclosure is improper unless it is made—

    (a)   with the consent of the person from whom it was obtained and, if different—
        (i)   the individual to whose affairs the information relates, or
        (ii)   the person for the time being carrying on the business to which the information relates;

    (b)   to facilitate the performance by a person mentioned in the first column of the table set out in Part I of Schedule 19 of a function mentioned in the second column of that table;

    (c)   in pursuance of a Community obligation;

    (d)   for the purpose of criminal proceedings in any part of the United Kingdom;

    (e)   in connection with the investigation of any criminal offence triable in the United Kingdom or any part of the United Kingdom;

    (f)   with a view to the institution of, or otherwise for the purposes of, civil proceedings brought under or in connection with—
        (i)   a competition provision; or
        (ii)   a specified enactment.

(3) A person guilty of an offence under this section is liable—

    (a)   on summary conviction, to a fine not exceeding the statutory maximum;

    (b)   on conviction on indictment, to imprisonment for a term not exceeding two years or to a fine or to both.

(4) Section 348 does not apply to competition information.

(5) 'Competition information' means information which—

    (a)   relates to the affairs of a particular individual or body;

    (b)   is not otherwise in the public domain; and

    (c)   was obtained under or by virtue of a competition provision.

(6) 'Competition provision' means any provision of—

    (a)   an order made under section 95;

    (b)   Chapter III of Part X; or

    (c)   Chapter II of Part XVIII.

(7) 'Specified enactment' means an enactment specified in Part II of Schedule 19.

352   Offences

(1) A person who discloses information in contravention of section 348 or 350(5) is guilty of an offence.

(2) A person guilty of an offence under subsection (1) is liable—

  (a)   on summary conviction, to imprisonment for a term not exceeding three months or a fine not exceeding the statutory maximum, or both;

  (b)   on conviction on indictment, to imprisonment for a term not exceeding two years or a fine, or both.

(3) A person is guilty of an offence, if, in contravention of any provision of regulations made under section 349, he uses information which has been disclosed to him in accordance with the regulations.

(4) A person is guilty of an offence if, in contravention of subsection (4) of section 350, he uses information which has been disclosed to him in accordance with that section.

(5) A person guilty of an offence under subsection (3) or (4) is liable on summary conviction to imprisonment for a term not exceeding three months or a fine not exceeding level 5 on the standard scale, or both.

(6) In proceedings for an offence under this section it is a defence for the accused to prove—

  (a)   that he did not know and had no reason to suspect that the information was confidential information or that it had been disclosed in accordance with section 350;

  (b)   that he took all reasonable precautions and exercised all due diligence to avoid committing the offence.

353   Removal of other restrictions on disclosure

(1) The Treasury may make regulations permitting the dislcosure of any information, or of information of a prescribed kind—

  (a)   by prescribed persons for the purpose of assisting or enabling them to discharge prescribed functions under this Act or any rules or regulations made under it;

  (b)   by prescribed persons, or persons of a prescribed description, to the Authority for the purpose of assisting or enabling the Authority to discharge prescribed functions.

(2) Regulations under this section may not make any provision in relation to the disclosure of confidential information by primary recipients or by any person obtaining confidential information directly or indirectly from a primary recipient.

(3) If a person discloses any information as permitted by regulations under this section the disclosure is not to be taken as a contravention of any duty to which he is subject.

Co-operation

354   Authority's duty to co-operate with others

(1) The Authority must take such steps as it considers appropriate to co-operate with other persons (whether in the United Kingdom or elsewhere) who have functions—

  (a)   similar to those of the Authority; or

  (b)   in relation to the prevention or detection of financial crime.

(2) Co-operation may include the sharing of information which the Authority is not prevented from disclosing.

(3) 'Financial crime' has the same meaning as in section 6.

PART XXIV

INSOLVENCY

Interpretation

355 Interpretation of this Part

(1) In this Part—

'the 1985 Act' means the Bankruptcy (Scotland) Act 1985;
'the 1986 Act' means the Insolvency Act 1986;
'the 1989 Order' means the Insolvency (Northern Ireland) Order 1989;
'body' means a body of persons—

(a)   over which the court has jurisdiction under any provision of, or made under, the 1986 Act (or the 1989 Order); but
(b)   which is not a building society, a friendly society or an industrial and provident society; and

'court' means—

(a)   the court having jurisdiction for the purposes of the 1985 Act or the 1986 Act; or
(b)   in Northern Ireland, the High Court.

(2) In this Part 'insurer' has such meaning as may be specified in an order made by the Treasury.

Voluntary arrangements

356 Authority's powers to participate in proceedings: company voluntary arrangements

(1) This section applies if a voluntary arrangement has been approved under Part I of the 1986 Act (or Part II of the 1989 Order) in respect of a company or insolvent partnership which is an authorised person.

(2) The Authority may make an application to the court in relation to the company or insolvent partnership under section 6 of the 1986 Act (or Article 19 of the 1989 Order).

(3) If a person other than the Authority makes an application to the court in relation to the company or insolvent partnership under either of those provisions, the Authority is entitled to be heard at any hearing relating to the application.

357 Authority's powers to participate in proceedings: individual voluntary arrangements

(1) The Authority is entitled to be heard on an application by an individual who is an authorised person under section 253 of the 1986 Act (or Article 227 of the 1989 Order).

(2) Subsections (3) to (6) apply if such an order is made on the application of such a person.

(3) A person appointed for the purpose by the Authority is entitled to attend any meeting of creditors of the debtor summoned under section 257 of the 1986 Act (or Article 231 of the 1989 Order).

(4) Notice of the result of a meeting so summoned is to be given to the Authority by the chairman of the meeting.

(5) The Authority may apply to the court—

(a)   under section 262 of the 1986 Act (or Article 236 of the 1989 Order); or

(b)   under section 263 of the 1986 Act (or Article 237 of the 1989 Order).

(6) If a person other than the Authority makes an application to the court under any provision mentioned in subsection (5), the Authority is entitled to be heard at any hearing relating to the application.

358   Authority's powers to participate in proceedings: trust deeds for creditors in Scotland

(1) This section applies where a trust deed has been granted by or on behalf of a debtor who is an authorised person.

(2) The trustee must, as soon as practicable after he becomes aware that the debtor is an authorised person, send to the Authority—

(a)   in every case, a copy of the trust deed;

(b)   where any other document or information is sent to every creditor known to the trustee in pursuance of paragraph 5(1)(c) of Schedule 5 to the 1985 Act, a copy of such document or information.

(3) Paragraph 7 of that Schedule applies to the Authority as if it were a qualified creditor who has not been sent a copy of the notice as mentioned in paragraph 5(1)(c) of the Schedule.

(4) The Authority must be given the same notice as the creditors of any meeting of creditors held in relation to the trust deed.

(5) A person appointed for the purpose by the Authority is entitled to attend and participate in (but not to vote at) any such meeting of creditors as if the Authority were a creditor under the deed.

(6) This section does not affect any right the Authority has as a creditor of a debtor who is an authorised person.

(7) Expressions used in this section and in the 1985 Act have the same meaning in this section as in that Act.

Administration orders

359   Petitions

(1) The Authority may present a petition to the court under section 9 of the 1986 Act (or Article 22 of the 1989 Order) in relation to a company or insolvent partnership which—

(a)   is, or has been, an authorised person;

(b)   is, or has been, an appointed representative; or

(c)   is carrying on, or has carried on, a regulated activity in contravention of the general prohibition.

(2) Subsection (3) applies in relation to a petition presented by the Authority by virtue of this section.

(3) If the company or partnership is in default on an obligation to pay a sum due and payable under an agreement, it is to be treated for the purpose of section 8(1)(a) of the 1986 Act (or Article 21(1)(a) of the 1989 Order) as unable to pay its debts.

(4) 'Agreement' means an agreement the making or performance of which constitutes or is part of a regulated activity carried on by the company or partnership.

(5) 'Company' means—

    (a)   a company to which section 8 of the 1986 act applies; or

    (b)   in relation to Northern Ireland, a company to which Article 21 of the 1989 Order applies.

360   Insurers

(1) The Treasury may by order provide that such provisions of Part II of the 1986 Act (or Part III of the 1989 Order) as may be specified are to apply in relation to insurers with such modifications as may be specified.

(2) An order under this section—

    (a)   may provide that such provisions of this Part as may be specified are to apply in relation to the administration of insurers in accordance with the order with such modifications as may be specified; and

    (b)   requires the consent of the Secretary of State.

(3) 'Specified' means specified in the order.

361   Administrator's duty to report to Authority

(1) If—

    (a)   an administration order is in force in relation to a company or partnership by virtue of a petition presented by a person other than the Authority, and

    (b)   it appears to the administrator that the company or partnership is carrying on, or has carried on, a regulated activity in contravention of the general prohibition,

the administrator must report the matter to the Authority without delay.

(2) 'An administration order' means an administration order under Part II of the 1986 Act (or Part III of the 1989 Order).

362   Authority's powers to participate in proceedings

(1) This section applies if a person other than the Authority presents a petition to the court under section 9 of the 1986 Act (or Article 22 of the 1989 Order) in relation to a company or partnership which—

    (a)   is, or has been, an authorised person;

    (b)   is, or has been, an appointed representative; or

    (c)   is carrying on, or has carried on, a regulated activity in contravention of the general prohibition.

(2) The Authority is entitled to be heard—

    (a)   at the hearing of the petition; and

    (b)   at any other hearing of the court in relation to the company or partnership under Part II of the 1986 Act (or Part III of the 1989 Order).

(3) Any notice or other document required to be sent to a creditor of the company or partnership must also be sent to the Authority.

(4) The Authority may apply to the court under section 27 of the 1986 Act (or Article 39 of the 1989 Order); and on such an application, section 27(1)(a) (or Article 39(1)(a)) has effect with the omission of the words '(including at least himself)'.

(5) A person appointed for the purpose by the Authority is entitled—

   (a)   to attend any meeting of creditors of the company or partnership summoned under any enactment;
   (b)   to attend any meeting of a committee established under section 26 of the 1986 Act (or Article 38 of the 1989 Order); and
   (c)   to make representations as to any matter for decision at such a meeting.

(6) If, during the course of the administration of a company, a compromise or arrangement is proposed between the company and its creditors, or any class of them, the Authority may apply to the court under section 425 of the Companies Act 1985 (or Article 418 of the Companies (Northern Ireland) Order 1986).

Receivership

363   Authority's powers to participate in proceedings

(1) This section applies if a receiver has been appointed in relation to a company which—

   (a)   is, or has been, an authorised person;
   (b)   is, or has been, an appointed representative; or
   (c)   is carrying on, or has carried on, a regulated activity in contravention of the general prohibition.

(2) The Authority is entitled to be heard on an application made under section 35 or 63 of the 1986 Act (or Article 45 of the 1989 Order).

(3) The Authority is entitled to make an application under section 41(1)(a) or 69(1)(a) of the 1986 Act (or Article 51(1)(a) of the 1989 Order).

(4) A report under section 48(1) or 67(1) of the 1986 act (or Article 58(1) of the 1989 Order) must be sent by the person making it to the Authority.

(5) A person appointed for the purpose by the Authority is entitled—

   (a)   to attend any meeting of creditors of the company summoned under any enactment;
   (b)   to attend any meeting of a committee established under section 49 or 68 of the 1986 Act (or Article 59 of the 1989 Order); and
   (c)   to make representations as to any matter for decision at such a meeting.

364   Receiver's duty to report to Authority

If—

   (a)   a receiver has been appointed in relation to a company, and
   (b)   it appears to the receiver that the company is carrying on, or has carried on, a regulated activity in contravention of the general prohibition,

the receiver must report the matter to the Authority without delay.

Voluntary winding up

365   Authority's powers to participate in proceedings

(1) This section applies in relation to a company which—

   (a)   is being wound up voluntarily;
   (b)   is an authorised person; and
   (c)   is not an insurer effecting or carrying out contracts of long-term insurance.

(2) The Authority may apply to the court under section 112 of the 1986 Act (or Article 98 of the 1989 Order) in respect of the company.

(3) The Authority is entitled to be heard at any hearing of the court in relation to the voluntary winding up of the company.

(4) Any notice or other document required to be sent to a creditor of the company must also be sent to the Authority.

(5) A person appointed for the purpose by the Authority is entitled—

    (a)   to attend any meeting of creditors of the company summoned under any enactment;

    (b)   to attend any meeting of a committee established under section 101 of the 1986 Act (or Article 87 of the 1989 Order); and

    (c)   to make representations as to any matter for decision at such a meeting.

(6) The voluntary winding up of the company does not bar the right of the Authority to have it wound up by the court.

(7) If, during the course of the winding up of the company, a compromise or arrangement is proposed between the company and its creditors, or any class of them, the Authority may apply to the court under section 425 of the Companies Act 1985 (or Article 418 of the Companies (Northern Ireland) Order 1986).

366   Insurers effecting or carrying out long-term contracts of insurance

(1) An insurer effecting or carrying out contracts of long-term insurance may not be wound up voluntarily without the consent of the Authority.

(2) If notice of a general meeting of such an insurer is given, specifying the intention to propose a resolution for voluntary winding up of the insurer, a director of the insurer must notify the Authority as soon as practicable after he becomes aware of it.

(3) A person who fails to comply with subsection (2) is guilty of an offence and liable on summary conviction to a fine not exceeding level 5 on the standard scale.

(4) The following provisions do not apply in relation to a winding-up resolution—

    (a)   sections 378(3) and 381A of the Companies Act 1985 ('the 1985 Act'); and

    (b)   Articles 386(3) and 389A of the Companies (Northern Ireland) Order 1986 ('the 1986 Order').

(5) A copy of a winding-up resolution forwarded to the registrar of companies in accordance with section 380 of the 1985 Act (or Article 388 of the 1986 Order) must be accompanied by a certificate issued by the Authority stating that it consents to the voluntary winding up of the insurer.

(6) If subsection (5) is complied with, the voluntary winding up is to be treated as having commenced at the time the resolution was passed.

(7) If subsection (5) is not complied with, the resolution has no effect.

(8) 'Winding-up resolution' means a resolution for voluntary winding up of an insurer effecting or carrying out contracts of long-term insurance.

Winding up by the court

367   Winding-up petitions

(1) The Authority may present a petition to the court for the winding up of a body which—

    (a)   is, or has been, an authorised person;

(b)   is, or has been, an appointed representative; or

(c)   is carrying on, or has carried on, a regulated activity in contravention of the general prohibition.

(2) In subsection (1) 'body' includes any partnership.

(3) On such a petition, the court may wind up the body if—

(a)   the body is unable to pay its debts within the meaning of section 123 or 221 of the 1986 Act (or Article 103 or 185 of the 1989 Order); or

(b)   the court is of the opinion that it is just and equitable that it should be wound up.

(4) If a body is in default on an obligation to pay a sum due and payable under an agreement, it is to be treated for the purpose of subsection (3)(a) as unable to pay its debts.

(5) 'Agreement' means an agreement the making or performance of which constitutes or is part of a regulated activity carried on by the body concerned.

(6) Subsection (7) applies if a petition is presented under subsection (1) for the winding up of a partnership—

(a)   on the ground mentioned in subsection (3)(b); or

(b)   in Scotland, on a ground mentioned in subsection (3)(a) or (b).

(7) The court has jurisdiction, and the 1986 Act (or the 1989 Order) has effect, as if the partnership were an unregistered company as defined by section 220 of that Act (or Article 184 of that Order).

368   Winding-up petitions: EEA and Treaty firms

The Authority may not present a petition to the court under section 367 for the winding up of—

(a)   an EEA firm which qualifies for authorisation under Schedule 3, or

(b)   a Treaty firm which qualifies for authorisation under Schedule 4, unless it has been asked to do so by the home state regulator of the firm concerned.

369   Insurers: service of petition etc. on Authority

(1) If a person other than the Authority presents a petition for the winding up of an authorised person with permission to effect or carry out contracts of insurance, the petitioner must serve a copy of the petition on the Authority.

(2) If a person other than the Authority applies to have a provisional liquidator appointed under section 135 of the 1986 Act (or Article 115 of the 1989 Order) in respect of an authorised person with permission to effect or carry out contracts of insurance, the applicant must serve a copy of the application on the Authority.

370   Liquidator's duty to report to Authority

If—

(a)   a company is being wound up voluntarily or a body is being wound up on a petition presented by a person other than the Authority; and

(b)   it appears to the liquidator that the company or body is carrying on, or has carried on, a regulated activity in contravention of the general prohibition,

the liquidator must report the matter to the Authority without delay.

371   Authority's powers to participate in proceedings

(1) This section applies if a person other than the Authority presents a petition for the winding up of a body which—

(a)   is, or has been, an authorised person;

(b)   is, or has been, an appointed representative; or

(c)   is carrying on, or has carried on, a regulated activity in contravention of the general prohibition.

(2) The Authority is entitled to be heard—

(a)   at the hearing of the petition; and

(b)   at any other hearing of the court in relation to the body under or by virtue of Part IV or V of the 1986 act (or Part V or VI of the 1989 Order).

(3) Any notice or other document required to be sent to a creditor of the body must also be sent to the Authority.

(4) A person appointed for the purpose by the Authority is entitled—

(a)   to attend any meeting of creditors of the body;

(b)   to attend any meeting of a committee established for the purposes of Part IV or V of the 1986 Act under section 101 of that Act or under section 141 or 142 of that Act;

(c)   to attend any meeting of a committee established for the purposes of Part V or VI of the 1989 Order under Article 87 of that Order or under Article 120 of that Order; and

(d)   to make representations as to any matter for decision at such a meeting.

(5) If, during the course of the winding up of a company, a compromise or arrangement is proposed between the company and its creditors, or any class of them, the Authority may apply to the court under section 425 of the Companies Act 1985 (or Article 418 of the Companies (Northern Ireland) Order 1986).

Bankruptcy

372   Petitions

(1) The Authority may present a petition to the court—

(a)   under section 264 of the 1986 Act (or Article 238 of the 1989 Order) for a bankruptcy order to be made against an individual; or

(b)   under section 5 of the 1985 Act for the sequestration of the estate of an individual.

(2) But such a petition may be presented only on the ground that—

(a)   the individual appears to be unable to pay a regulated activity debt; or

(b)   the individual appears to have no reasonable prospects of being able to pay a regulated activity debt.

(3) An individual appears to be unable to pay a regulated activity debt if he is in default on an obligation to pay a sum due and payable under an agreement.

(4) An individual appears to have no reasonable prospect of being able to pay a regulated activity debt if—

(a)   the Authority has served on him a demand requiring him to establish to the satisfaction of the Authority that there is a reasonable prospect that he will be able to pay a sum payable under an agreement when it falls due;

(b)   at least three weeks have elapsed since the demand was served; and

(c)   the demand has been neither complied with nor set aside in accordance with rules.

(5) A demand made under subsection (4)(a) is to be treated for the purposes of the 1986 act (or the 1989 Order) as if it were a statutory demand under section 268 of that Act (or Article 242 of that Order).

(6) For the purposes of a petition presented in accordance with subsection (1)(b)—

(a)   the Authority is to be treated as a qualified creditor; and
(b)   a ground mentioned in subsection (2) constitutes apparent insolvency.

(7) 'Individual' means an individual—

(a)   who is, or has been, an authorised person; or
(b)   who is carrying on, or has carried on, a regulated activity in contravention of the general prohibition.

(8) 'Agreement' means an agreement the making or performance of which constitutes or is part of a regulated activity carried on by the individual concerned.

(9) 'Rules' means—

(a)   in England and Wales, rules made under section 412 of the 1986 Act;
(b)   in Scotland, rules made by order by the Treasury, after consultation with the Scottish Ministers, for the purposes of this section; and
(c)   in Northern Ireland, rules made under Article 359 of the 1989 Order.

373   Insolvency practitioner's duty to report to Authority

(1) If—

(a)   a bankruptcy order or sequestration award is in force in relation to an individual by virtue of a petition presented by a person other than the Authority, and
(b)   it appears to the insolvency practitioner that the individual is carrying on, or has carried on, a regulated activity in contravention of the general prohibition,

the insolvency practitioner must report the matter to the Authority without delay.

(2) 'Bankruptcy order' means a bankruptcy order under Part IX of the 1986 Act (or Part IX of the 1989 Order).

(3) 'Sequestration award' means an award of sequestration under section 12 of the 1985 Act.

(4) 'Individual' includes an entity mentioned in section 374(1)(c).

374   Authority's powers to participate in proceedings

(1) This section applies if a person other than the Authority presents a petition to the court—

(a)   under section 264 of the 1986 Act (or Article 238 of the 1989 Order) for a bankruptcy order to be made against an individual;
(b)   under section 5 of the 1985 Act for the sequestration of the estate of an individual; or
(c)   under section 6 of the 1985 Act for the sequestration of the estate belonging to or held for or jointly by the members of an entity mentioned in subsection (1) of that section.

(2) The Authority is entitled to be heard—

(a)   at the hearing of the petition; and
(b)   at any other hearing in relation to the individual or entity under—
(i)   Part IX of the 1986 act;

      (ii) Part IX of the 1989 Order; or

      (iii) the 1985 Act.

(3) A copy of the report prepared under section 274 of the 1986 Act (or Article 248 of the 1989 Order) must also be sent to the Authority.

(4) A person appointed for the purpose by the Authority is entitled—

  (a)   to attend any meeting of creditors of the individual or entity;

  (b)   to attend any meeting of a committee established under section 301 of the 1986 Act (or Article 274 of the 1989 Order);

  (c)   to attend any meeting of commissioners held under paragraph 17 or 18 of Schedule 6 to the 1985 Act; and

  (d)   to make representations as to any matter for decision at such a meeting.

(5) 'Individual' means an individual who—

  (a)   is, or has been, an authorised person; or

  (b)   is carrying on, or has carried on, a regulated activity in contravention of the general prohibition.

(6) 'Entity' means an entity which—

  (a)   is, or has been, an authorised person; or

  (b)   is carrying on, or has carried on, a regulated activity in contravention of the general prohibition.

Provisions against debt avoidance

375 Authority's right to apply for an order

(1) The Authority may apply for an order under section 423 of the 1986 Act (or Article 367 of the 1989 Order) in relation to a debtor if—

  (a)   at the time the transaction at an undervalue was entered into, the debtor was carrying on a regulated activity (whether or not in contravention of the general prohibition); and

  (b)   a victim of the transaction is or was party to an agreement entered into with the debtor, the making or performance of which constituted or was part of a regulated activity carried on by the debtor.

(2) An application made under this section is to be treated as made on behalf of every victim of the transaction to whom subsection (1)(b) applies.

(3) Expressions which are given a meaning in Part XVI of the 1986 Act (or Article 367, 368 or 369 of the 1989 Order) have the same meaning when used in this section.

Supplemental provisions concerning insurers

376 Continuation of contracts of long-term insurance where insurer in liquidation

(1) This section applies in relation to the winding up of an insurer which effects or carries out contracts of long-term insurance.

(2) Unless the court otherwise orders, the liquidator must carry on the insurer's business so far as it consists of carrying out the insurer's contracts of long-term insurance with a view to its being transferred as a going concern to a person who may lawfully carry out those contracts.

(3) In carrying on the business, the liquidator—

(a) may agree to the variation of any contracts of insurance in existence when the winding up order is made; but

(b) mut not effect any new contracts of insurance.

(4) If the liquidator is satisfied that the interests of the creditors in respect of liabilities of the insurer attributable to contracts of long-term insurance effected by it require the appointment of a special manager, he may apply to the court.

(5) On such an application, the court may appoint a special manager to act during such time as the court may direct.

(6) The special manager is to have such powers, including any of the powers of a receiver or manager, as the court may direct.

(7) Section 177(5) of the 1986 Act (or Article 151(5) of the 1989 Order) applies to a special manager appointed under subsection (5) as it applies to a special manager appointed under section 177 of the 1986 act (or Article 151 of the 1989 Order).

(8) If the court thinks fit, it may reduce the value of one or more of the contracts of long-term insurance effected by the insurer.

(9) Any reduction is to be on such terms and subject to such conditions (if any) as the court thinks fit.

(10) The court may, on the application of an official, appoint an independent actuary to investigate the insurer's business so far as it consists of carrying out its contracts of long-term insurance and to report to the official—

(a) on the desirability or otherwise of that part of the insurer's business being continued; and

(b) on any reduction in the contracts of long-term insurance effected by the insurer that may be necessary for successful continuation of that part of the insurer's business.

(11) 'Official' means—

(a) the liquidator;

(b) a special manager appointed under subsection (5); or

(c) the Authority.

(12) The liquidator may make an application in the name of the insurer and on its behalf under Part VII without obtaining the permission that would otherwise be required by section 167 of, and Schedule 4 to, the 1986 Act (or Article 142 of, and Schedule 2 to, the 1989 Order).

377   Reducing the value of contracts instead of winding up

(1) This section applies in relation to an insurer which has been proved to be unable to pay its debts.

(2) If the court thinks fit, it may reduce the value of one or more of the insurer's contracts instead of making a winding up order.

(3) Any reduction is to be on such terms and subject to such conditions (if any) as the court thinks fit.

378   Treatment of assets on winding up

(1) The Treasury may by regulations provide for the treatment of the assets of an insurer on its winding up.

(2) The regulations may, in particular, provide for—

    (a)   assets representing a particular part of the insurer's business to be available only for meeting liabilities attributable to that part of the insurer's business;

    (b)   separate general meetings of the creditors to be held in respect of liabilities attributable to a particular part of the insurer's business.

379 Winding-up rules

(1) Winding-up rules may include provision—

    (a)   for determining the amount of the liabilities of an insurer to policyholders of any class or description for the purpose of proof in a winding up; and

    (b)   generally for carrying into effect the provisions of this Part with respect to the winding up of insurers.

(2) Winding-up rules may, in particular, make provisions for all or any of the following matters—

    (a)   the identification of assets and liabilities;

    (b)   the apportionment, between assets of different classes or descriptions, of—

        (i)   the costs, charges and expenses of the winding up; and

        (ii) any debts of the insurer of a specified class or description;

    (c)   the determination of the amount of liabilities of a specified description;

    (d)   the application of assets for meeting liabilities of a specified description;

    (e)   the application of assets representing any excess of a specified description.

(3) 'Specified' means specified in winding-up rules.

(4) 'Winding-up rules' means rules made under section 411 of the 1986 Act (or Article 359 of the 1989 Order).

(5) Nothing in this section affects the power to make winding-up rules under the 1986 act or the 1989 Order.

PART XXV

INJUNCTIONS AND RESTITUTION

Injunctions

380 Injunctions

(1) If, on the application of the Authority or the Secretary of State, the court is satisfied—

    (a)   that there is a reasonable likelihood that any person will contravene a relevant requirement, or

    (b)   that any person has contravened a relevant requirement and that there is a reasonable likelihood that the contravention will continue or be repeated,

the court may make an order restraining (or in Scotland an interdict prohibiting) the contravention.

(2) If on the application of the Authority or the Secretary of State the court is satisfied—

    (a)   that any person has contravened a relevant requirement, and

    (b)   that there are steps which could be taken for remedying the contravention,

the court may make an order requiring that person, and any other person who appears to have been knowingly concerned in the contravention, to take such steps as the court may direct to remedy it.

(3) If, on the application of the Authority or the Secretary of State, the court is satisfied that any person may have—

   (a)   contravened a relevant requirement, or
   (b)   been knowingly concerned in the contravention of such a requirement,

it may make an order restraining (or in Scotland an interdict prohibiting) him from disposing of, or otherwise dealing with, any assets of his which it is satisfied he is reasonably likely to dispose of or otherwise deal with.

(4) The jurisdiction conferred by this section is exercisable by the High Court and the Court of Session.

(5) In subsection (2), references to remedying a contravention include references to mitigating its effect.

(6) 'Relevant requirement'—

   (a)   in relation to an application by the Authority, means a requirement—
         (i)   which is imposed by or under this Act; or
         (ii)   which is imposed by or under any other Act and whose contravention constitutes an offence which the Authority has power to prosecute under this Act;
   (b)   in relation to an application by the Secretary of State, means a requirement which is imposed by or under this Act and whose contravention constitutes an offence which the Secretary of State has power to prosecute under this Act.

(7) In the application of subsection (6) to Scotland—

   (a)   in paragraph (a) (ii) for 'which the Authority has power to prosecute under this Act' substitute 'mentioned in paragraph (a) or (b) of section 402(1)'; and
   (b)   in paragraph (b) omit 'which the Secretary of State has power to prosecute under this Act'.

381   Injunctions in cases of market abuse

(1) If, on the application of the Authority, the court is satisfied—

   (a)   that there is a reasonable likelihood that any person will engage in market abuse, or
   (b)   that any person is or has engaged in market abuse and that there is a reasonable likelihood that the market abuse will continue or be repeated,

the court may make an order restraining (or in Scotland an interdict prohibiting) the market abuse.

(2) If on the application of the Authority the court is satisfied—

   (a)   that any person is or has engaged in market abuse, and
   (b)   that there are steps which could be taken for remedying the market abuse,

the court may make an order requiring him to take such steps as the court may direct to remedy it.

(3) Subsection (4) applies if, on the application of the Authority, the court is satisfied that any person—

   (a)   may be engaged in market abuse; or
   (b)   may have been engaged in market abuse.

(4) The court make an order restraining (or in Scotland an interdict prohibiting) the person concerned from disposing of, or otherwise dealing with, any assets of his which it is satisfied that he is reasonably likely to dispose of, or otherwise deal with.

(5) The jurisdiction conferred by this section is exercisable by the High Court and the Court of Session.

(6) In subsection (2), references to remedying any market abuse include references to mitigating its effect.

Restitution orders

382   Restitution orders

(1) The court may, on the application of the Authority or the Secretary of State, make an order under subsection (2) if it is satisfied that a person has contravened a relevant requirement, or been knowingly concerned in the contravention of such a requirement, and—

> (a)   that profits have accrued to him as a result of the contravention; or
> (b)   that one or more persons have suffered loss or been otherwise adversely affected as a result of the contravention.

(2) The court may order the person concerned to pay to the Authority such sum as appears to the court to be just having regard—

> (a)   in a case within paragraph (a) of subsection (1), to the profits appearing to the court to have accrued;
> (b)   in a case within paragraph (b) of that subsection, to the extent of the loss or other adverse effect;
> (c)   in a case within both of those paragraphs, to the profits appearing to the court to have accrued and to the extent of the loss or other adverse effect.

(3) Any amount paid to the Authority in pursuance of an order under subsection (2) must be paid by it to such qualifying person or distributed by it among such qualifying persons as the court may direct.

(4) On an application under subsection (1) the court may require the person concerned to supply it with such accounts or other information as it may require for any one or more of the following purposes—

> (a)   establishing whether any and, if so, what profits have accrued to him as mentioned in paragraph (a) of that subsection;
> (b)   establishing whether any person or persons have suffered any loss or adverse effect as mentioned in paragraph (b) of that subsection and, if so, the extent of that loss or adverse effect; and
> (c)   determining how any amounts are to be paid or distributed under subsection (3).

(5) The court may require any accounts or other information supplied under subsection (4) to be verified in such manner as it may direct.

(6) The jurisdiction conferred by this section is exercisable by the High Court and the Court of Session.

(7) Nothing in this section affects the right of any person other than the Authority or the Secretary of State to bring proceedings in respect of the matters to which this section applies.

(8) 'Qualifying person' means a person appearing to the court to be someone—

> (a)   to whom the profits mentioned in subsection (1)(a) are attributable; or
> (b)   who has suffered the loss or adverse effect mentioned in subsection (1)(b).

(9) 'Relevant requirement'—

(a) in relation to an application by the Authority, means a requirement—
   (i)   which is imposed by or under this Act; or
   (ii) which is imposed by or under any other Act and whose contravention constitutes an offence which the Authority has power to prosecute under this Act;
(b) in relation to an application by the Secretary of State, means a requirement which is imposed by or under this Act and whose contravention constitutes an offence which the Secretary of State has power to prosecute under this Act.

(10) In the application of subsection (9) to Scotland—

(a) in paragraph (a) (ii) for 'which the Authority has power to prosecute under this Act' substitute 'mentioned in paragraph (a) or (b) of section 402(1)'; and
(b) in paragraph (b) omit 'which the Secretary of State has power to prosecute under this Act'.

383 Restitution orders in cases of market abuse

(1) The court may, on the application of the Authority, make an order under subsection (4) if it is satisfied that a person ('the person concerned')—

(a) has engaged in market abuse, or
(b) by taking or refraining from taking any action has acquired or encouraged another person or persons to engage in behaviour which, if engaged in by the person concerned, would amount to market abuse,

and the condition mentioned in subsection (2) is fulfilled.

(2) The condition is—

(a) that profits have accrued to the person concerned as a result; or
(b) that one or more persons have suffered loss or been otherwise adversely affected as a result.

(3) But the court may not make an order under subsection (4) if it is satisfied that—

(a) the person concerned believed, on reasonable grounds, that his behaviour did not fall within paragraph (a) or (b) of subsection (1); or
(b) he took all reasonable precautions and exercised all due diligence to avoid behaving in a way which fell within paragraph (a) or (b) of subsection (1).

(4) The court may order the person concerned to pay to the Authority such sum as appears to the court to be just having regard—

(a) in a case within paragraph (a) of subsection (2), to the profits appearing to the court to have accrued;
(b) in a case within paragraph (b) of that subsection, to the extent of the loss or other adverse effect;
(c) in a case within both of those paragraphs, to the profits appearing to the court to have accrued and to the extent of the loss or other adverse effect.

(5) Any amount paid to the Authority in pursuance of an order under subsection (4) must be paid by it to such qualifying person or distributed by it among such qualifying persons as the court may direct.

(6) On an application under subsection (1) the court may require the person concerned to supply it with such accounts or other information as it may require for any one or more of the following purposes—

(a) establishing whether any and, if so, what profits have accrued to him as mentioned in subsection (2)(a);

(b)   establishing whether any person or persons have suffered any loss or adverse effect as mentioned in subsection (2)(b) and, if so, the extent of that loss or adverse effect; and

(c)   determining how any amounts are to be paid or distributed under subsection (5).

(7) The court may require any accounts or other information supplied under subsection (6) to be verified in such manner as it may direct.

(8) The jurisdiction conferred by this section is exercisable by the High Court and the Court of Session.

(9) Nothing in this section affects the right of any person other than the Authority to bring proceedings in respect of the matters to which this section applies.

(10) 'Qualifying person' means a person appearing to the court to be someone—

(a)   to whom the profits mentioned in paragraph (a) of subsection (2) are attributable; or

(b)   who has suffered the loss or adverse effect mentioned in paragraph (b) of that subsection.

Restitution required by Authority

384   Power of Authority to require restitution

(1) The Authority may exercise the power in subsection (5) if it is satisfied that an authorised person ('the person concerned') has contravened a relevant requirement, or been knowingly concerned in the contravention of such a requirement, and—

(a)   that profits have accrued to him as a result of the contravention; or

(b)   that one or more persons have suffered loss or been otherwise adversely affected as a result of the contravention.

(2) The Authority may exercise the power in subsection (5) if it is satisfied that a person ('the person concerned')—

(a)   has engaged in market abuse, or

(b)   by taking or refraining from taking any action has required or encouraged another person or persons to engage in behaviour which, if engaged in by the person concerned, would amount to market abuse,

and the condition mentioned in subsection (3) is fulfilled.

(3) The condition is—

(a)   that profits have accrued to the person concerned as a result of the market abuse; or

(b)   that one or more persons have suffered loss or been otherwise adversely affected as a result of the market abuse.

(4) But the Authority may not exercise that power as a result of subsection (2) if, having considered any representations made to it in response to a warning notice, there are reasonable grounds for it to be satisfied that—

(a)   the person concerned believed, on reasonable grounds, that his behaviour did not fall within paragraph (a) or (b) of that subsection; or

(b)   he took all reasonable precautions and exercised all due diligence to avoid behaving in a way which fell within paragraph (a) or (b) of that subsection.

(5) The power referred to in subsections (1) and (2) is a power to require the person concerned, in accordance with such arrangements as the Authority considers appropriate, to pay to the appropriate person or distribute among the appropriate persons such amount as appears to the Authority to be just having regard—

(a) in a case within paragraph (a) of subsection (1) or (3), to the profits appearing to the Authority to have accrued;

(b) in a case within paragraph (b) of subsection (1) or (3), to the extent of the loss or other adverse effect;

(c) in a case within paragraphs (a) and (b) of subsection (1) or (3), to the profits appearing to the Authority to have accrued and to the extent of the loss or other adverse effect.

(6) 'Appropriate person' means a person appearing to the Authority to be someone—

(a) to whom the profits mentioned in paragraph (a) of subsection (1) or (3) are attributable; or

(b) who has suffered the loss or adverse effect mentioned in paragraph (b) of subsection (1) or (3).

(7) 'Relevant requirement' means—

(a) a requirement imposed by or under this Act; and

(b) a requirement which is imposed by or under any other Act and whose contravention constitutes an offence in relation to which this Act confers power to prosecute on the Authority.

(8) In the application of subsection (7) to Scotland, in paragraph (b) for 'in relation to which this Act confers power to prosecute on the Authority' substitute 'mentioned in paragraph (a) or (b) of section 402(1)'.

385   Warning notices

(1) If the Authority proposes to exercise the power under section 384(5) in relation to a person, it must give him a warning notice.

(2) A warning notice under this section must specify the amount which the Authority proposes to require the person concerned to pay or distribute as mentioned in section 384(5).

386   Decision notices

(1) If the Authority decides to exercise the power under section 384(5), it must give a decision notice to the person in relation to whom the power is exercised.

(2) The decision notice must—

(a) state the amount that he is to pay or distribute as mentioned in section 384(5);

(b) identify the person or persons to whom that amount is to be paid or among whom that amount is to be distributed; and

(c) state the arrangements in accordance with which the payment or distribution is to be made.

(3) If the Authority decides to exercise the power under section 384(5), the person in relation to whom it is exercised may refer the matter to the Tribunal.

PART XXVI

NOTICES

Warning notices

387   (1) A warning notice must—

(a) state the action which the Authority proposes to take;

(b) be in writing;

(c) give reasons for the proposed action;

(d) state whether section 394 applies; and

(e) if that section applies, describe its effect and state whether any secondary material exists to which the person concerned must be allowed access under it.

(2) The warning notice must specify a reasonable period (which may not be less than 28 days) within which the person to whom it is given may make representations to the Authority.

(3) The Authority may extend the period, specified in the notice.

(4) The Authority must then decide, within a reasonable period, whether to give the person concerned a decision notice.

Decision notices

388 (1) A decision notice must—

(a) be in writing;

(b) give the Authority's reasons for the decision to take the action to which the notice relates;

(c) state whether section 394 applies;

(d) if that section applies, describe its effect and state whether any secondary material exists to which the person concerned must be allowed access under it; and

(e) give an indication of—

    (i) any right to have the matter referred to the Tribunal which is given by this Act; and

    (ii) the procedure on such a reference.

(2) If the decision notice was preceded by a warning notice, the action to which the decision notice relates must be action under the same Part as the action proposed in the warning notice.

(3) The Authority may, before it takes the action to which a decision notice ('the original notice') relates, give the person concerned a further decision notice which relates to different action in respect of the same matter.

(4) The Authority may give a further decision notice as a result of subsection (3) only if the person to whom the original notice was given consents.

(5) If the person to whom a decision notice is given under subsection (3) had the right to refer the matter to which the original decision notice related to the Tribunal, he has that right as respects the decision notice under subsection (3).

Conclusion of proceedings

389 Notices of discontinuance

(1) If the Authority decides not to take—

(a) the action proposed in a warning notice, or

(b) the action to which a decision notices relates,

it must give a notice of discontinuance to the person to whom the warning notice or decision notice was given.

(2) But subsection (1) does not apply if the discontinuance of the proceedings concerned results in the granting of an application made by the person to whom the warning or decision notice was given.

(3) A notice of discontinuance must identify the proceedings which are being discontinued.

390   Final notices

(1) If the Authority has given a person a decision notice and the matter was not referred to the Tribunal within the period mentioned in section 133(1), the Authority must, on taking the action to which the decision relates, give the person concerned and any person to whom the decision notice was copied a final notice.

(2) If the Authority has given a person a decision notice and the matter was referred to the Tribunal, the Authority must, on taking action in accordance with any directions given by—

(a)   the Tribunal, or
(b)   the court under section 137,

give that person and any person to whom the decision notice was copied a final notice.

(3) A final notice about a statement must—

(a)   set out the terms of the statement;
(b)   give details of the manner in which, and the date on which, the statement will be published.

(4) A final notice about an order must—

(a)   set out the terms of the order;
(b)   state the date from which the order has effect.

(5) A final notice about a penalty must—

(a)   state the amount of the penalty;
(b)   state the manner in which, and the period within which, the penalty is to be paid;
(c)   give details of the way in which the penalty will be recovered if it is not paid by the date stated in the notice.

(6) A final notice about a requirement to make a payment or distribution in accordance with section 384(5) must state—

(a)   the persons to whom,
(b)   the manner in which, and
(c)   the period within which,

it must be made.

(7) In any other case, the final notice must—

(a)   give details of the action being taken;
(b)   state the date on which the action is to be taken.

(8) The period stated under subsection (5)(b) or (6)(c) may not be less than 14 days beginning with the date on which the final notice is given.

(9) If all or any of the amount of a penalty payable under a final notice is outstanding at the end of the period stated under subsection (5)(b), the Authority may recover the outstanding amount as a debt due to it.

(10) If all or any of a required payment or distribution has not been made at the end of a period stated in a final notice under subsection (6)(c), the obligation to make the payment

is enforceable, on the application of the Authority, by injunction or, in Scotland, by an order under section 45 of the Court of Session Act 1988.

Publication

391   Publication

(1) Neither the Authority nor a person to whom a warning notice or decision notice is given or copied may publish the notice or any details concerning it.

(2) A notice of discontinuance must state that, if the person to whom the notice is given consents, the Authority may publish such information as it considers appropriate about the matter to which the discontinued proceedings related.

(3) A copy of a notice of discontinuance must be accompanied by a statement that, if the person to whom the notice is copied consents, the Authority may publish such information as it considers appropriate about the matter to which the discontinued proceedings related, so far as relevant to that person.

(4) The Authority must publish such information about the matter to which a final notice relates as it considers appropriate.

(5) When a supervisory notice takes effect, the Authority must publish such information about the matter to which the notice relates as it considers appropriate.

(6) But the Authority may not publish information under this section if publication of it would, in its opinion, be unfair to the person with respect to whom the action was taken or prejudicial to the interests of consumers.

(7) Information is to be published under this section in such manner as the Authority considers appropriate.

(8) For the purposes of determining when a supervisory notice takes effect, a matter to which the notice relates is open to review if—

  (a)   the period during which any person may refer the matter to the Tribunal is still running;
  (b)   the matter has been referred to the Tribunal but has not been dealt with;
  (c)   the matter has been referred to the Tribunal and dealt with but the period during which an appeal may be brought against the Tribunal's decision is still running; or
  (d)   such an appeal has been brought but has not been determined.

(9) 'Notice of discontinuance' means a notice given under section 389.

(10) 'Supervisory notice' has the same meaning as in section 395.

(11) 'Consumers' means persons who are consumers for the purposes of section 138.

Third party rights and access to evidence

392   Application of sections 393 and 394

Sections 393 and 394 apply to—

  (a)   a warning notice given in accordance with section 54(1), 57(1), 63(3), 67(1), 88(4)(b), 89(2), 92(1), 126(1), 207(1), 255(1), 280(1), 331(1), 345(2) (whether as a result of subsection (1) of that section or section 249(1)) or 385(1);

   (b)   a decision notice given in accordance with section 54(2), 57(3), 63(4), 67(4), 88(6)(b), 89(3), 92(4), 127(1), 208(1), 255(2), 280(2), 331(3), 345(3) (whether as a result of subsection (1) of that section or section 249(1)) or 386(1).

393   Third party rights

(1) If any of the reasons contained in a warning notice to which this section applies relates to a matter which—

   (a)   identifies a person ('the third party') other than the person to whom the notice is given, and

   (b)   in the opinion of the Authority, is prejudicial to the third party,

a copy of the notice must be given to the third party.

(2) Subsection (1) does not require a copy to be given to the third party if the Authority—

   (a)   has given him a separate warning notice in relation to the same matter; or

   (b)   gives him such a notice at the same time as it gives the warning notice which identifies him.

(3) The notice copied to a third party under subsection (1) must specify a reasonable period (which may not be less than 28 days) within which he may make representations to the Authority.

(4) If any of the reasons contained in a decision notice to which this section applies relates to a matter which—

   (a)   identifies a person ('the third party') other than the person to whom the decision notice is given, and

   (b)   in the opinion of the Authority, is prejudicial to the third party,

a copy of the notice must be given to the third party.

(5) If the decision notice was preceded by a warning notice, a copy of the decision notice must (unless it has been given under subsection (4)) be given to each person to whom the warning notice was copied.

(6) Subsection (4) does not require a copy to be given to the third party if the Authority—

   (a)   has given him a separate decision notice in relation to the same matter; or

   (b)   gives him such a notice at the same time as it gives the decision notice which identifies him.

(7) Neither subsection (1) nor subsection (4) requires a copy of a notice to be given to a third party if the Authority considers it impracticable to do so.

(8) Subsections (9) to (11) apply if the person to whom a decision notice is given has a right to refer the matter to the Tribunal.

(9) A person to whom a copy of the notice is given under this section may refer to the Tribunal—

   (a)   the decision in question, so far as it is based on a reason of the kind mentioned in subsection (4); or

   (b)   any opinion expressed by the Authority in relation to him.

(10) The copy must be accompanied by an indication of the third party's right to make a reference under subsection (9) and of the procedure on such a reference.

(11) A person who alleges that a copy of the notice should have been given to him, but was not, may refer to the Tribunal the alleged failure and—

    (a)   the decision in question, so far as it is based on a reason of the kind mentioned in subsection (4); or

    (b)   any opinion expressed by the Authority in relation to him.

(12) Section 394 applies to a third party as it applies to the person to whom the notice to which this section applies was given, in so far as the material which the Authority must disclose under that section relates to the matter which identifies the third party.

(13) A copy of a notice given to a third party under this section must be accompanied by a description of the effect of section 394 as it applies to him.

(14) Any person to whom a warning notice or decision notice was copied under this section must be given a copy of a notice of discontinuance applicable to the proceedings to which the warning notice or decision notice related.

394   Access to Authority material

(1) If the Authority gives a person ('A') a notice to which this section applies, it must—

    (a)   allow him access to the material on which it relied in taking the decision which gave rise to the obligation to give the notice;

    (b)   allow him access to any secondary material which, in the opinion of the Authority, might undermine that decision.

(2) But the Authority does not have to allow A access to material under subsection (1) if the material is excluded material or it—

    (a)   relates to a case involving a person other than A; and

    (b)   was taken into account by the Authority in A's case only for purposes of comparison with the cases.

(3) The Authority may refuse A access to particular material which it would otherwise have to allow him access to if, in its opinion, allowing him access to the material—

    (a)   would not be in the public interest; or

    (b)   would not be fair, having regard to—

        (i)   the likely significance of the material to A in relation to the matter in respect of which he has been given a notice to which this section applies; and

        (ii)   the potential prejudice to the commercial interests of a person other than A which would be caused by the material's disclosure.

(4) If the Authority does not allow A access to material because it is excluded material consisting of a protected item, it must give A written notice of—

    (a)   the existence of the protected item; and

    (b)   the Authority's decision not to allow him access to it.

(5) If the Authority refuses under subsection (3) to allow A access to material, it must give him written notice of—

    (a)   the refusal; and

    (b)   the reasons for it.

(6) 'Secondary material' means material, other than material falling within paragraph (a) of subsection (1) which—

    (a)   was considered by the Authority in reaching the decision mentioned in that paragraph; or

    (b)   was obtained by the Authority in connection with the matter to which the notice to which this section applies relates but which was not considered by it in reaching that decision.

(7) 'Excluded material' means material which—

    (a)   has been intercepted in obedience to a warrant issued under any enactment relating to the interception of communications;

    (b)   indicates that such a warrant has been issued or that material has been intercepted in obedience to such a warrant; or

    (c)   is a protected item (as defined in section 413).

The Authority's procedures

395   The Authority's procedures

(1) The Authority must determine the procedure that it proposes to follow in relation to the giving of—

    (a)   supervisory notices; and

    (b)   warning notices and decision notices.

(2) That procedure must be designed to secure, among other things, that the decision which gives rise to the obligation to give any such notice is taken by a person not directly involved in establishing the evidence on which that decision is based.

(3) But the procedure may permit a decision which gives rise to an obligation to give a supervisory notice to be taken by a person other than a person mentioned in subsection (2) if—

    (a)   the Authority considers that, in the particular case, it is necessary in order to protect the interests of consumers; and

    (b)   the person taking the decision is of a level of seniority laid down by the procedure.

(4) A level of seniority laid down by the procedure for the purposes of subsection (3)(b) must be appropriate to the importance of the decision.

(5) The Authority must issue a statement of the procedure.

(6) The statement must be published in the way appearing to the Authority to be best calculated to bring it to the attention of the public.

(7) The Authority may charge a reasonable fee for providing a person with a copy of the statement.

(8) The Authority must, without delay, give the Treasury a copy of any statement which it issues under this section.

(9) When giving a supervisory notice, or a warning notice or decision notice, the Authority must follow its stated procedure.

(10) If the Authority changes the procedure in a material way, it must publish a revised statement.

(11) The Authority's failure in a particular case to follow its procedure as set out in the latest published statement does not affect the validity of a notice given in that case.

(12) But subsection (11) does not prevent the Tribunal from taking into account any such failure in considering a matter referred to it.

(13) 'Supervisory notice' means a notice given in accordance with section—

    (a)   53(4), (7) or (8)(b);

    (b)   78(2) or (5);

    (c)   197(3), (6) or (7)(b);

    (d)   259(3), (8) or (9)(b);

(e)   268(3), (7)(a) or (9)(a) (as a result of subsection (8)(b));

(f)   282(3)(6) or (7)(b);

(g)   321(2) or (5).

396   Statements under section 395: consultation

(1) Before issuing a statement of procedure under section 395, the Authority must publish a draft of the proposed statement in the way appearing to the Authority to be best calculated to bring it to the attention of the public.

(2) The draft must be accompanied by notice that representations about the proposal may be made to the Authority within a specified time.

(3) Before issuing the proposed statement of procedure, the Authority must have regard to any representations made to it in accordance with subsection (2).

(4) If the Authority issues the proposed statement of procedure it must publish an account, in general terms, of—

(a)   the representations made to it in accordance with subsection (2); and

(b)   its response to them.

(5) If the statement of procedure differs from the draft published under subsection (1) in a way which is, in the opinion of the Authority, significant, the Authority must (in addition to complying with subsection (4)) publish details of the difference.

(6) The Authority may charge a reasonable fee for providing a person with a copy of a draft published under subsection (1).

(7) This section also applies to a proposal to revise a statement of policy.

PART XXVII

OFFENCES

Miscellaneous offences

397   Misleading statements and practices

(1) This subsection applies to a person who—

(a)   makes a statement, promise or forecast which he knows to be misleading, false or deceptive in a material particular;

(b)   dishonestly conceals any material facts whether in connection with a statement, promise or forecast made by him or otherwise; or

(c)   recklessly makes (dishonestly or otherwise) a statement, promise or forecast which is misleading, false or deceptive in a material particular.

(2) A person to whom subsection (1) applies is guilty of an offence if he makes the statement, promise or forecast or conceals the facts for the purpose of inducing, or is reckless as to whether it may induce, another person (whether or not the person to whom the statement, promise or forecast is made)—

(a)   to enter or offer to enter into, or to refrain from entering or offering to enter into, a relevant agreement; or

(b)   to exercise, or refrain from exercising, any rights conferred by a relevant investment.

(3) Any person who does any act or engages in any course of conduct which creates a false or misleading impression as to the market in or the price or value of any relevant

investments is guilty of an offence if he does so for the purpose of creating that impression and of thereby inducing another person to acquire, dispose of, subscribe for or underwrite those investments or to refrain from doing so or to exercise, or refrain from exercising, any rights conferred by those investments.

(4) In proceedings for an offence under subsection (2) brought against a person to whom subsection (1) applies as a result of paragraph (a) of that subsection, it is a defence for him to show that the statement, promise or forecast was made in conformity with price stabilising rules or control of information rules.

(5) In proceedings brought against any person for an offence under subsection (3) it is a defence for him to show—

    (a)   that he reasonably believed that his act or conduct would not create an impression that was false or misleading as to the matters mentioned in that subsection;

    (b)   that he acted or engaged in the conduct—

        (i)   for the purpose of stabilising the price of investments; and

        (ii) in conformity with price stabilising rules; or

    (c)   that he acted or engaged in the conduct in conformity with control of information rules.

(6) Subsections (1) or (2) do not apply unless—

    (a)   the statement, promise or forecast is made in or from, or the facts are concealed in or from, the United Kingdom or arrangements are made in or from the United Kingdom for the statement, promise or forecast to be made or the facts to be concealed;

    (b)   the person on whom the inducement is intended to or may have effect is in the United Kingdom; or

    (c)   the agreement is or would be entered into or the rights are or would be exercised in the United Kingdom.

(7) Subsection (3) does not apply unless—

    (a)   the act is done, or the course of conduct is engaged in, in the United Kingdom; or

    (b)   the false or misleading impression is created there.

(8) A person guilty of an offence under this section is liable—

    (a)   on summary conviction, to imprisonment for a term not exceeding six months or a fine not exceeding the statutory maximum, or both;

    (b)   on conviction on indictment, to imprisonment for a term not exceeding seven years or a fine, or both.

(9) 'Relevant agreement' means an agreement—

    (a)   the entering into or performance of which by either party constitutes an activity of a specified kind or one which falls within a specified class of activity; and

    (b)   which relates to a relevant investment.

(10) 'Relevant investment' means an investment of a specified kind or one which falls within a prescribed class of investment.

(11) Schedule 2 (except paragraphs 25 and 26) applies for the purposes of subsections (9) and (10) with references to section 22 being read as references to each of those subsections.

(12) Nothing in Schedule 2, as applied by subsection (11), limits the power conferred by subsection (9) or (10).

(13) 'Investment' includes any asset, right or interest.

(14) 'Specified' means specified in an order made by the Treasury.

398   Misleading the Authority: residual cases

(1) A person who, in purported compliance with any requirement imposed by or under this Act, knowingly or recklessly gives the Authority information which is false or misleading in a material particular is guilty of an offence.

(2) Subsection (1) applies only to a requirement in relation to which no other provision of this Act creates an offence in connection with the giving of information.

(3) A person guilty of an offence under this section is liable—

  (a)   on summary conviction, to a fine not exceeding the statutory maximum;
  (b)   on conviction on indictment, to a fine.

399   Misleading the Director General of Fair Trading

Section 44 of the Competition Act 1998 (offences connected with the provision of false or misleading information) applies in relation to any function of the Director General of Fair Trading under this Act as if it were a function under Part I of that Act.

Bodies corporate and partnerships

400   Offences by bodies corporate etc.

(1) If an offence under this Act committed by a body corporate is shown—

  (a)   to have been committed with the consent or connivance of an officer, or
  (b)   to be attributable to any neglect on his part,

the officer as well as the body corporate is guilty of the offence and liable to be proceeded against and punished accordingly.

(2) If the affairs of a body corporate are managed by its members, subsection (1) applies in relation to the acts and defaults of a member in connection with his functions of management as if he were a director of the body.

(3) If an offence under this Act committed by a partnership is shown—

  (a)   to have been committed with the consent or connivance of a partner, or
  (b)   to be attributable to any neglect on his part,

the partner as well as the partnership is guilty of the offence and liable to be proceeded against and punished accordingly.

(4) In subsection (3) 'partner' includes a person purporting to act as a partner.

(5) 'Officer', in relation to a body corporate, means—

  (a)   a director, member of the committee of management, chief executive, manager, secretary or other similar officer of the body, or a person purporting to act in any such capacity; and
  (b)   an individual who is a controller of the body.

(6) If an offence under this Act committed by an unincorporated association (other than a partnership) is shown—

  (a)   to have been committed with the consent or connivance of an officer of the association or a member of its governing body, or

(b)   to be attributable to any neglect on the part of such an officer or member,

that officer or member as well as the association is guilty of the offence and liable to be proceeded against and punished accordingly.

(7) Regulations may provide for the application of any provision of this section, with such modifications as the Treasury consider appropriate, to a body corporate or unincorporated association formed or recognised under the law of a territory outside the United Kingdom.

Institution of proceedings

401   Proceedings for offences

(1) In this section 'offence' means an offence under this Act or subordinate legislation made under this Act.

(2) Proceedings for an offence may be instituted in England and Wales only—

(a)   by the Authority or the Secretary of State; or
(b)   by or with the consent of the Director of Public Prosecutions.

(3) Proceedings for an offence may be instituted in Northern Ireland only—

(a)   by the Authority or the Secretary of State; or
(b)   by or with the consent of the Director of Public Prosecutions for Northern Ireland.

(4) Except in Scotland, proceedings for an offence under section 203 may also be instituted by the Director General of Fair Trading.

(5) In exercising its power to institute proceedings for an offence, the Authority must comply with any conditions or restrictions imposed in writing by the Treasury.

(6) Conditions or restrictions may be imposed under subsection (5) in relation to—

(a)   proceedings generally; or
(b)   such proceedings, or categories of proceedings, as the Treasury may direct.

402   Power of the Authority to institute proceedings for certain other offences

(1) Except in Scotland, the Authority may institute proceedings for an offence under—

(a)   Part V of the Criminal Justice Act 1993 (insider dealing); or
(b)   prescribed regulations relating to money laundering.

(2) In exercising its power to institute proceedings for any such offence, the Authority must comply with any conditions or restrictions imposed in writing by the Treasury.

(3) Conditions or restrictions may be imposed under subsection (2) in relation to—

(a)   proceedings generally; or
(b)   such proceedings, or categories of proceedings, as the Treasury may direct.

403   Jurisdiction and procedure in respect of offences

(1) A fine imposed on an unincorporated association on its conviction of an offence is to be paid out of the funds of the association.

(2) Proceedings for an offence alleged to have been committed by an unincorporated association must be brought in the name of the association (and not in that of any of its members).

(3) Rules of court relating to the service of documents are to have effect as if the association were a body corporate.

(4) In proceedings for an offence brought against an unincorporated association—

    (a)   section 33 of the Criminal Justice Act 1925 and Schedule 3 to the Magistrates' Courts Act 1980 (procedure) apply as they do in relation to a body corporate;

    (b)   section 70 of the Criminal Procedure (Scotland) Act 1995 (procedure) applies as if the association were a body corporate;

    (c)   section 18 of the Criminal Justice (Northern Ireland) Act 1945 and Schedule 4 to the Magistrates' Courts (Northern Ireland) Order 1981 (procedure) apply as they do in relation to a body corporate.

(5) Summary proceedings for an offence may be taken—

    (a)   against a body corporate or unincorporated association at any place at which it has a place of business;

    (b)   against an individual at any place where he is for the time being.

(6) Subsection (5) does not affect any jurisdiction exercisable apart from this section.

(7) 'Offence' means an offence under this Act.

PART XXVIII

MISCELLANEOUS

Schemes for reviewing past business

404   Schemes for reviewing past business

(1) Subsection (2) applies if the Treasury are satisfied that there is evidence suggesting—

    (a)   that there has been a widespread or regular failure on the part of authorised persons to comply with rules relating to a particular kind of activity; and

    (b)   that, as a result, private persons have suffered (or will suffer) loss in respect of which authorised persons are (or will be) liable to make payments ('compensation payments').

(2) The Treasury may by order ('a scheme order') authorise the Authority to establish and operate a scheme for—

    (a)   determining the nature and extent of the failure;

    (b)   establishing the liability of authorised persons to make compensation payments; and

    (c)   determining the amounts payable by way of compensation payments.

(3) An authorised scheme must be made so as to comply with specified requirements.

(4) A scheme order may be made only if—

    (a)   the Authority has given the Treasury a report about the alleged failure and asked them to make a scheme order;

    (b)   the report contains details of the scheme which the Authority propose to make; and

    (c)   the Treasury are satisfied that the proposed scheme is an appropriate way of dealing with the failure.

(5) A scheme order may provide for specified provisions of or made under this act to apply in relation to any provision of, or determination made under, the resulting authorised scheme subject to such modifications (if any) as may be specified.

(6) For the purposes of this Act, failure on the part of an authorised person to comply with any provision of an authorised scheme is to be treated (subject to any provision made by the scheme order concerned) as a failure on his part to comply with rules.

(7) The Treasury may prescribe circumstances in which loss suffered by a person ('A') acting in a fiduciary or other prescribed capacity is to be treated, for the purposes of an authorised scheme, as suffered by a private person in relation to whom A was acting in that capacity.

(8) This section applies whenever the failure in question occurred.

(9) 'Authorised scheme' means a scheme authorised by a scheme order.

(10) 'Private person' has such meaning as may be prescribed.

(11) 'Specified' means specified in a scheme order.

Third countries

405   Directions

(1) For the purpose of implementing a third country decision, the Treasury may direct the Authority to—

- (a) refuse an application for permission under Part IV made by a body incorporated in, or formed under the law of, any part of the United Kingdom;
- (b) defer its decision on such an application either indefinitely or for such period as may be specified in the direction;
- (c) give a notice of objection to a person who has served a notice of control to the effect that he proposes to acquire a 50% stake in a UK authorised person; or
- (d) give a notice of objection to a person who has acquired a 50% stake in a UK authorised person without having served the required notice of control.

(2) A direction may also be given in relation to—

- (a) any person falling within a class specified in the direction;
- (b) future applications, notices of control or acquisitions.

(3) The Treasury may revoke a direction at any time.

(4) But revocation does not affect anything done in accordance with the direction before it was revoked.

(5) 'Third country decision' means a decision of the Council or the Commission under—

- (a) Article 7(5) of the investment services directive;
- (b) Article 9(4) of the second banking co-ordination directive;
- (c) Article 29b(4) of the first non-life insurance directive; or
- (d) Article 32b(4) of the first life insurance directive.

406   Interpretation of section 405

(1) For the purposes of section 405, a person ('the acquirer') acquires a 50% stake in a UK authorised person ('A') on first falling within any of the cases set out in subsection (2).

(2) The cases are where the acquirer—

- (a) holds 50% or more of the shares in A;
- (b) holds 50% or more of the shares in a parent undertaking ('P') of A;
- (c) is entitled to exercise, or control the exercise of, 50% or more of the voting power in A; or
- (d) is entitled to exercise, or control the exercise of, 50% or more of the voting power in P.

(3) In subsection (2) 'the acquirer' means—

(a)   the acquirer;
(b)   any of the acquirer's associates; or
(c)   the acquirer and any of his associates.

(4) 'Associate', 'shares' and 'voting power' have the same meaning as in section 422.

407   Consequences of a direction under section 405

(1) If the Authority refuses an application for permission as a result of a direction under section 405(1)(a)—

(a)   subsections (7) to (9) of section 52 do not apply in relation to the refusal; but
(b)   the Authority must notify the applicant of the refusal and the reasons for it.

(2) If the Authority defers its decision on an application for permission as result of a direction under section 405(1)(b)—

(a)   the time limit for determining the application mentioned in section 52(1) or (2) stops running on the day of the deferral and starts running again (if at all) on the day the period specified in the direction (if any) ends or the day the direction is revoked; and
(b)   the Authority must notify the applicant of the deferral and the reasons for it.

(3) If the Authority gives a notice of objection to a person as a result of a direction under section 405(1)(c) or (d)—

(a)   sections 189 and 191 have effect as if the notice was a notice of objection within the meaning of Part XII; and
(b)   the Authority must state in the notice the reasons for it.

408   EFTA firms

(1) If a third country decision has been taken, the Treasury may make a determination in relation to an EFTA firm which is a subsidiary undertaking of a parent undertaking which is governed by the law of the country to which the decision relates.

(2) 'Determination' means a determination that the firm concerned does not qualify for authorisation under Schedule 3 even if it satisfies the conditions in paragraph 13 or 14 of that Schedule.

(3) A determination may also be made in relation to any firm falling within a class specified in the determination.

(4) The Treasury may withdraw a determination at any time.

(5) But withdrawal does not affect anything done in accordance with the determination before it was withdrawn.

(6) If the Treasury make a determination in respect of a particular firm, or withdraw such a determination, they must give written notice to that firm.

(7) The Treasury must publish notice of any determination (or the withdrawal of any determination)—

(a)   in such a way as they think most suitable for bringing the determination (or withdrawal) to the attention of those likely to be affected by it; and
(b)   on, or as soon as practicable after, the date of the determination (or withdrawal).

(8) 'EFTA firm' means a firm, institution or undertaking which—

(a)   is an EEA firm as a result of paragraph 5(a), (b) or (d) of Schedule 3; and

(b)   is incorporated in, or formed under the law of, an EEA State which is not a member State.

(9) 'Third country decision' has the same meaning as in section 405.

409   Gibraltar

(1) The Treasury may by order—

(a)   modify Schedule 3 so as to provide for Gibraltar firms of a specified description to qualify for authorisation under that Schedule in specified circumstances;

(b)   modify Schedule 3 so as to make provision in relation to the exercise by UK firms of rights under the law of Gibraltar which correspond to EEA rights;

(c)   modify Schedule 4 so as to provide for Gibraltar firms of a specified description to qualify for authorisation under that Schedule in specified circumstances;

(d)   modify section 264 so as to make provision in relation to collective investment schemes constituted under the law of Gibraltar;

(e)   provide for the Authority to be able to give notice under section 264(2) on grounds relating to the law of Gibraltar;

(f)   provide for this Act to apply to a Gibraltar recognised scheme as if the scheme were a scheme recognised under section 264.

(2) The fact that a firm may qualify for authorisation under Schedule 3 as a result of an order under subsection (1) does not prevent it from applying for a Part IV permission.

(3) 'Gibraltar firm' means a firm which has its head office in Gibraltar or is otherwise connected with Gibraltar.

(4) 'Gibraltar recognised scheme' means a collective investment scheme—

(a)   constituted in an EEA State other than the United Kingdom, and

(b)   recognised in Gibraltar under provisions which appear to the Treasury to give effect to the provisions of a relevant Community instrument.

(5) 'Specified' means specified in the order.

(6) 'UK firm' and 'EEA right' have the same meaning as in Schedule 3.

International obligations

410   International obligations

(1) If it appears to the Treasury that any action proposed to be taken by a relevant person would be incompatible with Community obligations or any other international obligations of the United Kingdom, they may direct that person not to take that action.

(2) if it appears to the Treasury that any action which a relevant person has power to take is required for the purpose of implementing any such obligations, they may direct that person to take that action.

(3) A direction under this section—

(a)   may include such supplemental or incidental requirements as the Treasury consider necessary or expedient; and

(b)   is enforceable, on an application made by the Treasury, by injunction or, in Scotland, by an order for specific performance under section 45 of the Court of Session Act 1988.

(4) 'Relevant person' means—

(a)   the Authority;

(b)   any person exercising functions conferred by Part VI on the competent authority;
(c)   any recognised investment exchange (other than one which is an overseas investment exchange);
(d)   any recognised clearing house (other than one which is an overseas clearing house);
(e)   a person included in the list maintained under section 301; or
(f)   the scheme operator of the ombudsman scheme.

Tax treatment of levies and repayments

411   Tax treatment of levies and repayments

(1) In the Income and Corporation Taxes Act 1988 ('the 1988 Act'), in section 76 (expenses of management: insurance companies), for subsections (7) and (7A) substitute—

'(7) For the purposes of this section any sums paid by a company by way of a levy shall be treated as part of its expenses of management.

(7A) "Levy" means—

(a)   a payment required under rules made under section 136(2) of the Financial Services and Markets Act 2000 ("the Act of 2000");
(b)   a levy imposed under the Financial Services Compensation Scheme;
(c)   a payment required under rules made under section 234 of the Act of 2000;
(d)   a payment required in accordance with the standard terms fixed under paragraph 18 of Schedule 17 to the Act of 2000.'

(2) After section 76 of the 1988 Act insert—

'Levies and repayments under the Financial Services and Markets Act 2000

76A.—(1) In computing the amount of the profits to be charged under Case I of Schedule D arising from a trade carried on by an authorised person (other than an investment company)—
(a)   to the extent that it would not be deductible apart from this section, any sum expended by the authorised person in paying a levy may be deducted as an allowable expense;
(b)   any payment which is made to the authorised person as a result of a repayment provision is to be treated as a trading receipt.

(2) "Levy" has the meaning given in section 76(7A).

(3) "Repayment provision" means any provision made by virtue of—
(a)   section 136(7) of the Financial Services and Markets Act 2000 ("the Act of 2000");
(b)   section 214(1)(e) of the Act of 2000.

(4) "Authorised person" has the same meaning as in the Act of 2000.

'Levies and repayments under the Financial Services and Markets Act 2000: investment companies

76B.—(1) For for the purposes of section 75 any sums paid by an investment company—

(a)   by way of a levy, or
(b)   as a result of an award of costs under costs rules, shall be treated as part of its expenses of management.

(2) If a payment is made to an investment company as a result of a repayment provision, the company shall be charged to tax under Case VI of Schedule D on the amount of that payment.

(3) "Levy" has the meaning given in section 76(7A).

(4) "Costs rules" means—
   (a)   rules made under section 230 of the Financial Services and Markets Act 2000;
   (b)   provision relating to costs contained in the standard terms fixed under paragraph 18 of Schedule 17 to that Act.

(5) "Repayment provision" has the meaning given in section 76A(3).'

Gaming contracts

412   Gaming contracts

(1) No contract to which this section applies is void or unenforceable because of—
   (a)   section 18 of the Gaming Act 1845, section 1 of the Gaming Act 1892 or Article 170 of the Betting, Gaming, Lotteries and Amusements (Northern Ireland) Order 1985; or
   (b)   any rule of the law of Scotland under which a contract by way of gaming or wagering is not legally enforceable.

(2) This section applies to a contract if—
   (a)   it is entered into by either or each party by way of business;
   (b)   the entering into or performance of it by either party constitutes an activity of a specified kind or one which falls within a specified class of activity; and
   (c)   it relates to an investment of a specified kind or one which falls within a specified class of investment.

(3) Part II of Schedule 2 applies for the purposes of subsection (2)(c), with the references to section 22 being read as references to that subsection.

(4) Nothing in Part II of Schedule 2, as applied by subsection (3), limits the power conferred by subsection (2)(c).

(5) 'Investment' includes any asset, right or interest.

(6) 'Specified' means specified in an order made by the Treasury.

Limitation on powers to require documents

413   Protected items

(1) A person may not be required under this Act to produce, disclose or permit the inspection of protected items.

(2) 'Protected items' means—
   (a)   communications between a professional legal adviser and his client or any person representing his client which fall within subsection (3);
   (b)   communications between a professional legal adviser, his client or any person representing his client and any other person which fall within subsection (3) (as a result of paragraph (b) of that subsection);

    (c)   items which—
        (i)   are enclosed with, or referred to in, such communications;
        (ii) fall within subsection (3); and
        (iii) are in the possession of a person entitled to possession of them.

(3) A communication or item falls within this subsection if it is made—

    (a)   in connection with the giving of legal advice to the client; or
    (b)   in connection with, or in contemplation of, legal proceedings and for the purposes of those proceedings.

(4) A communication or item is not a protected item if it is held with the intention of furthering a criminal purpose.

Service of notices

414   Service of notices

(1) The Treasury may by regulations make provision with respect to the procedure to be followed, or rules to be applied, when a provision of or made under this Act requires a notice, direction or document of any kind to be given or authorises the imposition of a requirement.

(2) The regulations may, in particular, make provision—

    (a)   as to the manner in which a document must be given;
    (b)   as to the address to which a document must be sent;
    (c)   requiring, or allowing, a document to be sent electronically;
    (d)   for treating a document as having been given, or as having been received, on a date or at a time determined in accordance with the regulations;
    (e)   as to what must, or may, be done if the person to whom a document is required to be given is not an individual;
    (f)   as to what must, or may, be done if the intended recipient of a document is outside the United Kingdom.

(3) Subsection (1) applies however the obligation to give a document is expressed (and so, in particular, includes a provision which requires a document to be served or sent).

(4) Section 7 of the Interpretation Act 1978 (service of notice by post) has effect in relation to provisions made by or under this Act subject to any provision made by regulations under this section.

Jurisdiction

415   Jurisdiction in civil proceedings

(1) Proceedings arising out of any act or omission (or proposed act or omission) of—

    (a)   the Authority,
    (b)   the competent authority for the purposes of Part VI,
    (c)   the scheme manager, or
    (d)   the scheme operator,

in the discharge or purported discharge of any of its functions under this Act may be brought before the High Court or the Court of Session.

(2) The jurisdiction conferred by subsection (1) is in addition to any other jurisdiction exercisable by those courts.

Removal of certain unnecessary provisions

416   Provisions relating to industrial assurance and certain other enactments

(1) The following enactments are to cease to have effect—

   (a)   the Industrial Assurance Act 1923;
   (b)   the Industrial Assurance and Friendly Societies Act 1948;
   (c)   the Insurance Brokers (Registration) Act 1977.

(2) The Industrial Assurance (Northern Ireland) Order 1979 is revoked.

(3) The following bodies are to cease to exist—

   (a)   the Insurance Brokers Registration Council;
   (b)   the Policyholders Protection Board;
   (c)   the Deposit Protection Board;
   (d)   the Board of Banking Supervision.

(4) If the Treasury consider that, as a consequence of any provision of this section, it is appropriate to do so, they may by order make any provision of a kind that they could make under this Act (and in particular any provision of a kind mentioned in section 339) with respect to anything done by or under any provision of Part XXI.

(5) Subsection (4) is not to be read as affecting in any way any other power conferred on the Treasury by this Act.

PART XXIX

INTERPRETATION

417   Definitions

(1) In this Act—

'appointed representative' has the meaning given in section 39(2);

'auditors and actuaries rules' means rules made under section 340;

'authorisation offence' has the meaning given in section 23(2);

'authorised open-ended investment company' has the meaning given in section 237(3);

'authorised person' has the meaning given in section 31(2);

'the Authority' means the Financial Services Authority;

'body corporate' includes a body corporate constituted under the law of a country or territory outside the United Kingdom;

'Chief executive'—

   (a)   in relation to a body corporate whose principal place of business is within the United Kingdom, means an employee of that body who, alone or jointly with one or more others, is responsible under the immediate authority of the directors, for the conduct of the whole of the business of that body; and
   (b)   in relation to a body corporate whose principal place of business is outside the United Kingdom, means the person who, alone or jointly with one or more others, is responsible for the conduct of its business within the United Kingdom;

'collective investment scheme' has the meaning given in section 235;

'the Commission' means the European Commission (except in provisions relating to the Competition Commission);

'the compensation scheme' has the meaning given in section 213(2);

'control of information rules' has the meaning given in section 147(1);

'director', in relation to a body corporate, includes—

    (a)   a person occupying in relation to it the position of a director (by whatever name called); and

    (b)   a person in accordance with whose directions or instructions (not being advice given in a professional capacity) the directors of that body are accustomed to act;

'documents' includes information recorded in any form and, in relation to information recorded otherwise than in legible form, references to its production include references to producing a copy of the information in legible form;

'exempt person', in relation to a regulated activity, means a person who is exempt from the general prohibition in relation to that activity as a result of an exemption order made under section 38(1) or as a result of section 39(1) or 285(2) or (3);

'financial promotion rules' means rules made under section 145;

'friendly society' means an incorporated or registered friendly society;

'general prohibition' has the meaning given in section 19(2);

'general rules' has the meaning given in section 138(2);

'incorporated friendly society' means a society incorporated under the Friendly Societies Act 1992;

'industrial and provident society' means a society registered or deemed to be registered under the Industrial and Provident Societies Act 1965 or the Industrial and Provident Societies Act (Northern Ireland) 1969;

'market abuse' has the meaning given in section 118;

'Minister of the Crown' has the same meaning as in the Ministers of the Crown Act 1975;

'money laundering rules' means rules made under section 146;

'notice of control' has the meaning given in section 178(5);

'the ombudsman scheme' has the meaning given in section 225(3);

'open-ended investment company' has the meaning given in section 236;

'Part IV permission' has the meaning given in section 40(4);

'partnership' includes a partnership constituted under the law of a country or territory outside the United Kingdom;

'prescribed' (where not otherwise defined) means prescribed in regulations made by the Treasury;

'price stabilising rules' means rules made under section 144;

'private company' has the meaning given in section 1(3) of the Companies Act 1985 or in Article 12(3) of the Companies (Northern Ireland) Order 1986;

'prohibition order' has the meaning given in section 56(2);

'recognised clearing house' and 'recognised investment exchange' have the meaning given in section 285;

'registered friendly society' means a society which is—

(a)   a friendly society within the meaning of section 7(1)(a) of the Friendly Societies Act 1974; and

(b)   registered within the meaning of that Act;

'regulated activity' has the meaning given in section 22;

'regulating provisions' has the meaning given in section 159(1);

'regulatory objectives' means the objectives mentioned in section 2;

'regulatory provisions' has the meaning given in section 302;

'rule' means a rule made by the Authority under this Act;

'rule-making instrument' has the meaning given in section 153;

'the scheme manager' has the meaning given in section 212(1);

'the scheme operator' has the meaning given in section 225(2);

'scheme particulars rules' has the meaning given in section 248(1);

'Seventh Company Law Directive' means the European Council Seventh Company Law Directive of 13 June 1983 on consolidated accounts (No. 83/349/EEC);

'threshold conditions', in relation to a regulated activity, has the meaning given in section 41;

'the Treaty' means the treaty establishing the European Community;

'trust scheme rules' has the meaning given in section 247(1);

'UK authorised person' has the meaning given in section 178(4); and

'unit trust scheme' has the meaning given in section 237.

(2) In the application of this Act to Scotland, references to a matter being actionable at the suit of a person are to be read as references to the matter being actionable at the instance of that person.

(3) For the purposes of any provision of this Act authorising or requiring a person to do anything within a specified number of days no account is to be taken of any day which is a public holiday in any part of the United Kingdom.

418   Carrying on regulated activities in the United Kingdom

(1) In the four cases described in this section, a person who—

(a)   is carrying on a regulated activity, but

(b)   would not otherwise be regarded as carrying it on in the United Kingdom,

is, for the purposes of this Act, to be regarded as carrying it on in the United Kingdom.

(2) The first case is where—

(a)   his registered office (or if he does not have a registered office his head office) is in the United Kingdom;

   (b)   he is entitled to exercise rights under a single market directive as a UK firm; and

   (c)   he is carrying on in another EEA State a regulated activity to which that directive applies.

(3) The second case is where—

   (a)   his registered office (or if he does not have a registered office his head office) is in the United Kingdom;

   (b)   he is the manager of a scheme which is entitled to enjoy the rights conferred by an instrument which is a relevant Community instrument for the purposes of section 264; and

   (c)   persons in another EEA State are invited to become participants in the scheme.

(4) The third case is where—

   (a)   his registered office (or if he does not have a registered office his head office) is in the United Kingdom;

   (b)   the day-to-day management of the carrying on of the regulated activity is the responsibility of—

      (i)   his registered office (or head office); or

      (ii)   another establishment maintained by him in the United Kingdom.

(5) The fourth case is where—

   (a)   his head office is not in the United Kingdom; but

   (b)   the activity is carried on from an establishment maintained by him in the United Kingdom.

(6) For the purposes of subsections (2) to (5) it is irrelevant where the person with whom the activity is carried on is situated.

419   Carrying on regulated activities by way of business

(1) The Treasury may by order make provision—

   (a)   as to the circumstances in which a person who would otherwise not be regarded as carrying on a regulated activity by way of business is to be regarded as doing so;

   (b)   as to the circumstances in which a person who would otherwise be regarded as carrying on a regulated activity by way of business is to be regarded as not doing so.

(2) An order under subsection (1) may be made so as to apply—

   (a)   generally in relation to all regulated activities;

   (b)   in relation to a specified category of regulated activity; or

   (c)   in relation to a particular regulated activity.

(3) An order under subsection (1) may be made so as to apply—

   (a)   for the purposes of all provisions;

   (b)   for a specified group of provisions; or

   (c)   for a specified provision.

(4) 'Provision' means a provision of, or made under, this Act.

(5) Nothing in this section is to be read as affecting the provisions of section 428(3).

420   Parent and subsidiary undertaking

(1) In this Act, except in relation to an incorporated friendly society, 'parent undertaking' and 'subsidiary undertaking' have the same meaning as in Part VII of the Companies Act 1985 (or Part VIII of the Companies (Northern Ireland) Order 1986).

(2) But—

    (a) 'parent undertaking' also includes an individual who would be a parent undertaking for the purposes of those provisions if he were taken to be an undertaking (and 'subsidiary undertaking' is to be read accordingly);

    (b) 'subsidiary undertaking' also includes, in relation to a body incorporated in or formed under the law of an EEA State other than the United Kingdom, an undertaking which is a subsidiary undertaking within the meaning of any rule of law in force in that State for purposes connected with implementation of the Seventh Company Law Directive (and 'parent undertaking' is to be read accordingly).

(3) In this Act 'subsidiary undertaking', in relation to an incorporated friendly society, means a body corporate of which the society has control within the meaning of section 13(9)(a) or (aa) of the Friendly Societies Act 1992 (and 'parent undertaking' is to be read accordingly).

421   Group

(1) In this Act 'group', in relation to a person ('A'), means A and any person who is—

    (a) a parent undertaking of A;

    (b) a subsidiary undertaking of A;

    (c) a subsidiary undertaking of a parent undertaking of A;

    (d) a parent undertaking of a subsidiary undertaking of A;

    (e) an undertaking in which A or an undertaking mentioned in paragraph (a), (b), (c) or (d) has a participating interest;

    (f) if A or an undertaking mentioned in paragraph (a) or (d) is a building society, an associated undertaking of the society; or

    (g) if A or an undertaking mentioned in paragraph (a) or (d) is an incorporated friendly society, a body corporate or which the society has joint control (within the meaning of section 13(9)(c) or (cc) of the Friendly Societies Act 1992).

(2) 'Participating interest' has the same meaning as in Part VII of the Companies Act 1985 or Part VIII of the Companies (Northern Ireland) Order 1986; but also includes an interest held by an individual which would be a participating interest for the purposes of those provisions if he were taken to be an undertaking.

(3) 'Associated undertaking' has the meaning given in section 119(1) of the Building Societies Act 1986.

422   Controller

(1) In this Act 'controller', in relation to an undertaking ('A'), means a person who falls within any of the cases in subsection (2).

(2) The cases are where the person—

    (a) holds 10% or more of the shares in A;

    (b) is able to exercise significant influence over the management of A by virtue of his shareholding in A;

    (c) holds 10% or more of the shares in a parent undertaking ('P') of A;

    (d) is able to exercise significant influence over the management of P by virtue of his shareholding in P;

    (e) is entitled to exercise, or control the exercise of, 10% or more of the voting power in A;

    (f) is able to exercise significant influence over the management of A by virtue of his voting power in A;

    (g) is entitled to exercise, or control the exercise of, 10% or more of the voting power in P; or

(h)   is able to exercise significant influence over the management of P by virtue of his voting power in P.

(3) In subsection (2) 'the person' means—

(a)   the person;
(b)   any of the person's associates; or
(c)   the person and any of his associates.

(4) 'Associate', in relation to a person ('H') holding shares in an undertaking ('C') or entitled to exercise or control the exercise of voting power in relation to another undertaking ('D'), means—

(a)   the spouse of H;
(b)   a child or stepchild of H (if under 18);
(c)   the trustee of any settlement under which H has a life interest in possession (or in Scotland a life interest);
(d)   an undertaking of which H is a director;
(e)   a person who is an employee or partner of H;
(f)   if H is an undertaking—
      (i)   a director of H;
      (ii)   a subsidiary undertaking of H;
      (iii)   a director or employee of such a subsidiary undertaking; and
(g)   if H has with any other person an agreement or arrangement with respect to the acquisition, holding or disposal of shares or other interests in C or D or under which they undertake to act together in exercising their voting power in relation to C or D, that other person.

(5) 'Settlement', in subsection (4)(c), includes any disposition or arrangement under which property is held on trust (or subject to a comparable obligation).

(6) 'Shares'—

(a)   in relation to an undertaking with a share capital, means allotted shares;
(b)   in relation to an undertaking with capital but no share capital, means rights to share in the capital of the undertaking;
(c)   in relation to an undertaking without capital, means interests—
      (i)   conferring any right to share in the profits, or liability to contribute to the losses, of the undertaking; or
      (ii)   giving rise to an obligation to contribute to the debts or expenses of the undertaking in the event of a winding up.

(7) 'Voting power', in relation to an undertaking which does not have general meetings at which matters are decided by the exercise of voting rights, means the right under the constitution of the undertaking to direct the overall policy of the undertaking or alter the terms of its constitution.

423   Manager

(1) In this Act, except in relation to a unit trust scheme or a registered friendly society, 'manager' means an employee who—

(a)   under the immediate authority of his employer is responsible, either alone or jointly with one or more other persons, for the conduct of his employer's business; or
(b)   under the immediate authority of his employer or of a person who is a manager by virtue of paragraph (a) exercises managerial functions or is responsible for maintaining accounts or other records of his employer.

(2) If the employer is not an individual, references in subsection (1) to the authority of the employer are references to the authority—

(a)   in the case of a body corporate, of the directors;
(b)   in the case of a parternship, of the partners; and
(c)   in the case of an unincorporated association, of its officers or the members of its governing body.

(3) 'Manager', in relation to a body corporate, means a person (other than an employee of the body) who is appointed by the body to manage any part of its business and includes an employee of the body corporate (other than the chief executive) who, under the immediate authority of a director or chief executive of the body corporate, exercises managerial functions or is responsible for maintaining accounts or other records of the body corporate.

424   Insurance

(1) In this Act, references to—

(a)   contracts of insurance,
(b)   reinsurance,
(c)   contracts of long-term insurance,
(d)   contracts of general insurance,

are to be read with section 22 and Schedule 2.

(2) In this Act 'policy' and 'policyholder', in relation to a contract of insurance, have such meaning as the Treasury may by order specify.

(3) The law applicable to a contract of insurance, the effecting of which constitutes the carrying on of a regulated activity, is to be determined, if it is of a prescribed description, in accordance with regulations made by the Treasury.

425   Expressions relating to authorisation elsewhere in the single market

(1) In this Act—

(a)   'EEA authorisation', 'EEA firm', 'EEA right', 'EEA State', 'first life insurance directive', 'first non-life insurance directive', 'insurance directives', 'investment services directive', 'single market directives' and 'second banking co-ordination directive' have the meaning given in Schedule 3; and
(b)   'home state regulator', in relation to an EEA firm, has the meaning given in Schedule 3.

(2) In this Act—

(a)   'home state authorisation' has the meaning given in Schedule 4;
(b)   'Treaty firm' has the meaning given in Schedule 4; and
(c)   'home state regulator', in relation to a Treaty firm, has the meaning given in Schedule 4.

PART XXX

SUPPLEMENTAL

426   Consequential and supplementary provision

(1) A Minister of the Crown may by order make such incidental, consequential, transitional or supplemental provision as he considers necessary or expedient for the general purposes,

or any particular purpose, of this Act or in consequence of any provision made by or under this Act or for giving full effect to this Act or any such provision.

(2) An order under subsection (1) may, in particular, make provision—

    (a) for enabling any person by whom any powers will become exercisable, on a date set by or under this Act, by virtue of any provision made by or under this Act to take before that date any steps which are necessary as a preliminary to the exercise of those powers;

    (b) for applying (with or without modifications) or amending, repealing or revoking any provision of or made under an Act passed before this Act or in the same Session;

    (c) dissolving any body corporate established by any Act passed, or instrument made, before the passing of this Act;

    (d) for making savings, or additional savings, from the effect of any repeal or revocation made by or under this Act.

(3) Amendments made under this section are additional, and without prejudice, to those made by or under any other provision of this Act.

(4) No other provision of this Act restricts the powers conferred by this section.

427   Transitional provisions

(1) Subsections (2) and (3) apply to an order under section 426 which makes transitional provisions or savings.

(2) The order may, in particular—

    (a) if it makes provision about the authorisation and permission of persons who before commencement were entitled to carry on any activities, also include provision for such persons not to be treated as having any authorisation or permission (whether on an application to the Authority or otherwise);

    (b) make provision enabling the Authority to require persons of such descriptions as it may direct to re-apply for permission having effect by virtue of the order;

    (c) make provision for the continuation as rules of such provisions (including primary and subordinate legislation) as may be designated in accordance with the order by the Authority, including provision for the modification by the Authority of provisions designated;

    (d) make provision about the effect of requirements imposed, liabilities incurred and any other things done before commencement, including provision for and about investigations, penalties and the taking or continuing of any other action in respect of contraventions;

    (e) make provision for the continuation of disciplinary and other proceedings begun before commencement, including provision about the decisions available to bodies before which such proceedings take place and the effect of their decisions;

    (f) make provision as regards the Authority's obligation to maintain a record under section 347 as respects persons in relation to whom provision is made by the order.

(3) The order may—

    (a) confer functions on the Treasury, the Secretary of State, the Authority, the scheme manager, the scheme operator, members of the panel established under paragraph 4 of Schedule 17, the Competition Commission or the Director General of Fair Trading;

    (b) confer jurisdiction on the Tribunal;

    (c) provide for fees to be charged in connection with the carrying out of functions conferred under the order;

    (d) modify, exclude or apply (with or without modifications) any primary or subordinate legislation (including any provision of, or made under, this Act).

(4) In subsection (2) 'commencement' means the commencement of such provisions of this Act as may be specified by the order.

428   Regulations and orders

(1) Any power to make an order which is conferred on a Minister of the Crown by this Act and any power to make regulations which is conferred by this Act is exercisable by statutory instrument.

(2) The Lord Chancellor's power to make rules under section 132 is exercisable by statutory instrument.

(3) Any statutory instrument made under this Act may—

   (a)   contain such incidental, supplemental, consequential and transitional provision as the person making it considers appropriate; and

   (b)   make different provision for different cases.

429   Parliamentary control of statutory instruments

(1) No order is to be made under—

   (a)   section 144(4), 192(b) or (e), 236(5), 404 or 419, or

   (b)   paragraph 1 of Schedule 8,

unless a draft of the order has been laid before Parliament and approved by a resolution of each House.

(2) No regulations are to be made under section 262 unless a draft of the regulations has been laid before Parliament and approved by a resolution of each House.

(3) An order to which, if it is made, subsection (4) or (5) will apply is not to be made unless a draft of the order has been laid before Parliament and approved by a resolution of each House.

(4) This subsection applies to an order under section 21 if—

   (a)   it is the first order to be made, or to contain provisions made, under section 21(4);

   (b)   it varies an order made under section 21(4) so as to make section 21(1) apply in circumstances in which it did not previously apply;

   (c)   it is the first order to be made, or to contain provision made, under section 21(5);

   (d)   it varies a previous order made under section 21(5) so as to make section 21(1) apply in circumstances in which it did not, as a result of that previous order, apply;

   (e)   it is the first order to be made, or to contain provisions made, under section 21(9) or (10);

   (f)   it adds one or more activities to those that are controlled activities for the purposes of section 21; or

   (g)   it adds one or more investments to those which are controlled investments for the purposes of section 21.

(5) This subsection applies to an order under section 38 if—

   (a)   it is the first order to be made, or to contain provisions made, under that section; or

   (b)   it contains provisions restricting or removing an exemption provided by an earlier order made under that section.

(6) An order containing a provision to which, if the order is made, subsection (7) will apply is not to be made unless a draft of the order has been laid before Parliament and approved by a resolution of each House.

(7) This subsection applies to a provision contained in an order if—

    (a)   it is the first to be made in the exercise of the power conferred by subsection (1) of section 326 or it removes a body from those for the time being designated under that subsection; or

    (b)   it is the first to be made in the exercise of the power conferred by subsection (6) of section 327 or it adds a description of regulated activity or investment to those for the time being specified for the purposes of that subsection.

(8) Any other statutory instrument made under this Act, apart from one made under section 431(2) or to which paragraph 26 of Schedule 2 applies, shall be subject to annulment in pursuance of a resolution of either House of Parliament.

430   Extent

(1) This Act, except Chapter IV of Part XVII, extends to Northern Ireland.

(2) Except where Her Majesty by Order in Council provides otherwise the extent of any amendment or repeal made by or under this Act is the same as the extent of the provision amended or repealed.

(3) Her Majesty may by Order in Council provide for any provision of or made under this Act relating to a matter which is the subject of other legislation which extends to any of the Channel Islands or the Isle of Man to extend there with such modifications (if any) as may be specified in the Order.

431   Commencement

(1) The following provisions come into force on the passing of this Act—

    (a)   this section;
    (b)   sections 428, 430 and 433;
    (c)   paragraphs 1 and 2 of Schedule 21.

(2) The other provision of this Act come into force on such day as the Treasury may by order appoint; and different days may be appointed for different purposes.

432   Minor and consequential amendments, transitional provisions and repeals

(1) Schedule 20 makes minor and consequential amendments.

(2) Schedule 21 makes transitional provisions.

(3) The enactments set out in Schedule 22 are repealed.

433   Short title

This Act may be cited as the Financial Services and Markets Act 2000.

SCHEDULES

SCHEDULE 1   Section 1

THE FINANCIAL SERVICES AUTHORITY

PART I

GENERAL

Interpretation

1   (1) In this Schedule—

'the 1985 Act' means the Companies Act 1985;
'non-executive committee' means the committee maintained under paragraph 3;
'functions', in relation to the Authority, means functions conferred on the Authority by
    or under any provision of this Act.

(2) For the purposes of this Schedule, the following are the Authority's legislative
functions—

   (a)   making rules;
   (b)   issuing codes under section 64 or 119;
   (c)   issuing statements under section 64, 69, 124 or 210;
   (d)   giving directions under section 316, 318 or 328;
   (e)   issuing general guidance (as defined by section 158(5)).

Constitution

2   (1) The constitution of the Authority must continue to provide for the Authority to
have—

   (a)   a chairman; and
   (b)   a governing body.

(2) The governing body must include the chairman.

(3) The chairman and other members of the governing body must be appointed, and be
liable to removal from office, by the Treasury.

(4) The validity of any act of the Authority is not affected—

   (a)   by a vacancy in the office of chairman; or
   (b)   by a defect in the appointment of a person as a member of the governing body or as
      chairman.

Non-excecutive members of the governing body

3   (1) The Authority must secure—

   (a)   that the majority of the members of its governing body are non-executive members;
      and
   (b)   that a committee of its governing body, consisting solely of the non-executive
      members, is set up and maintained for the purposes of discharging the functions
      conferred on the committee by this Schedule.

(2) The members of the non-executive committee are to be appointed by the Authority.

(3) The non-executive committee is to have a chairman appointed by the Treasury from among its members.

Functions of the non-executive committee

4 (1) In this paragraph 'the committee' means the non-executive committee.

(2) The non-executive functions are functions of the Authority but must be discharged by the committee.

(3) The non-executive functions are—

  (a) keeping under review the question whether the Authority is, in discharging its functions in accordance with decisions of its governing body, using its resources in the most efficient and economic way;
  (b) keeping under review the question whether the Authority's internal financial controls secure the proper conduct of its financial affairs; and
  (c) determining the remuneration of—
     (i)   the chairman of the Authority's governing body; and
     (ii) the executive members of that body.

(4) The function mentioned in sub-paragraph (3)(b) and those mentioned in sub-paragragph (3)(c) may be discharged on behalf of the committee by a sub-committee.

(5) Any sub-committee of the committee—

  (a) must have as its chairman the chairman of the committee; but
  (b) may include persons other than members of the committee.

(6) The committee must prepare a report on the discharge of its functions for inclusion in the Authority's annual report to the Treasury under paragraph 10.

(7) The committee's report must relate to the same period as that covered by the Authority's report.

Arrangements for discharging functions

5 (1) The Authority may make arrangements for any of its functions to be discharged by a committee, sub-committee, officer or member of staff of the Authority.

(2) But in exercising its legislative functions, the Authority must act through its governing body.

(3) Sub-paragraph (1) does not apply to the non-executive functions.

Monitoring and enforcement

6 (1) The Authority must maintain arrangements designed to enable it to determine whether persons on whom requirements are imposed by or under this Act are complying with them.

(2) Those arrangements may provide for functions to be performed on behalf of the Authority by any body or person who, in its opinion, is competent to perform them.

(3) The Authority must also maintain arrangements for enforcing the provisions of, or made under, this Act.

(4) Sub-paragraph (2) does not affect the Authority's duty under sub-paragraph (1).

Arrangements for the investigation of complaints

7 (1) The Authority must—

(a) make arrangements ('the complaints scheme') for the investigation of complaints arising in connection with the exercise of, or failure to exercise, any of its functions (other than its legislative functions); and

(b) appoint an independent person ('the investigator') to be responsible for the conduct of investigations in accordance with the complaints scheme.

(2) The complaints scheme must be designed so that, as far as reasonably practicable, complaints are investigated quickly.

(3) The Treasury's approval is required for the appointment or dismissal of the investigator.

(4) The terms and conditions on which the investigator is appointed must be such as, in the opinion of the Authority, are reasonably designed to secure—

(a) that he will be free at all times to act independently of the Authority; and

(b) that complaints will be investigated under the complaints scheme without favouring the Authority.

(5) Before making the complaints scheme, the Authority must publish a draft of the proposed scheme in the way appearing to the Authority best calculated to bring it to the attention of the public.

(6) The draft must be accompanied by notice that representations about it may be made to the Authority within a specified time.

(7) Before making the proposed complaints cheme, the Authority must have regard to any representations made to it in accordance with sub-paragraph (6).

(8) If the Authority makes the proposed complaints scheme, it must publish an account, in general terms, of—

(a) the representations made to it in accordance with sub-paragraph (6); and

(b) its response to them.

(9) If the complaints scheme differs from the draft published under sub-paragraph (5) in a way which is, in the opinion of the Authority, significant the Authority must (in addition to complying with sub-paragraph (8)) publish details of the difference.

(10) The Authority must publish up-to-date details of the complaints scheme including, in particular, details of—

(a) the provision made under paragraph 8(5); and

(b) the powers which the investigator has to investigate a complaint.

(11) Those details must be published in the way appearing to the Authority to be best calculated to bring them to the attention of the public.

(12) The Authority must, without delay, give the Treasury a copy of any details published by it under this paragraph.

(13) The Authority may charge a reasonable fee for providing a person with a copy of—

(a) a draft published under sub-paragraph (5);

(b)   details published under sub-paragraph (10).

(14) Sub-paragraphs (5) to (9) and (13)(a) also apply to a proposal to alter or replace the complaints scheme.

Investigation of complaints

8   (1) The Authority is not obliged to investigate a complaint in accordance with the complaints scheme which it reasonably considers would be more appropriately dealt with in another way (for example by referring the matter to the Tribunal or by the institution of other legal proceedings).

(2) The complaints scheme must provide—

    (a)   for reference to the investigator of any complaint which the Authority is investigating; and

    (b)   for him—

        (i)   to have the means to conduct a full investigation of the complaint;

        (ii)   to report on the result of his investigation to the Authority and the complainant; and

        (iii) to be able to publish his report (or any part of it) if he considers that it (or the part) ought to be brought to the attention of the public.

(3) If the Authority has decided not to investigate a complaint, it must notify the investigator.

(4) If the investigator considers that a complaint of which he has been notified under sub-paragraph (3) ought to be investigated, he may proceed as if the complaint had been referred to him under the complaints scheme.

(5) The complaints scheme must confer on the investigator the power to recommend, if he thinks it appropriate, that the Authority—

    (a)   makes a compensatory payment to the complainant,

    (b)   remedies the matter complained of,

or takes both of those steps.

(6) The complaints scheme must require the Authority, in a case where the investigator—

    (a)   has reported that a complaint is well-founded, or

    (b)   has criticised the Authority in his report,

to inform the investigator and the complainant of the steps which it proposes to take in response to the report.

(7) The investigator may require the Authority to publish the whole or a specified part of the response.

(8) The investigator may appoint a person to conduct the investigation on his behalf but subject to his direction.

(9) Neither an officer nor an employee of the Authority may be appointed under sub-paragraph (8).

(10) Sub-paragraph (2) is not to be taken as preventing the Authority from making arrangements for the initial investigation of a complaint to be conducted by the Authority.

Records

9   The Authority must maintain satisfactory arrangements for—

(a)   recording decisions made in the exercise of its functions; and
(b)   the safe-keeping of those records which it considers ought to be preserved.

Annual report

10   (1) At least once a year the Authority must make a report to the Treasury on—

(a)   the discharge of its functions;
(b)   the extent to which, in its opinion, the regulatory objectives have been met;
(c)   its consideration of the matters mentioned in section 2(3); and
(d)   such other matters as the Treasury may from time to time direct.

(2) The report must be accompanied by—

(a)   the report prepared by the non-executive committee under paragraph 4(6); and
(b)   such other reports or information, prepared by such persons, as the Treasury may from time to time direct.

(3) The Treasury must lay before Parliament a copy of each report received by them under this paragraph.

(4) The Treasury may—

(a)   require the Authority to comply with any provisions of the 1985 Act about accounts and their audit which would not otherwise apply to it; or
(b)   direct that any such provision of that Act is to apply to the Authority with such modifications as are specified in the direction.

(5) Compliance with any requirement imposed under sub-paragraph (4)(a) or (b) is enforceable by injunction or, in Scotland, an order under section 45(b) of the Court of Session Act 1988.

(6) Proceedings under sub-paragraph (5) may be brought only by the Treasury.

Annual public meeting

11   (1) Not later than three months after making a report under paragraph 10, the Authority must hold a public meeting ('the annual meeting') for the purposes of enabling that report to be considered.

(2) The Authority must organise the annual meeting so as to allow—

(a)   a general discussion of the contents of the report which is being considered; and
(b)   a reasonable opportunity for those attending the meeting to put questions to the Authority about the way in which it discharged, or failed to discharge, its functions during the period to which the report relates.

(3) But otherwise the annual meeting is to be organised and conducted in such a way as the Authority considers appropriate.

(4) The Authority must give reasonable notice of its annual meeting.

(5) That notice must—

(a)   give details of the time and place at which the meeting is to be held;
(b)   set out the proposed agenda for the meeting;
(c)   indicate the proposed duration of the meeting;

(d) give details of the Authority's arrangements for enabling persons to attend; and
(e) be published by the Authority in the way appearing to it to be most suitable for bringing the notice to the attention of the public.

(6) If the Authority proposes to alter any of the arrangements which have been included in the notice given under sub-paragraph (4) it must—

(a) give reasonable notice of the alteration; and
(b) publish that notice in the way appearing to the Authority to be best calculated to bring it to the attention of the public.

Report of annual meeting

12 Not later than one month after its annual meeting, the Authority must publish a report of the proceedings of the meeting.

PART II

STATUS

13 In relation to any of its functions—

(a) the Authority is not to be regarded as acting on behalf of the Crown; and
(b) its members, officers and staff are not to be regarded as Crown servants.

Exemption from requirement of 'limited' in Authority's name

14 The Authority is to continue to be exempt from the requirements of the 1985 Act relating to the use of 'limited' as part of its name.

15 If the Secretary of State is satisfied that any action taken by the Authority makes it inappropriate for the exemption given by paragraph 14 to continue he may, after consulting the Treasury, give a direction removing it.

PART III

PENALTIES AND FEES

Penalties

16 (1) In determining its policy with respect to the amounts of penalties to be imposed by it under this Act, the Authority must take no account of the expenses which it incurs, or expects to incur, in discharging its functions.

(2) The Authority must prepare and operate a scheme for ensuring that the amounts paid to the Authority by way of penalties imposed under this Act are applied for the benefit of authorised persons.

(3) The scheme may, in particular, make different provision with respect to different classes of authorised person.

(4) Up to date details of the scheme must be set out in a document ('the scheme details').

(5) The scheme details must be published by the Authority in the way appearing to it to be best calculated to bring them to the attention of the public.

(6) Before making the scheme, the Authority must publish a draft of the proposed scheme in the way appearing to the Authority to be best calculated to bring it to the attention of the public.

(7) The draft must be accompanied by notice that representations about the proposals may be made to the Authority within a specified time.

(8) Before making the scheme, the Authority must have regard to any representations made to it in accordance with sub-paragraph (7).

(9) If the Authority makes the proposed scheme, it must publish an account, in general terms, of—

    (a)   the representations made to it in accordance with sub-paragraph (7); and
    (b)   its response to them.

(10) If the scheme differs from the draft published under sub-paragraph (6) in a way which is, in the opinion of the Authority, significant the Authority must (in addition to complying with sub-paragraph (9)) publish details of the difference.

(11) The Authority must, without delay, give the Treasury a copy of any scheme details published by it.

(12) The Authority may charge a reasonable fee for providing a person with a copy of—

    (a)   a draft published under sub-paragraph (6);
    (b)   scheme details.

(13) Sub-paragraphs (6) to (10) and (12)(a) also apply to a proposal to alter or replace the complaints scheme.

Fees

17   (1) The Authority may make rules providing for the payment to it of such fees, in connection with the discharge of any of its functions under or as a result of this Act, as it considers will (taking account of its expected income from fees and charges provided for by any other provision of this Act) enable it—

    (a)   to meet expenses incurred in carrying out its functions or for any incidental purpose;
    (b)   to repay the principal of, and pay any interest on, any money which it has borrowed and which has been used for the purpose of meeting expenses incurred in relation to its assumption of functions under this Act or the Bank of England Act 1998; and
    (c)   to maintain adequate reserves.

(2) In fixing the amount of any fee which is to be payable to the Authority, no account is to be taken of any sums which the Authority receives, or expects to receive, by way of penalties imposed by it under this Act.

(3) Sub-paragraph (1)(b) applies whether expenses were incurred before or after the coming into force of this Act or the Bank of England Act 1998.

(4) Any fee which is owed to the Authority under any provision made by or under this Act may be recovered as a debt due to the Authority.

Services for which fees may not be charged

18   The power conferred by paragraph 17 may not be used to require—

    (a)   a fee to be paid in respect of the discharge of any of the Authority's functions under paragraphs 13, 14, 19 or 20 of Schedule 3; or

(b)   a fee to be paid by any person whose application for approval under section 59 has been granted.

PART IV

MISCELLANEOUS

Exemption from liability in damages

19   (1) Neither the Authority nor any person who is, or is acting as, a member, officer or member of staff of the Authority is to be liable in damages for anything done or omitted in the discharge, or purported discharge, of the Authority's functions.

(2) Neither the investigator appointed under paragraph 7 nor a person appointed to conduct an investigation on his behalf under paragraph 8(8) is to be liable in damages for anything done or omitted in the discharge, or purported discharge, of his functions in relation to the investigation of a complaint.

(3) Neither sub-paragraph (1) nor sub-paragraph (2) applies—

(a)   if the act or omission is shown to have been in bad faith; or
(b)   so as to prevent an award of damages made in respect of an act or omission on the ground that the act or omission was unlawful as a result of section 6(1) of the Human Rights Act 1998.

Disqualification for membership of House of Commons

20   In Part III of Schedule 1 to the House of Commons Disqualification Act 1975 (disqualifying offices), insert at the appropriate place—

'Member of the governing body of the Financial Services Authority'.

Disqualification for membership of Northern Ireland Assembly

21   In Part III of Schedule 1 to the Northern Ireland Assembly Disqualification Act 1975 (disqualifying offices), insert at the appropriate place—

'Member of the governing body of the Financial Services Authority'.

Section 22(2)   SCHEDULE 2

REGULATED ACTIVITIES

PART I

REGULATED ACTIVITIES

General

1   The matters with respect to which provision may be made under section 22(1) in respect of activities include, in particular, those described in general terms in this Part of this Schedule.

Dealing in investments

2   (1) Buying, selling, subscribing for or underwriting investments or offering or agreeing to do so, either as a principal or as an agent.

(2) In the case of an investment which is a contract of insurance, that includes carrying out the contract.

Arranging deals in investments

3   Making, or offering or agreeing to make—

(a)   arrangements with a view to another person buying, selling, subscribing for or underwriting a particular investment;

(b)   arrangements with a view to a person who participates in the arrangements buying, selling, subscribing for or underwriting investments.

Deposit taking

4   Accepting deposits.

Safekeeping and administration of assets

5   (1) Safeguarding and administering assets belonging to another which consist of or include investments or offering or agreeing to do so.

(2) Arranging for the safeguarding and administration of assets belonging to another, or offering or agreeing to do so.

Managing investments

6   Managing, or offering or agreeing to manage, assets belonging to another person where—

(a)   the assets consist of or include investments; or

(b)   the arrangements for their management are such that the assets may consist of or include investments at the discretion of the person managing or offering or agreeing to manage them.

Investment advice

7   Giving or offering or agreeing to give advice to persons on—

(a)   buying, selling, subscribing for or underwriting an investment; or

(b)   exercising any right conferred by an investment to acquire, dispose of, underwrite or convert an investment.

Establishing collective investment schemes

8   Establishing, operating or winding up a collective investment scheme, including acting as—

(a)   trustee of a unit trust scheme;

(b)   depositary of a collective investment scheme other than a unit trust scheme; or

(c)   sole director of a body incorporated by virtue of regulations under section 262.

Using computer-based systems for giving investment instructions

9   (1) Sending on behalf of another person instructions relating to an investment by means of a computer-based system which enables investments to be transferred without a written instrument.

(2) Offering or agreeing to send such instructions by such means on behalf of another person.

(3) Causing such instructions to be sent by such means on behalf of another person.

(4) Offering or agreeing to cause such instructions to be sent by such means on behalf of another person.

PART II

INVESTMENTS

General

10   The matters with respect to which provision may be made under section 22(1) in respect of investments include, in particular, those described in general terms in this Part of this Schedule.

Securities

11   (1) Shares or stock in the share capital of a company.

(2) 'Company' includes—

- (a)   any body corporate (wherever incorporated), and
- (b)   any unincorporated body constituted under the law of a country or territory outside the United Kingdom,

other than an open-ended investment company.

Instruments creating or acknowledging indebtedness

12   Any of the following—

- (a)   debentures;
- (b)   debenture stock;
- (c)   loan stock;
- (d)   bonds;
- (e)   certificates of deposit;
- (f)   any other instruments creating or acknowledging a present or future indebtedness.

Government and public securities

13   (1) Loan stock, bonds and other instruments—

- (a)   creating or acknowledging indebtedness; and
- (b)   issued by or on behalf of a government, local authority or public authority.

(2) 'Government, local authority or public authority' means—

- (a)   the government of the United Kingdom, of Northern Ireland, or of any country or territory outside the United Kingdom;

    (b)   a local authority in the United Kingdom or elsewhere;

    (c)   any international organisation the members of which include the United Kingdom or another member State.

Instruments giving entitlement to investments

14   (1) Warrants or other instruments entitling the holder to subscribe for any investment.

(2) It is immaterial whether the investment is in existence or identifiable.

Certificates representing securities

15   Certificates or other instruments which confer contractual or property rights—

    (a)   in respect of any investment held by someone other than the person on whom the rights are conferred by the certificate or other instrument; and

    (b)   the transfer of which may be effected without requiring the consent of that person.

Units in collective investment schemes

16   (1) Shares in or securities of an open-ended investment company.

(2) Any right to participate in a collective investment scheme.

Options

17   Options to acquire or dispose of property.

Futures

18   Rights under a contract for the sale of a commodity or property of any other description under which delivery is to be made at a future date.

Contracts for differences

19   Rights under—

    (a)   a contract for differences; or

    (b)   any other contract the purpose or pretended purpose of which is to secure a profit or avoid a loss by reference to fluctuations in—

        (i)   the value or price of property of any description; or

        (ii)   an index or other factor designated for that purpose in the contract.

Contracts of insurance

20   Rights under a contract of insurance, including rights under contracts falling within head C of Schedule 2 to the Friendly Societies Act 1992.

Participation in Lloyd's syndicates

21   (1) The underwriting capacity of a Lloyd's syndicate.

(2) A person's membership (or prospective membership) of a Lloyd's syndicate.

Deposits

22   Rights under any contract under which a sum of money (whether or not denominated in a currency) is paid on terms under which it will be repaid, with or without interest or a premium, and either on demand or at a time or in circumstances agreed by or on behalf of the person making the payment and the person receiving it.

Loans secured on land

23   (1) Rights under any contract under which—

(a)   one person provides another with credit; and

(b)   the obligation of the borrower to repay is secured on land.

(2) 'Credit' includes any cash loan or other financial accommodation.

(3) 'Cash' includes money in any form.

Rights in investments

24   Any right or interest in anything which is an investment as a result of any other provision made under section 22(1).

PART III

SUPPLEMENTAL PROVISIONS

The order-making power

25   (1) An order under section 22(1) may—

(a)   provide for exemptions;

(b)   confer powers on the Treasury or the Authority;

(c)   authorise the making of regulations or other instruments by the Treasury for purposes of, or connected with, any relevant provision;

(d)   authorise the making of rules or other instruments by the Authority for purposes of, or connected with, any relevant provision;

(e)   make provision in respect of any information or document which, in the opinion of the Treasury or the Authority, is relevant for purposes of, or connected with, any relevant provision;

(f)   make such consequential, transitional or supplemental provision as the Treasury consider appropriate for purposes of, or connected with, any relevant provision.

(2) Provision made as a result of sub-paragraph (1)(f) may amend any primary or subordinate legislation, including any provision of, or made under, this Act.

(3) 'Relevant provision' means any provision—

(a)   of section 22 or this Schedule; or

(b)   made under that section or this Schedule.

Parliamentary control

26   (1) This paragraph applies to the first order made under section 22(1).

(2) This paragraph also applies to any subsequent order made under section 22(1) which contains a statement by the Treasury that, in their opinion, the effect (or one of the effects)

of the proposed order would be that an activity which is not a regulated activity would become a regulated activity.

(3) An order to which this paragraph applies—

    (a)   must be laid before Parliament after being made; and

    (b)   ceases to have effect at the end of the relevant period unless before the end of that period the order is approved by a resolution of each House of Parliament (but without that affecting anything done under the order or the power to make a new order).

(4) 'Relevant period' means a period of twenty-eight days beginning with the day on which the order is made.

(5) In calculating the relevant period no account is to be taken of any time during which Parliament is dissolved or prorogued or during which both Houses are adjourned for more than four days.

Interpretation

27   (1) In this Schedule—

    'buying' includes acquiring for valuable consideration;
    'offering' includes inviting to treat;
    'property' includes currency of the United Kingdom or any other country or territory; and
    'selling' includes disposing for valuable consideration.

(2) In sub-paragraph (1) 'disposing' includes—

    (a)   in the case of an investment consisting of rights under a contract—
        (i)   surrendering, assigning or converting those rights; or
        (ii)   assuming the corresponding liabilities under the contract;

    (b)   in the case of an investment consisting of rights under other arrangements, assuming the corresponding liabilities under the contract or arrangements;

    (c)   in the case of any other investment, issuing or creating the investment or granting the rights or interests of which it consists.

(3) In this Schedule references to an instrument include references to any record (whether or not in the form of a document).

SCHEDULE 3   Sections 31(1)(b) and 37

EEA PASSPORT RIGHTS

PART I

DEFINED TERMS

The single market directives

1   'The single market directives' means—

    (a)   the first banking co-ordination directive;
    (b)   the second banking co-ordination directive;
    (c)   the insurance directives; and
    (d)   the investment services directive.

The banking co-ordination directives

2   (1) 'The first banking co-ordination directive' means the Council Directive of 12 December 1977 on the co-ordination of laws, regulations and administrative provisions relating to the taking up and pursuit of the business of credit institutions (No. 77/780/EEC).

(2) 'The second banking co-ordination directive' means the Council Directive of 15 December 1989 on the co-ordination of laws, etc., relating to the taking up and pursuit of the business of credit institutions and amending Directive 77/780/EEC (No. 89/646/EEC).

The insurance directives

3   (1) 'The insurance directives' means the first, second and third non-life insurance directives and the first, second and third life insurance directives.

(2) 'First non-life insurance directive' means the Council Directive of 24 July 1973 on the co-ordination of laws, regulations and administrative provisions relating to the taking up and pursuit of the business of direct insurance other than life assurance (No. 73/239/EEC).

(3) 'Second non-life insurance directive' means the Council Directive of 22 June 1988 on the co-ordination of laws, etc., and laying down provisions to facilitate the effective exercise of freedom to provide services and amending Directive 73/239/EEC (No. 88/357/EEC).

(4) 'Third non-life insurance directive' means the Council Directive of 18 June 1992 on the co-ordination of laws, etc., and amending Directives 73/239/EEC and 88/357/EEC (No. 92/49/EEC).

(5) 'First life insurance directive' means the Council Directive of 5 March 1979 on the co-ordination of laws, regulations and administrative provisions relating to the taking up and pursuit of the business of direct life assurance (No. 79/267/EEC).

(6) 'Second life insurance directive' means the Council Directive of 8 November 1990 on the co-ordination of laws, etc., and laying down provisions to facilitate the effective exercise of freedom to provide services and amending Directive 79/267/EEC (No. 90/619/EEC).

(7) 'Third life insurance directive' means the Council Directive of 10 November 1992 on the co-ordination of laws, etc., and amending Directives 79/267/EEC and 90/619/EEC (No. 92/96/EEC).

The investment services directive

4   'The investment services directive' means the Council Directive of 10 May 1993 on investment services in the securities field (No. 93/22/EEC).

EEA firm

5   'EEA firm' means any of the following if it does not have its head office in the United Kingdom—

    (a)   an investment firm (as defined in Article 1.2 of the investment services directive) which is authorised (within the meaning of Article 3) by its home state regulator;

    (b)   a credit institution (as defined in Article 1 of the first banking co-ordination directive) which is authorised (within the meaning of Article 1) by its home state regulator;

(c)   a financial institution (as defined in Article 1 of the second banking co-ordination directive) which is a subsidiary of the kind mentioned in Article 18.2 and which fulfils the conditions in Article 18; or

(d)   an undertaking pursuing the activity of direct insurance (within the meaning of Article 1 of the first life insurance directive or of the first non-life insurance directive) which has received authorisation under Article 6 from its home state regulator.

EEA authorisation

6   'EEA authorisation' means authorisation granted to an EEA firm by its home state regulator for the purpose of the relevant single market directive.

EEA right

7   'EEA right' means the entitlement of a person to establish a branch, or provide services, in an EEA State other than that in which he has his head office—

(a)   in accordance with the Treaty as applied in the EEA; and

(b)   subject to the conditions of the relevant single market directive.

EEA State

8   'EEA State' means a State which is a contracting party to the agreement on the European Economic Area signed at Oporto on 2 May 1992 as it has effect for the time being.

Home state regulator

9   'Home state regulator' means the competent authority (within the meaning of the relevant single market directive) of an EEA State (other than the United Kingdom) in relation to the EEA firm concerned.

UK firm

10   'UK firm' means a person whose head office is in the UK and who has an EEA right to carry on activity in an EEA State other than the United Kingdom.

Host state regulator

11   'Host state regulator' means the competent authority (within the meaning of the relevant single market directive) of an EEA State (other than the United Kingdom) in relation to a UK firm's exercise of EEA rights there.

PART II

EXERCISE OF PASSPORT RIGHTS BY EEA FIRMS

Firms qualifying for authorisation

12   (1) Once an EEA firm which is seeking to establish a branch in the United Kingdom in exercise of an EEA right satisfies the establishment conditions, it qualifies for authorisation.

(2) Once an EEA firm which is seeking to provide services in the United Kingdom in exercise of an EEA right satisfies the service conditions, it qualifies for authorisation.

Establishment

13   (1) The establishment conditions are that—

(a)   the Authority has received notice ('a consent notice') from the firm's home state regulator that it has given the firm consent to establish a branch in the United Kingdom;

(b)   the consent notice—

(i)   is given in accordance with the relevant single market directive;

(ii)   identifies the activities to which consent relates; and

(iii)   includes such other information as may be prescribed; and

(c)   the firm has been informed of the applicable provisions or two months have elapsed beginning with the date when the Authority received the consent notice.

(2) If the Authority has received a consent notice, it must—

(a)   prepare for the firm's supervision;

(b)   notify the firm of the applicable provisions (if any); and

(c)   if the firm falls within paragraph 5(d), notify its home state regulator of the applicable provisions (if any).

(3) A notice under sub-paragraph (2)(b) or (c) must be given before the end of the period of two months beginning with the day on which the Authority received the consent notice.

(4) For the purposes of this paragraph—

'applicable provisions' means the host state rules with which the firm is required to comply when carrying on a permitted activity through a branch in the United Kingdom;

'host state rules' means rules—

(a)   made in accordance with the relevant single market directive; and

(b)   which are the responsibility of the United Kingdom (both as to implementation and as to supervision of compliance) in accordance with that directive; and

'permitted activity' means an activity identified in the consent notice.

Services

14   (1) The service conditions are that—

(a)   the firm has given its home state regulator notice of its intention to provide services in the United Kingdom ('a notice of intention');

(b)   if the firm falls within paragraph 5(a) or (d), the Authority has received notice ('a regulator's notice') from the firm's home state regulator containing such information as may be prescribed; and

(c)   if the firm falls within paragraph 5(d), its home state regulator has informed it that the regulator's notice has been sent to the Authority.

(2) If the Authority has received a regulator's notice or, where none is required by sub-paragraph (1), has been informed of the firm's intention to provide services in the United Kingdom, it must—

(a)   prepare for the firm's supervision; and

(b)   notify the firm of the applicable provisions (if any).

(3) A notice under sub-paragraph (2) (b) must be given before the end of the period of two months beginning on the day on which the Authority received the regulator's notice, or was informed of the firm's intention.

(4) For the purposes of this paragraph—

'applicable provisions' means the host state rules with which the firm is required to comply when carrying on a permitted activity by providing services in the United Kingdom;

'host state rules' means rules—

    (a)   made in accordance with the relevant single market directive; and

    (b)   which are the responsibility of the United Kingdom (both as to implementation and as to supervision of compliance) in accordance with that directive; and

'permitted activity' means an activity identified in—

    (a)   the regulator's notice; or

    (b)   where none is required by sub-paragraph (1), the notice of intention.

Grant of permission

15   (1) On qualifying for authorisation as a result of paragraph 12, a firm has, in respect of each permitted activity which is a regulated activity, permission to carry it on through its United Kingdom branch (if it satisfies the establishment conditions) or by providing services in the United Kingdom (if it satisfies the service conditions).

(2) The permission is to be treated as being on terms equivalent to those appearing from the consent notice, regulator's notice or notice of intention.

(3) Sections 21, 39(1) and 147(1) of the Consumer Credit Act 1974 (business requiring a licence under that Act) do not apply in relation to the carrying on of a permitted activity which is a Consumer Credit Act business by a firm which qualifies for authorisation as a result of paragraph 12, unless the Director General of Fair Trading has exercised the power conferred on him by section 203 in relation to the firm.

(4) 'Consumer Credit Act business' has the same meaning as in section 203.

Effect of carrying on regulated activity when not qualified for authorisation

16   (1) This paragraph applies to an EEA firm which is not qualified for authorisation under paragraph 12.

(2) Section 26 does not apply to an agreement entered into by the firm.

(3) Section 27 does not apply to an agreement in relation to which the firm is a third party for the purposes of that section.

(4) Section 29 does not apply to an agreement in relation to which the firm is the deposit-taker.

Continuing regulation of EEA firms

17   Regulations may—

    (a)   modify any provision of this Act which is an applicable provision (within the meaning of paragraph 13 or 14) in its application to an EEA firm qualifying for authorisation;

   (b)   make provision as to any change (or proposed change) of a prescribed kind relating to an EEA firm or to an activity that it carries on in the United Kingdom and as to the procedure to be followed in relation to such cases;

   (c)   provide that the Authority may treat an EEA firm's notification that it is to cease to carry on regulated activity in the United Kingdom as a request for cancellation of its qualification for authorisation under this Schedule.

Giving up right to authorisation

18   Regulations may provide that in prescribed circumstances an EEA firm falling within paragraph 5(c) may, on following the prescribed procedure—

   (a)   have its qualification for authorisation under this Schedule cancelled; and

   (b)   seek to become an authorised person by applying for a Part IV permission.

PART III

EXERCISE OF PASSPORT RIGHTS BY UK FIRMS

Establishment

19   (1) A UK firm may not exercise an EEA right to establish a branch unless three conditions are satisfied.

(2) The first is that the firm has given the Authority, in the specified way, notice of its intention to establish a branch ('a notice of intention') which—

   (a)   identifies the activities which it seeks to carry on through the branch; and

   (b)   includes such other information as may be specified.

(3) The activities identified in a notice of intention may include activities which are not regulated activities.

(4) The second is that the Authority has given notice in specified terms ('a consent notice') to the host state regulator.

(5) The third is that—

   (a)   the host state regulator has notified the firm (or, where the EEA right in question derives from any of the insurance directives, the Authority) of the applicable provisions; or

   (b)   two months have elapsed beginning with the date on which the Authority gave the consent notice.

(6) If the firm's EEA right derives from the investment services directive or the second banking coordination directive and the first condition is satisfied, the Authority must give a consent notice to the host state regulator unless it has reason to doubt the adequacy of the firm's resources or its administrative structure.

(7) If the firm's EEA right derives from any of the insurance directives and the first condition is satisfied, the Authority must give a consent notice unless it has reason—

   (a)   to doubt the adequacy of the firm's resources or its administrative structure, or

   (b)   to question the reputation, qualifications or experience of the directors or managers of the firm or the person proposed as the branch's authorised agent for the purposes of those directives,

in relation to the business to be conducted through the proposed branch.

(8) If the Authority proposes to refuse to give a consent notice it must give the firm concerned a warning notice.

(9) If the firm's EEA right derives from any of the insurance directives and the host state regulator has notified it of the applicable provisions, the Authority must inform the firm of those provisions.

(10) Rules may specify the procedure to be followed by the Authority in exercising its functions under this paragraph.

(11) If the Authority gives a consent notice it must give written notice that it has done so to the firm concerned.

(12) If the Authority decides to refuse to give a consent notice—

    (a)   it must, within three months beginning with the date when it received the notice of intention, give the person who gave that notice a decision notice to that effect; and

    (b)   that person may refer the matter to the Tribunal.

(13) In this paragraph, 'applicable provisions' means the host state rules with which the firm will be required to comply when conducting business through the proposed branch in the EEA State concerned.

(14) In sub-paragraph (13), 'host state rules' means rules—

    (a)   made in accordance with the relevant single market directive; and

    (b)   which are the responsibility of the EEA State concerned (both as to implementation and as to supervision of compliance) in accordance with that directive.

(15) 'Specified' means specified in rules.

Services

20   (1) A UK firm may not exercise an EEA right to provide services unless the firm has given the Authority, in the specified way, notice of its intention to provide services ('a notice of intention') which—

    (a)   identifies the activities which it seeks to carry out by way of provision of services; and

    (b)   includes such other information as may be specified.

(2) The activities identified in a notice of intention may include activities which are not regulated activities.

(3) If the firm's EEA right derives from the investment services directive or a banking co-ordination directive, the Authority must, within one month of receiving a notice of intention, send a copy of it to the host state regulator.

(4) When the Authority sends the copy under sub-paragraph (3), it must give written notice to the firm concerned.

(5) If the firm concerned's EEA right derives from the investment services directive, it must not provide the services to which its notice of intention relates until it has received written notice from the Authority under sub-paragraph (4).

(6) 'Specified' means specified in rules.

Offence relating to exercise of passport rights

21   (1) If a UK firm which is not an authorised person contravenes the prohibition imposed by—

    (a)   sub-paragraph (1) of paragraph 19, or

(b)   sub-paragraph (1) or (5) of paragraph 20,

it is guilty of an offence.

(2) A firm guilty of an offence under sub-paragraph (1) is liable—

(a)   on summary conviction, to a fine not exceeding the statutory maximum; or
(b)   on conviction on indictment, to a fine.

(3) In proceedings for an offence under sub-paragraph (1), it is a defence for the firm to show that it took all reasonable precautions and exercised all due diligence to avoid committing the offence.

Continuing regulation of UK firms

22   (1) Regulations may make such provision as the Treasury consider appropriate in relation to a UK firm's exercise of EEA rights, and may in particular provide for the application (with or without modification) of any provision of, or made under, this Act in relation to an activity of a UK firm.

(2) Regulations may—

(a)   make provision as to any change (or proposed change) of a prescribed kind relating to a UK firm or to an activity that it carries on and as to the procedure to be followed in relation to such cases;
(b)   make provision with respect to the consequences of the firm's failure to comply with a provision of the regulations.

(3) Where a provision of the kind mentioned in sub-paragraph (2) requires the Authority's consent to a change (or proposed change)—

(a)   consent may be refused only on prescribed grounds; and
(b)   if the Authority decides to refuse consent, the firm concerned may refer the matter to the Tribunal.

23   (1) Sub-paragraph (2) applies if a UK firm—

(a)   has a Part IV permission; and
(b)   is exercising an EEA right to carry on any Consumer Credit Act business in an EEA State other than the United Kingdom.

(2) The Authority may exercise its power under section 45 in respect of the firm if the Director of Fair Trading has informed the Authority that—

(a)   the firm,
(b)   any of the firm's employees, agents or associates (whether past or present), or
(c)   if the firm is a body corporate, a controller of the firm or an associate of such a controller,

has done any of the things specified in paragraphs (a) to (d) of section 25(2) of the Consumer Credit Act 1974.

(3) 'Associate', 'Consumer Credit Act business' and 'controller' have the same meaning as in section 203.

24   (1) Sub-paragraph (2) applies if a UK firm—

(a)   is not required to have a Part IV permission in relation to the business which it is carrying on; and
(b)   is exercising the right conferred by Article 18.2 of the second banking co-ordination directive to carry on that business in an EEA State other than the United Kingdom.

(2) If requested to do so by the host stage regulator in the EEA State in which the UK firm's business is being carried on, the Authority may impose any requirement in relation to the firm which it could impose if—

(a) the firm had a Part IV permission in relation to the business which it is carrying on; and

(b) the Authority was entitled to exercise its power under that Part to vary that permission.

Section 31(1)(c)   **SCHEDULE 4**

                                   TREATY RIGHTS

                                    Definitions

1   In this Schedule—

'consumers' means persons who are consumers for the purposes of section 138;
'Treaty firm' means a person—

(a) whose head office is situated in an EEA State (its 'home state') other than the United Kingdom; and

(b) which is recognised under the law of that State as its national; and

'home state regulator', in relation to a Treaty firm, means the competent authority of the firm's home state for the purpose of its home state authorisation (as to which see paragraph 3(1)(a)).

                          Firms qualifying for authorisation

2   Once a Treaty firm which is seeking to carry on a regulated activity satisfies the conditions set out in paragraph 3(1), it qualifies for authorisation.

                              Exercise of Treaty rights

3   (1) The conditions are that—

(a) the firm has received authorisation ('home state authorisation') under the law of its home state to carry on the regulated activity in question ('the permitted activity');

(b) the relevant provisions of the law of the firm's home state—
   (i) afford equivalent protection; or
   (ii) satisfy the conditions laid down by a Community instrument for the co-ordination or approximation of laws, regulations or administrative provisions of member States relating to the carrying on of that activity; and

(c) the firm has no EEA right to carry on that activity in the manner in which it is seeking to carry it on.

(2) A firm is not to be regarded as having home state authorisation unless its home state regulator has so informed the Authority in writing.

(3) Provisions afford equivalent protection if, in relation to the firm's carrying on of the permitted activity, they afford consumers protection which is at least equivalent to that afforded by or under this Act in relation to that activity.

(4) A certificate issued by the Treasury that the provisions of the law of a particular EEA State afford equivalent protection in relation to the activities specified in the certificate is conclusive evidence of that fact.

Permission

4 (1) On qualifying for authorisation under this Schedule, a Treaty firm has permission to carry on each permitted activity through its United Kingdom branch or by providing services in the United Kingdom.

(2) The permission is to be treated as being on terms equivalent to those to which the firm's home state authorisation is subject.

(3) If, on qualifying for authorisation under this Schedule, a firm has a Part IV permission which includes permission to carry on a premitted activity, the Authority must give a direction cancelling the permission so far as it relates to that activity.

(4) The Authority need not give a direction under sub-paragraph (3) if it considers that there are good reasons for not doing so.

Notice to Authority

5 (1) Sub-paragraph (2) applies to a Treaty firm which—

  (a) qualifies for authorisation under this Schedule, but
  (b) is not carrying on in the United Kingdom the regulated activity, or any of the regulated activities, which it has permission to carry on there.

(2) At least seven days before it begins to carry on such a regulated activity, the firm must give the Authority written notice of its intention to do so.

(3) If a Treaty firm to which sub-paragraph (2) applies has given notice under that sub-paragraph, it need not give such a notice if it again becomes a firm to which that sub-paragraph applies.

(4) Subsections (1), (3) and (6) of section 51 apply to a notice under sub-paragraph (2) as they apply to an application for a Part IV permission.

Offences

6 (1) A person who contravenes paragraph 5(2) is guilty of an offence.

(2) In proceedings against a person for an offence under sub-paragraph (1) it is a defence for him to show that he took all reasonable precautions and exercised all due diligence to avoid committing the offence.

(3) A person is guilty of an offence if in, or in connection with, a notice given by him under paragraph 5(2) he—

  (a) provides information which he knows to be false or misleading in a material particular; or
  (b) recklessly provides information which is false or misleading in a material particular.

(4) A person guilty of an offence under this paragraph is liable—

  (a) on summary conviction, to a fine not exceeding the statutory maximum;

(b)   on conviction on indictment, to a fine.

Section 36   **SCHEDULE 5**

PERSONS CONCERNED IN COLLECTIVE INVESTMENT SCHEMES

Authorisation

1   (1) A person who for the time being is an operator, trustee or depositary of a recognised collective investment scheme is an authorised person.

(2) 'Recognised' means recognised by virtue of section 264.

(3) An authorised open-ended investment company is an authorised person.

Permission

2   (1) A person authorised as a result of paragraph 1(1) has permission to carry on, so far as it is a regulated activity—

(a)   any activity, appropriate to the capacity in which he acts in relation to the scheme, of the kind described in paragraph 8 of Schedule 2;

(b)   any activity in connection with, or for the purposes of, the scheme.

(2) A person authorised as a result of paragraph 1(3) has permission to carry on, so far as it is a regulated activity—

(a)   the operation of the scheme;

(b)   any activity in connection with, or for the purposes of, the operation of the scheme.

Section 41   **SCHEDULE 6**

THRESHOLD CONDITIONS

PART I

PART IV PERMISSION

Legal status

1   (1) If the regulated activity concerned is the effecting or carrying out of contracts of insurance the authorised person must be a body corporate, a registered friendly society or a member of Lloyd's.

(2) If the person concerned appears to the Authority to be seeking to carry on, or to be carrying on, a regulated activity constituting accepting deposits, it must be—

(a)   a body corporate; or

(b)   a partnership.

Location of offices

2   (1) If the person concerned is a body corporate constituted under the law of any part of the United Kingdom—

(a)   its head office, and

(b)   if it has a registered office, that office,

must be in the United Kingdom.

(2) If the person concerned has its head office in the United Kingdom but is not a body corporate, it must carry on business in the United Kingdom.

Close links

3   (1) If the person concerned ('A') has close links with another person ('CL') the Authority must be satisifed—

(a)   that those links are not likely to prevent the Authority's effective supervision of A; and

(b)   if it appears to the Authority that CL is subject to the laws, regulations or administrative provisions of a territory which is not an EEA State ('the foreign provisions'), that neither the foreign provisions, nor any deficiency in their enforcement, would prevent the Authority's effective supervision of A.

(2) A has close links with CL if—

(a)   CL is a parent undertaking of A;

(b)   CL is a subsidiary undertaking of A;

(c)   CL is a parent undertaking of a subsidiary undertaking of A;

(d)   CL is a subsidiary undertaking of a parent undertaking of A;

(e)   CL owns or controls 20% or more of the voting rights or capital of A; or

(f)   A owns or controls 20% or more of the voting rights or capital of CL.

(3) 'Subsidiary undertaking' includes all the instances mentioned in Article 1(1) and (2) of the Seventh Company Law Directive in which an entity may be a subsidiary of an undertaking.

Adequate resources

4   (1) The resources of the person concerned must, in the opinion of the Authority, be adequate in relation to the regulated activities that he seeks to carry on, or carries on.

(2) In reaching that opinion, the Authority may—

(a)   take into account the person's membership of a group and any effect which that membership may have; and

(b)   have regard to—

(i)   the provision he makes and, if he is a member of a group, which other members of the group make in respect of liabilities (including contingent and future liabilities); and

(ii)   the means by which he manages and, if he is a member of a group, which other members of the group manage the incidence of risk in connection with his business.

Suitability

5   The person concerned must satisfy the Authority that he is a fit and proper person having regard to all the circumstances, including—

(a)   his connection with any person;

(b)   the nature of any regulated activity that he carries on or seeks to carry on; and (c)　the need to ensure that his affairs are conducted soundly and prudently.

PART II

AUTHORISATION

Authorisation under Schedule 3

6　In relation to an EEA firm qualifying for authorisation under Schedule 3, the conditions set out in paragraphs 1 and 3 to 5 apply, so far as relevant, to—

(a)　an application for permission under Part IV;
(b)　exercise of the Authority's own-initiative power under section 45 in relation to a Part IV permission.

Authorisation under Schedule 4

7　In relation to a person who qualifies for authorisation under Schedule 4, the conditions set out in paragraphs 1 and 3 to 5 apply, so far as relevant, to—

(a)　an application for an additional permission;
(b)　the exercise of the Authority's own-initiative power under section 45 in relation to additional permission.

PART III

ADDITIONAL CONDITIONS

8　(1) If this paragraph applies to the person concerned, he must, for the purposes of such provisions of this Act as may be specified, satisfy specified additional conditions.

(2) This paragraph applies to a person who—

(a)　has his head office outside the EEA; and
(b)　appears to the Authority to be seeking to carry on a regulated activity relating to insurance business.

(3) 'Specified' means specified in, or in accordance with, an order made by the Treasury.

9　The Treasury may by order—

(a)　vary or remove any of the conditions set out in Parts I and II;
(b)　add to those conditions.

Section 72(2)　　　　　　　**SCHEDULE 7**

THE AUTHORITY AS COMPETENT AUTHORITY FOR PART VI

General

1　This Act applies in relation to the Authority when it is exercising functions under Part VI as the competent authority subject to the following modifications.

The Authority's general functions

2 In section 2—

(a) subsection (4)(a) does not apply to listing rules;
(b) subsection (4)(c) does not apply to general guidance given in relation to Part VI; and
(c) subsection (4)(d) does not apply to functions under Part VI.

Duty to consult

3 Section 8 does not apply.

Rules

4 (1) Sections 149, 153, 154 and 156 do not apply.

(2) Section 155 has effect as if—

(a) the reference in subsection (2)(c) to the general duties of the Authority under section 2 were a reference to its duty under section 73; and
(b) section 99 were included in the provisions referred to in subsection (9).

Statements of policy

5 (1) Paragraph 5 of Schedule 1 has effect as if the requirement to act through the Authority's governing body applied also to the exercise of its functions of publishing statements under section 93.

(2) Paragraph 1 of Schedule 1 has effect as if section 93 were included in the provisions referred to in sub-paragraph (2)(d).

Penalties

6 Paragraph 16 of Schedule 1 does not apply in relation to penalties under Part VI (for which separate provision is made by section 100).

Fees

7 Paragraph 17 of Schedule 1 does not apply in relation to fees payable under Part VI (for which separate provision is made by section 99).

Exemption from liability in damages

8 Schedule 1 has effect as if—

(a) sub-paragraph (1) of paragraph 19 were omitted (similar provision being made in relation to the competent authority by section 102); and
(b) for the words from the beginning to '(a)' in sub-paragraph (3) of that paragraph, there were substituted 'Sub-paragraph (2) does not apply'.

Section 72(3)   SCHEDULE 8

TRANSFER OF FUNCTIONS UNDER PART VI

The power to transfer

1   (1) The Treasury may by order provide for any function conferred on the competent authority which is exercisable for the time being by a particular person to be transferred so as to be exercisable by another person.

(2) An order may be made under this paragraph only if—

    (a)   the person from whom the relevant functions are to be transferred has agreed in writing that the order should be made;

    (b)   the Treasury are satisfied that the manner in which, or efficiency with which, the functions are discharged would be significantly improved if they were transferred to the transferee; or

    (c)   the Treasury are satisfied that it is otherwise in the public interest that the order should be made.

Supplemental

2   (1) An order under this Schedule does not affect anything previously done by any person ('the previous authority') in the exercise of functions which are transferred by the order to another person ('the new authority').

(2) Such an order may, in particular, include provision—

    (a)   modifying or excluding any provision of Part VI, IX or XXVI in its application to any such functions;

    (b)   for reviews similar to that made, in relation to the Authority, by section 12;

    (c)   imposing on the new authority requirements similar to those imposed, in relation to the Authority, by sections 152, 155 and 354;

    (d)   as to the giving of guidance by the new authority;

    (e)   for the delegation by the new authority of the exercise of functions under Part VI and as to the consequences of delegation;

    (f)   for the transfer of any property, rights or liabilities relating to any such functions from the previous authority to the new authority;

    (g)   for the carrying on and completion by the new authority of anything in the process of being done by the previous authority when the order takes effect;

    (h)   for the substitution of the new authority for the previous authority in any instrument, contract or legal proceedings;

    (i)   for the transfer of persons employed by the previous authority to the new authority and as to the terms on which they are to transfer;

    (j)   making such amendments to any primary or subordinate legislation (including any provision of, or made under, this Act) as the Treasury consider appropriate in consequence of the transfer of functions effected by the order.

(3) Nothing in this paragraph is to be taken as restricting the powers conferred by section 428.

3   If the Treasury have made an order under paragraph 1 ('the transfer order') they may, by a separate order made under this paragraph, make any provision of a kind that could have been included in the transfer order.

Section 87(5)   SCHEDULE 9

NON-LISTING PROSPECTUSES

General application of Part VI

1   The provisions of Part VI apply in relation to a non-listing prospectus as they apply in relation to listing particulars but with the modifications made by this Schedule.

References to listing particulars

2   (1) Any reference to listing particulars is to be read as a reference to a prospectus.

(2) Any reference to supplementary listing particulars is to be read as a reference to a supplementary prospectus.

General duty of disclosure

3   (1) In section 80(1), for 'section 79' substitute 'section 87'.

(2) In section 80(2), omit 'as a condition of the admission of the securities to the official list'.

Supplementary prospectus

4   In section 81(1), for 'section 79 and before the commencement of dealings in the securities concerned following their admission to the official list' substitute 'section 87 and before the end of the period during which the offer to which the prospectus relates remains open'.

Exemption from liability for compensation

5   (1) In paragraphs 1(3) and 2(3) of Schedule 10, for paragraph (d) substitute—

'(d) the securities were acquired after such a lapse of time that he ought in the circumstances to be reasonably excused and, if the securities are dealt in on an approved exchange, he continued in that belief until after the commencement of dealings in the securities on that exchange.'

(2) After paragraph 8 of that Schedule, insert—

'Meaning of "approved exchange"

9   "Approved exchange" has such meaning as may be prescribed.'

Advertisements

6   In section 98(1), for 'If listing particulars are, or are to be, published in connection with an application for listing,' substitute 'If a prospectus is, or is to be, published in connection with an application for approval, then, until the end of the period during which the offer to which the prospectus relates remains open,'.

Fees

7   Listing rules made under section 99 may require the payment of fees to the competent authority in respect of a prospectus submitted for approval under section 87.

Section 90(2) and (5)   **SCHEDULE 10**

COMPENSATION: EXEMPTIONS

Statements believed to be true

1   (1) In this paragraph 'statement' means—

- (a)   any untrue or misleading statement in listing particulars; or
- (b)   the omission from listing particulars of any matter required to be included by section 80 or 81.

(2) A person does not incur any liability under section 90(1) for loss caused by a statement if he satisfies the court that, at the time when the listing particulars were submitted to the competent authority, he reasonably believed (having made such enquiries, if any, as were reasonable) that—

- (a)   the statement was true and not misleading, or
- (b)   the matter whose omission caused the loss was properly omitted,

and that one or more of the conditions set out in sub-paragraph (3) are satisfied.

(3) The conditions are that—

- (a)   he continued in his belief until the time when the securities in question were acquired;
- (b)   they were acquired before it was reasonably practicable to bring a correction to the attention of persons likely to acquire them;
- (c)   before the securities were acquired, he had taken all such steps as it was reasonable for him to have taken to secure that a correction was brought to the attention of those persons;
- (d)   he continued in his belief until after the commencement of dealings in the securities following their admission to the official list and they were acquired after such a lapse of time that he ought in the circumstances to be reasonably excused.

Statements by experts

2   (1) In this paragraph 'statement' means a statement included in listing particulars which—

- (a)   purports to be made by, or on the authority of, another person as an expert; and
- (b)   is stated to be included in the listing particulars with that other person's consent.

(2) A person does not incur any liability under section 90(1) for loss in respect of any secuirities caused by a statement if he satisfies the court that, at the time when the listing particulars were submitted to the competent authority, he reasonably believed that the other person—

(a)   was competent to make or authorise the statement, and

(b)   had consented to its inclusion in the form and context in which it was included,

and that one or more of the conditions set out in sub-paragraph (3) are satisfied.

(3) The conditions are that—

(a)   he continued in his belief until the time when the securities were acquired;

(b)   they were acquired before it was reasonably practicable to bring the fact that the expert was not competent, or had not consented, to the attention of persons likely to acquire the securities in question;

(c)   before the securities were acquired he had taken all such steps as it was reasonable for him to have taken to secure that that fact was brought to the attention of those persons;

(d)   he continued in his belief until after the commencement of dealings in the securities following their admission to the official list and they were acquired after such a lapse of time that he ought in the circumstances to be reasonably excused.

Corrections of statements

3   (1) In this paragraph 'statement' has the same meaning as in paragraph 1.

(2) A person does not incur liability under section 90(1) for loss caused by a statement if he satisfies the court—

(a)   that before the securities in question were acquired, a correction had been published in a manner calculated to bring it to the attention of persons likely to acquire the securities; or

(b)   that he took all such steps as it was reasonable for him to take to secure such publication and reasonably believed that it had taken place before the securities were acquired.

(3) Nothing in this paragraph is to be taken as affecting paragraph 1.

Corrections of statements by experts

4   (1) In this paragraph 'statement' has the same meaning as in paragraph 2.

(2) A person does not incur liability under section 90(1) for loss caused by a statement if he satisfies the court—

(a)   that before the securities in question were acquired, the fact that the expert was not competent or had not consented had been published in a manner calculated to bring it to the attention of persons likely to acquire the securities; or

(b)   that he took all such steps as it was reasonable for him to take to secure such publication and reasonably believed that it had taken place before the securities were acquired.

(3) Nothing in this paragraph is to be taken as affecting paragraph 2.

Official statements

5   A person does not incur any liability under section 90(1) for loss resulting from—

(a)   a statement made by an official person which is included in the listing particulars, or

(b)   a statement contained in a public official document which is included in the listing particulars,

if he satisfies the court that the statement is accurately and fairly reproduced.

False or misleading information known about

6   A person does not incur any liability under section 90(1) or (4) if he satisfies the court that the person suffering the loss acquired the securities in question with knowledge—

(a)   that the statement was false or misleading,

(b)   of the omitted matter, or

(c)   of the change or new matter,

as the case may be.

Belief that supplementary listing particulars not called for

7   A person does not incur any liability under section 90(4) if he satisfies the court that he reasonably believed that the change or new matter in question was not such as to call for supplementary listing particulars.

Meaning of 'expert'

8   'Expert' includes any engineer, valuer, accountant or other person whose profession, qualifications or experience give authority to a statement made by him.

Section 103(6)   SCHEDULE 11

OFFERS OF SECURITIES

The general rule

1   (1) A person offers securities to the public in the United Kingdom if—

(a)   to the extent that the offer is made to persons in the United Kingdom, it is made to the public; and

(b)   the offer is not an exempt offer.

(2) For this purpose, an offer which is made to any section of the public, whether selected—

(a)   as members or debenture holders of a body corporate,

(b)   as clients of the person making the offer, or

(c)   in any other manner,

is to be regarded as made to the public.

Exempt offers

2   (1) For the purposes of this Schedule, an offer of securities is an 'exempt offer' if, to the extent that the offer is made to persons in the United Kingdom—

(a)   the condition specified in any of paragraphs 3 to 24 is satisfied in relation to the offer; or

(b)   the condition specified in one relevant paragraph is satisfied in relation to part, but not the whole, of the offer and, in relation to each other part of the offer, the condition specified in a different relevant paragraph is satisfied.

(2) The relevant paragraphs are 3 to 8, 12 to 18 and 21.

Offers for business purposes

3 The securities are offered to persons—

(a) whose ordinary activities involve them in acquiring, holding, managing or disposing of investments (as principal or agent) for the purposes of their businesses, or
(b) who it is reasonable to expect will acquire, hold, manage or dispose of investments (as principal or agent) for the purposes of their businesses,

or are otherwise offered to persons in the context of their trades, professions or occupations.

Offers to limited numbers

4 (1) The securities are offered to no more than fifty persons.

(2) In determining whether this condition is satisfied, the offer is to be taken together with any other offer of the same securities which was—

(a) made by the same person;
(b) open at any time within the period of 12 months ending with the date on which the offer is first made; and
(c) not an offer to the public in the United Kingdom by virtue of this condition being satisfied.

(3) For the purposes of this paragraph—

(a) the making of an offer of securities to trustees or members of a partnership in their capacity as such, or
(b) the making of such an offer to any other two or more persons jointly,

is to be treated as the making of an offer to a single person.

Clubs and associations

5 The securities are offered to the members of a club or association (whether or not incorporated) and the members can reasonably be regarded as having a common interest with each other and with the club or association in the affairs of the club or association and in what is to be done with the proceeds of the offer.

Restricted circles

6 (1) The securities are offered to a restricted circle of persons whom the offeror reasonably believes to be sufficiently knowledgeable to understand the risks involved in accepting the offer.

(2) In determining whether a person is sufficiently knowledgeable to understand the risks involved in accepting an offer of securities, any information supplied by the person making the offer is to be disregarded, apart from information about—

(a) the issuer of the securities; or
(b) if the securities confer the right to acquire other securities, the issuer of those other securities.

Underwriting agreements

7   The securities are offered in connection with a genuine invitation to enter into an underwriting agreement with respect to them.

Offers to public authorities

8   (1) The securities are offered to a public authority.

(2) 'Public authority' means—

(a)   the government of the United Kingdom;
(b)   the government of any country or territory outside the United Kingdom;
(c)   a local authority in the United Kingdom or elsewhere;
(d)   any international organisation the members of which include the United Kingdom or another EEA State; and
(e)   such other bodies, if any, as may be specified.

Maximum consideration

9   (1) The total consideration payable for the securities cannot exceed 40,000 euros (or an equivalent amount).

(2) In determining whether this condition is satisfied, the offer is to be taken together with any other offer of the same securities which was—

(a)   made by the same person;
(b)   open at any time within the period of 12 months ending with the date on which the offer is first made; and
(c)   not an offer to the public in the United Kingdom by virtue of this condition being satisfied.

(3) An amount (in relation to an amount denominated in euros) is an 'equivalent amount' if it is an amount of equal value, calculated at the latest practicable date before (but in any event not more than 3 days before) the date on which the offer is first made, denominated wholly or partly in another currency or unit of account.

Minimum consideration

10   (1) The minimum consideration which may be paid by any person for securities acquired by him pursuant to the offer is at least 40,000 euros (or an equivalent amount).

(2) Paragraph 9(3) also applies for the purposes of this paragraph.

Securities denominated in euros

11   (1) The securities are denominated in amounts of at least 40,000 euros (or an equivalent amount).

(2) Paragraph 9(3) also applies for the purposes of this paragraph.

Takeovers

12   (1) The securities are offered in connection with a takeover offer.

(2) 'Takeover offer' means—

    (a)   an offer to acquire shares in a body incorporated in the United Kingdom which is a takeover offer within the meaning of the takeover provisions (or would be such an offer if those provisions applied in relation to any body corporate);

    (b)   an offer to acquire all or substantially all of the shares, or of the shares of a particular class, in a body incorporated outside the United Kingdom; or

    (c)   an offer made to all the holders of shares, or of shares of a particular class, in a body corporate to acquire a specified proportion of those shares.

(3) 'The takeover provisions' means—

    (a)   Part XIIIA of the Companies Act 1985; or

    (b)   in relation to Northern Ireland, Part XIVA of the Companies (Northern Ireland) Order 1986.

(4) For the purposes of sub-paragraph (2)(b), any shares which the offeror or any associate of his holds or has contracted to acquire are to be disregarded.

(5) For the purposes of sub-paragraph (2)(c), the following are not to be regarded as holders of the shares in question—

    (a)   the offeror;

    (b)   any associate of the offeror; and

    (c)   any person whose shares the offeror or any associate of the offeror has contracted to acquire.

(6) 'Associate' has the same meaning as in—

    (a)   section 430E of the Companies Act 1985; or

    (b)   in relation to Northern Ireland, Article 423E of the Companies (Northern Ireland) Order 1986.

Mergers

13   The securities are offered in connection with a merger (within the meaning of Council Directive No. 78/855/EEC).

Free shares

14   (1) The securities are shares and are offered free of charge to any or all of the holders of shares in the issuer.

(2) 'Holders of shares' means the persons who at the close of business on a date—

    (a)   specified in the offer, and

    (b)   falling within the period of 60 days ending with the date on which the offer is first made,

were holders of such shares.

Exchange of shares

15   The securities—

    (a)   are shares, or investments of a specified kind relating to shares, in a body corporate, and

    (b)   are offered in exchange for shares in the same body corporate,

and the offer cannot result in any increase in the issued share capital of the body corporate.

Qualifying persons

16   (1) The securities are issued by a body corporate and are offered—

    (a)   by the issuer, by a body corporate connected with the issuer or by a relevant trustee;

    (b)   only to qualifying persons; and

    (c)   on terms that a contract to acquire any such securities may be entered into only by the qualifying person to whom they were offered or, if the terms of the offer so permit, any qualifying person.

(2) A person is a 'qualifying person', in relation to an issuer, if he is a genuine employee or former employee of the issuer or of another body corporate in the same group or the wife, husband, widow, widower or child or stepchild under the age of eighteen of such an employee or former employee.

(3) In relation to an issuer of securities, 'connected with' has such meaning as may be prescribed.

(4) 'Group' and 'relevant trustee' have such meaning as may be prescribed.

Convertible securities

17   (1) The securities result from the conversion of convertible securities and listing particulars (or a prospectus) relating to the convertible securities were (or was) published in the United Kingdom under or by virtue of Part VI or such other provisions applying in the United Kingdom as may be specified.

(2) 'Convertible securities' means securities of a specified kind which can be converted into, or exchanged for, or which confer rights to acquire, other securities.

(3) 'Conversion' means conversion into or exchange for, or the exercise of rights conferred by the securities to acquire, other securities.

Charities

18   The securities are issued by—

    (a)   a charity within the meaning of—
        (i)   section 96(1) of the Charities Act 1993, or
        (ii)   section 35 of the Charities Act (Northern Ireland) 1964,

    (b)   a recognised body within the meaning of section 1(7) of the Law Reform (Miscellaneous Provisions) (Scotland) Act 1990,

    (c)   a housing association within the meaning of—
        (i)   section 5(1) of the Housing Act 1985,
        (ii)   section 1 of the Housing Associations Act 1985, or
        (iii) Article 3 of the Housing (Northern Ireland) Order 1992,

    (d)   an industrial or provident society registered in accordance with—
        (i)   section 1(2)(b) of the Industrial and Provident Societies Act 1965, or
        (ii)   section 1(2)(b) of the Industrial and Provident Societies Act 1969, or

    (e)   a non-profit making association or body, recognised by the country or territory in which it is established, with objectives similar to those of a body falling within any of paragraphs (a) to (c),

and the proceeds of the offer will be used for the purposes of the issuer's objectives.

Building societies etc

19   The securities offered are shares which are issued by, or ownership of which entitles the holder to membership of or to obtain the benefit of services provided by—

  (a) a building society incorporated under the law of, or of any part of, the United Kingdom;

  (b) any body incorporated under the law of, or of any part of, the United Kingdom relating to industrial and provident societies or credit unions; or

  (c) a body of a similar nature established in another EEA State.

Euro-securities

20   (1) The securities offered are Euro-securities and no advertisement relating to the offer is issued in the United Kingdom, or is caused to be so issued—

  (a) by the issuer of the Euro-securities;

  (b) by any credit institution or other financial institution through which the Euro-securities may be acquired pursuant to the offer; or

  (c) by any body corporate which is a member of the same group as the issuer or any of those institutions.

(2) But sub-paragraph (1) does not apply to an advertisement of a prescribed kind.

(3) 'Euro-securities' means investments which—

  (a) are to be underwritten and distributed by a syndicate at least two of the members of which have their registered offices in different countries or territories;

  (b) are to be offered on a significant scale in one or more countries or territories, other than the country or territory in which the issuer has its registered office; and

  (c) may be acquired pursuant to the offer only through a credit institution or other financial institution.

(4) 'Credit institution' means a credit institution as defined in Article 1 of Council Directive No 77/780/EEC.

(5) 'Financial institution' means a financial institution as defined in Article 1 of Council Directive No 89/646/EEC.

(6) 'Underwritten' means underwritten by whatever means, including by acquisition or subscription, with a view to resale.

Same class securities

21   The securities are of the same class, and were issued at the same time, as securities in respect of which a prospectus has been published under or by virtue of—

  (a) Part VI;

  (b) Part III of the Companies Act 1985; or

  (c) such other provisions applying in the United Kingdom as may be specified.

Short date securities

22   The securities are investments of a specified kind with a maturity of less than one year from their date of issue.

Government and public securities

23   (1) The securities are investments of a specified kind creating or acknowledging indebtedness issued by or on behalf of a public authority.

(2) 'Public authority' means—

  (a)   the government of the United Kingdom;
  (b)   the government of any country or territory outside the United Kingdom;
  (c)   a local authority in the United Kingdom or elsewhere;
  (d)   any international organisation the members of which include the United Kingdom or another EEA State; and
  (e)   such other bodies, if any, as may be specified.

Non-transferable securities

24   The securities are not transferable.

General definitions

25   For the purposes of this Schedule—

'shares' has such meaning as may be specified; and
'specified' means specified in an order made by the Treasury.

Sections 111(2) and 115   SCHEDULE 12

TRANSFER SCHEMES: CERTIFICATES

PART I

INSURANCE BUSINESS TRANSFER SCHEMES

1   (1) For the purposes of section 111(2) the appropriate certificates, in relation to an insurance business transfer scheme, are—

  (a)   a certificate under paragraph 2;
  (b)   if sub-paragraph (2) applies, a certificate under paragraph 3;
  (c)   if sub-paragraph (3) applies, a certificate under paragraph 4;
  (d)   if sub-paragraph (4) applies, a certificate under paragraph 5.

(2) This sub-paragraph applies if—

  (a)   the authorised person concerned is a UK authorised person which has received authorisation under Article 6 of the first life insurance directive or of the first non-life insurance directive from the Authority; and
  (b)   the establishment from which the business is to be transferred under the proposed insurance business transfer scheme is in an EEA State other than the United Kingdom.

(3) This sub-paragraph applies if—

  (a)   the authorised person concerned has received authorisation under Article 6 of the first life insurance directive from the Authority;
  (b)   the proposed transfer relates to business which consists of the effecting or carrying out of contracts of long-term insurance; and

(c)   as regards any policy which is included in the proposed transfer and which evidences a contract of insurance (other than reinsurance), an EEA State other than the United Kingdom is the State of the commitment.

(4) This sub-paragraph applies if—

(a)   the authorised person concerned has received authorisation under Article 6 of the first non-life insurance directive from the Authority;
(b)   the business to which the proposed insurance business transfer scheme relates is business which consists of the effecting or carrying out of contracts of general insurance; and
(c)   as regards any policy which is included in the proposed transfer and which evidences a contract of insurance (other than reinsurance), the risk is situated in an EEA State other than the United Kingdom.

Certificates as to margin of solvency

2   (1) A certificate under this paragraph is to be given—

(a)   by the relevant authority; or
(b)   in a case in which there is no relevant authority, by the Authority.

(2) A certificate given under sub-paragraph (1)(a) is one certifying that, taking the proposed transfer into account—

(a)   the transferee possesses, or will possess before the scheme takes effect, the necessary margin of solvency; or
(b)   there is no necessary margin of solvency applicable to the transferee.

(3) A certificate under sub-paragraph (1)(b) is one certifying that the Authority has received from the authority which it considers to be the authority responsible for supervising persons who effect or carry out contracts of insurance in the place to which the business is to be transferred that, taking the proposed transfer into account—

(a)   the transferee possesses or will possess before the scheme takes effect the margin of solvency required under the law applicable in that place; or
(b)   there is no such margin of solvency applicable to the transferee.

(4) 'Necessary margin of solvency' means the margin of solvency required in relation to the transferee, taking the proposed transfer into account, under the law which it is the responsibility of the relevant authority to apply.

(5) 'Margin of solvency' means the excess of the value of the assets of the transferee over the amount of its liabilities.

(6) 'Relevant authority' means—

(a)   if the transferee is an EEA firm falling within paragraph 5(d) of Schedule 3, its home state regulator;
(b)   if the transferee is a Swiss general insurer, the authority responsible in Switzerland for supervising persons who effect or carry out contracts of insurance;
(c)   if the transferee is an authorised person not falling within paragraph (a) or (b), the Authority.

(7) In sub-paragraph (6), any reference to a transferee of a particular description includes a reference to a transferee who will be of that description if the proposed scheme takes effect.

(8) 'Swiss general insurer' means a body—

(a)   whose head office is in Switzerland;

(b)   which has permission to carry on regulated activities consisting of the effecting and carrying out of contracts of general insurance; and

(c)   whose permission is not restricted to the effecting or carrying out of contracts of reinsurance.

Certificates as to consent

3   A certificate under this paragraph is one given by the Authority and certifying that the host State regulator has been notified of the proposed scheme and that—

(a)   that regulator has responded to the notification; or

(b)   that it has not responded but the period of three months beginning with the notification has elapsed.

Certificates as to long-term business

4   A certificate under this paragraph is one given by the Authority and certifying that the authority responsible for supervising persons who effect or carry out contracts of insurance in the State of the commitment has been notified of the proposed scheme and that—

(a)   that authority has consented to the proposed scheme; or

(b)   the period of three months beginning with the notification has elapsed and that authority has not refused its consent.

Certificates as to general business

5   A certificate under this paragraph is one given by the Authority and certifying that the authority responsible for supervising persons who effect or carry out contracts of insurance in the EEA State in which the risk is situated has been notified of the proposed scheme and that—

(a)   that authority has consented to the proposed scheme; or

(b)   the period of three months beginning with the notification has elapsed and that authority has not refused its consent.

Interpretation of Part I

6   (1) 'State of the commitment', in relation to a commitment entered into at any date, means—

(a)   if the policyholder is an individual, the State in which he had his habitual residence at that date;

(b)   if the policyholder is not an individual, the State in which the establishment of the policyholder to which the commitment relates was situated at that date.

(2) 'Commitment' means a commitment represented by contracts of insurance of a prescribed class.

(3) References to the EEA State in which a risk is situated are—

(a)   if the insurance relates to a building or to a building and its contents (so far as the contents are covered by the same policy), to the EEA State in which the building is situated;

(b)   if the insurance relates to a vehicle of any type, to the EEA State of registration;

(c)   in the case of policies of a duration of four months or less covering travel or holiday risks (whatever the class concerned), to the EEA State in which the policyholder took out the policy;

(d) in a case not covered by paragraphs (a) to (c)—
    (i)   if the policyholder is an individual, to the EEA State in which he has his habitual residence at the date when the contract is entered into; and
    (ii) otherwise, to the EEA State in which the establishment of the policyholder to which the policy relates is situated at that date.

PART II

BANKING BUSINESS TRANSFER SCHEMES

7 (1) For the purposes of section 111(2) the appropriate certificates, in relation to a banking business transfer scheme, are—

(a) a certificate under paragraph 8; and
(b) if sub-paragraph (2) applies, a certificate under paragraph 9.

(2) This sub-paragraph applies if the authorised person concerned or the transferee is an EEA firm falling within paragraph 5(b) of Schedule 3.

Certificates as to financial resources

8 (1) A certificate under this paragraph is one given by the relevant authority and certifying that, taking the proposed transfer into account, the transferee possesses, or will possess before the scheme takes effect, adequate financial resources.

(2) 'Relevant authority' means—

(a) if the transferee is a person with a Part IV permission or with permission under Schedule 4, the Authority;
(b) if the transferee is an EEA firm falling within paragraph 5(b) of Schedule 3, its home state regulator;
(c) if the transferee does not fall within paragraph (a) or (b), the authority responsible for the supervision of the transferee's business in the place in which the transferee has its head office.

(3) In sub-paragraph (2), any reference to a transferee of a particular description of person includes a reference to a transferee who will be of that description if the proposed banking business transfer scheme takes effect.

Certificates as to consent of home state regulator

9 A certificate under this paragraph is one given by the Authority and certifying that the home State regulator of the authorised person concerned or of the transferee has been notified of the proposed scheme and that—

(a) the home State regulator has responded to the notification; or
(b) the period of three months beginning with the notification has elapsed.

PART III

INSURANCE BUSINESS TRANSFERS EFFECTED OUTSIDE THE UNITED KINGDOM

10 (1) This paragraph applies to a proposal to execute under provisions corresponding to Part VII in a country or territory other than the United Kingdom an instrument transferring all the rights and obligations of the transferor under general or long-term insurance policies, or under such descriptions of such policies as may be specified in the instrument, to the transferee if any of the conditions in sub-paragraphs (2), (3) or (4) is met in relation to it.

(2) The transferor is an EEA firm falling within paragraph 5(d) of Schedule 3 and the transferee is an authorised person whose margin of solvency is supervised by the Authority.

(3) The transferor is a company authorised in an EEA State other than the United Kingdom under Article 27 of the first life insurance directive, or Article 23 of the first non-life insurance directive and the transferee is a UK authorised person which has received authorisation under Article 6 of either of those directives.

(4) The transferor is a Swiss general insurer and the transferee is a UK authorised person which has received authorisation under Article 6 of the first life insurance directive or the first non-life insurance directive.

(5) In relation to a proposed transfer to which this paragraph applies, the Authority may, if it is satisfied that the transferee possesses the necessary margin of solvency, issue a certificate to that effect.

(6) 'Necessary margin of solvency' means the margin of solvency which the transferee, taking the proposed transfer into account, is required by the Authority to maintain.

(7) 'Swiss general insurer' has the same meaning as in paragraph 2.

(8) 'General policy' means a policy evidencing a contract which, if it had been effected by the transferee, would have constituted the carrying on of a regulated activity consisting of the effecting of contracts of general insurance.

(9) 'Long-term policy' means a policy evidencing a contract which, if it had been effected by the transferee, would have constituted the carrying on of a regulated activity consisting of the effecting of contracts of long-term insurance.

Section 132(4)   SCHEDULE 13

THE FINANCIAL SERVICES AND MARKETS TRIBUNAL

PART I

GENERAL

Interpretation

1   In this Schedule—

    'panel of chairmen' means the panel established under paragraph 3(1);
    'lay panel' means the panel established under paragraph 3(4);
    'rules' means rules made by the Lord Chancellor under section 132.

PART II

THE TRIBUNAL

President

2   (1) The Lord Chancellor must appoint one of the members of the panel of chairmen to preside over the discharge of the Tribunal's functions.

(2) The member so appointed is to be known as the President of the Financial Services and Markets Tribunal (but is referred to in this Act as 'the President').

(3) The Lord Chancellor may appoint one of the members of the panel of chairmen to be Deputy President.

(4) The Deputy President is to have such functions in relation to the Tribunal as the President may assign to him.

(5) The Lord Chancellor may not appoint a person to be the President or Deputy President unless that person—

    (a)   has a ten year general qualification within the meaning of section 71 of the Courts and Legal Services Act 1990;

    (b)   is an advocate or solicitor in Scotland of at least ten years' standing; or

    (c)   is—

        (i)   a member of the Bar of Northern Ireland of at least ten years' standing; or

        (ii) a solicitor of the Supreme Court of Northern Ireland of at least ten years' standing.

(6) If the President (or Deputy President) ceases to be a member of the panel of chairmen, he also ceases to be the President (or Deputy President).

(7) The functions of the President may, if he is absent or is otherwise unable to act, be discharged—

    (a)   by the Deputy President; or

    (b)   if there is no Deputy President or he too is absent or otherwise unable to act, by a person appointed for that purpose from the panel of chairmen by the Lord Chancellor.

Panels

3   (1) The Lord Chancellor must appoint a panel of persons for the purposes of serving as chairmen of the Tribunal.

(2) A person is qualified for membership of the panel of chairmen if—

    (a)   he has a seven year general qualification within the meaning of section 71 of the Courts and Leal Services Act 1990;

    (b)   he is an advocate or solicitor in Scotland of at least seven years' standing; or

    (c)   he is—

        (i)   a member of the Bar of Northern Ireland of at least seven years' standing; or

        (ii) a solicitor of the Supreme Council of Northern Ireland of at least seven years' standing.

(3) The panel of chairmen must include at least one member who is a person of the kind mentioned in sub-paragraph (2)(b).

(4) The Lord Chancellor must also appoint a panel of persons who appear to him to be qualified by experience or otherwise to deal with matters of the kind that may be referred to the Tribunal.

Terms of office etc.

4   (1) Subject to the provisions of this Schedule, each member of the panel of chairmen and the lay panel is to hold and vacate office in accordance with the terms of his appointment.

(2) The Lord Chancellor may remove a member of either panel (including the President) on the ground of incapacity or misbehaviour.

(3) A member of either panel—

(a)   may at any time resign office by notice in writing to the Lord Chancellor;

(b)   is eligible for re-appointment if he ceases to hold office.

Remuneration and expenses

5   The Lord Chancellor may pay to any person, in respect of his service—

(a)   as a member of the Tribunal (including service as the President or Deputy President), or

(b)   as a person appointed under paragraph 7(4),

such remuneration and allowances as he may determine.

Staff

6   (1) The Lord Chancellor may appoint such staff for the Tribunal as he may determine.

(2) The remuneration of the Tribunal's staff is to be defrayed by the Lord Chancellor.

(3) Such expenses of the Tribunal as the Lord Chancellor may determine are to be defrayed by the Lord Chancellor.

PART III

CONSTITUTION OF TRIBUNAL

7   (1) On a reference to the Tribunal, the persons to act as members of the Tribunal for the purposes of the reference are to be selected from the panel of chairmen or the lay panel in accordance with arrangements made by the President for the purposes of this paragraph ('the standing arrangements').

(2) The standing arrangements must provide for at least one member to be selected from the panel of chairmen.

(3) If while a reference is being dealt with, a person serving as member of the Tribunal in respect of the reference becomes unable to act, the reference may be dealt with by—

(a)   the other members selected in respect of that reference; or

(b)   if it is being dealt with by a single member, such other member of the panel of chairmen as may be selected in accordance with the standing arrangements for the purposes of the reference.

(4) If it appears to the Tribunal that a matter before it involves a question of fact of special difficulty, it may appoint one or more experts to provide assistance.

PART IV

TRIBUNAL PROCEDURE

8   For the purpose of dealing with references, or any matter preliminary or incidental to a reference, the Tribunal must sit at such times and in such place or places as the Lord Chancellor may direct.

9   Rules made by the Lord Chancellor under section 132 may, in particular, include provision—

(a)   as to the manner in which references are to be instituted;

(b)   for the holding of hearings in private in such circumstances as may be specified in the rules;

(c)   as to the persons who may appear on behalf of the parties;

(d)   for a member of the panel of chairmen to hear and determine interlocutory matters arising on a reference;

(e)   for the suspension of decisions of the Authority which have taken effect;

(f)   as to the withdrawal of references;

(g)   as to the registration, publication and proof of decisions and orders.

Practice directions

10   The President of the Tribunal may give directions as to the practice and procedure to be followed by the Tribunal in relation to references to it.

Evidence

11   (1) The Tribunal may by summons require any person to attend, at such time and place as is specified in the summons, to give evidence or to produce any document in his custody or under his control which the Tribunal considers it necessary to examine.

(2) The Tribunal may—

(a)   take evidence on oath and for that purpose administer oaths; or

(b)   instead of administering an oath, require the person examined to make and subscribe a declaration of the truth of the matters in respect of which he is examined.

(3) A person who without reasonable excuse—

(a)   refuses or fails—
(i)   to attend following the issue of a summons by the Tribunal, or
(ii)   to give evidence, or

(b)   alters, suppresses, conceals or destroys, or refuses to produce a document which he may be required to produce for the purposes of proceedings before the Tribunal,

is guilty of an offence.

(4) A person guilty of an offence under sub-paragraph (3)(a) is liable on summary conviction to a fine not exceeding the statutory maximum.

(5) A person guilty of an offence under sub-paragraph (3)(b) is liable—

(a)   on summary conviction, to a fine not exceeding the statutory maximum;

(b)   on conviction on indictment, to imprisonment for a term not exceeding two years or a fine or both.

Decisions of Tribunal

12   (1) A decision of the Tribunal may be taken by a majority.

(2) The decision must—

(a)   state whether it was unanimous or taken by a majority;

(b)   be recorded in a document which—
(i)   contains a statement of the reasons for the decision; and
(ii)   is signed and dated by the member of the panel of chairmen dealing with the reference.

(3) The Tribunal must—

    (a)   inform each party of its decision; and

    (b)   as soon as reasonably practicable, send to each party and, if different, to any authorised person concerned, a copy of the document mentioned in sub-paragraph (2).

(4) The Tribunal must send the Treasury a copy of its decision.

Costs

13   (1) If the Tribunal considers that a party to any proceedings on a reference has acted vexatiously, frivolously or unreasonably it may order that party to pay to another party to the proceedings the whole or part of the costs or expenses incurred by the other party in connection with the proceedings.

(2) If, in any proceedings on a reference, the Tribunal considers that a decision of the Authority which is the subject of the reference was unreasonable it may order the Authority to pay to another party to the proceedings the whole or part of the costs or expenses incurred by the other party in connection with the proceedings.

Section 162   SCHEDULE 14

ROLE OF THE COMPETITION COMMISSION

Provision of information by Treasury

1   (1) The Treasury's powers under this paragraph are to be exercised only for the purpose of assisting the Commission in carrying out an investigation under section 162.

(2) The Treasury may give to the Commission—

    (a)   any information in their possession which relates to matters falling within the scope of the investigation; and

    (b)   other assistance in relation to any such matters.

(3) In carrying out an investigation under section 162, the Commission must have regard to any information given to it under this paragraph.

Consideration of matters arising on a report

2   In considering any matter arising from a report made by the Director under section 160, the Commission must have regard to—

    (a)   any representations made to it in connection with the matter by any person appearing to the Commission to have a substantial interest in the matter; and

    (b)   any cost benefit analysis prepared by the Authority (at any time) in connection with the regulatory provision or practice, or any of the regulatory provisions or practices, which are the subject of the report.

Applied provisions

3   (1) The provisions mentioned in sub-paragraph (2) are to apply in relation to the functions of the Commission under section 162 as they apply in relation to the functions of the Commission in relation to a reference to the Commission under the Fair Trading Act 1973.

(2) The provisions are—

(a)   section 82(2), (3) and (4) of the Fair Trading Act 1973 (general provisions about reports);

(b)   section 85 of that Act (attendance of witnesses and production of documents);

(c)   section 93B of that Act (false or misleading information);

(d)   section 24 of the Competition Act 1980 (modifications of provisions about the performance of the Commission's functions);

(e)   Part II of Schedule 7 to the Competition Act 1998 (performance by the Commission of its general functions).

(3) But the reference in paragraph 15(7)(b) in Schedule 7 to the 1998 Act to section 75(5) of that Act is to be read as a reference to the power of the Commission to decide not to make a report in accordance with section 162(2).

Publication of reports

4   (1) If the commission makes a report under section 162, it must publish it in such a way as appears to it to be best calculated to bring it to the attention of the public.

(2) Before publishing the report the Commission must, so far as practicable, exclude any matter which relates to the private affairs of a particular individual the publication of which, in the opinion of the Commission, would or might seriously and prejudicially affect his interests.

(3) Before publishing the report the Commission must, so far as practicable, also exclude any matter which relates to the affairs of a particular body the publication of which, in the opinion of the Commission, would or might seriously and prejudicially affect its interests.

(4) Sub-paragraphs (2) and (3) do not apply in relation to copies of a report which the Commission is required to send under section 162(10).

Sections 165(11) and 171(4)   SCHEDULE 15

INFORMATION AND INVESTIGATIONS: CONNECTED PERSONS

PART I

RULES FOR SPECIFIC BODIES

Corporate bodies

1   If the authorised person ('BC') is a body corporate, a person who is or has been—

(a)   an officer or manager of BC or of a parent undertaking of BC;

(b)   an employee of BC;

(c)   an agent of BC or of a parent undertaking of BC.

Partnerships

2   If the authorised person ('PP') is a partnership, a person who is or has been a member, manager, employee or agent of PP.

Unincorporated associations

3   If the authorised person ('UA') is an unincorporated association of persons which is neither a partnership nor an unincorporated friendly society, a person who is or has been an officer, manager, employee or agent of UA.

Friendly societies

4 (1) If the authorised person ('FS') is a friendly society, a person who is or has been an officer, manager or employee of FS.

(2) In relation to FS, 'officer' and 'manager' have the same meaning as in section 119(1) of the Friendly Societies Act 1992.

Building societies

5 (1) If the authorised person ('BS') is a building society, a person who is or has been an officer or employee of BS.

(2) In relation to BS, 'officer' has the same meaning as it has in section 119(1) of the Building Societies Act 1986.

Individuals

6 If the authorised person ('IP') is an individual, a person who is or has been an employee or agent of IP.

Application to sections 171 and 172

7 For the purposes of sections 171 and 172, if the person under investigation is not an authorised person the references in this Part of this Schedule to an authorised person are to be taken to be references to the person under investigation.

PART II

ADDITIONAL RULES

8 A person who is, or at the relevant time was, the partner, manager, employee, agent, appointed representative, banker, auditor, actuary or solicitor of—

(a) the person under investigation ('A');
(b) a parent undertaking of A;
(c) a subsidiary undertaking of A;
(d) a subsidiary undertaking of a parent undertaking of A; or
(e) a parent undertaking of a subsidiary undertaking of A.

Section 203(8)   SCHEDULE 16

PROHIBITIONS AND RESTRICTIONS IMPOSED BY DIRECTOR GENERAL OF FAIR TRADING

Preliminary

1 In this Schedule—

'appeal period' has the same meaning as in the Consumer Credit Act 1974;
'prohibition' means a consumer credit prohibition under section 203;
'restriction' means a restriction under section 204.

Notice of prohibition or restriction

2   (1) This paragraph applies if the Director proposes, in relation to a firm—

(a)   to impose a prohibition;
(b)   to impose a restriction; or
(c)   to vary a restriction otherwise than with the agreement of the firm.

(2) The Director must by notice—

(a)   inform the firm of his proposal, stating his reasons; and
(b)   invite the firm to submit representations in accordance with paragraph 4.

(3) If he imposes the prohibition or restriction or varies the restriction, the Director may give directions authorising the firm to carry into effect agreements made before the coming into force of the prohibition, restriction or variation.

(4) A prohibition, restriction or variation is not to come into force before the end of the appeal period.

(5) If a Director imposes a prohibition or restriction or varies a restriction, he must serve a copy of the prohibition, restriction or variation—

(a)   on the Authority; and
(b)   on the firm's home state regulator.

Application to revoke prohibition or restriction

3   (1) This paragraph applies if the Director proposes to refuse an application made by a firm for the revocation of a prohibition or restriction.

(2) The Director must by notice—

(a)   inform the firm of the proposed refusal, stating his reasons; and
(b)   invite the firm to submit representations in accordance with paragraph 4.

Representations to Director

4   (1) If this paragraph applies to an invitation to submit representations, the Director must invite the firm, within 21 days after the notice containing the invitation is given to it or such longer period as he may allow—

(a)   to submit its representations in writing to him; and
(b)   to give notice to him, if the firms thinks fit, that it wishes to make representations orally.

(2) If notices is given under sub-paragraph (1)(b), the Director must arrange for the oral representations to be heard.

(3) The Director must give the firm notice of his determination.

Appeals

5   Section 41 of the Consumer Credit Act 1974 (appeals to the Secretary of State) has effect as if—

(a)   the following determinations were mentioned in column 1 of the table set out at the end of that section—
(i)   imposition of a prohibition or restrictions or the variation of a restriction; and
(ii)   refusal of an application for the revocation of a prohibition or restriction; and

    (b)   the firm concerned were mentioned in column 2 of that table in relation to those determinations.

Section 225(4)   **SCHEDULE 17**

THE OMBUDSMAN SCHEME

PART I

GENERAL

Interpretation

1   In this Schedule—
'ombudsman' means a person who is a member of the panel; and
'the panel' means the panel established under paragraph 4.

PART II

THE SCHEME OPERATOR

Establishment by the Authority

2   (1) The Authority must establish a body corporate to exercise the functions conferred on the scheme operator by or under this Act.

(2) The Authority must take such steps as are necessary to ensure that the scheme operator is, at all times, capable of exercising those functions.

Constitution

3   (1) The constitution of the scheme operator must provide for it to have—

    (a)   a chairman; and
    (b)   a board (which must include the chairman) whose members are the scheme operator's directors.

(2) The chairman and other members of the board must be persons appointed, and liable to removal from office, by the Authority (acting, in the case of the chairman, with the approval of the Treasury).

(3) But the terms of their appointment (and in particular those governing removal from office) must be seen as to secure their independence from the Authority in the operation of the scheme.

(4) The function of making voluntary jurisdiction rules under section 227 and the functions conferred by paragraphs 4, 5, 7, 9 or 14 may be exercised only by the board.

(5) The validity of any act of the scheme operator is unaffected by—

    (a)   a vacancy in the office of chairman; or
    (b)   a defect in the appointment of a person as chairman or as a member of the board.

The panel of ombudsmen

4   (1) The scheme operator must appoint and maintain a panel of persons, appearing to it to have appropriate qualifications and experience, to act as ombudsmen for the purposes of the scheme.

(2) A person's appointment to the panel is to be on such terms (including terms as to the duration and termination of his appointment and as to remuneration) as the scheme operator considers—

(a)   consistent with the independence of the person appointed; and
(b)   otherwise appropriate.

The Chief Ombudsman

5   (1) The scheme operator must appoint one member of the panel to act as Chief Ombudsman.

(2) The Chief Ombudsman is to be appointed on such terms (including terms as to the duration and termination of his appointment) as the scheme operator considers appropriate.

Status

6   (1) The scheme operator is not to be regarded as exercising functions on behalf of the Crown.

(2) The scheme operator's board members, officers and staff are not to be regarded as Crown servants.

(3) Appointment as Chief Ombudsman or to the panel or as a deputy ombudsman does not confer the status of Crown servant.

Annual reports

7   (1) At least once a year—

(a)   the scheme operator must make a report to the Authority on the discharge of its functions; and
(b)   the Chief Ombudsman must make a report to the Authority on the discharge of his functions.

(2) Each report must distinguish between functions in relation to the scheme's compulsory jurisdiction and functions in relation to its voluntary jurisdiction.

(3) Each report must also comply with any requirements specified in rules made by the Authority.

(4) The scheme operator must publish each report in the way it considers appropriate.

Guidance

8   The scheme operator may publish guidance consisting of such information and advice as it considers appropriate and may charge for it or distribute it free of charge.

Budget

9   (1) The scheme operator must, before the start of each of its financial years, adopt an annual budget which has been approved by the Authority.

(2) The scheme operator may, with the approval of the Authority, vary the budget for a financial year at any time after its adoption.

(3) The annual budget must include an indication of—

   (a)   the distribution of resources deployed in the operation of the scheme, and
   (b)   the amounts of income of the scheme operator arising or expected to arise from the operation of the scheme,

distinguishing between the scheme's compulsory and voluntary jurisdiction.

Exemption from liability in damages

10   (1) No person is to be liable in damages for anything done or omitted in the discharge, or purported discharge, of any functions under this Act in relation to the compulsory jurisdiction.

(2) Sub-paragraph (1) does not apply—

   (a)   if the act or omission is shown to have been in bad faith; or
   (b)   so as to prevent an award of damages made in respect of an act or omission on the ground that the act or omission was unlawful as a result of section 6(1) of the Human Rights Act 1998.

Privilege

11   For the purposes of the law relating to defamation, proceedings in relation to a complaint which is subject to the compulsory jurisdiction are to be treated as if they were proceedings before a court.

PART III

THE COMPULSORY JURISDICTION

Introduction

12   This Part of this Schedule applies only in relation to the compulsory jurisdiction.

Authority's procedural rules

13   (1) The Authority must make rules providing that a complaint is not to be entertained unless the complainant has referred it under the ombudsman scheme before the applicable time limit (determined in accordance with the rules) has expired.

(2) The rules may provide that an ombudsman may extend that time limit in specified circumstances.

(3) The Authority may make rules providing that a complaint is not to be entertained (except in specified circumstances) if the complainant has not previously communicated its substance to the respondent and given him a reasonable opportunity to deal with it.

(4) The Authority may make rules requiring an authorised person who may become subject to the compulsory jurisdiction as a respondent to establish such procedures as the Authority considers appropriate for the resolution of complaints which—

    (a)   may be referred to the scheme; and

    (b)   arise out of activity to which the Authority's powers under Part X do not apply.

The scheme operator's rules

14   (1) The scheme operator must make rules, to be known as 'scheme rules', which are to set out the procedure for reference of complaints and for their investigation, consideration and determination by an ombudsman.

(2) Scheme rules may, among other things—

    (a)   specify matters which are to be taken into account in determining whether an act or omission was fair and reasonable;

    (b)   provide that a complaint may, in specified circumstances, be dismissed without consideration of its merits;

    (c)   provide for the reference of a complaint, in specified circumstances and with the consent of the complainant, to another body with a view to its being determined by that body instead of by an ombudsman;

    (d)   make provision as to the evidence which may be required or admitted, the extent to which it should be oral or written and the consequences of a person's failure to produce any information or document which he has been required (under section 231 or otherwise) to produce;

    (e)   allow an ombudsman to fix time limits for any aspect of the proceedings and to extend a time limit;

    (f)   provide for certain things in relation to the reference, investigation or consideration (but not determination) of a complaint to be done by a member of the scheme operator's staff instead of by an ombudsman;

    (g)   make different provision in relation to different kinds of complaint.

(3) The circumstances specified under sub-paragraph (2)(b) may include the following—

    (a)   the ombudsman considers the complaint frivolous or vexatious;

    (b)   legal proceedings have been brought concerning the subject-matter of the complaint and the ombudsman considers that the complaint is best dealt with in those proceedings; or

    (c)   the ombudsman is satisfied that there are other compelling reasons why it is inappropriate for the complaint to be dealt with under the ombudsman scheme.

(4) If the scheme operator proposes to make any scheme rules it must publish a draft of the proposed rules in the way appearing to it to be best calculated to bring them to the attention of persons appearing to it to be likely to be affected.

(5) The draft must be accompanied by a statement that representations about the proposals may be made to the scheme operator within a time specified in the statement.

(6) Before making the proposed scheme rules, the scheme operator must have regard to any representations made to it under sub-paragraph (5).

(7) The consent of the Authority is required before any scheme rules may be made.

Fees

15   (1) Scheme rules may require a respondent to pay to the scheme operator such fees as may be specified in the rules.

(2) The rule may, among other things—

    (a)   provide for the scheme operator to reduce or waive a fee in a particular case;

    (b)   set different fees for different stages of the proceedings on a complaint;

    (c)   provide for fees to be refunded in specified circumstances;

    (d)   make different provision for different kinds of complaint.

Enforcement of money awards

16   A money award, including interest, which has been registered in accordance with scheme rules may—

    (a)   if a county court so orders in England and Wales, be recovered by execution issued from the county court (or otherwise) as if it were payable under an order of that court;

    (b)   be enforced in Northern Ireland as a money judgment under the Judgments Enforcement (Northern Ireland) Order 1981;

    (c)   be enforced in Scotland by the sheriff, as if it were a judgment or order of the sheriff and whether or not the sheriff could himself have granted such judgment or order.

PART IV

THE VOLUNTARY JURISDICTION

Introduction

17   This Part of this Schedule applies only in relation to the voluntary jurisdiction.

Terms of reference to the scheme

18   (1) Complaints are to be dealt with and determined under the voluntary jurisdiction on standard terms fixed by the scheme operator with the approval of the Authority.

(2) Different standard terms may be fixed with respect to different matters or in relation to different cases.

(3) The standard terms may, in particular—

    (a)   require the making of payments to the scheme operator by participants in the scheme of such amounts, and at such times, as may be determined by the scheme operator;

    (b)   make provision as to the award of costs on the determination of a complaint.

(4) The scheme operator may not vary any of the standard terms or add or remove terms without the approval of the Authority.

(5) The standard terms may include provision to the effect that (unless acting in bad faith) none of the following is to be liable in damages for anything done or omitted in the discharge or purported discharge of functions in connection with the voluntary jurisdiction—

    (a)   the scheme operator;

    (b)   any members of its governing body;

    (c)   any member of its staff;

    (d)   any person acting as an ombudsman for the purposes of the scheme.

Delegation by and to other schemes

19   (1) The scheme operator may make arrangements with a relevant body—

    (a)   for the exercise by that body of any part of the voluntary jurisdiction of the ombudsman scheme on behalf of the scheme; or

    (b)   for the exercise by the scheme of any function of that body as if it were part of the voluntary jurisdiction of the scheme.

(2) A 'relevant body' is one which the scheme operator is satisfied—

    (a)   is responsible for the operation of a broadly comparable scheme (whether or not established by statute) for the resolution of disputes; and

    (b)   in the case of arrangements under sub-paragraph (1)(a), will exercise the jurisdiction in question in a way compatible with the requirements imposed by or under this Act in relation to complaints of the kind concerned.

(3) Such arrangements require the approval of the Authority.

Voluntary jurisdiction rules: procedure

20   (1) If the scheme operator makes voluntary jurisdiction rules, it must give a copy to the Authority without delay.

(2) If the scheme operator revokes any such rules, it must give written notice to the Authority without delay.

(3) The power to make voluntary jurisdiction rules is exercisable in writing.

(4) Immediately after making voluntary jurisdiction rules, the scheme operator must arrange for them to be printed and made available to the public.

(5) The scheme operator may charge a reasonable fee for providing a person with a copy of any voluntary jurisdiction rules.

Verification of the rules

21   (1) The production of a printed copy of voluntary jurisdiction rules purporting to be made by the scheme operator—

    (a)   on which is endorsed a certificate signed by a member of the scheme operator's staff authorised by the scheme operator for that purpose, and

    (b)   which contains the required statements,

is evidence (or in Scotland sufficient evidence) of the facts stated in the certificate.

(2) The required statements are—

    (a)   that the rules were made by the scheme operator;

    (b)   that the copy is a true copy of the rules; and

    (c)   that on a specified date the rules were made available to the public in accordance with paragraph 20(4).

(3) A certificate purporting to be signed as mentioned in sub-paragraph (1) is to be taken to have been duly signed unless the contrary is shown.

Consultation

22   (1) If the scheme operator proposes to make voluntary jurisdiction rules, it must publish a draft of the proposed rules in the way appearing to it to be best calculated to bring them to the attention of the public.

(2) The draft must be accompanied by—

  (a)   an explanation of the proposed rules; and
  (b)   a statement that representations about the proposals may be made to the scheme operator within a specified time.

(3) Before making any voluntary jurisdiction rules, the scheme operator must have regard to any representations made to it in accordance with sub-paragraph (2)(b).

(4) If voluntary jurisdiction rules made by the scheme operator differ from the draft published under sub-paragraph (1) in a way which the scheme operator considers significant, the scheme operator must publish a statement of the difference.

Sections 334, 336 and 338   SCHEDULE 18

MUTUALS

PART I

FRIENDLY SOCIETIES

The Friendly Societies Act 1974 (c.46)

1   Omit sections 4 (provision for separate registration areas) and 10 (societies registered in one registration area carrying on business in another).

2   In section 7 (societies which may be registered), in subsection (2)(b), for 'in the central registration area or in Scotland' substitute 'in the United Kingdom, the Channel Islands or the Isle of Man'.

3   In section 11 (additional registration requirements for societies with branches), omit 'and where any such society has branches in more than one registration area, section 10 above shall apply to that society'.

4   In section 99(4) (punishment of fraud etc and recovery of property misapplied), omit 'in the central registration area'.

The Friendly Societies Act 1992 (c.40)

5   Omit sections 31 to 36A (authorisation of friendly societies business).

6   In section 37 (restrictions on combinations of business), omit subsections (1), (1A) and (7A) to (9).

7   Omit sections 38 to 43 (restrictions on business of certain authorised societies).

8   Omit sections 44 to 50 (regulation of friendly societies business).

PART II

FRIENDLY SOCIETIES: SUBSIDIARIES AND CONTROLLED BODIES

Interpretation

9   In this Part of this Schedule—

'the 1992 Act' means the Friendly Societies Act 1992; and
'section 13' means section 13 of that Act.

Qualifying bodies

10   (1) Subsections (2) to (5) of section 13 (incorporated friendly societies allowed to form or acquire control or joint control only of qualifying bodies) cease to have effect.

(2) As a result, omit—

   (a)   subsections (8) and (11) of that section, and
   (b)   Schedule 7 to the 1992 Act (activities which may be carried on by a subsidiary of, or body jointly controlled by, an incorporated friendly society).

Bodies controlled by societies

11   In section 13(9) (defined terms), after paragraph (a) insert—

'(aa) an incorporated friendly society also has control of a body corporate if the body corporate is itself a body controlled in one of the ways mentioned in paragraph (a)(i), (ii) or (iii) by a body corporate of which the society has control;'.

Joint control by societies

12   In section 13(9), after paragraph (c) insert—

'(cc) an incorporated friendly society also has joint control of a body corporate if—
     (i)   a subsidiary of the society has joint control of the body corporate in a way mentioned in paragraph (c)(i), (ii) or (iii);
     (ii)   a body corporate of which the society has joint control has joint control of the body corporate in such a way; or
     (iii)   the body corporate is controlled in a way mentioned in paragraph (a)(i), (ii) or (iii) by a body corporate of which the society has joint control;'.

Acquisition of joint control

13   In section 13(9), in the words following paragraph (d), after 'paragraph (c)' insert 'or (cc)'.

Amendment of Schedule 8 to the 1992 Act

14   (1) Schedule 8 to the 1992 Act (provisions supplementing section 13) is amended as follows.

(2) Omit paragraph 3(2).

(3) After paragraph 3 insert—

'3A.　(1) A body is to be treated for the purposes of section 13(9) as having the right to appoint to a directorship if—

(a)　a person's appointment to the directorship follows necessarily from his appointment as an officer of that body; or

(b)　the directorship is held by the body itself.

(2) A body ('B') and some other person ('P') together are to be treated, for the purposes of section 13(9), as having the right to appoint to a directorship if—

(a)　P is a body corporate which has directors and a person's appointment to the directorship follows necessarily from his appointment both as an officer of B and a director of P;

(b)　P is a body corporate which does not have directors and a person's appointment to the directorship follows necessarily from his appointment both as an officer of B and as a member of P's managing body; or

(c)　the directorship is held jointly by B and P.

(3) For the purposes of section 13(9), a right to appoint (or remove) which is exercisable only with the consent or agreement of another person must be left out of account unless no other person has a right to appoint (or remove) in relation to that directorship.

(4) Nothing in this paragraph is to be read as restricting the effect of section 13(9).'

(4) In paragraph 9 (exercise of certain rights under instruction by, or in the interests of, incorporated friendly society) insert at the end 'or in the interests of any body over which the society has joint control'.

Consequential amendments

15　(1) Section 52 of the 1992 Act is amended as follows.

(2) In subsection (2), omit paragraph (d).

(3) In subsection (3), for '(4) below' substitute '(2)'.

(4) For subsection (4) substitute—

'(4) A court may not make an order under subsection (5) unless it is satisfied that one or more of the conditions mentioned in subsection (2) are satisfied.'

(5) In subsection (5), omit the words from 'or, where' to the end.

References in other enactments

16　References in any provision of, or made under, any enactment to subsidiaries of, or bodies jointly controlled by, an incorporated friendly society are to be read as including references to bodies which are such subsidiaries or bodies as a result of any provision of this Part of this Schedule.

PART III

BUILDING SOCIETIES

The Building Societies Act 1986 (c.53)

17　Omit section 9 (initial authorisation to raise funds and borrow money).

18   Omit Schedule 3 (supplementary provisions about authorisation).

PART IV

INDUSTRIAL AND PROVIDENT SOCIETIES

The Industrial and Provident Societies Act 1965 (c.12)

19   Omit section 8 (provision for separate registration areas for Scotland and for England, Wales and the Channel Islands).

20   Omit section 70 (scale of fees to be paid in respect of transactions and inspection of documents).

PART V

CREDIT UNIONS

The Credit Unions Act 1979 (c.34)

21   In section 6 (minimum and maximum number of members), omit subsections (2) to (6).

22   In section 11 (loans), omit subsections (2) and (6).

23   Omit sections 11B (loans approved by credit unions), 11C (grant of certificates of approval) and 11D (withdrawal of certificates of approval).

24   In section 12, omit subsections (4) and (5).

25   In section 14, omit subsections (2), (3), (5) and (6).

26   In section 28 (offences), omit subsection (2).

Section 351   SCHEDULE 19

COMPETITION INFORMATION

PART I

PERSONS AND FUNCTIONS FOR THE PURPOSES OF SECTION 351

1   The Table set out after this paragraph has effect for the purposes of section 351(3)(b).

TABLE

Person	Function
1. The Commission.	Any function of the Commission under Community law relating to competition.
2. The Comptroller and Auditor General.	Any function of his.
3. A Minister of the Crown.	Any function of his under a specified enactment.

Person	Function
4. Director General of Telecommunications.	Any function of his under a specified enactment.
5. Director General of Gas Supply.	Any function of his under a specified enactment.
6. The Director General of Gas for Northern Ireland.	Any function of his under a specified enactment.
7. The Director General of Electricity Supply.	Any function of his under a specified enactment.
8. The Director General of Electricity Supply for Northern Ireland.	Any function of his under a specified enactment.
9. The Director General of Water Services.	Any function of his under a specified enactment.
10. The Civil Aviation Authority.	Any function of that authority under a specified enactment.
11. The Rail Regulator.	Any function of his under a specified enactment.
12. The Director General of Fair Trading.	Any function of his under a specified enactment.
13. The Competition Commission.	Any function of the Competition Commission under a specified enactment.
14. The Authority.	Any function of the Authority under a specified enactment.
15. A person of a description specified in an order made by the Treasury.	Any function of his which is specified in the order.

PART II

THE ENACTMENTS

1 The Fair Trading Act 1973

2 The Consumer Credit Act 1974

3 The Estate Agents Act 1979

4 The Competition Act 1980

5 The Telecommunications Act 1984

6 The Airports Act 1986

7 The Gas Act 1986

8 The Control of Misleading Advertisements Regulations 1988

9 The Electricity Act 1989

10 The Broadcasting Act 1990

11 The Water Industry Act 1991

12 The Electricity (Northern Ireland) Order 1992

13 The Railways Act 1993

14   Part IV of the Airports (Northern Ireland) Order 1994

15   The Gas (Northern Ireland) Order 1996

16   The EC Competition (Articles 88 and 89) Enforcement Regulations 1996

17   The Unfair Terms in Consumer Contracts Regulations 1999

18   This Act.

19   An enactment specified for the purposes of this paragraph in an order made by the Treasury.

Section 432(1)   SCHEDULE 20

MINOR AND CONSEQUENTIAL AMENDMENTS

The House of Commons Disqualification Act 1975 (c.24)

1   In Part II of Schedule 1 to the House of Commons Disqualification Act 1975 (disqualifying offices)—

(a)   omit—

'Any member of the Financial Services Tribunal in receipt of remuneration'; and
(b)   at the appropriate place, insert—

'Any member, in receipt of remuneration, of a panel of persons who may be selected to act as members of the Financial Services and Markets Tribunal'.

The Northern Ireland Assembly Disqualification Act 1975 (c.25)

2   In Part III of Schedule 1 to the Northern Ireland Assembly Disqualification Act 1975 (disqualifying offices)—

(a)   omit—

'Any member of the Financial Services Tribunal in receipt of remuneration'; and
(b)   at the appropriate place, insert—

'Any member, in receipt of remuneration, of a panel of persons who may be selected to act as members of the Financial Services and Markets Tribunal'.

The Civil Jurisdiction and Judgments Act 1982 (c.27)

3   In paragraph 10 of Schedule 5 to the Civil Jurisdiction and Judgments Act 1982 (proceedings excluded from the operation of Schedule 4 to that Act), for 'section 188 of the Financial Services Act 1986' substitute 'section 415 of the Financial Services and Markets Act 2000'.

The Income and Corporation Taxes Act 1988 (c.1)

4   (1) The Income and Corporation Taxes Act 1988 is amended as follows.

(2) In section 76 (expenses of management: insurance companies), in subsection (8), omit the definitions of—

'the 1986 Act';
'authorised person';

'investment business';
'investor';
'investor protection scheme';
'prescribed'; and
'recognised self-regulating organisation'.

(3) In section 468 (authorised unit trusts), in subsections (6) and (8), for '78 of the Financial Services Act 1986' substitue '243 of the Financial Services and Markets Act 2000'.

(4) In section 469(7) (other unit trust schemes), for 'Financial Services Act 1986' substitute 'Financial Services and Markets Act 2000'.

(5) In section 728 (information in relation to transfers of securities), in subsection (7)(a), for 'Financial Services Act 1986' substitute 'Financial Services and Markets Act 2000'.

(6) In section 841(3) (power to apply certain provisions of the Tax Acts to recognised investment exchange), for 'Financial Services Act 1986' substitute 'Financial Services and Markets Act 2000'.

The Finance Act 1991 (c.31)

5   (1) The Finance Act 1991 is amended as follows.

(2) In section 47 (investor protection schemes), omit subsections (1), (2) and (4).

(3) In section 116 (investment exchanges and clearing houses: stamp duty), in subsection (4)(b), for 'Financial Services Act 1986' substitute 'Financial Services and Markets Act 2000'.

The Tribunals and Inquiries Act 1992 (c.53)

6   (1) The Tribunals and Inquiries Act 1992 is amended as follows.

(2) In Schedule 1 (tribunals under supervision of the Council on Tribunals), for the entry relating to financial services and paragraph 18, substitute—

'Financial services and markets	18. The Financial Services and Markets Tribunal.'

The Judicial Pensions and Retirement Act 1993 (c. 8)

7   (1) The Judicial Pensions and Retirement Act 1993 is amended as follows.

(2) In Schedule 1 (offices which may be qualifying offices), in Part II, after the entry relating to the President or chairman of the Transport Tribunal insert—

'President or Deputy President of the Financial Services and Markets Tribunal'.

(3) In Schedule 5 (relevant offices in relation to retirement provisions)—

   (a)   omit the entry—

   'Member of the Financial Services Tribunal appointed by the Lord Chancellor'; and

   (b)   at the end insert—

   'Member of the Financial Services and Markets Tribunal'.

Section 432(2)   SCHEDULE 21

TRANSITIONAL PROVISIONS AND SAVINGS

Self-regulating organisations

1   (1) No new application under section 9 of the 1986 Act (application for recognition) may be entertained.

(2) No outstanding application made under that section before the passing of this Act may continue to be entertained.

(3) After the date which is the designed date for a recognised self-regulating organisation—

- (a)   the recognition order for that organisation may not be revoked under section 11 of the 1986 Act (revocation of recognition);
- (b)   no application may be made to the court under section 12 of the 1986 Act (compliance orders) with respect to that organisation.

(4) The powers conferred by section 13 of the 1986 Act (alteration of rules for protection of investors) may not be exercised.

(5) 'Designated date' means such date as the Treasury may by order designate.

(6) Sub-paragraph (3) does not apply to a recognised self-regulating organisation in respect of which a notice of intention to revoke its recognition order was given under section 11(3) of the 1986 Act before the passing of this Act if that notice has not been withdrawn.

(7) Expenditure incurred by the Authority in connection with the winding up of any body which was, immediately before the passing of this Act, a recognised self-regulating organisation is to be treated as having been incurred in connection with the discharge by the Authority of functions under this Act.

(8) 'Recognised self-regulating organisation' means an organisation which, immediately before the passing of this Act, was such an organisation for the purposes of the 1986 Act.

(9) 'The 1986 Act' means the Financial Services Act 1986.

Self-regulating organisations for friendly societies

2   (1) No new application under paragraph 2 of Schedule 11 to the 1986 Act (application for recognition) may be entertained.

(2) No outstanding application made under that paragraph before the passing of this Act may continue to be entertained.

(3) After the date which is the designated date for a recognised self-regulating organisation for friendly societies—

- (a)   the recognition order for that organisation may not be revoked under paragraph 5 of Schedule 11 to the 1986 Act (revocation of recognition);
- (b)   no application may be made to the court under paragraph 6 of that Schedule (compliance orders) with respect to that organisation.

(4) 'Designated date' means such date as the Treasury may by order designate.

(5) Sub-paragraph (3) does not apply to a recognised self-regulating organisation for friendly societies in respect of which a notice of intention to revoke its recognition order

was given under section 11(3) of the 1986 act (as applied by paragraph 5(2) of that Schedule) before the passing of this Act if that notice has not been withdrawn.

(6) Expenditure incurred by the Authority in connection with the winding up of any body which was, immediately before the passing of this Act, a recognised self-regulating organisation for friendly societies is to be treated as having been incurred in connection with the discharge by the Authority of functions under this Act.

(7) 'Recognised self-regulating organisations for friendly societies' means an organisation which, immediately before the passing of this Act, was such an organisation for the purposes of the 1986 Act.

(8) 'The 1986 Act' means the Financial Services Act 1986.

Section 432(3)   SCHEDULE 22

                                              REPEALS

Chapter	Short title	Extent of repeal
1923 c. 8.	The Industrial Assurance Act 1923.	The whole Act.
1948 c. 39.	The Industrial Assurance and Friendly Societies Act 1948.	The whole Act.
1965 c. 12.	The Industrial and Provident Societies Act 1965.	Section 8. Section 70.
1974 c. 46.	The Friendly Societies Act 1974.	Section 4. Section 10. In section 11, from 'and where' to 'that society'. In section 99(4), 'in the central registration area'.
1975 c. 24.	The House of Commons Disqualification Act 1975.	In Schedule 1, in Part III, 'Any member of the Financial Services Tribunal in receipt of remuneration'.
1975 c. 25.	The Northern Ireland Assembly Disqualification Act 1975.	In Schedule 1, in Part III, 'Any member of the Financial Services Tribunal in receipt of remuneration'.
1977 c. 46.	The Insurance Brokers (Registration) Act 1977.	The whole Act.
1979 c. 34.	The Credit Unions Act 1979.	Section 6(2) to (6). Section 11(2) and (6). Sections 11B, 11C and 11D. Section 12(4) and (5). In section 14, subsections (2), (3), (5) and (6). Section 28(2).
1986 c. 53.	The Building Societies Act 1986.	Section 9. Schedule 3.

Chapter	Short title	Extent of repeal
1988 c. 1.	The Income and Corporation Taxes Act 1988.	In section 76, in subsection (8), the definitions of 'the 1986 Act', 'authorised person', 'investment business', 'investor', 'investor protection scheme', 'prescribed' and 'recognised self-regulating organisation'.
1991 c. 31.	The Finance Act 1991.	In section 47, subsections (1), (2) and (4).
1992 c. 40.	The Friendly Societies Act 1992.	In section 13, subsections (2) to (5), (8) and (11). Sections 31 to 36. In section 37, subsections (1), (1A) and (7A) to (9). Sections 38 to 50. In section 52, subsection (2)(d) and, in subsection (5), the words from 'or where' to the end. Schedule 7. In Schedule 8, paragraph 3(2).
1993 c. 8.	The Judicial Pensions and Retirement Act 1993.	In Schedule 5, 'Member of the Financial Services Tribunal appointed by the Lord Chancellor'.

INDEX

References are to paragraph number

actuaries
  Financial Services Authority, and
    10.3
approval
  criteria   5.3.1
  employees, and   5.1
  procedure   5.3
  re-approvals   5.3.1
  recording   5.3.1
  senior management, and   5.3.2
  sole traders, and   5.3.1
authorisation
  'control', and   5.2.6
  definition   4.2
  EEA (European Economic Area)
    authorisation   5.2.4
  empty permission   5.2, 5.2.3
  methods   5.2
  notification threshold   5.2.6
  permission procedure   5.2.3
  threshold conditions   5.2.1
  transfers, and   5.2.7
  Treasury, and   5.2.5
  UK permission   5.2.2

Bank of England   1.2.4, 3.1
'Big Bang'   1.3
building societies   1.2.5
  Building Societies Protection
    Scheme   8.1

CISs *see* collective investment schemes
City fraud   7.1
clearing houses
  competition, and   11.2.4
  Financial Services Authority, and
    11.2.5
  fragmentation   11.2.6
  insolvency arrangements   11.2.2
  investigation   11.2.3
  notification requirements   11.2.3
  recognition   11.2
Code of Market Conduct (COMC)   7.5
collective investment schemes
  investigation   13.5

depositaries   13.2.1
  European Passports, and   5.2.4
  Financial Services Authority, and
    13.2.1
  marketing restrictions   13.3
    exceptions
      authorised schemes
        OEICs   13.4.2
        unit trusts   13.4.1
      exempt schemes   13.4.3
      recognised schemes   13.4.4
  investment trusts   13.2
  limited issue funds   13.4.2
  limited redemption funds   13.4.2
  OEICs (open-ended investment
    companies)   13.2
  open-ended investment companies
    (OEICs)   13.2
  operators   13.2.1
  Pooled Unauthorised Companies
    (PUNCs)   13.4.2
  PUNCs (Pooled Unauthorised
    Companies)   13.4.2
  trustees   13.2.1
  types   13.2
  unit trusts   13.2
COMC (Code of Market Conduct)   7.5
complaints
  Financial Ombudsman Scheme
    (FOS)   8.1.1, 8.2
  resolution schemes   8.1
  single system   8.1.1
compensation
  Financial Services Compensation
    Scheme (FSCS)   8.3.1
  schemes   8.1
  single system   8.1.2
conspiracy to defraud   7.1
consumer protection   3.3.1
'controlled functions'   5.3
corporate activities   4.3.4
credit unions
  regulation   4.1
cross-border services *see* European
  Passport

Delaware Effect   2.3.1

Department of Trade and Industry
    (DTI)   1.2.5
Deposit Protection Scheme   8.1
Designated Professional Bodies
    (DPBs)   3.1, 11.4
'distortion'   7.5.4
DPBs (Designated Professional
    Bodies)   3.1, 11.4
DTI (Department of Trade and
    Industry)   1.2.5

'economical with the truth'   7.2.1
'empty permission'   5.2, 5.2.3
'engaging in investment activity'   4.2.3
Euro-securities   12.5.1
European Convention on Human
    Rights   2.4
European Economic Area
    authorisation   5.2.4
European Passport
    collective investment schemes (CISs),
      and   2.2.4
    conduct of business rules, and   2.3.3
    credit institutions, and   2.2.2
    Delaware Effect, and   2.3.1
    development 2.1–2.2
    Financial Services Authority, and
      2.3.4, 9.3.7
    host State regulation, and   2.3.2
    insurers, and   2.2.1
    investment firms, and   2.2.3
    listing, and   2.2.4
    qualification   2.2.5, 5.2.4
    regulatory arbitrage, and   2.3.1
    transparency, and   2.3.1
    Treasury, and   5.2.5
exchanges
    competition, and   11.2.4
    definition   11.1
    Financial Services Authority, and
      11.2.5
    fragmentation   11.2.6
    function   11.1
    insolvency arrangements   11.2.2
    investigation   11.2.3
    notification requirements   11.2.3
    recognition   11.2
exempt persons   4.2.1
exemption order   4.3.1

'false or misleading impression'   7.5.3
Financial Ombudsman Scheme (FOS)
    8.1.1, 8.2

financial promotion
    definition   4.2.3
    see also marketing restrictions
Financial Promotions Exemptions
    Order   4.3.5
Financial Services and Markets Tribunal
    appeal   3.5
    Enforcement Committee, and   3.5
    jurisdiction   3.5
    legal aid, and   3.5.1
    proceedings   3.5.1
    structure   3.5.1
Financial Services Authority
    accountability
      competition, and   3.3.2, 3.4.3
      consumer representatives, and
        3.4.1
      immunity   3.4.4
      judicial review   3.4
      practitioners, and   3.4.1
      reports   3.4.2
        scope   1.5.1
      Treasury, and   3.4.2
    aims   1.6
    chairman   3.2
    challenges   1.6
    clearing houses, and   11.2.5
    collective investment schemes, and
      13.2.1
    compensation, and   8.3.1
    competition, and   3.3.2, 3.4.3
    complaints, and   3.4.4, 8.2.2
    composition   1.5.3
    constitution   3.2
    Consumer Panel   3.4.1
    consumer protection, and   3.3.1
    Designated Professional Bodies (DPBs),
      and   11.4
    DPBs (Designated Professional Bodies),
      and   11.4
    duties   3.3
    enforcement functions
      actuaries, and   10.3
      auditors, and   10.3
      civil enforcement   9.2.2
      disciplinary action
        cancelling a permission   9.3.6
        costs   9.3.4
        enforcement   9.3.2
        fines   9.3.4
        injunctions   9.3.5
      jurisdiction   9.3
      overseas regulators
        co-operation   9.37

Financial Services Authority – *cont*
  enforcement functions – *cont*
    disciplinary action – *cont*
      proceedings   9.3.1
      restitution   9.3.5
      standard of proof   9.3
      varying a permission   9.3.6
    Enforcement Committee   9.3.2
    insolvency proceedings and
      insurers   9.4.3
      powers   9.4.1
      rights   9.4.2
    investigations
      compulsion   10.2.1
      confidentiality   10.2.1
      inside the perimeter   10.2
      outside the perimeter   10.1
    market misconduct *see* market
      misconduct
    policing the perimeter   9.2
    prosecutions   9.2.1
    supervisory powers   9.3.1
  European Passport, and   2.3.4
  exchanges, and   11.2.5
  Financial Ombudsman Scheme (FOS),
    and   8.2.2
  Financial Services Compensation
    Scheme (FSCS), and   8.3.1
  functions   3.3
  funding   3.2
  immunity   3.4.4
  interim arrangements   1.5.2, 3.1
  internal structure   1.5.3
  judicial review, and   3.4
  legislative functions
    'additional' rules   6.2.1
    approved individuals
      Statements of Principle   6.5
    breach of rules   6.2.2
    client assets rules   6.4.2
    COBS (Conduct of Business
      Sourcebook)   6.3.3
    Conduct of Business Sourcebook
      (COBS)   6.3.3
    consultation procedures   6.2.4
    'customers'   6.3.2
    delegated powers   6.1
    evidential provisions   6.2.3
    'general' rules   6.2
    guidance   6.2.3
    Handbook   6.1
    Inter-Professionals Code (IPC)
      6.3.2
    IPC (Inter-Professionals Code)
      6.3.2
    modifications   6.2.2
    over-regulation, and   6.1
    PFBs (Principles for Businesses)
      6.3.1
    Principles for Businesses (PFBs)
      6.3.1
    procedural provisions   6.2.4
    Prudential Sourcebook   6.4.1
    reports   6.1
    stabilisation rules   6.4.3
    Statements of Principle   6.5
    Training and Competence Sourcebook
      6.4.4
    waivers   6.2.2
  Lloyd's, and   11.3
  objectives   1.6, 3.3, 3.3.1
  over-regulation   1.61
  Practitioner Forum   3.4.1
  principles   3.3, 3.3.2
  professional firms, and   11.4
  risks   1.6
  reports   3.4.2
  scope   1.5.1
  status   3.2
  structure   1.5.3
  systemic risk, and   3.3.1
  Treasury, and   3.4.2
  Tribunal
    appeal   3.5
    Enforcement Committee, and   3.5
    jurisdiction   3.5
    legal aid, and   3.5.1
    proceedings   3.5.1
    structure   3.5.1
Financial Services Compensation Scheme
    (FSCS)   8.1.2, 8.3
Financial Services and Markets Act
    (Regulated Activities) Order
  exclusions under   4.3.3
FOS (Financial Ombudsman Scheme)
    8.1.1, 8.2
friendly societies   1.2.6
  Friendly Societies Protection
    Scheme   8.1
FSCS (Financial Services Compensation
    Scheme)   8.1.2, 8.3

ICS (Investors Compensation
    Scheme)   8.1
IMRO (Investment Management
    Regulatory Organisation)   1.4.1
insider dealing
  defences   7.3.4

insider dealing – *cont*
  'inside information'   7.3.3
  'insiders'   7.3.2
  'relevant dealings'   7.3.1
insolvency   9.4
insurance
  brokers   1.2.5
  insolvency   9.4.3
  regulation   4.1
interim arrangements   1.5.2, 3.1
International Primary Markets
      Association   11.1
International Securities Markets
      Association (ISMA)   11.1
International Swaps and Derivatives
      Association   11.1
Investment Management Regulatory
      Organisation (IMRO)   1.4.1
investment trusts   13.2
Investors Compensation Scheme
      (ICS)   8.1
ISMA (International Securities Markets
      Association)   11.1

JMLSG (Joint Money Laundering Steering
      Group)   7.6
Joint Money Laundering Steering Group
      (JMLSG)   7.6

limited issue funds   13.4.2
limited redemption funds   13.4.2
listing
  admission   12.3
  announcements   12.3.3
  discontinuance   12.4
  liability   12.4.3–12.4.4
  particulars   12.3
  prospectus requirements   12.1,
      12.3.1
  Regulatory News Service (RNS)
      12.3.3
  RNS (Regulatory News Service)
      12.3.3
  Stock Exchange, and
      admission to trading   12.3.3
  suspension   12.4
  UKLA (UK Listing Authority)   12.2
  Listing Rules
    breach   12.4
Lloyd's   1.2.2, 3.1, 11.3
London Stock Exchange   1.2.1

'making misleading statements'   7.2.1
market abuse
  categories   7.4.1
  directors, and   7.4.2
  'indirect'   7.4.2
  Takeover Panel, and   7.4.2
'market manipulation'   7.2.2
market misconduct
  City fraud   7.1
  Code of Market Conduct (COMC)
      7.5
  COMC (Code of Market Conduct)
      7.5
  conspiracy to defraud   7.1
  'distortion'   7.5.4
  'economical with the truth'   7.2.1
  'false or misleading impression'
      7.5.3
  insider dealing
    defences   7.3.4
    'inside information'   7.3.3
    'insiders'   7.3.2
    'relevant dealings'   7.3.1
  liability   7.1
  'making misleading statements'
      7.2.1
  market abuse
    categories   7.4.1
    directors, and   7.4.2
    'indirect'   7.4.2
    Takeover Panel, and   7.4.2
  'market manipulation'   7.2.2
  money laundering   7.6, 10.4.3
  misleading statements and practices
      7.2
  'misuse of information'   7.5.2
  sanctions
    choice   10.4
    Enforcement Manual   10.4.1
    fines   10.4.1
    injunctions   10.4.1, 10.4.2
    prosecutions   10.4.1
    restitution   10.4.1, 10.4.2
marketing restrictions
  exception
    authorised firms   13.1.3
    exempt businesses   13.1.2
    private recommendations   13.1
  collective investment schemes, and *see*
      collective investment schemes:
      marketing restrictions
  commercial companies, and   13.1.1
misleading statements and practices
      7.2

'misuse of information' 7.5.2
money laundering 7.6, 10.4.3
mortgages
regulation 4.1
mutual recognition *see* European Passport

OEICs (open-ended investment
companies) 13.2
offers
listed securities *see* listing
unlisted securities 12.5
open-ended investment companies
(OEICs) 13.2
OTC (over-the-counter) operations
11.1
over-the-counter (OTC) operations
11.1

Panel on Takeovers and Mergers 1.2.3
pensions
occupational 3.1
perimeter
defining 4.2
policing 9.2
permission procedure 5.2.3
Personal Investment Authority (PIA)
1.4.1
PIA (Personal Investment Authority)
1.4.1
Policyholders Protection Scheme 8.1
Pooled Unauthorised Companies
(PUNCs) 13.4.2
private actions
outside the perimeter 10.5.1
within the perimeter 10.5.2
professional firms
regulation 11.4
public offers
listed securities *see* listing
unlisted securities 12.5
PUNCs (Pooled Unauthorised
Companies) 13.4.2

RCHs (Recognised Clearing Houses)
11.2
Recognised Clearing Houses (RCHs)
11.2
Recognised Investment Exchanges
(RIEs) 11.2
recognised professional bodies (RPBs)
1.4.1, 3.1

regulated activities 4.2.2
Regulatory News Service (RNS) 12.3.3
Restrictive Practices Court 1.3
RIEs (Recognised Investment
Exchanges) 11.2
RNS (Regulatory News Service) 12.3.3
RPBs (recognised professional bodies)
1.4.1, 3.1

securities
listed *see* listing
unlisted 12.5
Securities and Futures Authority
(SFA) 1.4.1
Securities and Investments Board
(SIB) 1.4.1, 1.4.3
self-regulating organisations (SROs)
1.4.1–1.4.3, 3.1
self-regulation 1.1–1.3
SFA (Securities and Futures
Authority) 1.4.1
SIB (Securities and Investments
Board) 1.4.1, 1.4.3
Single Market *see* European Passport
Society of Lloyd's 1.2.2, 3.1, 11.3
SROs (self-regulating organisations)
1.4.1–1.4.3, 3.1
statutory instruments 4.3
Stock Exchange 1.2.1
'Super Regulator'
creation 1.5 *see also* Financial
Services Authority
systemic banking collapse 1.6

Takeover Panel 1.2.3
TCAs (Threshold Conditions for
Authorisation) 5.2.1
Threshold Conditions for Authorisation
(TCAs) 5.2.1
Tradepoint 11.1
Treasury *see also* Financial Services
Authority

UKLA (UK listing Authority) 12.2
unit trusts 13.2

wholesale markets 4.3.4